D0919270

# NEW TESTAMENT THEOLOGY

## MANY WITNESSES, ONE GOSPEL

# I. HOWARD MARSHALL

**InterVarsity Press**
Downers Grove, Illinois

InterVarsity Press
P.O. Box 1400, Downers Grove, IL 60515-1426
World Wide Web: www.ivpress.com
E-mail: mail@ivpress.com

InterVarsity Press® is the book-publishing division of InterVarsity Christian Fellowship/USA®, a student movement active on campus at hundreds of universities, colleges and schools of nursing in the United States of America, and a member movement of the International Fellowship of Evangelical Students. For information about local and regional activities, write Public Relations Dept., InterVarsity Christian Fellowship/USA, 6400 Schroeder Rd., P.O. Box 7895, Madison, WI 53707-7895, or visit the IVCF website at <www.intervarsity.org>.

Biblical citations are taken from the NIV (Inclusive Language Edition) for the Old Testament and from the TNIV for the New Testament unless otherwise indicated.

Cover design: Cindy Kiple

Cover images: Erich Lessing/Art Resource, NY

ISBN 0-8308-2795-1

Printed in the United States of America ∞

Library of Congress Cataloging-in-Publication Data

Marshall, I. Howard.
  New Testament theology: many witnesses, one Gospel/I.
Howard
  Marshall.
    p. cm.
  Includes bibliographical references and index.
  ISBN 0-8308-2795-1 (hardcover: alk. paper)
  1. Bible. N.T.—Theology. I. Title.
  BS2397.M37 2004
  230'.0415—dc22

                                                              2004017266

| P | 18 | 17 | 16 | 15 | 14 | 13 | 12 | 11 | 10 | 9 | 8 | 7 | 6 | 5 | 4 | 3 | 2 | 1 |
| Y | 18 | 17 | 16 | 15 | 14 | 13 | 12 | 11 | 10 | 09 | 08 | 07 | 06 | 05 | 04 | | | |

*To Dai, Doug, Alan and Nathalie,*

*my sons- and daughter-in-law*

# Contents

# PREFACE

The aim of this book is to provide a guide to the theology of the New Testament that will be at a level and of a length suitable for use by students but will also be of use to all who are interested in the subject. In an era of increasingly lengthy books on every aspect of New Testament study, I have tried to be reasonably succinct and to produce a work of manageable scope.

Works on New Testament theology may be organized more in terms of theological themes as they are treated throughout the New Testament or more in terms of the theological teaching of the individual New Testament books. The approach taken here is to let each of the individual books of the New Testament speak for themselves and then to attempt some kind of synthesis of their teaching. Any approach has its drawbacks, and the weakness of this approach is that the reader will find discussion of, say, the church spread over various chapters and will need to make good use of the index. However, the great strength of this approach is that it lets the structure and the content of the discussion be shaped by what the individual writers were trying to say in the actual documents. In order to avoid repetition, some topics, which might be discussed equally well in other contexts, will generally be taken up in one place (e.g., the concept of the church as the body of Christ is discussed in the chapter on Ephesians, although it could also have been taken up in connection with Colossians).

In accordance with this aim of producing a book that will be helpful to students, the bibliographies have been deliberately confined to works in English that should for the most part be not too difficult to access. However, the two or three commentaries that I have listed for each book of the New Testament tend to be among the more solid ones available, and some of them may need at least a modest knowledge of Greek to get the most out of them. I see no point in providing exhaustive lists of literature (which I haven't read in any case) and offering no guidance as to which books should be priorities for the student. I have not listed books in other languages with one exception: I have given references to the main German theologies of the New Testament where appropriate (and very occasionally to other works that have influenced me).

Biblical citations are taken from the NIV (Inclusive Language Edition) for the Old Testament and from the TNIV for the New Testament unless otherwise indicated.

I am grateful to InterVarsity Press for their patience in waiting for the long-delayed completion of this book and for their efficient production.

*I. Howard Marshall*

# GENERAL BIBLIOGRAPHY

Alexander, T. Desmond, and Brian S. Rosner, eds. *New Dictionary of Biblical Theology.* Leicester: Inter-Varsity Press, 2000.

Balla, Peter. *Challenges to New Testament Theology: An Attempt to Justify the Enterprise.* Tübingen: Mohr Siebeck, 1997.

Bauckham, Richard J., ed. *The Gospels for All Christians: Rethinking the Gospel Audiences.* Grand Rapids, Mich.: Eerdmans, 1998.

Beker, J. Christiaan. *Paul the Apostle: The Triumph of God in Life and Thought.* Edinburgh: T & T Clark, 1980.

*Berger, Klaus. *Theologiegeschichte des Urchristentums.* Tübingen: Francke, 1994.

Boers, Hendrikus. *What Is New Testament Theology?* Philadelphia: Fortress, 1979.

*Bultmann, Rudolf. *Theology of the New Testament.* 2 vols. London: SCM Press, 1952-1953.

*Caird, G. B. *New Testament Theology.* Edited by L. D. Hurst. Oxford: Clarendon Press, 1994.

*Childs, Brevard S. *Biblical Theology of the Old and New Testaments: Theological Reflection on the Christian Bible.* Minneapolis: Fortress, 1993.

———. *The New Testament as Canon: An Introduction.* London: SCM Press, 1984.

*Conzelmann, Hans. *An Outline of the Theology of the New Testament.* London: SCM Press, 1969.

Dodd, C. H. *According to the Scriptures: The Substructure of New Testament Theology.* London: Nisbet, 1952.

Dunn, James D. G. *Christology in the Making.* London: SCM Press, 1980.

———. *The Theology of Paul the Apostle.* Grand Rapids, Mich.: Eerdmans, 1998.

———. *Unity and Diversity in the New Testament.* London: SCM Press, 1977.

Dunn, James D. G., and J. P. Mackey. *New Testament Theology in Dialogue.* London: SPCK, 1987.

Elwell, Walter, ed. *Evangelical Dictionary of Biblical Theology.* Grand Rapids, Mich.: Baker, 1996.

*Gnilka, Joachim. *Theologie des Neuen Testaments.* Freiburg: Herder, 1994.

*Goppelt, Leonhard. *Theology of the New Testament.* 2 vols. Grand Rapids, Mich.: Eerdmans, 1981, 1982.

*Guthrie, Donald. *New Testament Theology.* Leicester: Inter-Varsity Press, 1981.

Hafemann, Scott J., ed. *Biblical Theology: Retrospect and Prospect.* Downers Grove, Ill.: InterVarsity Press, 2002.

*Hahn, Ferdinand. *Theologie des Neuen Testaments.* 2 vols. Tübingen: Mohr Siebeck, 2002.

Hasel, Gerhard. *New Testament Theology: Basic Issues in the Current Debate.* Grand Rapids, Mich.: Eerdmans, 1978.

*Hübner, Hans. *Biblische Theologie des Neuen Testaments.* 3 vols. Göttingen: Vandenhoeck und Ruprecht, 1990-1995.

Hultgren, Arland J. *Christ and His Benefits: Christology and Redemption in the New Testament.* Philadelphia: Fortress, 1988.

Hunter, A. M. *Introducing New Testament Theology.* 1957. 2nd ed. Carlisle: Paternoster, 1997.

Hurtado, Larry W. *Lord Jesus Christ: Devotion to Jesus in Earliest Christianity.* Grand Rapids, Mich.: Eerdmans, 2003.

*Jeremias, Joachim. *New Testament Theology, Part One.* London: SCM Press, 1971.

*Kümmel, Werner G. *The Theology of the New Testament According to Its Major Witnesses.* Nashville: Abingdon, 1973; London: SCM Press, 1974.

*Ladd, George Eldon. *A Theology of the New Testament.* Grand Rapids, Mich.: Eerdmans, 1974. Second edition edited by D. A. Hagner, 1993.

Marshall, I. Howard. *Jesus the Savior: Studies in New Testament Theology.* London: SPCK; Downers Grove, Ill.: InterVarsity Press, 1990.

Marshall, I. Howard, Stephen Travis, and Ian Paul. *Exploring the New Testament.* Vol. 2. *The Letters and Revelation.* London: SPCK; Downers Grove, Ill.: InterVarsity Press, 2002.

Morgan, Robert. *The Nature of New Testament Theology.* London: SCM Press, 1973.

———. "Theology. New Testament". In *A Dictionary of Biblical Interpretation.* Edited by R. J. Coggins and J. L. Houlden, pp. 689-91. London: SCM Press; Philadelphia: Trinity Press International, 1990.

———. "Theology. NT". In *Anchor Bible Dictionary,* edited by David Noel Freedman, 6:437-83. New York: Doubleday, 1992.

*Morris, Leon. *New Testament Theology.* Grand Rapids, Mich.: Zondervan, 1986.

Räisänen, Heikki. *Beyond New Testament Theology: A Story and a Program.* London: SCM Press, 1990.

*Schmithals, Walter. *The Theology of the First Christians.* Louisville, Ky.: Westminster John Knox, 1997.

*Schweizer, Eduard. *A Theological Introduction to the New Testament.* London: SPCK, 1992.

Scobie, Charles H. H. *The Ways of Our God: An Approach to Biblical Theology.* Grand Rapids, Mich.: Eerdmans, 2003.

*Stauffer, Ethelbert. *New Testament Theology.* London: SCM Press, 1955. The original was published in Germany in 1941 but was not unsurprisingly unavailable to students elsewhere.

Strecker, Georg. *Das Problem der Theologie des Neuen Testaments.* Darmstadt: Wissenschaftliche Buchgesellschaft, 1975.

*——— . *Theology of the New Testament.* Berlin: de Gruyter; Louisville, Ky.: Westminster John Knox, 2000.

*Stuhlmacher, Peter. *Biblische Theologie des Neuen Testaments.* 2 vols. Göttingen: Vandenhoeck und Ruprecht, 1992, 1999.

———. "My Experience with Biblical Theology". In *Biblical Theology: Retrospect and Prospect.* Edited by Scott J. Hafemann, pp. 174-91. Downers Grove, Ill.: InterVarsity Press, 2002.

Thielman, Frank. *The Law and the New Testament: The Question of Continuity.* New York: Crossroad, 1999.

Via, Dan O. *What Is New Testament Theology?* Minneapolis: Fortress, 2002.

Walton, Steve, and David Wenham. *Exploring the New Testament.* Vol. 1. *The Gospels and Acts.* London: SPCK; Downers Grove, Ill.: InterVarsity Press, 2001.

Watson, Francis B. *Text and Truth: Redefining Biblical Theology.* Edinburgh: T & T Clark, 1997.

*Wilckens, Ulrich. *Theologie des Neuen Testaments.* 2 vols. Neukirchen: Neukirchener, 2002-.

Ziesler, J. A. "New Testament Theology". In *A New Dictionary of Christian Theology.* Edited by Alan Richardson and John Bowden, pp. 398-403. London: SCM Press, 1983.

*Zuck, Roy B., ed. *A Biblical Theology of the New Testament.* Chicago: Moody Press, 1994.

New Testament theologies asterisked above are referred to at the head of many chapter bibliographies by the name of the author.

# Abbreviations

| | |
|---|---|
| *ANRW* | *Aufstieg und Niedergang der Römischen Welt* |
| *BBR* | *Bulletin for Biblical Research* |
| *BJRL* | *Bulletin of the John Rylands University Library of Manchester* |
| *CBQ* | *Catholic Biblical Quarterly* |
| *CTJ* | *Canadian Theological Journal* |
| *DJG* | *Dictionary of Jesus and the Gospels* |
| *DLNTD* | *Dictionary of the Later New Testament and Its Developments* |
| *DNTB* | *Dictionary of New Testament Background* |
| *DPL* | *Dictionary of Paul and His Letters* |
| *EDBT* | *Evangelical Dictionary of Biblical Theology* |
| *EDNT* | *Exegetical Dictionary of the New Testament* |
| *EQ* | *Evangelical Quarterly* |
| *Int* | *Interpretation* |
| *JBL* | *Journal of Biblical Literature* |
| *JETS* | *Journal of the Evangelical Theological Society* |
| *JSNT* | *Journal for the Study of the New Testament* |
| NIV | New International Version |
| NRSV | New Revised Standard Version |
| *NTS* | *New Testament Studies* |
| REB | Revised English Bible |
| *SJT* | *Scottish Journal of Theology* |
| SNT (SU) | Studien zum Neuen Testament (und seiner Umwelt) |
| TNIV | Today's New International Version |
| *TynB* | *Tyndale Bulletin* |

# PART 1

## INTRODUCTION

# 1

# HOW DO WE DO
# NEW TESTAMENT THEOLOGY?

∽০∾

Before we can discuss how to write the theology of the New Testament, we need to say something about the legitimacy and possibility of the enterprise.

### The New Testament as an Object of Study

The most vocal contemporary critic of the enterprise is Heikki Räisänen, who makes four points to show why it must not and cannot be done.[1]

First, Räisänen claims that the historical and the theological must be kept separate. He argues that it is not the job of New Testament scholars as New Testament scholars to deal with theology; rather their sphere is history. The New Testament scholar can write a purely descriptive account of the early church, but nothing more. To write theology is to be prescriptive, and the New Testament scholar as such has no authority to prescribe anything to anybody.

Second, Räisänen also argues that the nature of the material confines us to writing a history of the religion of the early Christians. Here he is going back to the limited agenda set up a century ago by William Wrede.

Third, a study confined to the New Testament documents is said to rest on an artificial limitation; it is determined by a canonization process that represents a later theological decision and has no basis in the early history of the church.

---

[1]Heikki Räisänen, *Beyond New Testament Theology: A Story and a Program* (London: SCM Press, 1990).

Fourth, there is so much contradiction between the documents that a theology of the New Testament in the sense of a unified theological outlook common to the documents cannot be extracted from them.

Räisänen's arguments have been subjected to detailed and largely convincing criticism by Peter Balla.[2] Balla responds to his first point by arguing that there is no good reason why the theology of the first Christians cannot be the object of historical study, and that such historical study can be pursued without starting from a churchly standpoint or concluding with a statement of what the church ought to believe. The first of these two rejoinders is sound, but more needs to be said about the second one later.

Perhaps the simplest and most convincing response to Räisänen's second point is to note that no fewer than ten major presentations by highly competent New Testament scholars of widely differing theological persuasions have appeared in the last few years.[3] It is hard to believe that they were all united in doing something that is fundamentally illegitimate, and the existence of their works demonstrates that the enterprise is possible!

## The Problem of the Canon

More weight attaches to Räisänen's third point. At the outset there is the question whether the set of twenty-seven documents that are grouped together as the New Testament form a unified collection, one that is capable of being meaningfully distinguished from other documents of the period and is an appropriate object of study. Is it proper to examine the New Testament documents in their own right? Is it right to exclude, say, the apostolic fathers or the *Gospel of Thomas* or the *Gospel of Peter* from consideration? We can assemble some five arguments in favor of doing so, the first four of which appear to me to be sound.

First, these documents were recognized by later Christians as forming a collection of Scriptures akin to the collection of writings accepted by the Jews as their Scriptures. The shape of the collection and the core of its con-

---

[2]Peter Balla, *Challenges to New Testament Theology: An Attempt to Justify the Enterprise* (Tübingen: Mohr Siebeck, 1997).

[3]See the works by Klaus Berger, G. B. Caird, J. Gnilka, Ferdinand Hahn, Hans Hübner, George Eldon Ladd, Walter Schmithals, Georg Strecker, Peter Stuhlmacher and Ulrich Wilckens listed in the general bibliography. More works are known to be in preparation.

tents were essentially determined by no later than the end of the second century, although it took until A.D. 367 before we have the first extant statement of the list of books that was subsequently accepted almost universally as canonical.[4] We may grant that this process of gathering together these books and erecting a fence around them took place over a lengthy period of time after the books were written and that the books were not deliberately composed as a unified collection. Nevertheless, the fact that a consensus developed concerning them strongly supports the view that the early church was right to recognize that they had certain characteristics, which indicated that they formed a unity.

Second, the documents are the work of the earliest followers of Jesus, who were themselves, or stood in close relationship to, some of the original actors in the birth and growth of the church, and they all belong to the first Christian century.[5] There is thus a basis for seeing a possible unity in the relatively limited area and time within which they were composed.

Third, the New Testament documents constitute virtually the whole of the surviving Christian literature of the first century, although some of the apostolic fathers (*1 Clement; Didache*) probably belong to this period. The fact that there may be some overlap between the dates of the latest New Testament books and the earliest apostolic fathers (and other Christian literature of the same period) does not call in question the existence of the identifiable hard cores of both bodies of literature, just as a border dispute over the possession of Kashmir does not mean that the countries of India and Pakistan cannot be regarded as distinguishable entities. The basic distinction between first- and second-century Christian literature remains a valid one, even if the boundary is not sharply defined except by canon makers.

Fourth, there is a manifest unity of theme about the New Testament writings

---

[4]This statement is controversial but defensible. For varying points of view see the articles on canon by F. F. Bruce, *DJG*, pp. 93-100; Arthur G. Patzia, *DPL*, pp. 85-92; and Lee M. McDonald, *DLNTD*, pp. 134-44.

[5]I may be accused of making things easy for myself, but I very much doubt whether the possible exceptions, 2 Peter and the Pastoral Epistles (and certainly not Acts), are to be dated as late as the second century. See Steve Walton and David Wenham, *Exploring the New Testament*, vol. 1, *The Gospels and Acts* (London: SPCK; Downers Grove, Ill.: InterVarsity Press, 2001); I. Howard Marshall, Stephen Travis and Ian Paul, *Exploring the New Testament*, vol. 2, *The Letters and Revelation* (London: SPCK; Downers Grove, Ill.: InterVarsity Press, 2002).

in that they are all concerned in one way or another with Jesus and the religion that developed around him. To be sure, this does not necessarily imply that they all say the same things about this common theme and are in agreement with one another. Nevertheless, a corpus of writings with the same central theme must constitute a legitimate object of study.

Fifth, it has sometimes been argued that the writings show a quality of Christian thought that is not matched in the later literature. Clearly this is a subjective verdict, and there could be a case that some of the second-century writings (e.g., the *Epistle of Diognetus*) stand very close to them in spirit and quality, but as a broad verdict the statement is defensible. Even so, I would not want to put much weight on this argument.

Our claim, then, is that it makes sense in the light of canonization to ask whether there is a common, basic theology in the set of books that the early church canonized.

To adopt this procedure, of course, does not lead to excluding other works outside the New Testament from consideration. In elucidating the content of the New Testament and in reconstructing the history of the period it is essential to make use of all other relevant sources, including other early Christian literature. This approach was especially characteristic of Ethelbert Stauffer, who placed the New Testament in the context of what he called the "old biblical tradition" and appeared on occasion to be in danger of regarding this extracanonical material almost as if it were canonical.[6] If we are writing a history of the early church, then clearly all available sources are to be used; but if we are writing an account of the theology of the New Testament, then our task is to expound its contents, just as an exposition of the thought of Shakespeare will draw upon his writings but will do so in the context of the works of other Elizabethan playwrights, or an exposition of the founding fathers of the British Labor Party will draw upon their utterances but will do so in the context of other politicians of the time.[7]

### Problems of Occasionality, Diversity and Development

Turning now to Räisänen's fourth point, we have to face a number of difficul-

---

[6]Ethelbert Stauffer, *New Testament Theology* (London: SCM Press, 1955), p. 20.
[7]See further n. 13 on p. 26.

ties in our study that arise out of the nature and history of the documents under investigation.

First, the New Testament library does not contain any ready-made textbooks of theology. None of the books is written specifically as a theology in the sense of an account of the author's understanding of God and the world and their relationship to one another set out systematically in some detail. At least some of the writings are occasional or situational in that they were individually written on specific occasions to particular groups of people and give us what the writers thought to be relevant to these audiences. This is true, at least, of the letters of Paul. It is commonly thought that the Gospels were also written for specific individual communities, although this view may need some qualification.[8] And it is patent that Paul regarded some, if not all, of what he wrote to individual congregations as material that could be useful to other congregations. But even if the books were more than narrowly occasional, it remains true that none of them is a full and systematic exposition of its author's theology. It may, therefore, be impossible to analyze some of the writings with a view to determining the content of the author's theology, and there may be occasions when it is doubtful how far the author even had a formed theology. Nevertheless, the difficulty of the task is not in itself an argument against the attempt to reconstruct theology from works that are not specifically theological.

Second, there is considerable variety and diversity among the books that compose the New Testament.

The period of composition referred to earlier as "short" in comparison with the length of subsequent church history can be seen from a different perspective as a relatively lengthy one (as much as fifty years), and the writings come from a wide geographical area, stretching from Jerusalem to Rome.

The writings differ from one another in literary genre, and the individual genres—Gospels, letters and apocalypses—are notoriously hard to define in terms of their characteristics.

The writings show considerable variety of outlook among themselves, so

---

[8]Richard J. Bauckham, ed., *The Gospels for All Christians: Rethinking the Gospel Audiences* (Grand Rapids, Mich.: Eerdmans, 1998). While the main thesis is attractive, it may still leave room for the individual Evangelists being affected by the communities in which they lived and writing more particularly for them and their needs rather than deliberately trying to be catholic in their approach.

much so that some scholars would claim that they contain contradictory statements.

These points all raise the question whether there is sufficient unity of thought among the writings to justify examining them as a collection. But even if we cannot commence with the presupposition of unity of outlook, it does make sense historically to examine the corpus of earliest Christian literature in order to identify the theologies represented in it. This exercise would still be valid even if its result were to show that the supposed cohesion and unity are dubious. Whether we like it or not, there is such a collection of books as an object to be investigated.

Third, the writings are the fruit of a development in thinking that manifestly falls into at least two main stages.

*The first stage.* There is the very brief period of the activity of Jesus, terminated by his death in A.D. 30 or thereabouts. The four Gospels present themselves as historical records of this period, describing (as Luke puts it) what Jesus "did and taught".

*The second stage.* There is the period after Jesus' death during which his small group of followers increased in number and geographical extent, and formed congregations throughout the eastern Mediterranean world. They produced a literature that contains the Christian message, explained and applied to the needs of the first audiences. Their message, however, was not simply a continuation of what Jesus had taught but rather a proclamation about Jesus and his continuing significance. A superficial glance at the Gospels and the Letters shows that what Jesus taught and what his followers taught are far from being identical, no matter how much common ground there may be.

The division between the two stages is, of course, blurred by the fact that the Gospels were not written until the second stage (and, on the common view, comparatively late in it)[9] so that inevitably they reflect to some extent the interests and outlook of that period. There is therefore a tricky historical problem in attempting to discover exactly what Jesus said and did, and how he would have appeared to people in his lifetime. There is the further problem caused by the fact that the various writings come from different

---

[9]The universally accepted view is that Paul wrote his letters before the Evangelists wrote the Gospels.

times and places within the second stage, and we have the problem of trying to reconstruct the development of thought and their places within it. If we focus on the actual documents that compose the New Testament, we are dealing with items that stand in some kind of chronological development and cannot all be treated on the flat. And if we attempt to reconstruct the theology of the early church in the first century, we are even more committed to describing a rich tapestry of changing and developing ideas. But nothing here makes our task too complex to carry out or rules it out in principle.

## Approaches to the Task

Bearing in mind these three points concerning the diversity of the material, we can try to define our subject more precisely, and to help us in so doing we must catalog some of the recent approaches to it.

It may be helpful to attempt a tentative definition of the object of our concern: the aim of students of New Testament theology is to explore the New Testament writers' developing understanding of God and the world, more particularly the world of people[10] and their relationship to one another. That is a sufficiently broad definition to cover the subject matter and yet to exclude certain other things or at least to recognize their secondary character.

Thus it excludes the attempt to write a history of the early church except insofar as aspects of the history contribute to the theological understanding that we are seeking.

Equally, it excludes examining the New Testament simply as a piece of literature, although again a literary study is often relevant to a theological investigation.

It also marks a difference from a study of the religion of the early Christians, although the religion is significant for our purpose in that the religion gave rise to the theology and in turn the theology tended to shape the practice of the religion.

There would not be too great a difficulty in constructing a theology of, say, the Free Church of Scotland in the twentieth century; we would produce a description of the characteristic, mature understanding of a specific, reasonably homogeneous and comparatively small group of Christians who are self-con-

---

[10]But certainly not excluding the animals and the inanimate creation!

sciously aware of the need to be systematic in their theology and to base it firmly on the theology of the Reformation. A description of Anglican theology in the same period would be rather more difficult to produce in that there would be a much wider range of thinking and approach, with some groups in opposition if not contradiction to others, and yet there would be something that could be described as recognizably Anglican by contrast with Presbyterian or Roman Catholic theology.

But how does one deal with a period of birth and rapid growth in an extended family that comprises varied groups from Jews with their deep-rooted traditional beliefs to Greeks and Romans who had previously worshiped a variety of idols? There have been a number of approaches, some of which are more viable than others:

From what has already been said, it should be clear that we cannot simply lump all the books of the New Testament together indiscriminately and use them as a quarry for the stones, which we shall use to build our edifice. It would be possible to create a compilation of theological statements from the New Testament that was nothing more than a harmonizing assembly of quotations taken at random from any of its books. Such an approach would wrench the statements out of their contexts and lack the careful examination of their nuances to establish precisely what they were intended to affirm and imply. It would also assume that the quotations will all necessarily reflect the same point of view. But is a collection of texts a theology? There has to be some kind of arrangement. If so, how does one decide how to group the texts? To create a building rather than a cairn it is necessary to have some kind of plan or design.

Consequently, the first approach cannot in practice be separated from a second, accompanying tendency. This is to take over an existing plan such as is found in a textbook of systematic theology but without any firm evidence that this framework was in the minds of any of the New Testament authors. However, it has to be said that people who do this are usually quite convinced that their framework is that of the New Testament.

Two errors of method thus come together in this combination of approaches, the indiscriminate use of the books of the New Testament as if they all necessarily reflected identical thinking, and the use of a later framework as if it were that of the New Testament. The result can be distorting and anachronistic. It is fair to say that no serious student of the subject would take this route.[11]

A third possibility, which avoids the dangers just mentioned, is to examine the individual authors or the individual writings in the New Testament, to set out the teaching of each of them on the various topics and to lay them side by side, with or without some comparison of their contents. This is the route followed by G. B. Caird. He sets out his work in the form of what he calls a "conference" between the different New Testament authors on various themes that arise naturally out of the New Testament itself and are not imported from later theology. He then compares them with the teaching of Jesus.[12] I have no objections to this method, but Caird's description of it as a conference seems to me to be a misnomer. "Conference" is not the most appropriate word for his procedure in that the word normally conveys the idea of a discussion with the different participants responding to what one another says. For Caird it is not really possible to offer more than position papers from each of the speakers without any indication of how, say, John would have responded to Paul. But if we may evaluate what is done rather than the misleading description given to it, the objective is entirely worthy in that Caird has identified what appear to be the guiding themes of the New Testament writers themselves, rather than the themes of a book of systematic theology, and set out the teaching of the several authors on each of them.

A fourth possibility is to approach the subject historically by attempting to trace the development of the ideas that have been deposited in the extant writings. This is a legitimate and necessary enquiry that may help to bring order to an apparent chaos by showing how the various expressions of different ideas may be related genealogically to one another, and there has been some progress in carrying out this process for individual theological motifs.

---

[11]It would, of course, be hard to list any serious examples of this kind of approach by New Testament scholars. What I have described is rather a danger that is fairly well recognized. The work of Donald Guthrie, *New Testament Theology* (Leicester: Inter-Varsity Press, 1981), tends toward using the pattern of systematic theology, but the author is too perceptive to be in real danger of misrepresenting the New Testament teaching as a result. In fact, within his discussion of individual doctrinal topics he goes through the material by treating the various New Testament authors or areas one by one. One is more likely to meet this approach in older conservative works of systematic theology that are basically compilations of biblical material.

[12]G. B. Caird, *New Testament Theology*, ed. L. D. Hurst (Oxford: Clarendon, 1994), pp. 18-26.

   Somebody has commented that if you are trying to solve a chess problem, of the kind where you have a diagram of a board with a few pieces on it and have to work out the winning move for White, it is not necessary to know what moves led to the position on the diagram. If, however, you are a doctor dealing with a patient showing certain symptoms of illness, part of the diagnosis will certainly be taking a medical history of the patient in order to understand what may have led to the ambiguous symptoms and to prescribe the appropriate cure. Study of New Testament theology is more akin to medical diagnosis with its tracing of a case history than to solving a chess problem. We need some understanding of the history in order to place the theological statements in a proper context.

   The history to be explored will include the New Testament documents, the aim of the operation being to place them in some kind of chronological order so that the development of ideas can be pursued within the New Testament. But it will also look at what lies behind them so that the historical process can be properly reconstructed. If we adopt this approach, our concern cannot be limited to the theology of the New Testament writers but must extend to the underlying theology of the early church, including those Christians who have left no literary memorial of their own.[13]

   By way of example of this procedure we may note how Joachim Gnilka decided to include two sections on the theology of the hypothetical Gospel source Q and on the perhaps even more hypothetical pre-Markan passion nar-

---

[13]There are four other areas that have to be brought into the discussion.

   1. The non-Christian background against which the Christian theology developed. In what ways did the Christians take over ideas, motifs and vocabulary from the Jewish and the Greco-Roman world?

   2. The role of Jesus as the founder of Christianity. What did he do and teach, and how did it influence his followers and guide their thought?

   3. The complicated history of the early church before and alongside the written documents out of which developed the theology of the New Testament writers. What did Paul owe to those who were Christians before and alongside him?

   4. The path to the written documents was not one of smooth, unilinear development. Paul and John, for example, developed some of their ideas in reaction to groups who held ideas with which they disagreed, and some account of these other groups and their thinking must be included as part of the essential background information for understanding the New Testament authors.

   In order to keep this book to a reasonable size there will be little enough room here for the background material and particularly for introductory material that deals with the situations in and for which the different texts were composed.

rative in order to establish a basis for his consideration of how the Evangelists developed their ideas and what they meant by what they wrote. Regardless of whether we think that these hypothetical documents ever existed, the point at issue is simply that it is not possible to ignore the history whose literary deposit is found in the New Testament documents.[14]

Those who follow this route then find that their task is one that involves the two distinguishable stages of description and explanation. The description is the drawing out of the theological ideas expressed in the various writings. The explanation is the attempt to show how these ideas developed and thus how one author's theology is related to that of another. Writers on Paul find it necessary to ask what was thought by other people, including other Christian believers before and alongside him, so that they can see to what extent Paul is taking over common ideas and to what extent he is being original.

Such an approach is not free from risks. One possible danger is that what is produced may be not so much a theology of the New Testament as rather an archaeological investigation into the hypothetical sources that lie behind it. We may finish up with the theology of some early Christians rather than that of the New Testament authors.

A further danger is that we may simply chart a development without producing any kind of synthesis of the material. This type of approach can be more concerned to elucidate how doctrines developed than to examine the finished product for its own sake. Yet it is surely possible to be aware of these risks and to attempt to minimize the dangers of succumbing to them.

It seems that the route most traversed by recent travelers is some version of the fourth route, which uses a historical or developmental framework as the main guide to the journey and groups the individual New Testament authors or writings historically.

---

[14]See J. Gnilka, *Theologie des Neuen Testaments* (Freiburg: Herder, 1994), pp. 133-51. Strangely Gnilka also held that that an account of the theology held by Jesus is not part of a work on New Testament theology. We may well wonder what led him to include these hypothetical sources and omit the very historical Jesus himself. Ferdinand Hahn, *Theologie des Neuen Testaments*, 2 vols. (Tübingen: Mohr Siebeck, 2002), includes not only an account of the historical Jesus but also discussions of the early Aramaic-speaking church and the early Hellenistic-Jewish Christian communities. This distinction between two groups in the early church was developed in his earlier work on christology and has been much criticized, but it is maintained here in a somewhat more cautious manner.

## Getting Beneath the Surface

It would be possible simply to summarize the teaching of any of the various New Testament authors on the object of our concern and to do so with a sympathetic and nuanced understanding that considered statements in their context and in the light of their history. But such a summary would be like an artist's painting of the human body or even a sculptured figure, which may portray the surface ever so exactly but does not begin to explain why the body has the structure it has or how the different parts work or how the outward appearance reflects the inner workings and the shape of what lies below the surface. We need some kind of principles for organizing the mass of teaching contained in the New Testament so that the structure and underlying rationale of the thinking become apparent.

Although the use of such terms as *teaching* and *proclamation* indicates that we are largely concerned with deliberate formulations in words, it would be folly to assume that this is all that we must consider. The books of the New Testament do not simply record teaching but also tell the story of the religious experience of the Christians, and understanding the experience is part of the task, not least because the teaching arises out of the experience. Stauffer is one of the few New Testament theologians who includes a chapter on prayer in his *New Testament Theology*[15] and in so doing points up a blind spot in approaches that concentrate on proclamation and teaching. We are looking, therefore, not simply at teaching but also at an underlying history and an experience that express in their own way an understanding of our subject. So the theology of Paul is not simply a listing of what Paul says on the surface but rather an attempt to get at the contents of the mind that produced the literary deposit.

In essence, then, we are trying to grasp the understanding of God and his relationship to the world reflected in the various documents. We assume that the writer has such an understanding and that it comes to expression in a piecemeal or a more systematic manner in his[16] writing(s). It then becomes possible

---

[15]Stauffer, *New Testament Theology*, pp. 176-80.

[16]However much we may regret it, it remains the case that no New Testament writing can be confidently ascribed to the pen of a female writer. Attempts to do so for Hebrews and Revelation are scarcely successful. Therefore, I judge that it is permissible to use masculine pronouns in this context.

to analyze what is said in order to reconstruct this understanding.

The dangers of this process include that of systematization and tracing logical connections where these may be inappropriate; not all theologians had such orderly minds as Calvin! How do we avoid the temptation to project our systems onto the writers? There is also the temptation to bridge the inevitable gaps in our knowledge in ways that may be inappropriate or wrong; we can make the theology more complete and systematic than it actually was.

### Theologies and Theology

The implication of what we have said so far is that the initial task of a theology of the New Testament is to make a collection of the theologies that may be presumed to come to expression in its various documents. But is a theology of the New Testament or of the early church simply a collection of studies of the theologies of different believers brought together within the covers of one book, or must there not be some comparison between them to establish whether the several theologies form a unity, sharing the same basic understanding, however much they may differ in the ways in which they express it or in the details of the content?[17] It is surely the duty of the New Testament theologian to attempt some comparison of the outlooks of the writers in order to ascertain how far there is such an entity as *the* theology of the New Testament, and if so what this entity might be. Some writers assume the unity or begin by defending it and then proceed to use the whole of the New Testament as the basis for their study. Donald Guthrie offers summaries of the common teaching of the authors at the end of his depictions of their several understandings of each of the topics that he investigates. But some others offer the reader no such guidance.

Two related investigations need to be distinguished. The first is the attempt to relate the different theologies to one another by studying the development of theological thought and seeing where the various statements fit into it.[18] This task is immensely complex and speculative, and we shall not attempt to carry it out in any detail in this book. The other task is the comparison of the differ-

---

[17]See James D. G. Dunn, *Unity and Diversity in the New Testament* (London: SCM Press, 1977).

[18]This type of approach is classically adopted in the discussions of christology by Ferdinand Hahn, *The Titles of Jesus in Christology: Their History in Early Christianity* (London: Lutterworth, 1969), and Reginald H. Fuller, *The Foundations of New Testament Christology* (London: Lutterworth, 1965). Their work shows how speculative and difficult the task is.

ent theologies to establish the extent and nature of the unity and diversity.

Undoubtedly the main problem that faces the composer of a New Testament theology arises at this stage. It is the existence of variety within the writings. This may include the differences between different writers but also the fact of development and change within writings from the same author or from the same school of thought. That there are differences in modes of expression, in manners of thinking, in emphasis and so on is commonplace. There may also be contradiction, and for some modern authors the level of contradiction is such that we cannot speak of "New Testament theology" but only of "New Testament theologies" that may be in acute tension with one another.

There are some three possible ways of dealing with this kind of tension.

The first is to argue that it is totally irresolvable. Paul and James, for example, are opposed to one another, and there is no way that they can be made to agree.

The second way is to examine the alleged opposing statements or positions with care and to determine whether, when properly understood, they are in harmony with one another in what they affirm.

The third way is to determine whether, despite differences on the surface, there may be an underlying unity on a different level of perception.

Any of these three solutions may apply in individual cases, and not all problems will be solved in the same way.

It is the responsibility of the New Testament theologian to tackle this question. There must be two aspects to the discussion. On the one side, there is the duty of setting out the theologies of the several New Testament writers individually and sympathetically in all their difference and variety. On the other side, there is the duty of determining their relationship to one another, not just in terms of historical development but above all in terms of their theology: in what ways do they show a common mind and in what ways do they differ? Can we find a common outlook among them, and if so, how is it to be expressed?

Clearly the starting point must be to set out the thought expressed in the various documents, each for its own sake, before attempting any comparisons and detecting any tensions. It is a given fact that the New Testament comes to us in the form of discrete documents that are unrelated to one another except where one author may be responsible for a short series (like 1 and 2 Corinthians or Luke and Acts) or may write to different audiences (like Paul to different Christian congregations). In each case, therefore, the author is applying his theology to a different, specific situation. There is thus a strong case that the beginning of the analysis must be an examination of each individual document for its implications about the theology of the writer. Only thus will justice be done to the richness of each individual contribution.

But then the analysis must be carried further into comparison and synthesis as we see how the writings fit or do not fit together. Thus variety and possible unity must alike be the objects of investigation.

Our conclusion is thus that a theology of the New Testament has two tasks: First, it will investigate the way in which the theological thinking of the early Christians, as deposited in these documents, came into being, analyzing the theologies that come to expression in each of the several documents or in appropriate groups of documents.[19] Second, it will then enquire as to the existence and character of a possible synthesis that will bring out the common beliefs expressed in the documents and also show how they have individually developed these beliefs in different ways, so that we may see whether there is some kind of harmony between them or whether there are discords that cannot be resolved.

At the time when I originally wrote this chapter, there was no contemporary work that carried through this program in any detail. But now we have the work of Ferdinand Hahn, whose *Theologie des Neuen Testaments* comprises two substantial volumes, each of more than eight hundred pages, in which he deals first with the variety of the New Testament witnesses to Christ in a theological history of the material and then with the unity of the New Testament by means of a thematic presentation. Here, at last, we have an example of how the task might be done, but in far greater detail than is contemplated in the present work.

### Structuring the Material

It has already been said more than once that the New Testament does not contain any textbooks of theology; there are no detailed creeds or confessions. The material is largely unstructured and occasional. Can there, then, be such a thing as a theology behind any of the writings, or is such an entity an artificial de-

---

[19]As indicated above, in view of the complexity of the task and the limitations of space in an introduction to the topic, we shall concentrate attention on accurately describing and analyzing the theology of the various documents rather than attempting to provide a history of the development of the thought.

duction from this material? Are we in danger of replacing the teaching of the New Testament by a putative theology that is alleged to lie behind it?

Consider the analogy of the head teacher of a school who has to deal with various problems of conduct that arise among the pupils. Some matters are covered by a set of school rules that have been drawn up to cover likely contingencies and some unlikely ones. At other times situations arise on which the head has to make ad hoc decisions. These decisions could be simply arbitrary, but more probably they reflect some general rules or some basic principles of which the rules are regarded as specific applications. The head may state on occasion what these basic principles are, or they may be deducible from the particular decisions. So it would be possible at least in theory to work back from the head's decisions and occasional statements to an understanding of the principles accepted in the school and the ways in which they are applied.

At the risk of oversimplification it may be said that something similar can be done with the New Testament.[20] We can read the particular teaching and instruction that is given in the various books, and we can try to work back from that to the underlying body of belief and the ways in which it is being used. We can see which applications are occasional and which are so frequent and consistent that they are manifestly basic.

The application is a product of the underlying beliefs and the specific situation to which they are being applied, and therefore the same fundamental beliefs may have different applications, differently nuanced, from time to time. This approach has been most clearly articulated by J. C. Beker in his analysis of the theology of Paul.[21] Beker distinguishes between what he calls the coherent center and the contingent expression of Paul's theology. Paul has a set of beliefs that articulate his Christian experience, and these could be expressed in a systematic manner, but what we have from him is the contingent expression of these beliefs as they apply to the particular situations that he was called to address in his letters. So the task of New Testament theology is to examine the actual writings to see what coherent centers they express and to show how the centers find expression in the applications.

---

[20]One danger of my illustration is that it may suggest that the New Testament is essentially a book of rules to be followed.

[21]J. Christiaan Beker, *Paul the Apostle: The Triumph of God in Life and Thought* (Edinburgh: T & T Clark, 1980).

It may be helpful to elaborate the model by distinguishing three elements. First, a broad distinction can be made between the framework of a person's thinking and the specific thoughts developed within that framework. For example, there are certain types of ancient thought that presuppose the existence of a dualistic understanding of reality. Light and darkness, good and evil are familiar opposites, particularly when these are thought of as warring foes.[22] But within the framework of dualistic thinking there can clearly be different systems of belief. There may be some who believe in the ultimate victory of light or in the triumph of evil. There may be different views as to the origin of the dualism; in some schemes the dualism could find expression within individual human beings. And those who believe in the ultimate victory of good may do so on the basis of a belief that the future is predetermined by the good power.

It is therefore necessary to ascertain whether different writers have different frameworks of thought and to determine what factors constitute a writer's frame of thinking. There is a difference, for example, between a basically legal frame of reference in which God is thought of primarily as a lawgiver to his subjects and a basically personal one in which he is thought of primarily as a Father who has a familial relationship with his children. The first gives rise to moral teaching that is essentially in the form of rules, whereas the other may be more concerned with promoting the imitation of a character (Lk 6:36).

The distinction between framework and content is a fluid one. One person's teaching may now become another person's framework. For example, in the Old Testament God is rarely thought of as Father but more often as the initiator of the covenant with his people. In the teaching of Jesus to his disciples the thought that God is Father is introduced in a new way; it is one of his concerns to reveal this fact to his disciples. But in the early church the fact that God is Father is then taken completely for granted and has become part of the framework for Christian thinking. The framework has thus shifted, and what Jesus presented as a new (but not entirely new) understanding of God, that is, as part of the content of his teaching, is now part of the framework which does not need to be taught or defended but is taken for granted. Within the framework

---

[22]By contrast there are monistic systems of thinking which do not postulate an essential dualism. There are, of course, other forms of dualism, such as that between spirit and matter, which are different from the moral dualism referred to above.

there is scope for the presentation of further new ideas. So the New Testament writers grapple with the idea that within the framework of God's fatherhood there is a place for God the Son. Then once again the framework changes, so that eventually we have a trinitarian understanding of God over against a monistic framework.

The ways in which people think within their frameworks can then be explored. Here a further helpful distinction can be made between the main concern or concerns of the writer and the detailed outworking of the concern(s). By making this distinction we can pinpoint the focus of the thinking and avoid losing sight of the forest by only seeing the individual trees. For example, the detailed contents of the three Synoptic Gospels show considerable similarity and overlap, but attention to their main concerns helps us to recognize that they may have significant differences in the way in which they use their materials. Matthew emphasizes Jesus as a teacher, but John emphasizes him more as a revealer.

Framework, content or concern, and detailed outworking thus constitute the three categories that may be helpful to us. The distinctions between them are not sharp ones, but nevertheless they may be serviceable in attempting to analyze the thought of the New Testament writers.

## The New Testament and Mission

It will be helpful in our study to have some idea of where the focus of the New Testament writings is to be found. Is there something that binds them together beyond the fact that they belong to the same period of time? The obvious answer is that they are all concerned with Jesus and the repercussions of his activity. They belong within the literature of Judaism but form a specific part of it in that they all accept that Jesus is the representative of God through whom he is acting to bring salvation to the world. They offer, therefore, a Christian theology as distinguished from a purely Jewish theology. It is, then, the recognition of Jesus as Savior and Lord that gives them their common characteristic.

It may, however, be more helpful to recognize them more specifically as the documents of a mission. The subject matter is not, as it were, Jesus in himself or God in himself but Jesus in his role as Savior and Lord. New Testament theology is essentially missionary theology. By this I mean that the documents came into being as the result of a two-part mission, first, the mission of Jesus sent by God to inaugurate his kingdom with the blessings that it brings to people and to call people to respond to it, and then the mission of his followers called to continue his work by proclaiming him as Lord and Savior, and calling people to faith and ongoing commitment to him, as a result of which his church grows. The theology springs out of this movement and is shaped by it, and in turn the theology shapes the continuing mission of the church. The primary function of the documents is thus to testify to the gospel that is proclaimed by Jesus and his followers. Their teaching can be seen as the fuller exposition of that gospel. They are also concerned with the spiritual growth of those who are converted to the Christian faith. They show how the church should be shaped for its mission, and they deal with those problems that form obstacles to the advancement of the mission. In short, people who are called by God to be missionaries are carrying out their calling by the writing of Gospels, letters and related material. They are concerned to make converts and then to provide for their nurture, to bring new believers to birth and to nourish them to maturity.

Here what happens in Luke-Acts may serve as an example of what is true of the New Testament as a whole. W. C. van Unnik offered a convincing explanation of the relationship between the Gospel of Luke and the Acts of the Apostles.[23] He saw the Gospel as the record of the good news proclaimed by Jesus in word and deed, and he then characterized Acts as "the confirmation of the gospel", a record telling the story of the mission in such a way as to show how, when the gospel was proclaimed by the missionaries, it was seen to be truly the gospel in that it brought salvation to those who responded to it. The New Testament thus tells the story of the mission and lays especial emphasis on expounding the message proclaimed by the missionaries.[24]

A recognition of this missionary character of the documents will help us to see them in true perspective and to interpret them in the light of their intention.[25] They are at one and the same time the product of a dynamic process of evangelism and nurture, and the tools for accomplishing that pro-

---

[23]W. C. van Unnik, " 'The Book of Acts,' the Confirmation of the Gospel", *NovT* 4 (1960): 26-59.

[24]At the risk of estranging my colleagues in Old Testament studies, I would suggest that this characteristic shape of the New Testament distinguishes it from the Old Testament, where, although the missionary motif is by no means absent, it certainly could not be said to exercise a decisive influence over the action generally.

[25]Call it the author's intention or the text's intention, as you wish!

cess. It is the recognition of this organizing principle that enables us to have a coherent understanding of them. Essentially the New Testament is a collection of books that express the gospel or good news that was proclaimed in the Christian mission. Thus David Wenham suggests "that New Testament theology is all about the divine mission to the world", and he argues that it can be structured in terms of the context, center, community and climax of mission.[26]

Adoption of this guiding proposal means that we do not make the mistake of seeing the theology of the New Testament as primarily ecclesiastical or ecclesiological, that is, of seeing the central interest as being the church and its life and its structures, although that is not entirely mistaken. Recognition of the missionary orientation of the New Testament will alert us to a more dynamic view of the church as the agent of mission instead of the static view that we sometimes have. Nor is the interest of the New Testament primarily in christology for its own sake, but rather in the function of Christ as God's agent in bringing about reconciliation. We shall also be enabled to avoid a one-sided understanding of the Holy Spirit as the agent of sanctification and to pay proper attention to the Spirit's role in empowering and directing the church for mission and growth.

Elsewhere we shall have cause to note more than once the important and very helpful classification of three aspects of the action in the New Testament made by Stauffer; he notes the doxological, antagonistic and soteriological facets of what happens—the elements of glorifying God, overcoming evil and saving the lost.[27] There is a natural tendency to give primacy to the doxological on the grounds that the highest activity of human beings is to glorify God and even what God does is intended to increase his glory. That is correct, but since the glorification of God should be the ultimate aim of all our activity, a stress on glorification may fail to express what is especially characteristic of the New Testament, namely, that the specific way in which God is glorified is through mission. Ultimately the main concern of God's people

---

[26]In his contribution to George Eldon Ladd, *A Theology of the New Testament* (Grand Rapids, Mich.: Eerdmans, 1974; 2nd ed., 1993, ed. D. A. Hagner), pp. 712-13. For a history of the first Christians as specifically the history of mission see Eckhard J. Schnabel, *Early Christian Mission*, 2 vols. (Downers Grove, Ill.: InterVarsity Press, 2004).

[27]Stauffer, *New Testament Theology*, p. 28 and *passim*.

should be to glorify him, but recognition of this obligation does not require that this is the main theme of the New Testament; the New Testament is primarily about God's mission and the message that is associated with it. Similarly, the antagonistic motif is clearly of great importance, in that the powers of evil and death must be overcome if humanity is to be rescued, but this victory is not an end in itself: the triumph of the crucified must be proclaimed to humankind and become a reality for them—through mission. Again, soteriology is understood in a one-sided manner if attention is centered purely on the work of Christ as if it were an end in itself. It is significant that in Paul the fact of reconciliation achieved by the death of Christ and the proclamation of reconciliation by his messengers (leading to the human acceptance of reconciliation) belong together as the two essential and integral parts of God's saving action.

To identify the underlying rationale of the New Testament in this way is not to state what might be regarded as an arbitrary presupposition for study; rather it is a thesis to be tested by the investigation, a proposition to be tried out to see whether it is justified by the results of the study rather than a procrustean bed into which we try to fit everything regardless of whether it fits. The reader should understand, therefore, that this section of the introduction was written (as all good introductions should be) after the substance of the book was completed and it was becoming clearer what the results of the study were.

### The New Testament as Part of the Bible

The New Testament is not freestanding. Along with the Old Testament it forms part of the Christian Bible. It arose in the historical context of the work and teaching of Jesus and the development of the early Christian church. It stands at the beginning of the historical development of systematic, dogmatic theology. It remains to consider each of these three relationships and their relevance for the task.

If we consider the New Testament as part of the Bible, some important and unavoidable questions arise that lead in turn to two or three related tasks.

First, the early Christians saw themselves as the heirs of the religion expressed in the Old Testament and in Judaism. They came to think of themselves as standing in continuity with the people who worshiped the God of Abraham, Isaac and Jacob, and whose literary expression is what they came to call the Old

Testament.[28] An essential enquiry, therefore, is to determine the relationships between the two Testaments: in particular, how did the New Testament writers understand the Old Testament and make use of it?

Second, would it be possible and indeed preferable to write a biblical theology or theology of the whole Bible rather than simply a theology of either Testament? This would be a mammoth task, rendered the more difficult by the fact that Old Testament scholars don't show a lot of agreement about how to write a theology of their own Testament. Such a work would have the same problems that occur in dealing with either Testament on its own, the problem of dealing with a large body of literary works from a very wide period of time, with a wide range of literary forms and with a huge range of ideas, many of which may appear to be contradictory, some primitive and some more highly developed. Nevertheless, the aim is to be welcomed as representing a desirable goal, and there are at least two attempts to date to fulfill it.[29]

Third, a less ambitious task is indicated in the titles of books that attempt to write a biblical theology of the New Testament. What this means is that there is a recognition that the roots of the thinking of the New Testament writers lie in the Old Testament (and its transmission within the literature of Judaism) and that one task of the theologian is to lay bare the roots and to show how they have determined the way in which the tree has grown and borne fruit. The work of Hans Hübner is a detailed attempt to carry out this program, but with the tendency to concentrate on this aspect of New Testament theology only and to leave on one side other material. A broader and more satisfying approach is that of Peter Stuhlmacher, whose two-volume treatment is governed by the principle that "the theology of the New Testament is to be designed as a biblical theology of the New Testament that takes its origin from the Old

---

[28]Until comparatively recently among Christians the two parts of the Christian Bible have been known as the Old and New Testaments. Many people feel that this nomenclature implies a verdict upon the earlier Testament that is insensitive to those who also accept it as Scripture but do not accept the Christian faith. Hence the neutral term "Hebrew Bible" has come into use as a term that Jews and Christians can share. The term is not an entirely happy one in that its antithesis might appear to be the "Greek Bible", a term that however refers to the translation of the Hebrew Bible into Greek. Within this book, which is concerned with how Christians understand the earlier body of Scriptures we shall retain the traditional method of reference.

[29]Brevard S. Childs, *Biblical Theology of the Old and New Testaments: Theological Reflection on the Christian Bible* (Minneapolis: Fortress, 1993); Charles H. H. Scobie, *The Ways of Our God: An Approach to Biblical Theology* (Grand Rapids, Mich.: Eerdmans, 2003).

Testament and is open to it and is to be understood as a part of a biblical theology that considers the Old and New Testaments together."[30] Stuhlmacher is right: a study of New Testament theology should be concerned to trace the characteristics that arise out of the ingredients that have been worked and shaped to give it its present form.[31]

What is at issue perhaps is a question of focus. The present project would become unmanageable in length and would stray far outside the author's competence if it were to attempt a biblical theology of the Bible. However, a theology of the New Testament must surely be a biblical theology of the New Testament since there is no way that we can avoid the fact that the thinking of the New Testament writers is shaped by the Old Testament in two ways. The one is that they are all Jews, whether by birth or in their way of thinking, and therefore they are thinking within the framework of a Judaism that was shaped by the Old Testament. The other is that they make their own distinctive and deliberate forays into the Old Testament in order to develop their theology. The influence of the Old Testament is not that of an environment passively accepted but rather of a quarry enthusiastically mined.

It is appropriate here to refer to one of the shortest but most seminal books of modern New Testament study, C. H. Dodd's *According to the Scriptures*. Dodd did two things in this book. The first of them, widely recognized and debated, was his claim that rather than going to selected, isolated proof texts in the Old Testament, the New Testament writers went to selected fruitful areas within which they found material that they understood in a contextual manner. The second point, which is perhaps only now receiving due recognition, is that Dodd argued that this activity with the Old Testament formed what he called the "sub-structure" of New Testament theology, by which I take it he meant that the Old Testament provided the New Testament writers with the key categories and broad structure of a theology for which the major structure was given by the saving history which they interpreted so as to bring out its innate significance. The substructure is ad-

---

[30]Peter Stuhlmacher, *Biblische Theologie des Neuen Testaments*, 2 vols. (Göttingen: Vandenhoeck & Ruprecht, 1992, 1999), 1:5. A translation of this comprehensive work into English is an urgent necessity.

[31]The first and the third tasks are complementary in that the first asks how the New Testament writers understood the Old Testament and the third asks how the Old Testament influenced the thought of the New Testament writers.

mittedly much more determinative in some writings than in others, and it
may function in different ways, but of its presence and importance there can
be no doubt. It follows that an account of New Testament theology will inevitably offer a biblical theology in that we cannot avoid showing how the
biblical revelation as a whole is related to that particular cross-section we
call the New Testament.

### The Place of Jesus in New Testament Theology

It is well known that the most famous New Testament theology of the twentieth century, that of Rudolf Bultmann, deliberately put the teaching of Jesus on
one side as a presupposition of New Testament theology rather than as part of
its content and gave it the minimum of discussion.

There is a trivial sense, of course, in which Bultmann was right. If we are
writing a theology of the New Testament, Jesus was not one of its authors, and
therefore his thinking and teaching are not the thinking and teaching of a New
Testament author. Equally, when Bultmann included a much lengthier discussion of the kerygma of the earliest church and of the Hellenistic church, he consistently also made this part of the "Presuppositions and Motifs of New Testament Theology" rather than part of the theology itself.

However, there is a stronger argument, namely, that Jesus was not a Christian
theologian. Christian theology, it can be claimed, is the thinking of Christians
about Jesus, and it is not hard to defend the view that it is centered on his death
and resurrection and their implications; Jesus, however, was concerned with the
kingdom of God and only indirectly with himself, and only rarely with his own
future. Jesus, therefore, was doing something different from his followers, and
this is an additional reason for not regarding him as a Christian theologian.

Nevertheless, this argument can be refuted by the observation that the teaching of Jesus is taken up into the New Testament by the Evangelists in their Gospels. They considered it to be their task to relate much of what he said and, in
so doing, to accept it as part of their own message. We shall have to follow this
route. In a book on New Testament theology the emphasis must lie on the
teaching of the actual authors, but attention must also be paid to Jesus himself
as one of the major sources of their thinking. But how should this be done?

Here we must note that the Evangelists thought it important not merely to
record the teaching of Jesus but also to present his life story, or rather those

parts of it that they considered to be relevant to their audiences, at length and thematically in their Gospels.[32] It is highly significant that at a time when many of the letters had already been written and some were presumably known more widely than simply in their original destinations, there were Christian believers who felt that it was necessary to record how they saw and understood the life of Jesus. This shows, incidentally, that although one can be an early Christian theologian, like Paul, and say next to nothing about the life and teaching of Jesus, the early church was ultimately unsatisfied with this and the theology of the letters was seen in the wider context of the integration of the life and teaching of Jesus into the theological works that we know as the Gospels.[33] Thus the historical Jesus and his teaching find their way into the New Testament and so into its theology primarily through the medium of the Gospels.

We could say, then, that the historical Jesus is relevant to New Testament theology at three levels.

First, Jesus is the historical person whose activity and message, more than that of anybody else, formed and shaped the church, and therefore he has as much right to be heard for his own sake as Paul or John, and certainly far more than any hypothetical unknown figures who bridge the gap between him and the earliest New Testament writers.

Second, his historical activity is the starting point from which developed the whole Christian movement and its thought and practice, and therefore a study of his influence is appropriate. In this sense, Jesus is the presupposition of the theology of his followers.

Third, Jesus is the subject of reflection in the Gospels, and therefore the writings of the Evangelists must be considered as a significant part of the search for the theology of the New Testament.

In terms of these three levels of approach Bultmann treated the message of Jesus only at the second level. He somehow managed to overlook the third level

---

[32]It has become traditional to refer to this as the "ministry" of Jesus, probably on the basis of the way in which he spoke of his role as one of a "servant" (Gk. *diakonos*; Lat. minister). It may be better to think of it as his *mission*, since this term conveys more clearly the content of the activity of Jesus in his capacity as God's representative ("apostle", Heb 3:1) among human beings.

[33]To call the Gospels theological works is in no sense to deny that they are historical works concerned to relate what happened, and the remarkable thing in the case of the Synoptic Gospels at least is that the historical facts required so little interpretation in order to function as early Christian theology.

and thus provided a classical example of how a developmental approach to New Testament theology could blind a scholar to the need to look at the finished products. He also, of course, could be said to have amalgamated the first level with the second (rather than totally omitting it), but part of the reason for the brevity of his treatment lay in a combination of his skepticism regarding the greater part of the record and his conviction that the history of what Jesus did was irrelevant for Christian faith; what mattered was the existential challenge that came over in the few sayings that can be certainly traced to his lips.

It would seem, then, that the appropriate method to follow would be the admittedly repetitious one in which Jesus is discussed in his own right at levels one and two, but also the contributions of the Evangelists are discussed subsequently in their own right.[34] However, the first part of this task faces a serious practical difficulty, namely, to what extent it is possible to offer a justified and well-founded reconstruction of the work and message of Jesus without bursting the limits appropriate to a book on New Testament theology. Such a reconstruction is a major historical problem in terms of extent and complexity, and there is much to be said for treating it on its own rather than including it in a treatment such as the present one.[35] There continues to be a major difference in scholarship between those who hold that the Synoptic Gospels offer a substantially reliable picture of how Jesus acted and spoke, and those who believe that the Gospel accounts are unreliable and that the historical Jesus was significantly different from the Gospel portraits of him; I have expressed my consid-

---

[34]This is the path followed by Leonhard Goppelt, *Theology of the New Testament*, 2 vols. (Grand Rapids, Mich.: Eerdmans, 1981, 1982), who discussed Jesus in great detail in volume 1 of his work and included Matthew and Luke in volume 2. According to his editor, J. Roloff, he left no material on Mark because he did not consider himself able at this stage in scholarship to take a mature view of this Gospel.

[35]The danger is that to do justice to the historical problems means that they can dominate the discussion and prevent the scholar from ever reaching the theology! This happened with Joachim Jeremias, *New Testament Theology: The Proclamation of Jesus* (London: SCM Press, 1971), and to a lesser extent with Goppelt; yet the example of Stuhlmacher, *Biblische Theologie*, shows that this need not happen. Contrast the work of Ferdinand Hahn, who discusses the proclamation and work of Jesus without entering into the historical questions to any extent, with the result that some of his guiding principles (especially that the christological "titles" do not go back to Jesus himself) are simply stated without argument; in this case, however, the author had dealt with the matter at great length in his earlier monograph, *The Titles of Jesus*. Hahn takes an important step forward in asking not only what the message and story of Jesus were (insofar as the historian can reconstruct them) but also how they were incorporated in the witness of the disciples and the early church (Hahn, *Theologie*, 1: 43).

ered opinion in favor of the former possibility elsewhere, and I shall prescind from further detailed justification of it here.[36] I shall therefore compromise by taking the opposite option from that adopted by Bultmann and shall discuss the theology of Jesus as it is presented to us by the Evangelists on the well-founded assumption that the Synoptic presentations of Jesus are sufficiently close to historical reality to enable us to use them to understand his mission and message.[37]

## New Testament Theology and Systematic Theology

Problems of a different kind arise when we consider the relation of this investigation to the modern world. The systematic analysis of Christian beliefs is sometimes called dogmatic theology. This term is intended to describe a theology that is not so much a description of what Christians believe as rather what they ought to believe. There are such things as creeds and confessions, which have a prescriptive character within Christian communities. Is a work on New Testament theology descriptive or prescriptive? We need to distinguish here between a book on New Testament theology, which in itself cannot be prescriptive, and New Testament theology itself, which must have some relevance to the theology of Christian believers. What may be possible is to present the teaching of the New Testament and say that it is prescriptive, subject to the condition that the modern author has correctly understood and depicted it. But clearly it would only be prescriptive for those who belong to a community of faith that includes the author and all those who believe that the New Testa-

---

[36]See further chap. 2 below. A position that is essentially upheld by such a combination of scholars as John P. Meier, Gerd Theissen and Annette Merz, and N. T. Wright (to name only a few out of the many who could be cited) can confidently hold its own against the skeptical wing in the Jesus Seminar and such scholars as Marcus J. Borg and John Dominic Crossan. See I. Howard Marshall, *I Believe in the Historical Jesus* (Vancouver: Regent College Publishing, 2004); Marcus J. Borg, *Jesus: A New Vision* (San Francisco: Harper, 1987); John Dominic Crossan, *The Historical Jesus: The Life of a Mediterranean Jewish Peasant* (Edinburgh: T & T Clark, 1991); John P. Meier, *A Marginal Jew: Rethinking the Historical Jesus*, 3 vols. (New York: Doubleday, 1991, 1994, 2001); Gerd Theissen and Annette Merz, *The Historical Jesus: A Comprehensive Guide* (London: SCM Press, 1998); N. T. Wright, *Jesus and the Victory of God* (London: SPCK, 1996). J. D. G. Dunn, *Jesus Remembered* (Grand Rapids, Mich.: Eerdmans, 2003), offers a powerful presentation of the earliest memories of Jesus that comes to cautiously conservative conclusions.

[37]The reader will observe that I have not included the Gospel of John at this point. In view of the differences in "idiom" in the presentation of Jesus there, it is methodologically preferable to set it on one side and consider it separately from the Synoptic Gospels at a later point.

ment is, or rather is part of, Christian Scripture, which is true and authoritative for them and in their opinion ought to be so for humankind generally.[38]

Yet the prescriptive element is hard to eliminate. The modern author who believes that (some of) the statements in the New Testament are true will consider himself or herself to be passing on teaching that is true and valid for the readers. Equally there are modern authors who may point out the contradictions that they find within the New Testament and nudge the readers toward the statements that they consider to be more worthy of belief and away from those which are less acceptable. Or the modern author may feel free to interpret the statements in a way that the ancient author would not have recognized. And the modern author may be quite unconsciously constrained in these directions by forces of which he or she is unaware, being a child of the contemporary age. This particularly arises in relation to the ethical teaching of the New Testament, where the tendency to make it fit into one's own set of principles is all the stronger and the more difficult to detect.

The effect is that the author then becomes a deliberate interpreter of the New Testament as opposed to being the unconscious interpreters that we cannot avoid being. Authors may simply say that the teaching of the New Testament is to be taken as it stands and accepted by the church today. That in itself is a form of interpretation. They may also attempt some kind of process to reinterpret those parts of New Testament theology which they believe to be expressed in a time-bound manner so as to avoid misunderstanding, and they may try positively to re-express the message in such a way that it will speak to modern people. Provided that they are aware that this is what they are doing and are as self-conscious as possible about the procedure, then this approach is surely valid, if not unavoidable.[39]

The New Testament must be understood first of all and as far as possible on its own terms, as an expression of thought within the ways that were possible in the first century. These ways may be different from our own, shaped by subsequent centuries of intellectual development. Inevitably we tend to accept those ways of thinking that cohere with our own and to reject those that do

---

[38]The situation of the author is the same as that of Christian preachers who believe that they are called by God to proclaim and teach the gospel but recognize that this calling does not make them infallible.

[39]This seems to me to be the case whether or not one believes that the Bible is infallible in its teaching.

not. If the New Testament writers had not yet envisaged a heliocentric frame-work within which a spherical earth rotates round the sun but believed in a flat earth at the center of the universe, then there is no way that modern people[40] are going to share their physical framework of thought. But what do we do with the belief in the existence of God, which is confidently denied by many in the vanguard of modern thought, or the existence of supernatural actors and the reality of supernatural actions that might be denied by even more people? May there not be some extent to which the modern framework is challenged by the New Testament one?

Scholars who insist that New Testament scholars step out of their legitimate area when they write theology are recognizing that what is being done is in some sense prescriptive and are arguing that they should confine themselves to history. This distinction is ultimately based on the separation between historical and dogmatic theology that can be traced back to a famous essay by J. P. Gabler (1787).[41] However, it must be remembered that what motivated Gabler was the fettering of scholarship by the ecclesiastical orthodoxy of the time, and the value of his distinction was that it enabled scholars to study the theology of the New Testament unfettered by the need to provide an account that was in line with the theology of the contemporary church. But it is doubtful whether that danger is present today; granted that there are some institutions within which teachers must adhere to a party line, it is normally the case that scholars are not bound to any declarations of dogmatic theology that would prevent them from dealing honestly with the text. Rather there is the possibility of fruitful dialogue in which New Testament scholars can speak to the church and vice versa.

Balla's defense of the study over against the criticism of Räisänen is, as we saw, to claim that what we are providing is essentially a descriptive account of the theological thinking of the early Christians, that is, a historical task. I think that this is a fundamentally sound riposte. Nevertheless, some of us do under-

---

[40]I find it very hard to avoid the use of this term *modern* to refer to my contemporaries, even though some would insist that we have now moved on into a postmodern period. The thinking of all of us, whether we admit it or not, is shaped too significantly by contemporary thought, and it is this dif-ference between ancient thought and contemporary thought that I have primarily in mind when I use the word *modern* in a broad sense that does not exclude so-called postmodern thinking.

[41]J. Sandys-Wunsch and L. Eldredge, "J. P. Gabler and the Distinction Between Biblical and Dogmatic Theology: Translation, Commentary and Discussion of His Originality", *SJT* 33 (1980): 133-58.

take this task as Christians and do so within the context of the Christian community to which we belong. Doing theology is properly a Christian activity carried out ideally within the community of faith, as Francis Watson in particular has cogently and correctly argued.[42] But if what I have said about the freedom enjoyed by scholars within the church is true, then there is no need for scholars to keep their scholarship and their faith in separate compartments and never let either influence the other.

It follows that the approach to be taken here is in close sympathy with that advocated by Watson, who laments the fragmentation of the studies of Old Testament theology, New Testament theology and systematic theology to the detriment of each of the three enterprises.

## A Proposal Regarding Procedure

If we now put this all together, I suggest that the following guidelines are emerging for the construction of a New Testament theology.

The scope of the work is the books of the New Testament. The task is defined by the canon.

The books must be understood in the context provided by the Jewish Scriptures; the thought of the contemporary world, especially that of Judaism but not excluding the wider Hellenistic world; the development of early Christian thinking, including currents of theology rejected as well as those accepted by the New Testament authors; the later Christian writings which take us further along the trajectories that pass through the New Testament. The task must be conducted contextually and so biblically.

As the fundamental context for the development of early Christian thinking we must pay full attention to the activity and teaching of Jesus, while recognizing that the methodological problems are so great that they cannot be handled fully within the limitations of this book. The task must include jesusology as well as christology.

As a further part of the context we must handle the documents in the setting of the Christian mission by Jesus and by his followers out of which they have arisen. Our interpretation must be missiological.

The starting point must be the attempt to elucidate the theology of the in-

---

[42]Francis B. Watson, *Text and Truth: Redefining Biblical Theology* (Edinburgh: T & T Clark, 1997).

dividual documents as expressions of the writers' theology directed to specific occasions or purposes and from them to work back to the core beliefs. This is the stage of description.

At this and all stages it will be helpful to recognize the distinction between the assumed framework of a writer's theology, the central thrust of his theology and the more detailed outworking of it. Nevertheless, this heuristic tool must not be applied in an over-rigid manner. This is the stage of analysis.

When this has been done, it will be possible to explore to some extent the way in which these various expressions of theology have developed, while avoiding the temptation to be diverted into an attempt to write a history of New Testament theology. This is the stage of studying development.

It is important, however, to remember that we are dealing with a collection of books that was the object of canonization, and therefore it is essential to determine the ways in which these books display common beliefs and variety of beliefs and whether they constitute an essentially harmonious collection or stand in tension or even contradiction at various points. This is the stage of attempting synthesis.

A conceivable further stage is to discuss in what ways the theology as a whole and in its several parts has been and should be taken up into the dogmatic theology of the church. We may call this application. We shall have quite sufficient on our plate without attempting this further task, and in any case this is an area for cooperation between the New Testament scholar and the systematic theologian rather than for the former to attempt it alone.

In this book, then, I shall concentrate more on describing and analyzing the theologies of the New Testament books and their authors, and considering whether the evidence entitles us to speak of a unified theology of the New Testament. My procedure will be to start with the Synoptic Gospels and their presentation of the mission and teaching of Jesus, followed by Acts; the next major section of the book will be devoted to the Pauline letters, followed by the Johannine literature, and finally the remaining books of the New Testament.

## Bibliography

See the general bibliography.

Borg, Marcus J. *Jesus: A New Vision.* San Francisco: Harper, 1987.

Crossan, John Dominic. *The Historical Jesus: The Life of a Mediterranean Jewish Peasant.* Edinburgh: T & T Clark, 1991.

Dunn, James D. G. *Jesus Remembered*. Grand Rapids, Mich.: Eerdmans, 2003.

Marshall, I. Howard. *I Believe in the Historical Jesus.* Vancouver: Regent College Publishing, 2004.

Meier, John P. *A Marginal Jew: Rethinking the Historical Jesus*. 3 vols. New York: Doubleday, 1991, 1994, 2001.

Theissen, Gerd, and Annette Merz. *The Historical Jesus: A Comprehensive Guide*. London: SCM Press, 1998.

Wright, N. T. *Jesus and the Victory of God*. London: SPCK, 1996.

# PART 2

## JESUS, THE SYNOPTIC GOSPELS AND ACTS

# 2

# THE GOSPELS AND
# NEW TESTAMENT THEOLOGY

⤳◦⤸

No area of New Testament theology is easy, but the theology of the Gospels is particularly difficult since our study is beset by a complex of overlapping problems.

## *The Gospels and Their Sources*

At the outset there is the problem of distinguishing between what is common to all the Gospels and what is peculiar to the specific one under immediate consideration. Very often the differences are merely in emphasis and nuance, and there is the danger of exaggerating them so that the Gospels appear more different from one another than they are. For example, one might regard the motif that Jesus is a teacher as characteristic of Matthew, but it is attested and indeed front-staged in all the Gospels. Luke's Gospel may be preeminently the Gospel of prayer, but teaching about prayer is found in all the Gospels. The differences are most marked between John and the group of Synoptic Gospels,[1] but they all deal with recognizably the same figure of Jesus.

The similarities are due to the common dependence of the Gospels on the

---

[1]I use this accepted collective term for the Gospels of Matthew, Mark and Luke. It rests on the fact that the considerable similarities in order and content between these three Gospels make it possible and helpful for the student to have an arrangement of them in parallel columns so that the contents of any one Gospel can be conveniently compared with the similar material in the others. Such an arrangement is called a synopsis. While the exercise can be extended to include the parallel passages in the Gospel of John, the very considerable differences between it and the other Gospels set it apart from them.

traditions of the early church about Jesus as these have been mediated by inter-
mediate sources. The theological similarities of the Synoptic Gospels as well as
the narrative similarities are due to these interrelationships and use of common
materials. In what follows it will be assumed that Matthew and Luke each made
use of Mark, editing and incorporating the major portion of its contents, rather
more in the case of Matthew and somewhat less in the case of Luke. It will also
be assumed that Matthew and Luke both had access to sayings of Jesus together
with some narratives generally referred to by the symbol Q. Each Evangelist
also used materials that were not used by the others.[2]

The precise extent and nature of Q is dubious on two accounts. First, the
fact that neither Matthew nor Luke incorporated the whole of Mark into their
Gospels and the further fact that they were independently attempting to merge
their material from Q with that from Mark make it probable that neither writer
necessarily included the whole of Q in his Gospel and that consequently each
writer may include material that the other omitted. The Q material will have
included not only the texts that Matthew and Luke have in common, but also
material preserved by only one of them and material that was preserved by neither of them. Second, there is an ongoing debate about the composition and
development of Q, and no firm consensus has yet emerged on its nature and
shape. For myself, I tend to side with those who doubt the existence of Q as a
single document.[3] In view of the difficulty in establishing its contents on the
basis of comparison of Matthew and Luke, attempts to formulate its theology
with precision may seem to be rash.[4]

We thus have difficulties in attempting to characterize the theology of the
Evangelists in terms of what they have done with their sources. We can compare
Matthew and Luke with their putative source, Mark, and we can compare the

---

[2]The symbols M and L are sometimes used for the materials peculiar to Matthew and Luke respectively. Discussion of the origins of the materials used by Mark lies beyond our scope here.

[3]See most recently Maurice Casey, *An Aramaic Approach to Q: Sources for the Gospels of Matthew and Luke*
(Cambridge: Cambridge University Press, 2002). This view is to be carefully distinguished from that
of scholars who dispense altogether with Q and claim that Luke derived the non-Markan material
that he has in common with Matthew from Matthew itself. Even if we follow this latter group and
dispense with Q, we have still to account for the origin of the material in Matthew that is not based
on Mark.

[4]For a helpful introductory guide to the matters summarized here, see Steve Walton and David Wenham, *Exploring the New Testament*, vol.I, *The Gospels and Acts* (London: SPCK; Downers Grove, Ill.: Inter-
Varsity Press, 2001).

Matthean and Lukan versions of their other putative but lost source, Q, but the tasks must be done with great caution. It will clearly be better to analyze each Gospel in terms of its own narrative and discourse.

## The Gospels and Jesus

Next, we have the problem of the relation of the material in the Gospels to the career, deeds and teaching of Jesus. Since we do not know how Mark's material reached him and we do not have any firm evidence regarding the other sources used by Matthew and Luke, it could well seem that we should be profoundly agnostic regarding the authenticity of the picture of Jesus in the Gospels. Such an attitude, however, is unnecessarily pessimistic and indeed ill founded. Let us consider two of the possible distortions that could arise.

There is, first, the possibility that the Evangelists seriously modified the materials that they had and exercised their creativity in the way that they put together their Gospels and even in the composition of fresh material. This is a not uncommon view in some quarters of New Testament scholarship. It must suffice here to make the point that the pictures of Jesus in the Synoptic Gospels are very similar to one another and that the editing of the sources (Mark and Q) is very conservative; this encourages the view that the Evangelists, or at least Matthew and Luke, were not wild innovators.

But there is also, second, the possibility that the materials that the Evangelists inherited had already been significantly modified and in some cases created in the early church. Our earlier comment on the lack of consensus regarding the development of the Q material may be thought to point in this direction, with its implication that the process of transmission can no longer be satisfactorily traced. However, there are good grounds for assuming that the handing down of tradition in the early church was "controlled"[5], and the skepticism voiced above about Q was about the possibility or likelihood of establishing a complicated series of stages and layers in its composition. There is the strong possibility that the material substantially goes back to Jesus and that it was handed down faithfully without being manipulated within a very hypothetical Q community. This is admittedly a controversial stance to take, and it is adopted de-

---

[5]See Kenneth Bailey, "Informal Controlled Oral Tradition and the Synoptic Gospels", *Themelios* 20 (1995): 4-11.

spite awareness that a very different kind of view is taken, for example, by the so-called Jesus Seminar.

So long as we are looking at the theologies of the Evangelists at the level of their composition, different decisions about tradition history need not affect the matter overmuch, but once we ask about the development of their theologies and their relationship to what went on earlier, so soon do these questions become pressing.

When due allowance is made for the individual editing of the traditions by the Evangelists, we have in the Synoptic Gospels a faithful representation of how Jesus appeared to his earliest followers. Their memory of him stands up well to the tests for authenticity and inauthenticity that have been developed by critical scholars. The main area of dispute concerns the christological titles that occur on the lips of Jesus and other actors in the Gospels. All that I can do here is to reaffirm the position that I take, namely, that there are solid grounds for accepting the substantial authenticity of the tradition.[6] This section of the book will accordingly deal with two matters simultaneously, the mission and teaching of Jesus as the basis of early Christian theology, and the theological understanding of Jesus by the Evangelists.

### The Gospels and Other New Testament Writings

How is what the Evangelists were doing related to the other theological activities of the early Christians? Elsewhere in this book we look at a number of early Christians who expressed their theology in the form of letters to their fellow Christians. They were largely concerned with a figure who had appeared as a human being and been put to death but who was now risen from the dead and exalted to being beside God. From this position he had become a source of spiritual blessings, an object of devotion and worship, a spiritual being with whom some kind of personal relationship was possible, and a person who was expected to take a decisive role in future events associated with the consummation of God's purposes. In their accounts the career of this figure on earth from his birth to just

---

[6]Here I place myself alongside the position defended by Peter Stuhlmacher over against that represented, for example, by Ferdinand Hahn. The term "substantial authenticity" in the text recognizes, for example, that there are individual cases where titles have been added or subtracted in the tradition, or where the Evangelists have brought out more explicitly points that they believed to be implicit in their sources, or brought out the significance of what Jesus taught more pertinently for their readers.

before his death was in no way the focus of attention, although it was not ignored.

Now, however, we have the Evangelists writing at some point after the kind of theology just summarized was already in existence. Their style of writing is narrative, including discourse by Jesus, which is virtually foreign to the other New Testament writers; they stop at the resurrection of Jesus, although there are some predictions about events still to happen; and they go into detail about what this earthly being did and said, reporting teaching that does not appear to have been a part of the gospel proclaimed by the other early Christians, though not necessarily unknown to them. How, then, is what the Evangelists were doing related to the kind of Christianity represented by the Letters and their authors? Why are there at first sight so few points of contact between them? Do we have two rather different types of theology in the New Testament? The problem perhaps does not strike the average reader quite so strongly, because it is not strange to read the Gospels first, as their canonical order places them, and then to go on in historical order to see what the followers of Jesus did after his departure and how they tended to proclaim him rather than to repeat his proclamation. But if we consider things in the order of composition, then we see that the early Christians were proclaiming Jesus before they felt the need to write Gospels about what he had done and proclaimed, and we have this curious fact that the Letters tend to ignore what is of major concern to the Evangelists.

The problem is partially eased by a number of considerations. First, there is the fact that the disjunction between the two types of literature is not an absolute one. It is true that there does seem to be a curious reticence on the part of writers of letters not to cite directly what Jesus said, a reticence illustrated most clearly in the fact that the letters of John, which must come from the same stable as the Gospel, whether or not they are by the same author, do not refer to the teaching of Jesus whereas the Gospel is filled with his teaching.[7] However, at the same time there is a certain amount of allusion to what Jesus taught in some of the letters, notably in James and I Peter, and to some extent in Paul.[8]

---

[7]Or, at least, with what is presented as his teaching. The problem of the relationship between the discourses in John and the teaching of the historical Jesus need not be raised here. The point is simply that the Gospel presents what purports to be teaching of Jesus.

[8]See Seyoon Kim, "Jesus, Sayings of", in *DPL*, pp. 474-92; Graham N. Stanton, "Jesus Traditions", in *DLNTD*, pp. 565-79. There is no doubt that Paul, for example, knew at least some of the teaching of Jesus; the problem is why the writers of the Letters rarely cited it directly.

Second, it is most significant that the Gospel of Luke forms part of a two-volume work that goes on to tell the story of what happened after the death of Jesus in a way that is plainly intended to be understood as a continuation of the story in the Gospel. Luke had no difficulty in understanding what happened in the early church, with its proclamation about Jesus, as being in continuity with what Jesus had begun to do and to preach. Luke saw the story of Jesus as an essential part of his account of Christian origins.

Third, it would be wrong to assume that the material in the Gospels came into existence chronologically after the Letters, even if the Gospels themselves were composed later. Although the dates of composition of the Gospels are uncertain and there is a strong consensus that many, if not most, of the Letters were composed earlier, it is certain that the traditions behind the Gospels were contemporary with the period of letter writing. It is true that attempts have been made to argue that some Christian communities possessed only the preaching of people like Paul, while others possessed only the teaching of Jesus and paid scant account to his death, but these attempts fly in the face of all probability.[9]

These considerations reduce the size of the problem without altogether removing it. They suggest that the early Christians understood their movement as stemming from Jesus, that at first they handed down his story by word of mouth, perhaps as a "sacred story", and that with the spread of the church they began to feel the need to write down their foundational story.

---

[9]Walter Schmithals has developed the hypothesis that the early church tradition managed for many years without the "gospel" type of material. He holds that some traditions about the earthly Jesus were preserved in the Q traditions by a group of non-Christians, for whom the Q document functioned as their sole source of knowledge and input about him; since it does not mention the death and resurrection of Jesus, it is argued that these were not significant for them. Mark was then the first to bring together the preaching about the crucified and risen Lord and the traditions, many of them unhistorical and inauthentic, about the earthly Jesus. See *Das Evangelium nach Markus*, 2 vols. (Gütersloh: Gütersloher Verlagshaus Mohn/Würzburg: Echter Verlag, 1979), 1:61-70. To the best of my knowledge, he has won no adherents.

For a less extreme view see John S. Kloppenborg Verbin, *Excavating Q: The History and Setting of the Sayings Gospel* (Edinburgh: T & T Clark, 2000), pp. 369-79, who argues that Q's view is "different" from those of Paul and Mark.

# 3

# THE GOSPEL OF MARK

❦

Mark begins with a statement (Mk 1:1) whose reference is not crystal clear. It could mean "This book is the beginning of the good news about Jesus", or else "This (i.e., the immediately following story) is how the good news of Jesus begins". Either way, the verse makes clear that the following account is presented as "gospel" and that the subject is Jesus Christ, the Son of God. Both points are significant.

First, the story of Jesus is seen as a piece of good news; more specifically it is good news that comes from God and, in the light of the usage in Isaiah, the good news from God is concerned with salvation, that is, the well-being in the truest and fullest sense of human beings.[1]

Second, the story is about a specific person whose name was Jesus (a name that elsewhere is seen to be significant because it means "Yahweh saves") but who is also said to be "Christ", a term that here must retain its significance as a name with a meaning, namely, "Messiah"; thus it refers to a person anointed or appointed by God to a specific role, here probably to be the vice-regent in God's kingdom.[2] If the text of the Gospel translated in most versions is sound, the phrase "the Son of God" now follows, and

---

[1] In this context it might well be assumed that the good news is, however, simply for Jews (Mk 1:5).

[2] Here only in Mark do we have the combination "Jesus Christ" that is so common in Acts and the Letters. Although elsewhere "Christ" may have become more of a name than a meaningful title, the usage later in the Gospel requires that it retain its original significance here.

this states who Jesus is in an even more exalted manner.[3]

All of these terms were current in the church in Mark's time and earlier to express the status and role of Jesus. So what Mark is doing is going back to the beginning of how the early Christians came to believe this about Jesus. The story of Jesus functions as an explanation that, among other things, tells how Jesus presented himself and how his followers came to understand who he was and what he came to do. That, in simplified terms, is what the Gospel of Mark is about. The unfolding story will show us this process taking place.

### Mark's Theological Story

The beginning of Mark's narrative is constrained by the traditional framework, which saw the story of Jesus as "beginning from John's baptism" (Acts 1:22; 10:37). But this beginning itself is placed in a wider framework by seeing it as a fulfillment of the prophecy in Malachi 3:1 and Isaiah 40:3, a coupling of the prediction in the last prophetic book that God's coming would be preceded by that of his messenger and of a proclamation of God's coming in the wilderness. These prophecies were seen to be fulfilled in the appearance of John, nicknamed "the baptizer", whose story has a double significance.

On the one hand, he called people to repent of their sins and receive forgiveness, symbolized in a rite of religious washing with water; John's message received its urgency from his prophecy that he would be followed by another person who would carry out a similar rite but with the Holy Spirit. Mark does not have, perhaps does not know, the fuller form of John's words found in Matthew and Luke, which couple "fire" with the Holy Spirit, thereby probably denoting that the coming action would bring judgment upon the unrepentant and some kind of spiritual cleansing for the repentant. John's words in Mark evidently refer only to the promise of a spiritual cleansing.[4]

On the other hand, almost casually John's subjects for baptism include

---

[3]Some important manuscripts omit this phrase, and some doubt as to whether it is original is unavoidable (it is omitted in TNIV text and NRSV mg.; cf. Peter M. Head, "A Text-Critical Study of Mark 1.1 'The Beginning of the Gospel of Jesus Christ' ", NTS 37 [1991]: 621-29). In any case the immediately following statement in Mk 1:11 and other statements later in the Gospel show that this is how Mark understood the status of Jesus.

[4]John's prophecy does not appear to suggest that the forgiveness of sins offered in conjunction with his own water baptism was in any sense unreal or incomplete.

"Jesus from Nazareth in Galilee", introduced by a name with which readers would be familiar but apparently as an ordinary member of the crowd, yet nevertheless one to whom something remarkable happens. As he emerges from baptism with water, he experiences the Spirit coming down from above upon him and hears a voice identifying him as "my Son; with you I am well pleased". Although this event is not described as a baptism with the Spirit, it does look as though this is the baptism of the Spirit happening to the One who will baptize others with the Spirit. In the rest of the Gospel it may be assumed that Jesus does what he does and says what he says under the guidance and power of the Spirit, who is now permanently with him (Mk 1:12; cf. Mk 3:29). The incident is something like the calling of a prophet, but the language used is reminiscent of what God says to his anointed one (i.e., the king) in Psalm 2:7 and to his servant, on whom he puts his Spirit so that he may bring justice to the world, in Isaiah 42:1-4. The effect is thus to initiate Jesus into the office of God's coming king, since the Old Testament passages, or certainly Psalm 2, were by now understood as prophecies still awaiting fulfillment. A brief statement describes how Jesus is no sooner appointed to this office than he is brought by God into conflict with Satan, a name for the arch opponent of God and his plans, but is accompanied by angels who, it is to be assumed, strengthen him to oppose Satan (Mk 1:12-13).[5]

*A summary of the message.* All this so far, then, is the opening, the preliminaries that establish the appointment of Jesus to carry out his mission for God. The readers are privy to it, but not so the people of Galilee, who now witness the appearance of a man with a proclamation like that of the prophets. The prophets on the whole announced what God would do in the future, conditional upon the actions of the people; typically they pronounced prophecies of doom upon them because of their rebellion and idolatry, unless they repented, in which case there would be salvation instead of judgment. Jesus' teaching, however, is more in the language of fulfillment. "The time has come. The kingdom of God is near. Repent and believe the good news" (Mk 1:15). Probably Mark

---

[5]The story may seem odd. It refers to Jesus being tempted by Satan, whereas we might have expected that he would be opposed or that Satan would attempt to destroy him. It also refers enigmatically to Jesus being with the wild animals in the desert. And Jesus evidently needs angelic help to overcome his enemy. The impression given is of a story taken over by Mark that conveyed nuances going beyond his purpose.

wants his readers to understand the following points. First, just as the opening narrative indicated that prophecies were now being fulfilled, so Jesus announces to the people in general that the time of action has now come. Second, the action in question is the arrival of the kingdom of God. Third, this action is not primarily a threat but rather a piece of good news for those who hear it. Fourth, the proper response to it is repentance and faith.

This brief statement is of crucial importance for Mark and in some ways represents the text that is developed in the Gospel. More precisely, it sums up the proclamation of Jesus. Mark nowhere else tells us what Jesus said to the people at large when he took the initiative in giving a public proclamation; what he does give us are the usually brief responses of Jesus to particular questions or incidents and a collection of stories told by Jesus that are evidently his means of telling the message of the kingdom to the people.[6] Here alone do we have a summary of his message. It may seem strange that this is the one place where Mark tells us how Jesus addressed the people, particularly when we contrast the way in which in Acts we have several lengthy and somewhat repetitive accounts of what the apostles said in their public proclamation of the gospel. Mark's reticence is to be explained by a number of considerations. He may have been constrained by the amount of space at his disposal and the amount of broader material to be included. Again, the traditions available to him may not have given him any more information than this.[7] Further, Mark evidently believed that Jesus communicated with the people by means of parables, and he gives us several of these. And, finally, for Mark it was probably more important to present the role and identity of Jesus rather than his message.

Nevertheless, the question of the content of the message cannot be evaded. The term *kingdom* occurs with a theological sense no fewer than seventeen times in the Gospel. A kingdom in the ancient world is a geographical area and/or a people living in it that constitutes a unity in that it is governed by an all-powerful monarch. A parallel concept on a smaller scale is that of a household un-

---

[6]The other passages that contain fuller accounts of what Jesus said tend to be addressed to his followers who have responded positively to this message.

[7]Opinions differ as to whether Mark knew the material in Q; there are certainly sayings of Jesus in Mark which are doublets of Q sayings, but the differences in formulation suggest that Mark did not derive them from Q (i.e., from the common source that Matthew and Luke may be presumed to have used).

der the control of a householder. The term is used in various ways.

First, the kingdom is envisaged as something into which people may enter (Mk 9:47; 10:23-25; cf. Mk 14:25), and this realm appears to be the presence of God in a future state beyond death; people want to enter into "the age to come" as a blessed future when they depart this life.

Second, the kingdom is thought of as something that is to come in the future (Mk 9:1; 11:10; 15:43). The thought here is that somehow the future realm will become a reality here in this world, presumably a transformed world, so that the kingdom as transcendent and the kingdom as future are ideas that merge into each other. One might think of the heavenly rule of God into which people might enter through death becoming a reality by extending itself to take in this world.

Nevertheless, Jesus here says that the kingdom has drawn near. This remarkable announcement means that the kingdom promised for the future has already arrived or is about to arrive. The period of waiting is over. The heavenly rule of God is becoming a reality here in this world. This is the heart of the good news.

Third, the kingdom of God can be said to belong to certain people (children and those like them) in the sense that they are destined to become part of it (Mk 10:14) and to enjoy the privileges that it brings.

And, fourth, there is a secret about the kingdom that is shared with some people but not with others (Mk 4:10-12). This secret is made known to those who understand the parables told by Jesus.

The concepts of kingdom and household are also used of Satan (Mk 3:24-25). The world is regarded as the realm of Satan where people are under his control. To say that the kingdom of God is near is to suggest that a new realm is being set up under the control of God, and since at present Satan is in control this implies something like an invasion and the recovery of territory and people from the enemy who controls them. So one kind of language used by Jesus is that of conquest and deliverance of captives. At the same time, this is not the whole story; to some extent the captives are willing captives who need to shake themselves free of what binds them, and therefore the proclamation of Jesus includes the call to repentance.

But there is also the summons to belief in the good news. This element is crucial because what is happening is going to appear as something ambiguous, something that may not seem to be happening at all or to be happening otherwise than one might expect. The good news is from God, and therefore ultimately believing in the good news is believing that God is acting in what Jesus says and does.

*The mission in Galilee.* After this programmatic introduction Mark tells his story of Jesus' mission in a series of mostly brief episodes, in many of which the central or climactic feature is something said by Jesus. The initial incident is one in which he summons four fishermen to set aside their daily work and come with him to fish for people, and they for their part immediately obey (Mk 1:16-20). The story is told with intense brevity, and perhaps the overwhelming impression conveyed by it is that of the authority of Jesus, which is accepted by those who thus obey him.

In a large number of these short episodes Jesus does something unusual, generally by performing healings of various human disorders in a way that went beyond what people can normally do.[8] Thus doctors and surgeons can heal diseases and restore faculties by using various medicines and techniques whose effect normally takes time, but the stories about Jesus have him healing and restoring people simply by uttering a saying or command that has an instantaneous effect. These events would have seemed as wonderful to the people of the time as they would to us, and they suggested that some superhuman power was at work in him. This was also the case with people who appeared to be (as we would say) mentally deranged, suffering from delusions or feeling themselves to be possessed by alien powers. Such maladies were attributed to the person being taken over by a demonic power, and the cure was exorcism, that is, a command by a more powerful being to the demon to depart elsewhere. It is a story of this kind that opens up the narrative (Mk 1:21-28), and again the impression given is that of Jesus' unusual authority. At the same time the person cured, or rather the demonic spirit, attests that Jesus is "the Holy One of God", an unusual phrase that recognizes the source of Jesus' authority.

The story continues with accounts of specific healings of illness and skin disease, and generalizing comments about Jesus' travels round the area to speak

---

[8]For a full treatment of the historical and the theological aspects of the miracles in all the Gospels see Graham H. Twelftree, *Jesus the Miracle Worker: A Historical and Theological Study* (Downers Grove, Ill.: InterVarsity Press, 1999).

and to heal. An almost casual remark reveals that Jesus spent time in solitary prayer, and the reader is obviously meant to see in this practice the source of direction from God as to what he should do and the spiritual strength with which to accomplish it. In none of this is there anything particularly controversial, and the overwhelming impression conveyed by Mark is of a positive impact by Jesus arousing great popular interest.

But then controversy develops and becomes a major strand in the story. A series of incidents is described in which whatever Jesus does arouses opposition. He tells a paralyzed man that his sins are forgiven, thereby laying himself open to an accusation of usurping God's authority without any authorization to do so. Most peculiarly, he comments that this authority to forgive sins is attributed to "the Son of Man", a phrase that remains unexplained but is evidently understood to be a way of referring to himself (Mk 2:10, cf. Mk. 2:28).

He shows friendship to people marginalized by the respectable, religious society of the time because of a way of life that was, or was regarded as, incompatible with God's laws. He did not follow the strict religious practices of some Jews that involved abstention from food on certain days and from all kinds of work—the regulations were becoming all-embracing and unrealistic—on the seventh day of the week, which was regarded as a day of rest from all work. In particular he carried out one of his healings on the sabbath, and this was regarded as an unnecessary piece of "work". So from an early point, as Mark presents it, Jesus fell foul of people who evidently did not see in him an authoritative agent of God.

The story that continues to unfold thus has three strands entwined in it. First, there is the continuing activity of Jesus in speaking to the people and healing the sick in large numbers and their generally positive reception of him. Second, there is the development of opposition by upholders of a particularly legalistic form of Jewish religion.[9] And, third, there is his gathering together of a small group of men to be his companions and to share in the work that he was doing. These three strands are, as in any rope, intertwined with one another, and it is not too easy to separate them from one another, particularly since the

---

[9] I use the term *legalistic* here to refer to a form of religion that was characterized by the development of a rule mentality, with lots of minute regulations to be carried out and an emphasis on the paramount importance of keeping them.

audience of Jesus at any time was mixed in composition. We take up each of them in turn.

*Jesus and the people.* The activity of Jesus among the people can be categorized in terms of his teaching and his action.

Despite the often-repeated comment that Mark does not record much teaching of Jesus, he does in fact offer a substantial amount. One major section is in Mark 4, which contains five parables and parabolic sayings of Jesus from which we may gain some impression of how Mark envisages the kingdom of God as Jesus taught about it. The first parable (Mk 4:1-9) is the one that relates how a sower sows seed in four different types of ground; these produce varying amounts of growth—from none, through brief growth, to a variable yield of grain. Maybe the parable is so familiar to us that the broad application of it seems self-evident. The seed is the message of the kingdom, and it produces different results in different people, depending on whether external factors hinder its growth, but in some cases it grows as it should.

Nevertheless, even Jesus' closest associates did not understand the point of it and asked for an explanation. This is given in two stages. There is a general comment that an understanding of the mystery of the kingdom is given to some people, but others get nothing more than the stories, so that they are in the position of people who, for example, see a set of words in a foreign language that they can read but do not understand (Mk 4:10-12). But Jesus (or Mark) does not explain in any way how people come to be in one group rather than the other or how it is possible to pass from the uncomprehending to the comprehending group.

Then there comes a specific explanation of the parable to Jesus' friends (Mk 4:13-20). It is along the lines already indicated above. And it suggests that the parable may be a reflection of the experience of Jesus (confirmed by subsequent preachers) with his different audiences, but at the same time it is intended to be a call to the hearers to listen and to respond to the message.

The point of the next two sayings (Mk 4:21-25) is not certain. If they are still addressed to the Twelve, then they probably constitute a command to them to publicize what they hear about the kingdom and a warning to them to listen carefully to what they hear and not to ignore it.

The two remaining sayings compare the kingdom to the growth of a seed, which develops spontaneously without human intervention and becomes a plant or tree vast in size compared with the seed from which it sprang (Mk 4:26-32). This is most obviously interpreted to refer to the tremendous potential for growth of the kingdom despite its humble beginnings and the way in which it could easily be thought that God was not at work in a significant way in Jesus. This last point is perhaps illustrated in the way that, when Jesus returned to his home village of Nazareth, the people there could not believe that the local carpenter's boy was capable of doing what he was doing (Mk 6:1-6).

The recorded actions of Jesus are principally mighty works of the kind that were recorded at the outset of the Gospel, but some of them are even more impressive. They include the cure of a particularly violent demoniac; the healing of a woman with a hemorrhage; then, most remarkably of all, the raising to life of a child who died before Jesus could reach her (Mk 5); and, finally, two incidents in which Jesus was able to feed large numbers of people with tiny amounts of food that apparently were multiplied to provide enough for everybody (Mk 6:30-44; 8:1-10). The stories continue with an exorcism performed without seeing the demonized girl (Mk 7:24-30) and the cure of a deaf mute and a blind man (Mk 7:31-37; 8:22-26). Among other points two new features stand out in this series of stories. The one is that the stories contain echoes of material in the Old Testament—stories told about the activities of the prophets (Elijah and Elisha), statements about the power of God to quell nature and violent people, and prophecies about the coming time of peace and prosperity that God will bring about for his people. Jesus is understood as the prophet expected to come in the end time through whom God would exercise his transforming power. The other noteworthy feature is that some of these stories take place outside Judea and Galilee in territory inhabited overwhelmingly by non-Jews, and they give the impression that the coming of Jesus was not solely for the benefit of the Jews.

*Jesus in conflict.* Alongside this work among the ordinary people there is the development of conflict with the teachers of the law and the Pharisees who are seen as the religious establishment in the areas where Jesus worked.[10] Some of them attributed the superhuman powers of Jesus (whose reality apparently was

---

[10]The priests were based in Jerusalem and lived, when off duty, mostly in the surrounding area. Only when Jesus reaches Jerusalem do we hear of contacts with the Sadducees, who were the aristocratic leaders of the people, closely associated with the rich, priestly families that ran the temple.

not questioned) to black magic, as we would say, empowered by the ruler of the demons himself. Jesus regarded his mighty works as being done by the power of the Spirit of God and warned his opponents of the danger of scorning the power of God (Mk 3:22-30).

At this point Mark inserts the story of how King Herod Antipas put to death John the Baptist, who had spoken out against his dubious sexual ethics (Mk 6:14-29). The story is doubtless meant to cast a shadow over the story of Jesus, who will finish up in the same way if he too gets on the wrong side of the establishment. Preaching the kingdom of God carries a challenge to politicians. The occasion of the story is the way in which news about the activity of Jesus had reached the royal palace and was causing the superstitious king some uneasiness. Had John come back in some way to haunt him?[11]

But at this stage the direct opponents of Jesus come from the religious establishment. We have already noted how the synagogue religion, typified by the synagogue in Nazareth, was turning against Jesus. Is it significant that we do not hear again of Jesus entering a synagogue? Now it is the turn of teachers of the law and Pharisees who have come from Jerusalem—a sinister inspection— to note that Jesus' earlier looseness with regard to the minutiae of the law, as they had developed them, was corroborated by his indifference to the ritual washings before meals that were Pharisaic practice. These washings were not for purposes of hygiene, although they incidentally contributed to this, but for washing away the spiritual defilement that was believed to inhere in articles touched by sinners (especially Gentiles) or people who had been in contact with dead bodies or other sources of uncleanness. Jesus made a triple-pronged attack on the criticism leveled against him. First, he argued that these regulations were manmade and went beyond what Scripture required. Second, he accused his hearers of keeping these trivial rules while neglecting more important commands that were in Scripture. And, third, he attacked the whole idea that what people ate could make them religiously unclean; real uncleanness springs from immoral desires in a person's mind. Mark comments that the effect of Jesus' remarks was to show that the whole concept of unclean foods was flawed (Mk 7:1-23).

Finally, the Pharisees tried to get Jesus to perform some sign that would es-

---

[11]It is not clear in what sense Antipas thought that John could have been raised from the dead.

tablish beyond any doubt whether or not his authorization came from God, and in exasperation he refused to respond to them (Mk 8:11-13). His reference to them as "this generation" arouses echoes of the people of Israel during the wilderness wanderings when they refused to believe in God's power and obey him despite the signs and wonders that they had seen.

*Jesus and his disciples.* The third strand in the story is the interaction between Jesus and his close circle, the Twelve. The story shows how this group were with him constantly and were his standing audience. Mark relates how they were sent off on their own for a time to carry his message and to do the same kind of mighty works as he did over a wider range of country (Mk 6:6-13). But the story concentrates on their association with Jesus. In effect, the account bifurcates into stories of what Jesus did in the presence of anybody and everybody, and of what he did when only the Twelve were with him. We have noted how Jesus shared the meaning of the parables with them, and this pattern of public teaching followed by private explanation recurs. There are also a number of incidents where something remarkable happened when only they or some of them were present. There was an incident when they were crossing the Lake of Galilee; a storm blew up and subsided when Jesus commanded it to be still. The Twelve could only ask in wonder, "Who is this?" (Mk 4:35-41).[12] Again they were privileged observers when Jairus's daughter was brought back to life. When Mark relates the stories of the feedings of the large crowds, he makes no reference to the reaction of the crowds, but he does include a conversation in which Jesus rebukes the Twelve for not getting the message of the feedings (Mk 8:14-21). Mark also records another weird sea scene in which Jesus is seen by his disciples contravening nature by walking on the sea as if on dry land, and they do not know what to make of it (Mk 6:45-52).

*Recognition of Jesus as the Messiah.* The story of the disciples comes to something of a culmination in a series of scenes that literally occupy the center point in the Gospel (Mk 8:27—9:13). One way of summing up the Gospel so far is to say that the Twelve, who have been admitted to the secret of the kingdom, have been given a full account of the evidence on which one could decide what is going on, whether the kingdom really has come near. But the question that

---

[12]For this significant motif in Mark see Timothy Dwyer, *The Motif of Wonder in the Gospel of Mark* (Sheffield: Sheffield Academic Press, 1996).

they now face is not directly about the kingdom, but (picking up an earlier debate) who do people think that Jesus is, and more directly, who do the Twelve think that he is? The simple answer given by Peter is that Jesus is the Christ, a term that can only refer to the agent through whom God establishes the kingdom on earth.

It is probably true to say that the attainment of this insight represents the completion of the first part of what Mark saw as the aim of Jesus. He has gained the faith of a small group of people who understand what he is doing and accept him as the Messiah. It is also true to say that this is only the first part of the task and that it now needs to be followed by a second part. The Gospel will, as we know, go on to narrate the crucifixion of Jesus. Even though Jesus subsequently came to life again, nevertheless this course of events was not what people expected of the Messiah, and the resurrection could presumably be seen as an ad hoc intervention by God to deal with a plan that had gone dreadfully wrong. Mark therefore records how Jesus began to try to teach the Twelve that the Son of Man had to suffer, be killed and then come to life again. Accordingly, the recognition that he is the Messiah is immediately followed by this qualification or correction that says in effect: Yes, that is right, but the Messiah must suffer.

Two things follow in quick succession. The first is that the disciples and the crowds are told that the followers of Jesus must be prepared for the same kind of fate. Just as Jesus could be regarded as giving up the possibility of a life lived for his own enjoyment to face suffering and rejection by those opposed to his mission, so too his followers must be prepared to say no to their own desires and be prepared for self-sacrifice for his cause. Only so, it is said, will they eventually attain to a life that is really worth having.[13]

The second is that in an enigmatic saying (Mk 9:1) he promises that some of his hearers will live to see the kingdom of God come with power. The saying would appear to promise some kind of future event that will be recognizable as the coming of the kingdom (the sign that was not given to the Pharisees), but

---

[13]Jesus teaches that it is better to gain your own real life by being true to what you know is right, even though it costs you the benefits that come from sacrificing your principles (like a person who prefers to be honest in business although it means a lower standard of living) and that adherence to his cause (with the attendant deprivation and suffering) in this world will lead to attaining the life of the world to come. Clearly these two understandings of life merge with each other.

the narrative goes straight on to describe an event in which some of them had a private experience in which they had a vision of Jesus in heavenly glory along with Moses and Elijah (as his forerunners or models for his role) and heard the same heavenly voice that had spoken at the baptism of Jesus, affirming that Jesus was the Son of God (Mk 9:2-8). The vision would appear to function in the Gospel as a divine reaffirmation of Jesus despite the fact that he was going to suffer. In the closely associated brief conversation the fact that Elijah had appeared leads to an implicit identification of him with John the Baptist, who had already been put to death.[14] Here and frequently the point is being made that what is going to happen is no accident but forms part of a plan made by God that dictates what must happen and that has already been announced in Scripture.

*From Galilee to Jerusalem—prophecies of suffering.* How does the story now proceed? In many respects it seems to go on much the same way as it did in the first half of the Gospel. The transfiguration is followed by an abrupt return to ground level, where a particularly difficult example of exorcism takes place, but the story is told in such a way as to say something about the importance of faith in what God can do through Jesus and so about the importance of prayer. The interest is shifting from action among the people at large to instruction for the disciples, but always in the context of growing opposition to Jesus (Mk 9:14-29).

Jesus, therefore, repeats his statement about what is going to happen to him (Mk 9:30-32). If on the previous occasion Peter rebuked him for saying so, this time the reaction is one of incomprehension. A brief series of incidents follows in which Jesus teaches that one part of what it means to follow him is to give up claims to superiority over one another; it is more important to welcome (i.e., to honor) the most insignificant person in the ancient world (a child) than to seek honor for oneself. Even belonging to the group of disciples is of relative value. And there is strong condemnation for anybody who puts any obstacle in the way of others coming to faith (Mk 9:33-50).

Until now Jesus has been in Galilee, and Mark has made no mention of any travels south into Judea and Jerusalem, although the evidence of the Gospel of

---

[14]This is how Mt 17:10-13 understands the conversation, and there is no reason to suppose that Mark saw it otherwise.

John indicates that he had paid brief visits on the occasion of religious festivals, as the people were expected and required to do. Therefore, the transition that now takes place from Galilee to Judea via Transjordan (Mk 10:1) is all the more significant. In full cognizance of what is in store for him, Jesus chooses to go towards Jerusalem and his fate there. But the journey toward Jerusalem occupies a full chapter with a number of incidents in it.

There is another example of controversy with the Pharisees, this time concerning divorce (Mk 10:2-12). Divorce was an accepted practice, the only dispute being over what grounds sufficed to allow it. Jesus took his opponents back to the Scripture and used the principle of marriage established in Genesis 1 to relativize the permission given later by Moses for divorce and to prioritize the principle that marriage should be unbreakable. He drove the point home afterward to his disciples by his novel teaching that men who divorced their wives to remarry were guilty of adultery. There was obviously no attempt to be less controversial as Jerusalem loomed nearer!

Then he entered into the spirit of his earlier statement by welcoming children brought to him so that he might pray for them and by making them an example of the kind of person who will find entry into the kingdom of God (Mk 10:13-16). This little incident is evidently a foil to the much longer story of a rich man who felt unable to give away his possessions in almsgiving (a familiar practice in the Jewish religion) if that was the self-denial to which he was called. Self-denial is here made very concrete and practical. It is not easy for a person captivated by wealth to enter the kingdom. Indeed, nobody can enter without God having a hand in it. But for those who do so the ultimate reward is eternal life (Mk 10:17-31).

A third time[15] Jesus foretells his suffering in even greater detail to a group of disciples who are a mixture of astonishment and fear as he leads the way to Jerusalem. The incomprehension of the earlier occasions reaches its climax as in direct juxtaposition Mark places the request of James and John for a share in the dominion that they assume he will enjoy in the future. Jesus can only reply that this is not in his gift; all that he can do is invite them to share in his experience of suffering, which he characterizes as a cup and a baptism. The *cup*

---

[15]Not counting Mk 9:9-13, which is not a formal announcement in the same way as the other statements.

was an acknowledged metaphor for an experience of suffering, specifically of wrath from God; some of the Old Testament prophets used the picture of a drink that makes the recipient totally intoxicated (intoxication being understood as a thoroughly unpleasant and undesirable condition) and so is almost akin to a poison that kills. The term *baptism* seems to be a stretching of the term to denote a similar experience in terms of being engulfed in a flood or drowned in the sea. This is all that Jesus has to offer: to talk of greatness is incompatible with the divine way of things where people are called to serve, and Jesus exemplifies this with his willingness to die and give his life as a ransom for other people (Mk 10:32-45).

That is all that Jesus says at this point about the purpose or meaning of his death, other than the insistence that it will be no surprise but takes place in accordance with God's purpose "as it is written". It represents the rejection of a righteous person who trusts in God, and therefore it could be nothing more than the effect of evil opposition to God's messenger. But this statement picks up the language of ransom, which indicates that Jesus does something in dying akin to the making of a payment whereby slaves or prisoners are set free.

Finally, in this section, we have the last healing miracle performed by Jesus on a blind man who responds to his cure by following Jesus along the road. This miracle is meant to be seen as a visible paradigm of discipleship (Mk 10:46-52).

*Confrontations in Jerusalem.* The group of travelers is now outside Jerusalem, and Mark describes an arrangement to secure a colt for Jesus to ride into the city. There is a festive atmosphere about as those who accompany him stage a demonstration in his honor. To ride into the city is the mark of a king or a conqueror, and the companions of Jesus recognize this and proclaim the coming kingdom of David. For Mark the message is clear: Jesus is the messianic king, and this is his entry to his capital city. But, like the transfiguration, it is a moment of insight that is swiftly followed by the realities of the situation (Mk 11:1-11).

From this point two themes are developed. The first one is that of confrontation between Jesus and the various religious authorities in Jerusalem. It is foreshadowed in the little story of Jesus seeing a fig tree from which he should have been able to gather fruit, finding none, and uttering a curse against it, that is, a prayer that judgment would strike it. We are used by now to the fact that stories in Mark can be but do not always have to be symbolical, and that is true of this one.[16] Jerusalem should make a positive response to Jesus, but it is not going to do so, and it will come under judgment from God. Sandwiched in the middle of this incident[17] is an account of Jesus going into the temple and taking the offensive by a minor demonstration against the people trading there, alleging that the effect of their presence was to prevent people from fulfilling its true purpose, namely, prayer to God, and to make it a place of unscrupulous commerce. It is not surprising that the incident provoked the temple authorities to plot to get rid of him.[18] By now it has become apparent that Jesus does not only proclaim the kingdom of God and do works of compassion. He has also emerged as a critic of the existing religion of the people, which, it would seem, is not showing the kind of honor of God and his requirements that is associated with the kingdom (Mk 11:12-25).

Various groups of religious leaders now approach Jesus to challenge this upstart controversialist. The first question is a straight one about the source of Jesus' authority: that is to say, who, if anybody, has commissioned him to behave like this? Although Jesus refuses to answer directly, the implication of his answer is that, if they believed that John the Baptist was sent by God, so too was he (Mk 11:27-33).

Again Jesus takes the initiative with a parable, only this time it doesn't seem to need any explanation (Mk 12:1-12). The Old Testament picture of Israel as a vineyard (Is 5) is enhanced by bringing in the farmers who exploit it for their own ends (like the corrupt shepherds who look after the flock of God in Jer 23 and Ezek 34) and even despise the owner's son and kill him. People who behave like that will be brought to book—it would have been self-evident.

We can pass quickly over the questions about rendering tribute to Caesar with Jesus' response that one must give God and Caesar their dues, and about the nature of life after the resurrection, save to note that Jesus bases his answer on what he read in the Scriptures (Mk 12:13-27). More significant for under-

---

[16]It also has a significance in teaching the disciples about the efficacy of prayer.

[17]This is a familiar Markan technique that he employs for a variety of reasons, but often (as here) to enable two incidents to be interpreted in the light of each other.

[18]It must be remembered that execution was a much more common way of dealing with criminals in the ancient world than in our so-called civilized society.

standing the theology of the Gospel is the exchange with a friendly teacher of the law (they are not all against Jesus!) who agrees with Jesus on the importance of the law of love for God and one's neighbor (again taken from the Scriptures) over against the outward observances of the law (Mk 12:28-34).[19]

The exchanges come to a climax with Jesus once again challenging the authorities. The question concerns the Messiah (Mk 12:35-37). The hearers are left with a question: how can the Messiah be at one and the same time the descendant (son) of David, and therefore inferior to him, and yet his lord (since in Ps 110 David refers to him as "my lord")? There must be an answer to the question, and yet Mark does not supply it. How are the readers meant to answer it? The answer is presumably that the Messiah is a human being, descended from David, although the Davidic descent of Jesus is not mentioned in Mark, but he is either also descended from God or exalted by God and so made superior to David. Mark would probably have answered in terms of the second possibility.

In this way the confrontation between Jesus and the authorities has been built up. It will come to a head when an opportunity for arresting him presents itself. But before this, and interwoven with the story of the arrest, is the second theme of this section of the Gospel. It is introduced by the story of Jesus visiting the temple, where he sees an example of true devotion to God. He has already accused the temple authorities of misuse of its facilities. Now to his disciples he prophesies that the temple will be destroyed (Mk 13). It must be remembered that Jesus has spoken of the coming of the kingdom of God and of the judgment to be carried out by the Son of Man, and therefore it is natural for his hearers to associate the destruction of the temple with these events. The question put by them gives the opportunity for a statement by Jesus on what is going to happen in the future. Its length is indicative of its importance; only the chapter on teaching in parables is comparable. Its style is apocalyptic in the sense that it shares the imagery and subject matter of Jewish works in this genre. As it stands, it appears to be a prophecy of what must happen in the future right up to the end. A good deal of it is warning that various cataclysmic events will take place that are not necessarily signs that the end has come. In particular, followers of Jesus can expect suffering and rejection like their Master. But

---

[19]Note that the importance is relative, not absolute.

events will come to a climax with the appearance of "the abomination that causes desolation", and this is a signal that unprecedented suffering will take place in and around Jerusalem. False claimants to be deliverers will appear, but they are not to be trusted. Only after all this will there be cosmic signs (or whatever is meant by this language) and the appearance of the Son of Man to gather God's people together. All of this is near: the signs of the end happening will occur before this generation passes away. But since people do not know when it will happen, they must always be on the alert.

There is other material about judgment and the Son of Man in Mark, but this chapter nevertheless stands out as being remarkably different from anything else in Mark with its strange idiom. Yet any attempt to do justice to Mark's theology must somehow integrate it into the story.

*Passover meal, arrest, crucifixion and burial.* The story now resumes where it left off, so to speak. Sandwiched between the two parts of the account of the plot to do away with Jesus and the connivance of Judas is the incident in which an unnamed woman anoints Jesus, understood as an anticipation of his burial (and thus as confirming the imminence of his death) and as something that will be told wherever the gospel is preached (and thus as confirming that the story of Jesus will be told after his death) (Mk 14:1-11).

Jesus then holds a Passover meal with the Twelve (Mk 14:12-31). The meal becomes the occasion for again announcing that he will go to death, as has been foretold. But on this occasion Jesus shares bread and a cup with his disciples and uses them as symbols of his body and his blood that is to be poured out. The language again suggests death, with Jesus being compared with the sacrificial animal whose blood was sprinkled on the people at the initiation of the covenant made with Israel at Sinai. Jesus appears to be expressing his determination to go ahead to his death. He will do so alone, for his followers will be scattered, again understood as something foreseen in prophecy. And then comes the cryptic remark, "But after I have risen, I will go ahead of you into Galilee" (Mk 14:28). It will be picked up later!

The determination to follow God's purpose for him is severely threatened by the anguish of facing the impending horror of drinking the cup, during which Jesus is strongly enticed by his human weakness to avoid his fate but nevertheless steels himself to be resolute (Mk 14:32-42).

There follows almost immediately his arrest by the Jewish authorities, again interpreted as being what was laid down in Scripture and therefore as something that must happen (Mk 14:43-52). He is then judicially examined by the Sanhedrin (Mk 14:53-72), and Mark underlines the fact that no convincing grounds for condemnation could be found; even the threat of destroying the temple, like a modern terrorist conspiracy to blow up a government building, could not be made to stick. The high priest resorted to a direct question, "Are you the Christ?" to which Jesus said "I am" and proceeded to elaborate that they would "see the Son of Man sitting at the right hand of the Mighty One and coming on the clouds of heaven" (Mk 14:62). This was interpreted as a blasphemous statement, and he was condemned to death.

But since the Jews did not have the power to inflict capital punishment, the condemned prisoner had to be handed over to the Roman governor, Pilate, who is presented in Mark as condemning an innocent man (Mk 15:1-20). The charge now is clearly one of treason in that Jesus is understood to be claiming to be "the king of the Jews"; this is a political explanation of the significance of claiming to be "the Christ". Pilate does attempt to release Jesus by making use of his privilege of granting an amnesty at the Passover to a criminal, but this was rejected by the mob, who had been swayed by the authorities. The result was that a real criminal, Barabbas, was released instead.[20] Jesus, however, is dressed up like a king and mocked by the soldiery, in a scene of bitter irony, before being led out to execution.

The crucifixion is related in some detail with a number of implicit allusions to the Old Testament and to the earlier story in the Gospel, so that Jesus is depicted on the one hand as the kind of innocent sufferer typified in the Psalms (principally Ps 22; 69) and on the other hand as the person whose great claims for himself have failed to be fulfilled. The story finds its climax in the dying cry of Jesus, reflecting the sense of dereliction felt by the author of Psalm 22:1: God has forsaken him, and he dies unvindicated. Yet this tragic end is immediately followed by the comment of the centurion overseeing the execution who exclaims that this person was in reality the Son of God (Mk 15:21-39).

---

[20]Whether Mark would intend his readers to understand that Jesus was crucified in place of Barabbas appears on the whole to be unlikely. The point is rather to accentuate the innocence of Jesus and the rejection of him by the people.

The rest of the story describes how various women from among his friends were present at the scene and then one of his sympathizers, Joseph from Arimathea, saw to it that he received a decent, indeed an honorable burial (Mk 15:40-47).

However, when three of the women went to the tomb to complete the task of burial they found that although it had been closed in the normal way with a gigantic stone, this had been rolled aside and inside there sat a young man dressed in white. This description probably indicates an angel. He told the women that Jesus had risen and was not there. They were to go and tell his companions that he was going before them to Galilee and there they would see him. Utterly shaken by this experience, they came out of the tomb and said nothing to anybody (Mk 16:1-8).

And in this cryptic manner the story, as we have it, ends.[21] Opinions differ greatly as to whether this is Mark's intended conclusion or whether the story was meant to continue (presumably, as in the other three Gospels, with an account of the appearance of Jesus to his friends) but either was left unfinished or was accidentally cut short by the loss of the last page or so of the manuscript.[22] If this really is the end of the story, then the readers are left deeply puzzled, since this story was written at a point long after the event and any Christian readers would already know that Jesus did rise from the dead and did appear to his disciples. Mark has simply related the fact that Jesus did rise (or rather that this was reported to the women) and that he would meet his disciples in Galilee. Alternatively, Mark went on to tell a story that continued in much the same way as in the other Gospels and probably included at least one appearance of Jesus to his disciples and his commissioning of them.

---

[21]The brief account of what happened after the resurrection printed as Mk 16:9-20 is almost universally recognized to be a later addition by another writer; the best manuscripts of Mark conclude with Mk 16:8, and the following material shows stylistic differences and appears to be a summary based mainly on the contents of the other Gospels.

[22]For Mk 16:8 as the intended ending, see Morna D. Hooker, *A Commentary on the Gospel According to St. Mark* (London: A & C Black, 1991), pp. 391-94; for the view that the original ending has been lost, see R. T. France, *The Gospel of Mark: A Commentary on the Greek Text* (Grand Rapids, Mich.: Eerdmans; Carlisle: Paternoster, 2002), pp. 670-74; Robert H. Gundry, *Mark: A Commentary on His Apology for the Cross* (Grand Rapids, Mich.: Eerdmans, 1993), pp. 1012-21. I find the latter view more persuasive.

## *Theological Themes*

How are we to characterize what is going on theologically in this Gospel? I have presented the material in the form of a story, or rather as the analysis of a story to bring out the main elements in the plot. There was no other way in which Mark could deal with the material once it was recognized that the life of Jesus was significant for Christians. My analysis has shown that in broad terms the story has two main parts to it, a first part in which the identity of Jesus as the Messiah is recognized gradually, and a second part in which it is intimated that the Son of Man[23] must suffer and be raised from the dead and this intimation is fulfilled. We could say that Mark's theme is the Messiah and Son of God who proclaims the kingdom and who acts it out in ways that express who he is.[24]

The development of this story revealed three groups of people with whom Jesus interacted: the crowds who listened to him and saw what he did, his disciples, and the opposition. In some ways it is a very odd story. There is the enigmatic use of different terms, often called titles, to refer to Jesus, principally Messiah, Son of God and Son of Man; the puzzling manner in which Jesus spoke in ways that were incomprehensible to the crowds and even to the disciples despite the fuller teaching that they received; the unexplained use of "Son of Man"; the remarkably lengthy and detailed teaching about the future course of events leading up to the coming of the Son of Man; the way in which the story leads one to expect the resurrection appearances of Jesus and yet as we have it leaves the reader with a sense of frustration and mystique. At the end of this discussion we may well be left with a Gospel that remains mysterious rather than one whose questions have all been solved.

There have been several references to the Old Testament in our survey of the Gospel. From the beginning the progress of the plot is seen to fall in line with what had been said in Scripture (Mk 1:2),[25] and the motif keeps recurring to explain the course of the Son of Man (Mk 9:12; 14:21, 27, 49) and his forerunner (Mk 9:13), and the rebelliousness and lack of spiritual comprehension

---

[23]The alternation between the two titles in Mk 8:29/31 (and also in Mk 13:21-22/26 and Mk 14:61/62) should be noted.

[24]Note that this is not the same thing as the theme of the preaching and teaching of Jesus, which, as Mark tells us, is the kingdom of God.

[25]The crucial "as" in the phrase "as it is written" (NRSV) was transposed and rendered "and so" (Mk 1:4) in NIV, but TNIV has reverted rightly to the more literal translation.

of the people (Mk 4:10-12; 7:6; 11:17). References to events that must take place are to events in prophecy (Mk 8:31; 9:11; 13:7, 10). The main motifs in the Gospel—the kingdom of God and the Messiah—are drawn from Scripture. The allusions to Isaiah are particularly significant and indicate that the broad theme of the Isaianic new exodus, which is widely attested in the New Testament, has shaped Mark's presentation. What takes place in the story is the fulfillment of Scripture and specifically of its prophecies of future redemption through the coming of a messianic figure.

*The kingdom of God.* The kingdom of God is the main theological theme in the teaching of Jesus. It is so announced in Mark 1:15 as the content of the gospel. For Jesus the time has now come when it can be proclaimed as being at hand or near. In one group of sayings it is a realm into which people can enter rather than being cast into Gehenna, presumably after their death. Entry to it is always expressed in the future tense. But it is also something that "comes", as if the end of the present age is succeeded at some not too distant point by the new age replacing it. Right to the end of the Gospel godly people go on awaiting it (Mk 15:43). The present age is one of proclamation of it, but it is also apparently one of growth as the parables suggest. But if it is growing, then there must be a sense in which it is present. When Jesus says that it has drawn near, he may mean either that it has already come or that it is going to come soon.[26] Either way, something is happening in the present world.

William Telford finds that there are two different conceptions of the kingdom of God in Mark: the future, apocalyptic expectation and the present reality or experience in this world. He holds that Mark has modified the apocalyptic element, which is the original one in the teaching of Jesus, and played it down in light of the delay of the parousia. In other words, when the early Christians were disappointed by the failure of Jesus to come back, they began to lay more stress on the present working of God in the world and to see this as the

---

[26]The Greek verb here is ambiguous, and both interpretations have their supporters. Other texts in the Gospels support both possibilities. The parallelism with "the time has come" favors the former view; see, for example, Gundry, *Mark*, pp. 64-66. In some texts the kingdom is a future entity (Mk 9:1), whereas in others it is a present reality (Mt 10:7 par. Lk 10:9, 11; Mt 12:28 par. Lk 11:20; Lk 17:21; Mk 4:26-32). Probably the majority of scholars hold that the kingdom must be seen as both present and future, and try to find some way of expressing this paradox, for example, that the kingdom has been inaugurated but is still to be consummated.

coming of the kingdom. Mark thus interpreted the material in a "realized eschatological way". The church was turning away from the message proclaimed by Jesus to concentrate on his person instead. Thus Mark moves from eschatology to christology.[27]

But the tension in Mark is somewhat different. It is more between the kingdom as an eternal heavenly state into which people will enter and the kingdom as the dominion of God coming into being here in this world, whether in the near future or already in the time of Jesus. It is more a contrast between a transcendent spatial kingdom and an immanent dynamic kingdom that constitutes a space within this world in which God's blessings are realized.

In this connection the entry of Jesus to Jerusalem is highly significant, for here the people give praise for the one who comes in the name of the Lord, for the coming kingdom of our father David (Mk 11:9-10). This seems to suggest that the entry of Jesus to Jerusalem was seen as the entry of the Messiah and hence was an integral stage in the coming of the kingdom.

Already in Mark, therefore, the coming of the kingdom is closely linked with the coming of the Messiah, and the recognition that the Messiah is here is the recognition that the kingdom is being established. Can we go beyond this and say that for Mark Jesus is acting as Messiah (or king) but is not yet recognized and is rather rejected and crucified? To describe him, then, during his earthly mission as the Messiah-designate is inappropriate. The clear impression is that the kingdom has drawn near because the Messiah has appeared. What Jesus does is to announce the coming of the kingdom rather than his own coming as Messiah, but he speaks and acts with authority in such a way as to raise the question of who he is and what his role is in relation to the kingdom.

More than that, the association of the kingdom with Jesus' entry to Jerusalem strongly suggests that the suffering and death of Jesus are crucially related to its coming. The second half of the Gospel emphasizes the coming suffering and resurrection of Jesus and underlines the fact that his death took place in accordance with the plan of God. It is thus tied in with the divine

---

[27]William R. Telford, *The Theology of the Gospel of Mark* (Cambridge: Cambridge University Press, 1999), pp. 67-88, esp. pp. 76, 87.

purpose that leads to Jesus being equipped with the Spirit and announcing that the time of fulfillment has come. Only in the sequel to the third main passion prediction does it emerge that Jesus' giving of his life, that is, his death, is to function as the giving of a ransom for many. Within the same context Jesus refers to drinking the cup of divine wrath, and he uses the same metaphor in Gethsemane. To be linked with this are the words spoken at the Last Supper about his body and the pouring out of his blood, like the sacrifice that inaugurated the old covenant at Sinai (Ex 24). All of this adds up to a clear understanding of the death of Jesus as the means whereby people are delivered from sin and its dire consequences (Mk 9:42-50). For Mark the death of Jesus is by no means simply an expression of rejection of the Son of Man by sinners, an obstacle to the working of God; it is part of the work of God in bringing in the kingdom.

The people who respond to the call to discipleship have been given the secret of the kingdom. The parables in which this secret is revealed show an interesting alternation between those in which the principal actor is a person who sows seed (Mk 4:3-8) and those in which the principal object is the seed itself (Mk 4:26-32). The sower and the seed are both integral to the total picture. The coming of the kingdom is effected by the work of the Messiah. The kingdom consists of those who respond to the message in repentance and faith, and thereby come into the sphere of God's salvation and life.

Modern discussion of Mark has been dominated by the problem of the messianic secret. This problem arises from the fact that Jesus apparently endeavored to keep his identity as Messiah quiet by silencing people and demons who confessed who he was. Linked with this is the way in which he gave fuller teaching to his disciples in private and withheld it from the crowds and his opponents.[28] The passion predictions are made only to the disciples, although they are not specifically told to keep them secret.

---

[28]F. B. Watson, "The Social Function of Mark's Secrecy Motif", *JSNT* 24 (1985): 49-69, has argued that the secrecy is to be explained in terms of double predestination whereby the nonelect are kept from understanding the gospel and responding to it. This explanation seems to fall down on the passages where the gospel is proclaimed widely and it is implied that whosoever will may come (Mk 1:14-15). The secret of the kingdom is given to those who have already become disciples, and the interpretation of the parable of the sower is cast in terms of human response and satanic opposition rather than in terms of divine predestination; no theory of predestination is developed elsewhere in the Gospel.

The multifaceted nature of the secrecy probably requires a complex rather than one oversimple explanation.[29] Although modern scholarship has thought of this as a secret about the Messiah, in fact it is part of the secret about the kingdom. Jesus uses the word *mystery* or *secret* (Mk 4:11); a "mystery" in New Testament language is something that God has kept secret in the past but is now revealing to his messengers. So there has been a revelation of God's hitherto secret plan to the disciples who have committed themselves (however imperfectly at this stage) to Jesus, although their perception is limited. Full understanding of Jesus is gained by personal encounter and willingness to share his way in self-denial. It is important to stress that there is no indication that the disciples totally failed to understand what Jesus explained to them. Their story is one of gradual, fuller recognition of Jesus and his message. Mark sees Jesus as giving such instruction to people as they could comprehend (Mk 4:33). To be a disciple is to possess the mystery of the kingdom, i.e., to understand what is going on and to partake of it. It is to recognize Jesus as who he really is and to see that the kingdom really is present in him.

**Who Jesus is.** For Mark the Gospel is more about the messenger than the message. Who Jesus is takes priority over his message of the kingdom. The Messiah and the kingdom are correlative, and Mark majors on the Messiah.

Mark uses a variety of names or titles for Jesus. When he is telling the story, it is normal to refer to the protagonist simply by the name by which he was known, as Jesus. There does not appear to be any significant theological content

---

[29]In New Testament scholarship the problem of the messianic secret is constituted by the claim that the presentation of Jesus keeping his messiahship and associated matters a secret is historically improbable (e.g., how could the resuscitation of Jairus's daughter be kept quiet? What was the point of telling the demons not to reveal who Jesus was after they had already blurted it out?). An explanation of why Mark gave this purportedly improbable presentation is that it was intended to conceal the alleged historical fact that Jesus never claimed to be Messiah, but his later followers believed that he was the Messiah; this lack of an essential piece of evidence for his messiahship was covered up by the unhistorical presentation that he did claim to be the Messiah but did not let anybody know. For various reasons this kind of explanation (associated above all with W. Wrede) is untenable. Nevertheless, the question remains as to why Mark has emphasized this "secrecy". If we look for a historical explanation, the best view is still that Jesus did not wish to be misleadingly known by a title that he understood in a radically different way from the common conception of the Messiah as a military, national leader. But this may not fully explain why Mark emphasized the secret, especially in the light of its much lesser role in Matthew and Luke.

to the name. Three other main terms function as titles or descriptions for Jesus.[30]

*Christ*, the Greek equivalent of *Messiah*, appears in the opening words of the Gospel (Mk 1:1). It does not reappear until Peter's confession (Mk 8:29). Then it figures in the trial scene and in the irony of the cross where Messiah is synonymous with king of Israel (Mk 14:61; 15:32). However, other related language is used. The concept may also be present in the baptismal scene if Jesus is understood to be anointed by the Spirit (cf. Is 11:1-3). The concept of messiahship may also be associated with the title "Holy One of God" (Mk 1:24). More explicitly we also have "Son of David" (Mk 10:47; 12:35).

"Son of David" is tantamount to Messiah and is associated with the mighty work of healing the blind. Is this title implicitly criticized, as some have thought, in Mark 12:35-37? This would be unlikely; rather a riddle is presented that awaits resolution. The purpose of the pericope is to show that Jesus can flummox the scribes, whereas the readers have the secret of the kingdom/Messiah. For Mark the kingly associations of the term *Christ* indicate that it carries the sense of the person through whom God establishes his kingdom.

Alongside "Christ" we have "Son of God" used by various actors in the story (Mk 1:1—the author; Mk 1:11; 9:7—the voice of God; Mk 3:11; 5:7—demoniacs; Mk 13:32—which would be understood by the readers as a self-reference by Jesus; Mk 14:61—the high priest; Mk 15:39—a centurion at the death of Jesus). That this is the identity of Jesus is apparent to the readers from Mark 1:11 but not apparently to the others present at the scene. His identity is acknowledged by demons who are forbidden to make him known in Mark 3:11 but not in Mark 5:7 (it is unlikely that this is a private encounter between Jesus and the man himself in view of Mk 5:16); again it is confirmed by God to the inner group of disciples (Mk 9:7). Jesus alludes to himself by the title in the patent allusions in Mark 12:6 and in Mark 13:32. In Mark 14:61 "Son of the Blessed [God]" is used in apposition to "Christ" in a way that strongly suggests that the two terms are closely related. The manner of his death leads to the centurion's confession. "Son of God" suggests the closeness of Jesus as the

---

[30]The title of "Lord", which plays a significant part in postresurrection understanding of Jesus, has a minor role in Mark. When Jesus uses the term in Mk 11:3, this is not apparently a self-reference; in Mk 12:36-37 it occurs in a theological discussion of the relationship of the Messiah to David that is highly significant for future developments but stands isolated in the Gospel.

divine agent to God; one possibility is that the term appears at key points in the story (Mk 1:11; 9:7; 15:39) and brings out more deeply who the Messiah is.

Third, there is the enigmatic phrase "Son of Man". Whatever the origins of this phrase and its original reference,[31] for Mark the following points hold.

1. It is a self-reference by Jesus, and it is improbable that whatever it may have originally meant, it has any sort of inclusive or generic sense so that it may be used of statements that apply both to Jesus (the speaker) and to other people. Jesus is referring only to himself when he uses it.

2. It is the preferred term[32] for use in statements about the suffering, death and resurrection of Jesus (Mk 8:31; 9:12, 31; 10:33, 45; 14:21, 41).

3. It is also the preferred term for use about the future functions of Jesus coming in judgment, sitting at the right hand of God and coming to gather the people of God (Mk 8:38; 13:26; 14:62).

4. In two places (Mk 13:26; 14:62) there is a clear use of the language of Daniel 7:13, where the Son of Man comes with the clouds of heaven. Here at least it is this exalted figure who is in mind, and we may take it that Daniel 7 is understood as a prophecy that will be fulfilled in the future by Jesus in this role. Along with these two references we may link Mark 8:38, where the Son of Man comes in the glory of his Father with the holy angels. The element of judgment that is implicit in this text fits in with the references to a judgment scene in Daniel 7:10, 26.

However, the Danielic links to the other Son of Man sayings that refer to his

---

[31]For Mark and the other Evangelists "Son of Man" is a Greek phrase that refers to Jesus and is used only by him to refer to himself. There is debate over the precise sense in which it was used in the original Aramaic spoken by Jesus and to what extent the usage is original to him. Many scholars hold that it was a term of general application that could be used by a speaker to make statements true of people in general and therefore of himself in particular, and it was so used by Jesus; however, (they say) in those texts where it is used in statements that can refer only to the speaker, it is an addition made during the development of the gospel tradition. Others, including myself, hold that it was used by Jesus to refer to himself and that the influence of Dan 7 was present at this stage. See I. Howard Marshall, "Son of Man", in *DJG*, pp. 775-81.

[32]That is to say, we do not find another series of statements about these events using some other term (contrast Lk 24:26, 46). In particular the term *I* is not used in these statements.

present authority (to forgive sins and to control the sabbath) and to his death and resurrection are not very obvious. The former of these groups of sayings has parallels in Q material, and it is most probable that it reflects a mode of speech used by Jesus; in other words, it is traditional, and Mark has taken over the tradition. The latter group is peculiar to Mark, and the frequency of the statements (some six distinguishable occurrences) makes it peculiarly emphatic.

Would readers of the Gospel have been puzzled by this phrase? Here a distinction must be made between those reading the Gospel for the first time and encountering this unusual phrase in Mark 2:10 without any kind of explanation, and those reading the Gospel on a second or subsequent occasion who would be able to understand the earlier usages in the light of the later ones that provide unmistakable allusions to Daniel 7. It is also possible that some readers might have had knowledge of 1 Enoch, where the phrase is conspicuously used, but this must remain uncertain.

On two occasions a statement made to Jesus about the Christ is immediately followed by a statement made by him using this phrase, almost as if it were a correction of title (Mk 8:31; 14:62). One possible explanation for the "correction" may be that it is connected with Jesus' attitude to the term *Messiah.* Just as Jesus silences the demons when they use messianic terms with reference to him, so on the two occurrences when other people use the term of him, he effects this shift in terminology, almost as if there is something inappropriate about it. Yet there is no impropriety in using *Messiah* in Mark 9:41 and Mark 13:21, where it can refer to a future situation, or in Mark 12:35-37, where Jesus raises a puzzle about other people's usage of it. And we must not forget that Mark uses the term in the opening words of the Gospel with clear reference to Jesus. Neither Matthew nor Luke is so coy about it. Moreover, there does seem to be a climax in Peter's confession that Jesus is the Christ, and Mark 14:62 is quite affirmative (and in the present tense!) in Mark, whatever the corresponding statements in Matthew and Luke may be.

A further question is whether there is significance in the use of the three main titles in different contexts. Are they essentially synonymous, as the juxtaposition and alternation would suggest? Probably the fact that all three were applied to Jesus and were to some extent given fresh meaning through this application entails the likelihood that there was a tendency to assimilate them with one another. Nevertheless, there may be an appropriateness about the use of the individual titles. So, for example, the centurion's comment is from a Gentile and is the only possible one from him.

The dialogue with the high priest brings all three titles together and establishes that for Mark "Son of Man" is essential to an understanding of Jesus. One could say that the earliest usages of "Son of Man" indicate that it is a self-designation and that this self-designation is then identified as a reference to Daniel 7 and to the figure whom we find in 1 Enoch; moreover, here the inclusion of the allusion to Psalm 110:1 picks up on what is said about the Messiah in Mark 12:35-37 and makes it clear that the speaker is David's lord. The identification of Jesus as God's Son has already been made. It may be, then, that one of the advantages of "Son of Man" is that it is a term that functions as a self-designation and as a messianic title. Maybe perception of the messianic secret lies, at least in part, in the recognition that when Jesus speaks about the Son of Man he is identifying himself as the figure prophesied in Daniel 7.

Finally, the question arises as to how the terms are to be understood. William Telford makes a contrast between the more Jewish messianic type of understanding of Jesus and the Hellenistic "Son of God" understanding in which Jesus is more akin to a divine figure[33] and miracle worker. In this connection we need to consider the mighty works.

*The mighty works.* What has implicitly emerged from our survey is that the mighty works are essentially concerned with the authority and identity of Jesus rather than being simply signs of the presence of the kingdom of God. To be sure, these two possible functions naturally merge with each other, since the Messiah and the kingdom of God are correlates, but the emphasis is on the relation of the signs to the Messiah, whether to demonstrate who Jesus is or to afford grounds for opposition to him and rejection of him (cf. how the Pharisees want a sign from heaven to authenticate him). The mighty works arouse wonder (Mk 5:20). In a world where mighty works were accepted more easily

---

[33]The term *divine* is notoriously ambiguous, although attention is seldom drawn to this, and we might be better to avoid its use. In such a phrase as "divine voice" it refers to the voice of God, and a "divine messenger" is usually a messenger sent by God. But a "divine figure" is usually a person who in some way shares the nature or status of God. "Divine sonship" means that the person in question is in some sense a son of God (in contrast to a human being), but sometimes it means specifically that the person shares the nature and status of God. The word *divine (theios)* is not part of the New Testament christological vocabulary.

than they are today, the problem was not so much whether they actually happened but rather by what power they were done. Was the inspiration from the Holy Spirit or Beelzebul?

In line with his general thesis Telford argues that the term *Christ* is to be understood not in its Jewish nationalistic "Son of David" sense but "as a divine being who is to be identified with the community's exalted 'Lord'".[34] And "Son of God" refers to an epiphany of God in a "divine man" type of person who does mighty works rather than to a Davidic Messiah. If Mark accepts a Son of Man christology, the apocalyptic element is tempered by the stress on a suffering Son of Man.

The weakness in this thesis is its contrast between two aspects of the identity of Jesus that early Christians were capable of holding together. It may rather be the case that Mark tells the story of the Jesus who functioned in his lifetime as the Jewish Messiah and was understood or misunderstood in these terms by the people around him but who was then recognized by believers as the exalted Lord in the light of their postresurrection experience. What Mark does is to combine paradoxically the Jesus who performs mighty works and who will sit at the right hand of God with the Jesus who suffers and dies, and he insists that these two aspects are inextricably bound up with each other.

Part of Mark's purpose was to make it clear that Jesus is the Messiah who must suffer rather than a glorious, triumphant figure, and that discipleship therefore consists in readiness to bear the cross as he did. Mark is said to have counteracted a "theology [or, rather, christology] of glory" with a theology of the cross. A view diametrically opposed to this has been proposed by Robert H. Gundry, who holds that the Gospel was written for outsiders as an "apology for the cross", that is, to show that the Jesus whom the world rejected as a crucified, weak figure was in fact powerful and glorious. Despite Gundry's insistence that this proposal by itself fully explains Mark's theological purpose, it is more probable that the total message of the Gospel is such that readers with different needs would find appropriate answers to them in it.

*The future of the kingdom and the Messiah.* What is going to happen in the future? The amount of space devoted by Mark to the future is, as we have noted, almost disproportionate. It is presumably motivated by the needs of the readers

---

[34]Telford, *Theology*, p. 37.

and is an argument for seeing the Gospel as composed about A.D. 70.

Two themes intertwine in Mark 13. The first is the announced theme of the destruction of the temple and when it will happen. The second is the coming of the Christ/Messiah. A time is assumed when the Messiah is not here but may come. This would make sense for the readers of the Gospel who would know that the reference is to the time after his death when Jesus is no longer on earth. During this time they could see the fulfillment of the prophecies made by Jesus of false messianic claimants, natural disasters and wars, and persecution of Christians. People living in the time leading up to the war between the Jews and the Romans and especially during the war would certainly recognize the scenario. Part of the purpose of the chapter is to reassure the readers that these things were foretold and therefore are not out of God's control. There are also promises to the disciples (the "elect") that they will have divine help to withstand the temptations and suffering of this period. The fact that there will be such suffering is not explained in any way; it was an accepted fact that such sufferings would be, as it were, the birth pains of the new age (Mk 13:8). There is practical advice to the readers to flee from the scene of the danger symbolized by the appearance of "the abomination that causes desolation". This presumably refers to the desecration and destruction of the temple in Jerusalem. What follows thereafter is disputed. Traditionally Jesus is understood to go on to prophesy the coming of the Son of Man to gather together his disciples scattered all over the world, presumably into God's new world, the future manifestation of the kingdom of God. Some scholars, however, hold that the reference at this point is to the heavenly enthronement of the Son of Man, attested on earth by the fall of Jerusalem, which was understood as a judgment by the Son of Man, and by the worldwide mission of the church to gather together the new people of God; only at the end of the chapter (Mk 13:32-37) do we have a reference to that unknown time when the Son of Man will return for his waiting disciples.[35]

Mark 13 stands out as being very much on its own in the Gospel; yet it does take up the theme of the coming of the Son of Man that was adumbrated in Mark 8:38 and is reiterated in Mark 14:62. There is some tension here with a

---

[35]See especially France, *Gospel*, pp. 497-546; cf. R. T. France, *Matthew* (Leicester: Inter-Varsity Press, 1985), pp. 343-49; N. T. Wright, *Jesus and the Victory of God* (London: SPCK, 1996), pp. 320-68.

separate strand of teaching in the Gospel in which the resurrection of Jesus is foretold. In particular Jesus announces to his disciples that after he has risen he will go ahead of them to Galilee, and the women at the tomb are reminded of this message (Mk 14:28; 16:7). Nothing is said about the fulfillment of this promise, nor is it brought into relationship with the teaching in Mark 13. This may be a problem for us rather than for the original readers. They knew that Jesus was no longer on earth and that they were to look forward to his future coming. As for Mark's prediction of a temporary reunion in Galilee, the most reasonable solution is still that the original intended ending of the Gospel has not survived and that it related a meeting in Galilee (cf. Mt 28:16). Yet in a Gospel that has a strong element of mystery to it, the possibility cannot be excluded that Mark had some reason for not relating the resurrection appearances of Jesus.

*Response to Jesus.* Mark begins the Gospel with a stream of people flocking spontaneously to John to be baptized by him. Jesus commences his work by announcing the imminent arrival of the kingdom of God and urging people to repent and believe the good news. The summons to repentance picks up on John's baptism, but Jesus goes beyond John in announcing the good news. It is not clear in what way John's prophecy that Jesus would baptize with the Spirit is fulfilled; only in Mark 13:11 is it presupposed that the disciples will be inspired by the Spirit to speak courageously and appropriately under persecution. Here in Mark 1:15 the object of belief is the good news proclaimed by Jesus. However, the Gospel links belief in the good news closely to belief in the messenger. The language of discipleship and following Jesus is expressive of faith in him. Some of the mighty works are done for people who believe spontaneously or are encouraged to believe (Mk 2:5; 5:34, 36; 9:23-24; 10:52), and mighty works should lead to faith, although this may not happen (Mk 4:40). The opponents of Jesus want to see mighty works that would bring them to faith (Mk 15:32; cf. Mk 8:11-13). Thus for Mark people can become believers, but he does not explain how and why some do and others do not.

To "follow" Jesus is not necessarily the same thing as having faith in him and his message. The term is used literally of joining his group of companions and traveling with him with varying degrees of commitment (weak: Mk 2:15; 3:7; 5:24; strong: Mk 1:18; 2:14; 6:1). Jesus uses the term to indicate a close personal attachment to himself that demands total commitment (Mk 8:34; cf. Mk

10:28). The most common term to express this commitment is *disciple*, which is used with great frequency as a means of referring to the group of people who recognizably belonged to the entourage of Jesus and who could be presumed to be committed to him, even though the group could contain a Judas. Mark uses the term generally to refer to the traveling companions of Jesus who are to be identified with the Twelve (Mk 3:13-19). However, the group of people committed to Jesus is wider than the Twelve, who were especially chosen by Jesus apparently out of a larger number. The description in Mark 4:10, the call to a wider group to become followers of Jesus in Mark 8:34 and the example of Bartimaeus following Jesus (Mk 10:52)—these points all indicate that a larger group is intended. Nevertheless, in Mark the term *disciples* does appear to be restricted in reference to the group traveling with Jesus who from Mark 3 onward are the Twelve.[36]

The disciples function curiously in Mark. On the one hand, they are the recipients of Jesus' revelation concerning the kingdom of God and they receive teaching that he does not give to the crowds. They are a privileged group. On the other hand, they persistently show an inability to understand what Jesus is saying to them. It is implied that they ought to understand the parables (Mk 4:13), but they fail to do so. In various ways they behave ignorantly (like Peter in Mk 9:5-6) and without power (Mk 9:18). They are very human. At his arrest they all flee from the scene (Mk 14:50). This mixed evidence has been seen as indicating that Mark is severely critical of the disciples and that through them he is attacking the church leaders of his day.[37]

This explanation is quite unconvincing, since it is not clear why Mark should want to do this or exactly what he is criticizing. The picture is that of people learning what discipleship involves and fits in with the imperfections and need for growth found in the converts; only after the cross and resurrection does full understanding become possible. Thus the presentation is not unnatural; the puzzle is rather why Mark has not tended to idealize the first disciples and has rather gone out of his way to emphasize their slowness and lack of comprehension.

---

[36]The wider reference of the term is clearer in Lk 14:25-35.

[37]A key passage in all of this discussion is Mk 8:31-33, where Jesus teaches his disciples that the Son of Man must suffer and be raised and is reprimanded by Peter. But there is surely no way that this can represent a post-Easter attitude of Peter, since there could then be no denying that Jesus had in fact been crucified.

The issue is taken up by Telford, who argues that Mark develops this harsh picture of the disciples not merely for pastoral reasons (so that Mark can give teaching that offers encouragement and enlightenment) but also for polemical reasons in that he is opposing a christology and soteriology held by members of the Jerusalem church who saw Jesus as a royal Son of David who would shortly return and whose death they tended to ignore by contrast with his resurrection.[38]

There are some obvious weaknesses in this theory. Where is the evidence that would support the view that the primitive Jewish Christians held such a view of Jesus? And it is difficult to see the weaknesses of the disciples in the Gospel as being specifically linked to a mistaken christology; they are much wider than that.

The language used of discipleship at first tends to suggest that only the followers of Jesus (the disciples) can understand what he teaches and that they can do so only because it has been "given" to them by God. This would imply that there is a rigid distinction between those with Jesus and those "outside" (Mk 4:11), without it being clear how people may pass from one group to the other. Otherwise, however, the Gospel paints a picture of Jesus calling people to respond to his message and of some people coming to belief and discipleship without any indication of how they come to understand. The crucial teaching in Mark 4 seems to be better interpreted as saying that those who respond to the gospel go on to advance in knowledge of the kingdom of God in a way that is not possible for those who remain outside. If the latter hear Jesus teaching and do not respond, his teaching appears as parables or riddles that they hear without understanding. There is a puzzle as to why some respond positively and some negatively, and there is no answer to it. Mark is not saying that the former respond because God causes them to do so, whereas he passes over the others. But he is saying that persistent refusal to believe means that people are deprived of the opportunity to believe. There is a hardness of heart, by which is meant not tightfistedness but rather a blindness to truth, which is characteristic of the opposition to Jesus (Mk 3:5) and from which even disciples can suffer (Mk 6:52; 8:14-21).[39] One could be forgiven for sometimes wondering what it is

---

[38]Telford, *Theology*, pp. 151-63.
[39]Note that the language of "hardening" is not taken over by Matthew and Luke.

that distinguishes the disciples from the opposition! But at least there is some commitment on their part to Jesus (cf. the sentiment in Mk 9:24).

A further element in the people's reaction to Jesus that should not be overlooked is wonder and amazement coupled with fear. Mark seems to have a deeper sense of the numinous quality of the actions of Jesus than the other writers and brings out more fully this element of mystery that surrounds him. It may be that his stress on the messianic secret has some relation to this fact. He does not want his readers to think that everything can be grasped and easily explained.

## Conclusion

It may be premature at this point to attempt to characterize the theology of Mark since this needs to be done in comparison with that of the other Evangelists so that any distinctive elements stand out more clearly. Nevertheless, it may be helpful to summarize it in terms of its framework, main theme and detailed development.

The framework of Jesus' teaching, which is no doubt that of Mark, is provided by the current Jewish beliefs about the existence of God, the revelation of his will in the Scriptures and his choice of Israel as his people. Jesus accepted also the anthropology of Judaism with its belief in the reality of a spiritual dimension to human life and in the activity of spiritual agencies, both good (angels) and evil (demons and Satan). He also accepted the concept of two eras in human history, this present age and the coming age, which would be the era of God's perfect rule over his people.

The main theme of the Gospel is the identity of Jesus in his relationship to the kingdom of God. Mark spells this out in two stages. There is first the recognition of Jesus as Messiah and Son of God, with the evidence of the presence of the kingdom in and through the mighty works and his proclamation. Then there is the recognition that the Messiah must suffer and be raised from the dead, with the implications that this has for his followers. The kingdom will not come without suffering on the part of the Messiah and those who share in his task. Throughout the Gospel there is a sense of mystery: the Messiah is no ordinary, human person, and the Gospel is a secret revelation of who he is to those who are willing to accept the revelation and become his disciples, even though they are puzzled by it and even inclined to reject it.

At the risk of simplification and systematization we can summarize some significant elements in the detailed development of the main theme as follows.

1. Jesus presupposed that his audience consisted of people with needs, physical, social and spiritual. He criticized the religion associated with the Pharisees for its insistence on observance of the minutiae of the law, its concentration on outward observance regardless of the attitude of the heart and its lack of concern for those who did not live up to its standards.

2. Jesus' basic teaching, given in terms of this presuppositional framework, was concerned with this rule of God, understood as God's sovereign, gracious power operating in the world through himself to create a sphere of blessing for humankind and to overcome the power of Satan and destroy evil. It would be fully manifested in the near future, but it was already exercising its influence. His mission was to bring good news to the poor and needy, and to demonstrate the power of God at work in acts of healing and compassion. He attempted to bring sinners to a consciousness of their real condition in the sight of God.

3. His own role in this appeared to be like that of a teacher and prophet sent from God, but the way in which he spoke and acted with the sovereign power and authority of God raised the question whether he should be seen in the framework of Jewish expectations about the coming of the Messiah in the end time. He spoke about the coming and activity of the Son of Man, a phrase that was certainly understood messianically by his followers after his death and almost certainly so by himself. He thought of God as his father and prayed to him accordingly.

4. He closely identified himself with his cause, so that response to his message was expressed in terms of following him as disciples. Although he did not organize a new society of his followers, he did call some people to share closely in his mission.

5. He saw his task as the renewal of the people of Israel who had fallen away from a true relationship with God. Although he restricted his activity almost exclusively to the Jews, he showed a particular concern for the marginalized and did not exclude Gentiles from his concern.

6. He approved the summary of Jewish religion as wholehearted love for God and one's neighbor.

7. He carried his principles to the utmost limit by being willing to die for them. He saw that suffering not as something accidental but as part of his divinely destined vocation, and he regarded his sufferings as being in some way on behalf of other people and sacrificial and redemptive in effect.

8. He looked forward to the imminent consummation of God's rule, when humankind would be upheld or judged at God's bar in accordance with their response to himself.

## Bibliography

*New Testament Theologies:* (English) Ladd, pp. 228-36; Morris, pp. 95-113; Strecker, pp. 343-64; Zuck, pp. 65-86 (D. K. Lowery). (German) Berger, pp. 634-42 *et passim;* Gnilka, pp. 151-74; Hahn, I: 488-517; Hübner, 3:67-95; Stuhlmacher, 2:130-50.

Best, Ernest. *Following Jesus: Discipleship in the Gospel of Mark.* Sheffield: JSOT Press, 1981.

Evans, Craig A. *Mark 8:27–16:20.* WBC. Nashville: Thomas Nelson, 2001.

France, R. T. *The Gospel of Mark: A Commentary on the Greek Text.* Grand Rapids, Mich.: Eerdmans; Carlisle: Paternoster, 2002.

Geddert, Timothy J. *Watchwords: Mark 13 in Markan Eschatology.* Sheffield: JSOT Press, 1989.

Guelich, Robert A. *Mark 1–8:26.* Dallas: Word, 1989.

Gundry, Robert H. *Mark: A Commentary on His Apology for the Cross.* Grand Rapids, Mich.: Eerdmans, 1993.

Hooker, M. D. *A Commentary on the Gospel According to St. Mark.* London: A & C Black, 1991.

————. *The Message of Mark.* London: Epworth, 1983.

Marcus, Joel. *The Way of the Lord: Christological Exegesis of the Old Testament in the Gospel of Mark.* Edinburgh: T & T Clark, 1993.

Marshall, Christopher D. *Faith as a Theme in Mark's Narrative.* Cambridge: Cambridge University Press, 1989.

Martin, Ralph P. *Mark: Evangelist and Theologian.* Exeter: Paternoster, 1972.

Stonehouse, Ned B. *The Witness of Matthew and Mark to Christ.* London: Tyndale, 1959.

Telford, William R. *Mark.* Sheffield New Testament Guides. Sheffield: Sheffield Academic Press, 1995.

————. *The Theology of the Gospel of Mark.* Cambridge: Cambridge University Press, 1999.

Telford, William R., ed. *The Interpretation of Mark.* 2nd ed. Edinburgh: T & T Clark, 1995.

Twelftree, Graham H. *Jesus the Miracle Worker: A Historical and Theological Study.* Downers

Grove, Ill.: InterVarsity Press, 1999.

Watson, Francis B. "The Social Function of Mark's Secrecy Motif". *JSNT* 24 (1985): 49-69.

Watts, Rikki E. *Isaiah's New Exodus and Mark.* Tübingen: Mohr Siebeck, 1997.

# 4

# THE GOSPEL OF MATTHEW

&#8766;&#8762;&#8766;

I t is appropriate to proceed to the Gospel of Matthew rather than to the Gospel of Luke immediately after our treatment of the Gospel of Mark. In many ways Matthew is more similar to Mark than Luke is: Luke is less tied to the text and structure of Mark and has placed his Gospel in the context of a broader treatment of Christian beginnings. Matthew is more Jewish in outlook and to that extent closer to the ethos of Jesus and the earliest Christians. It is easier to understand Luke after having seen how Matthew has treated the story of Jesus, even though there are places where Luke may have an earlier outlook and account than Matthew.[1]

## Matthew's Theological Story

Matthew's theological story of Jesus is very close to that of Mark. He incorporates the vast majority of the individual story items in Mark. He keeps broadly to the same order in his narrative as in Mark, although there is a complex rearrangement of the material in the earlier chapters. He also sticks fairly closely to Mark's wording, although his tendency here is to abbreviate the accounts to some extent. The total impact of the material in parallel with Mark in his narrative is thus very much the same as it is in Mark, although the amount of additional material does cause us to see it in a different context, and there are numerous small changes and

---

[1]There is fairly broad agreement that the Gospel is to be dated after Mark. The general tendency is to argue that its authorship is unknown, although it may contain material ultimately stemming from Matthew, the disciple of Jesus. A strong case for authorship of the Gospel by Matthew is offered by R. T. France, *Matthew: Evangelist and Teacher* (Exeter: Paternoster, 1989), pp. 50-80, but most scholars hold that while this is possible, the arguments remain inconclusive.

additions that affect our understanding of it. Ideally, a proper treatment of the theological story of Matthew and likewise of Luke should cover the whole account in the same way and with the same detail as in the case of Mark, but this would take up a considerable amount of space and also inevitably entail a lot of repetition of their common emphases. Practically, the way forward will be to note the similarities and differences by comparison with Mark.

The basic structure of the Gospel is much the same as in Mark. It is noteworthy that Matthew uses the same form of words, "From that time on Jesus began to" in Matthew 4:17 and Matthew 16:21, and that this formula occurs at the beginning of Jesus' proclamation of the message of the kingdom[2] and at the point where he begins to teach his disciples about his imminent death. This suggests that Matthew shares the same basic *theological* two-part structure that Mark has in his Gospel, where the first part reveals who Jesus is and the second explains that he must suffer.[3] Another structure, however, is imposed on top of this one. This is a narrative structure that gives an alternation of action and discourse.[4]

*The birth, baptism and temptation of Jesus.* Matthew differs from Mark in providing a lengthy preface to the Gospel by the inclusion of the story of the birth of Jesus (Mt 1—2). This account contains two elements. It commences with a genealogical tree for Jesus, which begins with Abraham and traces the line that leads to the kings of Judah and on to Zerubbabel, and then through a series of otherwise unknown names until we reach Joseph, the husband of Jesus' mother, Mary. On the way through, four women are mentioned (Tamar, Rahab, Ruth and Uriah's wife, Bathsheba) who had irregular unions or were non-Jews. The effect of the genealogy is to root Jesus in the Jewish people and in its royal line, and to prepare the way for his irregular birth and for the inclusion of Gentiles in the people of God.[5]

---

[2]Instead of "kingdom of God" Matthew has the alternative form "kingdom of heaven" in nearly every case. This appears to be nothing more than a stylistic variant reflecting perhaps Jewish usage, although the phrase is not attested in Judaism before Johanan ben Zakkai; see W. D. Davies and D. C. Allison Jr., *The Gospel According to St Matthew* (Edinburgh: T & T Clark, 1997), 3:390-91.

[3]The theme of the rejection of Jesus is not absent from the first part of the Gospel (e.g., Mt 12:40), but it is not presented as explicitly as in the second part.

[4]The precise details of this structure, which are a matter of some debate, are not of essential importance for a study of the theology of Matthew.

[5]For Matthew, as for Luke, it is assumed that Joseph's acceptance of Jesus as if he were his own son legally entitled him to belong to this genealogy and so to be accounted as a descendant of David.

Then Matthew relates that Mary was found to be with child and that it was revealed to Joseph in a dream that this had come about by the Holy Spirit, with the clearly intended implication that Mary had not committed adultery or fornication with any other man. The child would be named Jesus, meaning "the Lord saves", and his birth would fulfill the Old Testament prophecy of a child of a virgin to be called Immanuel, meaning "God [is] with us". At the outset, therefore, Jesus is placed in the royal line of Judah, which strongly suggests that he is the Messiah, his role has to do with saving people from sin, and his presence is tantamount to that of God himself. This royal element is continued in the ensuing account of the birth and its aftermath, where the magi understand the child to be the king of the Jews, and Herod assumes that this is the "Christ". The motif that Jesus is the Son of God emerges almost incidentally in the story of the flight to Egypt with its "fulfillment" of Hosea 11:1. The rest of Jesus' childhood and youth is passed over without comment.

Matthew is now ready to pick up the story of the adult life of Jesus at the same point where Mark begins, namely, with the activity of John the Baptist and Jesus' baptism by him (Mt 3). The account illustrates well how Matthew works on his story. First, by including material from his other sources, such as the fuller account of the preaching of John (Mt 3:7-10, 14-15), he puts a greater stress on the judgment that awaits those who do not repent of their sins and voices a certain skepticism about the intentions of the Pharisees and Sadducees who came for baptism, both of which are themes that will recur. Second, he makes slight changes in the account given by Mark, such as the substitution of *"This is* my beloved son" for *"You are* my beloved son", which has the effect of turning a saying addressed primarily to Jesus in Mark into a public proclamation.

Similarly, Mark's very brief note that Jesus was tempted by Satan is replaced by a lengthier account of three attempts by the devil to tempt Jesus to disobey and distrust God (Mt 4:1-11). The resolute resistance and triumph of Jesus emerge more clearly in this alternative account.

*The manifesto of the teacher.* The preliminaries over, Matthew takes up the story of the work of Jesus in Galilee (Mt 4:12-25). Here, as earlier in the story of his birth, Matthew sees some kind of fulfillment of prophecy in the Old Testament and cites appropriate passages, usually with a specific formula that says that what happened took place in order to fulfill the prophecy. The effect of these citations is to show in some detail that significant events and activities in the life of Jesus correspond with Old Testament prophecies and types.[6] The message of Jesus is summarized even more briefly than in Mark as "Repent, for the kingdom of heaven has come near" (Mt 4:17).[7] The element of fulfillment in Mark's account of the message is contained in the preceding scriptural quotation from Isaiah 9:1-2. The command that identifies the message as good news ("gospel") and calls for belief in it is dropped but is effectively present in the following summary account of the mission of Jesus "proclaiming the good news of the kingdom and healing" (Mt 4:23).

Whereas Mark goes straight on into a set of episodes that would fill out this summary and that lead fairly quickly into the conflict raised by Jesus' teaching and healings, Matthew now places well up front the first of the five lengthy accounts of the teaching of Jesus that are so characteristic of this Gospel. By so doing he emphasizes that Jesus is a teacher who is at the same time a healer rather than vice versa. The Sermon on the Mount (Mt 5—7) is a carefully structured piece, extending to ninety-eight verses; it corresponds with a much briefer account in Luke 6:20-49 that runs to only thirty verses, although some of Matthew's material in his sermon is paralleled elsewhere in Luke. This procedure indicates the importance to Matthew of presenting the teaching of Jesus at length and in a reasonably systematic kind of way. As we saw, there is something similar in Mark 4 and Mark 13, but Matthew has gone much further in this respect.

The material is addressed to a group that comprises the crowds and the disciples of Jesus, the former term indicating those as yet uncommitted to him and his message, while the latter are those who have some kind of commitment, including some whose commitment may be very partial or nominal. It is striking, then, that the teaching is essentially for the followers[8] in that it includes the promises of Jesus to those who follow him but majors on the kind of conduct that is required by God of those who respond to the message of the kingdom of God. This is teaching for disciples, which at the same time is a summons to those not yet committed to Jesus and a glimpse into what they are letting themselves in for. In this way Matthew focuses on the kind of behavior that should

---

[6]Richard E. Menninger, *Israel and the Church in the Gospel of Matthew* (New York: Peter Lang, 1994), p. 71.

[7]The same message is attributed to John the Baptist in Mt 3:2.

[8]For example, Mt 5:13-16 can only be addressed to them.

be characteristic of disciples. Although Matthew is not lacking in material about the gracious, saving action of God, this sermon is a full-scale account of what is involved in repentance, a new way of life for those who respond to the message of Jesus.

Although the sermon is concerned with behavior rather than belief, nevertheless it makes theological assumptions and has theological implications. These must be briefly noted.

1. The kingdom of heaven is possessed by those who are poor in spirit and are persecuted for the sake of righteousness (Mt 5:3, 10). This means that they enjoy the benefits that are associated with the reign of God. Yet the other Beatitudes spelling out the promises in detail are in the future tense (Mt 5:4-9, 11-12). This recognizes the realities of the situation that the promises are not yet completely fulfilled but will be in the future. Nevertheless, the kingdom assuredly belongs here and now to the poor in spirit and there is certainly some sense in which it is already present and its blessings are already real (Mt 12:28).

2. Jesus asserts that the law and the prophets are not abolished but fulfilled by him and emphasizes the need for the practice and teaching of the least commandments in the context of the kingdom of heaven (Mt 5:17-20). He then proceeds to go through a number of commandments, all taken from the law, and gives teaching that takes them on to a higher level; if some of them are made redundant (e.g., Mt 5:38-39), the redundant command still remains in force as a kind of safety net. These examples are not of "least" commandments.[9] It is clear that for Jesus, as understood by Matthew, the law remains in force for his Jewish audience, but in the light of the antithetical teaching that follows it is the law as reinterpreted by Jesus that is now to be kept.

3. Jesus emphasizes the goodness of God as the heavenly Father and his care (Mt 6:8, 25-34). The teaching about his providential care is given in the context of encouragement for the disciples to trust in him. This fits in with the consistent teaching of Jesus elsewhere in the Gospels according to which the relationship of God as Father is always with those who are disciples and not with people in general. Jesus never speaks of God as Father except to his disciples.

---

[9]One might suppose that the term *least* is introduced with "commandments" in order to allow the play on words with "least in the kingdom of heaven" and is not to be taken too strictly.

The relationship is spiritual rather than being based on creation.

4. The goodness of God is seen in the way that he answers prayer and gives good gifts to his children (Mt 7:11). Here Matthew's version differs from that of Luke, according to which God will give the Spirit to those who ask him (Lk 11:13). It is unlikely that Matthew has changed an originally spiritual gift into one that is not so, and more probable that he has a more general expression that is primarily spiritual but does not exclude other kinds of answers to prayer.

5. The end of the sermon emphasizes the importance of obedience to the words of Jesus and to the will of God. Implicit here is the equation of the sayings of Jesus with the will of God, but the key point is that the Christian life is a matter of obedience and not just of faith. The sermon, accordingly, places together total faith in the goodness of God who answers prayer and total obedience to his will, which does not relax the commandments but rather lifts them to a higher plane of fulfillment that goes beyond simply obeying the letter of the law.

The sermon, then, expands the message that invites people to repent, and it does so by exhibiting the promises and the demands given to those who have accepted the message of the kingdom. In short, what an ongoing conversion to the way of Jesus entails is set in the context of God's fatherly care for disciples.

*The mission of Jesus—and his disciples.* After this manifesto Matthew basically uses the next two chapters of the Gospel (Mt 8—9) to cover some of the stories of Jesus' activity that we find in the early chapters of Mark (Mk 1—5) but without adhering too closely to Mark's order. Where Mark has used some of this material to illustrate the build-up of opposition to Jesus (Mk 2:1—3:6), Matthew appears to be less interested in this motif (but cf. Mt 9:34), and the stress is rather on the remarkable character of Jesus as healer, in accordance with prophecy (Mt 8:17), on his calls to discipleship and on his growing reputation. This comes to a climax at the end of Matthew 9, where the work is becoming too great for one person to accomplish. At this point, therefore, we hear that Jesus has appointed twelve disciples and now sends them out to extend his mission.

This sending is the occasion for the second main teaching section in the Gospel (Mt 10:5—11:1), which is concerned with instructions, warnings and encouragements for those engaged in mission. Although the teaching begins with material directly relevant to the mission of the Twelve there and then (Mt 10:5-15),[10] it becomes the locus in Matthew's systematic presentation of Jesus' teaching for bringing in other material that was more relevant to the disciples in the post-Easter situation (Mt 10:16-42).

The most remarkable features in the discourse are two verses peculiar to Matthew. In Matthew 10:5-6 the disciples are instructed not to go the Gentiles or to the Samaritans but to the lost sheep of Israel. The need for this command arises out of the realities of the geography: Galilee was heavily populated with Gentiles and was adjacent to Samaria, through which people would travel to Jerusalem. Theologically the mission has as its priority Israel and specifically the needy people in it (the marginalized and the poor). All the evidence points to the fact that the historical Jesus did focus his mission on the Jews, as the embarrassing incident in Mt 15:21-28 (note Mt 15:24 par. Mk 7:24-30) indicates. At the same time, there is an openness to Gentiles throughout the Gospel that indicates that for Matthew this limitation was confined to the mission of Jesus and was not binding on the early church. Consequently, although this chapter brings together teaching relevant for disciples on mission, the horizon at this point remains basically that of the lifetime of Jesus.

But the horizon is fuzzy. The thought of persecution in the Gentile world arises in Matthew 10:18-20, where Matthew has incorporated material from Mark 13. Then we have the puzzle of a second verse peculiar to Matthew (Mt 10:23), where the disciples are told that they will not finish going through the cities of Israel before the Son of Man comes. This saying appears to refer to the future coming of the Son of Man that is attested elsewhere in the Gospels and states that the task facing the disciples to Israel is too great to be completed before this final event; it would presumably envisage a mission that extends beyond the time of Jesus, and the Evangelists have no difficulties about Jesus being able to foretell events after his death. The statement would appear to be placed within the context of ongoing mission, and not of the immediate short-term mission of the disciples. This is certainly an odd statement in that the number of cities of Israel was not all that many, unless we are meant to include the many cities in the Diaspora where Jews lived. It is also odd in that, if it refers to the

---

[10]Matthew here follows the teaching in Mk 6 together with parallel material from Q.

postresurrection period, it retains the restriction to Jewish cities. The best explanation is that of W. D. Davies and Dale C. Allison Jr., who hold that Matthew saw in this saying a prophecy of the parousia of the Son of Man that would occur before the disciples had concluded their mission to the world, including Israel.[11] The saying is intended to be encouragement to those who experience persecution while on mission, and it reassures them that the Son of Man will come while they are still engaged on their task.[12]

*The growth of opposition and division.* The next section is also devoted to the activities of Jesus, principally to his teaching and the varied reactions to it (Mt 11—12). It contains Q material that is concerned with Jesus' relationship to John the Baptist and the contrast between the rejection that he found in the cities of Galilee and the acceptance of God's message by the disciples. Then it picks up the material in Mark 2—3 that was passed over earlier in the Gospel, supplementing it with Q material. In this section the opposition from the Pharisees, culminating in a murderous plot, is thematic.

Within this section it is noteworthy that the Evangelist now calls Jesus the "Christ" (Mt 11:2), thereby implicitly answering affirmatively the question of John the Baptist, "Are you the one who was to come?" Jesus' answer to the question refers to his mighty works and sees them as fulfilling what was prophesied in Isaiah 35 concerning the future era when God comes.[13] In a difficult saying a contrast is drawn between the previous era of the prophets and the law and the new era in which the kingdom of heaven is active (Mt 11:12-13).[14] John is identified clearly as the latter-day Elijah of Malachi 4:5-6.

The nature of God's work through Jesus is illumined in the important saying in which Jesus comments on the way in which God as Father reveals himself

---

[11]Davies and Allison, *Gospel*, 2:187-92.

[12]There is a minor inconsistency with Mt 24:14 (cf. Mk 13:10), which states that the gospel must "first" be preached to all nations. The inconsistency is resolved to some extent if "all nations" is not interpreted to mean "every single community".

[13]The reference to Is 35 and other associated texts is implicit; there is no formal quotation. The significant point is that what is prophesied there when God comes (Is 35:4) is understood to be fulfilled in the Messiah's coming. Hence Jesus is indeed Immanuel.

[14]The saying is ambiguous, and scholarly opinions differ as to whether the kingdom "has been forcefully advancing" (NIV) or "has been subjected to violence" (TNIV text; cf. NRSV text) and whether the "violent people" are straining to enter it (so apparently NIV) or to oppose it (TNIV; NRSV). The current trend is to accept the latter options; see, for example, Donald A. Hagner, *Matthew 1—13* (Dallas: Word, 1993), pp. 306-7. Either way, the kingdom is clearly active.

through the Son to those to whom the Son chooses to reveal him and then issues a general invitation to all who are burdened to come to him (Mt 11:25-
30). This saying is significant for christology and for soteriology. As it stands,
it clearly identifies Jesus as the Son, standing in the kind of exclusive, close relationship to the Father that is much more fully developed in the Gospel of
John.[15] It also indicates that knowledge of God and his will is mediated through
Jesus. This is linked with the fact that the wise people of this world have failed
to know God (cf. 1 Cor 1:18-25); God reveals himself to the "little children"
who are prepared to be taught.

The following chapter (Mt 12) then in effect deals with this closed attitude
of the Pharisees, who fail to appreciate what God is doing. Their opposition
stands in complete contrast with that of the people healed by Jesus who recognized him as God's agent. Two points arise here. First, Jesus warns the people
who are healed not to tell who he was (Mt 12:16). Here, as elsewhere (Mt 8:4;
9:30; 16:20; 17:9), Matthew has the same motif of keeping secret the identity
of Jesus as is found in Mark, but there are other cases where Matthew has not
preserved the motif, particularly with regard to the silencing of the demons.
The motif is thus not as prominent as in Mark, but it is certainly there. Second,
Matthew again takes the opportunity to cite Scripture that is fulfilled in the
mission of Jesus, in this case with a full quotation of Isaiah 42:1-4. The main
point of the quotation is to stress the meek and quiet mission of the Lord's Servant in the power of the Spirit (cf. Mt 11:28-30; 12:28), but the quotation also
carries two references to the nations that indicate that the mission of Jesus is
ultimately not confined to the Jewish people (cf. Mt 12:39-42).[16]

The third discourse section of the Gospel (Mt 13) comes appropriately at
this point as an extended comment on the way in which people respond, or fail
to respond, to God's message given by Jesus. It contains an enlarged set of parables as compared with Mark 4. As in Mark, the first parable, that of the sower,
is told simply as a story, and only afterward does it emerge that it is parabolic

---

[15] The relationship of the saying to the teaching of the historical Jesus is disputed. For a defense of its
authenticity see Ben Witherington III, *The Christology of Jesus* (Minneapolis: Fortress, 1990), pp. 221-
28.

[16] For the implications of this quotation see David Hill, "Son and Servant: An Essay on Matthean
Christology", *JSNT* 6 (1980): 2-16 (9-12), citing proposals by O. L. Cope; Richard Beaton, *Isaiah's
Christ in Matthew's Gospel* (Cambridge: Cambridge University Press, 2002).

of the kingdom of heaven. The remaining parables are all cases of "the kingdom of heaven is like" and invite the readers more directly to get beyond the story to the reality presented by it. It is significant that in the explanation of the parable of the sower there is a stress on the need for understanding the message (Mt 13:23, picking up on Mt 13:13, 15); as in Mark the disciples are regarded as having understood the message, whatever may be said about their lack of understanding on other occasions. Also, as in Mark, there may be the implication that Jesus began to speak in this way, which was not understood by everybody, only after people had begun to reject his message. Matthew's parables include two new ones, the tares and the dragnet, both of which are explained to refer to the final judgment, at which the people of the kingdom or "the righteous" will be glorified in the kingdom of God while the people of the evil one, those who cause sin and do evil, will be cast into eternal fire. More than the other Evangelists, Matthew stresses this element and uses strong language about the remorse and fury of the lost. At the same time, Matthew also depicts the joy of those who find the kingdom for themselves, like somebody finding a hidden treasure or a valuable pearl.[17]

*The revelation of Jesus as the Messiah.* In the next section devoted to the activity of Jesus, which covers Matthew 13:53—17:27, Matthew follows Mark rather more closely. The minor differences vary in significance. Thus Matthew 13:58 does not really paint Jesus' inability to work healing miracles in Nazareth any differently from Mark 6:5. A glance at a Synopsis shows that a good many differences are due simply to abbreviation. But there are also additions. The story of Jesus walking on the sea now includes the incident of Peter trying to emulate Jesus and failing. And where the disciples in Mark are filled with amazement and do not understand what is going on, in Matthew they worship Jesus as the Son of God. The element of "secret epiphany", which some scholars have traced in Mark, is thus all the stronger here.

In Matthew 15 there is some rearrangement of the material that may simply be in the interests of greater clarity. Opinions differ whether there is significance in the omission of Mark's comment that what Jesus said had the effect of declaring all foods clean (Mk 7:19). This is sometimes thought to fit in with a greater tendency to see Jesus as keeping the Jewish law and criticizing the

---

[17]The vocabulary of joy is almost absent from Mark (but see Mk 4:16).

Pharisees more for their failure to keep their own law and for their misinterpretation of it than for emphasizing the importance of the law. But it is rather more probable that Matthew is simply abbreviating Mark, and that his addition in Matthew 15:12-14 sufficiently indicates his rejection of the principle that foods can make people unclean.[18]

But the most important new material in this section comes in Matthew 16, in the section where Jesus asks his disciples who they think that he is. Peter's reply, "You are the Christ", is supplemented by the words "the Son of the living God" (Mt 16:16) and is followed by the lengthy saying of Jesus that comments that it is God who has revealed this to him, and then by the saying about Peter being the rock on which Jesus will build his church. The first part of this statement is not surprising in the light of Matthew 11:25-27, where it is the Father who reveals the Son to human beings. The second part is most plausibly interpreted as an identification of Peter as the rock.[19] Only here and in Matthew 18:18 does the term *church (ekklēsia)* occur in the Gospels. Its presence fits in with an interest in the Gospel in the disciples as forming a new community that is perhaps more pronounced than in the other Gospels; this community is obviously to be identified with the ongoing community of which Matthew and his readers were part. The same link is achieved by Luke through his compilation of his second volume.[20]

Peculiar to Matthew are the two following statements. First, the church will be invincible against all opposition. The "gates of Hades" is a reference to the powers of the underworld, which will attack the church.[21] The metaphor of the gate continues with a reference to Peter receiving the keys of the kingdom of heaven. The authority that Jesus has to "open the kingdom of heaven to all believers" is extended to his disciple. It is explicated in terms of teaching authority, so that Peter stands over against the Pharisees whose teaching is rejected. This is the strongest form of statement in which Jesus

---

[18]Cf. Menninger, *Israel*, pp. 124-26.

[19]But the view that the rock is the words of Jesus or the confession by Peter continues to find some support. See Chrys C. Caragounis, *Peter and the Rock* (Berlin: de Gruyter, 1990); for the more usual interpretation see, for example, Donald A. Hagner, *Matthew 14—28* (Dallas: Word, 1995), pp. 469-72.

[20]Mark knows that the disciples will reassemble with Jesus in Galilee after his resurrection, but otherwise he is rather silent about the church.

[21]Joachim Jeremias, *TDNT* 6:924-28.

hands on his own authority for the future to his disciples. It is important that the same statement about "binding and loosing" is made to all the Twelve in Matthew 18:18. The whole paragraph is crucial for its teaching that the church is in effect the new Israel, established by Jesus; the kingdom has been taken from its old leaders and given to a new people who will produce the appropriate harvest (Mt 21:43).[22]

*The community of disciples.* We can move straight from this section to the fourth teaching section in Matthew 18.[23] Here Matthew starts from the conversation about true greatness in the kingdom of heaven that he found in Mark 9:33-50. He sharpens it up by some omission of material and proceeds to bring together other teaching by Jesus that has to do with disciples in community. There is a stress on the importance of the "little ones", who must be humble believers rather than children (so also in Mt 11:25), that reminds us of Paul's urging the "strong" to show concern for the "weak" (1 Cor 8—10). Matthew's version of the parable of the lost sheep is oriented to the duty of disciples to care for erring believers rather than, as in Luke 15, to the justification of Jesus' mission to the tax collectors and sinners who typify the unconverted. In the second half of the chapter the problem of internal disputes between disciples occurs, and a procedure is established that aims to bring about recognition of one's fault and consequent reconciliation.[24] At the same time, the importance of cleansing the church of faults and disputes is recognized. This procedure may seem to stand in contradiction to the principle established by the parable of the wheat and the tares. However, in the parable the field is the world, not the church, and no interpretation is given to the instruction to the farm workers to let wheat and tares grow together until the harvest; this detail is simply part

---

[22]Nevertheless, Matthew does not explicitly identify the church as the new Israel; for John P. Meier, *The Vision of Matthew: Christ, Church and Morality in the First Gospel* (New York: Paulist, 1978), p. 55, it is Jesus who embodies the new Israel. France, *Matthew*, pp. 206-13, sees Jesus and the church as the fulfillment of Israel.

[23]There is nothing distinctive in the rest of Mt 16—17 that requires special comment from a theological angle. Matthew remains fairly close to Mark.

[24]The procedure described is reduced to essentials. It is assumed that the fault is clearly established. Opportunities for recognition and reconciliation are created, and it would be wrong to assume that only three opportunities need be given; the implication is rather that there comes a point when all reasonable attempts to heal the dispute have failed, and in that case the congregation must take action so that there is no continuing breach within the actual circle of the congregation. Nothing is said to imply that the exclusion is permanent and cannot be withdrawn.

of the scenery in the story and does not have any parabolic significance.

To the action of the congregation is attributed the same authority as was given to Peter.[25] A further reinforcement of the congregation's action is conveyed in the next statement, which assures a gathering of even two believers that their prayers will be answered; this is because if they gather together in the name of Jesus, he is with them and his prayers reinforce theirs (Mt 18:19-20). It is the Synoptic equivalent of John 16:23-24.

The procedure for dealing with faults by giving three opportunities for repentance to the offender is now followed by an instruction to the offended person to be prepared to forgive seventy-seven times. This teaching is reinforced by a parable whose meaning is dazzlingly obvious, provided we remember that in the language of parables "a king" is a fairly sure pointer to God. If this were not obvious in itself, the reference to a debt of ten thousand talents shows that we are not dealing with the real world of human beings.

This chapter demonstrates more than any other, perhaps, the pastoral aspects of Matthew's theology and his insight into the sheer grace of God toward sinners.[26]

*Jesus teaches in Jerusalem.* With this discourse we reach the end of the Galilean mission of Jesus; Matthew 19:1 marks the shift to Judea and Jerusalem, and from this point Matthew again runs parallel to Mark. There are a few significant differences. In Matthew 19:28-29 the promise that the disciples will be recompensed in the age to come for their self-denial in this age is supplemented by the saying (also found in Lk 22:28-30) that those who have followed Jesus will sit on twelve thrones judging the twelve tribes of Israel when the Son of Man comes. This saying is important as showing that the mission of Jesus is concerned with the renewal of Israel in the new age.

A second insertion is the parable of the workers in the vineyard (Mt 20:1-16), which reinforces the message about the grace of God that is given to those who need it rather than to those who deserve it. Such a parable as this, of course, is told to those who think that they especially deserve God's favor rather than to those who need it; it displays important resemblances to the parable of

---

[25] Consequently, there is no need for Peter to have a successor.

[26] Cf. Donald A. Hagner, "Righteousness in Matthew's Theology", in *Worship, Theology and Ministry in the Early Church*, ed. Michael J. Wilkins and Terence Paige (Sheffield: Sheffield Academic Press, 1992), pp. 101-20.

the two sons in Luke 15.[27] The same theme recurs later in the Matthean parable of the two sons (Mt 21:28-32).

Meanwhile, Jesus approaches ever closer to Jerusalem, and the shadow of the cross begins to become more pronounced, reminding the disciples that there will be no crowns or thrones for them without first drinking the cup of suffering with Jesus.[28] Yet there is a sense in which Jesus enters Jerusalem as already its king; it is Matthew who cites Zechariah 9:9 in connection with the entry and thus aligns himself with Luke and John in their identification of Jesus as the king—who is about to be rejected. The crowds, however, recognize him only as a prophet (Mt 21:11), whereas the children in the temple (cf. Mt 11:25!) recognize him as the "Son of David" (Mt 21:15).[29]

In the encounters with his opponents in Jerusalem, Matthew has a sharper form of the parable of the tenants. For him it culminates in the hearers themselves drawing the conclusion as to what the owner of the vineyard will do to the workers who murdered the son and thus laying themselves open to the prophecy that the kingdom of God will be taken away from them and given to a people who will produce the fruit (Mt 21:40-46). This is to be seen as a judgment primarily upon the Jewish leaders who will be replaced by the church or its leaders as the overseers of the people of God.[30]

At this point Matthew inserts yet another parable, that of the wedding banquet, which is concerned with the people who are invited into the kingdom of heaven (Mt 22:1-14); those originally invited make light of the invitation, whereas a very mixed bag of people, good and bad, are brought in. Nevertheless, it remains possible for people to come in and yet fail to show appreciation of their privilege; they are "in but not of the kingdom", and they will be uncovered at the final judgment. Matthew allows no complacency among his Christian readers.

---

[27]Davies and Allison, *Gospel*, 3:69.

[28]Matthew omits mention of the baptism that they must undergo, possibly because the saying appeared to be too cryptic.

[29]Surprisingly Matthew and Luke omit the phrase found in Mk 11:17 that the temple will be called a house of prayer for all the nations. This may reflect the fact that the temple was destroyed and the prophecy was not fulfilled literally.

[30]Opinions differ whether this verse is simply about a change of leadership or is also about the replacement of Israel by the church. The latter understanding is more probable (cf. Menninger, *Israel*, pp. 151-53). The word *replacement* is, however, inappropriate and open to misunderstanding. The point is that, now that the Messiah has been revealed, the faithful remnant within the nation of Israel will consist of those who accept Jesus as the Messiah (augmented by Gentile believers).

Matthew's major intrusion in the story at this point is his enlargement of the warning given in Mark 12:37-40 against the scribes into an extended warning that then develops into a series of accusations directed against the scribes and Pharisees, who are addressed as if they were present. Although the concern is largely with their inconsistent behavior, which combined punctilious observance of certain pious customs with a basic impiety, there are theological implications. There is a clear call to Jesus' followers to be consistent in their way of life. There is also a replacement of the scribes by one teacher, the Christ, and a denial of the title of "father" to human teachers. Coupled closely with this is an insistence on the brotherhood of all believers and a call to all to act as servants of one another. Any suggestion that the Twelve, for instance, have an exalted position because of their role (cf. Mt 19:28), is firmly denied.

Closely connected with this discourse but clearly separate from it is the final discourse in the Gospel that consists essentially of the teaching about the future in Matthew 24 (= Mk 13) supplemented by the three parables in Matthew 25. Thus there is some ambiguity as to whether the fifth and final discourse in the Gospel consists of Matthew 23—25 or simply of Matthew 24—25.[31]

Matthew 24 is fairly closely parallel to Mark 13, but it contains extra material from the Q tradition.[32] Matthew emphasizes the danger that some among the disciples may be tempted to fall away. He also comments that the coming of the Son of Man will be preceded by the appearance of his sign in heaven.[33] Nevertheless, the coming of the last day will still be unexpected and unpredictable, and Matthew includes strong warnings to disciples to be ready for that day and to live in such a way that they will not be caught unawares

---

[31]The general trend among scholars is to regard Mt 23 not as part of the fifth discourse but as an extended piece of teaching on its own. Nevertheless, the theme of judgment runs clearly through Mt 23—25.

[32]A major difference is the use of material parallel to Mk 13:9-13 already in Mt 10:17-22, but this does not seriously affect the flow of the passage.

[33]If the reference is to the parousia, then the sign probably functions as a warning to gather together for the final battle. France's interpretation of this section with reference to the fall of Jerusalem and the worldwide mission of the church fails to come up with a clear proposal for how the sign might be interpreted on this scenario; see R. T. France, *The Gospel According to Matthew: An Introduction and Commentary* (Leicester: Inter-Varsity Press; Grand Rapids, Mich.: Eerdmans, 1985), pp. 344-45.

and be liable to judgment instead of salvation.

This last point is developed in the three parables that follow. The first of them emphasizes the danger of not being ready at the time. The second stresses the need to occupy the intervening time in conduct that wins the Lord's approval. Alongside the stress on grace and on reward for the undeserving, there is still the recognition that entry into the kingdom is entry into a realm of service for God. The final "parable" is, of course, not a parable but a pictorial description of the final judgment, which is in the hands of the Son of Man, now clearly identified as "the king". It emerges that service to the king is what counts at the judgment, but this service is achieved by serving his brothers and sisters. On the one hand, people who may think that they are the king's servants but have failed to serve him because they did not serve his people are condemned. On the other hand, people who did not realize that they were serving the king in serving his people discover that they were serving him. Although the parable is commonly interpreted to mean that people can serve God or Christ unawares, the point would rather seem to be simply that the service of God or Christ takes place when the command to love one another and one's enemies is fulfilled, and the thought that this can happen unawares is not a point to be interpreted on its own.[34]

*The death and resurrection of Jesus.* For the last time we read "When Jesus had finished saying all these things". The final part of the Gospel then traces the story of the passion and the resurrection. Little needs to be said theologically about the former part of the story, since it is close to Mark and there are no particularly significant changes.[35] Thus, when Matthew's version adds that the blood of Jesus is poured out "for the forgiveness of sins" (Mt 26:28), this makes explicit what is implicit in the Markan account.

In the latter part of the story there are major matters to note. First, there is the story that at the death of Jesus there was an earthquake and the bodies of dead holy people were raised to life and appeared after Jesus' resurrection to

---

[34]To put it plainly, the parable is probably not meant to teach that people who have another or no religion will be saved at the last judgment simply through showing kindness to the needy, even if they had never believed in Christ, whether or not this possibility is taught elsewhere in the New Testament. The point is rather that service to the king's people is service to the king.

[35]The fact that according to some manuscripts Matthew gave the name of Barabbas as "Jesus Barabbas" (Mt 27:16-17 TNIV text; NRSV text) has literary rather than theological significance.

many people (Mt 27:52-53). Whether this is historical or not,[36] it is theological testimony to the fact that the death and resurrection of Jesus had decisive consequences for the fate of the dead. Until this point the resurrection of dead people was little more than a hope based on such prophecy as Daniel 12; now, it is claimed, there is a proleptic fulfillment of it.

Second, Matthew records the appearance of Jesus to the women who had visited the tomb (Mt 28:8-10). The promise that the disciples would see him is accordingly fulfilled, and indeed more than fulfilled. For the prophecy referred only to a sighting in Galilee to the disciples, but here there is already a fulfillment to the women in Jerusalem.

And third, when the disciples do see Jesus in Galilee, it is a numinous experience on a mountain at which they are moved to worship (Mt 28:16-20). The final words of Jesus to them are a declaration of tremendous authority; the Son of Man is now in effect seated on his throne. Therefore, the disciples must go now to all the nations and make disciples. They will baptize them in the combined name of the Father, Son and Spirit. They will teach them to keep the commands of Jesus. And they are assured of the presence of Jesus everywhere and for all time. Nothing could bring out more forcibly the supreme position of Jesus alongside God the Father, and at the same time the fulfillment of the Emmanuel prophecy at his birth.

### Theological Themes

In the second part of this discussion we endeavor to draw together what we have learned from our survey of the Gospel's theological story and to characterize the nature of the theology that is expressed by Matthew.

*Matthew's understanding of Jesus.* As in all the Gospels the center of Matthew's theology is Jesus. There is a clear understanding of Jesus as a genuine human being, but since it has no specific vocabulary dedicated to it, this is much more a basic feature of the narrative that can be taken for granted and therefore is in danger of being overlooked. In terms of designations for Jesus, Matthew's chris-

---

[36]The problem lies not in the possibility or otherwise of God raising the dead, but rather in the lack of any attestation of so unusual an event from other sources and of any effects produced by it; for different perspectives see Hagner, *Matthew 14—28*, pp. 849-52, and D. A. Carson, "Matthew", in *The Expositor's Bible Commentary*, ed. Frank E. Gaebelein (Grand Rapids, Mich.: Zondervan, 1984), pp. 581-82.

tology is not markedly different from that of Mark, with the same use of "Christ", "Son of God" and "Son of Man". But there are differences or changes of emphasis. Whereas Mark began his Gospel simply by designating its subject as Jesus Christ and the Son of God, Matthew has his birth narrative in which the significance of these terms emerges more clearly. The name Jesus is associated with salvation, although subsequently the theme is not really more prominent than in Mark.

The role of Jesus as Messiah is brought out by the quest of the magi and the equation that is made between the Christ and the king of the Jews. As in Mark, the term *king* is prominent in the passion narrative, but it is also used at the entry of Jesus into Jerusalem and especially with reference to his future role at the judgment. The traditional role of the king or a messianic figure as a shepherd of the people is taken over from Mark; it is to be traced in the motif of compassion for the shepherdless sheep in Matthew 9:36 (cf. Mk 6:34 in the context of the feeding of the five thousand),[37] and is also present in the description of the last judgment (Mt 25:32-33).

Particularly characteristic of Matthew is the identity of Jesus as "Son of David" that occurs in the first verse of the Gospel and is used especially in connection with healings performed by Jesus (Mt 9:27; 12:23; 15:22; 20:30-31 par. Mk 10:47-48); clearly in this context the conversation in Matthew 22:41-46 is not meant to be construed as a denial by Jesus of this designation as inappropriate, but it is rather an invitation to ponder the riddle of how David's son can also be his lord. Moreover, the role of the Son of David is seen to be significantly rewritten in the light of Jesus' compassionate actions for the needy.[38]

The exalted position of Jesus is further underlined by the much greater frequency of use of the address "Lord" (*Kyrie*), which is the normal address by sympathetic, committed people to Jesus, sometimes corresponding to the use of "Rabbi" in Mark. Although this term need be no more than a basic title of respect, the frequency of usage and the contextual indicators suggest that there is a rather greater degree of reverence in its use. Several people who come to Jesus are

---

[37]See also Mt 10:6; 15:24; 26:31; cf. Menninger, *Israel*, pp. 142-48.
[38]Cf. Leonhard Goppelt, *Theology of the New Testament* (Grand Rapids, Mich.: Eerdmans, 1981, 1982), 2:220-21.

said to show reverence to him *(proskuneō)*; this is the appropriate attitude to a king (Mt 2:2), and something of the same aura may surround the subsequent uses.[39] This motif reaches its climax in the final, postresurrection scene where Jesus is worshiped by the Eleven and proclaims his absolute authority.

Matthew's use of "Son of Man" is more prolific than Mark's, basically because he has more sayings of Jesus available to him. The general tendency that results is more of a stress on the identity of Jesus as the coming Son of Man and as a figure who is rejected on earth.[40]

Similarly, the use of additional source material leads to the greater prominence of "Son of God" in Matthew. The motif is implicit in the announcement of the birth of Jesus, which will take place by the Holy Spirit, and then emerges in the quotation from Hosea 11:1 in Matthew 2:15. In Mark the title is used only by nonhuman actors before the crucifixion, but in Matthew the disciples worship Jesus as the Son of God after the stilling of the storm (Mt 14:33), and Peter's confession at Caesarea Philippi includes this phrase (Mt 16:16). Moreover, Matthew includes the explicit statement of Jesus about the relationship of the Father and the Son and the latter's role in revelation of the Father (Mt 11:25-27). For Matthew, then, the recognition of Jesus as Son of God by human beings occurs more powerfully than in Mark, where it does not emerge until the confession of the centurion after the death of Jesus (Mk 15:39).[41]

There has been some discussion as to whether the concept of Messiah or that of Son of God has priority in Matthew's christology.[42] The debate is probably futile, and we should recognize that both lines of thought are essential for a full understanding of the role and status of Jesus.[43] Perhaps we are to see some development in the Gospel. At the outset Jesus is principally the messianic Son of David, thus emphasizing his role in relation to Israel, and his divine origin

---

[39]Cf. Mt 8:2; 9:18; 14:33; 15:25; 20:20; 28:9, 17. The term is also used in Mk 5:6 and, after the resurrection, in Lk 24:52. In each of the Synoptic Gospels there are isolated examples of people falling on their knees before Jesus (Mt 17:14; Mk 1:40; 10:17; Lk 5:8).

[40]Cf. I. Howard Marshall, *DJG*, pp. 776-77.

[41]In one or two places Matthew uses the term "the Son" rather than "the Son of God" or equivalents; see Mt 11:27; 24:36; 28:19. Since the Son of Man has God as his Father (Mt 16:27), Meier, *Vision*, pp. 82-83, 172, wants to argue that "the Son" is not necessarily equivalent to "the Son of God" but rather has connections also with "Son of Man", especially in Mt 24:36.

[42]For the latter view see especially Jack D. Kingsbury, *Matthew: Structure, Christology, Kingdom*, 2nd ed. (Minneapolis: Fortress, 1989).

[43]See, for example, J. Riches, *Matthew* (Sheffield: Sheffield Academic Press, 1996), pp. 88-93.

is stressed rather than his sonship. By the end of the Gospel he is named in a trinitarian formula as the Son of God, thus emphasizing his cosmic status for the world after the resurrection. But the difference is purely one of emphasis, and throughout the Gospel both lines of thought are held together.

Over against this tendency to exaltation, however, must be placed the identification of Jesus as the Servant of the Lord who works quietly and gently rather than by raising his voice (Mt 12:18-21, citing Is 42:1-4), and this is confirmed by the claim of Jesus to be gentle and humble (Mt 11:29; cf. Mt 21:5).[44] According to David Hill, Matthew gives content to the concept of Jesus as Son of God by his development of servanthood.[45]

The role of Jesus cannot be ascertained purely by a study of titles and designations. In particular, his role as teacher and miracle worker is of central importance and is not tied to any one type of christological designation. Two further possible aspects of his status that are not expressed in titles require consideration here.

First, there is the question whether the Jewish figure of Wisdom is significant for Matthew's christology. There is no dispute that on occasion Jesus speaks in the manner of a wise teacher, using the kind of sayings found in the wisdom tradition. Nor is there any dispute that Jesus is seen as an envoy (child) of Wisdom in Luke 7:35. However, Matthew 11:19 has the same saying in the form: "wisdom is proved right by her actions", which has been taken to imply an identification of Jesus with Wisdom.[46] There is also a puzzle with the saying of Jesus in Luke 11:49-51 which is said to emanate from "the Wisdom of God", who speaks in the first person; in Matthew 23:34-39, however, this saying is uttered by Jesus himself. Does this mean that Matthew silently identified Jesus as Wisdom? Similarly, Jesus speaks in a style that could be seen as typical of an utterance by Wisdom in Matthew 11:28-30, although we have no precise parallel elsewhere to confirm this supposition.

These pieces of evidence have been sufficient to persuade some scholars that for Matthew Jesus is seen in the role of Wisdom, but it is significant that there

---

[44]For a full exploration of the significance of the term, including especially its connections with justice, see Beaton, *Isaiah's Christ.*

[45]Hill, "Son".

[46]But is the saying really anything more than a comparison between Jesus and wisdom, or simply a proverbial saying?

is no clear use of the term as a title, and it cannot be said to play a major role in the Gospel compared with the other christological categories.[47] Certainly this identification would be appropriate in a Gospel that places so much stress upon Jesus as a teacher and emphasizes the divine origin and authority of his sayings (cf. Mt 8:8). It would also be appropriate in complementing the understanding of Jesus as the Son of God; in both cases we have a divine agent who is close to God.

More significant is the fact that Jesus may be seen as a counterpart to Moses with an authority that exceeds his.[48] This understanding of Jesus as a new Moses does justice to the major place that teaching has in the Gospel and fits in with the overall thrust of the Gospel as a work that is especially concerned with the relationship of Christianity to Judaism.[49]

*The gospel and Judaism.* It is now appropriate to observe how Jesus and his mission are understood within a Jewish context and in relation to Judaism in this Gospel. At the beginning of the Gospel the genealogy insists that Jesus is a descendant of Abraham as well as of David. Many aspects of his identity and his deeds, as well as of what happens to him, are related to prophecies in the Scriptures. Of all the Evangelists it is Matthew who focuses most on this point by his frequent use of the formal quotations introduced by such formulae as "This was to fulfill what was spoken through the prophet". There is no doubt that Matthew was responsible for this characteristic of his narrative, although some of the material used was traditional. The feature is thus not original to Matthew, but he formalizes it in a way that the other Evangelists do not. It is important for him to be able to show that Jesus fulfilled the Scriptures. But why is it important? One element may be apologetic, to prove that Jesus is indeed the expected deliverer, since his work corresponds with the job description provided by the prophets. That this was an element in early Christian apologetic is apparent from such a passage as Acts 17:2-3. At the same time, the usage enables the development of an understanding of the work of Jesus in terms of

---

[47]For a "high" estimate of Matthew's Wisdom christology, see Fred W. Burnett, *The Testament of Jesus-Sophia: A Redaction-Critical Study of the Eschatological Discourse in Matthew* (Lanham, Md.: University Press of America, 1981). For a much more restrained view, see Davies and Allison, *Gospel*, 2:295.

[48]Davies and Allison, *Gospel*, 3:718-21. More fully, Dale C. Allison Jr., *The New Moses: A Matthean Typology* (Minneapolis: Fortress, 1993).

[49]Another possibility is that Jesus is seen as embodying Israel (cf. Mt 2:15).

prophecy and fulfillment. A plan of God is being worked out in history, and the effect is to see the work of Jesus as the culmination of what God has been doing over the centuries past.

But to say this raises the question of the relation between the past and the present; more specifically it raises the question of the Jews in relation to this plan.

Matthew, like the New Testament writers generally, works with a scheme of promise and fulfillment, in which the coming of Jesus is seen as the fulfillment of the scriptural prophecies of the Messiah and the coming era of divine blessing. The effect of this understanding is to produce a broad division of history into two periods, that of the promise and that of the fulfillment. That Matthew shares this understanding is to be seen especially from Matthew 11:12-13, where there is a distinction between the time up to John the Baptist (when the Prophets and the Law were foretelling what would happen), and the period from John the Baptist onward (during which the kingdom of heaven is active).

There is, however, considerable debate over the fine-tuning of this basic insight. In his well-known discussion of Luke's understanding of history Hans Conzelmann argued that an original Christian understanding of time as divided into the past age and new age, with the assumption that the coming of Jesus heralded the imminent arrival of the new age, was reinterpreted by Luke into a scheme of three periods. The time of preparation was followed by the time of Jesus, which in turn is followed by the time of the church. In this way, Luke dealt with the problem caused by the increasing time gap between the coming of Jesus and the coming of the final consummation by interpolating the time of the church and by regarding the coming of Jesus as marking "the middle of time" rather than the inauguration of the end of time.[50]

Inevitably, the question has arisen as to whether Matthew shares a similar understanding of history. And if so, does he think basically in terms of two eras (promise and fulfillment) or of three (the times of Israel, Jesus and the church)? Or should we adopt a more complicated understanding with as many as five periods?[51] All things considered, it is probable that in Matthew, as in Luke, we should see a basic distinction between the time of promise and that of fulfill-

---

[50]Hans Conzelmann, *The Theology of Saint Luke* (London: Faber, 1960).
[51]For this last view see Scot McKnight, *DJG*, pp. 536-38.

ment but recognize that within the period of fulfillment there is an obvious subdistinction between the time of Jesus' ministry, which inaugurates the new age of the kingdom of heaven, and the time of the church, which continues what Jesus inaugurated.[52] John P. Meier argues strongly that for Matthew the death and resurrection of Jesus mark the key stage in the coming of the new age, with the apocalyptic events surrounding the resurrection of Jesus and the acknowledgment of Jesus as Son of God by the Gentile centurion and those with him.[53]

Closely associated with this question is that of the relationship of the Jews to the church. The scheme of the times of promise and fulfillment need in itself be no more than simply an account of the stages in the outworking of God's initiative for the salvation of the peoples of the world. But clearly there is a parallel problem raised by the existence of Israel as the people of God in the period of promise and the establishment of the church as the people who believed that the promises were being fulfilled in them. How are Israel and the church related? Or, more precisely, how are the Jews in the time of Jesus and the church related to the people of God? And linked with this are the important questions of the place of the Gentiles in the church and its mission, and the continuing validity or otherwise of the law of Moses.

*The law and the new righteousness.* By physical descent the Jews were the descendants of the people to whom the promises had been made in the Scriptures. Equally they were the people who had inherited the law of Moses, which they still regarded as binding. Then we have to remember that the Gospel was written at a time when a church had developed that included Jewish and Gentile Christians. Judaism certainly allowed for the entry of proselytes,[54] but on nothing like the scale on which Gentiles had flooded into the early church and certainly only on the understanding that they would accept the law of Moses in full. And, further, Judaism was dominated at the popular level by the attempts of the Pharisaic party to encourage minute observance of the law on all the people and not just on the priests. As we have already noted, these issues can be detected as part of the agenda in the Gospel of Mark, but they come to special prominence in Matthew. Scholars, to be sure, are divided over whether Mat-

---

[52]This analysis is similar to that of Kingsbury, *Matthew.*
[53]Meier, *Vision,* pp. 29-39.
[54]Cf. Mt 23:15. The much-debated question as to the nature and extent of "mission" among the Jews at this time can be left aside here.

thew is a Jewish-Christian or a Gentile-Christian Gospel. Suffice it to say that the evidence is puzzling, but there are far fewer puzzles if the former solution (which is the majority view) is adopted. On the whole, it is more plausible that the author is a Jewish Christian who writes the Gospel with the situation that has just been sketched very much in his mind.[55]

How, then, does the Gospel deal with these issues?

*Jesus and the law of Moses.* The teaching of Jesus was given historically to a Jewish audience, and there was little direct contact with Gentiles. Therefore, Jesus could naturally assume the context of Jewish piety and speak to people on the assumption that they continue to carry out Jewish religious practices (Mt 5:23-24; 6:1-17). It would have been anachronistic to do otherwise. His discussion of divorce is often thought to have been put in the context of the well-known scribal dispute over the grounds for divorce (Mt 5:31-32; 19:3). In this context the abolition of the law of Moses does not arise.[56]

Jesus can also tell his audience to obey what the scribes and the Pharisees tell them to do (Mt 23:2-3; cf. how approval is apparently given to the tithes on spices, Mt 23:23). This is frankly puzzling, for it stands in some tension with the rest of Jesus' teaching and even with the next verse, where the teaching of the scribes is characterized as "heavy loads"; moreover in Matthew 15:1-11 the tradition of the elders is contrasted with the command of God. One possibility is that Matthew 23:2-3 is heavily ironic. Another possibility is that Jesus is contrasting the reading of the law of Moses by the scribes and Pharisees with the way in which they interpreted and practiced it.[57]

*Radicalizing the law.* As already noted, Matthew records the teaching of Jesus that divides the history of God's dealings with his people into two stages, the period of the law and the prophets, and the time of the action of the kingdom of heaven (Mt 11:12). The former period is also the period of the giving of the law, which is understood here not as a way of salvation but rather as an expression of the way in which the people of God ought to live. Jesus' teaching about the law is twofold. On the one hand, he opposes the development of the tradi-

---

[55]For the view that Matthew was a Gentile, see (for example), Meier, *Vision*, pp. 17-25.

[56]On the interpretation of these contested passages see David Instone-Brewer, *Divorce and Remarriage in the Church: Biblical Solutions and Pastoral Realities* (Carlisle: Paternoster, 2003).

[57]So, for example, Frank Thielman, *The Law and the New Testament: The Question of Continuity* (New York: Crossroad, 1999), p. 61.

tion of the elders insofar as this was to be seen as in reality contrary to the command of God.[58] On the other hand, he developed his own teaching, which went beyond the law in its radical exposure of the need for obedience from the heart. Thus the law limited revenge to "an eye for an eye"; Jesus leaves that limit standing but insists that people should not take revenge at all and in that situation the law would be superfluous. The law forbade adultery; once again that law remains in force, but if people were to overcome lustful desires, the law would not be necessary. Where the law commanded love to neighbors, Jesus extended it to love to enemies. The whole law can be said to hang on the two great commandments to love God and your neighbor and your enemy. Thus the law is both internalized and radicalized. It is not abolished but is to be seen as an embodiment of these two radical commandments that involve people's motives as well as their outward behavior and that prioritize moral behavior over against the carrying out of ritual and ceremonial (cf. Mt 9:13; 12:7, citing Hos 6:6). Rather, then, the law is taken up into a new expression of the will of God as taught by Jesus, and at the end of the Gospel the disciples are to teach people "to obey everything that I have commanded you"—with no mention of the law.

Matthew gives a powerful impression of presenting the teaching of Jesus as a new law by the way in which he puts Jesus' teaching about the behavior of disciples up front and does so in a way which makes him appear as standing over against Moses. This could mean that he presents Jesus as a second Moses, giving a new Torah (based on the old, but going beyond it), or it could mean that he presents Jesus as doing something different from Moses. On the whole, the former is more likely, provided we recognize that what Jesus says is concerned with attitudes of the heart, and instruction about these is not "law" in the normal sense of the term.[59]

In this connection an important element in Matthew's vocabulary is *righteousness* and *righteous*.[60] The godly people of the past (Mt 13:17; 23:35) and the present (Mt 13:43, 49; 25:37, 46) are characterized as "righteous", which

---

[58]This way of putting it would imply that Jesus could well have approved of the tradition if it helped to clarify the law.

[59]We should not, to be sure, make the mistake of assuming that Moses was concerned purely with outward observances and not also with motives and a spiritual relationship to God.

[60]Matthew uses these two words twenty-three times, Mark two times, and Luke twelve times. For a balanced summary of the issues see Hagner, "Righteousness".

means quite simply that they lived according to the will of God as expressed in his commandments (as Lk 1:6 nicely puts it), even if they are persecuted for doing so (Mt 5:10). Matthew's main emphasis appears to be that the task of John (Mt 21:32) and Jesus (cf. Mt 3:15) is to teach and inculcate the way of life that is demanded by God's will and is closely associated with the kingdom of heaven (Mt 6:33). There has been considerable discussion of Matthew 5:6, 20. The latter verse requires the hearers to do more (or better) righteousness than the Pharisees if they want to enter the kingdom of heaven. This gives the impression that living righteously now is the condition or qualification for future entry into the kingdom. And it is closely linked to the teaching that people must practice even the least of the commandments. It is impossible that Jesus is going further down the line followed by the Pharisees with their emphasis on the trivial commandments, unless he is saying that one must keep the trivial commandments and also the major ones (as apparently in Mt 23:23); it seems more likely that Jesus is emphasizing the importance of keeping the law as a whole, and uses rhetorical, that is, hyperbolical, language to do so. In Matthew 5:6 the issue is whether hunger and thirst for righteousness is for the ability to do what God commands, that is, to be what God wants them to be, or is for righteousness in the Pauline sense of being accepted by God as "justified by faith", or (most probably) is a cry for justice to be shown to the oppressed (cf. Lk 18:3 for the motif). Matthew's version of the Beatitudes is on the whole concerned with things that God's people do rather than (as in Luke) with needs that are supplied and situations that are reversed, but this verse may be the exception to this generalization.

*The practicability of a new way of life.* The Gospels inculcate a radical code of behavior. The Sermon on the Mount in particular has often been thought to be too impractical and perfectionistic to be taken seriously, and it has even been suggested that its function is to show up human sinfulness rather than to present a viable code of behavior. What the Gospels do not seem to do is to promise divine help in living in the kingdom, such as we find in Paul's teaching about the function of the Holy Spirit or the power of the new life in union with the resurrected Lord. For Matthew the life and activity of Jesus is closely related to the Spirit. The Spirit is active in his conception (Mt 1:18, 20) and comes upon Jesus at his baptism (Mt 3:16), as prophesied by Isaiah (Mt 12:18). It is Matthew who records that Jesus cast out demons by the power of the Spirit of

God (Mt 12:28; Luke's "by the finger of God" conveys the same meaning), and this is confirmed by the saying in which Jesus regards blasphemy against the Holy Spirit as an unforgivable sin, the reference in the context being to the denial that what Jesus was doing was done by the power of the Spirit (Mt 12:31-32). But apart from the promise of baptism with the Holy Spirit and fire (Mt 3:11) and Jesus' promise that the Spirit of the Father would assist the disciples in times of persecution (Mt 10:20), there is nothing about any kind of life in the power of the Spirit.[61] What we do have, however, is the promise of Jesus to be with his disciples (Mt 18:20; 28:20; cf. Mt 1:23), which implies guidance for the church and enabling companionship on the task of mission and discipleship. Implicit in this promise may be the ability to live life according to the commands of Jesus.

*The kingdom of heaven.* The teaching of Jesus about the kingdom of heaven focuses on this righteousness or divinely willed behavior that its members should demonstrate. This raises the question whether Matthew thinks of a future kingdom that is entered by those who are qualified to do so or of a present kingdom in which its members behave in the ways that God commands. For Matthew the kingdom is undeniably future in the sense that people will enter it in the future. At the same time it is powerfully at work or powerfully opposed in the present time, and it grows like a tree or works like leaven; people can be "people of the kingdom" here and now. It would be possible to interpret discipleship to mean that people who follow Jesus and obey his teaching are disciples and will at a future time enter the kingdom, rather than that genuine discipleship of Jesus is the same thing as being in the kingdom here and now. Probably the decisive evidence is Matthew 23:13, which clearly refers to entry to the kingdom in the present tense. We have to reckon with the present reality and the future hope of the kingdom as a realm which people may be in.

*The God of the kingdom.* From the concept of the kingdom of heaven it is a natural step to consider the place of God in the Gospel. God is the character

---

[61]When Matthew relates Jesus' promise that God will give "good things" to those who ask him, whereas Luke records that God will give the Holy Spirit (Mt 7:11 diff. Lk 11:13), there is at least the possibility that Matthew has removed an original reference to the Holy Spirit. Cf. Max Turner, *Power from on High: The Spirit in Israel's Restoration and Witness in Luke-Acts* (Sheffield: Sheffield Academic Press, 1996), p. 340, for the possibility that Luke's text read "good Spirit".

who is most often neglected in studies of New Testament theology. This is not surprising, given the fact that the prime purpose of the New Testament is to express the missionary revelation of this God in Christ, with the risk that the emphasis may fall on the agent of revelation rather than upon the person revealed. To be sure, Matthew does make reference to the kingdom as the kingdom of the Son of Man (Mt 13:41; cf. the close link between the Son of Man as king and the kingdom in Mt 25:31, 34). He immediately follows this with a reference to "the kingdom of their Father" (Mt 13:43); there is evidently no conflict between these two expressions.

Archibald M. Hunter expressed the essential point neatly with his comment that "the King in the Kingdom is a Father", thereby indicating that it is within the new relationship of disciples to Jesus that God is experienced as Father who cares for their needs (Mt 6:25-34).[62] This characterization of God is not unknown by any means in the Old Testament and Judaism, but it was only with the teaching of Jesus that it became dominant to such an extent that the New Testament writers (such as Paul) can assume it as the normal way of understanding God. Matthew's Gospel more than Mark or Luke develops this new evaluation of God as Father. Mark uses the term of God a mere four times (three times of God as the Father of Jesus, and once of the heavenly Father of the disciples). Luke has it seventeen times. But Matthew has it forty-four times, frequently of God as the Father of Jesus but also of God as the Father of the disciples. It is probable that several of the references are due to Matthew using more widely an idiom that was certainly present in his sources as Jesus' characteristic way of speaking about God.

At the same time, the personal relationships into which God enters with disciples do not diminish his greatness (Mt 5:34-35), and Matthew emphasizes his activity as judge who will act against all evil and disobedience to his will. Matthew in fact holds together in a remarkable way the mercy and goodness of God and his strict judgment. The language used to express the results of the latter is strong, with references to the wicked being cast into outer darkness (Mt 8:12; 22:13; 25:30) or into the eternal fire of Gehenna (Mt 5:22; 18:8-9; 25:41; cf. the parabolic imagery in Mt 3:10-12 [John the Baptist's teaching];

---

[62]Archibald M. Hunter, *Introducing New Testament Theology*, 2nd ed. (Carlisle: Paternoster, 1997; originally 1957), pp. 31-33.

7:19; 13:40, 42, 50). This language is not unparalleled in the other Gospels (Mk 9:43, 48; Lk 3:9, 16-17) but on nothing like the scale in Matthew.

*Israel and the church.* In the light of all this, we can now see that the coming of Jesus constitutes a new age in which the kingdom is at work and the Messiah is present. The leaders of the Jews were the agents of God, and the kingdom belonged to them (Mt 21:43) in the sense that they had jurisdiction over it. But this jurisdiction will be taken from them and given to another group of people. Matthew speaks as if there is only one kingdom, and what takes place is a change in the people to whom it is promised. The Jewish leaders have forfeited that right. Had they responded positively to the Messiah it is conceivable that they might have sat on thrones ruling the twelve tribes of Israel. But that possibility never arose. It is the attitude to Jesus and his teaching that is decisive; as Luke's version states, Jesus is the stone over which people stumble and fall, and equally he is the stone that falls on people and destroys them (Lk 20:18).

The new people of the kingdom are, of course, the disciples of Jesus. Despite the fact that Jesus came for the lost sheep of the house of Israel and forbade his disciples to go to non-Jews (Mt 10:5; cf. Mt 15:24), there are signs in plenty that Matthew envisaged this new people as including the Gentiles. This is crystal clear in Matthew 24:14 and Matthew 28:19, which refer to a mission by the disciples in the future. It is also indicated by the fact that Matthew records material that points to the openness of the Messiah to the Gentiles: the visit of the magi, right up front in the Gospel; the prophecy of many coming from east and west into the kingdom (Mt 8:11); the mission of the Servant (Mt 12:18-21, especially Mt 12:18, 21); Jesus' eventual response to the Canaanite woman (Mt 15:21-28); the judgment on the sheep and the goats, which deals with people from "all the nations" (Mt 25:31-46). Consequently, the restriction of Jesus' mission and that of the disciples to the Jews can be understood only as a case of priorities and hardly of strategy.[63] Elsewhere in the New Testament some writers see a divine necessity for the kingdom to be proclaimed first of all to those to whom it had

---

[63]It is of course the case that, practically speaking, if Jesus had begun by going to the Gentiles, he would have lost all credibility with the Jews, but it is very doubtful whether this consideration was in the minds of the New Testament writers.

originally been promised; the Jews are "the subjects [sons] of the kingdom" (Mt 8:12),[64] and Jesus is concerned with the renewal of the people of God, which is then enlarged by being opened to all nations. If there is a rationale for the inclusion of the nations, it will lie in the biblical picture of the role of the Servant and of God's own people in being a light to the nations.

Further evidence that Matthew saw the kingdom of heaven as already present is to be seen in Jesus' teaching about the church. Matthew uses this term in two passages. In the latter (Mt 18:17) it evidently refers to a limited, local group of people, and in a Jewish context this could simply be a synagogue community. However, to Christian readers the word would undoubtedly signify a Christian congregation. This is particularly so, since this reference comes after the earlier one in Matthew 16:18, where the language is of a different kind. Here Jesus founds an *ekklēsia* that has a cosmic role in that it has the powers of death arrayed against it, and it or its leaders has the key that controls entry to the kingdom of heaven. As envisaged by Jesus, this community may have been small and insignificant by human standards, but in the light of the parables of the mustard seed and the leaven it is set for stupendous growth. Moreover, Matthew is concerned about how people relate to one another within this community. As we have seen, Matthew 18 is concerned with the relationships between disciples and specifically the pastoral concerns that people should not fall away and that it should be necessary to thrust them out. It can be presumed that the church and the disciples are the same entity. Nevertheless, the future tense may suggest that the church did not come into being until it was established under the leadership of Peter and the rest of the Twelve.

For Matthew, Israel finds its future in the church, the people who recognize that the Messiah has come. It is the sole entity that continues into the future; there cannot be any place for another church, which will withstand the onslaught of Hades. The position of the Twelve on their thrones as the judges of Israel indicates that the present leadership of Judaism have had their rule over the kingdom taken away from them. This does not mean that there is no future for Jews in the kingdom or that the church's mission goes solely to the Gentiles. The church or the new Israel consists of believing Jews and Gentiles; the disciples' mission is to all nations, which includes the Jewish nation. As Donald A.

---

[64]In Mt 13:38 the same phrase is used for those who respond to the teaching of Jesus.

Hagner puts it, "The church does not take the place of Israel; rather Israel finds its true identity in the church".[65]

## Conclusion

Matthew's theology is accordingly concerned very much with establishing the relationship of Jesus and the church to Judaism. His Gospel provides a foundation in the mission and teaching of Jesus for a church composed of Jews and Gentiles, called to a mission to all nations, including Jews, and conscious of itself as inheriting the gracious promises of God to his people in the Scriptures. It is probably a strongly Jewish-Christian audience that he has in mind, and his Gospel indicates powerfully that the law given by Moses is still valid in the sense that it has been taken up by Jesus and incorporated in his new teaching. So paradoxically the law continues to be valid, but only in the new form in which it is taught by Jesus.[66]

At the end of our discussion of Mark we endeavored to characterize his theology by analyzing it in terms of its framework, central theme and the detailed outworking of the theme. What happens when we attempt the same exercise for Matthew?

The framework of thought in Matthew appears to be essentially the same as in Mark, but Matthew is more overtly concerned with the Jewish people.

Matthew's main theme is the teaching of Jesus as the announcement of the coming of the kingdom of heaven, which requires a new way of life from its members, seen in a rejection of false religion and its replacement by a radical obedience to God's law expressed in love and compassion.

Analyzing this in greater detail and implicitly comparing it with Mark's presentation, we note the following significant elements.

1. Matthew underlines the way in which Jesus saw the people in their needy condition and attacked their religious leaders for their failure to carry out the religion that they taught.

---

[65]Donald A. Hagner, *NDBT,* p. 264. Here, as elsewhere in the New Testament, it is not a question of supersessionism, as if the church has replaced Israel and God's promises to Israel are no longer valid. On the contrary, God has renewed his covenant with his people; the elements of renewal include the fact that the Messiah has now come, and therefore acceptance of the covenant entails acceptance of the Messiah, and the opening up of the covenant people to include Gentiles who accept the Messiah.

[66]This raises the question whether Matthew saw different manners of fulfillment for Jewish and for Gentile Christians.

2. Jesus demonstrated the presence of the rule of God by his powerful acts of healing and compassion. He understood the character of God in terms of fatherhood toward those who respond to the good news of the kingdom of heaven.

3. Jesus' role is seen as a combination of being Messiah and Son of God in virtue of his birth, but he also functions like a new Moses in authoritatively teaching people God's law and as the humble yet powerful Servant of the Lord. He is seen as mediating the presence of God to people, and he himself is present spiritually with his followers (presumably this is a promise for the postresurrection period).

4. Jesus gathers followers and intends to raise up an *ekklēsia* on the foundation of his first followers. He anticipates the development of community life among them.

5. The Gospel looks forward to the ongoing mission to bring in Gentiles as followers of Jesus, although Jesus tended to restrict his activity and that of his earthly followers to the Jewish population. Although Jesus stated that the leadership of God's people would be taken from its present Jewish leaders, believing Jews still have their place in the new people of God.

6. The understanding of God's will as love is intensified by the inclusion of enemies as proper objects of love. There is also a stress on the need for true righteousness as opposed to empty piety.

7. The death of Jesus is seen as sacrificial and redemptive, leading to forgiveness of sins by God.

8. The reality of God's final judgment, carried out by the Son of Man and issuing in eternal bliss or condemnation, is emphasized.

Such a brief summary runs the risk of caricature. Nevertheless, it may suffice to indicate how the theology of Matthew essentially incorporates that of Mark but goes beyond it in significant ways.

### Bibliography

*New Testament Theologies:* (English) Conzelmann, pp. 144-49; Goppelt, 2:211-35; Ladd, pp. 213-28; Morris, pp. 114-43; Strecker, pp. 364-91; Zuck, pp. 19-64 (D. K.

Lowery). (German) Berger, pp. 677-85 *et passim;* Gnilka, pp. 174-96; Hahn, 1:518-46; Hübner, 3:96-119; Stuhlmacher, 2:150-74.

Allison, Dale C., Jr. *The New Moses: A Matthean Typology.* Minneapolis: Fortress, 1993.

Beaton, Richard, *Isaiah's Christ in Matthew's Gospel.* Cambridge: Cambridge University Press, 2002.

Blomberg, Craig L. *Matthew.* Nashville: Broadman, 1992.

Bornkamm, Günther, Gerhard Barth, and Heinz J. Held. *Tradition and Interpretation in Matthew.* Philadelphia: Fortress, 1963.

Burnett, Fred W. *The Testament of Jesus-Sophia: A Redaction-Critical Study of the Eschatological Discourse in Matthew.* Lanham, Md.: University Press of America, 1981.

Carson, D. A. "Matthew". In *The Expositor's Bible Commentary.* Edited by Frank E. Gaebelein, pp. 3-599. Grand Rapids, Mich.: Zondervan, 1984.

Davies, W. D., and Dale C. Allison Jr. *The Gospel According to St Matthew.* 3 vols. Edinburgh: T & T Clark, 1988-1997.

France, R. T. *The Gospel According to Matthew: An Introduction and Commentary.* Leicester: Inter-Varsity Press; Grand Rapids, Mich.: Eerdmans, 1985.

———— . *Matthew: Evangelist and Teacher.* Exeter: Paternoster, 1989.

Hagner, Donald A. "Matthew". In *NDBT,* pp. 262-67.

———— . *Matthew 1—13* and *Matthew 14—28.* Dallas: Word, 1993, 1995.

———— . "Righteousness in Matthew's Theology". In *Worship, Theology and Ministry in the Early Church.* Edited by M. J. Wilkins and T. Paige, pp. 101-20. Sheffield: Sheffield Academic Press, 1992.

Hill, David. "Son and Servant: An Essay on Matthean Christology". *JSNT* 6 (1980): 2-16.

Keener, Craig S. *A Commentary on the Gospel of Matthew.* Grand Rapids, Mich.: Eerdmans, 1999.

Kingsbury, Jack D. *Matthew: Structure, Christology, Kingdom.* 2nd ed. Minneapolis: Fortress, 1989.

Luz, Ulrich. *Matthew 1—7: A Commentary.* Minneapolis: Augsburg Fortress 1989.

———— . *The Theology of the Gospel of Matthew.* Cambridge: Cambridge University Press, 1995.

Meier, John P. *The Vision of Matthew: Christ, Church and Morality in the First Gospel.* New York: Paulist, 1978.

Menninger, Richard E. *Israel and the Church in the Gospel of Matthew.* New York: Peter Lang, 1994.

Mohrlang, Roger. *Matthew and Paul: A Comparison of Ethical Perspectives.* Cambridge: Cambridge University Press, 1984.

Przybylski, Benno. *Righteousness in Matthew and His World of Thought.* Cambridge: Cambridge

University Press, 1980.

Riches, J. *Matthew.* Sheffield: Sheffield Academic Press, 1996.

Stanton, Graham N. *A Gospel for a New People.* Edinburgh: T & T Clark, 1992.

———, ed. *The Interpretation of Matthew.* 2nd ed. Edinburgh: T & T Clark, 1995.

Stonehouse, Ned B. *The Witness of Matthew and Mark to Christ.* London: Tyndale, 1959.

Suggs, M. Jack. *Wisdom, Christology and Law in Matthew's Gospel.* Cambridge, Mass.: Harvard University Press, 1970.

Wilkins, Michael J. *The Concept of Disciple in Matthew's Gospel.* Leiden: E. J. Brill, 1988.

# 5

# LUKE-ACTS

❦

## *THE FORMER TREATISE*

❦

The Gospel of Luke and the Acts of the Apostles form two connected, successive parts of the one story of the life of Jesus and how his followers told the good news about him after his death and exaltation. This is clear from the way in which the second volume begins with a brief introduction that is clearly based on the introduction to the first volume in the manner of ancient multivolume works. Nevertheless, some scholars have detected differences between the two books that make them question just how unified the work of Luke is and whether there is essentially one and the same theology reflected in the two books.[1] Naturally there are differences between the messages of Jesus and his followers, and Jesus as a person living a human life is not the same as the exalted Lord; the question is whether Luke sees these two presentations in an appropriate harmony with each other. We must bear this question in mind as we work through Luke and Acts, but the nature of the material is such as to justify tackling the two books together.

### *Luke's Theological Story: Part 1*
I shall assume that Luke is telling his story of Jesus on the basis of Mark's Gos-

---

[1]There is no real doubt that one and the same author wrote both books despite some minor stylistic differences between them.

pel together with other source materials, some shared with Matthew and others peculiar to himself. Therefore, the main thread of the story is similar to that in Mark, and in many ways Luke shared his understanding of it. But, like Matthew, Luke is writing at greater length than Mark,[2] and the new material gives a different accent to the story quite apart from the ways in which Luke may edit the Markan material to express different nuances. There is also the fact that putting the Gospel into the context created by its sequel may affect the significance of the story.

*The overture (Lk 1—2).* At the outset Luke makes it clear that he is attempting to give an account of what actually happened based on reliable testimony and that he is doing so in order that his reader(s) may be sure that what they have been taught rests on a sound foundation. Already at this point we learn that Luke is concerned that the Christian message rests on historical events (Lk 1:1-4).

To be sure, the immediately following prelude to the story, an account of the births of John the Baptist and Jesus, contains elements that some people find it hard to accept as historical in the strictest sense of the term. Luke had no difficulty with telling stories of angelic visitations and what may look more like folklore than sober narrative. However, this is not the place to assess the historicity of the material; our concern is with what Luke was conveying by his account of it.

The theology of the story stands out plainly enough. There are two interlinked accounts of the announcements of the birth of Jesus and John, and then of their actual births and the immediately following events. Out of the blue the aged Zechariah and his wife learn that they are to be the parents of a son who will have the spirit and power of Elijah to prepare people for the Lord. Here the role assigned to John elsewhere in the Gospels (Mk 9:11-13) is brought right forward and emphasized. Likewise, Mary is told that she will be the mother of a child who will be called Jesus[3] and who will be the Son of the Most High, that is, of God, and who will rule eternally over the house of Jacob, that

---

[2]The lengths of the Gospels to the nearest one hundred words are Matthew, 18,300; Mark, 11,200; Luke, 19,400; John, 15,400. This means that Luke is 1.73 times the length of Mark, which is getting on for twice as long.

[3]The significance of the name is recognized by Matthew (Mt 1:21), but it is not clear whether Luke did so.

is, the Jews. This is basically a depiction of the Messiah, which picks up on the Old Testament description of him as having the relationship of a son to God (e.g., 2 Sam 7:14). The announcement is interpreted by Mary in terms of God acting in the world to bring down those who are evil and to satisfy the needy and to show concern and care for the Jews. However we understand the tenses in Mary's song in Luke 1:51-55, they are to be seen as an expression of what God will do through this person. The general picture is confirmed by Zechariah in his prophecy, which is again concerned with God's action for the sake of his people, Israel, and in some sense brings them salvation so that they can live godly lives in peace. The language brings out poignantly the nature of salvation in terms of forgiveness and light.

Then come the birth of Jesus and the revelation of his significance to a despised group of people—the shepherds—and the accent moves unmistakably to the future role of the child as a Savior. We are seeing a redefinition of the Messiah in terms of the Savior, and this is confirmed by the words of Simeon (Lk 2:30). But Simeon adds in a new element, which is that this salvation is not just for the people of Israel but is for all peoples; the point may be muted, but it is nonetheless definite. So while the accent lies on "the redemption of Jerusalem" (Lk 2:38), there is the potential for an event of wider import. The final episode describes how the young boy displays an unusual understanding of religion in the temple and refers to God as his Father (Lk 2:49). There is thus a complex of understandings of Jesus here. By this point the reader may realize that "Jesus" itself is a name connected with salvation. There is a multifaceted portrayal of what is going to happen, involving salvation, deliverance from enemies, forgiveness, peace, judgment upon the proud and the mighty (it is almost taken for granted that they owe their position to sinful behavior), and satisfaction for those who are hitherto empty and deprived. These are all the sorts of things that might plausibly be associated with the coming of God's order in society through his royal agent, the Messiah. The Messiah is understood to be the Son of God, and where in the Old Testament the Spirit rests upon the Messiah (Is 11:1-3; 61:1; cf. Lk 4:18), here the Spirit somehow also brings the Messiah to birth.

Whether it all happened exactly like this, or whether Luke has told the story in such a way as to provide a commentary on it in the light of later understanding, there can be no doubt as to the significance that he sees in the coming of

Jesus. The way in which the story is told indicates that these events are the fulfillment of what was promised in the Old Testament and that they are therefore part of the ongoing dealings of God in history; it is, therefore, appropriate that Luke relates at least this part of the story in a style that is closely related to that of the Jewish Scriptures.

*Jesus in Galilee (Lk 3:1—9:50).* All this is prologue or, in musical terms, overture. The story proper was known by Luke to begin with the activity of John (Acts 1:22; 10:37), and his careful dating is tied to that event. As with the reference to Caesar Augustus in Luke 2:1, the effect is to tie the story into world history, in a manner similar to the dating of the Old Testament prophets in the history of Israel. The account of John's preaching is fuller than in Mark or Matthew and includes some examples of how people who are repentant should live. In a mildly curious way the imprisonment of John is related as the conclusion to his personal preaching before the baptism of Jesus is related (Lk 3:20/21). The baptism of Jesus is related almost casually, as if to emphasize that the really significant element was the descent of the Spirit upon him while he was praying, together with the heavenly voice that confirmed that he was God's Son.[4]

These two elements reappear in the story of the temptation, where Jesus is led by the Spirit into the desert and is tempted to doubt his status as Son of God (Lk 4:1-13). When he returns from the desert, it is in the power of the Spirit, and the devil has used up his weapons for the time being.[5]

The story of the activity of Jesus begins with a scene in the synagogue at Nazareth that is generally interpreted as programmatic for what follows. It presents the work of Jesus as the fulfillment of prophecy, using Isaiah 61:1-2, and indicating that Jesus is God's anointed or appointed spokesperson to announce good news, expressed in terms of freedom, sight, deliverance and divine favor.

---

[4]The mention of Jesus' age and the inclusion of his line of descent at this point is awkward and is almost equivalent to a lengthy footnote. Unlike Matthew, Luke traces his descent all the way back to Adam, and there may well be some theological significance hidden in the structure of the line with its 11x7 names. At the very least there is probably some parallelism between Jesus (Lk 3:22) and Adam (Lk 3:38) as sons of God, but it is not developed.

[5]Hans Conzelmann developed from this basis his theory that the ministry of Jesus was depicted by Luke as a "Satan-free period" that lasted until Lk 22:3, when the devil again became active; see Conzelmann, *The Theology of Saint Luke* (London: Faber, 1960), p. 28. But evil activity instigated by the devil and the demons continues (Lk 13:16), and Luke's disuse of the vocabulary is not different from that of Matthew and Mark.

This could be said to spell out more concretely what was implied by the good news of the kingdom of God in Mark with a distinct emphasis on the benefits for those who are suffering. It is also the kind of proclamation that has the illocutionary effect of bringing into being what is announced, as when a powerful conqueror announces the overturning of the oppressive regime that previously existed. But the flow of the narrative is strange. Luke 4:22 is ambiguous as to whether there is admiration of Jesus or the sort of amazement that is inherently incredulous. Certainly by the end of the story, when Jesus has observed that prophets tend not to be accepted as such by their own people, his words are fulfilled in an act of mass violence against him from which he escapes because (as John would say) his hour had not yet come.

The motifs of bringing deliverance and healing in fulfillment of Old Testament promises by an anointed person[6] amid unbelief and opposition thus mark out the way in which the ensuing story is to be understood. Initially we have an account based on Mark and told in much the same way.[7] The same motifs of proclaiming the kingdom of God in word and deed, the calling of disciples and the rise of opposition are present. Whereas Matthew puts a lengthy discourse by Jesus right up front (contrast Luke's Nazareth scene), Luke has a shorter, parallel discourse at a later point, by which time it may be presumed that teaching for disciples and people attracted by his message would be appropriate. The content is shaped by the tradition available to Luke and is largely concerned with the behavior of disciples and would-be disciples, and the divine rewards and judgments that are promised to them. It presents a picture of a new society in which the oppressed are delivered and the well-off are deprived. Although the point tends to be implicit rather than explicit, it does seem that the well-off have achieved their position by evil behavior and that the deprived and oppressed are victims who call upon God to deliver them. This interpretation rests upon the way in which the language used had already acquired these associations from its use in the Old Testament.

---

[6]Although the anointed person in Is 60 appears to be the prophet, it would be difficult for the readers to avoid an allusion to the "royal" or kingly type of "Messiah". Cf. Lk 4:41, where the identification of Jesus as Son of God is taken to be tantamount to acknowledging that he is the Christ.

[7]A major variant is the story of the call of Simon (Peter) and his companions (Lk 5:1-11), which emphasizes the numinous character of Jesus as a wonder worker and the feeling of unworthiness beside him.

The interlude is followed by a rich variety of mighty works, including the resuscitation of a dead man (Lk 7:11-17); these provide evidence to convince the friends of the imprisoned John that Jesus really is the person promised in Jewish prophecy who brings about a new exodus, as described in Isaiah 35. But the package also includes forgiveness of a notorious sinner, which again raises the question of Jesus' identity. The story largely follows Mark, but Luke omits a major swath of material that results in the juxtaposition of the feeding miracle (echoes of Moses and Elijah!) with the question as to who he is.[8] In the ensuing story of the transfiguration Luke states that the subject of discussion between Jesus and the heavenly visitors was his "departure (Gk. *exodus*), which he was about to bring to fulfillment at Jerusalem" (Lk 9:31). Here the "departure" suggests that Jesus is on a journey that will take him via Jerusalem and death to his goal. In Luke 9:51 Luke also refers to the time of his being "taken up", which could also refer simply to death but more probably includes the idea of his ascension to heaven. How far Luke views the earlier part of Jesus' career as a journey that from this point has the definite goal of Jerusalem is not clear; it is rather a time of wandering with the aim of bringing the message and power of the kingdom of God.[9]

*Teaching on the way to Jerusalem (Lk 9:51—19:27).* From this point onward Jesus is portrayed much more as a teacher alternating between instruction of his followers and controversy with his opponents. It is hard to summarize this section of the Gospel, which contains many independent units, and there is no clear thread as the story develops; this is perhaps only to be expected in a story that reflects the life of an itinerant preacher who spoke ad hoc rather than giving a connected and orderly series of lectures developing a theme. However Luke has arranged the material available to him, he did not turn it into a systematic account of what Jesus taught under various heads.

A number of points with theological significance stand out. In the first section (Lk 9:51–11:13) the success of Jesus' followers as they go out indepen-

---

[8]Significantly this query is placed in the context of Jesus praying, a motif emphasized by Luke with the implication that Jesus' prayers are somehow related to his self-disclosure. See David Crump, *Jesus the Intercessor: Prayer and Christology in Luke-Acts* (Tübingen: Mohr, 1992).

[9]What follows in Lk 9:51 onward until Jesus reaches Jerusalem suggests that Jesus was still moving to and fro, but for Luke the ultimate, overriding goal is Jerusalem.

dently of him on mission is interpreted as the defeat of Satan (Lk 10:18). And Jesus sees himself as the Son of God who alone knows his Father and can share his knowledge with other people (Lk 10:21-22). The teaching that he gives stresses again the importance of love in which enemies are treated as neighbors (Lk 10:25-37) and of a relationship with God expressed in prayer to him as Father with the expectation that he will answer prayer by bestowing the gift of the Spirit (Lk 11:1-13).[10] It is important to recognize the character of God as a Father who wants to bestow good on his children and therefore to pray to him, as Jesus did.

In the next section (Lk 11:14-54) the issue is the unbelief of the Pharisees, as typical of the generation surrounding Jesus who attributed his mighty works not to the Holy Spirit but to Beelzebul, and they are told that the mighty works are done by the finger of God (cf. Ex 8:19 of the mighty deeds done by Moses and Aaron) and are a sign that the kingdom of God has arrived.[11] Such unbelievers profess that they would be convinced by a manifest heavenly sign confirming the divine mission of Jesus. But no sign will be given to them except the sign of Jonah, which is probably to be understood as his vindication by being raised from the dead (so explicitly in Mt 12:38-42). There ensues a briefer version of the denunciation of the Pharisees and scribes found in Matthew 23, somewhat differently arranged, and culminating in an attack on them for keeping out the people who are seeking the knowledge that leads to salvation.

Jesus then turns to his disciples in a section of teaching that deals principally with their readiness for the future and whatever it may bring (Lk 12:1—13:21). Their main concern must be readiness for God's judgment, and the dangers of hypocrisy and of failing to confess the Son of Man are emphasized. At the same time, they are encouraged by reference to God's care for them and his provision of the Holy Spirit. This point is reinforced by an injunction not to seek after the false security of wealth but to trust in the care of their Father. If they seek his kingdom, they will be supplied with whatever

---

[10]For this kind of prayer and divine response the disciples had in fact to wait until after the resurrection of Jesus.

[11]This remains the most plausible interpretation of this verse, despite Chrys C. Caragounis's claim that it means that the kingdom is just about to come ("Kingdom of God, Son of Man and Jesus' Self-Understanding", *TynB* 40 [1989]: 3-23, 223-38).

they need for daily living without having to worry over it. Their main concern should be to be like faithful servants continuing to do their duties in the temporary absence of the master. For Luke and his readers this parabolic saying presupposes the time of the church when Jesus is no longer physically with them. The end of the section (Lk 12:54—13:21) again has the crowds more in view and is concerned to inculcate a recognition that the present time is one of crisis during which people should be recognizing their sinfulness and repenting. Some people did recognize that what Jesus was doing was liberating Satan's captives, but others continued to refuse to do so. They presumably did not believe what Jesus was trying to say through his parables about the growth and spread of the kingdom.

Luke 13:22—14:35 is similarly mixed in content. Again there is the appeal to people to respond to Jesus' message before it is too late and a warning that those who heard him may find themselves excluded from the heavenly kingdom, while other people will take their place. This is doubtless a reference to the inclusion of Gentiles. But the general impression is that the refusal to accept the message is gathering strength, and this leads to Jesus' lament over Jerusalem's refusal to respond to him. The parable of the great banquet repeats the warning that if the Jews fail to respond to God's invitation, the Gentiles will take their places. At the same time, Jesus emphasizes that it is no easy option that he offers to people: to be a disciple is costly in terms of commitment, and it is dangerous to set out on the path of discipleship and then to give up along the way.

Throughout this section it has become apparent that Jesus' concern was for the outcasts of Jewish society (with this hint of future openness also to the Gentiles), and this concern is justified in Luke 15 with the three parables that speak of God's concern for the lost and then (in the parable of the two sons) raise in an open-ended kind of way the situation of those who identify themselves with the son who remained at home.

It has become obvious that one of the temptations that keep people out of the kingdom is the desire for wealth. Luke gathers together teaching on this theme in Luke 16; the second parable, that of the rich man and Lazarus, makes the point clearly enough, with its implication that the rich man had not used his wealth wisely. The first parable is perhaps not so clear, but certainly one lesson that it is meant to teach is the need to use wealth wisely in a way that befits those who are God's stewards.[12]

In the next section (Lk 17:1—18:8) there is further teaching for the disciples. The most important section theologically is that dealing with the coming of the kingdom of God (Lk 17:20-37), which appears to make a distinction between the coming of the kingdom, which does not come in a way that can be observed but is "in your midst" (Lk 17:21), and the coming of the Son of Man, which will be dazzlingly obvious when it happens. The meaning of Luke 17:21 is disputed, the best option in my view being that the kingdom is already present (rather than suddenly coming in the future) in the midst of the disciples (rather than being a spiritual entity "within" them).[13] To be distinguished from this presence of the kingdom is the future coming of the Son of Man, which will spell judgment for those who are not ready and waiting for him; on that day it will not be possible to escape. The coming is depicted in apocalyptic language. But here at any rate it may be significant that the coming is said to be like lightning or like what happened in the time of Noah and Lot, and its precise nature is left unspoken. The imagery of people being separated to different fates and of there being no time to do anything but flee without their possessions is that of a siege or invasion, and it could fit the Roman siege of Jerusalem, understood as a judgment brought about by the Son of Man. However, it is perhaps more likely that the imagery is used to bring out the separation caused by the final judgment and the need to be prepared for whenever it overtakes people.[14] Either way, the apocalyptic imagery is used in comparison rather than as direct description.

The immediately following parable of the unjust judge belongs to this section (Lk 18:1-8). It presumes the situation described in Luke 17:22 of longing for one of the days of the Son of Man and encourages the disciples to persevere in faith and prayer, even if it seems that God is never going into intervene in their difficult situation.

---

[12]Maybe the major puzzle in the chapter is not so much the interpretation of the first parable but rather the inclusion of Lk 16:16-18 with their shift of theme to the kingdom, the law and divorce. Taken on their own, the sayings are important as showing that for Luke the law is still valid despite the fact that the era of the kingdom has come; at the same time the teaching of Jesus sharpens up the law, as exemplified by his teaching on divorce.

[13]For different views see Darrell L. Bock, *Luke* (Grand Rapids, Mich.: Baker, 1994, 1996), 2:1414-19; John Nolland, *Luke* (Dallas: Word, 1993), 2:852-54.

[14]This must be the reference in the closely following verse Lk 18:8, and it is unlikely that the coming of the Son of Man would have different references in two adjacent verses.

There follows straightaway another parable about prayer, but with a different focus.[15] It introduces a section that deals with response to the message of Jesus. The tax collector recognizes his sinfulness, which Jesus assumes to be universal (cf. Lk 13:1-9) and casts himself on the mercy of God rather than depending upon self-righteousness. The children typify the attitude of humility and trust in God (cf. Lk 18:14!). The ruler is not prepared for the self-sacrifice demanded by Jesus, and even the Twelve do not fully understand all that will be involved for him, never mind for themselves. The blind beggar and Zacchaeus are paradigms of response to Jesus, whose mission is summed up as that of the shepherd who goes out to look for and to rescue those who are lost.

*The passion and resurrection (Lk 19:28—24:53)*. With this summative declaration we reach the end of the lengthy travel section, and the passion story now begins with a parable that appropriately reminds us that this is not the point at which the kingdom of God will appear; first, there will be a time of service for the disciples (cf. Lk 12:35-48). The story of Jesus in Jerusalem then unfolds on much the same lines as in Mark and Matthew. As in Matthew the entry of Jesus to Jerusalem is seen as the coming of the king: is Luke implying that there is a distinction between the coming of the kingdom and the coming of the king? Distinctive of Luke is the lament of Jesus over the fate that awaits a Jerusalem that did not recognize the coming of the King (Lk 19:41-44).[16]

Luke retains the so-called apocalyptic discourse of Mark 13. Despite considerable differences in wording, the general thrust is not dissimilar. Nevertheless, Luke's version speaks more clearly about the siege and destruction of Jerusalem and refers also to its ongoing subjection to its conquerors "until the times of the Gentiles are fulfilled" (Lk 21:24).[17] Only after that does the coming of the Son of Man take place, accompanied by cosmic signs.

Luke plainly expects a hard and difficult time for believers that could lead to abandonment of faith, and therefore there is again an appeal for perseverance in watchfulness and prayer.

Luke's account of the Last Supper differs from that in Mark and Matthew

---

[15]There is thus a topical connection between the end of one section of the Gospel and the next, but nevertheless there is a clear break and a change of subject.

[16]In Luke this statement in effect replaces the Markan story of the symbolical cursing of the fig tree.

[17]This enigmatic phrase refers to a period of Gentile (Roman) domination over Jerusalem that will not last forever. For attempts to link this motif with Rom 11:25-32 see Bock, *Luke*, 2:1680-82.

in two main respects.[18] First, there is the double saying before the sharing of the bread and the cup in which Jesus states that he will not eat or drink again until the Passover finds fulfillment in the kingdom of God and the kingdom of God comes. These sayings presuppose that there is some sense in which the kingdom is not yet present, and it is debated whether Jesus is referring to a new state of affairs brought about after his death or to some fulfillment in heaven. On the whole, the former view seems more likely.

Second, there is a rather lengthy set of statements after the meal by Jesus (Lk 22:21-38) that is concerned largely with the status of the disciples: they are not to seek greatness but to be content with humble service, and yet they are promised that in the kingdom of Jesus they will sit at his table and judge the tribes of Israel. The thought of falling away again emerges, but this time perseverance is made dependent in part at least on the prayer of Jesus. The language of conflict with Satan emerges again at this point.

Some of the distinctive material in this part of the Gospel is textually uncertain. This applies especially to the detail of Jesus being strengthened by an angel and sweating profusely what looked like drops of blood while he was praying (Lk 22:43-44). Although the detailed description of the trial and crucifixion of Jesus shows differences from Mark, these tend to be more concerned with the actual events than with their theological significance. Perhaps the most important of these is the way in which Jesus affirms that from that point onward the Son of Man would be seated at the right hand of God: the element of exaltation associated with the resurrection is emphasized (Lk 22:69). We have already noted the element of compassion for Jerusalem as it faces the judgment to come (Lk 22:27-31). During the crucifixion, there is the incident of the dying criminal who acknowledges the innocence of Jesus and is promised a place with Jesus in paradise, and also the textually insecure prayer of Jesus for the forgiveness of his executioners (Lk 22:34). The cry of dereliction in Matthew and Mark is omitted, and Jesus dies with an expression of trust in God on his lips (Lk 22:46). The general effect is to depict Jesus more as a martyr and a savior:

---

[18]Some textual authorities omit Lk 22:19b-20; the resulting shorter text would fit in with an understanding of Lukan theology in which the atoning significance of the death had next to no part. This shorter text is adopted by REB and some recent commentators, but the evidence for retention is indubitably stronger, even although defenders of the originality of the longer text have some difficulty in explaining how the omission took place.

there is nothing corresponding to the cries for vengeance found in accounts of other martyrs. It may seem surprising that the centurion at the cross comments that Jesus was "a righteous man" and not the "Son of God" (as in Mk 15:39).[19]

Like Matthew, Luke has accounts of the appearances of Jesus after the discovery of the empty tomb. The words of the "men" (i.e., angels) at the tomb say nothing of Jesus going to Galilee to meet his disciples (but refer instead to what he had said in Galilee), and this fits in with the fact that the appearances take place near and in Jerusalem. Thus with a kind of *inclusio* the Gospel begins and ends in Jerusalem with scenes in the temple. The first appearance story, that to the disciples walking to Emmaus, becomes an occasion for Jesus to explain the course of his events in his career as being a fulfillment of what was written in the Scriptures and reaches its climax in his identity becoming apparent to the travelers as they sit at table for an evening meal. The second appearance story to the Eleven and a wider group of disciples is again characterized by teaching that issues in a commission to continue the work of Jesus by acting as his witnesses, and the whole of this—the career of the Christ and the task of his witnesses—is again seen to be a fulfillment of Scripture. The final event, very briefly described, is that Jesus is taken up into heaven to the accompaniment of worship by the disciples.

### Theological Themes in the Gospel

At this point the commentator is caught in a dilemma, whether to draw together the threads of the theology of the Gospel or to proceed straightway to the continuation of the theological story in the Acts. For various reasons it is probably wiser to attempt a theological evaluation of the story so far. In view of the theological differences that some scholars have found between the Gospel and Acts, it makes good sense to sum up the teaching of the Gospel on its own. It is also helpful to have an assessment of the Gospel so that we can compare it with the other Gospels.

The opening two chapters of Luke set the stage for what is to follow, and a number of themes and characteristics of the Gospel can be recognized in

---

[19]The suggestion that *dikaios* here means "innocent" (NRSV text) is almost certainly wrong. More probably the point is to identify Jesus with the righteous and godly persecuted person in the wisdom tradition (Wis 2:10-24); see P. Doble, *The Paradox of Salvation: Luke's Theology of the Cross* (Cambridge: Cambridge University Press, 1996).

them. I shall take these up and develop them.

*History and the Gospel.* The opening verses announce the commencement of an orderly account, based on a reliable tradition, so that the readers may know that what they had been taught is certain. Thereby Luke indicates that his account is a kind of historical backing to the Christian message, which will strengthen existing faith and perhaps also lead to new faith. Although doubts have been expressed regarding the similarity of the prologue to the prologues of historical works, there is no doubt that the work as a whole fits broadly into the historical category and is not, for example, to be seen as historical fiction. It follows that Luke saw himself as more than the writer of a story that may or may not relate something that happened in the real world to which he belonged. The story has force only if it recounts what has sometimes been called "salvation-history".[20]

Luke's Gospel is not peculiar in this respect. The simple fact that Luke drew so much upon Mark demonstrates that Luke saw Mark as similar in character to his own work; and, we may add, it is equally obvious that Matthew also composed a work of similar character. Luke may be most self-consciously the historian, but all three Synoptic Gospels belong together to the same basic genre.

*God and his purpose.* The introduction to the Gospel makes it clear that in the history that is to be recorded God is active and takes the initiative through his various agents and other means which can include, for example, the way in which the casting of lots can be directed or used for his purpose (Lk 1:9). Throughout Luke's work there is a sense of a divine plan being put into effect, prophesied in the Scriptures (cf. Lk 1:69-70, 73-75) and involving Jesus in obedience to a destiny that he must fulfill. At the same time it needs to be emphasized that this plan is not worked out in a strictly deterministic manner.

---

[20]This is the point that Oscar Cullmann, *Salvation in History* (London: SCM Press, 1967), was concerned to establish over against Rudolf Bultmann's existential understanding of Christianity where it was only the proclamation that mattered and not any historical events to which it testified. Bultmann came dangerously near to saying that we are saved purely by the preaching of the gospel, and we neither can know nor should we even ask whether there was any factual basis for it. For Bultmann, the resurrection of Jesus does not appear to have been a historical event, and he was indifferent as to whether he was actually crucified. Cullmann's position remains valid over against the contemporary attempts to gloss over historical questions by emphasizing the function of the biblical narratives as "story". One can recognize the insights to be derived from appreciation of this element in the biblical material without surrendering the primary importance of the history that is related in the story.

People do behave quite normally and respond freely to God. In particular, they pray to God not only in praise and thanksgiving for what he does but also in petition to ask him to do things with the expectation that he will respond by answering them.[21] This Gospel emphasizes the place of prayer by Jesus and his disciples more than the others do. Nevertheless, there is no uncertainty that God's intended outcome to history will be brought to fruition. What has been prophesied will be fulfilled because the ultimate author of the prophecies has the ability to fulfill them. Consequently, events take place "as it is written" (Lk 3:4; 7:27; 18:31; 22:37) and will take place in the same manner (Lk 24:46-47). More than the other Evangelists Luke refers to the element of necessity that attaches to certain events and that constrains Jesus to obedience (Lk 2:49; 4:43; 13:16; 19:5); it is not surprising that this motif is connected particularly to the suffering, death and glorification of Jesus (Lk 9:22; 17:25; 22:37; 24:7, 26, 44).

*A people in need of salvation.* Luke's story commences with the people of Israel and is concerned with the renewal of a people that have fallen away from their God. John the Baptist will bring many of the people of Israel back to their God (Lk 1:16). Luke shares the common New Testament understanding that the people of God have by and large fallen away from him and constituted themselves sinners. The falling away is not universal, and there are people who are devout and keep God's commandments. They welcome what God purposes to do for his people.[22] But from the outset of John's preaching, it is presupposed that people are liable to God's judgment and need to repent. Luke takes the view shared by other early Christians with various sectarian Jewish groups that the people as a whole, and especially their leaders, had fallen away from God. When Jesus contrasted the righteous with those whom they regarded as sinners, he was plainly speaking ironically (Lk 5:32). In the earlier part of his mission, however, sin is not particularly prominent in the teaching of Jesus, and a variety of other human needs are the main object of his attention. There is an increasing sense that failure to recognize and respond to God's message through Jesus

---

[21]There is nothing here or anywhere else in the New Testament to indicate that the prayers were predetermined by God to take place with the result that he would not be answering prayer but rather carrying out a plan that included the making of the prayer and his subsequent action.

[22]There is accordingly no suggestion that such people would continue to be accounted righteous by God if they spurned the Messiah.

and to Jesus himself is the most characteristic expression of sin (Lk 9:26; 10:8-15; 11:29-32; 12:8-10, 54-59; 13:34; 16:30-31).

*God's agents.* The coming of John and Jesus takes place by a divine intervention that bursts the bounds of ordinary human events. In both cases apparently impossible things happen, the birth of a child to elderly, childless parents, and the birth of a child to a woman who is a virgin. Thus, like Matthew but unlike Mark, Luke is concerned to relate the story of how Jesus came into the world in a way that marked him out as no ordinary human being but as the Son of the Most High.

God acts throughout this narrative by means of agents. Messages are conveyed by Gabriel, the angel of the Lord (Lk 1:11, 19, 26), but when human beings are God's agents, the Holy Spirit fills them so that they can convey God's messages (Lk 1:15, 67). The Holy Spirit is said to be upon Simeon and reveals a divine message to him (Lk 2:25-26). John the Baptist will be filled with the Spirit even from his birth (Lk 1:41), and the birth of Jesus takes place because the Holy Spirit came upon Mary (Lk 1:35). However, the Spirit does not come upon Jesus himself until his baptism by John (Lk 3:22). His subsequent activity is empowered by the Spirit (Lk 4:1, 14, 18; 10:21; cf. Lk 11:20). The promise of Jesus that the Spirit will help his followers in time of persecution (Mk 13:11) is broadened out: the Spirit is promised to all who ask God for this gift (Lk 11:13; contrast Mt 7:11).

*Salvation.* The main theme of the opening section of the Gospel is the action of God the Savior to bring a Savior, Christ the Lord, to his people (Lk 1:47; 2:11). The coming of John is seen as the first step in raising up "a horn of salvation", that is, a powerful source of salvation, for God's people (Lk 1:69). The action is celebrated in traditional language as the redemption or deliverance of Israel from its enemies. Such affirmations could certainly be taken literally to refer to the coming of a Messiah who would cast out the enemies of the people, ruled as they were by a foreign power, perhaps doubly so in that Herod the Edomite was a client of the Roman Empire. They refer to the scattering of the proud and the exaltation of the humble in what could be a social revolution. Yet the rest of the story hardly encourages such an interpretation in that this is not how things work out. On the contrary, what lies ahead of Jerusalem is continued and increased suffering at the hands of its enemies, although this is interpreted as judgment upon it for its sins. Just as there is a use of apocalyptic imagery to convey the signifi-

cance of future events, so too the language of warfare and victory can be used metaphorically to celebrate the redemptive activity of God. Some of the imagery used
by Christians today (or until recently) uses the language of military triumph and
social revolution, but few people take it literally.

The same problem of interpretation arises throughout the Gospel. The
Nazareth manifesto of Jesus could be taken in literal terms of release of the oppressed and recovery of sight for the blind, and good news for the poor could
refer to economic alleviation (Lk 4:18-19). Yet the story is not primarily about
these things: certainly there are signs and wonders that bring sight to some
blind people and healing to some sick people, but there is no overcoming of the
wicked by force, and the deliverance brought by Jesus is basically spiritual with
wider effects.

*Mercy and judgment.* The offer of salvation is very much for the poor (Lk
4:18; 7:22). On the one hand, these are the most needy people, and the promises made to them are bound up with their particular plight, which amounted
to deprivation in many aspects of life. Literal poverty and other wants go hand
in hand. The gospel is good news for the poor. There is no need to repeat here
the evidence of Jesus' concern, as reflected in Luke, for the sinners and for
women and other marginalized and despised groups, including Samaritans and
foreigners.

On the other hand, the poor are seen as those who are most open to the message of Jesus. The revelation is not accepted by the strong and the wealthy but
by the little children who have no standing and make no claims for themselves
(Lk 10:21).

So the effect of the message is to bring into the open the division in society
(Lk 12:51-53) and at the same time to produce some realignment: not all the
rich people reject the message (Zacchaeus!), and not all the needy accept it (the
impenitent criminal!). Those who are wealthy and strong face judgment, but the
poor and weak find salvation. The theme of reversal is more prominent in Luke
than elsewhere.[23]

Luke thus expresses the two sides of God's nature. On the one hand, there
is his mercy shown toward the needy who have not been treated with compassion by their fellow human beings. Strangely, Luke's use of "mercy" *(eleos)* as

---

[23]See John O. York, *The Last Shall Be First: The Rhetoric of Reversal in Luke* (Sheffield Academic Press, 1991).

an attribute of God is confined to the birth narratives (Lk 1:50, 54, 58, 72, 78), and elsewhere his use of related language is not significantly different from that in the other Gospels. The impression that we receive of the divine care for the needy depends more on the way that the story is told than upon a developed language for mercy and grace (Lk 15:20).

On the other hand, the judgment of God upon sin is also prominent. It is not as strongly developed as in Matthew, but the same motifs are present (Lk 11:50-51; 12:20, 45-48, 57-59; 13:1-9, 22-30; 16:19-31; 17:26-37).

*Promise and fulfillment.* The framework within which Luke operates is similar to that which we saw in Matthew, namely, the period of promise and that of fulfillment, with the latter being seen as consisting of the time of Jesus and that of the church. In the Gospel the distinction is simply into the two basic periods. This is clear from Luke 16:16, where the contrast is between two periods of proclamation. In the former period, the Law and the Prophets were the controlling factors. From then on, the good news of the kingdom is being proclaimed. This proclamation continues after the death and resurrection of Jesus, as the followers of Jesus also make the kingdom the object of their preaching (Acts 8:12; 19:8; 20:25; 28:23, 31), although there is a shift in accent as the theme is expounded more in terms of the king (Acts 17:7) and the call to repentance with the offer of forgiveness of sins (Lk 24:47). Luke, like Mark and Matthew, thus identifies the theme of the preaching of Jesus as the kingdom of God, but at the same time he uses more of the vocabulary of salvation to indicate its significance. Within the birth stories the significance of Jesus is that he will reign over the house of Jacob in a kingdom that will never end (Lk 1:33).

As we noted in discussion of Matthew, a somewhat different scheme was developed by Hans Conzelmann, who distinguished three periods in salvation history, the time of Israel, the time of Jesus and the time of the church, with the time of Jesus forming the center of time, so that an earlier Christian understanding of the coming of Jesus as inaugurating the end of time was modified in the light of the delay of the imminent parousia to allow for a significant interval between the times of the first and second comings of Jesus. On this view, the second coming is relegated to the distant future and ceases to be as relevant a factor in Christian thinking as in the earliest period of the church. Conzelmann's view has been highly influential and continues to have its supporters; however, it is vulnerable to criticism.[24] It is very doubtful whether Luke was an innovator in replacing an imminent eschatological understanding with a salvation-historical understanding of God's action in the world, and the distinctions drawn by Conzelmann between the time of Jesus and the time of the church are hard to sustain. Rather, it would seem that the early Christians thought of the period of the coming of Jesus as the decisive action of God in fulfilling his promises of salvation, which then became effective in the witness of the church.[25] That is to say, the early church's theology was "salvation-historical" right from the start, and it is questionable whether it was ever significantly determined purely by the hope of the imminent return of Christ.

*Jesus the Savior.* Luke presents the same basic christology as in the other Synoptic Gospels. The opening announcement of the birth of Jesus brings together the name Jesus, divine sonship and Davidic descent in much the same way as we saw in Matthew 1—2. The body of the Gospel confirms these three basic aspects of who Jesus is. The messiahship is a thread running through the Gospel. It is closely linked with the concept of Jesus as God's prophet. It is true that the anointing in Luke 4:18 is apparently a prophetic anointing.[26] However, the fact that anointing was much more characteristic of the appointment of priests and kings, and the nature of the task here assigned to the prophet strongly suggest that the roles of the prophet and the anointed king are assimilated to one another. Prophetic traits characterize the work of Jesus in all the Synoptic Gospels, but in the case of Luke there is a strong Elijah-Elisha typology that confirms that he is seen as a counterpart to these two prophets. Jesus also describes his activity as a fulfillment of the prophecies of the coming age of divine blessing (Lk 7:22; Is 35), and this raises the possibility that he is to be seen as the end-time prophet like Moses, who again is a messianic type of figure.[27] By the time we reach Luke 7:39 it is not surprising

---

[24]See especially Joseph A. Fitzmyer, *The Gospel According to Luke* (New York: Doubleday, 1981, 1985), 1:179-87.

[25]We shall see later how the saving event was understood by Paul and other writers to embrace the coming of Jesus *and* the witness of his followers.

[26]The anointing of prophets is only rarely attested in the Old Testament (1 Kings 19:16; Is 61:1).

[27]By this loose description I mean an agent who is active in bringing about the future blessings promised by God. No such figure is mentioned explicitly in Is 35, but the passage should be read in conjunction with the later material about the Servant of Yahweh.

that Simon the Pharisee is wondering whether Jesus is a prophet.[28]

The task of Jesus is defined in prophetic terms. He is preeminently a proclaimer of God's word, announcing the good news of the kingdom of God and accompanying the message by signs that indicate that the kingdom is present in power (Lk 24:19). It is a mission of compassion toward the needy but also of denunciation and judgment upon those who are willfully blind and unrepentant, and yet it is also accompanied by expressions of deep sorrow for the latter group because of the judgment that they are bringing upon themselves. The Lukan Jesus is not unlike Jeremiah in this respect. The pain felt extends to those around Jesus (Lk 2:35; see also Lk 23:27, 48-49).

But as the story proceeds, the disciples of Jesus are forced to go further than defining Jesus in prophetic terms when they see him able to command the winds and the water (Lk 8:25). So in Luke, again as in Mark and Matthew, the confession of Peter is that Jesus is the Messiah. And again, as in Mark, Jesus goes on to tell his disciples that the Son of Man must suffer. In this Gospel Jesus has already used this designation in Luke 5:24, Luke 6:5, 22 and Luke 7:34, with reference to himself apparently as a human figure who is said to have, or is implied to have, authority but who is also the object of some scorn and opposition. To this point and beyond "Son of Man" may appear to be nothing more than a self-designation, "the man" used as a roundabout way of referring to oneself. From Luke 12:8 onward the term is used with increasing frequency to refer to a specific figure who has a role at the last judgment and who will come to the earth or be revealed. If there is a pattern of any kind in this development of the usage, it could well be accidental. For in any case on a second or subsequent reading of the Gospel readers would recognize that the use of the designation identified Jesus with this coming figure, and they would probably understand it in terms of the account in Daniel 7, perhaps as developed in I Enoch.

The uses of "Son of Man" in Luke are largely taken over from the traditions that the author has inherited; there is some doubt in the case of those sayings that do not have Synoptic parallels (Lk 17:22; 18:8; 19:10; 21:36; 22:48;

---

[28]The text is uncertain; a tiny group of significant manuscripts have "the prophet". The narrative implies that Simon did think that the description fit Jesus, until he began to have doubts because Jesus allowed himself to be touched by a woman with a bad reputation; a real prophet would have had supernatural knowledge of her character.

24:7) as to whether Luke has introduced the term, but these generally fit into the established pattern. Luke does not have the "ransom" saying about the Son of Man in Mark 10:45, and it may be that we should see Luke 19:10 as a kind of replacement for it, expressing in a different idiom the role of Jesus as the shepherd who saves the lost sheep.

One point that might easily be missed is Luke's use of the term *Lord (kyrios)*. Used in the vocative form *(kyrie)*, this is a respectful form of address that might be no more than a formal courtesy (like "sir" in English) but could also be used to a person who was superior in wealth, position or authority. It is scarcely used to address Jesus in Mark (Mk 7:28), but is more frequent in Matthew (sometimes equivalent to "rabbi") and in Luke. But Luke also uses it several times (from Lk 7:13 onward) as a narrator's way of referring to his main character. Later it was a normal way for Christians to refer to Jesus as their Lord, often in combination with other names and titles, and at this stage the coincidence with the fact that the standard way of referring to God was as "the Lord" must have had some influence on the significance that was attached to it. Luke appears to be anticipating the later church usage by recognizing that Jesus had God's authority as a teacher and as the doer of mighty works. But the motif may well go deeper. C. Kavin Rowe has argued that there is a pervasive ambiguity through Luke-Acts with respect to the use of *kyrios* for God and Jesus, so that there is an identity between the bearers of the title that points in a trinitarian direction.[29]

Although Luke has not included Mark 10:45, a saying that is most probably to be understood in the light of the concept of the Servant of Yahweh, the Servant motif is found elsewhere in the Gospel, particularly in the formal quotation from Isaiah 53:12 in Luke 22:37. It is also probable that the text of Isaiah 61:1-2 cited in Luke 4:18-19 was understood as a reference to the Servant, since it shares characteristic motifs found in the earlier, explicit Servant texts. And the motif of humble service is certainly commended by Jesus (Lk 22:26-27).

As elsewhere, the variety of designations used for Jesus suggests that a number of traditional roles and types are seen as coming to fulfillment simulta-

---

[29]C. Kavin Rowe, "Luke and the Trinity: An Essay in Ecclesial Biblical Theology", *SJT* 56 (2003): 1-26.

neously in him, and each of them from this time on is reshaped in the light of the fulfillment into something new. We might compare the way in which, let us say, a local competition to write a musical composition in a particular form attracts a number of entries that are fairly pedestrian and predictable in character. However, one unknown genius submits a piece that does fit more or less into the form but is nevertheless fresh and original and shows that the particular form chosen is capable of being developed in ways that nobody had previously imagined.

*Mission to Israel and the Gentiles.* The character of the career of Jesus is best summed up as mission. Already in the birth narratives key figures act as witnesses to the advent of salvation; Simeon's words of praise are meant to be heard by those around and not just by God, and Anna spoke about the child to the people. The task of John the Baptist is summed up as preaching good news (Lk 3:18), and the words of Isaiah 61:1 make the same point for Jesus (Lk 4:18; cf. Lk 4:43; 8:1; 16:16; 20:1). The theme is, to be sure, already there in Mark, where Jesus preaches the good news of God (Mk 1:14-15; cf. Mk 8:35; 10:29), and this is good news is to be proclaimed in the future in all the world (Mk 13:10; 14:9). Similarly, when the disciples go out on mission, they preach the good news and heal everywhere (Lk 9:6): it is the message of the kingdom of God that is good news (Lk 9:2). The importance of mission is underlined by the fact that Luke records the two missions of the Twelve and the seventy-two, and the numerical symbolism indicates that mission to Jews and Gentiles is foreshadowed in these accounts.

The mission is primarily to Israel, where not only those generally recognized as sinners but all alike are seen to be in need. Put otherwise, the proclamation of the kingdom of God demands a response by all people, in the same way as Roman citizens or provincials who were already subject to the emperor might be required to take a fresh oath of loyalty to him under pain of penalty.[30] The message of the kingdom thus has the effect of compelling people to renew their commitment to God. To do so, of course, involves accepting that Jesus really is the agent of God, authorized to demand allegiance on his behalf, in the same kind of way as John the Baptist was understood as a genuine prophet (cf. Lk

---

[30]It has been conjectured that the census mentioned in Lk 2:1 might be identified with such an oath of allegiance imposed by Augustus on Judea (Josephus *Antiquities* 16.290; 17.42).

20:1-8). It is not surprising that the question of Jesus' authority was frequently raised.

As we have observed, the Gospel has a strongly Jewish flavor and significantly begins and ends in the temple. There are indications throughout that the ultimate scope of salvation includes the Gentiles. This is especially apparent in Luke 2:32 and Luke 3:6 but also in the occasional contacts between Jesus and those outside Israel (the Roman centurion, Lk 7:1-10; the Samaritan leper, Lk 17:11-19), and it becomes explicit in Luke 24:47. The mission of the seventy-two is symbolic of the mission to all the nations, even though in context it is directed to Israel. It may be significant that Luke has omitted the story of the Syro-Phoenician woman (Mk 7:24-30), although this incident is merely one part of a longer section that Luke has chosen to omit from Mark's account.

*The saved people.* The mission of John the Baptist was declared by Gabriel to involve bringing back many of the people of Israel to the Lord and turning their hearts from disobedience to the wisdom of the righteous (Lk 1:16-17). Response to the messages of John and Jesus was expressed in repentance, a concept that figures more prominently in Luke than in the other Gospels; the term is significantly added in Luke 5:32 and expresses the fundamental response to God in Luke 13:1-9 (cf. Lk 10:13; 15:7). Luke emphasizes that such repentance and conversion must be wholehearted and is to be a lifelong commitment rather than something ephemeral (Lk 8:13-15; 9:57-62; 14:25-35). In the passages cited the danger of turning back or giving up is accented: salt that loses its saltiness cannot be restored.[31]

Luke's attitude to the law as the way of life for believers is a matter of debate. In the birth narratives the leading characters are implicitly praised for the fact that they keep the commandments of God and carry out the duties prescribed by the law (Lk 1:6, 59; 2:21-24, 27, 39, 41). As in Mark 10:17-21, a question about inheriting eternal life is answered in terms of what is written in the law (Lk 10:25-29); but if this answer may seem to suggest that keeping the law is all that is needed, Luke's later parallel to Mark's story shows that following Jesus and self-denial are also integral to the answer (Lk 18:18-30). Luke's key saying is in Luke 16:16-17 (cf. Mt 5:17-20; 11:12-13). Here, as in Matthew, it is stated that it is impossible for the least stroke of a pen to drop out of the

---

[31]The language is probably hyperbolical rather than to be taken over-literally.

law. Luke also has the statement of Jesus that requires attention to the payment
of tithes as well as to the justice and the love of God (Lk 11:42). These sayings
would suggest that for Jesus the law remains in force. However, as happens
more broadly in Matthew 5, the saying about the validity of the law is immediately followed by a representative example of Jesus forbidding what the law
allowed and made provision for, namely, divorce. Although the point is not developed in Luke, it appears that for him what continues to be valid is the law
as newly understood by Jesus. Luke does not have Jesus' teaching about the
things that defile people (Mk 7:1-23). This teaching came in the longer section
of Mark that Luke has omitted;[32] Luke may have seen the teaching in Luke
11:39-41 (cf. Mt 23:25-26) as making much the same point. Also Luke does
not have the lengthy, systematic presentation of the teaching of Jesus in relation
to the law that is found in Matthew 5, and the general impression gained from
Matthew that Jesus corresponds typologically to Moses is not so apparent in
Luke.[33]

*The everlasting kingdom.* Almost by definition the reign of the Messiah is
"forever" (Lk 1:33). Therefore, although much of the teaching is about the
present rule of God and the realization of salvation here in this world during
the lifetime of Jesus, Luke inevitably shares in the belief in the future coming
of the Messiah to bring God's purposes to completion. Where Mark has the
one discourse about the future (Mk 13; cf. Mt 24—25), Luke has two (Lk
17:20-37; 21). He has Jesus speak much less cryptically and more openly
about the forthcoming destruction of Jerusalem and its remaining desolate
until the times of the Gentiles are fulfilled. And, although some scholars
have thought that he makes a clear distinction between that event and the
far distant parousia of the Son of Man, nevertheless he makes it very clear
that people must at all times live in readiness for that event and not be taken
unawares by it (Lk 21:34-36). His account of the resurrection appearances
also brings out much more emphatically the way in which the followers of
Jesus have the task laid upon them of being witnesses to Jesus in the intervening period.

---

[32] There is no reason to suppose that Luke had theological reasons for omitting this particular section
of the narrative; it fell away as part of the overall omission of this part of Mark.

[33] Luke does have a Moses typology, as we have seen, but it is concerned more with the idea of Moses
as a messianic figure than as a lawgiver.

## Conclusion

Our survey has shown how the theological emphases in this Gospel arrange
themselves naturally around the broad theme of the purpose of God to bring
salvation to Jews and Gentiles alike through the activity of his missionary agent,
Jesus, who functions as prophet and Messiah. These motifs can also be found
in Mark and Matthew but presented somewhat differently. If Jesus is a prophet
in Luke, he is more of a teacher in Matthew. Matthew and Mark present Jesus'
message more in terms of the kingdom of God/heaven, whereas Luke has a
more salvific thrust.

As in the case of Matthew, we can say that Luke operates within the same
framework of thought as Mark.

If we try to sum up the main theme of Luke in a sentence, we may say that
the main theme is the coming of the Savior who brings salvation to the needy.

Developing this brief summary in more detail we can list some significant
elements in it as follows.

1. Jesus assumes the need and sinfulness of human beings in much the same
way as Mark and Matthew.

2. Luke reports faithfully the teaching of Jesus about the rule or sovereign
power of God, but he brings out the way in which this action conveys salvation
to people. The continuity between what Jesus offered in his lifetime and what
the church preached after his resurrection is made the more obvious. There is
some stress on the importance of repentance on the part of sinners.

3. The role of Jesus is similar to that in Matthew, again based on his birth,
but there is more stress on his authoritative position as Lord, even before his
resurrection and exaltation.

4. He calls disciples and sends them out to share his mission.

5. His mission is primarily to Israel, but from the beginning it foreshadows
the wider mission to the Gentiles.

6. There is perhaps more overt stress on the compassion of Jesus for the
poor and needy, and this reinforces the command to love that is given to his
disciples.

7. Jesus' death is to be seen as sacrificial and redemptive.

8. Luke's view of the future is much the same as in Mark and Matthew.

## Bibliography

*New Testament Theologies:* (English) Ladd, pp. 236-45; Morris, pp. 144-221; Strecker, pp. 392-417; Zuck, pp. 87-166 (Darrell L. Bock). (German) Berger, pp. 697-707; Gnilka, pp. 196-225; Hahn, 1:547-83; Hübner, 3:120-51; Stuhlmacher, 2:174-99.

Beck, Brian E. *Christian Character in the Gospel of Luke.* London: Epworth, 1989.

Bock, Darrell L. *Luke.* 2 vols. Grand Rapids, Mich.: Baker, 1994, 1996.

——— . *Proclamation from Prophecy and Pattern: Lukan Old Testament Christology.* Sheffield: Sheffield Academic Press, 1987.

Bovon, François. *Luke 1: A Commentary on the Gospel of Luke 1:1–9:50.* Minneapolis: Fortress, 2002.

——— . *Luke the Theologian: Thirty-three Years of Research (1950-1983).* Allison Park, Penn.: Pickwick Press, 1987.

Conzelmann, Hans. *The Theology of Saint Luke.* London: Faber, 1960.

Crump, David. *Jesus the Intercessor: Prayer and Christology in Luke-Acts.* Tübingen: Mohr, 1992.

Cullmann, Oscar. *Salvation in History.* London: SCM Press, 1967.

Doble, Peter. *The Paradox of Salvation: Luke's Theology of the Cross.* Cambridge: Cambridge University Press, 1996.

Fitzmyer, Joseph A. *The Gospel According to Luke.* 2 vols. New York: Doubleday, 1981, 1985.

——— . *Luke the Theologian: Aspects of His Teaching.* London: Geoffrey Chapman, 1989.

Green, Joel B. *The Gospel of Luke.* Grand Rapids, Mich.: Eerdmans, 1997.

——— . *The Theology of the Gospel of Luke.* Cambridge: Cambridge University Press, 1995.

Marshall, I. Howard. *The Gospel of Luke: A Commentary on the Greek Text.* Exeter: Paternoster, 1978.

——— . *Luke: Historian and Theologian.* 3rd ed. Exeter: Paternoster, 1988.

Moessner, David P. *Lord of the Banquet: The Literary and Theological Significance of the Lukan Travel Narrative.* Minneapolis: Fortress, 1989.

——— , ed. *Jesus and the Heritage of Israel: Luke's Narrative Claim upon Israel's Legacy.* Harrisburg, Penn.: Trinity Press International, 1999.

Nolland, John. *Luke.* 3 vols. Dallas: Word, 1989, 1993, 1993.

Rowe, C. Kavin. "Luke and the Trinity: An Essay in Ecclesial Biblical Theology". *SJT* 56 (2003): 1-26.

Tannehill, Robert C. *The Narrative Unity of Luke-Acts: A Literary Interpretation.* Vol. I. *The Gospel According to Luke.* Philadelphia: Fortress, 1986.

Tuckett, Christopher M. *Luke.* Sheffield: Sheffield Academic Press, 1996.

Verheyden, J., ed. *The Unity of Luke-Acts.* Louvain: Louvain University Press, 1999.

York, John O. *The Last Shall Be First: The Rhetoric of Reversal in Luke.* Sheffield: Sheffield Academic Press, 1991.

# 6

# LUKE-ACTS

❧❀❧

## *THE SEQUEL*

❧❀❧

It is difficult to overemphasize the theological significance of the fact that Luke, unlike the other Evangelists, saw his Gospel as the earlier part of a two-volume work. This verdict stands firm regardless of whether Luke had the second volume in mind at the time when he compiled the first (as I believe to be the case) or decided later that the Gospel needed to be complemented. But the precise nature of the relationship between the two volumes is complex. It is most probable that Luke is providing the Christians of his time, as represented by Theophilus, with an account of Christian origins that serves to confirm the reliability of the gospel that is being preached and taught. The preaching is thus backed up by an appeal to the facts on which it is based, as handed down by the people in the best position to know what had happened. But this story of Christian origins has two parts.

On the one hand, there is the story of Jesus, culminating in his death and resurrection. This was certainly the basis of the early Christian preaching, but whether the mission and teaching of Jesus was a central part of the content has been questioned.[1] It is notorious that, according to Acts, the only occasion on

---

[1]Compare the small amount of reference to the story of the mission and teaching of Jesus in the New Testament letters.

which any extended reference is made by a preacher to the life of Jesus is in Peter's sermon[2] to Cornelius (Acts 10:36-43). Nevertheless, it is probable that reference was made to it more widely.[3] In Acts 1—9 the gospel had been preached to Jews in Jerusalem who had some familiarity with the story; now in Acts 10 it is preached to Gentiles who have only a scanty knowledge of what had happened. In any case, a good deal of the preaching is concerned with the condemnation, crucifixion and resurrection of Jesus, which occupies a substantial part of the Gospel.

On the other hand, there is the second part of the divine program laid down in prophecy, that repentance and forgiveness of sins should be preached to all nations, beginning from Jerusalem (Lk 24:47). In a full account of the basis for the gospel it was necessary to show how this second, equally crucial, part of God's plan was fulfilled. In particular, Acts shows how under divine guidance that aspect of God's plan which concerned the Gentiles was fulfilled, so that God might have "a people for his name" including Jews and Gentiles (Acts 15:14). This plan did not intend that the Jews were henceforward excluded from the people of God, but it included those Jews who believed in the gospel.

It can be seen that each of the two parts of Luke's work implies the other, and neither is complete in itself.

Questions arise in the case of Acts similar to those that arise in the Gospels in their relation to what Jesus taught and believed. Acts professes to give an account of the preaching and life of the earliest Christians and then of Paul in particular. Many scholars argue that the picture of Paul's theology differs considerably from that which we find in his letters and represents the work of somebody who did not fully know or understand Paul and has given a somewhat inaccurate account of him.[4] If, then, Luke was not well informed about somebody nearer in time to him, how much more likely it is that he was even

---

[2]I would gladly use some other term than *sermon* with all the misleading associations that contemporary usage attaches to it, but I have been unable to think of an apt substitute. *Speech* is not much better.

[3]Luke is capable of repeating important stories for emphasis (the conversion of Cornelius; the conversion of Saul) and of mentioning only once activities that can be reasonably assumed to have been standard practice.

[4]This verdict on Luke's account of Paul's theology is generally accompanied by a critique of his story of Paul's career as being one-sided and inaccurate.

less knowledgeable about the theology and life of the earliest Christian believers. The way is then open to argue that Luke's picture rests upon little hard evidence and represents his own idealization of that period or a reading back of the preaching and attitudes of his time into the earlier times. What is the nature of Luke's theology, and how does it relate to the actual theologies of the characters in the story?

I side with those who take a high view of Luke's historical reliability in Acts, but this does not mean that the theology of the author of Acts is to be simply identified with that of any of the characters in the narrative, nor does it deny that Luke's reconstruction of their positions may be open to question in detail.[5]

## Luke's Theological Story: Part 2

*The story lines.* Whereas the three Synoptic Gospels consist of many small units (with a few larger ones) that have been worked together editorially into a story with a certain amount of progress and development,[6] the narrative in Acts is much more of a connected narrative told in chronological order. Various story lines make up the plot. Of all the books of the New Testament it is Acts that most clearly exemplifies the relationship of the theology of the early church to its mission. Acts is the story of a mission, in the course of which we learn the theological content of the gospel and the theology on which the mission to Jews and Gentiles rested.

There is the story of how the witnesses to Jesus began their task in Jerusalem, spreading out to Judea and Samaria and then into the wider world until at last they reached Rome (Acts 1:8). It is the story of how the word of God grew territorially.

Roughly corresponding with this story is the way in which the gospel first

---

[5]As in the case of the historical Jesus, the limits of this volume prevent a detailed discussion of this position. The major commentary of C. K. Barrett presents a reasoned case for a moderately critical evaluation of Luke's work; see C. K. Barrett, *Acts* (Edinburgh: T & T Clark, 1994, 1998). Scholars who have a higher estimate of his historical reliability include Joseph A. Fitzmyer, Jacob Jervell and Ben Witherington III. See further Steve Walton and David Wenham, *Exploring the New Testament*, vol. I, *The Gospels and Acts* (London: SPCK; Downers Grove, Ill.: InterVarsity Press, 2001), pp. 285-90; I. Howard Marshall, *Acts* (Sheffield: Sheffield Academic Press, 1992).

[6]Granted that there is a simple overall scheme in the Gospels based on chronology and geography, it is still the case that there is little detailed development of a plot, and many of the individual pericopae could be and were related in a different order (contrast Matthew and Mark in the first halves of their Gospels).

reached Aramaic-speaking Jews, then the group of Greek-speaking Hellenists in Jerusalem, then non-Jews, beginning with the Samaritans and the Ethiopian traveler, and finally reaching Gentiles in a wide sweep from Caesarea to Antioch, to Cyprus and Galatia, to Asia, to Macedonia and Achaia, and finally to Rome.[7] This is a story of cultural spread.

Simultaneously with this account of the spread of the gospel and the growth of the church, there takes place the development of Christian theology and in particular the way in which the church had to cope with the twofold problem of the opposition to the gospel from the Jewish leaders and of the admission of uncircumcised Gentiles into the people of God. It is important to emphasize that this is a problem with two sides to it and that Luke is not concerned solely with the status of Gentile believers but also with the response or lack of response of the Jews.[8] It is part of the genius of Luke to be able to present this theological problem and its resolution through the medium of the story of the early church.

Our task now is not to retell these stories as such but rather to search out the theological story that is being conveyed by Luke.

*Transition and preparation.* Acts commences naturally enough with a recapitulation of the closing of the Gospel but in such a way as to make it a new beginning.[9] Some crucial theological points are made. First, for the time being the task of the followers of Jesus is worldwide witness to him. Whatever is meant by the restoration of "the kingdom to Israel", it is "not yet" and meanwhile witness must be borne to Jesus (Acts 1:6-8). Second, the disciples need the power of the Holy Spirit for their task, just as Jesus was empowered by the Spirit and other actors in Luke 1—2 were filled with the Spirit to prophesy concerning his coming. Third, the hope of the restoration of the kingdom is in effect replaced by the hope of the return of Jesus. Fourth, the number of witnesses to the resurrection of Jesus had to be made up to the original number of twelve apostles; the symbolism of the number, presumably reflecting the twelve

---

[7]Luke of course knows that there were believers in Rome before Paul reached there, but he has chosen to make the coming of Paul the climax of Acts.

[8]For the central role of Israel in Luke's theology see David P. Moessner, ed., *Jesus and the Heritage of Israel: Luke's Narrative Claim upon Israel's Legacy* (Harrisburg, Penn.: Trinity Press International, 1999).

[9]Cf. Mikeal C. Parsons, *The Departure of Jesus in Luke-Acts: The Ascension Narratives in Context* (Sheffield: Sheffield Academic Press, 1987).

tribes of Israel (cf. Lk 22:30), was important. The task is variously described as "leadership" (TNIV) or "oversight" (NRSV) (Gk. *episkopē*), "service" (Gk. *diakonia*), "apostleship" and "witness". The first of these terms is derived from Psalm 109:8, and its use may suggest that Luke saw the task of the apostles as similar to that of the later "overseers" (traditionally "bishops"; cf. Acts 20:28).

The promise of power is fulfilled in the descent of the Spirit upon the disciples; it is altogether more probable that the Spirit came upon the entire group of disciples rather than just upon the Twelve (cf. Acts 2:16-18). The descent of the Spirit should probably be seen as having some correspondences to the giving of the law at Sinai, although Luke has done little if anything to draw attention to the analogy. For him it is more important that the event is the fulfillment of Joel's prophecy concerning the last days in which the saving action of God is extended to cover all kinds of people, young and old, male and female, and salvation is available to all who call on the Lord's name.

For the moment the audience is international but Jewish. Only the variety of languages spoken perhaps hints at a symbolism of the nations of the world.[10]

*Witness to the resurrection.* We are now given an example of what the first Christians did in public: through Peter as their spokesperson they gave witness to the resurrection of Jesus. The essence of Peter's public statement is that despite his divine accreditation Jesus had been put to death by the Jewish leaders but God had raised him to life and exalted him to heaven, a clear token that God confirmed his position as Lord and Christ. Although Jesus had been handed over to the authorities in fulfillment of God's purpose and his foreknowledge of what would happen, Peter accused his hearers of responsibility for the crucifixion and hence of guilt for it. Yet they could be pardoned for their sins through repenting and submitting to baptism, and they would receive not only forgiveness but also the gift of the Spirit. The reasoning appears to be that the people share in the guilt of their leaders unless they dissociate themselves from their action. It is not explained how forgiveness comes "in the name of Jesus Christ", but Peter identifies Jesus as the Lord in Joel 2:32 who has the power to save. The promise of the Holy Spirit is tied to the prophecy of John the Baptist that

---

[10]It is assumed that these Jews speak the vernacular of their several countries, although presumably many of them would know Greek as the common language of the eastern Mediterranean world; only some of them will have known Hebrew or Aramaic.

the Messiah would baptize with the Spirit, and Peter asserts that Jesus received this gift on his exaltation to God's right hand.

The rationale for these statements is not immediately obvious to the reader: how does Peter know that Jesus is now at God's right hand, that this position makes him Lord and Christ and that he has received the Spirit? The probable answer to the first two questions for Luke is that he has previously recorded Jesus' use of Psalm 110:1, which would be understood as a prophecy fulfilled in him, and, if Jesus had ascended to heaven, this would be the occasion on which this happened. In any case, resurrection and exaltation are associated in Judaism (*1 Enoch* 62:14-16; *2 Baruch* 51:5, 10; *T. Benj.* 10:6, 9, with a scriptural basis in Dan 12:1-3).[11] As for the gift of the Spirit to Christ, this may reflect an understanding of Psalm 68:18 (cf. Eph 4:8) taken to mean "you have received gifts for humankind".[12]

It is clear that Jesus Christ is still active in that baptism is performed in his name and is efficacious. Healings are also performed in his name, which means that his agents operate by his power and not by their own authority (Acts 3:6). The work of the apostles is thus a continuation of the work of Jesus whereby the signs of the kingdom of God are manifested and salvation is made effective in people's lives through the preaching of his followers. Although Jesus is not physically present, his work goes on. The content of the message, however, has shifted in that, while Jesus proclaimed the rule of God and called people to be his disciples, his followers tell people about him and how he was the person through whom life was being bestowed in response to a faith that was related to him (cf. Acts 3:16; 4:9-10). In this way Jesus is more obviously the object of proclamation than in the Gospel, although it must be insisted that he is both the proclaimer and the proclaimed in both parts of Luke's work.

A variety of expressions are used to indicate the status and role of Jesus. Peter can refer to Jesus as being a prophet like Moses (Deut 18:15-19; Acts 3:22-23). Such a prophet is no ordinary prophet but rather the leader of the people, as Moses was. The description clearly applies to Jesus in his earthly life, as the

---

[11]K. L. Anderson, "The Resurrection of Jesus in Luke-Acts" (doctoral thesis, Brunel University, 2000), p. 171.

[12]Cf. Max Turner, *Power from on High: The Spirit in Israel's Restoration and Witness in Luke-Acts* (Sheffield: Sheffield Academic Press, 1996), pp. 280-89, where a series of parallels with Moses' reception of the law is worked out.

Gospel has indicated, but here it seems to refer also to his continuing activity. It is to be noted in passing that in view of his exalted rank anybody who does not listen to him will be cut off from the people of God; being a member of the Jewish people is not in itself an adequate qualification for remaining in God's favor now that the prophet has come.

The statements about actions being performed in the name of Jesus are highly significant. These must be heard against the Old Testament background in which it is the name of Yahweh that functions in this kind of way, and the inevitable conclusion is that here the name of Jesus functions in the same way as the name of Yahweh and indeed replaces it. He alone is the channel through which salvation is available (Acts 4:12).

At the same time, we have the other principal divine agent, the Holy Spirit, who also functions prominently in the early part of Acts. As already noted, the Spirit fills the apostles who utter God's message. The effect of the filling is apparently to give courage to them to stand up in the midst of threatening audiences, as Jesus had promised, but also in more encouraging situations. And it would seem that the Spirit must also have something to do with the content of what is said in the same way as the content of prophecy was mediated by the Spirit. Christian preaching and witness is accordingly a continuation of the prophetic activity of Jesus and the witnesses to him in the Gospel.

The activity of Jesus and of the Spirit as God's agents does not mean that God retreats into the background and is not directly involved in what goes on. Throughout Acts it is insisted that what happens in and through Jesus is due to the plan of God, which is being carried out. It is he who allowed Jesus to be crucified and who raised him from the dead. It is he who gave the Spirit to Jesus to pour out on believers. It is his calling to salvation that is expressed in the preaching (Acts 2:39). When the disciples are released from prison, it is to God that they pray for action (Acts 4:24-30), and it is only rarely that prayer is addressed to Jesus. Despite the fact that Jesus is also given the title of "Lord" and that people call on him for salvation, God remains the Lord to whom people pray. Because of his sovereign power and purpose the Christians have confidence that, whatever the opposition, the work to which he has called them will go on successfully. This point is even attributed to a leading Pharisee who recognizes that if the apostles' activity is of God, then the Sanhedrin cannot thwart it (Acts 5:38-39).

*The spreading mission—to the uncircumcised.* The story in Acts is the story of this ongoing activity of God that human beings can oppose and attempt to thwart but that will nevertheless proceed as God purposes. The details of its progress are not our present concern, although they testify to this direction and empowering by God that we have already seen exemplified in the earliest chapters of Acts. Much more significant for our purpose is the way in which the early Christians are found to be testifying about Jesus to people other than Jews. This happens in various ways. Apparently of his own accord Philip goes to Samaria, but then he is specially directed by an angel to meet up with an Ethiopian official. Saul is deliberately commissioned by God to go to Gentiles as well as to the people of Israel. Peter is brought into contact with the Gentile centurion Cornelius through a series of dreams and visions of divine origin. People from Cyprus and Cyrene speak spontaneously to Greeks about Jesus. And then the floodgates open and the resulting mixed church of Jews and Gentiles in Antioch deliberately sends out, at God's direction, two missionaries who discover an audience of Gentiles that wants to hear their message (Acts 13:7). Luke thus makes it clear that the mission to Gentiles is carried on in response to varied stimuli, but is above all due to God's direction of events. It was, of course, foreordained by God, who had foretold through the prophets that "repentance for the forgiveness of sins will be preached in his [Christ's] name to all nations, beginning at Jerusalem" (Lk 24:47). The wording here indicates very clearly that the Jews are included as much as are the Gentiles.

There may, therefore, have been little problem for the early Christians in seeking to win Gentiles as Christian proselytes rather than simply as Jewish proselytes, and we do not in fact hear of any opposition in principle to this, although there may have been lukewarmness about actually doing it. What caused difficulty was the question whether such converts needed to fulfill all the other requirements of the Jewish religion like ordinary Jewish proselytes. Even before they were converted, there were of course the practical problems associated with meeting and eating with Gentiles. In the case of Cornelius, as Luke tells the story, Peter was assured in a dream that, whatever had been the case in the past, God no longer required his people to abstain from so-called unclean foods, and by implication from association with so-called unclean people. The Holy Spirit came upon Cornelius and his family, uncircumcised as they were, and they were baptized there and then. The implication is that circumcision was not required. Later, other Gentiles became Christian believers without having been circumcised at Antioch, and this became the pattern on Paul's first missionary campaign. But if Gentiles became believers in Israel's Messiah, why should they not be required to be circumcised and keep the rest of the law, as proselytes did? It can be well understood that the case of the conservative Jews in the church was a strong one.

The theological answer to it is given in Acts 15, where the question has now become quite sharply that of whether Gentiles could be saved without being circumcised.

The first part of the answer was what we might call pragmatic: large numbers of Gentiles had already become believers and received the gift of the Spirit without being required to be circumcised. God evidently did not take circumcision into account when apportioning gifts of the Spirit. It is not clear whether the so-called Judaizers believed that God should not give the Spirit until after circumcision, or that, if he did bestow it, then the position must be regularized by subsequent circumcision.

A second part of the answer, again given by Peter, was that the law was an unbearable yoke that could not save people anyhow (Acts 15:10). As Paul put it, "through [Christ] everyone who believes is set free from every sin, a justification you were not able to obtain under the law of Moses" (Acts 13:39). Although that might be construed to mean that the law of Moses saved from some sins and Christ dealt with the remainder, it is altogether more probable that the force is exclusive: Christ saves from all sins, from none of which the law of Moses could save. If the law was impotent to save, there was no need for Gentiles to keep it.

Third, Peter insisted that "through the grace of the Lord Jesus we believe [in order] to be saved", whether Jews or Gentiles (Acts 15:11).[13] Here an antithesis is implicit between grace and faith on the one side and performance of the law on the other side. Whether or not these words were actually said on the occasion, they undoubtedly represent Luke's view that salvation is by grace and faith and not by keeping the law. The point may be put with less depth than in the

---

[13]For this translation see John Nolland, "A Fresh Look at Acts 15.10", *NTS* 27 (1980-81): 105-14. The Greek could also mean "we believe it is through the grace of our Lord Jesus that we are saved, just as they are" (TNIV). The main point, that salvation is by grace, is not affected.

letters of Paul, but there is fundamental agreement.

We again note the significant fact that Jews are regarded as being as much in need of salvation by grace through faith as are Gentiles. The way to salvation is the same for both groups. The Messiah is regarded as a Savior with complete power to save those who believe, and he alone has the power to save. Nobody else or nothing else can save, and no supplementation or prior conditions are needed. The verdict of the apostolic council is therefore that circumcision is not required of Gentiles; they are not to be burdened with it. Nevertheless, certain requirements are laid upon the Gentiles: abstinence from food sacrificed to idols, from blood (i.e., meat not slaughtered in the Jewish manner), from the meat of strangled animals, and from sexual immorality. These requirements are often thought to reflect certain regulations laid down in Leviticus 17—18 for Jews and Gentiles living in the land of Israel, and they ensured that the main barriers to fellowship in the church would be removed: Gentiles would not be forcing Jewish Christians to eat food prepared in unacceptable ways, nor would they be living in sexual immorality. These rules represent something of a compromise perhaps, and they may have been applicable only in areas thought to belong to the land of Israel at its widest extent.[14] They assume that Jewish Christians will go on living in their traditional ways, and later in Acts Paul is represented as doing so. Whether Luke's view is that Jewish Christians should or must continue to live in this way is a moot point.

The significant point from all this is that for Luke Gentiles do not need to be circumcised and to keep the Jewish law as it applied to Jews; they do not have to become Jewish proselytes. However, it was not necessary for Jewish Christians to give up their way of life under the Jewish law, for instance by not circumcising their infants.

*The divine plan.* This expansion of the people of God raises afresh the question of the place of the Jews in God's plan. Luke deals with this issue at some length in two passages, the speeches of Stephen in Acts 7 and of Paul in Acts 13.

---

[14]So Markus Bockmuehl, *Jewish Law in Gentile Churches: Halakhah and the Beginning of Christian Public Ethics* (Edinburgh: T & T Clark, 2000), pp. 49-83. Frank Thielman, *The Law and the New Testament: The Question of Continuity* (New York: Crossroad, 1999), pp. 156-58, is skeptical of the connection with Lev 17—18 and thinks that the decree is more of a pragmatic compromise to make it easier for strict Jewish Christians to have fellowship with Gentile believers.

Stephen's speech is set in a context of accusations that he has been speaking against the temple and the law, alleging that Jesus would destroy the temple and change the customs (i.e., the way of life according to the law) laid down by Moses. His reply is cast in the form of a historical survey from the call of Abraham onward in which he traces the line of God's dealings with Israel. The speech abounds in detail and makes numerous subsidiary points along the way. The providential care of God for his people emerges. The movement of the people and their ancestors into and out of the Promised Land is recorded. Major attention is devoted to Moses, who was sent to be a ruler and judge of the people. Like Joseph before him, he was rejected by the people despite God's choice of him, and their rejection extended to the worship of God, which they replaced by idolatry. Yet despite their lapses the people had the traveling tabernacle of God in the wilderness and then in the Promised Land until it was replaced by the temple built by Solomon. At this point Stephen asserts that God does not dwell in houses made by human hands and attacks the Jews for failing to obey the prophets. The speech thus accuses them, rather than the Christians, of disobedience to God, seen in their rejection of the prophets, culminating in the killing of Jesus, and disobedience to the law. It appears to suggest that God is not tied to a temple built in a single place but moves with his people wherever they go. The speech falls short of stating that God now dwells in a new building not made with hands, that is, the church composed of believing people, but it comes near to doing so. Nothing is said here about the Messiah, although there is a typology sitting there, waiting to be developed with respect to Moses as the ruler and deliverer or redeemer of the people.

The story is repeated and extended from a different point of view in Acts 13. The period up to Moses is passed over swiftly and attention is directed to God's provision of leaders for the people, the judges, Saul and David. Then there is a rapid transit to David's descendant Jesus, who was put to death by the rulers and then raised from the dead. The resurrection of Jesus is seen as the fulfillment of God's promises to the Jews in Scripture. As in Acts 2, the prophecies about life after death were demonstrably not fulfilled in the case of David, but in the case of Jesus, and this confirms that he was the heir of David concerning whom the prophecies were made.

Between them, these two speeches sum up the past history of the Jews as one of rejection of leadership provided by God, leading up to the rejection of Jesus and his vindication by God. The rejection of Jesus is thus the final part in a pattern of behavior that stretches back to the beginning. Yet, despite the past rejection, Jesus is sent first of all as the Savior for the Jews, and it is only after their rejection of him that the apostles turn to the Gentiles. In the plan of God there is a priority in the offer of the gospel to the Jews. And this pattern repeats itself throughout Acts as the apostles go first to whatever Jews there are in any given location. To be sure, the initial audience often includes proselytes and God-fearers; the lines are not hard and fast. This fits in with Paul's expressed belief that the gospel was first for the Jews (Rom 1:16).

It emerges that although the Jews have a record of failure to recognize God's agents and keep his commandments, nevertheless the Messiah is sent first to them (Acts 3:26), and Luke maintains this priority in his account of the mission (Acts 13:46). Indeed, he comes dangerously near to suggesting that it is only when and because the Jews reject the gospel that the missionaries turn to the Gentiles. It is difficult to believe that this is what he means to say, and it would seem more likely that the point is to state that the Gentiles will replace unbelieving Jews as the people of God without implying that they will be evangelized only if the Jews disbelieve.

*Mission in an ever-wider field.* By the end of Acts 15, accordingly, the theological story in Acts has reached this point, that the gospel is offered to Jews first and also to Gentiles, out of whom a people is being formed who believe and are saved. From here onward the story is that of Paul's mission and his imprisonments. Acts is so arranged, however, that Paul's mission was already established before Acts 15, and the rest of the story is an extension of the events in Acts 13—14. What does the second half of Acts add to the story that has so far been told?

First, the story explores at greater length what happens when Paul comes into contact with Gentiles who have no connections with Judaism. This point had already emerged earlier in Acts 13:6-12 and Acts 14:8-20. In the latter story, set in Lystra, Paul and Barnabas meet up with worshipers of pagan gods, and the recorded part of their message deals with the reality of the one living God, the Creator. In the past he had left the Gentiles to themselves, although not without providing graciously for their needs and so giving evidence of his existence and his kindness. This theme is more fully developed in the scene at

Athens, where again the message is concerned with the reality of the one God who does not need human worship but who has appointed the life of the nations in such a way that people should be able to find him without falling into idolatry. The guilt of the world, which has failed to appreciate the signals of God's reality, stands revealed, and judgment confronts all. History has moved to its climax with the revelation of the One through whom God will exercise this judgment.

Above all, the story relates the way in which the mission proceeds under the guidance and care of God. To some extent it does little more than add marginal notes to what has preceded. Its main purpose could be said to be to provide further evidence of the divine approval for the mission of Paul to the Gentiles. Luke's purpose is to demonstrate the progress of the Word of God.

In passing, we should note the significance of the story of Apollos and the disciples at Ephesus. In both cases we have people who appear to have known only the baptism of John and to have had some Christian instruction. The need for fuller instruction in the gospel, as understood by Paul, is expressed. In the case of Apollos, it is a moot point whether he had received the Spirit. The phrase "fervent in spirit" (Acts 18:25) should probably be understood as "fervor in the Spirit" (TNIV mg.).[15] Certainly Luke does not record that he received Christian baptism. In the case of the disciples at Ephesus it is emphasized that they had not received the Spirit, and in view of this lack they were baptized and had hands laid on them, after which the Spirit came upon them with evidential signs. Thus the importance of right doctrine and of the gift of the Spirit is underlined.

By the end of Acts 20 the mission of Paul has reached its preliminary conclusion, to be followed by his arrest and imprisonment. The address by Paul to the church leaders at Miletus consequently acts as a kind of closure to the story so far, and it provides a survey of how Paul saw his missionary work, which is also intended as a model for local congregational leaders. It sums up his message directed to Jews and Greeks as the gospel of God's grace, culminating in an appeal for repentance and faith in the Lord Jesus. It lays the foundation for that appeal in the purchase of the church by God with his own blood (Acts 20:28).[16] This

---

[15]Turner, *Power from on High*, p. 389.

[16]The reference can only be to the blood of Christ. To speak of this as God's own blood (TNIV) may

strongly suggests that the church is something new, and that suggestions that
Luke simply envisaged a continuing people of God, enlarged by the inclusion of
the Gentile believers, are not altogether accurate. There is in fact a new people of
God, in continuity with the old but now composed of believers in the Messiah.
The coming of Christ marks a new beginning. Language appropriate to the people of God in the previous age can be applied to it, such as the flock of God (Acts
20:28) or the holy ones (the "sanctified", Acts 20:32).

*Paul as a prisoner—and still a missionary.* But the story is not yet complete,
and eight chapters (roughly a quarter of the book) still remain. These are concerned with Paul as a prisoner and a number of theological motifs emerge.

First, it is evident that even as a person under arrest, in prison and in captivity generally Paul continues his mission and is effective in Christian witness. It
is difficult to avoid the impression that Luke has devoted so much space to this
aspect of Paul's life in order to express the harsh realities under which Christians may be called to live out their lives and bear witness to Christ. Paul's principle that "we must go through many hardships to enter the kingdom of God"
(Acts 14:22) is exemplified at length in his own life. God remains in ultimate
control and, although he allows Paul (like Jesus) to suffer, nevertheless his suffering can be used to forward the gospel. Appearances before judges become an
occasion for testimony (Acts 9:15). Paul is even slated to appear before the
highest tribunal, that of the emperor in Rome, but there is no authentic record
of this event either in Acts or elsewhere. But if he is not upheld by human beings, he is nevertheless seen to be vindicated in other ways. The lengthy story
of his journey to Rome is no doubt told partly for its vivid interest but also
because the deliverance of the ship from disaster and the subsequent protection
of Paul from being poisoned by a snake are indications that God looks upon
him with favor (cf. expressly Acts 27:24; 28:6).

Second, the accounts of Paul's public appearances and the legal proceedings
provide the occasions on which he can reply to the accusations against him,
which were that he was teaching everywhere against the Jewish people, their law
and the temple (Acts 21:28). Paul therefore recounts yet again different aspects
of his own story of how he came to be a witness to Jesus Christ.

---

seem surprising, and many commentators retranslate the Greek as "with the blood of his own
[one]" (cf. NRSV), which is a possible rendering but certainly unusual.

In the first appearance (Acts 22:1-21) the story is of what God or Christ did and said in calling Paul to be a witness from being a persecutor and how he was specifically told to leave Jerusalem and go to the Gentiles. It is the word *Gentiles* that leads to the crowd's interruption of his speech; the story of Paul's Jewish religious zeal and of the role of the respected Jew, Ananias, in his conversion appears to have been at least tolerable, but after that a wave of anti-Gentilism erupted.

On the second occasion for public speech, before the Sanhedrin (Acts 23), Paul elects to stand on the Jewish credentials of his career, emphasizing that his beliefs were those of Judaism, specifically of the Pharisees, in that he believed in the hope of the resurrection; on this point the Pharisees differed significantly from the Sadducees, who denied the possibility of resurrection. Again the continuity of Christian belief with that of one strand of Judaism is maintained.

On the third occasion, Paul again emphasizes that his way of life was in line with Jewish piety in respect of ritual observance of the law and works of love (almsgiving), and again he affirms the hope of the resurrection (Acts 24:10-21; cf. Acts 23:6).

Finally, in Acts 26 Paul appears before the Roman governor Felix and the Jewish king Agrippa. Once again the Christian message is argued to be a fulfillment of the hope of the Jews. True, Paul had at one time rejected and resisted it, but now he had had personal experience of the resurrected Jesus and recognized him as Lord. From him he had been commissioned to be a witness and had been promised that he would be protected from his Jewish attackers and be sent to witness to the Gentiles so that they might become members of God's people, provided that they repented and turned to God.

All the way through, therefore, Paul protests his loyalty to Judaism and the Jewish way of life, and yet he insists that his calling was to bear witness to Jesus to Gentiles and Jews. In the present context the question of whether these repentant Gentiles also needed to keep the law and live by it is not raised. The emphasis is rather on the fact that being Christians does not entail that Jewish believers forsake the law.[17]

---

[17]Does this clash with the account earlier in Acts where Peter learned that no foods are unclean and (by implication) that no people are unclean? It would seem that in practice there was some relaxation of the law for Jewish believers.

Despite this insistence that Christianity is not incompatible with a Jewish way of life, Paul remains the object of attack. But this leads on to the question of what he had done wrong that constituted an offense in the eyes of the Romans. The Romans come into the picture because there was an outbreak of public disorder involving Paul. At first it seems that Paul is responsible for it (particularly if, as alleged, he had brought Gentiles within the forbidden area in the temple), but then he emerges as the object of mob violence, and the question is whether he has done anything under Roman law that constitutes an offense. The answer is given by the lawyer Tertullus, who accuses Paul of being a troublemaker belonging to the Nazarene sect who had tried to desecrate the temple. Paul's response is to challenge the lack of evidence for the latter charge (which disappears from view) and to admit that he has a sectarian set of beliefs within Judaism. The effect of the subsequent examinations is to emphasize that Paul is thereby doing nothing wrong that falls within Roman jurisdiction and is entitled to be set at liberty. But he remains in custody with the case unsettled, and eventually he appeals to Caesar rather than allow his case to revert to a Jewish court. The theological point at issue is thus that Paul's beliefs cannot be regarded as a criminal offense under Roman law, even if the Roman officials do not treat him entirely fairly.

The Jewish opposition to Paul continues to the end of the book. When Paul reaches Rome, two things are surprisingly underplayed. The first is the relationship of Paul to the existing Christian believers in and around Rome; they are there in the vicinity (Acts 28:14-15, but we hear nothing of Paul meeting with believers in Rome. The second thing is the outcome of the judicial process. According to one reading of Acts, Luke has already given sufficient hints that Paul was martyred in Rome and does not need to address the fact explicitly (Acts 20:23-24, 38; cf. Acts 21:10-14). According to another the outcome was successful and Paul was released. For Luke this is not a matter of importance. Rather the book ends with a picture of Paul continuing to proclaim a gospel, to which testimony is borne in the Jewish Scriptures. Some Jews believe, and others reject the message. In the case of the latter the prophecy in Isaiah 6:9-10 is fulfilled. So Paul turns, as on past occasions, to the Gentiles with a better hope of acceptance.

Does this mean that the mission to Jews no longer continues? The point is debated, but the more probable view is that God's salvation remains available to any Jews who will repent and believe the good news.

## Theological Themes in Acts

*God and his purpose.* We have already observed the centrality of God in Acts as the initiator of the action, foretelling what is to happen in broad terms in Scripture, though with special application to the Christ, and then in more precise detail through various agents, heavenly and human.[18] For some scholars this implies that the course of the story is predetermined, almost set by an impersonal fate, and is so to an extent that is perhaps beyond that in any other writer in the New Testament. An element of necessity ("it must happen") hangs over the story, in the Gospel and in Acts, but more markedly in the latter.

As we have seen, however, this element is not consistent. We need to draw a clear distinction between determinism, in which God controls what is to happen, and divine guidance, in which God tells people what to do or encourages them in what they are doing; we can also distinguish broadly between the determinism of actions in detail and general predictions of what may happen. There are times in Acts when people do things by their own initiative and other times when they act under a divine guidance that can amount to compulsion (Acts 20:22),[19] and of course there are occasions when things happen to them (like storms at sea) over which they have no control. This mixture of kinds of motivation suggests that a predetermined course of action in detail is hardly what Luke is reporting.

It is certainly true that the authorities who acted against Jesus did "what your power and will had decided beforehand should happen" (Acts 4:28), even though they committed wicked acts in doing so (Acts 2:23), but this does not entail that all wicked acts were planned beforehand, still less initiated, by God. In a couple of cases the positive responses of people to the gospel may appear to have been predetermined by God (Acts 13:48; 16:14; cf. Lk 24:45), but the possibility of disobedience to the divine call is raised by Paul (Acts 26:19-

---

[18]See especially John Squires, "The Plan of God", in *Witness to the Gospel: The Theology of Acts*, ed. I. Howard Marshall and David Peterson (Grand Rapids, Mich.: Eerdmans; Carlisle: Paternoster, 1998), pp. 19-39.

[19]Acts 16:6-7, however, probably means no more than that God told them not to do something and they obeyed.

20),[20] and on other occasions there is nothing to suggest that the response of people to the gospel was other than their own decision (e.g., Acts 2:37).

The motif, then, is not developed so consistently as to result in absolute determinism, but the impression of God's plan and purpose being carried out remains dominant. It functions to encourage the readers that God's purpose will be carried out, despite whatever opposition and suffering there may be.

*According to Scripture.* The plan of God is particularly foretold in Scripture. Of all the New Testament writers it is perhaps Luke who is most articulate on the fact that the establishment of the church and its mission is the object of prophecy and that this event is therefore closely tied to the coming of the Messiah in the plan of God. That is why Luke wrote the Gospel and the Acts. There is a very considerable use of Scripture in Acts, particularly in the speeches of the various characters rather than in the narrative framework. An important part of the Scriptural material is, of course, used in what we may call an apologetic manner to demonstrate from Scripture what the Messiah would be and do and then to argue that only Jesus fits the personal profile and the job description (Acts 17:2-3, 11). But it is also of special importance for Luke that the creation of the church of Jews and Gentiles could be seen to be prophesied in Scripture (Acts 13:47; 15:16-18). The outpouring of the Spirit that initiated the formation of the church is clearly foretold in Scripture in a passage that also anticipates people calling upon the Lord for salvation (Acts 2:17-21).[21]

*Salvation history.* These two factors, God's plan and the laying out of it in Scripture, entail that Luke envisages a "history of salvation". This phrase can be understood to convey various nuances. As used by Oscar Cullmann, the concept of "salvation-history" emphasizes that God's salvation issues from his

---

[20]This is doubtless a figure of speech (*litotes*), but it does raise the question whether Paul, at least according to Luke, could have resisted God's appointment of him as his "chosen instrument" (Acts 9:15).

[21]For fuller detail see Darrell L. Bock, "Scripture and the Realization of God's Promises", in *Witness to the Gospel: The Theology of Acts*, ed. I. Howard Marshall and David Peterson (Grand Rapids, Mich.: Eerdmans; Carlisle: Paternoster, 1998), pp. 41-62. See further Darrell L. Bock, *Proclamation from Prophecy and Pattern: Lukan Old Testament Christology* (Sheffield: Sheffield Academic Press, 1987); Mark L. Strauss, *The Davidic Messiah in Luke-Acts: The Promise and Its Fulfillment in Luke's Christology* (Sheffield: Sheffield Academic Press, 1995); and my contribution to a forthcoming commentary on the use of the Old Testament in the New Testament (ed. Gregory K. Beale and D. A. Carson) to be published by Baker.

deeds in history, from events that are to be understood as divine actions, such as the freeing of the Israelites from captivity in Egypt and later in Babylon and supremely in the coming, death and resurrection of Jesus. This insistence on God's mighty acts in history stands over against any suggestion that people are saved essentially through an act of preaching that refers to little or nothing in the way of divine action and engenders an existential decision by the hearers, no doubt made possible only by the preaching of Christ but dangerously near to being not much more than a human decision.[22]

At the same time, the phrase envisages an ongoing activity of God stretching throughout the story told in the Old Testament, so that the coming of Jesus is the appropriate climax to what has gone before by way of anticipation and fore-telling. Scripture thus becomes the heritage of a church whose roots lie firmly in the past activity of God in raising up a people for himself. This attitude rules out any kind of theological Marcionism that rejects the Old Testament from Christian Scripture.[23]

But also there is the implication that God's activity continues into the future in an ongoing history of Christian mission, of which Luke has reported only the first stage.

As we have previously observed, it has been claimed that Luke developed this understanding as a response to the "delay of the parousia". The earliest Christians, it is argued, regarded the coming of Christ as inaugurating the last days and expected the coming of the Son of Man (identified with Jesus) and the arrival of the new age almost immediately. For them the coming of Jesus marked in effect the end of history. But time went by, and the expected climax did not materialize. The church needed to revise its theology of two ages with the Christ event as the dividing line, and what we see in the work of Luke is an interpretation in which salvation history continues into the future until the distant parousia. The time of the church and its mission fills the gap that has opened up between the coming of Christ and the end of time, and the presence of the Spirit and its activity functions theologically as a kind of re-placement of the parousia. Thus the coming of the Spirit is the Lukan solu-

---

[22]See the discussion on p. 141 n. 20 of the opposing positions of Rudolf Bultmann and Oscar Cullmann.

[23]It is ironic that Marcion adopted Luke, of all the Gospels, as his preferred Gospel, though not without considerable amputative surgery.

tion to the disappointment caused by the delay of the parousia, and the parousia, now shunted off into the distant future, loses its former significant
role as the dominant factor in Christian theology.

We have already seen that this interpretation is vulnerable in other ways. To
our earlier criticisms must now be added the fact that it is very dubious whether
the early church was so dominated by the expectation of the parousia. It is much
more likely that the kind of view here attributed to the later theology of Luke
was in fact present from a very early stage indeed. Certainly, the experience of
the Holy Spirit as the decisive evidence of the reality of the new age goes back
as far as we can trace. We should understand history more in terms of two eras,
those of Israel (characterized by partial realization and by promise) and that of
Christ and the church (characterized by fulfillment and continuing promise).
There is obviously a distinction between the times before and after the resurrection of Jesus and Pentecost, but these are two stages in the period of fulfillment. And, further, it is simply not the case that for Luke the parousia has lost
its significance for the early Christians by being postponed indefinitely. Finally,
John Nolland has warned us against understanding salvation history in three
sharply delineated periods; instead there are what he calls repetitions and escalation.[24]

*The Christ event.* Within this broad period of fulfillment there are three major
events, the Christ event,[25] the coming of the Spirit, and the mission of the
church.

First, there is the coming of the one whom Luke uniquely calls "the Lord's/
God's Messiah" (Lk 2:26; 9:20; Acts 4:26; the phrase parallels the more familiar "Servant of the Lord", Acts 3:13, 26; 4:27, 30). Something of Luke's understanding of Jesus in Acts has already emerged earlier in the chapter. For Acts
the resurrection, ascension and glorification of Jesus are of particular significance. Luke alone of the Evangelists describes the ascension as a separate event
from the resurrection, and both events are significant. The resurrection is im-

---

[24]John Nolland, "Salvation-History and Eschatology", in *Witness to the Gospel: The Theology of Acts,* ed.
   I. Howard Marshall and David Peterson (Grand Rapids, Mich.: Eerdmans; Carlisle: Paternoster,
   1998), pp. 70-76.
[25]I regret this cumbersome, impersonal phrase, but some vocabulary is needed to express the sum total
   of Christ and what he did, that is, to include the coming of the person and the activity that he performed.

portant because it establishes the triumph of God over death in the case of Jesus and gives a firm basis for the hope of resurrection that the Christians shared with the Pharisees. The ascension is important because it establishes the position of Jesus as Lord and Messiah (Acts 2:33-36). For Luke the Messiah is the authoritative ruler in the kingdom of God. For such a person the title of "Lord" is appropriate in any case, but the alternation between Jesus and God as "Lord" in Acts and the use of "God language" (such as "name") with reference to Jesus serve to establish some kind of functional equivalence between Jesus and God, that ties in with the fact that Jesus is also recognized as the Son of God (Acts 9:20; 13:33).

Some scholars regard Acts as seeing Jesus as exalted to this rank for the first time by the ascension; this is an example of the kind of christology known as "adoptionism" or a two-stage christology in which there is a difference between the status of Jesus before and after the resurrection.[26] This understanding is refuted by the way in which the child Jesus is established as the Son of God from his birth (Luke 1:32) and throughout the Gospel and by the way in which Luke can refer to Jesus as "Lord" when narrating the story in the Gospel.[27] Luke thus appears to share the typical humiliation/exaltation christology in which the earthly Jesus is the Lord appearing in the humble guise of the servant and unrecognized by people generally. But we do not need to appeal to the Gospel for proof of the case. The resurrection of Jesus is not simply the result of God's decision to raise a good man; rather he was the Holy One whom death could not hold (cf. Acts 2:24).

When Peter refers to Jesus as simply "a man" (Acts 2:22), he is expressing how Jesus appeared during his lifetime (Acts 5:28). There must be some significance in the fact that the final judgment will take place through the man whom God has appointed and set apart by raising him from the dead rather than by God or some heavenly agent (Acts 17:31).

Within Acts the brief descriptions of the life of Jesus serve to show that God

---

[26] It has been suggested that Acts 3:20 might mean that Jesus would not be installed as Messiah until his return; for now he is the messiah-designate. This unlikely interpretation, however, would only be possible in a pre-Lukan source, since in Acts 3:18 it is the Christ who is the subject of suffering.

[27] Lk 7:13, 19; 10:41 et al. Human characters in the Gospel do not refer to Jesus as "Lord" in his lifetime, except in Lk 1:43, 76; 19:34, although they address him as "Lord" in a way that is open to a deeper nuance than mere respect.

was working salvation through him and that he was not recognized but rather opposed by those who put him to death. This human opposition was thwarted by God in raising him from the dead, and in any case it was allowed for within God's plan. But an explanation of why God allowed it and what purpose, if any, it served is surprisingly absent from the apostolic preaching. Certainly in Acts 20:28 the church is "bought" by God and made his special possession by "blood" which (however we understand the phrase; see pp. 167-68) can only be a reference to the blood of Jesus and hence to the death of Jesus. This ties in with the retention of the reference to the body and blood of Jesus in Luke 22:19-20.[28] For Luke the resurrection and ascension of Jesus establish his position as the author of salvation who dispenses repentance and forgiveness of sins (Acts 5:30-31).

The implied human situation is accordingly one of sinfulness and guilt. In the case of the Jewish authorities this is summed up in their rejection of Jesus, and the implication is that the people share in this guilt unless they actively repudiate what was done to Jesus and accept him as Messiah and Lord. In the case of the Gentiles, they are assumed to live in ignorance of God and their salvation lies in turning to him and repenting of their idolatry. It has been argued that what is really wrong with the Gentiles is nothing more than ignorance and that therefore they need to be "helped" rather than "saved", but this interpretation cannot survive the black picture of Gentile sin that emerges from Acts.[29]

*Salvation and the Holy Spirit.* A major blessing of salvation is thus forgiveness of sins, or in Pauline language, justification (Acts 13:38-39), with its positive counterpart, eternal life (Acts 13:46). Put otherwise, people are brought out of darkness into light (Acts 26:18), and the language characteristic of Jesus is retained in references to entry into the kingdom of God. Now it lies within the authority of God to forgive sin, and this authority has been shared with Jesus. God works through his agent. But Acts, as we have noted, is virtually silent on the place of the death of Jesus in this, although we know from the rest of the New Testament, and not least from earlier traditions embedded in the letters, that "Christ died for our sins".

Alongside forgiveness of sins the gift of the Holy Spirit is also an essential

---

[28]For the omission of Lk 22:19b-20 in some textual authorities, see p. 139 n. 18.

[29]See Christoph Stenschke, "The Need for Salvation", in *Witness to the Gospel: The Theology of Acts,* ed. I. Howard Marshall and David Peterson (Grand Rapids, Mich.: Eerdmans; Carlisle: Paternoster, 1998), pp. 125-44.

component of the experience of salvation (Acts 2:38). In two instances the apparent absence of the Spirit is treated as a situation that must be remedied, namely, in the cases of the Samaritan believers who had received Christian baptism and of the disciples at Ephesus who had received John's baptism (Acts 8:14-17; 19:1-7). In a further case the gift of the Spirit preceded Christian baptism (Acts 10:44-48). In both of the former cases laying on of hands was applied to the converts, but there is no mention of it elsewhere in relation to other converts.[30]

The fragmentary and apparently inconsistent evidence is used by some Pentecostalist and charismatic interpreters to argue the twofold case that for Luke the gift of the Spirit may be or even normally is an experience subsequent to conversion and forgiveness and that it is not so much an aspect of salvation as rather an equipping of the believer for Christian service. However, although it is not said expressly that the converts on the day of Pentecost received the Spirit there and then, this is the natural inference from Acts 2:38.[31]

There is, of course, no doubt whatever that the Spirit in Acts is primarily associated with guidance and empowerment for Christian mission and proclamation. Individual believers are filled with the Spirit when they are about to speak in the name of Christ, just as for Paul the power of the Spirit makes the words of evangelists effective in the hearts of the hearers (1 Thess 1:5; 1 Cor 2:4). Nor is there any felt tension when a person who is already filled with the Spirit receives a further filling (Acts 6:5; 7:55).

Despite these fillings subsequent to conversion, there should be little doubt that it is normal in Luke's eyes for all believers to receive the gift of the Spirit at conversion and that it is considered anomalous when this does not happen. It would also seem that early Christians did experience phenomena that were understood to be indicative of the presence of the Spirit, including on occasion the gift of tongues or of prophecy or simply a sense of joy (Acts 13:52). Such manifestations may not always have been authentic; we know from Paul and John that not every message that was claimed to be Spirit-inspired was necessarily so and that Spirit utterances needed to be tested, and the same will have been true of other experiences of the Spirit. The gift of the Spirit was part of

---

[30]Laying on of hands was also practiced when commissioning people for mission (Acts 13:3).

[31]Cf. Turner, *Power from on High*, p. 359.

the promise of salvation (Acts 2:38) and therefore functioned to create assurance of salvation; in Acts, Luke is almost completely silent about the effects of the Spirit in Christian growth—there is nothing of the mood of Romans 8:1-17—but he does associate the Spirit with joy (Acts 13:52).

*The church, Jews and Gentiles.* The experience of salvation is tied up with entry into the church. The fundamental theological question in Acts concerns the relationship of the church to Israel and the Gentiles. Luke significantly refers to Christian believers as "disciples", thereby indicating that there is a basic continuity between the followers of Jesus before Easter and the believers thereafter. He also indicates clearly that there is an entity called Israel that consists of Jews and proselytes. To them God has sent the Messiah, and salvation lies in acceptance of the Messiah. Failure to do so is tantamount to apostasy from Israel. At the same time Gentiles become members of the people of God through faith in the Messiah, and thus there arises a new situation in which the people of God consists of circumcised Jews and uncircumcised Gentiles. The early church did not find it easy to come to grips with this situation terminologically and practically. The use of the term *Israel* to refer to the church as the "new Israel" developed only gradually, and the tendency was to use *Israel* as a term for the Jewish people (Acts 2:22; 4:10; 5:21). There is also the question, which may be no more than one of nuance, as to whether the Gentiles are admitted to the existing people of God or whether believing Jews and Gentiles form a new people of God that stands in continuity with the old.[32]

We have already seen that for Luke believing Jews continue to follow the law of Moses with regard to circumcision and to other matters, including the making of vows and the offering of sacrifices. Any suggestion that Paul was advocating a non-Jewish way of life for Jews is repudiated (Acts 21:24). At the same time, there appears to be a weakening of Jewish attitudes so far as the question of foods and association with Gentiles is concerned. For their part Gentiles in at least some areas are required to make some concessions that would make it easier for Jewish believers to have fellowship with them. As we have noted, it is sometimes said that in these matters Luke is something of a pragmatist and

---

[32]The former position is particularly associated with the work of Jacob Jervell, *The Theology of the Acts of the Apostles* (Cambridge: Cambridge University Press, 1996). The difference between it and the latter (and preferable) view may not be all that great. Nevertheless, important differences do arise over the continuing role of the law for Jewish and Gentile believers.

does not set out defined principles.[33] The truth is more likely that he was describing a church that was wrestling with practical problems and moving in a pragmatic kind of way at different speeds in different areas, and we should not expect to find Luke's description of it to be altogether consistent and free from tension.

*Leaders and missionaries.* Luke's theology is selective in its interests. He is not over-concerned with the structure of the church. Yet it is important in his eyes that the early church had a full complement of twelve apostles, and they appear to be symbolical figures whose mission is essentially to bear witness to Israel concerning the Messiah. The question of their rule over Israel (Lk 22:30) is not raised again, except perhaps in Acts 1:6, and their function is rather that of witness. After Acts 15 they fade out of the story. This is because the interest shifts to the Gentile mission and to its most significant missionary, Paul. Paul and Barnabas are termed "apostles" in Acts 14:4, 14, and particularly in the latter verse the use of the title seems quite deliberate. It is the only indication that Luke knows (as he must have done) that this was Paul's preferred designation, and elsewhere he reserves the designation for the Twelve. It seems likely that Luke concentrates on the function of the Twelve as establishing the continuity in the church with the pre-Easter period. He is quite clear that the leadership of the church in Jerusalem was in the hands of the Twelve together with a group called "elders" who appear suddenly in Acts 11:30 without a word of explanation. But there is no reason why Luke should not have recognized the extension of the term apostles to other Christians engaged in mission.

We have also to bear in mind another development. At the beginning it was natural for the Christians in Jerusalem to think of themselves as "the church" with some kind of jurisdiction or authority over other groups of Christians. But increasingly with the spread of the church other congregations would arise who would see themselves as relating more to the founding missionaries or as independent groups in fellowship with other Christian congregations. Clearly Paul did not think of the congregations that he founded as being under the control of the church in Jerusalem. These are relationships and questions that Luke

---

[33]See especially Stephen G. Wilson, *The Gentiles and the Gentile Mission in Luke-Acts* (Cambridge: Cambridge University Press, 1973).

does not specifically raise, but they form part of the scene that he was attempting to describe and interpret.

What is important for Luke is the function of the apostles as witnesses to Christ and the saving events. It has been proposed that only the apostles actually function as witnesses in the strict sense of the term and that the task of other and later believers is to repeat the apostolic witness rather than to be witnesses themselves.[34] This may be a correct account of how Luke uses the terminology, but it sounds somewhat pedantic, and we should allow a softened use of the term *witness* to apply to people who were not themselves eyewitnesses of Christ but have nevertheless proved for themselves the reality of salvation. Paul falls strictly outside the Lukan qualifications for apostles (he had not been with Jesus during his earthly life), and so the term *witness* is already in his case being used in a somewhat broader sense (Acts 22:15).

## Conclusion

The framework of Luke's theology in Acts is identical with that in the Synoptic Gospels in that it is shaped by contemporary Judaism. At the same time, the setting of the story in the wider Greco-Roman world brings out more clearly the way in which the Christian understanding of reality stands in contrast to the polytheistic idolatry of the time; there is a critique of idolatry, although the reality of evil spiritual powers is assumed.

The main theme is that God has raised and exalted the crucified Jesus to be the Messiah and Lord through whom forgiveness and the Holy Spirit are offered to all who call on the Lord. In this way a people of God is being formed of believing Jews and Gentiles that stands in continuity with Israel but has now been reconstituted around the Messiah. The followers of Jesus are committed to carrying out God's plan for his salvation to be preached to the whole world.

Developing this theme in greater detail we note the following significant elements.

1. All people, whether Jews or Gentiles, are commanded to call upon the Lord Jesus to be saved. This applies to Jews, who are otherwise reckoned to be

---

[34]See Peter Bolt, "Mission and Witness", in *Witness to the Gospel: The Theology of Acts*, ed. I. Howard Marshall and David Peterson (Grand Rapids, Mich.: Eerdmans; Carlisle: Paternoster, 1998), pp. 191-214, especially pp. 210-12.

guilty by association with their leaders of the death of Jesus, and to Gentiles, who are understood to be sinners.

2. The Gospel was about what Jesus began to do and to teach. In Acts he continues to be active as the Lord who has the power to save and to bestow the gift of the Spirit to all people. Repentance and faith, expressed in submission to baptism are the appropriate response to the proclamation.

3. The exaltation of Jesus shows him to be the Messiah and Lord, commissioned by God to pour out the Spirit and sharing functions with God to such an extent that it is not always clear whether the term *Lord* refers to God the Father or to Jesus.

4. Continuity with the earthly mission of Jesus is seen in the preservation of the term *disciples* for converts, but a church consciousness develops, and the development of congregations with leadership is traced. The mission is primarily in the hands of the twelve apostles, but this group is augmented in numerous ways, for example, by the Seven and by Paul and his associates.

5. The mission begins with Jews but soon spreads to Gentiles; they form one people of God, but the Gentiles are not required to be circumcised.

6. Jewish believers continue to practice their own law and customs, but the Gentile believers are not required to do more than would be expected of Gentiles living alongside Jews.

7. Little is said about the function of the death of Jesus in achieving salvation, and more stress is placed on his authoritative position as the exalted Lord.

8. The hope of the parousia is not abandoned, but all the stress in Acts lies on the missionary responsibility of the church in the present age.

## Bibliography

See also the bibliography for Luke.

*New Testament Theologies:* (English) Conzelmann, pp. 144-49; Goppelt, 2:266-88; Ladd, pp. 311-56; Morris, pp. 144-221; Strecker, pp. 392-417; Zuck, pp. 87-166 (Darrell L. Bock). (German) Petr Pokorny, *Theologie der lukanischen Schriften* (Göttingen: Vanden-hoeck und Ruprecht, 1998); Gnilka, pp. 196-225; Hübner, 3:120-51; Stuhlmacher, 2:174-99.

Anderson, K. L. "The Resurrection of Jesus in Luke-Acts". Doctoral thesis, Brunel University, 2000.

Barrett, C. K. *Acts.* 2 vols. Edinburgh: T & T Clark, 1994, 1998, especially "The Theology of Acts" (2:lxxxii-cx).

Bock, Darrell L. *Proclamation from Prophecy and Pattern: Lukan Old Testament Christology.* Sheffield: Sheffield Academic Press, 1987.

Bruce, F. F. *The Book of the Acts.* 2nd ed. Grand Rapids, Mich.: Eerdmans, 1988.

Buckwalter, H. Douglas. *The Character and Purpose of Luke's Christology.* Cambridge: Cambridge University Press, 1996.

Doble, Peter. *The Paradox of Salvation: Luke's Theology of the Cross.* Cambridge: Cambridge University Press, 1996.

Franklin, Eric. *Christ the Lord: A Study in the Purpose and Theology of Luke-Acts.* London: SPCK, 1975.

———. *Luke: Interpreter of Paul, Critic of Matthew.* Sheffield: Sheffield Academic Press, 1994.

Jervell, Jacob. *The Theology of the Acts of the Apostles.* Cambridge: Cambridge University Press, 1996.

Kee, Howard C. *Good News to the Ends of the Earth: The Theology of Acts;* London: SCM; Philadelphia: Trinity Press International, 1990.

Maddox, Robert. *The Purpose of Luke-Acts.* Edinburgh: T & T Clark, 1982.

Marshall, I. Howard. *Acts.* Sheffield: Sheffield Academic Press, 1992.

———. "'Early Catholicism' in the New Testament". In *New Dimensions in New Testament Study.* Edited by Richard N. Longenecker and Merrill C. Tenney, pp. 217-31. Grand Rapids, Mich.: Zondervan, 1974.

Marshall, I. Howard, and David Peterson, eds. *Witness to the Gospel: The Theology of Acts.* Grand Rapids, Mich.: Eerdmans; Carlisle: Paternoster, 1998.

Moessner, David P., ed. *Jesus and the Heritage of Israel: Luke's Narrative Claim upon Israel's Legacy.* Harrisburg, Penn.: Trinity Press International, 1999.

Morris, Leon. "Luke and Early Catholicism". *WTJ* 35 (1973): 121-36.

O'Neill, J. C. *The Theology of Acts in Its Historical Setting.* 2nd ed. London: SPCK, 1972.

Penney, John M. *The Missionary Emphasis of Lukan Pneumatology.* Sheffield: Sheffield Academic Press, 1997.

Shelton, James B. *Mighty in Word and Deed: The Role of the Holy Spirit in Luke-Acts.* Peabody, Mass.: Hendrickson, 1991.

Squires, John T. *The Plan of God in Luke-Acts.* Cambridge: Cambridge University Press, 1993.

Stenschke, Christoph W. *Luke's Portrait of Gentiles Prior to Their Coming to Faith.* Tübingen: Mohr Siebeck, 1999.

Strauss, Mark L. *The Davidic Messiah in Luke-Acts: The Promise and Its Fulfillment in Luke's Christology.* Sheffield: Sheffield Academic Press, 1995.

Turner, Max. *The Holy Spirit and Spiritual Gifts Then and Now.* Carlisle: Paternoster, 1996.

————. *Power from on High: The Spirit in Israel's Restoration and Witness in Luke-Acts.* Sheffield: Sheffield Academic Press, 1996.

Wilson, Stephen G. *The Gentiles and the Gentile Mission in Luke-Acts.* Cambridge: Cambridge University Press, 1973.

————. *Luke and the Law.* Cambridge: Cambridge University Press, 1983.

# 7

# THE THEOLOGY OF THE
# SYNOPTIC GOSPELS
# AND ACTS

In our examination of the three Synoptic Gospels and Acts we have not been able to avoid some elements of comparison between them, since we analyzed the theology of Matthew in the light of its assumed dependence on Mark and then we looked at Luke in relation to Mark and Matthew, and we also looked to some extent at the relationship between Luke and Acts. There are several dimensions to the consideration of the Gospels: their relationships to one another, their relationship to Jesus and the Jesus tradition, and the relationship of their pictures of Jesus to those held by the early church or to Luke's depiction of it. To these we should add a fourth dimension: their relationship to the Gospel of John.

Since the purpose of this book is to expound the theology or theologies of the New Testament writers rather than to attempt a history of the development of thought, I shall not attempt to discuss in any detail how the picture presented in the Gospels relates to the historical reality of the mission of Jesus. I have already indicated that I see no reason to deny that the Gospel accounts are firmly rooted in reliable traditions. Discussion of the relation of Johannine theology to that in the Synoptic Gospels will be undertaken after we have analyzed the Johannine literature. So our present task is to continue our comparative study of the theologies of the Synoptic Gospels and to compare them with the theological picture presented by Acts. The aim is not to write a synthesis of them in detail but to enquire whether they belong harmoniously together.

A comparison of the three Gospels to each other naturally shows a complex web of likenesses and differences. In the discussions of Matthew and Luke I have already indicated that there appears to be a considerable amount of general agreement between them in their theological presentations. We now need to explore this area more thoroughly and see whether this initial impression is justified. I have to admit that I am probably the kind of person whose bias or temptation is to see the likenesses and play down or not notice the differences, and therefore my observations may tend to be one-sided. But I am nevertheless impressed by the essential harmony that exists between the theologies of the three Gospels. They all tell the story of Jesus in similar ways; this is at once obvious from the large number of pericopes that they have in common and especially from the way in which many of the sayings of Jesus show a high degree of verbal agreement. To be sure, there are significant differences in wording and in the overall impression given, not least by the variations in context and positioning. A fair amount of difference could be characterized as change in emphasis, topics that are central in some Gospel or Gospels being marginal in others. For example, Mark's "messianic secret" does not figure so prominently in the later Gospels but is not wholly absent, and Luke's interest in prayer is muted, but again not absent, in the other Gospels. But despite these and other individual features, there is a good case that the Gospels offer essentially the same theology of the mission and teaching of Jesus.

How is Luke's theology in Acts to be categorized in relation to that of the Gospels? We remind ourselves once again that Acts is the second part of a work composed of two parts, and we must distinguish between the time of Jesus and that of his witnesses. Luke is thereby indicating with all clarity that these two times belong closely together and that it is not sufficient simply to tell the story of Jesus. It is also necessary to show to Christians how we got from the time of Jesus to where we are now. Some scholars argue that Luke was looking back on the period of Christian origins from a later date toward the end of the first century, by which point it was possible to see the time up to Paul's arrival in Rome as constituting the origin and basis of the Christian church and its ongoing mission. For other scholars Luke was telling the story up to the juncture at which he stood, not very long after Paul had reached Rome. Clearly he saw this as a decisive point in the divine program, but emphatically not as the end of the story. Not only was he writing with a living hope of the return of Christ, but also he was well aware that the Christian mission had not yet fulfilled the task of bringing its witness to Christ to "the ends of the earth" (Acts 1:8).[1]

This approach goes beyond that of the other Evangelists, who apparently wrote only Gospels. As we have already seen, this does not require that Luke had a new understanding of salvation history that included for the first time the age of the church; rather, he was demonstrating that the purpose of God included not only the coming of the Messiah but also the establishment of the Christian mission of witness to the gospel. To that extent his theology can be regarded as more consciously ecclesiastical than that of the other Evangelists.

This has suggested to some scholars that Luke's outlook belongs to early catholicism with its understanding of the church as an institution dispensing salvation and characterized by the development of hierarchical organization and the beginnings of ecclesiastical office. This understanding, however, is plainly inappropriate to Luke, who is not interested in church organization and office and who is concerned with the progress of the Word rather than with the church. Rather Luke is concerned, like the other Evangelists, to explain to believers how the Christian way started by telling them the story of their beginnings.

The theology of Acts is thus essentially a theology of mission, describing the mission of the early church and powerfully implying that this must continue to be the nature of the church, even if there is opposition and persecution.

What we must now ask is whether the theological position in the Gospel is the same as that in Acts: are the two books consistent theologically? I shall argue that the answer to this question is a straightforward affirmative, qualified

---

[1]The suggestion that the reference is to Rome should be rejected; we should think rather of the far west as it was then conceived, ancient Gades (modern Cadiz); see E. Earle Ellis, "'The End of the Earth' (Acts 1:8)", *BBR* 1 (1991): 123-32.

The principal argument against this conclusion is that the task in Acts 1:8 was given to the apostles as the witnesses to Jesus and that this witness was confined to them and Paul. Paul can be regarded as having in principle reached the end of the earth by preaching in "Rome as representative of the whole world" (C. K. Barrett, *Acts*, 2 vols. [Edinburgh: T & T Clark, 1994, 1998] 1:80-81; cf. Peter Bolt, "Mission and Witness", in *Witness to the Gospel: The Theology of Acts*, ed. I. Howard Marshall and David Peterson [Grand Rapids, Mich.: Eerdmans; Carlisle: Paternoster, 1998], pp. 191-214, especially pp. 210-12). But this argument rests on a narrow understanding of witness, ignores the fact that Paul was not present to receive the commission in Acts 1 and has to contend with the linguistic arguments given by Ellis.

by the reminder that Luke is doing two different things. In the first book he is giving an account of the earthly life and work of Jesus, and in the second he is relating what early Christians believed about him after his resurrection. This change of perspective inevitably means that there are differences, but only such as would be historically expected. The basic structure of the theology in the two books is the same.

We proceed, therefore, to some further comparison of the Gospels with one another and of Acts to the Gospel of Luke and to the other Synoptic Gospels.

*The identity of Jesus—in the Gospels.* The beginning of each Gospel is particularly important in setting the expectations of the reader. Mark's story of Jesus begins rather abruptly with Jesus coming from Nazareth to be baptized, whereas Matthew and Luke each have a birth story that indicates his divine origin in clear terms and leads the readers to see Jesus as the Son of God and the Messiah from the outset. But is not that precisely what Mark tells his readers in his opening words: "The beginning of the gospel about Jesus the Messiah", who is identified by God as "my Son, whom I love" (Mk 1:1, 11)?[2] We gain the impression that, more than Matthew and Luke, Mark is inviting his readers to accompany the original contemporaries of Jesus in their journey of discovery to ascertain who the carpenter from Nazareth really was. Matthew and Luke are more inclined to take the status of Jesus for granted and to concentrate on what he said and did.

The differences also become apparent at the end of the story. All three Gospels contain the same forward-looking announcements that the Son of Man must die and be raised from the dead. In the case of Mark we cannot be certain whether he deliberately concluded with the discovery of the empty tomb, leaving his readers to ponder its significance, or whether he included some account of resurrection appearances. Matthew portrays essentially the (re)appearance of a figure who is now glorified and majestic, and is the object of worship; he claims omnipotence and issues his lordly command, which is cosmic in its scope. Luke's portrayal is rather more domestic, and Jesus appears as another human being (admittedly unrecognized at first) who is prepared to discuss crucifixion, resurrection and messiahship with his disciples, and who then reap-

---

[2]See chap. 3 n. 3 (58) for the problem of whether the phrase "Son of God" is an authentic part of Mk 1:1.

pears in another meal scene where he gives instruction rather than commands. Yet the element of worship is not absent from Luke, and the lordly figure in Matthew calls his disciples "my brothers". The paradoxical motifs of lordship and brotherhood are common to the two Gospels. And all three Gospels have the same stupendous discovery of an open tomb with an angelic presence.

The christology that develops between these two poles shows the same mixture of constants and varied emphasis. There is no need to show that Jesus is a human being; that is taken for granted, and at this point there was no threat of docetism to be resisted.[3] Mark is concerned to show Jesus as the Messiah in the main thread of the story and then specifically as the suffering One. But divine sonship is at least as important a category; while in some cases it may simply be an alternative to messiahship, a number of passages show that it does refer to a particular relationship to God that is peculiar to Jesus.[4] We have seen how Mark avoids direct naming of Jesus as Messiah and stresses his unwillingness to be made known whether by demons or other people. Much more frequent is the term "Son of Man" which, as the Gospel stands, is open to understanding in the light of Daniel 7 and the later apocalypses based upon it (4 Ezra; 1 Enoch), although Mark may also be aware of it as a phrase that could be used as a self-designation identifying the user as a human being like other human beings. In the former sense the phrase identifies Jesus as a figure who is presently humble and humiliated but whose authority will one day be openly revealed and exercised. Other people address Jesus with the respect appropriate to a teacher but sometimes go beyond it (Mk 10:47-48, but contrast Mk 10:51).

This general pattern recurs in the other two Gospels. But it would be true to say that in each of them the identity of Jesus is presented less ambiguously to the reader. In Matthew we saw more use of "Son of David" as an address by people who see him as Messiah and able to perform mighty works. The deeper

---

[3]Docetism (from Gk. *dokeō*, "to seem") is the belief that the earthly Jesus was not a real human being but was rather a divine figure temporarily transformed to appear like a human being in the kind of way in which Greek gods might assume a human body in order to take part in human life. The representation of the risen Jesus as a real human being with flesh and bones in Lk 24 is a different kind of matter; there the point is that the risen Jesus is not an insubstantial ghost, whereas docetism is concerned with his nature before his death.

[4]The statements in Mk 1:11; 9:7; 13:32; 14:61 do not leave room for any other sons of God alongside Jesus.

sense of such addresses is reflected in the more frequent references to people showing reverence to him. Similarly, in Matthew and Luke there is a usage of *kyrie* as an address to Jesus that on occasion suggests a deeper reverence than simply that due to a teacher in the Jewish context. Matthew also has the important name Immanuel for Jesus signifying that in him "God is with us", and this must be read in the light of the promise in Matthew 18:20 that Jesus will be with people gathered together in his name. At this point the horizon is opened up to the period when Jesus is no longer physically on earth (cf. Mt 28:20).

Various other ways in which Jesus is understood are significant. The concept of Jesus as a new Moses is found in Matthew but is not explicit in the other Gospels; however, it significantly reappears in Acts 3:22-23. Another important theme is that of Jesus in relation to Wisdom. As we saw, the evidence in this regard is somewhat ambiguous. In Matthew, Jesus speaks on occasion in the manner of wisdom, but I tend to side with those who think that an identification of him with Wisdom is only weakly present, if at all. Identification with the Servant of Yahweh (Is 40—55) is implicit in Mark 10:45 (Mt 20:28) and is explicit in the scriptural citations in Matthew 8:17, Matthew 12:17-21 and Luke 22:37. The picture thereby presented has two facets in that it brings out the status and mission of Jesus as Yahweh's appointed agent but also his humiliation and suffering as the rejected messenger.

*The place of Scripture.* From what has been said it will be clear that the question of Jesus' identity is raised and answered with reference to the Jewish Scriptures, by looking for what could be regarded as prophecies and patterns that would be fulfilled by the coming One and observing elements in the words and deeds of Jesus that indicate that he does in fact correspond to the scriptural descriptions. This approach is particularly characteristic of Matthew, whose Gospel contains numerous lengthy quotations accompanied by the statement that what was happening in Jesus took place in order that the Scripture might be fulfilled. These citations are placed there by Matthew as narrator, and he uses them to explain to his readers the full significance of who Jesus is and what he does, and also to show that God had a plan or pattern waiting to be carried out and has now brought it about. These citations, which come mostly in the first half of the Gospel, are to be distinguished from the way in which Jesus and occasionally other speakers may refer to Scripture in the course of debate and explanation; in these cases the interest is somewhat less in prophecy and more in respect of God's requirements of his people. In Luke we find a pattern of citing texts that are taken to refer to the coming Messiah and specifically to his death and resurrection, and then arguing that they are fulfilled by Jesus. This procedure is ascribed to the early preachers in Acts (typically, Acts 17:3) but is also found in the Gospel where the risen Jesus expounds the Scriptures concerning the Messiah in this way (Lk 24:25-27, 44-46) and also finds prophecies of the mission of the church (Lk 24:47-48). There is also a rich use of Scripture, making use of allusions and biblical language rather than formal citations, in the birth stories of John and Jesus, part of which probably reflects the actual way in which people composed fresh poetry and songs on the basis of biblical material. The stories of the death of Jesus are likewise phrased with scriptural allusions. Matthew and Luke are carrying further what we already find in Mark's Gospel, where Jesus and the narrator cite and allude to Scripture. Running through all three Gospels, even when actual citations and allusions are not made, there is the strong sense that Jesus is there to accomplish a divine purpose foretold and laid down in Scripture.

*The identity of Jesus—the Gospels compared with Acts.* In Acts Jesus is presented in the way that one would expect in a sequel to the Gospel of Luke. The Gospel has prepared the way for Acts by presenting Jesus as the Messiah and Son of God whose identity is jeopardized by his death on the cross. The story ends with his resurrection and entry into glory, which are seen to have been in line with Scripture. So the task of mission goes on, aiming at bringing people to acknowledge Jesus as the Messiah. Already in the Gospel the theme of Jesus is the kingdom of God, but the emphasis lies on the salvation that is associated with the establishment of God's rule through the Messiah, and the resulting appeal is to repentance and discipleship. Now the same general pattern is seen in Acts. It is confirmed that Jesus is the Messiah through the resurrection. The proclamation of the kingdom, already shared by the disciples, naturally continues through them, and it is inevitable that the accent shifts from the kingdom to the Messiah. Can one remotely imagine anything else happening than this? It is certainly an important shift in accent, but the message is still essentially the same: it is about the new way in which God is acting to establish his rule. Therefore, it can still be presented as in effect a call to discipleship, seen in the continuation of this term for those who respond to the message. *Disciple* is very rarely used by speakers in Acts (Acts 15:10) and is an authorial term. Significant in this respect is Acts 14:21, where Luke uses the verb "to make disciples" to clarify what evangelism is. Naturally, the character of discipleship shifts from adherence to an earthly leader to whatever is involved in the new postresurrection setting. The essence is a recognition that the earthly person, Jesus, was in fact the Messiah and that his rule continues, even though he is translated to heaven and is no longer physically present.

There is a difference in theological idiom in that Matthew conceives of Jesus being spiritually present with the disciples (as also in John; see Mt 1:23; 18:20; 28:20), whereas in Acts there is rather a series of interventions from heaven through angels, visions and heavenly voices; nevertheless, the Lord (Jesus) promises to be with Paul (Acts 18:10). Similarly, in Acts the Holy Spirit is both with the disciples continually and comes upon them on special occasions. But this twofold way of representing spiritual realities is also found in Paul's writings. The two modes are not incompatible with each other.

In the Gospels the evidence that Jesus is the Messiah is threefold. First, there is the character of Jesus in his authoritative teaching and proclamation of the kingdom in word and deed: he acts as the Messiah. Second, there is the appeal to Scripture to confirm that he corresponds to the picture presented there. And, third, there is the confirmation supplied by the resurrection. Essentially the testimony of the resurrection is to three things: the fact of Jesus being alive; the fact that this corresponded with his prophecies and with Scripture; and the fact that only God could have brought it about, thereby implicitly declaring Jesus to be the Messiah. In the Gospels this testimony is largely confined to the resurrection narratives. It is hardly prominent in Mark, where the emphasis is on the reunion of the disciples with Jesus in Galilee (Mk 16:7; cf. Mk 14:28). In Matthew there is more emphasis on overcoming the doubts of the disciples as to whether Jesus had really been resurrected, but there is also the vision of the omnipotent Lord. In Luke there is much more stress on the argument from the correspondence between the scriptural picture of the Messiah and the role of Jesus.

When we turn to Acts, we find the same elements present, but there is a new one, the witness of those who have seen the resurrected Jesus, and there is considerably more exploration of the scriptural evidence for the role of the Messiah. In the spoken material there is little about the earthly life of Jesus. That there was space in the preaching for the earthly life is seen in the sermon to

Cornelius (Acts 10:37-39), and it may well be that, having told the story in the Gospel, Luke saw no need to repeat it in Acts. The fact that Jesus was a human being emerges naturally. He is identified as the prophet like Moses and also as the servant of God in a manner that is parallel to the use of this term for the king (Acts 4:25) in the Old Testament but specifically echoes the usage in Isaiah 40—55.

In Acts, Luke majors on the scriptural evidence for the death and resurrection of Jesus. The extraordinary character of the resurrection and the need to overcome the scandal of the cross would inevitably have overshadowed the story of what Jesus said and did. The concern in the sermons is to offer the needed confirmation that Jesus is the Messiah, but the status of "Lord" is specifically added to this. This is a clarification of the role of the Messiah, but at the same time it detaches christology from expression in purely Jewish terms. Jesus is now the exalted and glorified Lord (Acts 2:33; 3:13; 5:31), envisaged as seated beside God in heaven (Acts 2:34; 7:55-56) with a future role as judge of the world (Acts 17:31). This new placement signifies that he is now in a position of authority that he did not exercise or did not exercise in the same way in his earthly life. Prayer is addressed to him (Acts 7:59), and mighty works are done in his name (Acts 3:6; 4:10, 30; 16:18; cf. Mk 9:38-41; Lk 10:17). Inevitably it is this exalted Lord who occupies center stage.

There is thus a natural development in christology from the Gospels to Acts, once it is believed that God raised Jesus from the dead and exalted him.[5]

*The understanding of God.* The most significant feature in the theology (in the narrow sense) of the Gospels is the way in which the understanding of God as Father becomes central and develops distinctively. For disciples of Jesus, as for Jesus, God is experienced as a loving Father who cares for his children and with whom they have an intimate personal relationship expressed in prayer. This relationship is admittedly not stressed in Mark, where there are but three refer-

---

[5]I have discussed the continuity and development between Luke and the other Gospels and Acts on the assumption that we see the beginning of christology in the accounts in the Gospels and then the further development of it in the light of the resurrection and fuller consideration in Acts. The historical question arises most acutely in this connection, since it is commonplace with many scholars to argue that the historical Jesus did not use later christological language at all. Scholars who take this position attribute a much greater degree of creativity to the early church. I am also assuming that the christology expressed in Acts is essentially that of the early church, while recognizing that to some extent the presentation has been shaped by Luke.

ences to God as the Father of Jesus (Mk 8:38; 13:32; 14:36) and one as the Father of the disciples (Mk 11:25), yet one of these is of crucial importance with its use of *Abba*. The picture is markedly different in Luke and especially in Matthew, where God is frequently referred to by Jesus as "my father" or as "your father". A characteristic locution of Jesus is reflected in this language, even if some of the usage is editorial.

In Acts this understanding of God is marginal. The locution is confined to statements by the risen Jesus (Acts 1:4, 7) and Peter (Acts 2:33), but this is explicable in the light of the lack of statements addressed directly to believers about their spiritual relationship with God. This corresponds with the way in which in the Gospels Jesus generally spoke about God in terms of his fatherhood only to his disciples.

In all the Gospels the mission of Jesus takes place according to God's will as it is already revealed in Scripture. The advent of Jesus, the nature of his task, his rejection and crucifixion, and his resurrection are all regarded as events that must take place because God has planned them and laid down in Scripture the pattern that Jesus must follow. The formal way in which Scripture is used for this purpose varies from Gospel to Gospel, but the underlying understanding is the same. Scripture forms the framework within which theology is done in each case, and Scripture is also determinative in establishing the way of life expected by God from the followers of Jesus. Scripture is interpreted by Jesus in such a way that his teaching could be said to incorporate it and to stand over it.

This motif of God as the sovereign initiator of all that is done in and through Jesus is central in Acts. Luke's teaching in the Gospel and Acts further indicates how the mission of the disciples to preach the gospel to Jews and Gentiles is part of this same plan and foretold in Scripture.

Prayer to this God is integral to the life of Jesus and his followers. All of the Synoptic Gospels record that Jesus prayed and expected his disciples to pray, as was indeed only natural in the context of Jewish religion. Prayer includes joyful thanksgiving (Mt 11:25-26 par. Lk 10:21), appeals to God to do mighty works, request for guidance and strength, intercession for opponents, confession of sin, and petition, based on the assurance that God is a loving Father to the disciples who will answer their prayers, even if the desired answer is not immediately forthcoming. The picture in Acts is essentially similar but can include prayer addressed to Jesus (Acts 7:59).

*Human sin and need.* In the Gospels the mission of the Messiah is to proclaim in word and deed the coming of the kingdom of God. The establishment of God's rule is to be seen as the overcoming and defeat of Satan and his rule, resulting in the deliverance of those held captive by him, whether through demon possession or illness or sin or through social marginalization resulting from the misuse of power. It thrusts Jesus into opposition against those whose activities contribute to injustice and a noncompassionate society. He speaks out strongly in condemnation of the leaders in Jewish society for their failure to care for the people.

On the whole, there is less of this element in Acts. The accent shifts to the sin of the people in general but especially, so far as the Jews are concerned, in their rejection of Jesus as the Messiah. Such a shift was only to be expected, granted the centrality of Jesus in the proclamation of the early Christians.

*The message of Jesus and discipleship.* In Mark the activity of Jesus is specifically identified as the proclamation of the kingdom of God, and it raises the question as to who Jesus is. This proclamation is characterized as gospel or good news. It brings healing to the ill and the disabled, delivers people from Satan and the demons, and offers forgiveness to sinners. It also leads to a fresh statement of how life should be lived. Response to it is understood in terms of repentance and faith but more weight is placed on discipleship, that is, personal commitment to Jesus and all that flows from that, and on self-denial and totality of commitment to Jesus and the gospel. The terms "eternal life" and "being saved" are also employed to signify the benefits that come to those who are disciples.

Essentially the same picture is presented in Matthew. Here the nature of the new life is spelled out in much greater detail. There is fuller recognition that a new community life will develop among the followers of Jesus.

In Luke there is more emphasis on salvation and the benefits of discipleship, sufficiently so to justify the view that this is a major motif for him. Whereas in Mark salvation is more tied to final deliverance and entry into the heavenly kingdom of God (Mk 10:26), in Luke it is something to be experienced here and now (Lk 19:9). Yet it is hard to identify any essential difference from Mark. One might say that Luke has put a name to what is going on in Mark.

When we move forward into Acts, "being saved" is the characteristic expression for the benefit that comes to believers. A term that had a specific application to deliverance from final judgment takes on a much broader meaning to signify the wholeness of deliverance and the positive conferring of blessings from God. The message of the apostles can still be summed up as preaching the kingdom, but it is also the message of salvation (Acts 13:26; 16:17).

There is clearly a shift in emphasis if the move is from declaring the kingdom of God in the sense of affirming his kingly rule to announcing salvation in the form of blessings from God for those who respond to the message, and the diminished use of kingdom language in Acts might be thought to suggest that this is happening. Yet Acts 17:7 clearly testifies to the former motif being part of the message. Acts 28:31 forms an *inclusio* with Acts 1:3 to indicate that the message of the kingdom is now understood more and more as teaching about the Lord Jesus Christ.

*Discipleship and community.* From the beginning there is a community of disciples of Jesus in Acts that quickly expands in Jerusalem and is characterized by communal activities. Wherever Christians travel in Acts, they form communities that meet together; it can be safely presumed that the activities ascribed to the Jerusalem Christians were typical of the new communities that formed. Consequently, there is a new association called "the church", and the individual communities within it are known as "churches".

There is virtually nothing of this in the Gospels. There is a group of close associates of Jesus, male and female, who itinerate with him, but we hear nothing of people who respond to his message forming themselves into distinctive communities in their own towns and villages. The word *church* is not used, except in Matthew 16:18 and Matthew 18:17. The latter of these references might suggest that the formation of such groups was in the mind of Jesus. Otherwise, we learn nothing about the way of life of those who responded to the message. It is to be presumed that they continued to live according to Jewish religion and custom (cf. Mt 5:23-24), but nothing is made of this point.

The Evangelists cannot be accused of anachronistically reading back the life of the church into the pre-Easter period. Here we have a sharp distinction between before and after Easter.

*The death of Jesus.* The coming of the kingdom and the announcement of salvation take place in the Gospels simply by the decision of God. The rejection and death of Jesus are seen as the expression of opposition to God's plan. Nevertheless, the whole process of rejection, death and resurrection is recorded as taking place because it must happen as prophesied in Scripture. Now this might be interpreted to mean that God foreknows the fact of human opposition and how he will respond to it, and therefore the ultimate basis for the "must" lies in the reality of human opposition. But this will hardly do. Moreover, the rationale for the "must" cannot lie simply in the fact that "it is written" in Scripture but in the fact that Scripture testifies to the plan and purpose of God. The necessity lies in what God has determined. There is no explanation as to why God does not intervene to prevent Jesus from suffering (cf. the vivid question in Mt 26:53).

So what was this divine purpose? All of the Evangelists record the Last Supper at which Jesus symbolically interpreted his impending death as a sacrificial action related to the establishment of the covenant. Luke clarifies that this was the new covenant. The death is understood to be for the benefit of many people, including the disciples of Jesus, and Matthew adds that it was for the forgiveness of sins. The Matthean addition creates an echo of the opening scenes in the Gospels where John's baptism was for the forgiveness of sins. This incident, placed conspicuously at the beginning of the work of Jesus, is reinforced by the earlier statement in Matthew that Jesus would save his people from their sins (Mt 1:21) and by the statement by Zechariah that John would prepare the way for the Lord "to give his people the knowledge of salvation through the forgiveness of their sins" (Lk 1:77). The theme recurs at the end of Luke in the instruction to the disciples concerning the future proclamation (Lk 24:47). Within the narrative sin is a concern occasionally in Mark (Mk 2:9-10; 3:28-29; 11:25) and rather more frequently in the other Gospels, and people described as "sinners" appear with some frequency, especially in Luke. Does God forgive sins simply because people repent of them and endeavor not to sin in the future? The Jewish ethos with its sacrificially based worship indicates that it was taken for granted that the offering of sacrifice[6] was necessary for the removal of sin and for the inauguration of a covenant. Hence Jesus' interpretation of his death as a sacrifice on behalf of the people is appropriate. Here we may find the ultimate basis for the necessity of his death, tying in with the statement of purpose in Mark 10:45 (Mt 20:28).

Luke does not record the scene in Mark 10:35-45. This may be partly be-

---

[6]I use the term in a broad sense to include the scapegoat ritual on the Day of Atonement.

cause he has parallels to the sayings of Jesus in it in Luke 12:50 and Luke 22:24-27 (see also Lk 19:10). The latter of these, however, is concerned purely with servanthood and the example of Jesus and has nothing about his self-giving as a ransom. Here, however, it is important to note that there are other examples of Luke omitting material in the Gospel and replacing it with something equivalent, though not necessarily identical, in Acts;[7] it could be that Acts 20:28 should be seen as fulfilling this function.

Turning to Acts, we find there that the rejection and death of Jesus is a theme in the sermons, where it is argued that, although it was the deed of wicked people, nevertheless it occurred in accordance with God's set purpose and that it was followed by God's act in raising Jesus from the dead (something that God was bound to do in the light of his promises to the Messiah expressed prophetically in the Psalms). The purpose of the sermons is to overcome the obstacle to recognition of Jesus as the Messiah created by his rejection and death: it is argued that God overcame the death by raising and exalting Jesus, thus vindicating him, and that in any case the death itself, though carried out by sinners acting sinfully, nevertheless took place by God's purpose. The sermons do not explain what that purpose might have been. It is one thing to say that God was not taken by surprise and had quickly to devise a rescue scheme but rather had planned that the death should happen; it is another thing to state what his purpose in so planning was. Since the sermons are concerned primarily with the basic point of overcoming the scandal of the cross, it was less important to develop the thought of redemptive suffering at this point. What does happen is that the sermons declare the exaltation of Jesus by God to be a Savior for Israel (Acts 5:31): the authority that God has to forgive and to save is transferred to Jesus. Only in the one place (Acts 20:28) is reference made to the church being bought with the blood of Jesus. With the exception of the cup saying, therefore, there is no other explicit reference to the sacrificial character of the death of Jesus in Luke-Acts. Luke's account of the teaching of the early church can thus be said to be in line with what is said in the Gospel and indeed to rep-

---

[7]Luke has no equivalent to Mk 13:32 in the Gospel, but there is an equivalent in Acts 1:7; cf. the theme of Mk 7 (omitted in the Gospel) with that of Acts 10—11, and the omission of Mk 14:58-59 from the trial scene in the Gospel with an equivalent in Acts 6:13.

resent what the early Christians are likely to have taught, but it is striking
that the motif of Christ dying for our sins, which we have ample reason to
believe was part of the early preaching, is virtually absent from Acts.[8]

Various explanations for its absence have been proposed. One is that the
early preaching to Jews had to concentrate on overcoming the scandal of the
cross (1 Cor 1:23), and Acts gives one way in which this was achieved. A second
is that the development of a theology of the cross as saving event may well have
taken some time, and Luke presents the earliest stages of teaching.[9] True, we
cannot set the development very late in the light of 1 Corinthians 15:3, but it
must be remembered that developments did not proceed at the same speed everywhere. Third, it is clear that some early church statements of a creedal or
kerygmatic nature did not expressly mention the death of Christ for sins or sinners. Thus Philippians 2:6-11 refers to the cross but says nothing about its
salvific effects; 1 Thessalonians 1:9-10 refers to the resurrection but not the
cross; 1 Timothy 3:16 is concerned purely with the vindication of Christ. It is
not in dispute that these statements stand alongside others of equal age that do
refer to Christ's death for sinners (and there are more of these), but it is simply
being maintained that despite the existence of the latter the gospel could be formulated in other terms. Nevertheless, it is strange that Peter and Paul are not
depicted as taking up the motif of Christ's death for sinners. An earlier strand
of preaching that majored on the identity of Jesus as the now exalted Messiah
and therefore as the future judge and present Savior is entirely conceivable and
plausible. And the preaching to peoples with little or no previous contact with
Judaism would very naturally begin with a pointer away from polytheism to the
one God.

It is most unlikely that Luke rewrote the apostolic message by carefully removing all reference to the cross as the means of salvation at a time when this
was to the best of our knowledge universally accepted. What motives would he

---

[8]The explanation offered by some scholars that the language of Mk 10:45 and the Supper sayings
represents later church theology read back into the time of Jesus is unsustainable. The evidence for
the early development of the redemptive, sacrificial understanding of the death of Jesus in the early
church and the arguments for the authenticity of the Gospel material cannot be easily set aside.
[9]The problem remains, however, that Luke's presentation of the preaching of Paul in the second half
of Acts shows no development beyond the early preaching of Peter and that Paul's description of the
gospel that he preached in Corinth includes "Christ died for our sins" (1 Cor 15:3).

have had for so doing? What he has presented is an understanding of Jesus as the exalted Messiah to whom God has given the authority to confer salvation and the gift of the Spirit. It is fundamentally the identity of Jesus as the Messiah that he sees as the issue in the early speeches. The burden of proof must lie on those who would argue that the earliest preaching was fundamentally different from this presentation.[10]

If there is plausibility in this argument, then we can see that the earliest preaching of Jesus was an appropriate development from the way in which the story of Jesus is told in the Gospels. The identity of Jesus as the Messiah, now exalted by God, continued to be the basic point in debate and evangelism with the Jews.

*The Holy Spirit.* In the Gospels there is a common acceptance of the role of the Spirit in the inspiration of scriptural authors, conferring on them prophetic insight (Mk 12:36 and par.). This role continues in the activity of contemporary persons who give Spirit-inspired commentary on events (Lk 1—2). Since the resting of the Spirit on the Messiah was promised in the Old Testament, it is appropriate that Jesus receives the Spirit at his baptism at the outset of his work so that he is guided by the Spirit and his mighty works are empowered by the Spirit (and not the result of satanic or demonic influence). This basic understanding is nuanced in various ways. Mark gives us the bare essentials. Matthew and Luke cite scriptural backing (Mt 12:18; Lk 4:18). Parallel references in Matthew and Luke show that expressions about the power of God have the same force (cf. Mt 12:28; Lk 11:20). Luke's manner of expression may suggest that Jesus enjoys the power of the Spirit rather than that he is controlled by the Spirit. Matthew and Luke associate the conception of Jesus with the activity of the Spirit. Luke has a distinctive vocabulary of being filled with the Spirit (Lk 1:15, 41, 67; 4:1). There might seem to be some tension between the concept of Jesus as a person who needs the Spirit to accomplish his mission (like a human agent of God) and as the Son of God who has all the insight and power that he needs for his task. It can be assumed that the Evangelists were constrained by the Old Testament picture of the Messiah on whom the Spirit rests

---

[10]There is some reason to believe that the understanding of the death of Jesus as being for sins did not develop in the very earliest days of the church. We might compare how the Thessalonian church did not appreciate the full significance of the resurrection for believers who had died until Paul found that he needed to explain it to them in 1 Thess.

and saw no incongruity in the Son of God receiving the Spirit of God.

All the Gospels record the prophecy by John that the stronger One will baptize with the Spirit (and with fire, according to Mt and Lk). Only Luke is in a
position to show that this prophecy was fulfilled in the early church (Acts
11:16). The teaching of Jesus makes but brief mention of the Spirit enabling
disciples to say the right things when they are persecuted and put on trial, and
there is an interesting variant in Luke 21:15, where Jesus himself promises to
give them "words and wisdom". In the light of Acts 2:33 this suggests that the
heavenly role of Jesus as the dispenser of the Spirit is in mind. It seems clear
that the Spirit is not bestowed on the disciples during the time of Jesus. The
exceptions are the actors in Luke 1—2 who function like Old Testament
prophets in announcing the birth of the Messiah and possibly the disciples who
receive "power" from Jesus for their mission (Lk 9:1; but Mt and Mk simply
have "authority").[11] There is also the promise of Jesus that the Father will give
the Spirit to those who pray to him in Luke 11:13 (where Mt has "good
things");[12] there is nothing in the context to suggest that the disciples could not
pray there and then for the gift. The picture is thus basically consistent
throughout the Gospels. The Spirit is active in the life and work of Jesus as the
Messiah, and to some extent in other people, but the Baptist's promise of baptism with the Spirit waits to be fulfilled.

In Acts the mood is set at the beginning by the central place given to the
powerful descent of the Spirit at Pentecost, which is clearly identified as the fulfillment of the prophecy of baptism with the Spirit (Acts 1:5). Since the coming of the Spirit upon the household of Cornelius is also identified as baptism
with the Spirit, it is clear that the pentecostal gift is given to all believers and
not just to the original recipients. The citation from Joel favors this understanding, and it is confirmed by Peter's words to the crowd in Acts 2:38. This is the
new element in Acts as compared with the Gospels.

In the Gospels the Spirit is primarily concerned with equipping individuals
for the messianic mission. This role persists in Acts, where the majority of references are to the work of mission. Individuals are filled with the Spirit before

---

[11]There might seem to be some tension between authority and power, but both expressions could be
used to refer to the divine enabling to do mighty works. Compare how prophecies and mighty works
are also done in the name of Jesus (Mt 7:22-23; Mk 9:38-39; Lk 10:17).

[12]Luke's reference to the Spirit is more likely to represent what Jesus actually said.

they speak and bear witness, so that rejection of their testimony can be said to be resistance to the Spirit (Acts 7:51). Guidance is given by the Spirit and by other heavenly agents. At the same time reception of the Spirit is evidently the sine qua non of being a Christian and is the clear mark that God has accepted recipients into his people (Acts 15:8). It follows inescapably that the Spirit is not only the agent of mission but also the mark of belonging to Christ. There is a tension in that some individuals are said to be full of the Spirit (Acts 6:3, 5, 8; 7:55; 11:24) in a way that might suggest that there are degrees of possession (the Seven appear to be more "spiritual" than the rank and file of believers out of whom they are chosen), and there is the phenomenon of "filling" people who already have the Spirit for specific tasks (Acts 2:4/4:8; 9:17/13:9). Evidently the baptism of the Spirit is a permanent endowment of believers, a mark of belonging to the new covenant, and is common to them all. It equips them all for the mission, but this is entirely compatible with specific endowments for particular occasions. Like the Gospels, Acts says little about the functions of the Spirit in relation to what we might call the spiritual life of the individual and the community, but this motif is not entirely absent, and a one-sided insistence that the Spirit is purely the Spirit of prophecy and mission in Acts is unjustified. Nor is it correct to argue that the baptism with the Spirit is a later experience that tends to be detached from the initial act of belief in Christ. The onus lies on those who would argue that the promise in Acts 2:38 was not fulfilled there and then.

*Jesus, Israel and the Gentiles.* Mark's Gospel presents a mission by Jesus among the Jews, although various features suggest that it was written for an audience who needed to be instructed about Judaism. He enters non-Jewish territory from time to time and has contacts with non-Jews, but little is made of this. In his teaching he criticizes the practice of the teachers of the law, but the criticism is directed against the traditions of the elders and not against the law itself. When Mark comments that by his teaching he declared all foods clean, this looks like a criticism of current practice. The implications of the condemnation uttered in the parable of the vineyard are not followed through explicitly. A mission to Gentiles throughout the world is anticipated at a later stage.

There is general agreement that Matthew's Gospel thematizes the issue. The matter of obedience to the law is taken up, and it is probably fair to say that the law, or, rather, the law as interpreted by Jesus, is understood to be binding on disciples. Jesus has not come to abolish the law. The main thrust of the Sermon on the Mount is to give teaching that deepens the law by dealing with attitudes and motives in a way that calls for a radical lifestyle governed by love. It is assumed that people continue to live by the Jewish religion, offering sacrifices in the temple. Nevertheless, there is a strong criticism of the Jewish leaders for their failure to obey God and to recognize the coming of the Messiah. The kingdom will be taken from them and given to others. The Jews are compared unfavorably with the Gentiles who will believe, and the mission to Gentiles is anticipated over and over again, even though the mission of Jesus and his disciples is essentially limited to Jews during his lifetime. The Gospel concludes with a tremendous emphasis on making disciples of the nations.

Luke likewise respects the fact that Jesus went primarily to the Jews but in various ways points forward to the mission to the Gentiles; the symbolism of the seventy-two witnesses is unmistakable. Like Matthew, he assumes that Jesus' audience continue to keep the law.

In Acts, Luke traces the story of a church that in many ways found it hard to adjust to mission to the Gentiles, so that opposition continued on the part of some. There is one new people of God. There is debate as to how far this new people is required to keep the law. The decisive point that Gentiles are not required to be circumcised stands firm; this is an issue never raised one way or the other in the Gospels, where the only circumcision ever mentioned is that of Jesus.

*Eschatology.* Eschatology, in the broad sense of teaching about the final events in God's plan for the world, features fairly prominently in the Gospels. The kingdom of God was thought of as the final intervention of God into human history to establish his rule and bring its opposition to naught. At the same time it was understood as the eternal state, so that to talk of the kingdom was to talk of the transcendent sphere where God reigns eternally. For Jesus to announce that the kingdom of God was near or had arrived was to signal the initiation of the end events. His teaching also contained sufficient information about the final judgment and the preceding times of stress to make people feel that the end was near. In fact, the immediate future was one of increasing breakdown of society in Judea and further afield, culminating in the horrific events of the war with Rome, which must inevitably have seemed to people like the onset of final doom. Yet at the same time it seems to have been possible to think of "business as usual". Right up to Mark 8 the impression given is much more that Jesus is announcing a new state of affairs in this-worldly terms, in which he is bringing healing to individuals and to society through mighty works that indicate God is at work in an unusual way. The teaching of Jesus about human life is thus a combination of rules and norms for ordinary human life and of calls to whole-hearted commitment to the Messiah, whatever the cost in self-denial and readiness for loyalty to death in the face of opposition.

Alongside this is also the promise of some kind of vindication. On the one hand, Jesus prophesies that he himself will somehow survive being put to death. On the other hand, there is a prophecy of the coming of the Son of Man with language that suggests final judgment. James and John proceed to ask for seats beside Jesus when he enters his glory. Did they think that they would be martyred, pass straight to heaven and join Jesus there, or did they think that he would be resurrected and then the new world would begin on earth? The arrival of Jesus in Jerusalem is heralded as being associated with the coming messianic kingdom. Was the messianic kingdom thought of as a temporary stage before the final reign of God? Then comes Mark 13, in which Jesus speaks of the destruction of the temple and a period in which they will be without him, since people will be claiming to be "he".[13] Much the same picture is presented in Matthew and Luke.

There is very little of this in Acts. When the disciples ask a question that is presumably concerned with eschatology, the time of the restoration of the kingdom to Israel, they are in effect told that this is none of their business. Their task is to be witnesses to Jesus "to the ends of the earth" (Acts 1:6-8), a saying that implies a considerable period of time initiating a task that has not been completed by the end of the book. The promise of the return of Jesus stands firm, but it does give the impression of being less imminent or at least not immediate (Acts 3:20). Yet the last days have begun, in that the Spirit has been poured out. Heaven is near, in that Stephen has a vision that takes him within sight of it (Acts 7:55-56). But thereafter the interest is centered on the mission, particularly to the Gentiles. The message includes warning about the

---

[13]However we identify "he", it would hardly seem possible for such a figure to appear alongside Jesus. The traditional interpretation—that Jesus is no longer present and pretenders to his role appear— is probably right.

day of judgment by Jesus (Acts 10:42; 17:31). But that is all. Acts does not deal extensively with the issue. Whatever the chronological relationship of the composition of Acts with the war against Rome and the fall of Jerusalem, it is silent on the matter—in stark contrast to Luke 21, where the fall of Jerusalem is unambiguously thematized (contrast the more opaque language in Mark and Matthew).[14]

Luke, then, respects the way in which apocalyptic prophecy was a known part of the teaching of Jesus, but in Acts he presents a picture in which it is of marginal importance for a church primarily engaged in mission and facing human opposition.

### Conclusion

From this comparison we can confirm that the presentations of Jesus and his message in the three Gospels are strikingly similar to one another. The presentation of the theology of the early Christians in Acts can be understood as a straightforward development from that in the Gospel, although there are some vital new understandings as well. In other words, the kind of theology depicted in Acts is what we would expect from a group of followers of the earthly Jesus who believed that he was risen from the dead and still active among them. The differences between Acts and the Synoptic Gospels demonstrate clearly enough that the teaching of Jesus has not been assimilated to that of the early church. The vital distinction between Jesus' proclamation of the kingdom and the early church's proclamation of Jesus is carefully preserved. This is all the more noteworthy, granted that the temptation to assimilate the teaching of Jesus to that of the early church must have been quite strong.

What we have, then, are two theologies, that of Jesus and that of his followers (as depicted by Luke), which express the same underlying structure and content but do so in different idioms. On the one hand, we have the message of Jesus announcing the kingdom of God as something that is coming to pass in the here and now, a message that offers deliverance from the powers of evil to the oppressed and to sinners, brings entry into a new relationship with God as

---

[14]The problem cannot be solved by dating Acts a long time after A.D. 70, since Luke's Gospel must be dated reasonably close in time to Acts, and it does focus on the issue. Might the presence of apocalyptic in the Gospel and its absence from Acts parallel the situation in the Johannine literature, where apocalyptic is present in Revelation but absent from the Gospel of John?

Father, and promises eternal life. Jesus is more than simply a proclaimer of what God is doing; he is the agent through whom he acts by the power of the Spirit, and his position as Son of Man, Messiah and Son of God emerges as the story is told by the Evangelists. His message requires a response of commitment in discipleship to Jesus and a new way of living that goes beyond the requirements of the Mosaic law. Jesus is God's missionary bringing this message to the Jews in order that Israel might be restored to be truly and not just nominally God's people, but there is an openness to Gentiles even if this is not fully exploited at this stage. His mission runs foul of opposition from the Jewish leaders, which sets in train a series of events purposed by God through which he is rejected, crucified and then vindicated by God raising him from the dead. This is how the Evangelists see Jesus, and their presentation rests firmly on reliable traditions of his life and teaching.

On the other hand, we have the theology of the early Christians. The resurrection of Jesus and their experience of the Spirit confirm for them that the message of Jesus is true and that he is now confirmed by God as Messiah and Lord. He is therefore now active from heaven through a variety of agencies. Their discipleship continues, and they are aware of a continuing obligation to mission to bring Israel to a recognition of the Messiah. So their proclamation shifts in emphasis from the kingdom to the Messiah, and consequently it is not so much a repetition of what he proclaimed as rather a proclamation of him. They carry out their mission by the power of the same Holy Spirit who is now a vital part of the experience of all the followers of Jesus. With the shift away from the emphasis on the kingdom of God there comes an increased emphasis on the experience of salvation and eternal life, including the forgiveness of sins and the reception of the Spirit. A combination of events, in which divine guidance is perceived, leads them to a rapidly expanding mission among the Gentiles that takes the missionaries all over the Roman world and creates problems regarding the place of the Jewish law and practices for the converts. Opposition to the new movement leads to martyrdom, imprisonment and threats of death, so that it is recognized that the path taken by Jesus must also be the path for his followers.

Comparing these two statements we can see their essential identity as we bear in mind the great difference that the death and resurrection of Jesus made to the experience of his followers. There is an extensive range of agreement in broad structure and detailed content between the Synoptic Gospels and Acts in their theology so that they belong harmoniously together. And although we have not attempted to argue the case in detail, there is good reason to suppose that this reflects the fundamental agreement between Jesus and the first Christians.

This is not to say that there was necessarily complete harmony between three congregations nurtured on Matthew, Mark and Luke-Acts respectively, any more than there is today between Christian congregations today who would all profess to accept the historical creeds of the church but who differ on lesser issues. But there is sufficient agreement on basic issues for us to affirm that the Synoptic Gospels are the work of Evangelists who have a harmonious understanding of Jesus, and that in Acts we have a picture of the theology of the early Christians that can be plausibly seen to stand in continuity with that in the Gospels.

This leaves us with two major questions that still remain to be discussed. On the one hand, we shall have to ask how the theology in the remaining Gospel, that of John, is to be understood since it appears to present a rather different understanding of the teaching of Jesus. And, on the other hand, there is the important question of comparing the theology of the early Christians as depicted in Acts and the theology of Paul and other early Christians. It will be appropriate to begin our treatment of these two questions with an analysis of the theology of the Pauline letters.

## Bibliography

Tannehill, Robert C. *The Narrative Unity of Luke-Acts: A Literary Interpretation.* Vol. I. *The Gospel According to Luke.* Philadelphia: Fortress, 1986.

———. *The Narrative Unity of Luke-Acts: A Literary Interpretation.* Vol. 2. *The Acts of the Apostles.* Philadelphia: Fortress, 1990.

Verheyden, Jozef, ed. *The Unity of Luke-Acts.* Louvain: Louvain University Press, 1999.

# PART 3

## THE PAULINE LETTERS

# 8

# THE LETTER TO
# THE GALATIANS

∽∘∾

Our study of Paul's theology will take up the letters ascribed to him in something like the chronological order of their composition[1] and will cover both the letters about whose Pauline authorship there is no real doubt and those about which there is continuing scholarly debate.[2] This procedure is appropriate since, even if some of the letters are not directly from the hand of Paul, they are from followers who claimed to be continuing his work and were certainly strongly influenced by his theology.

We begin, then, with Galatians and immediately are plunged straight into

---

[1]Needless to say, this is a controverted issue. The oldest surviving letter of Paul is either 1 Thessalonians or Galatians, with the majority of scholars opting for the former. I belong to the small band, including F. F. Bruce and Richard N. Longenecker, that opts for the latter; see F. F. Bruce, *The Epistle of Paul to the Galatians* (Exeter: Paternoster, 1982); Richard N. Longenecker, *Galatians* (Dallas: Word, 1990).

Scholars who favor a later dating of Galatians claim that its theology is more mature than that of 1 Thessalonians and stands much closer to that of Romans. The view adopted here is that the differences compared with 1 Thessalonians are better explained by the fact that in Galatians Paul had to develop his understanding of certain aspects of the gospel more explicitly and polemically against opponents than was the case in Thessalonica, where this opposition was not present. In any case using Galatians as our introduction to Paul has the advantage of taking us straight into the heart of his theological thinking. See James D. G. Dunn, *The Theology of Paul's Letter to the Galatians* (Cambridge: Cambridge University Press, 1993), p. 133: "Within the Pauline corpus, therefore, Galatians has a primary place as the first extant statement of Paul's distinctive theology."

[2]To the latter group belong 2 Thessalonians, Colossians, Ephesians, 1 and 2 Timothy, and Titus. For discussion of the issues, see I. Howard Marshall, Stephen Travis and Ian Paul, *Exploring the New Testament*, vol. 2, *The Letters and Revelation* (London: SPCK; Downers Grove, Ill.: InterVarsity Press, 2002).

controversy—at two levels. The controversy is not only that carried on by Paul in debate with his readers, on which he apparently thrived, but also the modern controversy about what exactly was happening.

## The Controversy Behind Galatians

Galatians is the one letter of Paul to a church that does not begin with some kind of thanksgiving to God, usually for the spiritual progress of the readers, but dives immediately into controversy. From the letter it is readily apparent that the believers in the several congregations in Galatia were largely, but not exclusively, Gentiles; some of them may well have been former attenders at the Jewish synagogues without having become full converts to Judaism through taking the step of being circumcised. But now they were being powerfully encouraged by some group of people to be circumcised and to observe various special days and seasons (these must be Jewish festivals; Gal 4:10). The letter is a sustained effort to argue them out of yielding to this pressure and it does so by reminding them of the true nature of the gospel and its benefits.

Why was this pressure being exerted, and what lay behind it? There was a group of people evidently moving around the several congregations established by Paul and trying to shift the thinking and practice of his converts. They are generally nicknamed "Judaizers" on the basis of the Greek verb used in Galatians 2:14. According to J. Louis Martyn they constituted a missionary movement that aimed to convert Gentiles to a law-abiding version of the gospel.[3] In any case, they were Jewish Christians, and their understanding of the gospel was that the Christian movement was in effect an opening up of Judaism and the Jewish people to accommodate Gentiles.[4] In their eyes the problem was that Paul was preaching about the coming of the Messiah and claiming that all that was needed to become a member of God's people was to believe in Jesus. Circumcision and the keeping of other aspects of the law were not necessary for Gentiles.

This question had arisen earlier in Antioch and elsewhere where uncircum-

---

[3]J. Louis Martyn, *Theological Issues in the Letters of Paul* (Edinburgh: T & T Clark, 1997), pp. 7-24.

[4]This is the universally held view. Or at least it was until the recent monograph by Mark Nanos, *The Irony of Galatians: Paul's Letter in First-Century Context* (Minneapolis: Fortress, 2002), which argues that the problem came from pressure by Jews rather than Jewish Christians. The jury is still out on this issue.

cised Gentiles were becoming Christian believers (cf. Gal 2:11-14). It created
a practical problem for the Jewish believers because a central part of congregational life was the common meal at which the death of Jesus was remembered.
Jews practiced a rigid separation from non-Jews, and this was especially so in
that Jews would not eat with Gentiles or eat food prepared by them that did
not fulfill the Jewish regulations about ritual cleanliness; both the Gentiles and
their foods were considered "unclean", as the story of Peter in Acts 10 vividly
brings out.[5] But to partake in church meals meant that Jews were now expected
to eat with uncircumcised Gentiles who were "unclean". It would be difficult
for Jewish Christians to shake off centuries of avoiding such occasions and also
to stand up to the criticism that would inevitably come their way from non-
Christian Jews who might be prepared to tolerate their eccentric beliefs about
Jesus but who drew the line sharply at their non-Jewish practices. Indeed, it may
well be that it was the sheer force of the pressure from non-Christian Jews that
was the ultimate motivation for the Judaizers. Surely the simple solution was
that Gentiles who became Christians should be circumcised and keep the law,
just as these Jewish Christians evidently were doing, and then everything would
be all right. The solution was obvious and compelling. It is no wonder that its
advocates were on to a winning line in the Galatian churches.[6]

The argument of the Judaizers carried two further corollaries.

First, if it was true that believing in Jesus was not enough for full entry
into the people of God, there was the further consequence that Paul must be
regarded as mistaken if not deliberately distorting the gospel in the views that
he was preaching. Was he really a true Jew, faithful to his ancestral heritage?
True, he claimed to be an apostle, but from where did he derive his authority?
It had not been given to him by any human body. He had no sound basis for

---

[5]There is controversy about just how rigid the Jews were on this matter; see the different stances of
James D. G. Dunn, *Jesus, Paul and the Law: Studies in Mark and Galatians* (London: SPCK, 1990), pp. 129-
82, and Philip F. Esler, *Galatians* (London: Routledge, 1998), pp. 93-116.

[6]Although the issue of common meals is mentioned by Paul in the letter only with reference to the
situation in Antioch, it can be assumed that Paul's opponents (as we must call them) would have
raised this issue in his congregations also.

We need to distinguish carefully between the Antioch problem whose starting point was fellowship between Jews and Gentiles at communal meals and the problem in Galatia, which is couched in
terms of acceptance of circumcision and other requirements of the law. It can be presumed that the
requirement for fellowship in Antioch was the same as was being demanded in Galatia, although the
question of meals together is not raised in the Galatian setting: it is merely one aspect of the problem.

his preaching. He was not to be trusted.

A second point made by the opposition was probably that if people did not keep the law, how could they live lives that were consistent with the moral quality of behavior demanded by it? Surely people who rejected the law would also reject its moral demands? From I Corinthians 5:11 and I Corinthians 6:9-11 we know that Gentile sins persisted among Gentile converts in the church. Paul's counterargumentation here (Gal 5:13-26) would seem to require that this sort of objection to his gospel was being put forward.

But why should the Jewish Christians (or some of them) have been so eager to fulfill the law? Earlier interpreters argued that the purpose of keeping the law, whether by Jews or Gentiles, was to acquire merit (not a Pauline word) in the sight of God, that is, to pile up a record of good deeds done and wrong deeds avoided on the basis of which God would justify sinners despite their previous bad record. Many more recent interpreters, among whom E. P. Sanders is preeminent, have argued that this interpretation rests on a misunderstanding of Judaism.[7] In Judaism individuals were situated within God's covenant people on the basis of his electing grace; they were not required to keep the law in order to get in, but once in they kept the law in order to stay in; keeping the law was the response to grace rather than the condition of it. This position has been refined to say that the essence of the "works of the law" that people were required to keep was that they were the marks or badges of belonging to God's people and served the function of erecting a boundary around them. What Paul objected to was the setting up of this boundary, which meant that Gentiles had to keep the law in order to be counted among the people of God.[8]

---

[7]E. P. Sanders, *Paul, the Law and the Jewish People* (Philadelphia: Fortress, 1983); this work rests on the basic research in his *Paul and Palestinian Judaism* (Philadelphia: Fortress, 1977); cf. Dunn, *Jesus.*

[8]The debate has to some extent been sidetracked by the introduction of the term *merit*, which surfaced much more at the time of the Reformation. This is not a term that is used in Galatians. Rather it is simply asserted that people must fulfill God's requirements expressed in the law in order to be saved, and it so happens that these requirements (or some of them) had become the marks of Jewish identity and served to throw a fence around the people of God.

But once the wearing of a badge becomes a requirement, it has clearly become a condition for salvation and is not merely something that you can do if you please. Further, from Gal 6:14 (cf. Phil 3:3-4) it emerges that these were things in which people put their confidence instead of in Christ and his death, and it is very difficult to see how this confidence could be distinguished from self-confidence in that these are human actions (the "flesh"). We have here at least the seeds of the later doctrine of merit against which the Reformers reacted so strongly and rightly.

It may be that the underlying motivation of the Judaizers was concerned with Jewish national identity and the forcing of the marks of Jewish identity onto Gentiles. Circumcision, festivals and eating "clean foods" were among the central symbols (along with the temple) that defined Judaism. So the Judaizers felt that their Jewish identity was threatened by Paul's gospel, which in effect opened up the Jewish religion to Gentiles without requiring them to accept the defining marks of Judaism and which could be regarded as questioning the importance of those symbols for Jews.[9] There could, therefore, have been social reasons for the impositions on the Gentiles; but these would have been defended with biblical and theological arguments, such as the fact that Abraham, the father of the people, was circumcised. It may also be, as Philip Esler has argued, that the Jewish Christians had taken up and developed the Old Testament terminology of "the righteous" as a self-description that expressed their identity as the true people of God.[10]

Paul debates the issue on the biblical and theological level because he sees in the imposition a real threat to the character of the gospel. He reasserts that Gentiles do not need to "follow Jewish customs" (Gal 2:14), that is, keep the law, which prescribes these defining marks, in order to get right with God but simply to believe in Jesus. The argument is conducted on a theological level through and through.

### The Theological Story

Paul's letter is a passionate response to this situation. We shall find our way into its theology by following through the main lines of the argument.

*Paul's authority and the "other gospel" (Gal 1:1—2:13).* In the opening greeting Paul announces two themes that will be developed at greater length later. The first is that he has an authority that derives from Jesus Christ and God, and that is therefore implicitly superior to any merely human authority (Gal 1:1). The second and main point is a reminder that Jesus Christ has dealt with the problem caused by human sin (Gal 1:4). Paul's main concern is with the gospel and how people are saved or rescued from their present predicament in this evil age (Gal 1:4, 6-9).

---

[9]Cf. the accusation in Acts 21:21.
[10]Esler, *Galatians*, pp. 143-45 and *passim*.

The basic statement of the gospel is, then, that Christ gave himself for us (Gal 1:4; repeated in Gal 2:20; 3:13). All through the letter deliverance and benefit (Gal 5:2) are ascribed to what Christ has done—he redeems (Gal 4:5) and sets free (Gal 5:1), and through faith in him people are "justified" (Gal 2:17). Implicitly a new age has begun.

Paul then characterizes the message of his opponents as "another gospel", as if there could indeed be such a thing (Gal 1:6-9). The point of this is twofold. First, it shows that the opponents were saying that people had to accept their teaching in order to be saved (as in Acts 15:1). Circumcision and law-keeping were not simply desirable extras but were indispensable, and the problem of table fellowship was only part of the real issue. Second, by calling it a "gospel" Paul implies that it was a message that they considered to be authoritative and of divine origin, and there is the further implication that they considered his message to be merely human in origin.

Hence the first part of Paul's defense is to insist that he received his message for the Gentiles directly from Jesus Christ, and he was in no way dependent upon human beings for it (Gal 1:11—2:10). The message was part of his call to apostleship given by Jesus and God (Gal 1:1). This insistence by Paul would have carried no weight with non-Christian Jews and demonstrates that his debate is with Christian Jews who agreed with him on christology but without sharing the implications that he saw in it.

Paul is particularly anxious to insist that his calling was entirely due to divine agency and he goes out of his way to claim that none of the existing apostles in Jerusalem had anything to do with conferring authority on him. He was independent of Jerusalem but fully recognized by the leaders there. What happened was that when he went up to Jerusalem and told them about the gospel that he had been preaching for the past fourteen years—a significantly long time!—they warmly accepted what he was doing because they recognized that God had made him the apostle to the Gentiles alongside Peter as the apostle to the Jews.

Paul's argument so far, then, is that he got his message from God and that the existing apostles did not lay any additional requirements down for his converts, but rather they encouraged him strongly in his mission (Gal 2:1-10). Those who opposed him, therefore, could not call his personal authority and that of his message in question by doubting his calling or by claiming that he was out of harmony with the leaders of the church in Jerusalem. Yet there was a lapse in their agreement when Peter came to Antioch at a later stage and was persuaded by "certain people . . . from James" to withdraw from eating with Gentiles (Gal 2:11-14). This led to a confrontation in which it is generally assumed that Paul was the loser in that he failed to persuade Peter, but it is not evident why he should mention it if it was not to his advantage to do so.[11] Since there is no sign anywhere of any lasting rift between Paul and Peter but every indication that Paul regarded him as a fellow worker in the gospel (I Cor 3:21-23; 9:5),[12] we may take it that the disagreement was temporary.[13]

Paul begins to relate what he said to Peter, but somewhere along the line it becomes an argument addressed to the readers, and the focus shifts from his authority to the nature of the gospel.[14]

*Paul's exposition of the gospel (Gal 2:14—6:18).* What are the main lines of the argument?

Paul claims that Jewish Christians like Peter and himself know that they themselves are "justified" or "made righteous" by faith in Christ and not by observing the law (Gal 2:14-16). Christians were agreed that a person could be put right with God or enter into a right relationship with him or be counted as "righteous" only through believing in Jesus Christ and not by observance of the Jewish law. For Paul this was common ground for Peter and himself, and this must be the implication of the agreement reached at Jerusalem in Galatians 2:1-10, at least as Paul saw it. The point of mentioning it seems to be to assure the readers that Peter and himself were in agreement on this point. The implication

---

[11]It is often said that Paul does not conclude his account of the argument with Peter in Gal 2 because he was the loser. On the contrary, as Mark Nanos suggested to me in conversation, it is unlikely that Paul would have recounted any part of the story if he had been worsted in the argument or failed to carry the agreement of Peter; why should he make any mention of what would have been an embarrassment to him?

[12]Here I differ radically from the interpretation that goes back at least to Ferdinand C. Baur: that there were rival Petrine and Pauline parties in the early church with different understandings of the gospel; cf. chap. 30 n. 18 (p. 698).

[13]Paul's argument may simply be "this was what they originally agreed and they were wrong to go back on it later", or "it is true that they did go back on it temporarily but Peter and Barnabas did recognize the force of my argument to them". Another suggestion is that Paul misunderstood the extent of the agreement between Peter and James and himself (Hübner, 2:64 n. 77, citing the work of B. Holmberg). We do not know for certain when the rift was healed, but I think that it was probably before the composition of Galatians.

[14]The TNIV text does not terminate the quotation until the end of Gal 2:21, but there is a marginal note that it may close at the end of Gal 2:14 (so NRSV).

is that justification is also by faith in Jesus Christ for Gentiles, and the corollary is that, if observing the law does not lead to justification, then it should not be necessary for Gentiles. They do not need to keep the law in addition to believing in Christ.

The next part of the argument is difficult (Gal 2:17-21). Paul appears to be saying that if Christian believers do go back to keeping the law of Moses and fail to keep it, this would mean that belief in Christ leads people into sin, something that Christians can hardly believe. Here the point may be that if people go back to keeping the requirements of circumcision, Jewish festivals and so on, they are not going to be able to do so fully and completely but in some respects will fall short and will thereby be sinners in terms of the law's requirements. In fact, believers have died with Christ and so passed out of the sphere in which the law has authority over them.[15]

Next, Paul appeals to experience (Gal 3:1-5). The evidence of Christian salvation is the experience of receiving the Spirit, which Paul confidently claims his readers had received before and apart from circumcision and keeping the law.[16] What Paul condemns is adding the "flesh" to the Spirit. Here *flesh* refers to things done by human beings in their own strength in contrast to what God does for them. Paul is on firm experiential ground in that the converts received the Spirit when they believed in Christ long before the demand for observance of the law had been thrust upon them.[17] So works of the law are not needed in order to receive the Spirit, and for Paul it would appear that reception of the Spirit is not only indispensable for being a Christian but also is the fundamental effect of faith.[18] Paul will return to the experience of the Spirit in Galatians 4:6.

Characteristic of this letter is the way in which the use of Scripture dominates much of the discussion, almost providing the structure of the argument as well as the basis for it.[19] The process starts in earnest when Paul appeals to

---

[15]Cf. the fuller discussion in Rom 7:1-6.

[16]Compare how he uses the same kind of chronological argument with respect to Abraham in Rom 4:9-12.

[17]Paul's point is similar to his argument that Abraham was justified by faith long before the law of Moses was given (Rom 4).

[18]The question whether the experience might have been fallacious is not raised. Paul assumes that it is self-evidently authentic.

[19]Hübner, 2:57.

Scripture (Gal 3:6-14), where Abraham was justified by his faith before he was circumcised and before the law had been given, and he was told that God's promise was for him and his descendants. If Abraham was justified by faith, the promise of blessing to all nations through him must be on the same principle.

The alternative route to blessing advocated by his opponents is to try to get right with God by dependence on keeping the law. But to do so is to come under a curse. This curse rests on people who try to keep the law but do not keep all its commands and prohibitions, this being a principle taken from the law (Deut 27:26). In what is virtually a parenthesis (Gal 3:11-12) Paul seems to combine two lines of argument. First, he comments that Scripture upholds the principle of justification by faith (Hab 2:4). The law fails in not being based upon this scriptural principle of faith but upon works. It follows that for Paul the law was not meant to be a means of justification or to give life (Gal 3:21) but had some other function, despite the fact that here it is said that people who do its commandments will live by them. Second, in any case, nobody is able to keep the law. Paul does not say this outright here (but see Rom 3:9-20), but it is clearly assumed in his comment that everybody who depends on works of the law is under its curse (Gal 3:10). Everybody who tries to keep it stands under its curse, and the law has no means of delivering people from its own curse. But Christ has delivered those who believe by taking this curse on himself.[20] By believing in Christ in this way the blessing promised to and experienced by Abraham is received by Christians, and it is identified as the experience of the Spirit. Thus faith is the means by which we obtain a benefit that has been secured for us by somebody else, namely, Christ.

The promise to Abraham, then, is fundamental. The later arrival of the law (i.e., the law of Moses) cannot alter the covenant that had been made (Gal 3:15-18). Paul assumes that the promise to Abraham and his descendants, once made, cannot be set aside.

So, if the law was not intended to replace or cancel the promise, what was its purpose, given as it was by God (Gal 3:15-25)? It had a temporary function until Christ came. This was to be a kind of guardian to the Jews, like the slave who supervised children in a wealthy Roman household on their way to and from school. The law was not opposed to the promise because it was never in-

---

[20]Compare how Paul will also say that Christ became sin for us (2 Cor 5:21).

tended to be an alternative way of life, and it had a different purpose. It was there to lead people to Christ by making them realize that they were sinners. Paul repeats that the law was not able to give life and righteousness (Gal 3:21). Everybody is held captive by sin, as Scripture testifies, and the purpose of the law is to be in charge of us for the period until faith comes.[21] It would seem that the purpose of the law was to identify for people what they were and were not to do and to that extent to keep them from sin; but it was also there to make people conscious of their sin until God's way of putting people right by faith was revealed.

But now the situation is different (Gal 3:21-29). A new age has come with Christ, and the temporary function of the law has ceased. Those who believe in Christ are now children of God, regardless of whether they are Jews or Greeks, and constitute one people in Christ. This point is elaborated in Galatians 4:1-7. Believers are adopted as God's sons and daughters instead of being like slaves under bondage to keeping the law. And with sonship come the privileges associated with it and especially the gift of the Spirit now and the status of being heirs to what God will give them in the future. This is a new experience, one that is not found under the law, and it therefore constitutes a fresh argument that salvation does not come by means of the law.

So far Paul has basically been addressing the situation of the Jews under the law.[22] But now two things happen. First, attention shifts to the Gentiles who are being encouraged to be circumcised (Gal 4:8-11). Paul sees an analogy between their pre-Christian state and that of the Jews under the law. They had known what it was to be slaves to their false gods and idols before they became believers. Surely they do not want to return to slavery, this time not to their false gods but to the Jewish law. From this point (and this is the second shift in the discourse) Paul begins to use the language of entreaty as well as that of argument. He pleads with the Gentile readers of his letter not to yield to persuasion to adopt the Jewish law, since what was true of the Jews before the coming of Christ would now apply to them also (Gal 4:12-20).

Perhaps they do not realize what is involved. So he develops a picture out of

---

[21]This period could be both historical of the Jewish people from Moses until Christ and personal of the life of the individual from coming under the law to conversion.

[22]Up to Gal 4:7 it is principally (but not exclusively—cf. Gal 3:28) the situation of the Jews that is in mind.

Scripture, that of Abraham who had two sons, one by a slave and one by a free woman (Gal 4:21-5:1). The former corresponds to the law and to the Judaism that is still in slavery to it, while the latter corresponds to the "Jerusalem" that is to come, the realm of promise and freedom.[23]

With the mention of *freedom* Paul moves on into a discussion of the way in which accepting circumcision and the law is to move back into bondage, since to do so is to cease to trust in Christ and to rely instead on the keeping of the law. The law is a taskmaster, requiring total obedience and threatening death to those who fail to render it. By contrast, the life of God's children is one of freedom (Gal 5:2-15). The freedom, however, is not freedom to sin but is deliverance from the requirements of the law and from the power of sin in order to keep the fundamental commandment, which is to love.

But how are people to live out this commandment of love (Gal 5:16-26)? Here Paul draws a contrast between the flesh, that is, human nature in its weakness and liability to yield to temptation, and the Spirit as the power that enables people to demonstrate the qualities of godly character. The evil nature is there with its passions. But believers need not yield to the pull of this nature and can experience a new life in which they are led by the Spirit.

Paul here speaks of people who are pulled to and fro by the flesh and the Spirit so that they cannot do what they want to do (Gal 5:17). Does this reduce believers to the level of an object like a rugby ball with a scrum of opposing players fighting over it to gain possession? Does Paul mean that not even the Spirit can enable believers to do what they want to do? Clearly believers do have an active role in the struggle; otherwise Paul would not address imperatives to them. J. Louis Martyn makes the important point that Paul is writing to believers who already have the Spirit and is not urging them to "get" the Spirit. He interprets the difficult verse 17 to be addressed to believers who are trying to serve Christ and the law at the same time and find themselves achieving nothing as a result. Although they are trying to fulfill the law, they are in fact coming under the dominion of the flesh.[24] The law cannot enable them to overcome the flesh. The solution is to follow the guidance of the Spirit exclusively.

---

[23]The difficulties that modern readers have with this sort of allegory are diminished when we realize that the point of this discussion lies in assertion rather than argument.

[24]Martyn, *Theological Issues*, pp. 251-78.

The remainder of the letter is encouragement and summing up (Gal 6:1-18). There is practical instruction on how to behave in this situation of temptation to abandon Christ for the law. In particular, there is a warning against living so as to please the flesh. Whether this refers to evil doing in general or to the growth of sinful boasting by those who try to keep the law (cf. Gal 6:13-14) is not clear. Finally, Paul evidently takes the pen from his scribe to make a final appeal in which he questions the motives and consistency of those who would woo the readers away from Christ and his cross (Gal 6:11-18). For himself, he is not concerned about boasting or about pleasing other people, since he has died with Christ.

### Theological Themes

Such is the theological argument in brief summary. We now need to identify and develop some of the themes that arise in it.

*Salvation history and the gospel.* It is clear from the outset of this letter that Paul is concerned about the gospel as something that is preached (Gal 1:11). It is a "word" to which people respond, but the response is not simply acceptance of the word (Gal 1:9) but faith in the person to whom it bears witness, to Jesus crucified (Gal 2:20). Therefore, right away we can affirm that Paul's understanding of Christianity is both salvation-proclamatory[25] and salvation-historical. It is also salvation-receptive. This means that the gospel is more than simply a story that may or may not have a factual counterpart. The gospel is the interpretation of what happened (Gal 3:1), but it is an interpretation in that it makes plain what happened, or rather, as we might say, "what really happened". "A man died on a cross" is certainly what happened, and this is true as a partial description. "Christ . . . gave himself for our sins" (Gal 1:3-4) is a statement of what really happened, but it is a statement that depends on an understanding of the event that goes beyond mere visual observation and that is made within a framework of thinking within which such a statement is a genuine possibility.[26] At the same time the message is intended to be persuasive and to lead to a faith commitment by those who hear it.

---

[25]I use this term in preference to "existential", which creates a false contrast with "salvation-historical".
[26]It is a grammatical statement that does not break the rules within a particular grammar, by contrast with other statements that might belong to a different "grammar".

The framework of Paul's thinking is determined by this "salvation history".[27] God has been active in making promises and fulfilling them since the time of Abraham. Meanwhile, there have arisen the problems of the law, understood as the way to life by at least some Jews who have encouraged Gentiles to be circumcised and keep the Jewish festivals. Paul's theology is centered on the death of Jesus as the way in which people are redeemed from the curse imposed by the law, upon faith as the appropriate response to the action of God, and upon the Spirit as the power through which people live a life that pleases God through fulfilling the single commandment to love their neighbors.

Paul's theology thus operates within a scheme of the old era and the new era that is brought about by the coming of Christ and becomes a reality for people when they believe in him. This theology draws material from the Jewish Scriptures and deals with problems that arise in a Jewish context.

But there is great stress on the need for truth (Gal 2:14); the interpretation of events must be in accordance with truth. This is operative on two levels. One level is that of correct understanding of the gospel. The other is that of correct behavior. Manifestly these two belong together. At the heart of Galatians is the threat posed by "another gospel" that required adherence to the Mosaic law by Gentiles as an integral part of their response. This involved acceptance of a way of life that required adoption of circumcision, Jewish food regulations and Jewish festivals. Alongside this, however, was the common temptation on the part of converts to persist in the breaches of divinely taught morality that were characteristic of sinful humanity in general, whether Jewish or Gentile. Paul did not believe that proclamation of the Mosaic law and the need to obey it could deal with the impulses that led to sin. He proclaimed a gospel that was too great to be reduced to a single motif. It had two central aspects. The one was the announcement of justification purely on the grounds of the bearing of the curse by Jesus and received purely on the basis of faith and not by keeping the law. The other aspect was the promise to believers of the Spirit by whose working in their lives they could overcome the power of the flesh. So the gospel offered not only a new rela-

---

[27]B. W. Longenecker, *The Triumph of Abraham's God: The Transformation of Identity in Galatians* (Edinburgh: T & T Clark, 1998).

tionship with God but also a transformation of nature.

*Justification.* Paul introduces a key set of terms that dominate his argument with Judaizers. The basic issue, as he sees it, is how a person is "justified". This word is a translation of a Greek verb *(dikaioō)* that is related to the adjective *just (dikaios)* and the noun *justice (dikaiosynē)*. More commonly we want to translate these last two Greek words as "righteous" and "righteousness", since these are more all-encompassing than the terms just and justice, which have a rather narrower application to being fair and impartial. Unfortunately when we require a corresponding verb and abstract noun, the English language forces us to switch to "justify" and "justification" (rather than the nonexistent "rightify" and "rightification").[28] *Justify* and *justification,* then, refer to the process of making a person righteous.

But there is a further linguistic problem here in that this phraseology can refer to two distinguishable activities. On the one hand, it could refer to changing the character of a person with evil motives and actions so that he or she thinks and acts in a righteous way. Sometimes the term "a righteous person" is used more of people who are of such a character that they can be expected to do righteous actions from righteous motives. On the other hand, the phraseology could refer to changing the verdict on a person who has done wrong and declaring that the person is righteous despite the wrong he or she has done. There is general agreement that when Paul uses the verb *justify* he is referring to this latter action of declaring a wrongdoer to be nevertheless in the right with God rather than to the action of changing a person's character so that the person begins to act righteously. Paul is talking about how people who have done wrong in God's sight can be accepted by him as righteous in the sense that he no longer holds the wrong against them and establishes a positive relationship with them. Thus the term *righteous* comes to convey the idea of being in a right relationship with God. But at the same time it is obvious that even if this is what the verb means, it is not enough for God simply to forgive past failures; somehow there must also take place a change in the character of persons so that they do become righteous in their motives and

---

[28]Kendrick Grobel experimented with the verb "to rightwise" in his English translation of Rudolf Bultmann's *New Testament Theology,* and Martyn has adopted "rectify" and "rectification", which to my mind carry rather too much of their scientific overtones and are less personal.

actions.[29] So the question arises whether justification is in effect nothing more than forgiveness and does not do something to the character of those justified.[30]

Paul's assumption here as in Romans is that apart from Christ nobody has this righteous status with God. He did not need to argue this in the case of the Gentiles. His main problem was with Jews who assumed that the law was their means of obtaining such a status. Consequently the motif of justification appears mainly in those letters where this problem arises.

*The cross and its effects.* Paul's argument depends on the fact accepted by both himself and his readers, though not necessarily by the Judaizers, that the death of Christ really does save completely from sins. He states that Christ did something that has the effect of delivering people from their existing situation. That situation is expressed in terms of "deliverance from this present evil age", "redeeming us from the curse of the law" and "redeeming those under the law", to which we may add deliverance from being "under the control of sin" (Gal 3:22). It goes without saying that Paul here has in mind the fact that Christ suffered death.[31] Later he describes how the Son of God became a human being and was born "under the law" so that he could deliver people who were under the law (Gal 4:4-5). Although it is not said directly here, in the light of Galatians 3:6 another way of putting the result of Christ's death is to say that as a result of it righteousness is "credited" to people who believe. "Righteousness"

---

[29]The term *righteous* can have various shades of meaning. Paul takes it for granted that nobody is righteous as it were "by nature": all have sinned. He is therefore especially concerned with the question of people's relationship to God or their status in his eyes and how it is possible for people who are not righteous in their motives or deeds to be accounted by God as righteous. Hence the emphasis on the justification of the ungodly. But Paul is also concerned that people should actually be righteous and do righteousness. Hence for Paul the concept of being righteous oscillates between having a status in which God does not condemn us (because the problem of our unrighteousness has been dealt with) and thinking and acting in a righteous way.

[30]As we have seen, Esler, *Galatians*, p. 167, wants to interpret this language primarily as a means of expressing privileged identity. The "righteous" have "a desirable set of qualities and gifts and a desirable destiny". This may well be true, but it does not require that we abandon the important theological significance of the terms. It is a weakness in Esler's treatment that he virtually ignores the evidence of Romans for Paul's usage of the terms.

[31]It is important that Paul simply assumes the significance of the death of Jesus. In Gal 2:15-16 he comments that this is common ground with other Christians. Consequently, the basic understanding of salvation through the death of Jesus as a means of redemption from sin must have been attained at a date prior to the writing of this letter.

here means the status of not being guilty.[32]

Redemption means deliverance achieved at a cost, and it is most naturally understood as delivering people from the curse or judgment that they are under because they have not kept the law. In what is perhaps the clearest New Testament statement of what is generally called "substitution", Paul says that people who stand under the curse (Gal 3:10) are delivered from that curse because Christ has delivered them by himself coming under the curse.[33] For Paul it is evidently possible for somebody else to suffer the effects of a curse on behalf of lawbreakers and to release them from the consequences that would otherwise fall on them. This raises two problems.

First, is it possible for the curse imposed upon one person to be borne by somebody else in place of them? Can the curse of the law, or, in our phraseology, the guilt due to sin, be transferred? Guilt here means liability to judgment because of sin, and the problem is whether this liability can be undertaken by somebody else. For Paul it clearly was not a problem. He obviously saw no problem in the rescue of one person by another, particularly when this action springs out of love. Such an act of rescue could endanger the life of the rescuer, as when somebody rescues a drowning person from a dangerous sea and perishes in so doing. Christ did something analogous to this in that he became a human being and himself lived under the law. His mission was to redeem people from being under the law and its curse. Consequently, Paul's thought seems to be not so much of transfer of guilt as rather of deliverance from a power that holds us in its grip.[34] Later he develops the concept of Christ as becoming one with the human race by being born of woman and being born under the law (Gal 4:4-5). He sees no difficulty in one person identifying closely with a group and then rep-

---

[32] At least from the Reformation onward it has been common to interpret this positively by speaking of the righteousness of Christ being "imputed" to the sinner. But whether it is the righteous status of Christ that is actually attributed to the sinner here in Galatians is not altogether clear. The point will recur in discussion of Rom 4:3 (see p. 312 n. 10) and 2 Cor 5 (see p. 296); cf. Phil 3:9.

[33] By this time the recognition had developed that the deaths of outstanding individuals as martyrs could deliver the nation from the divine wrath that was conspicuously evident from time to time (4 Macc 17:21). Hence the way was open for Christians to assert that Jesus perfectly fulfilled this kind of role in virtue of who he was, namely the Messiah and the Son of God.

[34] Nevertheless, elsewhere he does hold that we are guilty before God and liable to his wrath. Perhaps surprisingly there is no mention of his wrath in Galatians.

resentatively bearing the curse for them.[35]

A second apparent difficulty is that the fact that somebody else became a curse for the wrongdoer may do nothing to change the attitude or character of the wrongdoer, for example, by inducing feelings of remorse for the wrong action or a resolve not to do it again. It is not surprising that some people have felt that substitution of one person for another in this way is immoral and have therefore questioned whether this is Paul's rationale. Three points may be made in response.

The first is to remind ourselves that what Paul is talking about here is something that becomes effective only when people have faith. Although the term is often used absolutely without an object (Gal 3:22), it is clear that it is faith in God (Gal 3:6) or Christ (Gal 2:16) that is meant. Sometimes Paul speaks of "faith in Jesus Christ" (literally "the faith of Jesus Christ"; Gal 2:16, 20; 3:22). However, an important contemporary interpretation of Paul's words is that this phrase should be interpreted as "the faithfulness displayed by Jesus Christ". On this view believers are justified and saved by appropriating the faith[fullness] of Christ rather than by fulfilling the works required by the law. But it is difficult to see how this notion would function in Paul's argument: in what sense was Christ faithful to God or how did Christ put his faith in him in a way that is relevant to the argument?[36]

The second point is a reminder that earlier Paul says that he has been "crucified with Christ" (Gal 2:20). The implication of this is that Paul has somehow shared in the death of Jesus on the cross, which was the event in which he became a curse. Consequently, Paul does not see the death of Jesus merely as the death of another person, which God as the lawgiver accepts in place of the death of the sinner. Rather he sees the death of Jesus as a death that includes the sinner who is crucified with Christ; the "gospel" element is that the sinner is counted to have died, although he or she has not in fact suffered death as a penalty with all its pain and receives life. And the effect of this

---

[35]Transfer of guilt is not part of Paul's language, but he expresses something very like it in 2 Cor 5:21.

[36]For the case for this interpretation see especially Richard B. Hays, *The Faith of Jesus Christ: An Investigation of the Narrative Substructure of Galatians 3:1–4:11* (Chico, Calif.: Scholars Press, 1983; rev. ed., Grand Rapids, Mich.: Eerdmans; Dearborn, Mich.: Dove Booksellers, 2002), and Bruce W. Longenecker, *Triumph*; for the argument against it see James D. G. Dunn, *The Theology of Paul the Apostle* (Grand Rapids, Mich.: Eerdmans, 1998), pp. 379-85. See further pp. 336-37.

death is that they have "crucified" their sinful flesh with its desires (Gal 5:24).

Third, this close relationship is also expressed by statements about believers being "in Christ" or being "baptized into Christ" (Gal 3:27-28), phraseology which in at least some of its occurrences denotes a very close relationship between believers and Christ. The charge, therefore, that substitution allows people to avoid the judgment on their sin without any real change on their part being involved is sufficiently refuted. The nature of faith is such that it unites a person with Christ in a very real way.

*Paul's message and the Jewish Scriptures: Abraham.* To a great extent the development of Paul's argument depends upon an appeal to what Scripture teaches about Abraham. There are two features about this argument that may cause difficulty.

The first is concerned with the promise that all the nations would be blessed through Abraham. Part of what Paul means is that God will justify the Gentiles in the same way as Abraham, namely, by faith. The promises were made to Abraham and his descendants, specifically the descendants through Isaac, but Paul knows that the promise included the Gentiles. He therefore has to conclude that the descendants are the people who share the character of Abraham as believers in God, regardless of whether they are physically his offspring or not; believing Gentiles are included, whereas unbelieving physical descendants are excluded. By using the term in a nonliteral sense Paul can assert that Jewish and Gentile believers are included in the one offspring or "seed" of Abraham; the language speaks of "seed" (singular), not "seeds" (plural).

But second, the way in which Paul reaches this conclusion is not clear until we note that the formulation of the promise in Genesis 22:18 is "through your offspring all nations on earth will be blessed". When Paul says in Galatians 3:14 "that the blessing given to Abraham might come to the Gentiles through Jesus Christ", he may well be echoing and interpreting this text. Paul further interprets the term *seed* (singular) to refer to one individual who is "Christ". It is often held that the attempt to tie down the term to refer to one person is vulnerable to the comment that "seed" (singular) could equally well be a collective noun referring to Abraham's descendants generally. This objection can be overcome when we remember that by "Christ" here Paul means "the Christian community composed of Jews and Gentiles" who are "one in Christ" (Gal 3:28; cf. I Cor 12:12) and are the "body of Christ". Consequently, in Galatians 3:29 it is precisely because the readers belong to Christ that they are collectively the seed of Abraham. The church is understood as the new Israel of God (Gal 6:16), composed as it is of Jews and Gentiles who accept Jesus as the Messiah.[37]

One way of expressing what is going on in Galatians is to say that Paul is concerned with the problem of identity and deals with it in a radical way by asserting a new Christian identity that is distinct from how the Judaizers wished to understand it. Christian believers are the seed of Abraham in view of their sharing Abraham's faith by believing in Christ (of which baptism was the outward sign) and by living a life in the Spirit that issues in "faith working through love".[38]

***Paul's message and the Jewish Scriptures: The law.*** For Paul nothing more was needed than this in order to be justified. He makes a contrast between believing in Christ and doing what the law requires; he tells the Galatians that they are trying to be justified by the law (Gal 5:4) and that they should know that "a person is not justified by observing the law" (Gal 2:16). God's blessings come by faith, not by observing the law. The expression "observing the law" is literally "by the works of the law", which means "doing what the law requires".[39] So evidently the Judaizers thought that justification was by doing what the law requires. Paul simply saw Jews and Gentiles alike as in need of justification (because all have sinned) and insisted that the only way was through faith in Christ, and not through observing the law.

But why is justification not by the works of the law? Here Paul is difficult.

---

[37] The interpretation of Gal 6:16 is disputed. Nowhere else does Paul refer to the church as "Israel", although he comes near to it in Rom 9:6, where he distinguishes the "real" Israel from the nation of Israel. Consequently some scholars argue (less probably in my view) that here the reference is to pious Jews or to Jewish Christians; see the discussion in Bruce, *Galatians*, pp. 273-75.

[38] Cf. John M. G. Barclay, *Obeying the Truth: A Study of Paul's Ethics in Galatians* (Edinburgh: T & T Clark, 1988), pp. 93-94.

[39] The Hebrew equivalent of this phrase has turned up in the Qumran document 4QMMT, where it refers to the detailed interpretation of the law to apply it to life. These works were not required to enter into the covenant (that was by birth followed by circumcision for males) but were essential for staying in. At Qumran, however, the position was ambiguous. Justification was by the grace of God to sinners, but doing the works of the law led to the reckoning of righteousness. Cf. briefly Martin G. Abegg Jr., in *DNTB*, pp. 709-11.

He insists that the law is not able to give life and was not meant to do so (Gal 3:21). But we can see why people thought that obedience to it would bring life. The law appears to promise life to those who keep it (Gal 3:12, citing the promise in Lev 18:5; also cited in Rom 10:5). Paul evidently accepts this, but he juxtaposes it with the comment that the righteous person will live by faith. He is convinced that the law cannot give life. Only the Spirit can give life, as he will affirm in 2 Corinthians 3:6. There is a fundamental difference between the law, which can only demand, and the Spirit, who can empower.

Two things need to be distinguished. The first is that the law laid down the kind of conduct required by God, and therefore life lay in following it. In that sense it was the doing of the law that led to life. The other thing is that the law was not able to give life, since there was nothing about it that enabled people to keep its commandments. People were thrown back on their own imperfect ability.

What Paul says may seem to go against the currently popular "new perspective" on Judaism as a religion of grace and election, in which people enter into salvation by God's grace rather than by keeping the law and merely keep the law in order to stay in or as a mark of belonging.

This current picture probably needs correction. Paul is making a revaluation of Judaism and stressing that God's election of Israel as a people is worth nothing if it does not issue in faith in Christ on the part of its members (Rom 9:4-5). Paul, like many other Jews of his time, held what we may call a remnant theology. On this view, whatever may be said in favor of "covenantal nomism"[40] with its assertion that all Jews were "in" the covenant through the grace of God, it was nevertheless recognized by some Jews that to greater or less extent the people were tainted with sin and apostasy and needed to get right with God by some kind of performance, usually by following the precepts of some particular teacher or group. The straightforward, orthodox way was to keep the law and so to be "righteous".[41]

In fact, Paul presupposes that all people, Jews and Gentiles, are in a situation

---

[40]This is the phrase used by E. P. Sanders, *Paul, the Law and the Jewish People* (Philadelphia: Fortress, 1983), to characterize his understanding of Judaism. See my discussion in chap. 18 (pp. 444-50).

[41]Mark A. Elliott, *The Survivors of Israel: A Reconsideration of the Theology of Pre-Christian Judaism* (Grand Rapids, Mich.: Eerdmans, 2000).

from which they need to be delivered; they are living in "the present evil age" (Gal 1:4).[42] From a Christian point of view, of course, there are blessings which they do not possess until they are saved, notably the reception of the Holy Spirit (Gal 3:14), sonship (inclusive of daughtership; Gal 4:5) and a promised inheritance (Gal 3:18, 22). But apart from that, so far as the Jews are concerned, they are evidently sinners and breakers of the law (Gal 2:17-18), and as breakers of the law they are under a curse (Gal 3:10). Something needs to be done to bring them salvation. It is easy to understand that fervent keeping of the law was seen to be necessary. Likewise, when we take non-Jews into account, the way into the Jewish people was by doing what the law laid down, namely, circumcision and all that followed it. Grace and works could thus go together, in that grace was inviting people to do certain things in order for Gentiles to get in and for Jews to stay in.

But if Paul insisted that justification was not by the law, this still leaves the question of the proper function of the law. It was enacted after Abraham in the time of Moses, and Paul's claim is that the coming of the law could not cancel the promise made to Abraham. We can agree in general that once a promise is made, it cannot or should not be cancelled unless there are some powerful reasons for doing so.

What, then, was the purpose of the law? For Paul states quite clearly that the Jews were placed under it. The answer given here would seem to be that by putting God's commands before people which they could not keep (as their history had shown), the law was pronouncing a condemnation upon them that should lead them to turn to Christ for justification by faith. The law was thus intended to act like the slave who was responsible for guiding children safely to school by directing people to their need for Christ. Throughout this period before Christ came, the Jews were certainly meant to keep the law, so far as they could. But this was a temporary function, and with the coming of Christ believers are no longer under the supervision of the law. The law can be understood as God's provision for his people by which they were to live until Christ came. But justification is on the basis of

---

[42]Cf. Longenecker, *Triumph*, pp. 35-58. Some recent writers, especially N. T. Wright, *The New Testament and the People of God* (London: SPCK, 1992), pp. 268-71, also claim that Paul was taking up the view that Israel was still in exile, from which Christ was the deliverer; cf. James M. Scott, ed., *Exile: Old Testament, Jewish and Christian Conceptions* (Leiden: E. J. Brill, 1997).

faith in Jesus Christ and not by the works of the law. Evidently the teaching of Paul's opponents was that works of the law were still required, presumably alongside faith in Christ. But Paul argues that if the law is taken as the way to life, then full obedience is still required (Paul's interpretation of Lev 18:5). People who do not keep the law are under a curse (Gal 3:10, citing Deut 27:26). It follows that the law was never intended as the way to life (Gal 3:21).

It would seem that what Paul is trying to say is that it is the misuse of the law as a means of justification that is the problem, and this misuse is not inherent in the law but is due an interpretation put upon it. The real purpose of the law is given in Galatians 3:19: it was meant to take care of Israel presumably by keeping them from sinning and by providing the means of atonement until Christ came.

All of this raises a number of further problems to which it is not too easy to give answers.

First, how were people saved or how did they become righteous during the period of the law, and why did God introduce this temporary measure? Paul appears to suggest that faith came only when Christ came. He speaks of the period "before faith came", as if the intervening period was not one of faith. The time from the giving of the law to Moses at Sinai to the coming of Christ is regarded as a temporary period during which the way of faith is apparently suspended and obedience to the law is what matters. The position of Paul's readers is that they were under the law and under its curse until Christ came and delivered them (Gal 4:5). They were slaves bound to keep God's law. This is apparently true whether they were Jews or Gentiles who had not heard of God and worshiped idols. There is a parallelism between being under the law and being under the elements of the world. It was the principle in the time of Abraham, but during the period of the law it does not seem to have been an option until it reappeared with the coming of Christ.

But it is very hard to believe that Paul meant this, since his appeal to David as a witness to justification by faith in Romans 4 suggests that he was well aware of the principle being alive during the period of the law. And did Paul interpret the statement in Habakkuk 2:4 as a strict future or as a logical future? It seems that Paul is thinking specifically of faith *in Christ* as the means of justification, although he clearly holds that Abraham was justified by faith.

Second, it is perhaps surprising that Paul does not refer directly here to the fact that the Jews had an elaborate sacrificial system provided under the law for dealing with sins, and at the time of writing Galatians this system continued to operate. Why, then, was anything else required? When Paul says that justification is not possible through the law, is he saying that the sacrificial system did not effect anything? There is almost total silence on this point in Paul. He does take up the imagery of sacrifice and apply it to Jesus in Romans 3, and he also comments there that God passed over sins committed in the past on the basis of the sacrifice of Christ; so it may be that Paul believed that the sacrifices "worked" for the Jews because of God's "passing over" of sins. He apparently regarded judgment as suspended because of the sacrifice of Christ (this seems to be the point of Rom 3:25), but in Galatians the point is not cleared up.[43] He could have said that the sacrifices worked during the era of the law but are now obsolete since Christ has come.[44]

Paul, then, does not specifically discuss how people were justified before the coming of Christ. He presumably believed that they were forgiven for their transgressions of the law by the means provided in the law, namely, the sacrificial system. When he refers to the law as something that could not give life, he may be thinking of circumcision and the festivals and other requirements (such as purity laws) and not of the sacrificial system at the temple (which he never mentions), or he may be arguing that the law simply pointed forward to the coming of Christ, in virtue of which people who believed might be saved even though Christ had not yet come. Or again he may have believed that the sacrificial system could cope only with unwitting sins and not with deliberate disobedience.

Third, what place, if any, has the law in the life of the believer? Paul has already denied that it is necessary to keep the law—focused in circumcision and the keeping of Jewish festivals—in order to be justified. He has argued that the law had a role in the past until Christ came, but Christ has done something that

---

[43]Here in Galatians Paul may be implicitly making a distinction between the sacrifices as a God-given means of atonement separate from the law and the works of the law carried out by individual Jews as a means of justification.

[44]This is the answer supplied by the writer to the Hebrews, and it may well have been shared by other Christians.

has changed the situation. The solution appears to be that he sees the law as brought to completion by Christ in the single command given in the Torah, "You shall love your neighbor as yourself" (Gal 5:14; cf. Rom 13:8-10),[45] and he commands his readers to use their freedom from the law to keep that commandment in the power of the Spirit. For Paul the commandment to love (and all the commandments that are summed up in it) retain their validity for believers. In effect, the various commands in the law can be seen as the applications of that single command, and therefore it is perfectly possible for Paul to go back to them and cite them approvingly.

It would seem, therefore, that when Paul talks about dying to the law, he must mean dying to the Mosiac law as a means of justification. To fulfill the love command in the freedom given by the Spirit is not a means of gaining life and righteousness but an expression of the fact that one has them. Some scholars, to be sure, argue that in Paul's mind the law had no continuing validity for believers, but this will hardly stand in view of his positive affirmations of it in Romans; it remains as something that is taken up into the law of Christ.[46]

The matter would be eased if we could find evidence that Paul made a distinction between the moral and ritual aspects of the law. Was it primarily the latter that he had in mind when he talked of justification by the works of the law? Certainly it is circumcision and festivals that he specifically mentions in this context. But it has to be admitted that he does not distinguish very clearly between the moral commandments in the law and those which are concerned with the ritual aspects of the Jews' relationship with God.

*The Spirit.* Finally, we must consider the role of the Holy Spirit. If the cross predominates in Galatians 1—3, the Spirit predominates in Galatians 4—6. Indeed, the only references to the Spirit in the first half of the letter are in Galatians 3:1-5, 14. Here Paul bases part of his argument on an appeal to the readers' experience of the Spirit that had taken place before the Judaizers had come on the scene and they had begun to flirt with keeping the law. They had not been required to keep the law in order for God to give manifestations of

---

[45]Martyn, *Theological Issues,* pp. 233-49.

[46]I see no reason to believe that Paul underwent a substantial change of mind between Galatians and Romans.

the Spirit in the congregations. The reception of the Spirit is understood to be the blessing of Abraham, that is, the blessing promised to Abraham, which comes to the Gentiles through the redemption wrought by Christ.

For Paul the difference between those under the law and those under grace is that the former are like slaves and the latter are like sons and daughters to God. Their new status is ascribed to two factors. On the one hand, they become children of God through faith in Christ (Gal 3.26). Faith is expressed in the act of baptism. Baptism is "into Christ", which appears to mean that through this act the person is brought into a spiritual relationship with Christ, which can also be expressed in terms of being clothed with Christ. On the other hand, God sends the Spirit of his Son into the hearts of his children. This appears to mean that the Spirit is sent in response to faith and that the Spirit then makes the status of sonship effective by enabling believers to address God as their Father.[47] Elsewhere the Spirit can be described as a seal that confirms God's ownership of his people, and this is not so different from what is said here. Here the stress is more on the assurance that the Spirit gives to believers that God is now their Father.

The Spirit is also connected with the hope of righteousness in Galatians 5:5; the thought is that people who are being made righteous by the Spirit here and now have the hope of final justification from God.

The fullest and most important passage about the Spirit is Galatians 5:16-25, where the Spirit who has been given to believers desires that certain qualities be produced in their lives; the Spirit can be thought of as a life-giving principle that creates "fruit", specific results which are identified as the practice of various types of Christian conduct—the demonstration of love, joy, peace and so on. Believers are to let the Spirit do these things in their lives.

But what about the contrasting list of activities which are ascribed to the "flesh" of believers, that is, to their existing, sinful character? These things are contrary to the law, and therefore they fall under the category of prohibitions to be obeyed under the law and also under the new era of grace. But the law cannot help people to refrain from them; it can only tell them what not to do. The implication is that the Spirit not only produces in people the positive

---

[47]The alternative is that it is the Spirit who makes people believers, but this does not seem to be what Paul says here or in Rom 8.

fruits of character (which are not prohibited by the law)[48] but also enables them to keep the prohibitions. Paul, however, puts the point differently by saying that believers have crucified the flesh and its desires. He sees the crucifixion of the believer with Christ as including a death to sinful desires; the dead person is dead to all stimuli, including temptations to do wrong actions.

## Conclusion

Implicit in the gospel that is at the heart of Galatians is an understanding of Jesus as the Son of God sent into the world to redeem people from the curse of the law, and of God's Spirit sent into the hearts of believers to make them children of God. But what we might call the ontology of the Son and the Spirit is not in itself an object of enquiry and exposition. These were apparently not disputed issues in this context; there is a clear, fully formed, understanding of who Jesus is that must have been shared by Paul and his readers, but it is not discussed for its own sake. Equally undisputed is the way in which the coming of the Spirit to all believers can be taken for granted. The theological argument is concerned with other, controversial issues.

## Bibliography

*New Testament Theologies:* (English) Childs, pp. 297-310. (German) Hübner, 2:57-111.

Barclay, John M. G. *Obeying the Truth: A Study of Paul's Ethics in Galatians.* Edinburgh: T & T Clark, 1988.

Barrett, C. K. *Freedom and Obligation: A Study of the Epistle to the Galatians.* London: SPCK, 1985.

Bassler, Jouette M., ed. *Pauline Theology.* Vol. I. *Thessalonians, Philippians, Galatians, Philemon.* Minneapolis: Fortress, 1994 (articles by J. D. G. Dunn, B. R. Gaventa and J. L. Martyn).

Belleville, Linda L. " 'Under Law': Structural Analysis and the Pauline Concept of Law in Galatians 3.21 – 4.11". *JSNT* 26 (1986): 53-78.

Bruce, F. F. *The Epistle of Paul to the Galatians.* Exeter: Paternoster, 1982.

Ciampa, Roy E. *The Presence and Function of Scripture in Galatians 1 and 2.* Tübingen: Mohr Siebeck, 1998 (cf. his article in *NDBT*, pp. 311-15).

Dunn, James D. G. *The Theology of Paul's Letter to the Galatians.* Cambridge: Cambridge Uni-

---

[48]When Paul says this, he may be implying that the law does not tell people positively to show these qualities. But that would be to overlook the positive command to love that is contained in the law.

versity Press, 1993.

Esler, Philip F. *Galatians.* London: Routledge, 1998.

Hays, Richard B. *The Faith of Jesus Christ: An Investigation of the Narrative Substructure of Galatians 3:1–4:11.* Chico, Calif.: Scholars Press, 1983. Rev. ed., Grand Rapids, Mich.: Eerdmans; Dearborn, Mich.: Dove Booksellers, 2002.

Longenecker, Bruce W. *The Triumph of Abraham's God: The Transformation of Identity in Galatians.* Edinburgh: T & T Clark, 1998.

Longenecker, Richard N. *Galatians.* Dallas: Word, 1990.

Martyn, J. Louis. *Theological Issues in the Letters of Paul.* Edinburgh: T & T Clark, 1997.

Nanos, Mark. *The Irony of Galatians: Paul's Letter in First-Century Context.* Minneapolis: Fortress, 2002.

Sanders, E. P. *Paul, the Law and the Jewish People.* Philadelphia: Fortress, 1983.

Sloan, Robert B. "Paul and the Law: Why the Law Cannot Save". *NovT* 33 (1991): 35-60.

Witherington, Ben, III. *Grace in Galatia: A Commentary on St. Paul's Letter to the Galatians.* Edinburgh: T & T Clark; Grand Rapids, Mich.: Eerdmans, 1998.

# 9

# The Letters to the Thessalonians

There is universal agreement that Paul wrote the first of the two letters addressed to the church at Thessalonica, and probably a majority opinion at the present time that the second letter is by a later writer. I do not share this opinion of 2 Thessalonians,[1] but in order not to prejudge the issue we shall begin by considering the two letters separately.

## *1 Thessalonians*

First Thessalonians was written to a group of newly converted Christian believers who were probably drawn largely, but not exclusively, from the Gentile population of the town (cf. Acts 17:1-9). They do not appear to have been the target of the Judaizers who dominate the letter to the Galatians and consequently the tone of the letter is rather different. Paul's concern is much more to encourage a congregation that was suffering outside pressure to abandon their faith (1 Thess 3:5) and to develop their Christian way of life. There is also a major section about the problems caused by some misunderstanding regarding the parousia or future coming of the Lord. Thus the broad structure of the letter is comparatively straightforward.

---

[1]A significant supporter of Pauline authorship is Abraham J. Malherbe, *The Letters to the Thessalonians* (New York: Doubleday, 2000). Karl P. Donfried (and I. Howard Marshall), *The Theology of the Shorter Pauline Letters* (Cambridge: Cambridge University Press, 1993), assigns the letter to one of Paul's companions, probably Timothy.

***The theological story.*** *Paul's relationship with the congregation (1 Thess 1:1—3:13).* The first half of the letter is devoted to encouragement and forms an extended thanksgiving into which Paul weaves an account of his relationships with the congregation since it was founded. He is able to encourage them by reminding them of the reality of their conversion and of the way in which they had stood up to persecution. He describes at length the care and concern that his fellow missionaries and he had shown to them, both while they were in Thessalonica and then during the subsequent period when he sent Timothy to keep in touch with them.

Paul begins the letter with a prayer report (1 Thess 1) that serves to encourage his readers and express his confidence in them as he meditates on their conversion experience, which was characterized by Spirit-inspired preaching and Spirit-inspired response to the message (1 Thess 1:5, 6). Using phraseology that is probably based on the kind of things said by the missionaries, he outlines briefly the nature of their conversion from idolatry to serve the living God and their attitude of expectancy toward the future coming of Jesus who will rescue them from the coming wrath. Then in a closely related section (1 Thess 2:1-16) he goes on to comment more fully on the actions and motives of the missionaries as they brought the gospel to Thessalonica.

The major aim in this part of the letter is to give encouragement to believers who are under pressure to give up their faith. Paul refers to their experience of suffering and compares the situation of the readers with that of the congregations in Judea, where "the Jews" had killed Jesus and the prophets and driven out the apostles who wished to evangelize the Gentiles (1 Thess 2:12-16). This kind of action had accompanied Paul and his companions on their travels. It was often instigated by Jews, but not exclusively, and it was generally a matter of unofficial action rather than involving the official action of the appointed magistrates and other persons in civil authority, although they had to deal with cases when Christian believers were the subject of accusations to them. In the ancient world, where policing was much less efficient than in many modern countries, it was comparatively easy for people to take the law into their own hands.

Paul comments that this was something that he had told them would happen. His language suggests not simply that he could see on a human level that it was inevitably going to happen, but rather that it was something that was part of the destiny of believers (I Thess 3:3), in other words, something that God had willed or allowed to happen.[2] In this connection he reveals his belief in the activity of "Satan", a supernatural being opposed to God.

Meanwhile, one part of his response to it is to pray for the congregations. He prays specifically that he and his companions may be able to visit them and encourage them despite the obstacles (I Thess 3:10). He puts his prayers into words in the letter, sharing with the readers what he is praying for them (I Thess 3:11-13; 5:23-24) and asking them in turn to pray for him (I Thess 5:25).

The other part of his response is to encourage the readers. Despite the strength of the attacks, Paul is confident about them. They are standing firm "in the Lord" (I Thess 3:8). Because of this Paul can confidently encourage them to stand fast because they have superior power at their disposal (cf. I Thess 3:2-3).

*Instruction for the congregation (1 Thess 4:1—5:28).* The second half of the letter is then teaching for the church, the kind of things that Paul would have said if he had been able to visit the church. It falls into three parts. First, there is teaching on the need to grow in holiness and brotherly love (I Thess 4:1-12). Second, there is specific teaching about the worries that the congregation had about what would happen at the return of Christ; this reassurance about the resurrection of Christians who had already died merges into further encouragement to godly lives so that they are ready and waiting for the Lord when he comes (I Thess 4:13—5:11).

Finally, there are some practical instructions for their life together as a congregation (I Thess 5:12-28). Paul emphasizes the need for harmony and love, and also throws a brief flash of light on a congregation in which the Spirit was active through prophecy and other means (I Thess 5:19; cf. I Cor 12; 14).

*Theological themes. Mission and apostleship.* More directly perhaps than any other New Testament document, I Thessalonians arises out of the missionary work of Paul in that it is written to a group of fairly recent converts and bases its appeal to them in large measure on an account of how they became Christians. The story of their conversion is intended to encourage them to continue to believe despite the opposition that they were facing and which (if 2 Thess is also

---

[2]Admittedly he does not say this here in so many words (cf. Acts 14:22).

directed to them) was destined to become even fiercer.

The responsibility for encouraging people to become Christians rests on the apostles, people with a special commission from God to proclaim the good news; put at its simplest, an apostle is a missionary. The passage says a lot about the commitment of the missionaries to their work and their loving concern for their converts. Although this is written by one of them, the tone is far from any boasting or self-satisfaction about themselves and the quality of their work. Nevertheless, it emerges that the apostles could have made claims for themselves, presumably for their keep and travel, which could have been burdensome for the congregation—and have been within their rights in doing so—but they had refrained from doing so.

The task of the apostles was primarily speaking. Elsewhere, however, Paul talks about "the marks of a true apostle" (2 Cor 12:12) and indicates that the speaking was accompanied by miraculous signs such as are related in Acts (Gal 3:5). These appear to have been part of the experience of salvation, which could meet bodily and spiritual need and also served to accredit the missionaries. When Paul refers here to the coming of the gospel "also with power", the power may well have been manifested in miraculous signs.

While Paul emphasizes the importance of the work of the Holy Spirit in the task of evangelism, nevertheless he also stresses that it was through human words that God spoke, and it is clear that he was prepared to use the resources of rhetoric to persuade people to accept the message. This point must be made, of course, in the context of his general repudiation of human wisdom and rhetoric in I Corinthians 2:4-5, but nevertheless he must be measured by what he actually did as well as by what he said that he was doing.

*The gospel.* The content of the speaking is summed up as "the gospel" (I Thess 1:5; 2:2, 4, 8-9; 3:2). Originally meaning "good news", the word never loses this sense, but it tends to be defined more by its content than its character and becomes a term that refers primarily to the basic Christian message about Jesus Christ. This message is summed up in traditional language in I Corinthians 15:3-5, and it centered on the death and resurrection of Jesus. The death of Jesus is there stated to have taken place "for our sins" and, here in this letter, "for us", and its effect is that people receive salvation instead of experiencing the wrath of God (I Thess 5:9-10). The message is not discussed in any detail in this letter, presumably because it was not in dispute.

There is an apparent problem in that in I Corinthians the center of the gospel is clearly the past event of the death and resurrection of Jesus, whereas here in this letter the effect of conversion is that people wait for Jesus coming from heaven. Throughout the letter there is a stress on this event such as is not found elsewhere in the writings of Paul. This raises the question whether there was an earlier stage in Paul's thought when the future coming of Jesus[3] was more central in his theology than his death and resurrection.

This is probably not the case in view of two considerations. First, there is a category difference between the event that brings about salvation and the content of salvation. In this letter the death and resurrection of Jesus function as the basis for future hope (I Thess 4:14; 5:9-10), and in I Corinthians, where Paul emphasizes that the gospel is centered on the death and resurrection of Jesus (I Cor 15:3-5), he can also write at great length about the future resurrection of believers. The hypothesis of development thus rests partly on a misunderstanding of the different functions of the two events. The basis of the gospel is the death and resurrection of Jesus, but the content of the gospel includes the promise of the new age inaugurated by the parousia of Jesus.

Second, we may make some deductions from Paul's account of how the hearers responded to the message (I Thess 1:9-10). What they heard evidently included an assertion of the reality of the true God and of his Son (cf. I Cor 8:5-6) and a declaration of the resurrection of Jesus (cf. I Cor 15:3-5) and of his significance as a deliverer from the wrath to come (Rom 5:9). When Paul further affirms that Christians believe that Jesus died and rose again, that he is the source of salvation (I Thess 5:9) and that he died for them so that they might live together with him (I Thess 5:10), it can be taken for granted that these statements of common Christian belief rested on what he had preached to the Thessalonians. It is clear that the gospel preached to the Thessalonians is the same gospel as is reflected elsewhere in Paul's writings.

*Conversion.* The response to the gospel message is "turning to God". This is natural language to use of erstwhile pagans who had worshiped idols, less appropriate of Jews who already believed in God. But much more common is the

---

[3]This is often referred to by the transliterated Greek word *parousia* ("coming, arrival").

term *faith*, which signifies a complex of trust, commitment and obedience directed toward God and his Son, Jesus. Faith is referred to so often and so casually that it was clearly the principal mark of Christians in their relationship toward God. This is all the more remarkable in that while faith is also a characteristic attitude in the Old Testament and is not unknown in other religions, there does not appear to have been any other religion in which it was so central and characteristic that the term "the believers" could become the normal way of referring to the adherents.

It is quite possible to describe the process of conversion on a human level: apostles and their companions tell people about what God has done to save them through the death and resurrection of Jesus and urge them to have faith, and people respond to this message by an act of faith that is the starting point for a continuing relationship. It does not greatly alter the mechanics of the process when Paul claims that the message comes as the Word of God and not simply as a human message. But Paul also describes it as a process in which the Holy Spirit was operative in the proclamation of the message and in the reception of it: the converts welcomed the message with the joy given by the Holy Spirit. He can also comment on how the evidence that God has chosen the readers is to be seen in the way in which the gospel came to them and they responded to it.

Behind the conversion of the readers, then, there lies the initiative of God, expressed in terms of his "calling" of them (1 Thess 2:12; 4:7; 5:24). Paul also uses the term *election* or *choice* (1 Thess 1:4) to express the fact that the readers now belong to God as his people. It is customary to regard election as signifying the divine choice or selection that then issues in God's call to salvation,[4] but it appears to be the case that the term *elect* is always applied to those who have actually become members of God's people rather than to those whom God has predestined to salvation before they have actually received it. What Paul is referring to here is the fact that God's choice of the readers is seen in the way in which they have accepted the gospel.[5]

The effect of the preaching of the gospel and the conversions that ensued was the establishment of a "church" or congregation (1 Thess 1:1), a term

---

[4]Donfried, *Theology*, p. 29.
[5]I. Howard Marshall, "Election and Calling to Salvation in 1 and 2 Thessalonians", in *The Thessalonian Correspondence*, ed. R. F. Collins (Louvain: Louvain University Press, 1990), pp. 259-76.

that is significant in identifying the readers as standing in continuity with
the people of God in the Old Testament, although this thought is not developed here. The letter's chief concern is the spiritual progress of this community.

*Steadfastness.* Paul is particularly conscious in this letter of the activity of
Satan, alias "the tempter" (I Thess 3:5), who is also able to bend human
situations to achieve his evil purposes (I Thess 2:18). It is probably impossible to reduce Paul's conceptions here to simple terms; the picture is a complicated one in which Satan appears to have freedom to tempt people and
yet can be thwarted by the overriding power of God, but why God doesn't
simply defeat him once and for all is never asked; all that Paul knows is that
God can defeat his enemies and that one day he will do so completely (cf.
2 Thess).

The frequent references in the letter to prayer indicate that Paul believes that
situations and people are changed through prayer, the rationale obviously being
that God responds to what his people ask him to do.

So we have the paradoxical tension between the ways in which the perseverance of believers is simultaneously dependent on their own steadfastness and
on the activity of God. This is brought out in the description of them as
"standing firm in the Lord" (I Thess 3:8). This phrase indicates that their situation is to be seen from a higher than human angle. It expresses their reliance
on the Lord to keep them, and this reliance is well founded.

The note of being "in the Lord" runs through the letter, right from the beginning where in a striking phrase the church is said to be "in God the Father and the
Lord Jesus Christ" (I Thess 1:1; cf. 2 Thess 1:1; Col 3:3). This form of words is
a variant of the much more common "in Christ" and equivalent expressions (such
as "in him"). This distinctive phrase is characteristic of Paul from his earliest writings.[6] Sometimes it is simply the appropriate construction after a verb (I Thess
3:8). At other times it is used adverbially to characterize the close relationship between believers and Christ, and the way in which their lives must be determined
by him as the crucified and risen Lord (cf. I Thess 4:1; 5:12, 18). It is also used
more adjectivally with the same kind of force, but with the implication that there

---

[6]The use of this phrase in I Thessalonians is quite varied and does not suggest any immaturity or lack
of development in Paul's theological vocabulary. Cf. 2 Thess 1:1, 12; 3:4, 12.

is some kind of spiritual bond between the readers and Christ (1 Thess 2:14; 4:16).[7] Here the stress is on the basis of the believers' firm standing. They rest on God, on his promises and his power. The crucial point is the characterization of God as being faithful (1 Thess 5:24; cf. 2 Thess 3:3); this is a note that recurs explicitly in later letters (1 Cor 1:9; 10:13; 2 Cor 1:18) but underlies Paul's theology.

*Sanctification.* A further concern for the readers is summed up in this letter in the concept of holiness (1 Thess 4:1-12). This term can be used to signify the position or character that believers already have in that they are God's people and also the expression of that character as they grow and develop in their faith. All the soldiers on parade wear the uniform that marks them out as soldiers, but some are still raw recruits and others are trained and experienced, and the goal is all that become trained soldiers through and through and not simply in appearance. It is here that the biblical inspiration of Paul's theology is most marked in a letter that is singularly short of direct allusions to the Old Testament.[8] The development of holiness, it is clearly implied, is related to God's gift of the Holy Spirit to the readers.

The specific concept of holiness is more prominent in 1 Thessalonians than elsewhere in Paul (1 Thess 3:13; 4:3-4, 7; 5:23; cf. 2 Thess 2:13). Twice it is linked with blamelessness and expresses the condition that Paul prays will be that of the readers at the day of the Lord (1 Thess 3:13; 5:23). It is practically expressed in sexual purity, which is not understood (as it often was in the ancient world) as asceticism and abstinence from sexual relationships but rather as faithfulness in marriage and the absence of passionate lust (1 Thess 4:3-8).

Alongside holiness stand the three foundational facets of Christian character, faith, love and hope (1 Thess 1:3; cf. 5:8).[9] These form a traditional triad that recurs in the New Testament and sum up the relationships of believers to

---

[7]Similar language is used in John, but there it is often used reciprocally—believers are in Christ and he is in them. This appears to be more the language of close spiritual union.

[8]Max Turner, *The Holy Spirit and Spiritual Gifts* (Carlisle: Paternoster, 1996), pp. 108-10, has stressed that the wording of 1 Thess 4:8 reflects Ezek 36:27; 37:6, 14 and thus testifies to Paul's understanding of the Spirit as life-giving and re-creative. There is other phraseology based on the Old Testament in the letter, such as the use of "Lord" as a title for Jesus and the references to the "word of the Lord" (1 Thess 1:8; cf. Jer 1:4), the "day of the Lord" (1 Thess 5:2) and the "coming" of Christ (based ultimately on the OT hope of the coming of God in judgment and salvation (e.g., Is 40:10; Joel 3:14).

[9]Donfried, *Theology*, pp. 53-58.

God, other people and the future.[10] In this letter, broadly speaking, 1 Thessalonians 1—3 are concerned with faith, 1 Thessalonians 4:1-12 with love, and 1 Thessalonians 4:13—5:11 with hope. Faith is initially the attitude of acceptance of the reality of God and commitment to him that is the hallmark of conversion (1 Thess 1:8). But it is equally an ongoing attitude of trust and commitment based on the conviction that Jesus died and rose again (1 Thess 4:14), so much so that *believers* is an appropriate and characteristic term for referring to Christians (1 Thess 1:7; 2:10, 13). It is the continuation of their faith that matters to Paul (1 Thess 3:2, 5, 6-7, 10). Faith is closely linked with love (1 Thess 3:6; 5:8), but the latter term also stands on its own to express the attitude that believers should have to one another (1 Thess 4:9-10). Finally, the one Greek word also conveys the sense of "faithfulness" (cf. the way we talk of "keeping faith" with somebody), and with this particular nuance it expresses the character of God himself as utterly reliable (1 Thess 5:24).

*The resurrection and the parousia.* Of all the Pauline letters 1 Thessalonians and 2 Thessalonians stand out for the way in which they are dominated by the future. The content of conversion is that people not only serve God now but also wait for his Son to come from heaven (1 Thess 1:9-10). The missionaries' work in bringing them to faith will be recognized when the Lord comes (1 Thess 2:19-20), and their longing is that their converts will be blameless and holy at that time (1 Thess 3:13; 5:23). The letter contains the longest thematic section on the subject of any Pauline letter (1 Thess 4:13—5:11). The parousia is thus a significant sanction for Christian living in terms of reward and joy but also of destruction and judgment.

Paul assumes that some of his readers could be alive when the event takes place, and he seems to expect that this will in fact be the case. He uses the preacher's "we" in this connection, which includes himself as a possible member of the class (1 Thess 4:15, 17). Such an expectation, if seriously held, must have had a very powerful influence on the outlook of those who held it, even if it is hard for modern Christians to enter into it.[11]

---

[10]But they cannot be sharply separated; hope is an aspect of faith, and love can be directed to God and other people.

[11]The coming of Jesus has not, of course, taken place within the time that the early Christians envisaged. The first-century taunt that the lengthening delay was in fact to be interpreted as an indication that the hope was an empty one becomes all the more sharp as the years continue to go by. The New Testament writers, however, emphasize that nobody knows the time planned by God, and it has been ob-

Two thematic points control Paul's discussion. The first is the fear that some of the community who had already died or who might die in the interim would be at a disadvantage and be excluded from participation in the events surrounding the parousia. Paul's response is to insist that in fact living believers will come second, since those who died in Christ will be raised from the dead and will meet with the Lord before those still alive are caught up to meet him.[12] The language is apocalyptic in that it speaks in terms of a literal raising of the dead, an audible and presumably visible return of the Lord from heaven, and a literal rapture of believers to meet him "in the air". From the way in which Paul writes it seems that the readers were familiar with the concept of the parousia but that somehow they were not familiar with the concept of the resurrection of believers who had died.[13] Paul, therefore, had to reassure them by stressing that if people had "fallen asleep" while being in a relationship with Christ, it surely followed that when Christ returned they would be wakened and would be with him; just as he had died and was resurrected, so too would they. The sounding of the trumpet seems to represent pictorially the summons of the angel to God's chosen people to assemble together, and it is assumed that the call goes to the dead as well as to the living.

The second point in Paul's discussion is concerned with the timing of the event and the need for readiness for it. Paul believed that the parousia would naturally come as a surprise to people who were not waiting for it and did not believe that it would happen; consequently, they would not be ready for it, and it would come unwelcomely to them as judgment. But Christians who knew that it would happen would not be taken by surprise, that is to say, although they might be surprised by the unexpected arrival at a time that could not be precisely forecast, they would be ready and prepared for it. Instead of it coming like a thief in the night, it would be more like the ring at the door by the taxi

---

served that nobody ever delimited the time period within which the parousia must take place (Arthur L. Moore, *The Parousia in the New Testament* [Leiden: E. J. Brill, 1966]).

[12] Paul bases his statement on a saying (lit. "word") of the Lord (1 Thess 4:15). This is understood by perhaps a majority of commentators to be a reference to a prophetic utterance (whether to Paul or to somebody else), but I prefer the view that it is an allusion to teaching by the earthly Jesus.

[13] No fully convincing explanation of this has yet been offered, but all preachers know that sometimes a congregation can fail to take in what they think they have explained clearly. If the Thessalonian Christians were expecting the parousia as a genuine imminent possibility, then the deaths of some of their number could easily have baffled them, so that they were not able to come to terms with the situation and apply what they had learned to it.

driver for people who are already dressed with their bags packed. Therefore, the practical point is that Christians should always be in a state of spiritual readiness, so that they will not be ashamed to meet their Lord.

## 2 Thessalonians

In many ways the content of the second letter ostensibly addressed by Paul to the same congregation is similar to that in the first letter, and there are notable echoes in the wording. If the letter was not written shortly afterward by Paul, it was written by somebody who had steeped himself in 1 Thessalonians and was using it as a quarry. Three main theological interests dominate the letter and shape its structure.

*The church under persecution (2 Thess 1:1-12)*. The letter begins with the spiritual state of the readers who are presented as making growth in the three areas that were considered important in the first letter, faith, love and steadfastness, despite the fact of continuing attacks on them from outside. This circumstance leads straight into a theological discussion of persecution with regard to the persecuted and those who attacked them. It has to be remembered that we are observing a situation in which people could be in genuine fear for their lives and property because of their Christian profession, and it was not exaggerated to compare their position with that of Jesus (1 Thess 2:14-16).

It is therefore not surprising that Paul could speak of God judging those who were hostile to his people and regarding them as fit only to be cast out from his presence when it came to the day of judgment. Again, therefore, we observe that the concept of judgment on unbelievers is a basic plank in Paul's theology. It is counterbalanced by his belief in the very different destiny of Christians. They will in effect be recompensed for their sufferings by being given relief from them and by sharing in the glory of the risen Christ. Thus the wrong done by the persecutors is righted by both the punishment of the offenders and the recompense of the sufferers.

With this hope in mind, it is natural that Paul should pray for the believers so that they may not be tempted away from their faith but may rather live in such a way that they will obtain the promised recompense, or as he puts it, so that the way in which they live will redound to the credit of Christ and also lead to their sharing in his glory (2 Thess 1:5-12).

*The day of the Lord (2 Thess 2:1-17)*. The second concern of the letter is that some of the congregation were being led to believe that the coming of Jesus was very near, that they were living in "the day of the Lord", by which Paul means that climactic period of history in which the parousia was about to take place. Having read I Thessalonians, we can readily appreciate how hopes of an imminent future crisis and climax could easily have been fuelled so that people felt able to affirm that they really were living "in the last time". Consequently, Paul had to disabuse them of false hopes. In what is perhaps the most cryptic passage in the Pauline letters, he states that despite all that has been said about the day of the Lord coming unexpectedly and soon, nevertheless the coming of Christ must be preceded by other events that (it is implied) had not yet happened. There will be some kind of "rebellion" and the rise of a powerful opponent to God who will deceive people into unbelief. At present, the letter says, this opponent has not yet appeared because of some kind of restraining power. We need not attempt to identify more precisely what Paul was talking about. For our purpose it is sufficient to observe that somehow or other he claimed to know the rough order and nature of future events. Presumably he or somebody else claimed insight from a prophetic revelation, just as Jesus had spoken in a broadly similar way about the future.

There is thus the belief that the future course of events is known to God and that he may reveal aspects of it to people. The importance of prophecy must not be underestimated. For the early Christians the course of the struggle between God and his adversaries is mapped out, but not yet fully revealed, and it is against this background that they live their Christian lives.

The author and the readers of this letter evidently see nothing strange in this excursion from what we would regard as normal discourse into this mode of apparently fanciful description. We would like to know how literally they understood it. The only part of the story that gets beyond what could be literal is the splendor of the coming of Christ with a powerful breath in his mouth to destroy enemies like a dragon in fable. A man taking his seat on a throne in a temple and producing counterfeit miracles that take people in is perfectly conceivable, and such things have happened.

Over against this picture of people deceived by the power of Satan, which is a Pauline motif found elsewhere (2 Cor 4:3-4), we have the situation of Christian believers who are assured of God's choice of them to be saved. Their salvation has come about through the work of God's Spirit (cf. I Thess 1:5-6) and at the same

time through their belief in the "truth", the gospel message. Therefore they can
be encouraged to stand firm in their faith and not to be swayed by teachings that
are contrary to those of Paul. Once again, as in I Thessalonians the paradox of
divine protection and the need for human perseverance is sharply put.

*The place of prayer (2 Thess 3:1-18).* The third part of the letter is concerned
with practical aspects of the life of the church and its mission. Of theological significance is Paul's request for prayer for himself and his work. Again the paradox
is present: he is confident of the faithfulness and protecting power of God (2
Thess 3:3), and yet he requests prayer for the progress of the mission and for his
own safety (2 Thess 3:1-2). Equally he expresses confidence that his readers will
remain faithful and yet prays to God to enable them to persevere (2 Thess 3:4-5).

## The Character of the Theology

*The absence of major motifs.* The theology of I Thessalonians is marked out by its
comparative simplicity compared with that of the so-called Hauptbriefe, the
principal letters of Paul (Rom; I—2 Cor; Gal), but it is in no way inconsistent
with them. The features to which I have drawn attention are constants that we
shall find to be paralleled elsewhere in Paul. The differences emerge when we
observe the features that are missing or play little part, such as the Pauline vocabulary of flesh, body, sin, circumcision, law, works, righteousness/justifica-
tion, and the concept of dying and rising with Christ. But much of this vocabulary is associated with the struggle of Paul against opposition from so-called
Judaizers, who insisted on the need for Gentiles to keep the law in order to be
truly part of God's people, and there is a good case that the development of
these themes in other letters is an outworking of the basic Pauline understanding of salvation which is presented in this letter. There is, therefore, no real
problem about fitting I Thessalonians into Paul's correspondence in between
the other letters.[14]

We have noted the strategic position that is occupied by the motif of the
parousia and the associated future judgment; although not absent from Paul's
other letters, it is not so prominent as it is here. But, as we have noted already,

---

[14]The standard explanation is that Paul wrote I Thessalonians early in his career, before he had de-
veloped his thought fully. See, for example, Udo Schnelle, *The History and Theology of the New Testament
Writings* (London: SCM Press, 1998), pp. 50-55. Cf. Karl P. Donfried, *Paul, Thessalonica and Early
Christianity* (London: T & T Clark, 2002), pp. 69-98.

this does not mean that it was the central concept of the gospel; rather it was the inescapable horizon within which the Christians live. The essential elements of life in Christ in the here and now are integral to Paul's theology in the letter.

*Differences between 1 and 2 Thessalonians.* The scale of our discussion in this book does not permit detailed treatment of the subtle differences that some scholars have found between 1 and 2 Thessalonians. The key points are

1. It is argued that in 2 Thessalonians the parousia is preceded by signs and is not imminent, whereas in 1 Thessalonians it takes the world by surprise and could occur at any time.

2. It is argued that 2 Thessalonians appeals to "Paul's" teaching and example in an un-Pauline way.

3. The delay of the parousia has given rise to doubt and to a loss of any sense of mission in 2 Thessalonians.

4. The picture of Jesus emphasizes judgment and remoteness.[15]

These points are all dubious and incapable of substantiation. The second letter reflects a situation in which people had been sorely tested by persecution, and the picture of Jesus emphasizes his role as judge precisely because of this situation.[16] If Paul is reacting to an extremist misinterpretation of his teaching in the earlier letter, it is not surprising that he has to emphasize the fact that the signs of the times have been misread.

*Significant characteristics.* A number of themes receive special emphasis in these two letters.

First, there is the strong future orientation. One can understand the thematizing of the topic in view of the misunderstanding and questions in the church, but quite apart from that the parousia occupies a central place in Paul's under-

---

[15]Cf. E. Krentz, "Through a Lens: Theology and Fidelity in 2 Thessalonians", in *Pauline Theology*, vol. I, *Thessalonians, Philippians, Galatians, Philemon*, ed. Jouette M. Bassler (Minneapolis: Fortress, 1994), pp. 56-57, on the concentration on this aspect of the role of Jesus. See, however, Robert Jewett, "A Matrix of Grace. The Theology of 2 Thessalonians as a Pauline Letter", in 1:63-70, for some balancing considerations.

[16]On the authenticity of 2 Thessalonians see also John M. G. Barclay, "Conflict in Thessalonica", *CBQ* 55 (1993): 512-30, who suggests that the church saw current disaster as the manifestation of God's wrath (the day of the Lord) against their persecutors and drew false conclusions about the imminence of the parousia that Paul had to counter sharply.

standing of the Christian life (1 Thess 1:10; 2:19; 3:13; 5:23). This stress is quite different from the virtual absence of the concept in Galatians. Part of the reason for this absence is undoubtedly the concentration on the problems of the law and the Spirit in Galatians, where there is much less reflection of the character of the gospel as preached to Gentiles and of the prayers of Paul for the spiritual progress of his converts and the development of the mission.

A second theme is that of holiness as the preferred term for expressing that quality that God wishes to bring about in his people. This may be tied up with the predominantly Gentile character of the church; the inclusion of former Gentiles in a Christian movement that was firmly rooted in Judaism required that their lifestyle was thoroughly acceptable within that environment. The example of the church in Corinth demonstrates how difficult it could be to set aside ways of life that were acceptable enough among non-Christian Gentiles (1 Thess 4:5) but that were unacceptable in a church that was powerfully influenced by the spirituality and morality of Judaism.

Third, there is the missionary context of both letters with the frequent allusions to the conversion of the readers and to the ongoing mission of Paul in other places for which he seeks their prayers. The mission and the resulting conversions take place despite considerable opposition, but Paul's faith in the Lord as the one responsible for the mission gives him confidence that it will be successful.

### Bibliography

*New Testament Theologies:* (German) Hübner, 2:41-56, 376-77.

Barclay, John M. G. "Conflict in Thessalonica". *CBQ* 55 (1993): 512-30.

Bassler, Jouette M. "Peace in All Ways: Theology in the Thessalonian Letters: A Response to R. Jewett, E. Krentz, and E. Richard". In *PT* I, pp. 71-85.

Bassler, Jouette M., ed. *Pauline Theology.* Vol. I. *Thessalonians, Philippians, Galatians, Philemon.* Minneapolis: Fortress, 1994. (abbreviated as *PT* I).

Bruce, F. F. *1 and 2 Thessalonians.* Waco, Tex.: Word, 1982.

Collins, Raymond F. *Studies on the First Letter to the Thessalonians.* Louvain: Louvain University Press, 1984.

Collins, Raymond F., ed. *The Thessalonian Correspondence.* Louvain: Louvain University Press, 1990.

Donfried, Karl P. (and I. Howard Marshall). *The Theology of the Shorter Pauline Letters.* Cambridge: Cambridge University Press, 1993), pp. 1-113.

Donfried, Karl P. *Paul, Thessalonica* and *Early Christianity*. London: T & T Clark, 2002.

Jewett, Robert. "A Matrix of Grace. The Theology of 2 Thessalonians as a Pauline Letter". In *PT* I, pp. 63-70.

Krentz, E. "Through a Lens: Theology and Fidelity in 2 Thessalonians". In *PT* I, pp. 52-62.

Malherbe, Abraham J. *The Letters to the Thessalonians*. New York: Doubleday, 2000.

Marshall, I. Howard. "Election and Calling to Salvation in 1 and 2 Thessalonians". In *The Thessalonian Correspondence*. Edited by R. F. Collins, pp. 259-76. Louvain: Louvain University Press, 1990.

————. "Pauline Theology in the Thessalonian Correspondence". In *Paul and Paulinism: Essays in Honor of C. K. Barrett*. Edited by M. D. Hooker and S. G. Wilson, pp. 173-83. London: SPCK, 1982.

Morris, Leon. *Word Biblical Themes: 1, 2 Thessalonians*. Waco, Tex.: Word, 1989.

Richard, Earl J. "Early Pauline Thought. An Analysis of 1 Thessalonians". In *PT* I, pp. 39-51.

————. *First and Second Thessalonians*. Collegeville, Minn.: Liturgical Press, 1995.

Wanamaker, Charles A. *The Epistles to the Thessalonians*. Grand Rapids, Mich.: Eerdmans; Exeter: Paternoster, 1990.

# 10

# THE FIRST LETTER
# TO THE CORINTHIANS

❦

Paul's two letters to the church at Corinth cover many issues, theological, ethical and pastoral. The first of the two letters appears at first sight to have a wide variety of separate themes, and at certain points Paul moves sharply from one topic to another, sometimes giving the impression of taking up *seriatim* issues raised by the readers with him.[1] The Corinthian church evidently contained people who were in disagreement with one another and with Paul on various matters, and his theological convictions come to expression as he shapes his contingent answers to their several arguments. It has been cogently claimed that the letter forms a unified answer to the problems raised by these divisions that had arisen within the church rather than dealing with a loose set of topics with little relation to one another.[2] The result is a letter that is deeply theological in its application of the doctrine of the cross to the situation.

## The Theological Story
*Greeting and prayer report: The strengths of the congregation (1 Cor 1:1-9).* The letter begins with a greeting that expresses the Christian status of the recipients. Three motifs stand out.

---

[1] In I Cor 5:9-10 the writing of an earlier letter by Paul is attested, and I Cor 7:1 indicates that the Corinthians also wrote to Paul and raised various points with him. The headings in I Cor 8:1; 12:1; I Cor 16:1, 12 may suggest topics of enquiry by the Corinthians.

[2] See Margaret M. Mitchell, *Paul and the Rhetoric of Reconciliation: An Exegetical Investigation of the Language and Composition of 1 Corinthians* (Tübingen: Mohr Siebeck, 1992; reprint ed., Louisville, Ky.: Westminster/ John Knox, 1993).

First, the readers are addressed as people who are sanctified and called to be holy—language that we recognize from 1-2 Thessalonians as depicting the way in which believers form part of the people of God and are called to express their standing in their manner of life.

Second, this is immediately followed by an account of what Paul can especially give thanks to God for in the congregation; he singles out the influence of God's grace in their lives, which finds expression in spiritual gifts.[3] The discussion in 1 Corinthians 12—14 indicates that this was indeed a characteristic of the congregation.

Third, we also note that Paul refers to the expectation of the revelation of Christ, that is, the parousia, which he qualifies by reminding the readers that they will need to be blameless on that day (1 Cor 1:4-9).

All of these motifs remind us of 1 Thessalonians and indicate the strength of the theological connection between the letters.[4] They also establish points to which Paul will return as he develops his discourse.

*Divisions, the cross and the Spirit (1 Cor 1:10—4:21).* From this assessment of the strengths of his readers, Paul passes straight to the issue that causes most concern; as in Galatians, he wastes little time in getting down to the heart of the matter. The main problem in the church was divisions manifesting themselves in quarrels. Church meetings, we may presume, were the scene of arguments and strong differences of opinion. There is still no consensus among scholars on exactly what was happening, but I shall assume the view that members of the church, perhaps from different house groups, were identifying themselves as partisans of different Christian leaders, specifically Apollos, who had worked in Corinth, and Cephas, alias Peter, who may have visited Corinth. Some of the members probably tried to respond to the rivalry by saying "But we belong to Christ" and putting themselves above this worldly discussion. All attempts to identify three or four distinguishable points of view associated with the groups have failed, but it is clear that there was difference of opinion on various issues, involving some fairly serious deviations from Paul on some issues.

---

[3]The term for "spiritual gifts" is *charismata*, which is related to "grace" (*charis*) rather than to "spirit" (*pneuma*).

[4]Although the "holiness" language is particularly to the fore in 1-2 Thessalonians, it continues to play an important role in Paul's other letters. However, it is missing from Galatians.

The direct response to this situation and the underlying spiritual problems extends to the end of I Corinthians 4; Paul's appeal goes considerably beyond simply saying "Grow up and stop bickering!" Thereafter the discussion shifts to the specific theological and practical issues on which there were differences between Paul and some of the church. Here Paul makes three points.

First, some members of the church were putting their human idols on pedestals. Paul saw this not only as boasting about human beings but also as a subtle way of boasting about oneself ("I must be superior to other people because I support the best leader!"). He therefore had to emphasize that the various leaders were merely servants of God, each doing the specific task assigned to them, and consequently none was superior to any other. Even if a particular leader has authority in the church, that does not make him or her anything other than a servant of God, responsible to him. It appears that some people were using their professed loyalty to other leaders as a way of evading their responsibility to Paul, who did expect a loyalty to himself as their father in the gospel equipped with authority from God. Out of this discussion, therefore, there comes a profound discussion of the nature of Christian leadership, and specifically of apostleship.[5]

Second, some people attached importance to the identity of the person by whom they were baptized. To Paul this was a matter of no significance whatever, and he congratulated himself that he had in fact baptized very few people in Corinth. He considered that his task was to preach a gospel that was about a crucified Christ, a Christ crucified in weakness and therefore not an object of boasting in the normal sense of the term. The implication is that if the Savior was prepared to be so humbled, his servants and followers cannot indulge in pride.[6]

Third, some people evidently prized wisdom and eloquence as qualities or abilities to be sought after, and they may have judged Paul for his apparent lack of them (cf. 2 Cor 10:10). He therefore insisted that his preaching of the gos-

---

[5]Presumably Paul and Peter are the only apostles in mind. Apollos was evidently not an apostle. (He could not have fulfilled the description in I Cor 9:1-2, and he is not mentioned there.)

[6]The Greek verb *kauchaomai* can be used in a good or bad sense. It is used with reference to that in which one puts one's confidence. One may "boast", or rather "exult", and put one's trust in the Lord and his gracious deeds, but not boast in the sense of putting one's confidence in one's own achievements, being arrogant over against other people or being self-satisfied.

pel was not intended to display these qualities and that any power attaching to it came from the Holy Spirit as he preached in a manner that befitted the theme of a crucified Messiah. Only so could faith be dependent upon God's power rather than upon human wisdom. He insisted that there was a divine wisdom, however foolish it appeared to human beings, but that it was recognized as such only by people who possessed the Spirit of God and who could therefore appreciate what was taught by the Spirit. Paul is here referring to a wisdom that he communicated to those who were "mature" believers and had developed the capacity for spiritual truth.

It was precisely this lack of spiritual maturity that had led to the boasting about different Christian leaders. The converse is not to regard them all with indifference and lack of respect but rather to recognize that all the leaders belong to all the congregation as God's servants and stewards and to rejoice in this fact.

From this discussion we can now see that the crucial elements in Paul's theology that he brings to bear on this situation are the weakness of Christ on the cross, which is nevertheless the only means of salvation; the concept of a divine wisdom, which is identified with Christ; and the work of the Spirit in revealing God's wisdom to believers who possess the Spirit.

*Sexual ethics and litigation (1 Cor 5:1—6:20).* In the next section of the letter the focus shifts to ethical issues, specifically incest, litigation and, more generally, sexual ethics. There are three sections.

The first topic is a case of incest between a man and his stepmother (1 Cor 5:1-13). The situation was extraordinary in that in Paul's view the congregation were proud of what was happening. There are five significant features of Paul's response.

First, there is an insistence that the church must act in discipline against the offender (evidently against the man and not the woman).

Second, the form that the discipline takes is not simply the exclusion of the member from the church,[7] which might be sufficient as a declaration of abhorrence of the action, but a "handing over to Satan", which may lead to the man's ultimate salvation. The congregational meeting is conceived of as a spiritual court in which Christ is present and also Paul is there "in spirit", and the man

---

[7]This was certainly part of what was to happen (1 Cor 5:13).

is solemnly handed over to Satan. What happens, therefore, is more than a human action by the church. There is a spiritual dimension to its activities.

Third, the presence of the sinner is regarded as a contaminating influence that can lead the rest of the church into sin. Toleration of it is a blemish that renders the whole church sinful. The case is seen as an extreme example of sin that in less serious cases is dealt with by a withdrawal of fellowship, from the sinful members.[8]

Fourth, Paul reminds them that some "obvious" sins are incompatible with Christian faith and exclude people from the kingdom of God (1 Cor 6:9-10).

Fifth, Christian believers are delivered from such sins and their contaminating effects through the event that is comprehensively described as washing, sanctification and justification. The clear implication is that the consequences of such sins in the past are cancelled out and that believers (should) no longer commit them.

This theological exposition relating to sexual issues is interrupted by a related theme, namely, believers engaging in litigation with fellow believers before secular courts (1 Cor 6:1-11). This reveals that greed and cheating are going on between believers, and greedy persons and swindlers are included in the list of sinners who will not enter the kingdom. The extraordinary feature, which emerges almost as an aside, is that believers should not take their differences to secular courts and allow them to have jurisdiction over them; they should remember that one day the saints will judge the world. This is presumably a reference to the way in which when Christ comes to judge the world he will be accompanied by "the saints", an expression that sometimes refers to angels or other heavenly beings and sometimes to believers.[9]

Then Paul returns to the theme of sexual immorality, but now in more general terms (1 Cor 6:12-20). We come back to the pride of some of the congregation in their sexual behavior. They evidently believed that "anything was permissible" for believers and took pride in following out this principle over against, perhaps, the law-abiding behavior of traditionally minded Jewish Christians. Paul clearly did not agree. He insisted that the body was meant for the Lord and not for sexual immorality. He was not advocating celibacy. Since

---

[8]Exclusion from the church meal is meant.
[9]Cf. Mt 19:28; Lk 22:29-30; 2 Thess 1:10. First Thess 3:13 is ambiguous.

the Lord had blessed marriage, to take part in marriage was in no way incompatible with devotion to the Lord, but to give one's body to a prostitute went against the command of the Lord. The point is backed up with various arguments that are fired in rapid succession.

First, the body will be raised from the dead by God, and in view of this prospect the believer cannot use it for sinful purposes.

Second, the bodies of believers belong to Christ and therefore should not be united to sinners.

Third, Paul seems to regard sexual sin as going deeper than other sins since it involves a union between two human bodies. He would not have regarded the body as merely physical in view of its destiny. The body is more than physical; it is the living entity that is the person.

Fourth, the body is the dwelling place of the Holy Spirit—again indicating that the body is something more than purely physical.

Fifth, the body of the believer in any case belongs to Christ who has bought it at a high price—that is, by his death.

Paul does not work these points into a single, coherent system but hammers them home as different aspects of what it means to be a Christian believer in relation to God, Christ and the Spirit.

*Problems regarding marriage (1 Cor 7).* First Corinthians 7 then takes up the related matter of marriage and legitimate sexual relationships. Over against people who rejected sexual relationships of any kind, Paul upheld the practice of marriage, not least in view of the fact that it channeled sexual impulses that might otherwise be uncontrollable into a divinely authorized setting; he upheld the full legitimacy of physical sexual relationships within marriage, over against some people who favored so-called platonic relationships.[10]

While seeing value in remaining unmarried, Paul consistently saw nothing wrong in widowers and widows remarrying. Following the teaching of Jesus, he rejected divorce and required divorcees to remain unmarried or to return to their former partners. He recognized the special situation of believers married

---

[10]It may seem surprising that the same congregation included people who indulged in sexual immorality with prostitutes and those who favored celibacy and sexual inactivity. The former group probably consisted of expagans who had not given up their preconversion way of life. The latter group typified an ascetic outlook, not uncommon in the ancient religious world, that believed in suppressing bodily impulses in order to achieve what they regarded as a spiritual salvation.

to unbelievers.[11] In this case, he allowed separation at the behest of the unbelieving partner. In this situation he probably regarded the believer as free to enter into a second marriage with a believer.[12]

Paul asserts a general principle that people should stay in the state they are in, whether married or unmarried, and extends this to include slave and free. His reasoning is that it is more important to keep God's commands in whatever situation one finds oneself. Behind this lies the statement that the time is short and the world is passing away, and therefore people should live without being tied to the things of the world, whether what they already have or what they are desirous of having. The generally accepted view is that what Paul has in mind is the imminence of the parousia, which renders the time short for making any long-term plans and imposes urgency upon believers in dealing with the Lord's affairs. But it may be that there was a local crisis in Corinth that overshadowed the situation.[13] In any case he was more generally conscious of the shortness of the time at people's disposal and the need to be fully consecrated to God's service in the use of it. Again the need for believers to be "holy" is crucial (1 Cor 7:34 NRSV; cf. 1 Cor. 7:14.)[14]

We thus see that underlying Paul's practical advice lie such factors as the obligation to live a holy life in obedience to known commands of God or the Lord Jesus; awareness of the future coming of the Lord, and concern for the work of the Lord. To some extent he relies on his cognition of God's will in these matters as an apostle entrusted with revelation from God.

*Food and idolatry (1 Cor 8:1—11:1).* The next major section has a single theme but with digressions. It concerns the question whether Christians may eat food, specifically meat, that has been first offered as a sacrifice to a pagan

---

[11] Although Paul would have counseled believers not to enter into marriage with unbelievers, there were numerous situations that could result in a believer finding himself or herself married to an unbeliever (e.g., through conversion of one of the partners after the marriage or through an arranged marriage).

[12] David Instone-Brewer, *Divorce and Remarriage in the Church: Biblical Solutions and Pastoral Realities* (Carlisle: Paternoster, 2003), pp. 96-106.

[13] Cf. Bruce S. Winter, *After Paul Left Corinth: The Influence of Secular Ethics and Social Change* (Grand Rapids, Mich.: Eerdmans, 2001).

[14] 1 Cor 7:14 is somewhat enigmatic with its references to unbelieving marriage partners and children being made holy. See Anthony C. Thiselton, *1 Corinthians* (Carlisle: Paternoster; Grand Rapids, Mich.: Eerdmans, 2000), pp. 527-33, who adopts the view that the believing partner's holy way of life exerts a positive influence on the unbelieving partner and the children.

god or idol. To do so could be understood as an expression of worship to the idol. It could of course be argued that since idols do not exist and there is only one God (and also, importantly, one Lord), one can eat such meat without it symbolizing anything. Sacrifice is an empty action that makes no difference to the meat. However, this basic freedom has to be severely qualified.

First, while Paul sees nothing wrong in eating meat in somebody's home[15] or in purchasing it at the meat market, the situation is different with eating it in a pagan temple. In this case there is participation in a pagan rite, and although the strong Christian may protest that the rite is meaningless, Paul believes that there are demonic powers at work in pagan worship, and one is inevitably sharing in this worship, which is intolerable to God.

Second, behind this judgment lies Paul's reading of the story of Israel in the wilderness, where idolatry and sexual immorality overtook people who had enjoyed all the blessings of God's care for them at the exodus. Paul is concerned at how easily people can yield to temptation. While God will not let people be tempted beyond what they can bear, there is such a thing as playing with fire and getting your fingers burned.

Third, those who really think that idols exist and that taking such food is a form of worship may be led by the example of other Christians to eat the meat and in so doing to go against their own conscience and commit what is for them a sin.[16]

A significant point that emerges is the expression of concern for other believers who may be led into sin by a person's action that in itself is not harmful. Sin is taken seriously: it can lead to destruction, which can only mean divine judgment. Therefore, the believer must be governed by love for others, and the claims of love override the claims of personal freedom. I am not always free to do what I want and what is in itself legitimate if the superior demands of love for other believers intervene.

To illustrate and reinforce the point, Paul devotes the whole of I Corinthians 9 to the way in which he has voluntarily limited his freedom as an apostle

---

[15] But not if the meat is explicitly said to have been offered to an idol, that is, where the origin of the meat has become a conscious issue.

[16] It is a sin for them in that it expresses a breaking of the Ten Commandments in their deliberately going against conscience by worshiping an idol. It is not a sin for the strong Christians in that they are not worshiping an idol but eating innocuous meat.

to claim what he could rightfully claim, principally in the area of entitlement to financial and material support from the congregations. He firmly insists on the rights of the apostles and then equally firmly insists that he has refused to take his rights, all as part of his willingness to surrender his freedom in order to win people for Christ. He has his eyes fixed not on rewards in this life but on the heavenly crown of approval from his Lord. This does not mean that he is a calculating seeker of his own interests, reckoning that it is good policy to forego present, trivial rewards in the light of a future, eternal and far weightier reward, a person who knows which side his bread is buttered on. It is clear rather that he is principally motivated by the desire to glorify God and to win others for Christ.

*The conduct of congregational meetings (1 Cor 11:2-34).* From the danger of visits to pagan shrines with restaurants attached, Paul turns to conduct in the church meeting. Two issues are dealt with comparatively briefly, followed by the larger issue of spiritual gifts in and out of the church meeting.

The first issue is the (to modern eyes) trivial one of the demeanor of women in the church meeting. Paul's argumentation, including his reference to angels, is still not completely explained to everybody's satisfaction.[17] It can easily appear bizarre. Understanding is complicated by the word play on "head", which can refer both to a person's literal head and to a person to whom one stands in some kind of relationship.[18] Some women were praying or prophesying with their heads uncovered, which appears to mean without some kind of head covering such as was worn by some women at the time. For some reason lack of a head covering is dishonoring to a woman's head (her husband), whereas a man's lack of head covering is dishonoring to his head (Christ)—at least, while one is praying or prophesying. The doctrine of creation is invoked, with man being the image and glory of God, while woman is the glory of man. The issue appears to be the problem of gender differentiation and the honoring of one's head rather than the subordination of wives to husbands.

The second issue is the problems at the church meeting with its common meal. Some people had sufficient provisions to be able to eat and drink to ex-

---

[17]See Francis B. Watson, "The Authority of the Voice: A Theological Reading of 1 Cor 11.2-16", *NTS* 46 (2000): 520-36.

[18]The significance of "headship" is disputed. See Thiselton, *1 Corinthians*, pp. 812-22.

cess, whereas others went hungry; this was expressive of and furthering a social division in the church between the rich and the poor, with the result that people were not recognizing the church as church, where there is neither Jew nor Greek, neither free nor slave, and (Paul would have added here) neither rich nor poor. It is likely that the religious aspect of the meal was getting lost or ignored in the mix of conviviality, frustration, envy and grumbling that was going on.

Paul had already mentioned in passing the incompatibility of eating at idolatrous feasts and at the Lord's Supper, since the latter involved sharing in the body and blood of Christ and united the participants with one another as one body (1 Cor 10:16-17). Here he deals with the issue first of all by citing the account of the Last Supper held by Jesus, which evidently functioned as the foundational story for what the church did. The tradition establishes the nature and function of the church meal. Paul emphasizes again that at this meal believers partake of bread, which represents the body of Christ for them, and of the cup, which represents the new covenant in his blood, so that they remember Jesus and proclaim his death.

Second, from this he draws the conclusion that it is possible at this sacred occasion to partake unworthily. The unworthiness manifestly lies in the conduct that accompanies the meal whose sacred character underlies the incongruity of acting sinfully at the table. It arose out of a failure to recognize the body. This could mean failing to recognize that the bread represents the body of Christ dying on the cross. It could also mean a failure to recognize that the church gathered together is the body of Christ; lack of love for fellow members has theological significance. The emphasis is then on the church as a body of equals, within which setting social barriers should be pulled down. Either way, the sin is of shocking proportions and Paul does not hesitate to say that the Lord can act in judgment against those who sin, as is demonstrated by the illness and premature death of some of the congregation.[19] Such appalling consequences are to be understood as warnings from the Lord, so that those who have sinned and those who observe them may be warned to turn from sin, committed or contemplated.

*Spiritual gifts and people (1 Cor 12—14).* Closely connected with the topic of

---

[19]We need not doubt that there were people who suffered in this way in Corinth. The hard point for modern readers is the interpretation of these cases by Paul as examples of divine judgment.

church meetings is that of spiritual gifts *(pneumatika)* or "grace gifts" *(charismata)*, which receives major attention. These were Spirit-inspired qualities or the actions facilitated by them that functioned as forms of ministry or service within the congregation, or as spiritual exercises that benefited the person exercising them. Within the latter category falls the gift of tongues, the capacity to speak, apparently in praise of God, in a language or languages unknown to the speaker or the hearers. This was of spiritual benefit to the participant, whether as an experience that stimulated assurance of salvation or as a means of fellowship with God. Within the former category fell most of the other gifts, which included prophesying, healing, teaching and so on. Paul had various concerns.

He was aware that phenomena of this kind did not necessarily originate from the Spirit and that similar phenomena existed among pagans. Therefore, it was essential to ensure that activity in the church was genuinely Christian. Granted that a person could not make the Christian confession "Jesus is Lord" except when led by the Spirit, it was also the case that a person might make statements that were clearly not Spirit-inspired (such as "Cursed be Jesus") and that were presumably inspired by evil spirits.

We have, therefore, a situation in which various forms of activity were ascribed to the effects of inspiration, whether Christian or otherwise. Not all allegedly Spirit-inspired behavior was necessarily what it seemed to be, and this seems to have applied in particular to the utterances of prophets (I Cor 14:29; cf. I Jn 4:1-6). It was necessary to "test" the utterances. The alternatives were presumably that the utterances were either purely human or else demonically inspired.

There was a tendency in the congregation to regard some gifts as intrinsically more valuable than others or as expressing the higher worth of those who exercised them. Paul therefore took up the analogy of the parts of the body so as to emphasize that gifts might be varied and some more useful than others. But this did not affect the worth of the gifts and their bearers, all of whom were equally parts of the same body and all of whom depended in varying ways upon one another. All gifts were inspired and empowered by the same divine source. There was a tendency to pride and spiritual arrogance on the part of some of the believers, so that there were aspirations to have some gifts rather than others.

Faced by this rivalry, Paul developed as a centerpiece to the discussion his analysis of the necessity and nature of love as a quality without which the possession of spiritual gifts was valueless, and as a quality that ruled out all thoughts of superiority and rivalry, whether with regard to spiritual gifts or anything else whatever. In the last analysis, faith, hope and love are what matter, and these alone will survive into the world to come.

Paul was concerned that people were striving after the gifts, notably tongues, which may have helped them personally in their spiritual lives but brought no help to other people present in the congregation because they could not understand what was being said and could even lead nonbelievers to think that the Christians were out of their minds. He therefore expressed a strong preference for the gift of prophecy, which did communicate to other people, and insisted that tongues should not be practiced in the church meeting without the accompanying activity of interpretation.

Since tongues and prophecy were being exercised to excess in the meeting and people were in effect shouting one another down, he called for restraint and order in the exercise of both gifts, and for the proper place to be given to other activities, such as hymns and words of instruction, alongside revelations, tongues and interpretations.

In a very problematical addition at the end (1 Cor 14:34-35) he insists that women should be silent in the church meetings because the law requires them to be submissive. Since he has already allowed that women could pray and prophesy, both of which were oral activities, the purport of this instruction is not clear. The Gordian knot is cut by those who argue on text-critical and other grounds that the paragraph is an interpolation in the letter.[20] Those who hold that it is authentic suggest that the women were being excluded from the examination of prophecies (particularly if the prophets were their husbands) or maybe from asking questions aloud, which were a distraction from the meeting.[21] The point is to avoid conduct regarded as shameful in the church.[22]

*Affirmation of the resurrection (1 Cor 15).* The theme shifts abruptly from the

---

[20]Gordon D. Fee, *The First Epistle to the Corinthians* (Grand Rapids, Mich.: Eerdmans, 1987), pp. 699-708; Richard B. Hays, *First Corinthians* (Louisville, Ky.: John Knox Press, 1997), pp. 245-49.

[21]It is possible that against a Jewish background some of the women were less well educated and instructed than the men. See, for example, Ben Witherington III, *Conflict and Community in Corinth: A Socio-Rhetorical Commentary on 1 and 2 Corinthians* (Grand Rapids, Mich.: Eerdmans; Carlisle Paternoster, 1995), pp. 287-88; Thiselton, *1 Corinthians*, pp. 1146-62.

[22]It is fair comment that if the participation of women in the church meeting is no longer considered shameful today, there is no impediment to it.

Christian meeting to Christian belief in I Corinthians 15, which is the most sustained discussion in the New Testament of the resurrection of Christian believers. The theme does not get announced until I Corinthians 15:12, where it emerges that some[23] of the congregation say that there is no resurrection of the dead. From what Paul says in reply this must have been a denial that physically dead people are brought back to life. It may have included the belief that Christians had been brought to life spiritually at their conversion and that resurrection was nothing more than this.

Paul's response to this claim falls into various parts.

He begins by asserting that the resurrection of Jesus was an integral part of the basic gospel that he and all the other apostles preached. Moreover, it was attested by a large group of reliable witnesses that they had seen Jesus alive after his death. The Corinthian believers shared in this belief. Otherwise Paul had preached to no effect and their salvation was in question.

This one attested case was sufficient to establish the fact that dead people can be raised from the dead. The argument, repeated from different angles, is that if the dead cannot be raised, then Christ was not raised, but it is foundational to Christianity that Christ was raised.

Simultaneously Paul argues that the resurrection is the essential presupposition for belief in the forgiveness of sins and for any Christian hope for the future, including hope for those who have died.

From this basis Paul then develops the thought that the resurrection of Christ is the first stage in the process of bringing life to the world and conquering the power of death and all that is opposed to God. He develops a forecast or prophecy of Christ reigning until he returns and the dead are raised, and then, as it were, handing over the spoils of his victory to his Father.

Paul argues that various forms of Christian conduct are inconsistent if the dead are not raised, such as the willingness to forego transitory pleasures in this world for the sake of a life after death. He also includes the curious practice of "baptism for the dead", which appears to mean baptism in order to share in eternal life.

---

[23]It may be worth observing that throughout the correspondence Paul's differences are with "some" of the congregation (and not necessarily the same group all the time) and not with the congregation as a whole.

Finally, he deals with the possible objection to the resurrection of the dead that the event was inconceivable. He compares the resurrection of dead bodies, buried in the ground, with the way in which apparently dead seeds are sown in the soil and then burst into a new and glorious life. A perishable body is "sown" and an incorruptible, eternal one springs from it. The new body is necessarily "spiritual", which appears to mean that it is not made of perishable flesh but has an everlasting composition. And all this takes place somehow in and through Christ, who rose from the dead to become a life-giving spirit, conveying eternal life and resurrection to his followers.

*Closing matters (1 Cor 16)*. Finally, 1 Corinthians 16 is concerned with domestic matters such as the collecting of money to help the poor in Jerusalem and the work of Paul and his helpers. Right at the end we have a remarkable reference to people who do not love the Lord; they stand under a curse. This is followed by a cry of "Maranatha", the Aramaic phrase for "Come, O Lord" or "Our Lord has come",[24] which looks like a backup to the threat, presumably directed against persistent sinners in the church who needed to be disciplined.

## Theological Themes

Our survey has endeavored to highlight the theological aspects of a letter that is concerned as much with Christian behavior as with Christian belief. We have unearthed a framework of thinking that is strange to modern readers, with its acceptance of a world in which the Holy Spirit and Satan and demonic spirits can influence and affect human behavior, in which the ending of the world is taken for granted, and in which dead people can be brought back to life in a new and imperishable manner. These beliefs need to be emphasized because they are part of the total picture of what early Christians believed, and we must not develop a partial view based on what we want or do not want to find there.

*The center of the gospel.* Paul's exposition makes use of a number of statements

---

[24]The Aramaic phrase transliterated into Greek letters is ambiguous, like the answer of the arrogant lady who, when asked who she was, said haughtily, "I am one of the directors' wives", but was misunderstood as, "I am one of the director's wives". In the absence of punctuation marks, who is to know which interpretation is right? Here the Aramaic form could be either imperative or indicative depending on how the phrase is divided up. The imperative form *(marana tha)* is generally considered to be more likely (NRSV text; TNIV) and to be a prayer for the parousia of Jesus rather than his immediate presence with the congregation; the indicative form, though perfect *(maran atha;* cf. NRSV mg.), is best understood as a future tense, affirming that the Lord will come.

that are best understood as materials that he has inherited and has passed down because of their authoritative character.[25] In particular, a debate over whether the resurrection of Jesus is a cardinal Christian belief is settled by an affirmation of the gospel that Paul had received and then passed on to the congregation (I Cor 15:1-5). A number of points emerge from this citation.

First, this passage is of crucial importance in that it demonstrates by its vocabulary of receiving and passing on that Paul's theology was tied to traditions that were accepted as authoritative by himself and his readers. In an earlier passage dealing with the warrant for celebrating the Lord's Supper he ascribes the origin of the tradition to the Lord Jesus (I Cor 11:23-26); here, although the whole passage shows signs of its traditional origin, the accent is on what the Lord said and did.

Second, Paul cites a summary of the main contents of the gospel, acceptance of which leads to salvation. That is to say, Paul claimed that the gospel, as he preached it, was identical with that which had been handed down to him by other believers, and in the context we may conclude with confidence that it was shared by the other apostles whom he names.[26]

Third, the center of the gospel is the affirmation that Christ died for our sins according to the Scriptures and was raised from the dead. The crucifixion and resurrection of Christ are utterly central. It is surely more than coincidence that the other traditional passage introduced by a similar rubric contains the words of the Lord at the Last Supper, which were understood as a proclamation of his death, that is, as a proclamation of the significance of his death. His body given in death was "for you", and through the shedding of his blood a new covenant was inaugurated.

Fourth, in the first passage the crucifixion and resurrection of Christ are affirmed to be "according to the Scriptures". This phrase suggests that they happened "just as the Scriptures foretold", a statement that affirms that they had to happen because this was part of the purpose of God already communicated

---

[25]However, Paul is not necessarily tied down to a precise, fixed form of words. The principal passages are I Cor 8:5-6; 11:23-26; 15:3-5; cf. I Cor 7:10; 9:14.

[26]There is no clash with Paul's statement in Gal 1:11-12 that he did not receive the gospel from a human source. There he is referring rather to the manner of his conversion through a direct revelation of Jesus Christ. See James D. G. Dunn, *Unity and Diversity in the New Testament* (London: SCM Press, 1977), pp. 66-67.

to the prophets, and that these events, the execution of a man presumably guilty of some capital crime and the subsequent rumors that he had been seen alive after his death, were to be explained as the death and resurrection of the Messiah: that is to say, the explanation or interpretation of these events was fixed in principle by the prophetic teaching. We might have expected a fuller use of the Scriptures by Paul in this way, both some reference to the actual passages that he had in mind at this point and also fuller use of citations from Scripture elsewhere in the letter to explain other aspects of the gospel. Nevertheless, at point after point it can be seen that his theology is deeply formed by his knowledge of the Scriptures.[27] Similarly, Paul can occasionally quote other sayings of Jesus to back up his argument (1 Cor 7:10; 9:14).

Paul's emphasis on the cross as the center of the gospel in this passage is significant in itself for the rest of the letter and indeed for his theology as a whole. It implies that the center of the gospel was not the parousia of Jesus, the coming of the Lord for which prayer is offered at the end of the letter. Whether or not the very earliest Christians centered their attention on the hope of the imminent return of Jesus and then slowly realized that God's timescale was more elongated than theirs, the content of Paul's gospel was certainly not the prophecy that Jesus was coming back. The future coming was not the saving event in itself. Paul's interest was in what had already happened, the death and resurrection of Jesus.

***The cross and the divisions in the congregation.*** For Paul the heart of the church's activity lay in the proclamation of the message of the cross, and he used this fact to deal with the disunity that was rampant in the congregation. The religion to which Christ was the gateway had opened up as a realm in which the practice of spiritual gifts had become the most prized characteristic, and there was rivalry between people and pride depending on which were regarded as the highest and showiest gifts. Christianity was in danger of becoming a religion of revelation of God's secrets through gifted people. It was thus becoming a reli-

---

[27]Paul's overt appeals to scriptural texts are curiously scattered through his writings for reasons that are not wholly clear. For the case that, even where Scripture is not directly cited, its influence underlies Paul's thought in ethical teaching in this letter see Brian S. Rosner, *Paul, Scripture and Ethics: A Study of 1 Corinthians 5–7* (Leiden: E. J. Brill, 1994; reprint ed., Grand Rapids, Mich.: Baker, 1999); on the other side, see Christopher M. Tuckett, "Paul, Scripture and Ethics: Some Reflections", *NTS* 46 (2000): 403-24.

gion of spiritual achievement, of pride and human position.

Against all such pretensions Paul uses the message of the cross to utter a decisive no. This is rather different from but not unrelated to the message of the cross in 1 Corinthians 15 and elsewhere where the stress is on Christ dying for us, Christ becoming a curse for us, Christ being the means of redemption from sin. Here the death of Christ is seen rather as an expression of weakness and shame, the last extremity in humiliation, and yet paradoxically it is also the expression of divine power. Interestingly, Paul does not refer to the resurrection in this context as the means by which the apparent defeat of Christ by the powers of evil is turned into victory by the radical reversal wrought by God. Rather, Paul sees in the cross the paradigm of the way in which God works by doing something which in the eyes of the world is foolish and weak. The same rationale is evident in Philippians 2:6-11, where the one who was equal with God takes the form of a servant and submits to death, death on a cross, wording that finds an echo in Paul's reference here to the crucifixion of the Lord of glory (1 Cor 2:8). We are thus dealing with a motif that is absolutely fundamental in Paul's theology. It is the method by which God works. The message of the cross is to human eyes foolish and a stumbling block. The folly is by contrast with what the world regards as wise. There is nothing clever about a message that concerns an executed criminal, nothing philosophical. Equally the cross is offensive to a world that looks for respectability and even assumes that God will be manifested by showy, miraculous interventions that compel belief.

Yet for Paul it is wise and powerful. How so? Paul does not explain. He sees in the cross a paradigm of God's behavior in pulling down the wise and mighty and exalting the foolish and weak people of the world. That is why God behaves in this way. Christ is now powerful; he was crucified in weakness, but he lives by the power of God (2 Cor 13:4). So the weakness of God displayed in the cross is in the end stronger than human strength, and this strength is manifested in the resurrection. Nevertheless, the paradox is not resolved in this way in 1 Corinthians 1—4.

The cross, then, is the expression of God's power and wisdom. These cannot be appreciated by mere human beings who measure things by their own standards. Therefore, the effect of the cross is to call into question what human beings regard as powerful and wise. Equally this relativizes the people who think themselves to be, or are perceived by others as, strong and wise. Nobility of birth, position due to wealth, human eloquence and philosophical skill—all count for nothing. If in Romans Paul will insist that nobody can raise their head in God's presence through works of the law, here he insists that nobody can do so on grounds of power or wisdom.

The motif of wisdom plays a significant role here; there are far more references to it in I Corinthians 1—3 than anywhere else in the New Testament. This doubtless arises from the context of the congregation in a city where sophists (philosophers and orators) flourished and learning was a mark of status. Most of what Paul says about wisdom is a critique of human wisdom that has failed to find God by its own efforts and that stands under God's judgment. Preachers of the gospel do not persuade people by means of human wisdom, that is, by what seems wise in the eyes of the world.[28] God's way of salvation may seem to be foolish to the world, but in reality the crucifixion of the Savior is an expression of God's kind of wisdom. Paul can say that as far as we are concerned wisdom is identified with Christ.[29]

The relevance of this to the divisions in the congregation is developed in I Corinthians 3:1-4 and I Corinthians 4:6-21. People who are taken up with position and pride and quarrel with one another over these things are not in a position to appreciate the divine wisdom properly. Only when they stop their boasting and become humble will they be in a position to accept what God has to say to them in his wisdom. They claim to be wise, strong and honored, but they do not realize that this is not the Christian way, which does not look for worldly wisdom and honor. A look at the missionaries and their situation should have convinced them otherwise! They are seen as the scum of the earth, of no reputation and no importance!

So the congregation is meant to live by the paradigm of the cross in that it renounces human power and wisdom as qualities in which it can boast and by which other people measure it. Instead, like the apostles, it must have a different scale of values, adopting the wisdom and power of God, which are of no value

---

[28]Yet this does not entirely rule out the use of rhetorical skills, as is clear from the evidence of their use by Paul and other writers.

[29]This is not the same thing as a wisdom christology that sees the Christian understanding of Jesus as being developed in part from the Old Testament and Jewish concept of Wisdom as God's companion and helper in creation. This influence may have been present elsewhere, but it does not seem to have affected the present discussion.

in human eyes, and looking only for God's rewards, which are real enough.

Here, then, at the nerve center of Paul's theology is a full-scale exposition of the way in which the function of the cross is to tear down human pride and make people live to please God. This is not to replace one form of pride and boasting with another, as if it were all right to seek God's rewards and to aspire to excel in them. So soon as people think in that manner, they have fallen back into worldly standards.

*Apostles, ministers, servants.* Out of this discussion arises Paul's understanding of the role and status of the missionaries (1 Cor 3:5—4:5). These are people whose task is to plant congregations and encourage their growth (the field metaphor) or to lay a foundation and build a congregation on it (the building metaphor). According to both metaphors they are sharing in God's work, for the foundation is a "given" from God and the actual growth is produced by God. Thus there is a complex interaction of God and his human agents that defies analysis. Although there is to be no human evaluation and assessment of the workers, nevertheless the metaphor of reward and loss is used to indicate that they are responsible to God for the quality of their work. There is, accordingly, an element of human responsibility to God for what is done.[30] The nature of the relationship with God is thus that of stewards, people with delegated responsibility; they are given their orders, so to speak, but it is their responsibility as to how they are to carry them out in accordance with the general guidance that they have been given.

Paul and the other Christian workers can thus lay claim to considerable authority, and this becomes apparent in the strong line that he takes in 1 Corinthians 5 with respect to the sexual offender; the congregation is here commanded how it is to act.

Yet Paul can feel the need to defend himself and to justify his position. He does this in 1 Corinthians 9, where he is defending his practice with regard to accepting or not accepting his keep from the congregation. The point of this discussion is not to defend his position as an apostle, which was undisputed, but rather to demonstrate the way in which he did not claim any rights that arose from it so that he might be an example to the congregation in regard to

---

[30]This would not sit easily with the idea that everything that they do has been foreordained by God. Note also that, despite all that is said about the workers not being under human judgment, there are manifestly cases where this must have taken place and did. Pastors who pay no attention to the justifiable criticisms made by members of their congregations are irresponsible.

the denial of one's rights for the benefit of the other members. He therefore has to stress that he was an apostle and so entitled to certain rights before he can go on to claim that he has surrendered his rights. The marks that demonstrate that he is an apostle are that he had seen Jesus and that he had founded the congregation. The former of these points entails that he had been commissioned by God, as is made clear in Galatians 1:15-17.

*Jesus Christ, his status and role.* The discussion of Christ crucified that sets the tone for the letter raises the question of the place of Christ in the remainder of the letter. About his present status there is no doubt. Although he was crucified in weakness, he now lives in power (2 Cor 13:4), and he is the Lord.

Paul uses this term particularly when the authority of Jesus over the church is in view, and he does so, for example, when referring to teaching by the earthly Jesus (1 Cor 7:10; 9:14). He also uses the same term when he is referring to the supreme position of Jesus alongside God the Father. In 1 Corinthians 8:5-6 it is generally agreed that Paul is using already-formed phraseology to juxtapose God the Father and the Lord, Jesus Christ, as the only divine figures over against the so-called gods and lords of the non-Christian world, beings, whether real (like the emperor) or imaginary (like the numerous deities in the polytheistic world) who were accorded this status by their worshipers. Here, without considering explicitly how the figure of Jesus Christ, who had lived in the world, might be identified with the Lord who was the agent of creation, Paul affirms that Jesus is and was the Lord.[31] Elsewhere the title of "Lord" is appropriately employed when Old Testament language is being used and interpreted as a reference to Jesus (1 Cor 10:9) or when a fixed usage is being invoked (e.g., in the references to the Lord's Supper, 1 Cor 10:21; 11:23-31). The Christian confession is likewise that "Jesus is Lord" (1 Cor 12:3). And it is as the Lord that he will return in glory (1 Cor 1:7; 4:5). In general *Lord* is used when the authority of Jesus is invoked (1 Cor 7:17).[32]

---

[31]Although Phil 2:9-11 links the title of Lord with the exaltation of Jesus, Paul was evidently not aware of any tension with his statement here.

[32]The lordship of Christ is stated alongside his ultimate submission to God the Father (1 Cor 15:28). There is a paradox between the statement elsewhere that Christ is equal to the Father, although he renounced that equality to become a servant (Phil 2:6-7) and this statement of subordination. The language of sonship implies the submission of the Son to the Father. There is a similar combination in John, where the Son shares the glory of the Father and yet does what the Father tells him to do.

But when writing about other aspects of the role of Jesus in relation to the church, Paul regularly uses the term *Christ*. The church is the body, not of the Lord, but of Christ (1 Cor 6:15; 12:12, 27), and it is Christ who was crucified, except in 1 Corinthians 2:8, where the enormity of the outrage is depicted: they crucified *the Lord of glory*. There is an interesting juxtaposition in 1 Corinthians 6:13-17, where the lordship of Christ is deliberately invoked in the context of the incompatibility between being members of Christ and indulging in sin. Where Jesus is the source of life and blessings, the tendency is to use *Christ*. This is why the name Christ is used in 1 Corinthians 15 rather than *Lord*, even though the focus is on the resurrection: it is precisely the union of believers with Christ now and then at the resurrection of the dead that is the issue rather than the position of Christ as the coming Lord.

Paul seems to use the term as a name, and his preference for it rather than for Jesus is significant. It suggests that the identity of Jesus as the Messiah had become so natural that, on the one hand, it was easy to use the title as a name (just as happened with the reigning Roman emperor who was Caesar), and, on the other hand, there was no need to reckon with any other possible claimants for the position, since there were and could be none. Moreover, in Christian usage it would seem that the original associations of the title in Judaism were retreating somewhat into the background and the significance of the name was being defined in terms of the role that was being enacted by Jesus.[33]

*The Holy Spirit.* The Spirit plays a significant role in the theology of this letter. At the outset Paul gives thanks to God for the grace given to his readers. He refers to various gifts, specifically speaking and knowledge, which are part of a broader range of *charismata* bestowed on them (1 Cor 1:5-7). Although the Spirit is not expressly mentioned at this point, there is no doubt that these gifts, here said to be given "in Christ", are the gifts imparted by the Spirit, who comes into a living relationship with individual believers and bestows different gifts upon them. This conclusion is justified by the way in which Paul does go on to speak about knowledge in 1 Corinthians 2 and relates it to the Spirit, and then by the way in which in 1 Corinthians 12 the same gifts are attributed to

---

[33]Paul's use of the term *Son* with reference to Jesus here, as elsewhere, is comparatively sparse. In 1 Cor 15:28 the point is that even the Son remains subject to God the Father. It is not so clear why in 1 Cor 1:9 believers are called into fellowship specifically with "his Son Jesus Christ our Lord".

the one Spirit. Teaching involving the Spirit is found especially in these two places.

*The Spirit and revelation.* Paul works from the assumption that the only entity that knows how a person thinks is that person's own spirit, by which he presumably means their own conscious mind. He makes the bold analogy that the same is true of God; human beings cannot know his mind unaided. Therefore, if they are to know his thoughts, he must reveal them to him, just as people can know what I really think (as opposed to their guesses, which may be mistaken) only if I tell them. This is the privileged position of the believer to whom God has given his Spirit and is now able to understand what God says through his apostles and prophets. Other people may hear the same words and either fail to understand what is being said or refuse to accept their truth. Such people are said to be "natural" (*psychikos*, lit. "soulish"; TNIV despairs of finding a suitable equivalent and paraphrases with "without the Spirit"). To them what God says—specifically, in the message of the cross—is foolishness.

*The Spirit and conversion.* The agency of the Spirit in the life of believers is attested in I Corinthians 6:11, where the changes wrought in their lives take place "in the name of the Lord Jesus Christ and by the Spirit of our God". It is probable that all three changes, washing, sanctifying and justifying, are to be seen as aspects of becoming a Christian. The process of conversion thus takes place in virtue of what Christ has done but at the same time the Spirit is the agent in applying what Christ has done to the individual.

But the Spirit is not an outside agent. The Spirit is said to be "in" believers. If the Spirit is conceived as a spiritual person capable of being everywhere, then there is no problem about regarding the Spirit as being present in Christian believers, all of them and wherever they happen to be. The concept of God's presence in the world was a familiar one in Judaism and has its roots in the Old Testament, where God was present in the temple and his Spirit was envisaged as being in or with individual members of his people (I Sam 10:10; Ps 51:11; Is 61:1). So here the metaphor of the temple is applied to individual believers (I Cor 6:19) and to the congregation as the place in which the Spirit of God is resident (I Cor 3:16).

An apparently less personal picture is presented in I Corinthians 12:13, where Paul comments that all of the congregation have drunk the one Spirit. The metaphor is not that of people drinking with their mouths but rather that of plants in a field being sprinkled with rain or being watered by the farmer (cf. I Cor 3:7-8), and it draws upon the imagery in Isaiah 32:15. What is poured out is not something with merely external effects: just as the plants absorb the moisture, so the members of the congregation receive the Spirit into themselves. The effect is that they receive charismata, the spiritually enabling gifts of God associated with particular functions that they are called upon to perform in the congregation. These charismata can be attributed to the Spirit, the Lord and God, thereby indicating that no hard and fast line can be drawn between the activities of the different persons to whom Paul assigns divine status, and equally the terminology for the gifts can be quite fluid.

At the same time Paul regarded some members of the congregation in Corinth as lacking in the Spirit and therefore not able to receive and understand his message (I Cor 3:1). This lack of the Spirit was evidenced by the failure to develop in Christian character; they were still dominated by their non-Christian character and were like mere infants who had not grown as Christians. Evidently, therefore, Paul conceived of a process of developing fuller insight thanks to the working of the Spirit. Clearly Paul believed that there was such a thing as spiritual development and progress in which people were more and more enabled by the Spirit to appreciate and understand the mind of God, but that this development could be arrested by sub-Christian forms of behavior, specifically envy and quarrelling. He also believed that people could return to making spiritual progress through repentance and turning away from these sins.[34]

*The life of the congregation.* The common life of the congregation is the main theme of this letter. We have already seen that for Paul its divisiveness was a sign of spiritual immaturity. But what was it meant to be like?

Paul develops a concept of believers being the body of Christ. It already emerges in I Corinthians 6:15, where he states that the individual bodies of Christians are members of Christ; the underlying assumption is that Christ has a body composed of various parts. The same imagery is employed in I Corinthians 10:17, where the fact that believers share together in one loaf at the Lord's Supper is symbolic of their constituting one body. It follows that they

---

[34]This is yet another example of the paradox that the New Testament seems at times to ascribe whatever happens in the illumination, conversion and spiritual progress of believers to the Spirit and at other times to recognize their personal responsibility and ability.

should not enter into relationships, specifically through eating food offered to idols, that are incompatible with their solidarity and union with Christ. The concept is developed at length in I Corinthians 13. Collectively believers can be compared with a body, with many different parts, each of which has its own individual function but interrelated and meant to serve one another and promote the well-being of the body as a whole. Thus unity and diversity are both emphasized, but the diversity is in the service of the unity. The description here might appear to be no more than an analogy (the congregation is *like* a body), but Paul states that the readers are the body *of Christ* (I Cor 12:27; cf. I Cor 11:29; 12:12) and indicates that they are incorporated into this body through the Spirit at baptism (I Cor 12:13). Moreover, it is not the Corinthian congregation by itself that is the body of Christ; the body must comprise all believers everywhere (cf. Rom 12:4-5).

As throughout the New Testament the congregation consists of people who are referred to simply as "believers" or "saints", and the word that sums up their distinctive attitude is "faith" (I Cor 2:5; 14:22-23; 15:11, 14, 17; 16:13). To be a Christian is the result of beginning to have faith (I Cor 3:5; 15:2.) The beginning of faith is marked by baptism. Paul makes an offhand reference to it in I Corinthians 1:13-17; he cannot even remember whom he personally baptized! What is more important than being a person who baptizes is being a preacher of the gospel. There may well be an allusion to the symbolism of baptism in the description of Christians as people who have been washed, sanctified and justified (I Cor 6:11),[35] but the symbolism is fleeting, as Paul rather gives a comprehensive statement of various facets of the change in their lives. Out of these three terms it is in fact the second one (sanctified), which provides the other characteristic self-description of Christians alongside "believers" (I Cor 1:2; 6:1, 2; 14:33; 16:1, 15).[36]

Those who believe are also described as "the saved" (I Cor 1:18, 21; 15:2), but this motif is not developed in I Corinthians except in relation to mission. We should note, however, that being saved is contrasted with perishing, and the language is used of the way in which believers escape the destruction that

---

[35] Cf. the reference to redemption, righteousness and sanctification in I Cor 1:30. The symbolism of watering plants in I Cor 12:13 may suggest that affusion rather than immersion was one mode of baptism.

[36] Holiness is not, however, thematized so strongly as in 1-2 Thessalonians.

falls upon shoddy work at the last judgment (1 Cor 3:15).

In no other letter is the place of the Spirit in the life of the congregation discussed so fully as here. The ground is prepared in 1 Corinthians 1:7, where the presence of spiritual gifts in the congregation is applauded. The Spirit is seen to be the agent in conversion and the means whereby God's revelation is received. But in 1 Corinthians 12 the Spirit is the source of various gifts. These are placed in parallelism with "services" and "sources of power" in a way that suggests that the three terms refer to essentially the same things from different aspects. "Gifts" recurs in 1 Corinthians 12:9 as the ability to work healings (cf. 1 Cor 12:28, 30). The word thus conveys the idea of a divine equipping or empowering to perform acts that would otherwise not be possible.[37] The use of "powers" in relation to "works of power" (dynameis) affords a close parallel. The gifts described are related to apprehension of God's words and powers so as to act as his agents. They equip people to act on behalf of God, thus serving him and acting as his agents. Very broadly, the actions are similar to those carried out by Christ in his earthly life with the help of the Spirit. The fact that they can be counterfeited does not call in question the reality of the genuine article. The tests may not be infallible, but there are certain guidelines—denial of Christ and perhaps lack of accompanying love are among them.

Congregational meetings accordingly are occasions on which God may communicate in word and deed with his people through the agency of any of their number according as they are given his gifts to enable them to function on his behalf with spiritual insight and power.[38] This has crucial importance for our understanding of the function of congregational meetings. Little is said in the New Testament about their function being a Godward action of worship. Rather they are primarily occasions when God communicates with his people in such a way that he is truly present with them through his Spirit who is in his people individually and so collectively. The outsider who comes in rightly concludes that God is among them. Clearly this realization should lead to a sense of awe and worship; praise and prayer are offered to the Lord,

---

[37]Since the topic in 1 Cor 12—14 is gifts of the Spirit, nothing is said about the place of natural abilities and activities within the congregational setting. It would be mistaken to conclude that everything that goes on in a Christian meeting is dependent upon the special gifts of the Spirit.

[38]At least one gift, namely, tongues, may contribute more to the edification of the individual, and its exercise in the congregation is open to misuse unless the gift of interpretation is also exercised.

but these are responses to the presence and activity of God.

We may compare the twofold function of the Lord's Supper. On the one hand, it is a form of proclamation of the Lord's death, a presentation of the gospel. On the other hand, it represents a participation in the body and blood of Christ. There is a real communion with God the Son. Essentially God acts and people receive.

The picture presented here fits in with that in I Thessalonians 5:19-20, where the Spirit was not to be quenched and prophecies were not to be treated with contempt. Charismata also appear in Romans 12, where the recipients are encouraged to use them in the appropriate way depending on what their gifts are. Here they are listed as prophecy, service, teaching, exhortation, sharing, caring/leading, showing mercy. Tongues is not mentioned here. There is more emphasis on mutual care and love in practical ways.

A problem appears in the vying by the congregation for the gifts that they considered to be of greater worth and carrying greater prestige. Paul deals with this problem in two ways. On the one hand, he insists that all gifts are necessary in the congregation, and therefore there is to be no ranking of them, since each has its place. On the other hand, he relativizes them all by his insistence on the superiority of love. Yet he cannot avoid a certain ranking of the gifts in that one should desire to prophesy rather than to speak in tongues. And he recognizes that apostles, prophets and teachers stand at the head of a list in which significantly tongues is mentioned last. So, although the body metaphor stresses that all are necessary and essential, nevertheless some are more valuable than others.

While Paul insists that the gifts are given by God as he wills, he can nevertheless encourage people to desire the gifts, especially prophecy. This indicates that the divine apportionment of the gifts is somehow related to the prayers of the people; compare how in 2 Corinthians Paul could pray for the removal of his "thorn" and had to have a divine answer that in effect justified God's refusal to do so. There is some interaction between God and the suppliant. This is further evident in the fact that the person on whom a gift is bestowed evidently retains control of its use: the spirits of the prophets are subject to the prophets. People with the gift of tongues may refrain from exercising it in appropriate circumstances. The linking of the gifts with service indicates that the possession of the gift carries with it the obligation to use it in the service of God as he directs.

*The resurrection of Christ and of believers.* No other letter discusses so fully the question of the resurrection. Surprisingly the motif occurs only once in the earlier part of the letter, where the parallelism between God's raising of the Lord and of us is used in an argument against fornication (1 Cor 6:14). Since the point that is at issue is that the body is for the Lord, already at this point the assumption is that raising is an activity that is concerned with the bodies of believers; no other kind of resurrection would be relevant to the argument here. It is this point that is developed in 1 Corinthians 15.

The chapter breaks into two parts. In the first of these the resurrection of the body is not explicitly within Paul's sights (1 Cor 15:1-34). His first concern is whether dead people are raised, a point denied by some of his readers. It is difficult to be sure precisely what the issue was, but we can be certain that the denial concerned a future bodily resurrection of believers, since this formed an integral part of Paul's teaching (1 Thess 4:13-18).

Paul's argument is complex. He first establishes that the content of the gospel as preached to the Corinthians and as believed by them included at its center the event of Christ's resurrection, and he maintains that the preaching rested on the testimony of those who had seen him.

Then he moves on to challenge those who deny the resurrection of believers by insisting on the resurrection of Christ. His argument is that one person in particular, Christ, cannot have risen if there is no resurrection of dead people. If that were the case, he comments almost in passing, then Christian faith is pointless and empty because it is based on the assumption that Christ rose. The gospel is empty, and faith is empty and leads nowhere. There is no hope for those who died believing in Christ; if not even Christ rose, what chance is there for anybody else? There is also no forgiveness of sins. This point also emerges in Romans 4:24-25, where justification is granted to those who believe in the God who raised Jesus from the dead; Jesus was handed over to death because of our sins and was raised from the dead so that we might be justified. For Paul the death of Christ by itself would not have had saving efficacy. There had to be the evidence that God accepted the death of his Son as an efficacious offering, and the resurrection is understood as the act of acceptance.

Paul then passes to the offensive by asserting the implications of Christ's resurrection, which he has in effect already established by the testimony lying behind the kerygma and by showing how it is integral to the Christian faith. He moves from Christ's resurrection to that of believers by understanding the former as the firstfruits of the latter. The point of the illustration is that the first part of the harvest to be collected is by definition the first part of the larger harvest that is sure to follow. Putting the point differently, what the offering of the firstfruits signifies is that the harvest has begun. The point is not so much that the firstfruits carries with it the promise of more to follow, as that the reaping of the firstfruits is the signal that the harvest as a whole has begun. This is the significance of the resurrection of Jesus: the general resurrection of God's people has commenced! This leaves the question: how does Paul know that the resurrection of Jesus is not a one-time event involving only one person? And how does he know the future course of events that he lays out here? The answer to the former question lies in the way in which Paul understands believers to be united with Christ (cf. especially Rom 5—6); the answer to the latter question seems to depend on a special revelation of this "mystery" to Paul (1 Cor 15:51).

Paul in fact tackles two topics here. The one is the resurrection of believers as an integral part of Christian hope. The other brought in almost casually is the final defeat of the powers of evil arrayed against God and his people. This is clearly equally important, since there can be no lasting salvation so long as these powers are still free and active. Paul draws on Psalm 8:6 for his scriptural proof that the Christ will be the agent of victory over the powers. Later in the chapter he also resorts to the Old Testament for his basis for including death among these powers as "the last enemy" to be defeated.

Only, then, in the second part of the chapter (1 Cor 15:35-57), is the question of the body raised. It may well be a response to an objection to Paul's teaching that cast doubt on the possibility of resurrection by pouring scorn on the idea of a bodily resurrection. Maybe the thought is that a human body is perishable, so what is the point of resurrecting it. Paul's reply is first to use the analogy of sowing where the seed dies and is raised to life in a very different form as a plant. There is a whole variety of different kinds of flesh and body. So a new kind of body at the resurrection is not surprising. It will be incorruptible and spiritual. Here Paul is probably arguing from what he understood to be the nature of the risen Christ. Certainly he goes on to work out his doctrine in terms of likeness to Adam and to Christ.

### Conclusion

First Corinthians is remarkable among Paul's letters for the number of different theological issues that are raised. Although we have seen interesting links with Paul's teaching in I Thessalonians, there is a set of new issues that are developed much more fully. What stands out particularly is the place of the cross, or rather of Christ crucified, as the determinator of Christian behavior. This was a significant counterbalance to any tendencies to depend on human ideas or even to isolate the Spirit as the determining factor in Christian experience.[39] To this letter we also owe the fullest treatment of the resurrection in the New Testament. And nowhere else is the topic of spiritual gifts treated in such depth. There is also the development of the ecclesiastical concept of the body of Christ. It is interesting to note how these emphases all arise from the specific nature of the situation in the church with its tendencies to prize human wisdom and spiritual charismata and to deny the future resurrection of believers. First Corinthians is thus a particularly good example of the way in which the local problems determine the agenda for Paul, although the answers that he gives are his own. But we do not gain the impression that Paul is creating new theological ideas in response to these questions, as if he had never thought of them before. Rather, he seems to work from an existing theology that he calls into service and develops appropriately to deal with the particular way in which theological and ethical problems were posed to him.

We may also observe the way in which appeals to different sources of theology stand side by side. He is conscious at times of being inspired by the Spirit and recognizes the existence of other prophets in the congregation; he also makes appeal to accepted formulations of doctrine in wording that was becoming a fixed tradition, and he can also be influenced by Scripture. At other times, he seems to be exercising a Christian mind illuminated and determined by his knowledge of Christ.

## Bibliography

*New Testament Theologies:* (German) Hübner, 2:112-208.

Barrett, C. K. *The First Epistle to the Corinthians.* London: A. & C. Black, 1968.

Brown, Alexandra R. *The Cross and Human Transformation.* Minneapolis: Fortress, 1995.

---

[39]See Raymond Pickett, *The Cross in Corinth* (Sheffield: Sheffield Academic Press, 1997); H. Drake Williams III, "Living as Christ Crucified: The Cross as a Foundation for Christian Ethics in I Corinthians", *EQ* 75 (2003): 117-31.

Fee, Gordon D. *The First Epistle to the Corinthians.* Grand Rapids, Mich.: Eerdmans, 1987.

Furnish, Victor Paul. *The Theology of the First Letter to the Corinthians.* Cambridge: Cambridge University Press, 1999.

Hay, David M., ed. *Pauline Theology 2: 1 and 2 Corinthians.* Minneapolis: Fortress, 1993.

Hays, Richard B. *First Corinthians.* Louisville, Ky.: John Knox Press, 1997.

Martin, Dale B. *The Corinthian Body.* New Haven, Conn.: Yale University Press, 1995.

Mitchell, Margaret M. *Paul and the Rhetoric of Reconciliation: An Exegetical Investigation of the Language and Composition of 1 Corinthians.* Tübingen: Mohr Siebeck, 1992; reprint ed., Louisville, Ky.: Westminster John Knox, 1993.

Pickett, Raymond. *The Cross in Corinth.* Sheffield: Sheffield Academic Press, 1997.

Rosner, Brian S. *Paul, Scripture and Ethics: A Study of 1 Corinthians 5–7.* Leiden: E. J. Brill, 1994; reprint ed., Grand Rapids, Mich.: Baker, 1999.

Thiselton, Anthony C. *1 Corinthians.* Carlisle: Paternoster; Grand Rapids, Mich.: Eerdmans, 2000. See also his article in *NDBT,* pp. 297-306.

Tuckett, Christopher M. "Paul, Scripture and Ethics. Some Reflections". *NTS* 46 (2000): 403-24.

Watson, Francis B. "The Authority of the Voice: A Theological Reading of 1 Cor 11:2-16", *NTS* 46 (2000): 520-36.

Williams, H Drake, III. "Living as Christ Crucified: The Cross as a Foundation for Christian Ethics in 1 Corinthians". *EQ* 75 (2003): 117-31.

Winter, Bruce S. *After Paul Left Corinth: The Influence of Secular Ethics and Social Change.* Grand Rapids, Mich.: Eerdmans, 2001.

Witherington, Ben, III. *Conflict and Community in Corinth: A Socio-Rhetorical Commentary on 1 and 2 Corinthians.* Grand Rapids, Mich.: Eerdmans; Carlisle: Paternoster, 1995.

# 11

# THE SECOND LETTER
# TO THE CORINTHIANS

❧

Second Corinthians is an intensely personal letter. It is largely concerned with Paul's relationship with the congregation and with his personal circumstances, these two points being closely intertwined. Essentially the first part of the letter (2 Cor 1—9) is intended to prepare the way for a forthcoming visit; it prepares the ground by explaining the chain of events involving a person who had in some way grieved Paul and prevented him from visiting the church until there had been some kind of reconciliation. In the second part (2 Cor 10—13) Paul defends himself against a group who disparaged his apostolic mission and who appear to have constituted a threat to him.

Although there is no manuscript or other external evidence that 2 Corinthians was ever anything other than one single letter composed of the present thirteen chapters, scholars dispute the integrity of the letter. The major point at issue is whether 2 Corinthians 10—13 form part of the same letter as 2 Corinthians 1—9 or part of a separate letter that may have preceded or followed it. If this section was a separate letter, it was written very close in time to the main letter, and it will prove to be possible to discuss both parts of the letter as we now have it in the same chapter without any mishandling of the material.[1]

---

[1]The Pauline authorship of the material is not in any doubt, except that a number of scholars have proposed that 2 Cor 6:14—7:1 is a non-Pauline interpolation; see the defense of this section in Margaret E. Thrall, *A Critical and Exegetical Commentary on the Second Epistle to the Corinthians* (Edinburgh: T & T Clark, 1994, 2000), 1:25-36. See further David R. Hall, *The Unity of the Corinthian Correspondence* (London: T & T Clark International, 2004).

### The Theological Story: 2 Corinthians 1—7

*Paul's experience of suffering (2 Cor 1:1—2:13).* The first part of the letter opens in an unusual way with a thanksgiving to God for his intervention in Paul's life, although Paul generalizes what he says to include his readers. Evidently in some way Paul had been near to death, probably as a result of persecution, but had been delivered from it in a manner that he could ascribe only to God. He draws the broader point that not only he but his readers know what it is to suffer as a result of their faith but also to experience the comfort of God in the midst of their afflictions. Such experiences lead to a greater trust in God as the faithful deliverer of his people, but in some mysterious way God's intervention is related to the prayers of his people for one another. Paul and his readers are thus united with one another through their sufferings, comfort and prayers (2 Cor 1:1-7).

Paul then moves over to his specific situation with regard to the church, defending his behavior as holy and sincere and not dictated by worldly wisdom (note the echoes of the opening of 1 Corinthians). It appears that he had been accused of changing his plans in his own interests, saying that he would visit Corinth and then not doing so. But, being Paul, his defense of himself against this charge brings in the fact of God's faithfulness and sincerity; in Christ we have the fulfillment of God's promises, what we might call God's yes in which he does what he has promised. It is this faithful God who works in Paul and his converts, and therefore Paul does not vacillate. He did change his plans, but it was not out of self-interest but because it would not have helped his readers. It would have caused them pain that Paul would gladly spare them. Instead Paul had written a letter that had moved things significantly toward reconciliation. The congregation had been moved to take disciplinary action against the person who had wronged Paul, and now it was possible to go on to the next stage, to forgive and comfort the offender, who was gripped by sorrow for what had happened (2 Cor 1:8—2:13).

*The ministry of the new covenant (2 Cor 2:14—7:1).* This leads Paul from his personal account of his relationship with the congregation into a lengthy section in which he discusses theologically the implications of the recent events, only to resume the personal account in 2 Corinthians 7:2.[2] The section is par-

---

[2]Not surprisingly, some scholars have argued (unconvincingly) that 2 Cor 2:14—6:13 is an interpolation from another letter (on 2 Cor 6:14—7:1 see above).

ticularly dense theologically, and the train of thought is not easy to summarize.

Essentially Paul begins to think about the calling of the apostles and missionaries of Christ to spread knowledge of him, a knowledge that may lead to life and salvation or to death and judgment, depending on the reaction of the hearers. With such eternal consequences dependent on the presentation of the gospel a high responsibility is placed on the preachers. Paul claims that he lives up to this and is not in the work for personal profit. This may sound like self-defense to his opponents, but in fact he does not need any defense or commendation because the readers themselves are evidence of his authentic ministry. *Ministry (diakonia)* is a key word here, to signify the task of being God's agent doing his work. And for this work God adequately equips his servants (2 Cor 2:14—3:3).

Paul then moves into an exposition of the nature of the work of God's servants, which he presents as a glorious service in comparison with the service of the old covenant. Here we have a contrast between the old covenant, which brought condemnation in that it imposed commandments that people were not able to keep, and the new covenant, which brings the gift of the Spirit whereby people are given life. Paul regards the task of mediating the old covenant by Moses as being associated with glory, seen in the physical radiance of Moses' face when he had spoken with God, and argues that the new covenant must all the more be associated with glory. He develops the point further by commenting that the Israelites were unable to gaze directly at the glory of Moses, who therefore used to wear a veil to hide it. From this he draws the (to our minds) strange corollary that this signifies the inability of the Israelites to understand the covenant given by Moses; only when a person turns to "the Lord" is the veil taken away and he or she has the capacity to understand what God is saying. In this context the term *Lord* signifies the Spirit of God, who brings freedom (an echo of Paul's controversies over the law) and a transformation of believers into the divine likeness and glory (2 Cor 3:4-18).

All of this exposition seems to have as its main thrust the dignity of the calling of the apostles within the context of God's calling; it is emphatically not intended to be a basis for human glorying or boasting in a worldly manner but rather to emphasize the glory of the task rather than of the servants.

Nevertheless, the exposition serves to reinforce the confidence of the apostles even when they face opposition and apparent failure in their work. It implies that they do not need to use worldly ways to achieve their ends. When there is failure and people do not respond positively to the gospel, this can be attributed to a satanic blindness to the gospel.[3] In fact, through the work of the missionaries the glory of Christ is revealed to those who believe (2 Cor 4:1-6).

And all of this happens despite the frailty, weakness and mortality of the missionaries as they face all kinds of obstacles and opposition. God makes his power and glory known through weak human beings. In this they resemble Jesus, who submitted to death but was raised to life. So too there is a sense in which the missionaries are always dying in order to bring life. It is this knowledge that God brings life through death that encourages the missionaries to press on with their task in faith. Physically and outwardly they may be facing suffering and death, but all the time their vision is pinned on the God who will bestow life on them and those who respond to their gospel (2 Cor 4:7-18).

This point is so important that Paul enlarges upon it to assure his readers as well that even though their human bodies may perish, nevertheless they have a heavenly body prepared by God. He uses the contrast between a movable, perishable tent and a permanent building or house to make his point. In this way he stresses that the future destiny of the believer is not some kind of bodiless existence and that the gift of the Spirit already received by believers is a down payment, the first installment of what is to come. (Paul appears to think of the new "spiritual" body as already in process of formation "in" the believer, rather like the development of the butterfly within the chrysalis.)[4] There is thus an impermanence about life in the present body, and it is not to be compared with the future life, which brings us nearer to the Lord. With such a hope believers can be confident and indeed enthusiastic for the future, and their main responsibility is to live now in a way that will please the God before whom they will one day be judged (2 Cor 5:1-10).

Out of all this now emerges the apostle's concern for the congregation at Corinth. Paul hopes that this exposition of the nature of apostleship, which has led into the character of Christian existence as such, will commend his work to those who have had doubts about it and want some other kind of leadership.

---

[3] Paul does not complicate the basic issue by bringing in the possibility that sometimes apostles and other missionaries may be poor communicators.

[4] See n. 19 below.

Whatever he does springs from the love of God, which drives him to urge people to reconciliation with God. And here he inserts one of the most profound statements of the gospel. Two crucial images are used.

The one is mentioned almost in passing: it is the picture of a new creation. This motif has already been used by Paul in Galatians 6:15 to describe the new situation in which the difference between the circumcised and the uncircumcised is no longer of any significance. Scholarship is divided on whether the metaphor is more individualistic (the converted person is a new creature, and status as circumcised or uncircumcised is irrelevant) or more communal and cosmic (there is a new society in which such a distinction no longer matters).[5] Here the thought is concerned with the way in which people are evaluated: in the new creation Christ is no longer seen from a worldly point of view, and the same will apply to other people.

The other picture, developed more fully, is that of reconciliation, in which a diplomat brings about peace between two estranged parties. No usual diplomat this: Christ is the agent through whom God himself acts in such a way that the sins that have separated people from God no longer count against them and cut them off from God's friendship; by identifying himself with sinners (literally, with sin), and dying for them. Christ has made it possible for sinners to be regarded as righteous and to have a right standing with God. This is the gospel for sinners, but here Paul is applying it to the members of the congregation who have been rejecting him and with him the gospel. The reading of the letter to them gives them the opportunity to respond to God's call here and now (2 Cor 5:11—6:2).

In a final section he again defends his colleagues and himself as people who have undergone every kind of hardship in the cause of the gospel and have undertaken their task in dependence upon God and with utter commitment. This is not the style of imposters and timeservers! Through it all there runs the paradox of strength in weakness and weakness in strength (2 Cor 6:3-10).

The soliloquy about Paul and his companions ends with a further appeal to reconciliation (2 Cor 6:11-13). It is immediately followed by a call to separation from unbelievers who would lead them into sin and so separate them from

---

[5]See Moyer V. Hubbard, *New Creation in Paul's Letters and Thought* (Cambridge: Cambridge University Press, 2002), who adopts the former possibility.

the God who lives in their midst. Here, as at other points, we detect hints that the injunctions issued in I Corinthians needed to be repeated (cf. I Cor 8—10). The need for the congregation to be holy is paramount (2 Cor 6:14—7:1).

*Paul's story resumed (2 Cor 7:2-16).* After this long meditative and exhortatory section Paul returns to the story of the events leading up to the letter at the point at which he had turned from it back in 2 Corinthians 2:14. Picking up on his protestations of honorable conduct in the intervening passage he again appeals for reconciliation and then describes how his colleague Titus had brought him news of the sorrow and repentance of the congregation that had revived his drooping spirits and encouraged him to write this letter in anticipation of his visiting them.

### The Theological Story: 2 Corinthians 8—9

Sudden shifts of theme are not uncommon in Paul's letters to Corinth. With the theme of reconciliation concluded for the time being, Paul turns to the issue of a major gift that he was gathering together for the poor in the church at Jerusalem by means of a collection of money from his congregations. It is probably fair to conclude that the congregation had lost its enthusiasm for the donation during the period of strained relations with Paul, and that the theme is thus not entirely separate from what has preceded.[6] What we have here is an appeal for generosity and a discussion of the practical arrangements for ensuring that the money reaches its destination without any suspicions of mismanagement, but these points are made on the basis of a theology of giving.

The fundamental basis of the theology is the example of Jesus, who became poor so that others through his poverty might become rich. The language is metaphorical of the self-emptying of the incarnation, although it has also been held that it refers rather to Jesus' assumption as a human being of a frugal way of life (2 Cor 8:9). It emerges incidentally from the form of Paul's statement that poverty is not a good in itself, an ascetic ideal to be cultivated for its own sake; rather it is a condition that is voluntarily endured in order that the lot of

---

[6]Nevertheless, the view that 2 Cor 8—9 constitute parts of one or more separate letters that have been incorporated in 2 Corinthians continues to find support. Thrall, *Commentary*, 1:36-43, holds that 2 Cor 9 is probably a separate communication.

other people who are poor may be enriched (2 Cor 8:13-15).

A further point that is made is that God enriches people so that they may have the resources to help other people; they are gifted with riches by God so that they have the means to be generous (2 Cor 9:10). The suggestion is not that people simply give what is spare out of their abundant possessions, for the people singled out for praise are those who gave despite being comparatively poor themselves (2 Cor 8:1-5).

And, third, the effect of the giving will be praise to God from the recipients of the bounty that ultimately stems from him. There is what Ethelbert Stauffer would call a "doxological" motive for the action (2 Cor 9:13-15).

### The Theological Story: 2 Corinthians 10—13

Then comes a surprise! Despite the reconciliation announced earlier, there is evidently still a group of people who think that Paul adopts worldly methods rather than (presumably) God's methods in his work. There follows a lengthy defense of himself.

There is rather less straight theology in this section of the letter, which is concerned much more with Paul's opponents and with his response to them on a more human kind of level. Nevertheless, there are statements of theological significance. There is the concept of mission and pastoral care as a spiritual conflict that does not depend only on the use of human arguments but also on simply preaching Christ as Lord (2 Cor 10:3-6; cf. 2 Cor 4:1-6). We are reminded again that apostles are people with authority in the congregation (2 Cor 10:8), not only to preach the gospel but also to build up the congregations that they have founded. Paul can even refer to "the marks of a true apostle", which include signs, wonders and miracles (2 Cor 12:12); this is a fleeting reference that throws light on Galatians 3:5 and indicates that Luke was not romancing when he credited the apostles with miraculous powers in the narrative in Acts. They are the delegates of Christ for this purpose, but always within the limits that Christ has set for them. Nevertheless they are entirely in the hands of God and should not commend themselves (2 Cor 10:12-18).

The missionary task can thus be seen metaphorically as the presentation of the congregation to Christ as its Lord, like a chaste virgin to her husband (cf. Eph 5:25-32); presumably this presentation takes place at the parousia, and therefore there is an ongoing apostolic task of preserving the congregation from error, sin and disloyalty to Christ (2 Cor 11:2-3).[7]

This task is not easy because of the presence of false missionaries, whether people who falsely claim to be apostles or people who act falsely as apostles. Paul does not scruple to call them emissaries of Satan (2 Cor 11:14-15) because they tolerate sin in the congregation (this seems a fair implication from 2 Cor 12:21) and promote a "different gospel". They must also have been pressing for some kind of Judaizing practices. Paul responds to these missionaries whom he dubs "super-apostles" (2 Cor 11:5; 12:11) in several ways.

Paul could indulge in self-commendation by talking in a worldly fashion about how much he has undergone for the sake of the gospel, and he does do so. In particular he picks up on their self-commendation and replies to it by ironically descending to their level in putting forward his grounds for boasting (2 Cor 11:21—12:10). He claims to have worked harder than them (cf. 1 Cor 15:10) and to have undergone more humiliating experiences. But he stresses that though he could even boast of having visions of paradise, yet at the same time he was subjected to some intense weakening experience from which he could get no respite, except that God promised that he would experience his grace in the midst of his weakness. Here we have a vivid glimpse into Paul's personal prayer relationship to God.

Having defended himself, Paul exercises his authority in the congregation. He fears that when he visits them again he may be humiliated, that is, that his exultation and confidence in them may prove to have been misplaced, and he issues a stern warning that action will be taken against sinners. The authority displayed in 1 Corinthians 5 will be exercised again. For there is a limit to the weakness of the apostles: Christ, who died in weakness, is now alive by the power of God and exercises his authority through the apostles. But Christ is also alive in the members of the congregation, and indeed his presence is the test of whether they are truly believers (2 Cor 13:1-4). Let them test themselves to see whether Christ is in them (2 Cor 13:5). Evidently, then, there is a form of Christian assurance of salvation that is related to self-examination.[8]

Finally, it is noteworthy how the letter ends with a benediction that refers to

---

[7]The metaphor also figures in Rev 19:6-9 and Rev 21, where the people of God, also metaphorically understood as the holy city, new Jerusalem, are the bride of the Lamb in the new creation.

[8]As against any suggestion that Christian assurance depends solely upon the faithfulness of God's promises in Scripture.

Jesus Christ, God and the Spirit (2 Cor 13:14). Jesus Christ and God are the sources of grace and love; "the fellowship of the Holy Spirit" can only mean participation in the Holy Spirit and not a fellowship brought about by the Holy Spirit.[9] This threefold way of referring to divine blessings is anticipated to some extent in I Corinthians 12:4-6 and will occur again. It shows that a tendency to see God in a threefold way was developing perhaps quite unconsciously in the light of Christian experience.

## Theological Themes

If there is a single theme that seems to dominate this letter, it is that of the mysterious and paradoxical combination of suffering and joy, life and death that suffuses the life of the Christian believer and is particularly exemplified in the life of Paul as a Christian missionary. There is much to be said for C. K. Barrett's characterization of the three major letters of Paul:

> I believe that the church in our generation needs to rediscover the apostolic Gospel; and for this it needs the Epistle to the Romans. It needs also to rediscover the relation between this Gospel and its order, discipline, worship and ethics; and for this it needs the First Epistle to the Corinthians. If it makes these discoveries, it may well find itself broken; and this may turn out to be the meaning of the Second Epistle to the Corinthians.[10]

Although this comment is concerned with the contemporary church as it reads the letters in their canonical order, it is an apt analysis of the impact of these three key compositions. Second Corinthians is the work of a man who is broken by his experience and yet in this brokenness is aware of the healing power of God.

*The God of comfort.* It is appropriate, then, to begin with God. As has recently—and at long last—come to be realized, there is a central theology in Paul's letters, in that the Christian God is their focus. Jesus Christ has not replaced God at the center of Christian religion but rather has brought Christians to a new understanding of God as Father through his relationship to him as Son. This concept of fatherhood is basic for Paul's experience and understanding. Thus it is significant that the letter begins with God, God as the source of

---

[9]Cf. Thrall, *Commentary,* 2:916-19.
[10]C. K. Barrett, *The First Epistle to the Corinthians* (London: A & C Black, 1968), pp. v-vi.

apostleship (2 Cor 1:1), God as the lord of the church (2 Cor 1:1) and God as the source of grace and peace for his people (2 Cor 1:2). Then straightaway Paul plunges into praise of this God as the source of compassion and comfort in the sufferings that he has been enduring (2 Cor 1:3). The suffering was real and physical and contained the threat of death. We should not spiritualize it or in any way trivialize it. It was a situation that from a human point of view was hopeless and therefore utterly depressing and desperate. Yet in that situation Paul came to appreciate that he could still rely on the God who raises the dead. That resurrection might be expressed (as on this occasion) in rescue from his lethal situation, or in resurrection through physical death to eternal life. Either way, he had divine assurance that his life was not of so little account that it could be snuffed out without any trace remaining beyond the record of his achievements in the memory of his friends and their continuing affection for him.

God, therefore, is the God who can bring comfort, a hope and faith that rest on two facts. The one is that he had exemplarily raised Jesus from the dead, the supreme paradigm of the fact that he brings life in the midst of death. The other is that he is a God of grace and compassion who cares for his people. But a third fact should be added alongside these two foundational ones that relate to his power and love, namely, his faithfulness (2 Cor 1:18; cf. 1 Cor 1:9; 10:13; 1 Thess 5:24; 2 Thess 3:3; 2 Tim 2:13). It is a key element in the character of God that he will continue his relationship with his people and will not abandon them at any point to death and destruction. Here and now this God is present in the midst of his people, so that they form a living temple for the living and active God (2 Cor 6:16).

*Jesus Christ—suffering and powerful.* Each of these aspects of the character of God is accordingly related to Christ. Paul is more or less incapable of thinking of God apart from Christ. Thus the life-giving power of God is seen primarily in the resurrection of Christ, and it is on this basis that Paul affirms the resurrection of believers (2 Cor 4:14). Equally, the grace of God is nothing other than that grace that was shown by Christ in becoming poor that others might become rich (2 Cor 8:9); it is significant that in this section of the letter Paul moves freely from the grace of God to the grace of Christ (2 Cor 8:1; 9:8, 14). This is further apparent in the closing blessing, which parallels the grace of Christ with the love of God. On the whole, Paul prefers to speak of the grace rather than the love of God (for the latter see Rom 5:5, 8; 8:35, 39; cf. Rom 15:30; 2 Cor 5:14; 13:11, 13; Eph 3:19; cf. Col 1:13; 2 Thess 3:5). It would seem that the former word, *grace*, brings out more explicitly the way in which God's love contains the elements of spontaneous compassion for the needy and the undeserving. As for the faithfulness of God, Paul sees this as expressed in Christ, who is the proof that God fulfills his promises. Evidently Paul sees all the promises made by God through the prophets as at last coming to fulfillment in Christ.

Christ, then, occupies a twofold position in this letter. On the one hand, he is the archetypical exemplar of the mystery of death and life, suffering and power, humiliation and exaltation. On the other hand, he is the agent of reconciliation and new life. We consider the first of these statements here.

The precise significance of 2 Corinthians 8:9 with its reference to his assumption of poverty is disputed. Certainly the main point that is being made concerns the immense generosity of the divine grace in Christ that led him to "poverty". The traditional rendering is that this is a contrast between the "riches" that he originally possessed before the incarnation compared with the "poverty" that he assumed by becoming a mere mortal and taking the role of a slave (Phil 2:7). An alternative view is that the reference is to "the radical impoverishment of a degrading and humiliating death in which everything was taken from him"; his "riches" signify "his enjoyment of God's fellowship and his complete submission to his will".[11] In both cases, the fact that Jesus was literally poor gives parabolic expression to the spiritual reality. James D. G. Dunn lays stress on the parallel with 2 Corinthians 6:10, which he sees as a contrast between spiritual wealth and material poverty. The parallel is to be granted, and the question at issue is really whether the "riches" of Christ include his enjoyment of God's fellowship before the incarnation. Nothing that Dunn and Jerome Murphy-O'Connor say about the imagery precludes this possibility, and a decision hangs on whether Paul's understanding of Christ elsewhere includes the concept of his preexistence. At the same time, the language of poverty does not immediately suggest death as such, and the point of 2 Corinthians 6:10 is

---

[11]Jerome Murphy-O'Connor, *The Theology of the Second Letter to the Corinthians* (Cambridge: Cambridge University Press, 1991), p. 83, following James D. G. Dunn, *Christology in the Making* (London: SCM Press, 1980), pp. 121-23.

surely to suggest that the outward poverty of the apostles concealed their inner wealth that they could share with others, whereas here the crucial point is that Christ laid aside his riches to become poor. Thus the parallel proposed is not an exact one. When Paul refers earlier in 1 Corinthians 2:8 to the crucifixion of the Lord of glory, it is more likely that he is referring to the actual status of Christ at the time rather than to his future status. The traditional rendering of the verse remains the more probable one.[12]

What is not in dispute on any reading is that the human life and death of Jesus were characterized by poverty and weakness, by the opposite of that which would be expected in the case of a mighty Savior. In the case of Jesus, the weakness and vulnerability to death were replaced by the power associated with the resurrection when God raised him from the dead. Here, as elsewhere, it is the case that Jesus rose not by his own power but rather by the power of God; the weakness is complete. The pattern here appears to be one of weakness followed by power rather than of power displayed in the midst of weakness.

*Sin and the work of the missionaries.* Human life is characterized not only by the kind of weakness that we have already noticed but by the fact of sinfulness. We are thus brought to a consideration of the fact of sin in the community. The Corinthian correspondence is particularly concerned with this aspect of the life of believers, although surprisingly the term is found only in 2 Corinthians 5:21. However, the first part of the letter is concerned with some person in the congregation who had offended in such a way that he had suffered some kind of discipline or punishment imposed by the congregation. Furthermore, the task of the Christian missionaries is to spread the message of Christ, which radiates life or death to those who hear it. To know Christ brings life; to reject him incurs death. Unbelievers are blind to the light given by Christ and are perishing. The familiar categorization of humanity is thus part of the assumptions that surface periodically in this letter. The categories are not fixed in the sense that nobody can pass from one to the other.

Rather, Paul sees himself as engaged in a task of persuasion in which he will use all legitimate means, controlled as he is by the love of Christ. Two major concepts open up this possibility. Both of them rest upon what has been achieved by the death of Christ.

---

[12]Cf. Thrall, *Commentary*, 2:532-34.

*The new creation.* The first concept is that of a new creation. Paul begins by establishing that as a result of Christ's death people now live not for themselves but for Christ. Behind this statement lies the universally accepted understanding of the death of Jesus as in some sense a death on behalf of all people. From this statement Paul draws the conclusion that all people who join themselves to Jesus (elsewhere he makes it clear that this takes place through the act of faith in Christ) are joined to him in his death and resurrection, so that they can be said to have died and risen like him (cf. Gal 2:20). This sets them free from the old self-centered life, which is a life of sin and rebellion against God, and enables them to live for Christ. This leads him to affirm that he, and we, now see people in a new way. A fleshly understanding of people is ruled out; thus he now no longer views people who are in Christ in the same way as once he knew Christ, that is, in a worldly way that failed to recognize him as the Messiah and agent of God's new creation. He now knows Christ as the firstfruits from the dead. Thus a new creation has begun in Christ, and if anybody is "in Christ", it follows that this person is part of this creation and is to be understood in "new creation" terms. Paul uses this same terminology in Galatians 6:15 as if it were accepted language that his readers would understand: there is now a new world in which the old categories of circumcised and uncircumcised no longer count for anything, for God has made all things new through the resurrection of Jesus.

*Reconciliation.* The second concept is that of reconciliation. Paul sees himself as God's ambassador who appeals to people to be reconciled to God. This appeal is directed in the first instance to those who are sinners and unbelievers, but Paul apparently uses this language here in a derived sort of way to make an appeal for harmony and peace within the congregation and with himself.

Paul, then, passes on a message that comes from God and offers reconciliation to those who are his enemies. The basis for the offer, that which makes it credible that reconciliation really is on offer, is that God was in Christ reconciling the world to himself, not counting their sins against them. This is explained further by the statement that God made Christ, who had no sin, to be sin for us, so that we might become the righteousness of God.

Here the language of diplomacy provides the framework for Paul's expression of the nature of being saved or put right with God. The term *reconciliation* is used for a two-sided action. On the one side, God is said to have reconciled

us to himself through Christ and then passed on to us (i.e., believers) the agency
of reconciliation: it is the church's task to announce what is in effect an amnesty
to sinners. But, on the other side, the message that is passed on does not simply
say, "Everything is now all right, because God has reconciled the world to himself"; rather it says, "We urge you on behalf of Christ: be reconciled to God".
Sinful humanity is thus called to respond to God's initiative, and it is evident
that without the answering response no reconciliation can take place. The offer
must be accepted; peaceful relationships must be initiated. The clear implication is that if people do not respond to the gospel, they continue to live in
alienation from God.

The need for reconciliation manifestly springs from the fact that people
have committed sins against God. These are a barrier in that, on the one hand,
they are acts of rebellion against God, and, on the other hand, they are grounds
for condemnation by God, who holds the sins against people. The ground of
reconciliation is the fact that Christ became sin. The choice of the abstract
noun was inevitable, since, if Paul wished to assert the way in which Christ became one with sinners, he could not say that Christ became a sinner, which
would have been seriously misleading. He therefore chose to say that Christ became one with sin. An identification of Christ with sinners is effected whose
purpose is that a kind of exchange could take place. If Christ became one with
sinners, this had as its goal that sinners might become one with him who was
sinless and righteous and thus share in his sinlessness and righteousness.

It is impossible to understand how this transfer could take place if we do not
take into account the statement immediately above that "one died for all, and
therefore all have died". Elsewhere in Paul the crucial act of Christ for other
people is also his death. Here it is made clear that his death is equivalent to the
death of other people. Since again Paul regards the "wage" or due recompense
for sin as death (Rom 6:23; cf. Rom 5:12), it would seem to be inescapable that
he regarded the death of Jesus as his reception of the wage for sin, after the due
payment of which nothing further stands against the sinner. In the one death
of Jesus there takes place the death of all sinners who align themselves with him.

Here, then, we have an explicit statement of how reconciliation is achieved
using the language of trespass alongside that of reconciliation. The common
understanding of this is that reconciliation is possible when the penalty appropriate to the offense has been paid. The difficulty with this explanation for

many people is that once an offense has been committed, it is not obvious that payment of the penalty, especially by a third party, in any way reduces the guilt of the offender or signals a change in the offender from rebellion to acceptance.[13] It seems, therefore, that this explanation by itself is inadequate.

Another complementary possibility is that what Christ did was to display full obedience to God in contrast to the disobedience of sinners, and that he did so the point of death (Phil 2:8), so that his positive act of obedience somehow cancels out the sin, or provides that with which sinners can now identify themselves, thereby coming out from under their condemnation to death. Margaret E. Thrall makes the important point that the saving act is not limited to the death of Christ but must include his resurrection in a meaningful way. She suggests, following Morna D. Hooker, that through the resurrection Christ was vindicated by God as righteous, and that this righteous status is shared with sinners.[14]

The thought at this point is thus quite complex, and we should avoid any oversimple explanation of how reconciliation is achieved. The significance of the motif is that it demonstrates that God deals with sinners not simply on the legal level, as might be thought from a superficial understanding of justification, but also on a personal level in which the judge enters into a personal relationship with those who are justified and forgiven.

*The life of believers: Weakness and strength.* In the case of believers Paul appears to teach not only that present weakness will be followed by future resurrection but that the power of God is manifested here and now in the midst of weakness. This is certainly the case in 2 Corinthians 4, which stresses the fact of present inward renewal and life at work in the Corinthian believers.[15] Paul particularly stresses that involvement in the work of mission is what opens up believers to this experience, but clearly this is by no means exclusively the case. When he

---

[13]Cf. the discussion of these points as they arose in Galatians (pp. 223-26).

[14]Cf. Thrall, *Commentary*, 1:439-44; Morna D. Hooker, "Interchange in Christ", *JTS* n.s. 22 (1971): 349-61. Hooker correctly explains the result of Christ's death but is in danger of underplaying the role of Christ as substituting in his death for sinners, on which the possibility of interchange rests.

[15]When Paul says that death is at work in us, but life in you, this is not meant in absolute terms. The point is that the "death" of Paul is what leads to the "life" experienced by the Corinthians, and it does not mean that they are exempt from death as they share in Paul's ministry of the gospel or that Paul does not share in the life brought by the gospel. The contrast here is the broad one between missionaries and converts.

cites himself as an example of strength in the midst of weakness in 2 Corinthians 12:7-10, there is no suggestion that this is purely an apostolic experience.

What, then, do weakness and strength signify? The weakness would appear to be the circumstances of the believer seen from a worldly point of view: a body vulnerable to weariness, injury, disease and death, a social situation that may be one of poverty and lack of esteem, deprivation perhaps of a home, marriage and a family—all of them things that indicate that they are nothing in the eyes of other people. The strength is then the experience of the grace of God that enables them to cope with this situation and to accept it, the inner experiences of communion with God that impart a sense of being loved and of consequent joy, and the power to communicate the gospel effectively and thus bring life to other people. In what may seem a surprising manner, the spiritual effectiveness can include the apostolic capacity to show "the marks of a true apostle—signs, wonders and miracles" (2 Cor 12:12), the very things that might be regarded as worldly strengths and the basis for human boasting.

Spiritual communion and apostolic effectiveness are not dependent upon human position and possessions. Therefore, people should realize that the gospel is a divine and not a human power, and there is nothing special about the messengers of the gospel. Yet the tendency to assess people in human terms is a constant temptation and source of sin. Nevertheless, Paul still claims that there is something special about the service of the gospel that derives from the character of its content.

Here again is the paradox. On the one hand, the messengers of the gospel are likened to the captives who are being led in the victorious general's celebratory procession to humiliation and death. That this is the picture behind 2 Corinthians 2:14 is now firmly established.[16] It is an extraordinary picture of humiliation that ties in with the other descriptions of the despised situation of the missionaries (1 Cor 4:13). On the other hand, the missionaries are the messengers of the new covenant. Paul draws a remarkable comparison between the

---

[16]See Scott J. Hafemann, *Suffering and the Spirit: An Exegetical Study of 2 Corinthians 2:14—3:3 Within the Context of the Corinthian Correspondence* (Tübingen: Mohr-Siebeck, 1986); reprinted as *Suffering and Ministry in the Spirit: Paul's Defense of His Ministry in 2 Corinthians 2:14—3:3* (Carlisle: Paternoster, 2000). The alternative view, that the messengers share in the triumph as the general's colleagues, does not appear to be tenable.

service of the old covenant and the new. He notes how glory was associated with the former, exemplified in the story of the brightness that illuminated the face of Moses as a result of his talking face to face with God. He draws the conclusion that if the old covenant was accompanied by glory, how much more true must this be of the new covenant, not least in view of the fact that the old covenant brought condemnation whereas the new covenant brings life.

The language is bold and pretentious: what is its cash value? Paul brings it down to earth by insisting that all believers similarly behold the Lord and so reflect his glory as they are transformed into his likeness (2 Cor 3:18). The glory is seen by looking at the face of Jesus (2 Cor 4:6). But this does not bring us much further on, for the language is still metaphorical. We seem to have two spiritual concepts, looking at Jesus and being transformed into his likeness. How would Paul have explained these? This question is rightly raised by Thrall, who suggests that believers could "see" Jesus in the lives of people like Paul and in the visible bread and wine of the eucharist, and possibly in some kind of inward vision, and that the transformation of believers has the effect of making them more Christlike in their character.[17] It would be difficult to better these suggestions. The description of this process may seem unduly exalted, but it serves to enhance the significance of what is going on in the life of the believer.

Importantly, by putting things in this way, Paul in effect brings the missionaries down to the level of the ordinary Christians. Or rather he does not claim any special privilege for the former that is not shared by the latter. Yet this does not mean that there is not something special about the ministry of the gospel. It has a surpassing glory to it. But it is the ministry rather than the ministers that is glorious.

*Death, judgment and transformation.* The life of believers experiencing this continuous transformation leads in the end to a state of eternal glory by comparison with which the present sufferings are considered light and brief. Paul's development of this point is one of the more controversial aspects of the letter. In 2 Corinthians 5:1-10 he makes a number of statements that are reasonably clear and others that are more difficult to elucidate.

First, the destruction of our temporary earthly tent will be followed by the

---

[17]Thrall, *Commentary*, I:284-85.

acquisition of a permanent, heavenly dwelling.[18] The implication appears to be that this is physical death without surviving to the parousia, the problem that is also discussed in I Thessalonians 4.

Second, the metaphor of receiving new clothing allows Paul to affirm that the dead will not be in a state of nakedness, generally understood to mean the survival of the soul without some kind of body to incorporate it, and to make the point in passing that it would be preferable if the new clothing could be added on top of the existing clothing without having to take off the former. Taken literally, this metaphor might appear to clash with that used in 2 Corinthians 4:16, which suggests that while the outward body is decaying there is an inward life that is being renewed. But there may be harmony between them, in that what Paul is now thinking of is an appropriate habitation for the renewed inward life, and it would be easier if this new habitation could simply envelop the existing person without having to go through the process of dying and sloughing off the old body.[19]

Third, there appears to be an anticipation of this new dwelling in the fact that the Holy Spirit is already given to believers as a first installment of the new life. Again there may be some tension, in that the gift of the Spirit might more plausibly be linked to the renewal of the inward person inside the old body of the believer. It is probably best not to push too hard into tension Paul's two pictures of the eternal inward person developing inside the temporary outward body and of the temporary earthly tent being replaced by the eternal house.

Fourth, Paul sees the future state as a preferable one, in that we who are in the body are "absent from the Lord" and walk by faith. Although expressed in absolute terms, this statement must be understood in a relative sense; it is a case of comparative distance from the Lord, and Paul would not have denied that the Lord is with his people in the body.

---

[18]Note that the dwelling is heavenly; the concept of a new earth is not used here. Or did Paul share the imagery of Rev 21:2, where the new Jerusalem comes down from heaven to the new earth?

[19]It is also possible that Paul thinks of the "inward person" who is renewed as identical with the "heavenly dwelling", but this is much less likely.

Earlier in my discussion of 2 Cor 4, I used the familiar analogy of the "old" body of the caterpillar that turns into a chrysalis, inside which the "new" body of the butterfly develops, and then the "old" body is cast aside. The analogy is helpful, but it is not an exact one, and it does not take into account the fact that in 2 Cor 5 the inward person that is developing inside the old body now needs a new body in which it can be embodied.

Fifth, the prospect places a spiritual requirement upon all people to do what pleases the Lord, since all must appear before his judgment and be judged for what they have done while in the body.

The most problematic aspect of this account concerns when and how this change takes place. According to I Corinthians 15, the clothing of the perishable, corruptible believer with imperishable immortality takes place at the parousia of Christ (1 Cor 15:50-55), and this is in tune with I Thessalonians 4, where the resurrection of the dead is associated with the parousia. However, according to Philippians 1:20-26 Paul looked forward to the prospect at death of being with Christ. There are various attempts to solve this tension.

One view is to regard those who die as being "asleep" in Christ and not conscious of the intervening time until the parousia and their resurrection; people remain asleep for differing lengths of time depending on the time intervals between their deaths and the parousia.[20] A major problem with this attractive solution is that in the ancient world the dead were generally thought of as being in some kind of conscious state while they waited for whatever was to happen to them; the solution sounds too modern for Paul.

A second view is that what Paul is talking about here is the certainty of future provision at the parousia for the dead, although they will remain "naked" until that date but nevertheless with the Lord. This view takes "we have" in 2 Corinthians 5:1 to mean in effect "we have waiting for us".

A third view is that Paul understood the assumption of the heavenly, spiritual body to take place at the moment of death rather than after some length of time at the parousia.[21] An obvious objection to this hypothesis is the simple fact that the time interval between the writing of 1 and 2 Corinthians is remarkably short for such a major reorientation in his thinking.[22] Various responses have been made to this objection, such as that "2 Corinthians 5, written from the perspective of the individual Christian, envisages transformation

---

[20]F. F. Bruce, *1 and 2 Corinthians* (London: Oliphants, 1971), p. 204.

[21]Cf. Thrall, *Commentary*, 1:373-80.

[22]There is, of course, the alleged difference between the timing of the parousia in I Thessalonians (any time now) and in 2 Thessalonians (various events must precede the day of the Lord), which also must have arisen within a short space of time. But it can be fairly confidently affirmed that 2 Thessalonians offers a qualification of what is said in I Thessalonians rather than a contradiction in the timing.

at death, while I Corinthians 15, expressing the corporate hope of the Church, places the resurrection at the second advent".[23]

We need to bear in mind that for Paul the time gap between death and the parousia was probably conceived in years rather than centuries or millennia, and therefore it would not have been the problem for him that it is for us. Elsewhere when Paul talks of those who are asleep (I Thess 4:14-15), he is using language that is compatible with the dead being with Christ and aware of it (Phil 1:21-23). Here also the crucial element is that believers who have died are "at home with the Lord" (2 Cor 5:8), and it is this relationship that matters more than the problems raised by trying to harmonize what is said in different passages using varying imagery.

*The old and the new covenants.* For Paul believers constitute the temple of the living God (2 Cor 6:16); the Old Testament promises of God's presence in the midst of his people are fulfilled in believers. This statement is not made to draw a contrast with Judaism but rather to contrast the Christians with the unbelievers and to show how it is incompatible for believers to participate in idolatry.

Similarly, there does not appear to be any deliberate contrast with contemporary Judaism in the lengthy section in 2 Corinthians 3 where Paul develops the thought that Christian apostles and missionaries are servants of the new covenant (2 Cor 3:6).[24] Since this covenant is associated with the Spirit rather than with the written "letter", that is, the law, its servants can expect to be empowered by the Spirit for a service that is more glorious than the service of the old covenant. The associations of the old covenant with Mount Sinai and the giving of the law in awesome fashion could be said to be glorious, as reflecting the majesty and splendor of God, but this covenant brought condemnation rather than life because it exposed sin but could not cure it. Moreover, it was temporary. By contrast the new covenant that brings life through the power of the Spirit and is eternal is the more glorious and its service is correspondingly glorious, although its servants are in themselves weak and hard-pressed people.

Paul makes a further point by noting how Moses covered his face with a veil

---

[23]Murray J. Harris, *Raised Immortal: Resurrection and Immortality in the New Testament* (London: Marshall, Morgan and Scott, 1983), p. 101.

[24]The only other Pauline reference to the new covenant is in the Last Supper narrative at I Cor 11:25. The contrasting old covenant is found in 2 Cor 3:14. See further the references to two covenants in Gal 4:24.

to prevent it being seen. He sees in this a picture of the way in which when the law is read there is a kind of veil over the hearts of the hearers so that they cannot fully understand what God is saying. When people turn to the Lord, the veil is removed and they are able to understand. Christian believers see the Lord directly and as a result they are changed through gazing on the Lord. The new covenant thus brings about a developing and lasting glorification of believers that contrasts with the temporary glorification of Moses when he received the law from the Lord.

In this remarkable way Paul develops the idea of the superiority of the new covenant.

*Boasting.* As we have seen, 2 Corinthians is a letter full of the paradoxical juxtaposition of weakness and strength, exemplified in Christ, in the experience of Paul as a missionary, and in the lives of ordinary believers. There is a cruciform shape to Christian experience, in which being conformed to the death of Jesus and sharing in his resurrection life are thought of not only as a temporal sequence (dying now, resurrection to follow) but also as simultaneous. Moreover, the life and the corresponding power and glory are entirely the gift of God. The implication of all this is that there is no place for boasting in the Christian life. The vocabulary of pride and boasting is particularly characteristic of 2 Corinthians. Paul is able to boast or, better, exult in his converts at Corinth because of what God is doing in their lives (2 Cor 7:4), and he can express his confidence in them to other people (2 Cor 8:24; 9:2-3). But there is another kind of boasting in oneself and one's work for the Lord that can involve comparisons with other people. Faced by opponents who evidently denigrated him, Paul had to resort to some kind of self-defense in the interests of the gospel. This led him into a difficult area. He refers to the possibility of expressing confidence and pride on a human level (2 Cor 11:18), but when he does so, he proceeds to list not the kind of achievements of which other people were proud, but rather what he considered to be weaknesses and humiliating situations, such as fleeing ignominiously from Damascus. Even if he could refer to receiving visions of the Lord, he refuses to boast of them, but only of his weaknesses. Instead he talks about his "thorn in the flesh", a weakness that persisted despite his longing to be rid of it. He had to learn to be "strong in weakness". Even then he is not saying that he can be proud of having the spiritual stamina to cope with ongoing weakness, but he simply says that in weakness he experiences divine grace.

## Conclusion

The theology of this letter, then, is intensely concerned with Paul's experience as it developed in the context of a recalcitrant congregation and opposition from other missionaries. It is above all a theology of suffering by one who is qualified by experience to talk about it. The experience of suffering alluded to at the beginning of the letter evidently had a profound effect upon Paul.[25] The fragility of the life of the believer is always in view. It is a combination of ordinary human weakness as a creature of flesh with the weakness involved in identification with Christ in his vulnerability and suffering on behalf of humankind. But such a life is sustained by the new life that is already being imparted by God and that will be fully experienced in the renewal of the body.

## Bibliography

*New Testament Theologies:* (German) Hubner, 2:209-31.

Barrett, C. K. *A Commentary on the Second Epistle to the Corinthians.* London: A. & C. Black, 1973.

Belleville, Linda L. *Reflections of Glory: Paul's Polemical Use of the Moses-Doxa Tradition in 2 Corinthians 3:1-18.* Sheffield: Sheffield University Press, 1991.

Furnish, Victor Paul. *2 Corinthians.* New York: Doubleday, 1984.

Hafemann, Scott J. *Suffering and the Spirit: An Exegetical Study of 2 Corinthians 2:14—3:3 Within the Context of the Corinthian Correspondence.* Tübingen: Mohr-Siebeck, 1986. Reprinted as *Suffering and Ministry in the Spirit: Paul's Defense of His Ministry in 2 Corinthians 2:14—3:3.* Carlisle: Paternoster, 2000.

Hanson, Anthony Tyrrell. *The Paradox of the Cross in the Thought of St. Paul.* Sheffield: Sheffield Academic Press, 1987.

Harris, Murray J. *Raised Immortal: Resurrection and Immortality in the New Testament.* London: Marshall, Morgan and Scott, 1983.

Harvey, A. E. *Renewal Through Suffering.* Edinburgh: T & T Clark, 1996.

Hay, David M., ed. *Pauline Theology, 2: 1 and 2 Corinthians.* Minneapolis: Fortress, 1993.

Hubbard, Moyer V. *New Creation in Paul's Letters and Thought.* Cambridge: Cambridge University Press, 2002.

Martin, Ralph P. *2 Corinthians.* Waco, Tex.: Word, 1986.

Murphy-O'Connor, Jerome. *The Theology of the Second Letter to the Corinthians.* Cambridge:

---

[25]See especially A. E. Harvey, *Renewal Through Suffering* (Edinburgh: T & T Clark, 1996), for an exposition of this point.

Cambridge University Press, 1991.

Pate, C. Marvin. *Adam Christology as the Exegetical and Theological Substructure of 2 Corinthians 4:7—5:21.* Lanham, Md.: University Press of America, 1991.

Tannehill, Robert C. *Dying and Rising with Christ: A Study in Pauline Theology.* Berlin: de Gruyter, 1967.

Thrall, Margaret E. *A Critical and Exegetical Commentary on the Second Epistle to the Corinthians.* 2 vols. Edinburgh: T & T Clark, 1994, 2000.

Young, Frances, and David F. Ford. *Meaning and Truth in 2 Corinthians.* London: SCM Press, 1987.

# 12

# THE LETTER TO THE
# ROMANS

❦

James D. G. Dunn's book on *The Theology of Paul the Apostle* is organized around the letter to the Romans as a template that provides its structure since this is the most systematic of all Paul's letters in its presentation of his theology. Nevertheless, the letter arose out of a particular set of circumstances, and this means that, like all Paul's letters, it offers a presentation of aspects of his basic theology appropriate to those circumstances and shaped by them. The intense concentration on the topic of justification in the earlier chapters is motivated by the situation, even if this term is an important expression of what was central in Paul's thought.

The elements that make up the situation and the relative significance of each of them continue to be a matter of debate. As a letter addressed to Rome, it introduces Paul and his particular understanding of the Christian message to a congregation that he had not founded, although the length of the list of people greeted in Romans 16 indicates that he had a rather good knowledge of the congregation and its problems.[1] At the same time, coming as it does at the point where Paul was about to journey to Jerusalem for what (so far as we know) was the last time, the letter may reflect some of the concerns in his mind at this decisive juncture in his career. The crucial problem

---

[1] I assume that Rom 16 was originally part of the letter to Rome and is not a letter, or part of a letter, addressed to elsewhere.

is the place of Jews and Gentiles in God's plan of salvation and their relationship to one another. This practical problem emerges particularly in the closing, practical section of the letter (Rom 12—16, especially Rom 14—15),
where the "strong" and "weak" believers appear to be basically Gentile and
Jewish respectively. The body of the letter is concerned with the nature of the
gospel for Jews and Gentiles, and it takes up in a fresh way the issues that
surfaced in Galatians. On what terms does God accept Gentiles, and what is
the place of the Jewish law in this matter? And if we now have a church in
which on the whole Gentiles are responding positively to the gospel but Jews
by and large are not, how do we understand the position of the Jews as the
descendants of the Israel that was named by God as his chosen people in the
Scriptures? Broadly speaking, these two themes are tackled in Romans 1—8
and Romans 9—11 respectively.

It could be argued that this is really a question relating to God and his righteousness: is he dealing justly with all of humanity in justifying the ungodly
Gentiles and apparently no longer being faithful to his promises to the chosen
people, the Jews? In short, Romans might be seen as a theodicy.[2]

### The Theological Story

*Greeting and prayer report (Rom 1:1-17).* Romans begins with the lengthiest
greeting of any Pauline letter (Rom 1:1-7). It introduces Paul as a person set
apart by God to be a missionary of the gospel. The stress on his divine calling
is reminiscent of Galatians 1, where it is developed all the more fully, and is intended to underscore the divine authority that attached to his message. It is important that his gospel is promised in the Scriptures, and Scripture will be
quoted extensively in this letter at crucial points, since this is the authority of
greatest significance in debates concerning Israel and the Gentiles. The content
of the gospel is Jesus whose status is that of Messiah and Son of God, facts confirmed by his physical descent and his divinely wrought resurrection. The purpose of the gospel and of Paul's missionary work is to call together a people

---

[2]This is essentially the influential approach of N. T. Wright. It is certainly one aspect of the complex
purpose of the letter. See N. T. Wright, "The Letter to the Romans: Introduction, Commentary and
Reflection", in *The New Interpreter's Bible*, Leander E. Keck et al. (Nashville: Abingdon, 2002), 10:393-
770; also N. T. Wright, *The Climax of the Covenant: Christ and the Law in Pauline Theology* (Edinburgh: T &
T Clark, 1991).

drawn from all the peoples of the world[3] who are obedient to God but whose obedience springs from faith. The rest of the letter will develop this basic theme.

First, however, in the prayer report Paul thanks God for the faith of the addressees and describes his own prayers that he may be able to visit them (Rom 1:8-17). The report of the prayer quickly gives way to commentary. Paul believes that his hoped-for visit will be to their mutual benefit. It was not to take place for some time, as a result of Paul's arrest and imprisonment in Jerusalem, and therefore from our point of view it was providential that he wrote at such length to expound the kind of things that he believed that the congregation needed to hear. The impression is unavoidable that Paul felt the need to present the gospel according to his particular understanding of it to help a church that was strategically placed in the main city of the Roman Empire.

The theme is now restated much more precisely in terms of the content of the gospel. It is a message about Jesus, as we have learned already, that is powerful in conveying salvation to those who believe. Whether Jews or Gentiles, people need to be saved, and they can be saved through faith. And salvation is concerned with the fact that in the gospel there is a revelation of the possibility of righteousness that comes from God and that depends entirely on faith and therefore not on something else, as Scripture testifies. Clearly the emphasis of this thematic statement is on salvation as something that comes from God and is received by faith. Salvation is redefined in terms of righteousness. And this experience of righteousness by faith is for both Jews and Gentiles: "surprise, surprise", as we might say, for those who thought that the Jews as Jews already possessed it by virtue of being Jews and that Gentiles could have it provided that they adopted and obeyed the law.[4]

**The gospel according to Paul (Romans 1:18—8:39).** *Universal sin and guilt (Rom 1:18—3:20).* The first part of the letter is devoted to a development of the background to the gospel, the fact that God's wrath is directed against all sin-

---

[3]It is generally assumed that the reference here is to Gentiles as the special target of Paul's mission, but Paul's concern for the Jews also is powerfully expressed throughout the letter.

[4]One may put the former of these points otherwise by adopting the view popularized by Wright that there was a perception that the Jews were still in exile and needed deliverance from God, which for Paul would come through acceptance of the Messiah and the new relationship with God that he was offering to them.

ners, and that it therefore extends to all people, because all of them are sinners. In the remainder of Romans 1 the focus is clearly on the Gentiles. The issue is the revelation of God in nature rather than in the history of Israel or in the Scriptures, which ought to have been recognizable by people at large. We may speak of a revelation being given by God, but one that did not receive recognition by those for whom it was intended. This is demonstrated in the fact of idolatry, which testifies to people's failure to recognize God as God. In making idols they were worshiping creatures rather than the Creator. The result, which God brought about in his wrath, was that their lives were taken over by sins that destroy human life and that in the end lead to death as God's final judgment on them. It is not actually said that all people are guilty of all these sins. But what is emphasized is that failure to acknowledge God leads to sinfulness.

It would be easy for people who are relatively free from such serious sins to scorn those who do fall into them. From this point (Rom 2:1) Paul increasingly has the Jews in mind, as he fully has from Romans 2:17 onward. He argues that even those who do not fall into the grosser sins nevertheless sin in other ways and are equally culpable. If they do not experience God giving them up to the degrading way of life described in Romans 1, but rather experience his patience, they should see this as a merciful act intended to encourage and permit repentance. Lack of repentance will lead to divine judgment when people will be recompensed depending on whether they have sought the rewards that God gives by doing good or have followed self-seeking ways. And this judgment will be upon all people, both Jews and Gentiles.

At this point Paul introduces the fact of the law, given by God through Moses to the Jews: Does possession of the law not give the Jews an advantage over Gentiles? This is strongly denied, essentially on the grounds that it is obedience to what one knows of God's requirements that matters. Even Gentiles can obey God since what the Mosaic law requires is known inwardly to them.[5] Therefore, the day of judgment will deal with people who knew what

---

[5]Paul is no doubt thinking of the general requirements laid by God upon all people and not of the special requirements laid upon Israel in the law of Moses. And he is not saying that Gentiles keep God's requirements all the time but that isolated acts of obedience do happen. Whether he is thinking of Gentiles in general or specifically of Christian Gentiles (so Simon J. Gathercole, "A Law unto Themselves: The Gentiles in Romans 2:14-15 Revisited", *JSNT* 85 [2002]: 27-49), his point that Gentiles can obey God without knowing the law of Moses stands.

they should have done and did or did not do it.

In view of all this, it follows that Jews should examine themselves as to whether they keep the commandments of the law. Certainly Jews as Jews do observe one of the main requirements of the law, circumcision, but that one act counts for nothing if it is not accompanied by obedience to the other commandments, and Gentiles, who are not required to be circumcised, who obey the requirements of the law are in just as good a position as Jews or better. In the end what matters is not physical circumcision but the corresponding spiritual attitude of true obedience to God.

This does not mean that there is no value in being a Jew; the Jews were privileged with the gift of God's words in Scripture. And the fact that some of them did not believe does not nullify God's covenant with the Jews as his people.[6] Yet none of this makes the Jews any better than the Gentiles. The truth is that Jews and Gentiles alike are sinners, and by this Paul does not mean simply that sinners can be found just as much among Jews as among Gentiles; he means that everybody without exception is a sinner, as Scripture attests, and stands under the threat of judgment

From this there follows the all-important conclusion that people cannot get right with God by observing the law. All that the law does is to make people aware of their sin in that it labels as sinful the conduct that they practice. (Thus the law, for example, explicitly states that adultery is forbidden by God, thus confirming what people know in their hearts but may fail to acknowledge.) Possession of the law does not preserve people from sinning.

*Justification by grace through faith (Rom 3:21-31).* Universal sin and guilt are accordingly established. Equally, universal inability to get right with God has been asserted. The way is prepared for the central statement of the letter, which is that God has now revealed a righteousness that comes through faith in Jesus Christ. Although the term *righteousness* can on occasion mean the quality of treating people fairly that is demonstrated by God (and that might include his provision of salvation), here it indicates the status that God will confer on people and that they cannot gain by observing the law. If the noun is open to ambiguity, this is not the case with the verb, which describes people being justified

---

[6]Here Paul briefly introduces the important theme to which he will return for full-length treatment in Rom 9—11.

by the action of God. To be justified is to be put into a right relationship with God, in which the sins that persons have committed are no longer counted against them and consequently they can enter into a relationship with God characterized by peace and not by wrath. The way in which this happens is summed up in four significant terms.

First, it occurs through the *grace* of God, by which is meant his favorable attitude toward sinners, even though they have sinned and done nothing that can compensate for their sin. Grace is mercy toward sinners.

Second, there is an act of *redemption*, which signifies deliverance from the situation in which sinners find themselves, both the sin and its attendant consequences. Here the language of deliverance from a superior power that enslaves people is employed; in the language of Romans 6:23, sin is like a master who pays death as the wage to his servants, but God sets people free from that master and gives them what they have neither earned nor deserved, eternal life.

Third, the redemption is possible because God put Jesus forward "as a sacrifice of atonement" (Gk. *hilastērion*). This much-debated term may be a noun referring to the lid of the ark, or box, of the covenant in the tabernacle on which was sprinkled the blood of sacrifices by which atonement was made for the sins of the people (Lev 16:14), or it may be used adjectivally to signify the effect of that blood as *propitiatory* or *expiatory*.[7] These two technical terms indicate respectively that the effect of the blood is to satisfy the wrath of God against sin or to cancel out the sins that excite that wrath. However, it is unwise to create a dichotomy between these two actions, since each expresses an aspect of the nature of sacrifice. The points that need to be emphasized are that it is God who provides this remedy for the sins committed against himself and that, however the matter be understood, the effect of the action is to deliver sinners from the wrath to which they would otherwise be exposed at the last judgment. It is the blood of Jesus that achieves this effect; that is, it is the death of Jesus that delivers sinners from their sin and its consequences, and this means that this death

---

[7]These two interpretations come to much the same thing, since the ark of the covenant was the place where propitiatory or expiatory rites were carried out. The term was also used in 4 Macc 17:21-22 to describe the effect of the death of the Jewish martyrs in sacrificial terms as averting the wrath of God from the apostate nation to which they belonged. It is a matter of debate whether Paul's thought is related more to the sacrificial system or to the theology of martyrdom. See, for example, Douglas J. Moo, *The Epistle to the Romans* (Grand Rapids, Mich.: Eerdmans, 1996), pp. 231-36.

functions in a way analogous to that of the animal sacrifices described at length in the Scriptures. If so, it would follow, although Paul does not state it explicitly (as is done, however, in Hebrews) that the animal sacrifices are now redundant.

Fourth, it is through the *faith* of individuals that justification becomes a reality in their lives.

Various consequences are drawn from this basic statement. First, this action establishes the righteousness of God in the sense of his justice, in that earlier sins had been passed over unpunished.[8] Paul does not relate the death of Jesus here to the sacrifices offered under the law. It is not stated whether they had intrinsic power to atone for sin during the time when the law was in operation or whether they had this power in virtue of the fact that they symbolized the sacrifice of Christ.

Second, there is one way of justification for Jews and Gentiles, since justification does not depend upon observance of the Jewish law. Here Paul is thinking principally of circumcision.[9] Faith is equally available to both groups.

Third, the effect of this is to exclude what Paul calls "boasting", a term that combines the nuances of trusting or being confident in something and of regarding it as a human achievement, and of thinking oneself superior to other people who have not achieved it (cf. Phil 3:3-4). "Boasting" here is shorthand for "boasting in the law" (the possession of it and the fulfilling of it). That could suggest that the law no longer counts. On the contrary, Paul argues that his approach upholds the law, in the sense that he sees the law as prophetic of God's action in Christ, and thus the law is seen to be validated by God as prophecy that is fulfilled.

*The justification of Abraham (Rom 4:1-25).* The basic proposition has now been stated. It is amplified and defended in various ways in Romans 4—8.

---

[8]Presumably Paul is thinking here of the way in which mercy was displayed to the Jews (Rom 2:4) and the full penalty was not exacted from people in general. Death did not follow immediately upon sin, despite Gen 2:17 NRSV.

[9]Again he says nothing about the observance of the sacrifices in the temple. Part of the explanation of this may be that he was dealing with the situation in the Diaspora, where Jews could not sacrifice because they were geographically distant from Jerusalem but they did keep the other aspects of the law. (This explanation is not wholly satisfying, since considerable numbers of Jews did go to Jerusalem on pilgrimage, and this event must have meant a great deal to them, just like a Muslim pilgrimage to Mecca.)

In Romans 4 Paul tackles the question as to which side in the argument is taken by one of the principal witnesses in the debate. This is Abraham, the father of the Jewish people, who was understood by the Jews to have been put in the right with God by what he did (his "work") when he obeyed God's commands, including particularly the sacrifice of Isaac; moreover, Abraham was the first to practice circumcision in accordance with God's command, thus observing a preeminent element in the law even before the time of Moses. Paul's response to this objection is to cite the text that says that "Abram believed the LORD, and he was credited it to him as righteousness" (Gen 15:6). His interpretation of the text is that this speaks of righteousness as a gift given by God rather than as an obligation that God had to give to somebody who had worked to deserve it. The text could be taken to mean that Abraham demonstrated faith in God instead of confidence in his performance of the works of the law, specifically circumcision, and this faith was seen by God as the right thing to do; that is to say, in believing in God Abraham was acting righteously. Or we may say that God granted a righteous status to Abraham in response to his trustful acceptance of what God said.[10] Elsewhere in Scripture it is stated that God himself decides not to count people's sins against them without any word about these people doing anything to deserve it (Ps 32:1-2).

Further, the chronology is important. This declaration was made to Abraham before he was circumcised and therefore was not made because he had been circumcised. So circumcision was not the means of justification but a seal or confirmatory mark of his new status. It follows that circumcision is not required for justification, and therefore Jews and Gentiles are on the same footing, provided that they believe and regardless of whether they are circumcised.[11]

Consequently there is a sense in which Abraham can be seen as the father of

---

[10]Some interpreters take this to mean that the righteousness belonging to Christ is "imputed" to the sinner. Certainly justified sinners are "clothed in righteousness divine" as they boldly "approach the eternal throne" (Charles Wesley), and to say that this is the righteousness of Christ may be a fair inference from the language about putting on Christ, but it goes beyond what Paul actually says. The question of whether Christ's own righteousness is imputed to the justified sinner is currently the subject of lively debate in North America. See Mark Husbands and Daniel J. Treier, eds., *Justification: What's at Stake in the Current Debates* (Downers Grove, Ill.: InterVarsity Press, 2004).

[11]An objector could of course have responded that circumcision as the subsequent seal of justification was mandatory for all believers, Jews and Gentiles. Paul would have doubtless have rejected the objection. In any case, circumcision of male Jews normally took place in infancy before they came to the point of belief.

all believers, both the Jews, who were physically descended from him, and the Gentiles, insofar as they all follow his example of faith. This accords with the Scripture that speaks of Abraham as the father of many nations (Gen 17:5). Paul thus resorts to the concept of spiritual fatherhood in order to account for the fulfillment of this scriptural promise to Abraham. He sees that the promise will work only if justification is by faith and not by keeping the law.

Finally, Paul reverts to Abraham's faith and demonstrates that he was a superb example of believing against all the odds in God's power to do what he promised. He is the counterpart to those who believe in the God who did the impossible again when he raised Jesus from the dead. In a brief comment it is asserted that the resurrection of Jesus is part of the saving event. If Christ died for our sins, that is, because our sins made it necessary, he was also raised for our justification, that is, in order to bring it about. By this Paul indicates that the resurrection is an integral part of the saving event and not just simply the restoration of Jesus to life after he had performed the all-important act of dying for sin. Specifically, Jesus raises dead people to life, as Ephesians 2 brings out especially. The effect of sin is not just to render people liable to judgment but also to place them in a state of captivity from which they need to be set free. Paul's concern is not simply with guilt and subsequent judgment, as is so often assumed.

*Justification and future salvation (Rom 5:1-11).* With Romans 5 Paul returns to consider the situation brought about by God's act of justification. It is noteworthy that justification is what takes place in their personal relationships with God when people believe rather than what happened at the point when Christ died.[12] Paul expatiates on the effects of justification. Essentially it issues in a new relationship with God that is one of peace, whereas formerly it was one of enmity. Enmity is a two-way relationship in which people may be opposed to God and disobey him, and he may be opposed to them because of their disobedience. But now the enmity is ended, and people can have confidence to come into the presence of God, as for example when they want to pray to him. This new relationship will culminate in sharing in the glory of God, which sinners had failed to achieve (Rom 3:23; cf. Phil 3:21). It is true that there are obstacles

---

[12]Contrast redemption and reconciliation, which occurred objectively when Christ died and rose and which take effect subjectively when people believe. Paul never speaks in this way of justification.

to such a hope, principally in the suffering that is part of human existence,[13] but such suffering is a means of developing a mature character, and it is offset by the fact that believers know God's love as an inward experience conveyed to them by the Holy Spirit.[14]

The fact of God's love is confirmed by the nature of Christ's death, in that he died for those who were ungodly and sinners, whereas in normal life people tend to give their lives only for those who are righteous and good.

As for the future hope, this also rests on the death of Jesus. If God has acted in Jesus to justify sinners, there is all the more reason to suppose that he will save those who have been justified at the final judgment. Put otherwise, if God reconciled his enemies to himself through the death of Jesus, how much more will he accept his friends at the final judgment? In this significant paragraph we note how Paul has a tendency to reserve the term *save* for God's action at the final judgment, so that salvation tends to be primarily a future expectation, whereas for believers justification is a past event with continuing effects. Paul also uses the language of reconciliation in a way very similar to that of justification to indicate the restoration of good relations between two sides previously at enmity with each other. As with justification, so reconciliation is achieved through the death of Jesus. Two aspects of this may appear to be somewhat paradoxical.

First, although God the Father and Christ are at one in their saving purpose, nevertheless the language of reconciliation and sacrifice can suggest that somehow Christ took the part of sinners in seeking reconciliation from God or acted the part of a middleman or mediator between God and sinners. The same is true when we hear of Christ or the Spirit interceding for us (Rom 8:26-27, 34).[15]

Second, although the attitude of God to sinners is one of grace and mercy and, as God, he has freedom to forgive (cf. Rom 4:7-8), nevertheless he can bring about justification and reconciliation only through the death of Jesus whom he gave up for human salvation. It has sometimes been proposed that the death of Jesus was necessary only for the sake of human beings, to convince

---

[13]Having announced this theme, Paul will return to it in Rom 8:18-39.

[14]This is the first mention of the Spirit in this letter in relation to believers (apart from Rom 2:29).

[15]This is why it is important that Jesus is a human being, representing humanity to God, as Rom 5:12-21 will explain in detail.

them that God was ready to forgive and by this display of selfless love to encourage them to respond and thus to remove any barriers on the human side. However, the overwhelming impression from the New Testament is that the necessity lay on God's side and that he had to do something before he could confer salvation. Again this might be understood in the sense that humanity lay captive to a superior power that it was necessary for God to defeat in order to set the prisoners free, but this is an inadequate explanation; alongside it we have the vocabulary of sacrifice that speaks of something done by God to deal with the problem of guilt and liability to judgment. When in Galatians Paul writes of Christ bearing the curse of the law, or in 2 Corinthians of Christ being made sin for us, he is expressing the concept of judgment being borne on behalf of humanity by Christ.

*Adam and Christ: Comparison and contrast (Rom 5:12-21).* The function of the second part of Romans 5 is to stress the universal availability of righteousness and life through Christ. The Scriptures recorded the story of how the first human being, Adam, had sinned[16] and consequently a sentence of death was passed upon him. As a result sin and death spread to the entire human race. Paul evidently concludes the universality of sin from the universality of death among humanity. What is not clear is how the sin of the rest of the human race is related to that of Adam. Adam sinned before the promulgation of the law of Moses, and sin is not reckoned where there is no law; this must mean that specific sins later punished under that law were not taken into account earlier. The real problem lies in the ambiguity of the last clause of Romans 5:12, which may simply mean that death came upon all people "because all sinned" (TNIV; NRSV) but has been taken to mean that all people were somehow "in Adam" when he sinned, and his sin passed to them, and they were "made sinners" (Rom 5:19). Be that as it may, it does not alter the fact that through one person sin infected the entire race.

But now comes the contrast for whose sake Paul introduced the comparison with Adam. Christ is also a man, and by his righteous deed there comes life for all people. The comparison is one-sided, for the greatness of the gift of life far exceeds the effects of one person's disobedience. Paul becomes positively lyrical as he explores the way in which the effect of Christ's deed far outweighs that of

---

[16]In company with Eve, but here the blame is put on Adam alone. Contrast 1 Tim 2:14.

Adam's sin. Where, then, does the law of Moses fit in to this, since Paul has built his case on the time from Adam to Moses? It makes no real difference. It slips into the history of the human race and makes sin the more obvious and the more blatant, in that there is now a lengthy list of specific deeds that count as sinful and so stand under judgment. But grace is greater than sin!

*Death and new life for believers (Rom 6:1-23).* It is hard to believe that any serious person would draw the conclusion that if grace is able to cancel out all sins, then we should go on sinning, because, the more we sin, the more scope there is for God to show his grace (Rom 6:1). It could be that the question is more a reductio ad absurdum that Paul places on the lips of people who want to uphold the continuing significance of the law. In any case, the point that Paul now picks up is that, despite the possibility of justification extending to cover all our sins, the recipient of justification is under obligation not to persist in sin.

The response to the question is essentially twofold. The second part of the answer will come in Romans 8, where Paul takes up the theme of life in the Spirit. The first part of the answer is to argue from the nature of Christian baptism as a rite to which all believers had submitted. John the Baptist had drawn a contrast between his baptism with water and the baptism that the Messiah would accomplish with the Spirit (cf. Acts 1:5). However, the early Christians did not speak of baptism with the Spirit but of baptism "into Christ" (Gal 3:27) or "in(to) the name of Christ". By this phrase they signified that baptism brought the believer into some kind of relationship to Christ. Paul also spoke of believers being "in Christ", a phrase that also signified a close relationship with him. Putting these two types of language together, we can see how baptism into Christ would be understood as drawing the believer into a spiritual relationship with him. This enables Paul to draw the consequence here that the baptized were baptized into the death of Christ and even buried with him. It could be said, therefore, that they died with Christ.

From this two things followed. The first was that the baptized could be said to have died to their old life in which they were under captivity to sin. If a slave owner dies (let us assume that there is no heir), then his former slaves are free since they no longer have a master to obey. But the same result follows if not the master but the slaves die. Once they have died, he has no authority over them because they are deaf to his commands and unable to obey them. So Paul claims that believers have died to their old master, sin, and are under no obligation to sin any longer. They cannot be forced to sin. They have freedom.

But this would be no freedom if the believers were simply dead rather than passing through death into a new sphere of existence. The second point that Paul makes, therefore, is that just as Christ rose from death to new life, so too believers who are united with him share in his resurrection. This is true in two ways. Ultimately, they will share in his resurrection when they are raised from physical death to new life or, if they are still alive at the parousia, are transformed. Prior to this, however, they are raised up spiritually to live a new life in which they can regard themselves as dead, so far as sin is concerned, but alive to God and therefore now responsive to him as their new master. Therefore, although they still live in this world, they now have a hidden life with God that transforms the way in which they live in the world.[17]

It follows that believers are no longer under duress to obey sin. But they are under obligation to obey God (or, negatively, to resist sin), and therefore they must consecrate themselves to him.

So far all is comparatively simple. But then at the end of Romans 6:14 Paul tags on by way of further explanation "Because you are not under the law, but under grace". This reminds us that underlying the discussion is the problem of the law of Moses. Paul's emphasis was on salvation by grace, and he saw this as being by faith rather than by law. Judaism had no difficulty with understanding salvation as being by grace, but it understood grace to be consonant with law: those who had become God's people by grace were now to keep his law as the condition of remaining so. Paul rejected this view because he believed that grace excluded the works of the law. He therefore drew antitheses not only between faith and works but also between grace and law. The action of God's grace did not require obedience to the law.

But this way of putting things was vulnerable to the criticism that if people were under grace and not under law, then it would not matter if they went on sinning. Paul had already answered this criticism by insisting that believers are under obligation to obey God, but he goes over the ground again so that the objection can be thoroughly refuted. Essentially he repeats the point that be-

---

[17]The understanding of baptism as identification with Christ in his death has sent scholars chasing for an explanation of its origins, with recourse to the mystery religions being a particularly congenial hunting ground. The exposition above tries to show how an explanation can be developed much more simply in terms of the implications of other basic theological motifs developed by Paul.

lievers are now slaves to God and therefore under obligation to obey him, just
as Jews were under the obligation to obey the law. But during the time when
Jews were under obligation to obey the law and Gentiles to the law written in
their hearts, they did not do so. They were slaves to sin because the law was
powerless to make them obey itself, and their lives produced a harvest of deeds
that stood under God's judgment. But now, as those who have been set free
from sin, they are under obligation to God and they will do what is good and
right. The result will be eternal life rather than the death that sin pays as its
wage; this could be understood as the wage for good deeds, but Paul insists that
it is God's free gift and not a reward that he is under obligation to pay.

*The impotence of the law (Rom 7:1-25).* Out of this statement arises the vital
question of the proper function of the law, which is tackled in Romans 7. In
the first part of the chapter Paul has yet another attempt to explain the relationship of the believer to the law. This time instead of the analogy of slavery he
uses that of marriage. A wife is bound by marriage to her husband so long as
he lives, but when he dies she is legally free of her obligation and may now
marry somebody else. Paul regards Jews as formerly "married" to the law and
under obligation to obey it. Then, whereas in the illustration the husband died,
in the application the "wife" dies and passes out of the realm of obligation to
her former husband; transferred by death and resurrection into a new sphere,
where the law no longer has force, the believer is now free to "marry" a new
"husband", namely, Christic.[18] Thus in the application the situation is exactly the
same as with the slave who dies to one master and rises to new life to serve another.

However, a slightly different point is being made. The point at issue now
is that before becoming believers people were under obligation to obey the
law; it had rightful authority over them, whereas the point in Romans 6 was
more that the slave was controlled by sin and unable to disobey. In Romans
6 Paul did not take up the question of the authority of the law, as we might
have expected, but dealt with the actual captivity of people to sin. Now his
point is that they were under the rightful authority of the law, but once they
have become believers the law has no longer authority over them: Christ and

---

[18]The shift from the husband dying to the wife dying has caused problems for some commentators,
but it is not too difficult to cope with.

the law stand in antithesis to one another. But juxtaposed with this argument is the one that had already been used in Romans 6, namely, that the law did not succeed in its aim of preventing sin; on the contrary, it functioned to stimulate sinful passions (see Rom 7:7-12). The written code of Moses could not stop people from sinning but rather made things worse. There is, however, a new way, that of the Spirit, and with the Spirit's aid believers can bear fruit that is pleasing to God.

With this statement about the law effecting sin in people, Paul might be thought to have come dangerously near to denigrating the law, a sure way to lose his argument with the people who thought that the law was necessary in order to prevent sin. Is the law itself sin, that is, is it on the side of sin? Paul's answer can only be no. Rather, the law functions to bring dormant (or, as Paul calls it, "dead") sin to expression so that its sinful character becomes apparent. Dormant in Paul was the tendency to covet. It was the knowledge of the law that forbade covetousness, which roused that sinful tendency into action and made Paul covet and made him realize that he was a sinner. So the law that was intended to produce life ("This do and you shall live") led to death. There was nothing sinful about the law, but it did stimulate evil desires into action and place Paul under condemnation. And yet, it was not really the law that "killed" Paul. On the contrary, it was the sinful nature in him, which the law exposed for what it really was. Paul, therefore, upholds the law very positively in Romans 7:12.

The remainder of the chapter goes into the question of sin more fully. Although Paul has elsewhere compared the written law code that kills with the Spirit that gives life (2 Cor 3:6), here he declares that the law is spiritual whereas he himself is "unspiritual" (lit. "I am of the flesh") and a slave to sin. There has been endless debate as to who is meant by "I" here and to what period in a person's life reference is being made. Paul here is clearly speaking on behalf of people generally and not just about his own experience.[19] The use of the present tense, as compared with the past tense in Romans 7:7-12, has led to the suggestion that Paul is here referring to his present life as a be-

---

[19] The long popular view that Paul was speaking about other people and not about himself, that is, that by "I" Paul was referring to anybody other than himself, is utterly implausible. See Gerhard Theissen, *Psychological Aspects of Pauline Theology* (Edinburgh: T & T Clark, 1987), pp. 177-265.

liever, with some division of opinion as to whether the reference is to the Christian life as it normally is or when the believer is abnormally made captive by sin. There is no doubt that most believers do experience such occasions in their life. But is the description also true of nonbelievers? Some would want to argue that unbelievers do not have the desire to do what is good, still less to carry it out, and therefore this cannot be a description of them. But this is simply not true. The Roman poet Ovid said more or less exactly the same thing as Paul says here.[20] Rather what Paul is doing here is to insist that a person may know what is good, because the law lays it down, and want to do it, and yet be unable to do so. The reason for the failure does not lie in the law but rather in the fact that the person lives "in the flesh" and is controlled by sin. There is no hope of deliverance—except through Christ: thus, anybody may experience the captivity described here, but only the believer has the key to freedom.

Here, then, we find the most focused account of Paul's understanding of human nature. Human beings have minds that can understand and even approve of God's law,[21] but they have bodies composed of various parts that are prone to sin and disobedience. This does not mean that sin is purely a matter of actions by the body; the covetousness mentioned in Romans 7:7-8 is a sin of the mind, which is part of the body as a whole. The body is made of physical substance, here broadly called "flesh". Paul used this term, which carries the nuance of the perishability and weakness of the body, to express that weakness that cannot resist the enticements of temptation to do wrong, and therefore he can draw a contrast between the mind, which serves God's law, and the flesh, which serves sin.[22]

*The Holy Spirit and future glory (Rom 8:1-39).* In Romans 8 Paul shows how

---

[20]"I see and approve the better things, but pursue the inferior things" (Ovid *Metamorphoses* 7.19-21). See Moo, *Romans,* pp. 442-51.

[21]Paul does not say that this attitude of approval is universal and present all the time. People can also rebel against God's law.

[22]From this it might be assumed that there is a simple dualism in humanity, so that people have good minds and sinful bodies, and one might draw the further conclusion that the mind does not need to be saved, but the body does. It is unlikely that Paul would have agreed. The "flesh" controls the whole life of a person, and the flesh/mind antithesis is not to be pressed. Elsewhere Paul recognizes that the mind needs to be renewed along with the body (Rom 12:1-2). Nor would Paul have agreed that the mind could be saved apart from the body. Ultimately the person is seen as an indivisible whole, and salvation consists in the resurrection of the body.

the conflict is resolved. Romans 8:1 should be seen as a conclusion drawn from Romans 7:25a with Romans 7:25b as a parenthesis. There is deliverance from the sinful body through Jesus Christ, and this means that believers no longer stand under condemnation because of their sin. Paul seems to have two things to say here. First, he is concerned with that fate of death, which is God's judgment upon sinners. The law could do nothing to stop people sinning and therefore from facing this judgment.[23] But God sent Jesus to be a sin offering, and his death is the means of dealing with sin. Second, Paul asserts that the Spirit of life comes into the lives of believers and enables people to live according to the Spirit and so to fulfill what the law requires. This would suggest that people who approve what the law says are now able to put their desires into action.

Paul now develops this thought in a lengthy comparison between the people who live in accordance with the flesh, that is, who follow the sinful desires that arise in a mind that is controlled by sin and whose destiny is death, and people who live in accordance with the Spirit, that is, who are guided and controlled by the Spirit so that they do what is in conformity with God's will and in the end attain eternal life. Just as sin can control people and make people to do wrong, so also the Spirit can control people and make them do what is right and good. This latter situation is that of all believers, since nobody who belongs to Christ lacks the Spirit.

Despite all this believers still sin—as they know from personal experience! So what is wrong? Evidently the control of the Spirit is not automatic. Paul has to remind believers not to live in obedience to their sinful nature but to kill their sinful desires by the Spirit. It seems that believers have some kind of freedom to decide which master they will follow; the Spirit sets them free to live by the Spirit, but they must make the decision to submit to the Spirit.

Obedience to the Spirit, then, leads to life. Paul expands positively on this thought by stating that those who are led by the Spirit are children of God. For a further function of the Spirit is to bring about adoption of believers into the family of God. It is because believers have the Spirit that they feel able to call God "Father", and as such they are promised as their

---

[23] As we noted in our discussion of Galatians, Paul did not see the Jewish sacrificial system as dealing with this problem during the time when the law was in force.

future inheritance a share in the glory of Christ.[24]

The exposition now takes what may appear to be a surprising turn.[25] If the main problem faced up until now in the letter has been sin, now attention is switched to the problem of the suffering endured by believers, and Paul develops the thought of the contrast between present suffering and future glory. He places this in the context of the perishable and fallen world that will be restored by God in due time. The renewal of the world is an integral part of hope in the Judeo-Christian tradition. Believers suffer from the decay and weakness of their bodily lives. They experience the reality of salvation but they are caught in the tension of "the now and the not yet", in that salvation is not yet fully realized. They live by hope, which implies that things are not all they should be now, and their weakness extends even to their inability to pray properly, but the Spirit is there to pray for them to God.[26]

More than this, Paul has the firm conviction that God has a plan for believers that consists in bringing them to share the glory of Christ (Rom 8:17). He has predestined that believers will be brought to this goal,[27] and therefore he takes the appropriate steps to bring it about, from calling them to final glorification.[28]

---

[24]Strictly speaking, an inheritance is what a person promises that their heirs will receive in the future when the person dies. The picture has to be broadened out when it is applied to God; it refers to what God has promised to his sons and daughters in the future with no suggestion that he dies.

[25]If we are surprised, then somehow we have misunderstood what Paul is aiming to do. The fact is that Paul is extremely conscious of the reality of suffering in human life, both as a result of our existence as frail human beings in a fallen universe and as a result of direct attacks upon Christian believers, and he is conscious of the way in which such suffering may tempt people to abandon their Christian faith. *Suffering* becomes thematic in 2 Corinthians, and *illness* and *death* in Philippians, and *persecution* is prominent in 1-2 Thessalonians. It was a basic insight of Paul that Christ had to suffer before he could enter into his glory (this way of putting it stems from Lk 24:26), and that for Christians it could not be any different.

[26]Paul recognizes the paradox here, in that God the Father does not need to be persuaded to answer the prayers of his people, and therefore intercession by one person in the Godhead to another is superfluous. The language, therefore, must be seen as deeply metaphorical to make it plain that God is on the side of believers.

[27]In this passage the term *predestination* refers to God's purpose of future glorification of his people, carried out by his sequence of calling, justifying and glorifying. It is to be differentiated from his foreknowledge, which is his prior knowledge that he will have such a people; here this prior knowledge may be collective (God foreknows that he will have a church) rather than individual (God foreknows and calls only certain individuals).

[28]When Paul uses the past tense "he glorified", he is possibly looking back on the entire process from a future vantage point when it has been completed, or he is thinking of a process that is already taking place (cf. 2 Cor 3:18). The passage does not state that God's plan is necessarily carried out for each individual who is called, and it obviously does not imply that some people might want salvation and yet not be called by God.

All of this leads up to a rhetorical conclusion in which Paul insists that believers need not fear any force opposed to them bringing suffering and even death, for with God on their side—a God, moreover, who loves them—there is not the remotest chance of success for their opponents.[29] Their hope rests on the faithfulness of the God who loved them so much that he gave his Son.

*Israel and the Gentiles (Rom 9—11).* Up to this point Paul has expounded his gospel, which promises salvation to Jews and Gentiles solely on the basis of faith. One major problem already faced by Paul in defending it was the question of the place of the Jewish law, which appeared to be swept aside by it, but Paul argued that his approach upheld the law.

A second problem is expressed initially in a remarkably personal manner. This was Paul's deep disappointment at the way in which the gospel was not accepted by so many of the Jewish people, whereas there was a much more enthusiastic Gentile response. Paul felt a tremendous sense of grief over this, since his fellow countrymen were depriving themselves of salvation. At the same time, their failure to respond constituted something of an embarrassment for Christians: why was it that Jesus was rejected by his people if he really was the Messiah, as Christians maintained?[30] Paul does not ask the question in precisely this form, but his wrestling with his personal sense of grief and his attempt to account for the unbelief of the Jews leads to a discussion that is a crucial part of the defense of his understanding of the gospel and of the purpose of God.

The bottom-line question, then, that Paul is posing is whether the failure of the Jews to respond to the gospel indicates that God has not kept his promise (Rom 9:6a) and has rejected his people (Rom 11:1). Whatever else he does in this part of the letter, Paul does try to answer this question. Paul develops a twin-track response to this accusation.

First, he comments on the promises. God is not to be convicted of failure to keep his promises. It was not the case that God promised that all Israelites (i.e.,

---

[29] Assurance of future salvation thus depends upon the love and faithfulness of God rather than upon some divine decree; Paul pins everything on the love of God revealed in Christ.

[30] The unbelief of the Jews was all the more surprising because they had received so many religious privileges in time past and because the Messiah was humanly descended from them. If the immediately following doxology in Rom 9:5b is to be attached to Christ (NRSV mg; TNIV text), it balances his human descent with his divine identity; however, the interpretation of this difficult phrase is disputed, and some scholars regard it as a separate exclamation.

the physical descendants of Jacob) would be included in the people of the Messiah. Certainly God's promises were made to Abraham and his offspring, but Paul notes that even then physical descent was not everything. For God was free to choose whom he would favor, and acceptance by him does not depend on physical descent. Just as believing Gentiles could be regarded as spiritually Abraham's offspring (Rom 4:11), so conversely physical descent was not necessarily a qualification for being part of his offspring. This could be seen literally in the narrowing down of the line of descent first through Isaac and not Ishmael and then through Jacob and not Esau. This demonstrated that the inheritance was not due to a qualification based on human works but was entirely dependent on God's call. The descendants of Abraham were not the natural children but the children called into being by God's promise. So, in the present time, it would seem, by analogy, that it is not belonging to the physical nation of Israel that matters but response to God's call, which goes to Jews and Gentiles.

Paul goes even further. He states that ultimately God is entitled to show mercy to some people and also harden some so that they do not believe. And he has the right to do so because he is God with freedom and authority to do as he pleases, like a potter deciding the destiny of his pots.

This may seem to challenge human freedom and to take away the blame from human beings who resist God. Not so. For Paul, God showed patience to those who were the objects of his wrath and makes known his mercy to those whom he has destined for glory, namely, the believers from the Jews and the Gentiles. God has accepted as his people those who formerly were not his people; in Hosea this refers to Jews who had rebelled against God and forfeited their position as his people, but he would bring them back to himself. Paul sees here a principle that extends beyond the Jews to the Gentiles.

Nevertheless, those who would be saved in this way would be only a small proportion of the whole of Israel, and the rest of the nation were in danger of going the way of Sodom and Gomorrah—to total destruction.

So Paul appears to be saying that the unbelief of so many Israelites is consistent with God's promises to the descendants of Abraham since these promises were never intended to include everybody, and God has acted in mercy to save a people composed of Israelites and Gentiles.

But now (Rom 9:30) the second line of argument is beginning to emerge. It is concerned with human response. What in fact has happened is that the Gentiles who in the past had not sought after righteousness had attained it, whereas the Jews, who had a past history of seeking after righteousness, had failed to attain it. The explanation of the difference, however, is not traced to divine choice at this point but to the fact that the Gentiles had responded to Christ with faith, whereas the Jews on the whole had tried to get right with God by the works of the law. They had a zeal for God, but it was misdirected in that they thought that the works of the law would lead them to righteousness and so to a right relationship with God. If righteousness was to be gained by the law, it was only on condition of keeping the law, which as Galatians tells us is not a possibility for sinners. There is another way to righteousness for Jews and Gentiles. It consists in believing that Jesus rose from the dead and so is confirmed to be Messiah and Son of God and openly acknowledging him as Lord.

Two important comments are made. The first is that Paul repeats the note of personal concern about Israel, but this time he tells us that he prays to God for their salvation. Clearly, therefore, he does not think in terms of a predetermination by God limiting the number of those who will be saved, although salvation still remains dependent on God's initiative. Second, he stresses how vital it is that the gospel be preached so as to give people the opportunity to believe. Faith comes as a consequence of hearing the message, but it is possible to hear and not to believe. The Jews have heard but by and large have not believed, whereas the Gentiles have believed.

The "by and large" is important. There were many Jews, including Paul, who believed. It follows that God has not totally rejected his people and prevented them from being saved. There always has been a small group of Israelites whose admission to God's saved people was due to grace and therefore not to their works. The rest of Israel have been "hardened" like Pharaoh so that they cannot hear and believe. This is to be understood as a judgment upon them for their unbelief. It is important to recognize that Paul is discussing the Israelites as a collective group and is not thinking primarily of all the individuals who compose it. Consequently there was no barrier in the way of individual Jews hearing the gospel and responding to it, but for the time being there has been a general hardening of hearts against the gospel, and God has in effect "given them up" to it, just as he gave up sinful Gentiles to the effects of their sin (Rom 1:24, 26, 28).

Paul wants to say that God has acted in judgment against Israel, but this does not mean that he has finally rejected them. The coming of salvation to the Gentiles could have the effect of making the Jews envious and so turning to the same source of salvation. Paul evidently believes, then, that the hardening is not absolute and despite it some Jews may be saved here and now. And to that end Paul was working among Jews and Gentiles.

There could be a tendency for the believing Gentiles to have superior feelings to the unbelieving Jews, and Paul warns against this. They are now part of God's people only by grace and must not become boastful of their faith; that would be a sin as bad as that of boasting of one's works. The Gentiles are reminded that they have been grafted into the olive tree that is Israel, whereas the unbelieving branches have been cut off. This metaphor indicates clearly that for Paul the church is firmly in continuity with God's people in the past.

Moreover, branches that have been cut off can be grafted back in. And Paul believes on the basis of a divine revelation backed up by Scripture that when the mass of the Gentiles have come to faith, the hardening of the Jews will come to an end, and there will be mercy for them.[31] So all Israel will be saved, by which Paul means the Jews in general. He is not saying that all people will be saved, but that all who believe will be saved.[32]

So Paul answers his question by stating that it can be seen that God has kept his promise to Israel, once it is realized that God's purpose encompasses those Israelites who believe and are Abraham's children spiritually as well as by physical descent but does not include those descendants of Jacob who do not believe, specifically those who have "pursued the law as the way of righteousness", who have heard the good news but not accepted it. There has always been a believing remnant in Israel, and if at present the mass of the people are hardened against acceptance of the gospel, the time will come, once the Gentile response is complete, for Israel to experience God's mercy, and thus finally all Israel will be saved. God's promise is irrevocable. Despite all that has been said about the freedom of God to accept or reject as he chooses, nevertheless, the last word is that God's purpose is to offer mercy to all, whether or not they accept it.

*Living the new life (Rom 12—15).* The remainder of the letter falls into the general area of application, spiritual and ethical. It depends ("Therefore", Rom 12:1)

---

[31]Some scholars deduce from this what they call a "national future" for Israel; I cannot find this in the text, which is concerned purely with people becoming believers.

[32]This is quite clear from the insistence on belief in Rom 11:23.

on the doctrinal statements made in the earlier part of the letter, which have tended to emphasize the grace and mercy of God. But, whereas earlier the stress lay upon the appropriate response of faith and not of works, there is now a shift to gratitude, to the rendering of a thank offering to God that consists in the dedication of the readers to God. There will now be a new way of living, not dictated by this sinful world but by minds transformed by God. Paul utilizes briefly the metaphor of the body, developed much more fully in I Corinthians 12, to argue that in Christ the members of a congregation belong to one another and serve one another in different ways depending on the grace (i.e., the gifting of the Holy Spirit) given to them. In line with this concept of mutuality he develops an ethic of love that culminates in a repudiation of taking revenge on other individuals for their wrongdoing against one another. Such acts will be judged by God.[33]

The motif of love is crucial for Paul (Rom 13:8-10). Love is seen as the way in which the law is fulfilled, since all the commandments can be regarded as the outworking of the command to love one's neighbor. The implication of this statement is that the requirements of the law are to be fulfilled by Christians, although they are not under the law but under grace. But the commandments in question are all moral commandments, and despite the lack of a clear differentiation in Paul's writings the hypothesis that in practice Paul saw a distinction between the moral commands and the Jewish ritual commands may be the best way to deal with the problem.

Also noteworthy here is the way in which Paul urges a new life on the basis of the fact that salvation (i.e., the final manifestation of salvation at the coming of Christ) is now nearer in time than formerly (Rom 13:11-14). Why should this be a sanction? Essentially the point is that the night of darkness is about to be succeeded by the light of day. Believers already belong to the day and should be ready at all times for its arrival lest they be found asleep and are excluded from it; this is much the same argumentation as in I Thessalonians 5:1-11. The imagery enables Paul to condemn the kind of sins associated with night and to urge people to put on appropriate clothing for the day. Again, it is im-

---

[33] A brief section in Rom 13 develops a theology of the state that acknowledges the existence of the rulers and their authority, which derives from God. The question of what happens when the rulers do not behave in accordance with God's justice is not raised; the norm is for subjects to obey them. Nor does Paul raise the question of the consent of the subjects to their rulers. It would have been an academic irrelevance in the situation of the Roman Empire.

plied that the choice between doing good and evil lies in their hands.

In Romans 14:1—15:13 the practical issue of believers living together in the same congregation is raised. The congregation included people who differed in their attitude to the observance of festivals and to food, in a way that was similar to but not identical with the issue discussed in 1 Corinthians 8—10. Paul establishes the right of both sides to live in their own way since both types of practice can be seen as driven by the desire to honor God, and there must be freedom for difference of opinion over how this is to be done.[34] The important thing is that, whatever people do, they act in such a way as to honor the Lord[35] and also to behave lovingly toward their Christian brothers and sisters. There are more important things than what people eat or drink. God's kingdom is concerned with establishing a community in which mutual peace and harmony, doing what is right and rejoicing in God's gifts are made possible through the influence of the Holy Spirit.

This section, then, is a plea for unity in the congregation so that people can glorify God together. God's intention, confirmed by Scripture, is that Jews and Gentiles together should glorify God. Christ came as a servant of the Jews to confirm God's promises to Abraham and their other ancestors, but these promises include the place of the Gentiles among the worshipers of God.

Finally, Paul comments that what he has written arises out of his concern for the conversion of the Gentiles, which he sees as a kind of offering that he is to bring to God as his particular service (Rom 15:14-33). The service, however, is not something that Paul does. Rather it is Christ who works in him by the Spirit. In this way he has been able to preach the gospel over the whole area between Jerusalem and the west of Greece, and he can now extend his sights to include the west of the known world, provided that his friends pray for him that he may avoid from trouble in Jerusalem and be able to travel to Rome and then on to Spain. We know that there was trouble in Jerusalem and that Paul's visit to Rome was delayed—and he came as a prisoner. Whether he traveled west subsequently is not something that can be certainly established, but neverthe-

---

[34]This is admittedly risky, for it is very easy for people to convince themselves that their inherited habits or their prejudices are honoring to God.

[35]It is important that Paul refers to God and the Lord (Jesus) side by side in this context. It is Christ who has been appointed by God as the Lord who is judge of all people, and therefore they are answerable to him.

less the gospel did make its way (2 Tim 2:9). The letter concludes with a lengthy doxology that sums up in a fresh way some of the main doctrinal teaching about the gospel that God had long planned, announced through the prophets and finally revealed so that all the nations might come to faith.

## Theological Themes

*The main concerns.* We have seen that many of the principal themes of Paul's theology are covered in this letter. Essentially Paul is expounding and defending his mission to the Gentiles and the gospel on which it was based, but always in the context that the gospel is "first for the Jew". He shows that all people, Jews and Gentiles, are sinners under divine judgment, and all can be justified through faith in Christ apart from the requirement to be circumcised and keep the rest of the law. This is possible because of the death of Jesus, understood as an act of redemption with the power to deal with the sins that make people guilty and liable to God's wrathful judgment. The pattern of faith as the means to justification is established from the case of Abraham. Any suggestion that justification by faith rather than by obeying the law results in an immoral life of disobedience to God's will is refuted by the fact that believers are set free from bondage to sin by their union with Christ and the gift of the Spirit. They are under obligation to live a new life of obedience to God that issues in corresponding fruit.

All this raises the question of the law and the suspicion that Paul is disparaging it. This suggestion is rejected inasmuch the law is God's law. It does not cause sin but rather exposes the sin that is already there latent in people's lives, but it cannot enable people to overcome sin; for this to be possible the power of God's Spirit is needed, so that law and Spirit form a kind of antithesis. There is accordingly an obligation on believers to live by the Spirit and no longer by their old nature, which is dominated by sin.

Paul faces up to the disappointing fact that the Jews have not responded to the gospel in the same way or to the same extent as the Gentiles, although some have done so. This does not mean that God has rejected his chosen people, but rather they have refused to accept that a right relationship with him comes through acceptance of what he has done in Christ rather than through their efforts to please him by the works of the law. This steadfast refusal can be understood as being due to a hardening that is a divine judgment on those who did not believe for a temporary period during which the mission to the Gentiles is successfully proceeding. Paul believes that once the full number of the Gentiles have responded to the gospel, then the Jewish people by and large will see what they have been missing and will then be saved.

Finally, Paul develops an ethic of love for the life of Jews and Gentiles together in the church. This in effect fulfils the law but at the same time allows for diversity in practice on some issues, always provided that diversity is accompanied by mutual loving concern for those who think and behave differently.

Such, in briefest outline, is the main theological concern of Paul in the letter. In the course of developing it a wide range of other topics are inevitably brought to expression.

*The sovereignty of God.* We have already noted that from one angle Romans can be understood as a theodicy, a justification of God when he is understood as the God and Father of Jesus Christ and of Christian believers. Paul's concept of God in Romans is of a sovereign being with authority and power over all the universe. He stresses the love of God toward sinners, issuing in his sending of his Son to save them (Rom 5:6-8), and toward believers, expressed in his power to deliver them from all the hostile forces arrayed against them and to bring them ultimately to that state of glory that he has foreordained for them (Rom 8:31-39). He also takes it for granted that God will judge those who are hostile to him and subject them to his wrath at the final judgment. The fact that salvation is dependent upon God's sovereign power and love creates a number of tensions that we must recognize while conceding that human beings cannot fully resolve them. Two areas in particular require attention.

*The problem of sin and sanctification.* The first is the problem of sin and sanctification. Left to themselves, all people are under the domination of sin, and although they may want to break free and may on occasion do what is good and right, nevertheless they cannot escape from sin and ultimately from death. The effect of believing in Christ is that people are delivered from the power of sin; they can be said to be "dead" to its authority over them, and they are now set free to obey God (Rom 6:19-23). Such freedom of the believer is not freedom in the sense of a permission or license to do what they like; rather, it is liberation from the power of sin so that they have the potential to become obedient to God.

Thus believers have it in their power to obey God, thanks to the power of the Spirit, which replaces the power of sin in their lives. But at the same time they may fall back under the domination of sin and need to be warned against doing so.

There is thus a paradoxical situation in which believers can be controlled by the Spirit of God, without which they cannot fulfill God's will, and yet they have to be commanded to do so and warned against the danger of succumbing again to sin. This is the same situation that we saw in Galatians 5, where believers are told that if they walk by the Spirit, they will not fulfill the desires of the flesh, but nevertheless they have to be urged to walk by the Spirit. Here in Romans believers can be said to have died with Christ and to be people who walk by the Spirit, and yet they have to be commanded not to yield to sin and to be told that they must not follow the flesh but the Spirit (Rom 6:13; 8:12-13). And Paul evidently knows that there is an experience of knowing what is good and yet not doing it, from which he can be delivered by Christ (Rom 7:24-25).

No explanation is given as to how it is that believers who have been crucified and raised with Christ and have received the Spirit still fall into sin and need to be exhorted not to sin. There is a tension here between divine empowering and the human freedom that can evidently choose not to do righteousness. We can also recognize that divine power can work on human lives in response to prayer, with the implication that this would not happen apart from prayer; Paul genuinely believes that the prayers of his readers can significantly alter what happens to him (Rom 15:30-32).

*The problem of election and faith.* Related tensions arise with regard to belief and unbelief and the will of God. There are passages that are traditionally taken to mean that God has chosen beforehand those whom he intends to save, calls them and then brings about the whole process that leads to their justification and eventual glorification (Rom 8:29-30). The implication would appear to be that in some way he also brings about the fact that they respond to the gospel with faith, although this is not in fact said. Similarly, it is said that God can harden certain people so that they do not respond to him, from Pharaoh to the present generation of unbelieving Jews who reject the way of salvation by faith (Rom 9:18; 11:7-10, 25; cf. 2:5).[36]

---

[36]In the case of the latter, at least, the hardening is a temporary judgment upon unbelief. The hardening is only "in part" (Rom 11:25); some Jews are not hardened and so are free to respond to the gospel. And the temporariness is with respect to the people as a whole. Did Paul envisage the turn in Israel affecting the same people as were now opposed to the gospel, or was he thinking of a new generation who would not share the unbelief of their parents and ancestors (on the analogy of the Israelites who came out of Egypt and died in the wilderness but their children entered the promised land)?

One overall approach to these passages is that associated particularly with Augustine and Calvin. They build on the statements that refer to God's choosing of people to be saved and his preparation of others for destruction and postulate that God has total control of human beings and chooses some for salvation but passes over others. The latter are left to the judgment that falls upon their sins, since they are held to be responsible for their sins, and God may even harden them in their unbelief. The former are those and those alone for whom Christ died, and God brings them to faith and repentance so that they are justified and preserves them in faith so that they do not fall away from their status as his people. The offer of salvation is thus not universal in the sense that God gives the opportunity of salvation for all people; although upholders of this view insist that the death of Christ would be adequate for all, they nevertheless hold that Christ died only for the people chosen by God to be saved. Yet this does not mean that anybody who wants to believe is prevented from doing so because they have not been chosen; but people want to believe and do believe because of the hidden working of God. He is working out a program in history whereby the Israelites as a whole are hardened and do not believe, while the Gentiles by and large come to faith, and then eventually the hardening of the Israelites comes to an end and "all Israel" are saved.

This understanding of Paul's theology is widely held because it seems to allow the reader to take much of what he says in an obvious and literal sense.

However, the difficulties in accepting it as the underlying rationale of Paul's thought are many.[37]

First, it goes against the clear teaching in this letter and elsewhere that the death of Christ is universal in its scope and not confined in its intent to a limited number of beneficiaries (Rom 5:18; 11:32).[38]

---

[37]In order to make this interpretation plausible resort must be had to a philosophical concept of compatibilism, the hypothesis that total divine control of human actions and human freedom to act and so to be held responsible can coexist. Whether this hypothesis is tenable is a highly controversial matter. Other proposals have been offered. A different kind of solution to the problem was offered by Jacob Arminius, who held that God's election of human beings to salvation was dependent upon his foreknowledge of what they would freely do. More recently some philosophers have made use of the mediaeval concept of middle knowledge as a way of reconciling divine foreknowledge and human freedom. The complexity of the issues and the lack of a consensus can be seen from James K. Beilby and Paul R. Eddy, eds., *Divine Foreknowledge: Four Views* (Carlisle: Paternoster, 2001).

[38]I. Howard Marshall, "For All, for All My Saviour Died", in *Semper Reformandum: Studies in Honour of Clark H. Pinnock*, ed. Stanley E. Porter and Anthony R. Cross (Carlisle: Paternoster: 2003), pp. 322-46.

Second, it makes God out to be unjust in that he arbitrarily dispenses mercy to some and not to others.[39] It is true that Paul defends God's freedom to do so (Rom 9:15), but his point is rather that human beings cannot compel God to be merciful, and not that God is arbitrary in his exercise of mercy.

Third, Paul's language of predestination refers either to what God purposes to do with people who have come to faith or to his purpose of creating a people for himself rather than to his purpose to save some specific individuals and not others.[40]

Fourth, he prays to God that Israel may behave differently (Rom 10:1).[41] But, if God has predetermined the whole course of history, Paul's prayer would be pointless. The alternative is that even Paul's prayers were preordained by God, as were God's responses to them. In that case, however, prayer is not really prayer; the divine-human relationship ceases to be a relationship between persons and becomes more like the enactment of a dramatic script.

Fifth, Paul describes how God can appeal to the obstinate people and be disappointed by their lack of response in a way that would be inconsistent with his having hardened them (Rom 10:21). He also refers to people not persisting in their unbelief as if it were within their own power whether or not to believe (Rom 11:23). He also tries to make Israel envious of the Gentiles so that they will also want to believe (Rom 11:14). But if everything was foreordained by God, then God would have had to foreordain that the Israelites would not believe and that he would punish them for what he had foreordained that they would do by hardening them (since their lack of belief was their own fault) and

---

[39]The point at issue is not that God chooses one individual (like Paul, Gal 1:15) rather than another for a particular purpose, nor that he is free to do as he chooses (Rom 9:21), but rather that he is presented as choosing one person to be saved and another to be lost despite the fact that both are equally in need of salvation. See Marshall, "For All".

[40]Although the term *elect* is often assumed to refer to people not yet brought to faith who are destined to come to faith (as well as those who have come to faith), in Pauline usage it refers to people who have already come to faith. The term *elect* (Rom 8:33; 11:7; 16:13; Col 3:12) is not applied to potential believers but only to actual believers who have obtained salvation (see chap. 9 n. 5). When Paul speaks of those whom God foreknew in Rom 8:29, he is referring to God's plan to save a people for himself, without implying that God has foreordained which specific individuals will form part of that company; he is saying that his purpose for such people is ultimately to glorify them.

[41]This presupposes that God can influence people to believe in response to prayer. But Paul does not say, and never says, "God's purpose is that X should be saved, but in order that this should happen he instigates me to pray for X so that he can 'answer' the prayer which he has put into my heart to pray."

that then he would bring about their conversion.[42] God's purposes can be carried out by individuals who are apparently acting freely, and yet Paul can also refer to the activity of Satan in opposing the work of God and temporarily thwarting his plans (I Thess 2:18; cf. Rom 16:25).

Sixth, as we saw, from about Romans 9:30 onward Paul speaks of human actions of response or failure to respond to God's initiative without giving any indication that these were predetermined by God.[43] He never writes as though his preaching would lead to the salvation of a predetermined group of hearers who would certainly believe once they heard the message because God had predetermined it. By the end of Romans 9 Paul describes how the Gentiles have attained righteousness through faith, whereas Israel failed to secure righteousness because they chose the way of the law instead of the way of faith. At this point he is attributing the salvation of the one and the condemnation of the other to the presence and absence of faith respectively, but he does not say that this was because God chose to give faith to the Gentiles and to withhold it from Israel.

These observations demonstrate that this way of understanding Romans is problematic.[44] When all is said and done, we are left with a mystery beyond our total comprehension, but we can at least recognize that some solutions to it raise intractable problems. The mystery is partly due to the impossibility of understanding the relationship between God and human beings, but it is also the mystery of the nature and working of evil. All interpreters must recognize that the universe is fallen and the power of evil is active, and that we cannot explain its origin in a universe created by a sovereign God; that God has plans and can work to bring them to completion; that he treats people as persons and not as things; that there is such an activity as prayer to which God makes genuine responses; that he wants all people to be saved and come to a knowledge of the truth; and that he certainly works in human lives by the Spirit.

Somehow Paul is trying to express his theology in the light of these factors that are ultimately beyond human understanding, because we cannot fully understand either evil or God. It is, therefore, not surprising that he makes state-

---

[42]On this view, it would be hard to deny that God was responsible for human sin and unbelief.

[43]Apart, of course, from when he hardens those who have already sinned.

[44]See further Ben Witherington III with Darlene Hyatt, *Paul's Letter to the Romans: A Socio-rhetorical Commentary* (Grand Rapids, Mich.: Eerdmans, 2004), pp. 236-74.

ments that may appear contradictory or paradoxical or that, if taken on their own and absolutized, can be misleading. Paul holds together his beliefs in the sovereignty and freedom of God and his working out of his purpose for peoples and individuals while at the same time affirming that people are saved or lost depending on whether they believe or not. He recognizes that it is the Spirit who opens hearts to receive the gospel, but yet people appear to have it in their power whether they believe or not, whether they fall away or persist in belief (i.e., it is possible to resist the Spirit, Acts 7:51).

We thus have a set of statements that indicate that people attain righteousness because they believe and do not attain it because they disbelieve. The failure of Israel in general to attain righteousness is not attributed to God but to their disbelief.

Yet at the same time Paul can quote Scripture to the effect that God has hardened those who did not believe for a temporary period. He also uses the metaphor of the potter and the vessels to argue that human beings cannot complain to God about the destinies that he has in mind for them.[45] In theory at least since all are sinners, they are treated with justice if they are judged and condemned by God, but he can show mercy if he chooses. Yet his ultimate purpose is to show mercy to all, whether or not it is accepted, and mercy must be justly executed in that it is bestowed on all who are in the same piteous condition and not restricted to a limited number.

God has not rejected Israel in the sense that the door has been finally closed against belief in the Messiah because of the rejection so far. There is a remnant chosen by grace (this means the Jewish Christians who believe) whose salvation does not depend on works. There can be a hardening of people so that they do not attain to salvation, but this hardening is not necessarily final and irrevocable. In fact once the Gentiles have "come in", there will be a change and mercy will be shown to all Israel. This can only mean that there will be Israelites who believe; it is fundamental with Paul that righteousness is available on no other basis than faith. We then have to conclude either that God gives Israel the opportunity to believe through the gospel being proclaimed to them, or he causes

---

[45]When this metaphor is used in Jer 18 it refers to the potter's ability to change his plans for a particular lump of clay dependent upon how the clay behaves. It is not said that how the clay behaves is dependent upon God making it so behave.

them to believe. Some of the phraseology suggests the former: Romans 11:23 "if they do not persist in their unbelief", since they were "broken off because of unbelief" (Rom 11:20), not because God made them disbelieve so that he could break them off![46]

*Righteousness and faith.* Paul's understanding of the gospel in this letter is expressed in terms of righteousness and justification. But what is meant by righteousness and in particular by the righteousness of God? In some passages the term must refer to the justice and fairness of God (Rom 3:5). At other times it refers to an entity that God credits to human beings and appears to mean that quality or standing in virtue of which their sins are not counted against them and they have a good relationship with God. Here it is closely related to the doing of what is right in God's eyes as opposed to doing what is evil. It is the closeness of these two concepts that leads to misunderstandings. The failure of the Jews according to Paul was that they sought a righteous standing with God by doing the works of the law (Rom 9:30-31), whereas God credits righteousness to those who do not work but trust in him as the one who justifies the ungodly (Rom 4:1-5). Yet this does not mean that people are not obliged to do what God requires and to present themselves to him to do what is righteous (Rom 6:13, 19). The distinction between doing good works or righteous deeds in order to be in good standing with God or to win his favor and doing them because one is already in good standing with God is a valid one.

The crucial factor on the human side in justification is faith. Often this term is used by Paul without specifying the object of the faith since he wants to draw the contrast between believing and working as two opposing ways of getting right with God. However, he does talk of having faith or believing in God (Rom 4:3, 5, 24; 9:33; 10:11) and of having faith in Christ (Rom 10:14).

There is an ongoing debate about the phrase "the faith of Jesus Christ", which might be interpreted to mean "faith in Jesus Christ" or "faith shown by Jesus Christ" (Rom 3:22, 26).[47] Certainly Paul can refer to the faith(fulness)

---

[46]Paul may be thinking of a change in the same people because he has a limited time horizon, whereas we tend to think of a change in future generations of the Jews. Equally Paul does not seem to take into account the problem that we have of why for long years God ignored the Gentiles and allowed people to die without having heard the gospel or enjoyed its benefits. This is a real problem of theodicy.

[47]See p. 225 n. 36.

of God in contrast to human lack of faith(fulness) (Rom 3:3), but that is in the context of whether God keeps his side of the covenant even if the people are unfaithful to him. But to speak of the faithfulness of Christ in the context of his death for sinners (Rom 3:22) is more elusive. A possible clue is in Romans 5:19, where the obedience of Christ is the means of justification by contrast with the disobedience of Adam that led to condemnation. Obedience and faith are connected in Romans 1:5; 16:26. In Romans 3:26 the person who depends on the faith of Jesus could be understood as the person who depends on the faithfulness shown by Jesus in dying or as the person who depends on faith in Jesus. The latter understanding is much more probable in view of Paul's usage elsewhere of phrases with *ek* to signify the quality by which they live (Rom 2:8; 4:16 and especially Rom 9:30). Such faith is essentially trust in God's promises, as in the case of Abraham, and hence reliance on him rather than on oneself or one's own deeds.

*Israel and the Gentiles.* We have already looked at some of the issues surrounding Jews and Gentiles in our consideration of the sovereign purposes of God. Romans is particularly concerned with the nature of the church composed of believing Jews and Gentiles and how these two groups should live together. But it does so on the basis of theological considerations. For Paul, then, the non-Jews are described in the first chapter as people who should have known God from his revelation in the created order but had failed to do so and turned to sinful and idolatrous practices that God used to become an ongoing judgment upon them. They thus formed part of the sinful humanity that stood under God's wrath. But the gospel preached by Paul on the basis of divine revelation offered them justification and new life on the basis of faith and not on the basis of keeping the Jewish law, as Judaism would have required of them. Paul regarded them as being engrafted into the people of God, Israel, and was worried lest they should develop feelings of spiritual superiority to nonbelieving Jews.

As for the Jews, Paul argued that they did not have a superior position by virtue of possession of the law unless they kept it and that they were all sinners just like the Gentiles. Physical descent from Abraham and circumcision did not guarantee them a place in the people of God. But since they had in fact fallen under sin and the law could not save them, they needed to be justified by faith, just like the Gentiles. It is impossible to understand what Paul says in any other sense than that Jews and Gentiles alike can be justified only by faith in Christ.

Paul thinks of "Israel" as the people of God with a temporal dimension in that this body begins from Abraham and stretches down through his descendants, at first in the specific line of succession through Isaac and Jacob and the patriarchs, but, at least in the vision of the prophets, open to Gentiles. The coming of the Messiah, Jesus, would appear to bring out into the open the fact that not all physical descendants of Abraham lived by faith and therefore cut themselves off from Israel in God's sight, and that Gentiles who believed were thereby included in the people of God. Although Paul can describe believing Gentiles as the children of Abraham, he appears to reserve the term *Israel* for the Jews, but he clearly distinguishes between the Jewish people and Jews who believe; the latter are the true Israel.[48] However, he does use the metaphor of the olive tree from which some branches are broken off and into which a wild shoot is engrafted. The olive represents the people of God, from which God cuts off those Israelites who do not believe and into which he inserts those Gentiles who do.

It is important to note this because it makes clear that there is no straight supersessionism in the sense that the church replaces Israel as the people of God; rather the believing Gentiles are engrafted into believing Israel. But there is a development in that the people of God are now defined by faith in Christ and not by the marks of Jewish identity (physical circumcision, Jewish festivals, other Jewish practices). But this believing people of God have existed since Abraham. Nevertheless, they seem to have been always a minority in Paul's eyes, a "remnant", and in his time the mass of the people had been hardened and did not believe. But this hardening would not last forever, and Paul looked to a day when the hardening would cease and Jews would respond to the deliverer who would "turn godlessness away from Jacob" (Rom 11:26).

The fact that Paul speaks of "all Israel" being ultimately saved raises the question of what is called universalism. This is the doctrine that all people will

---

[48]This distinction is found in Rom 9:6a, where "all who are descended from Israel" refers to the physical descendants of Jacob, that is, Israelites (Rom 9:4; 11:1), and Rom 9:6b, where Paul is evidently thinking of those who are "really" Israel, that is, those who truly belong to God's people. Rom 9:27 distinguishes between the totality of the people and the smaller number (the "remnant") who will be saved. Similarly Rom 9:31 refers to the people who have not attained righteousness (cf. Rom 10:19, 21; 11:2, 7, 25, which all refer to Israel generally as disobedient and disbelieving). When Paul finally says that "all Israel will be saved", he is thinking of this sinful people and prophesying that ultimately there will be a massive turning back to God thanks to the coming of the deliverer.

ultimately be brought into the people of God, with none being left permanently subject to his wrath. Did Paul believe that all Jews and Gentiles would be finally saved and reconciled to God? There is also Paul's comment that just as one man's sin led to condemnation for all people, so one man's righteous act has resulted in justification and life for all (Rom 5:18, 19). These passages have been taken to imply that God will bring about the salvation of all people; since, however, salvation is by faith, what he will do is to cause all people finally to believe through some kind of postmortem persuasion and reformatory judgment. The fatal difficulty with this interpretation is that there is not the slightest indication in the texts of any such action. The final judgment, with the issues of life or death, is never presented as other than final. The texts must be understood in some other way that does justice to the total context of Paul's teaching. The point of Romans 5 is much more to demonstrate by the analogy of all becoming sinners through Adam's sin that all can be saved through the righteous action of one person, Jesus Christ; Romans 5:18 thus refers to what is potentially available for all, provided that they believe. In Romans 11, Paul is thinking of those who are still living; those who have already died are not within his sights at this point. He conceives of the full number of the Gentiles being saved, by which he evidently means all those Gentiles who are going to be saved; and by "all Israel" he apparently refers to all those Israelites who are going to be saved.[49] He can say this because he believes that God's purpose is to save Gentiles and Jews in great numbers.[50]

*The law of Moses.* The problem of Paul's attitude to the law is one that has already surfaced in Galatians. The Jews were distinguished from other people by the covenant that God had made with them at Sinai, thus ratifying his earlier choice of Abraham and of Jacob, and with this covenant there came the law committed to Moses by which they were to live as God's people. Paul was concerned with the reality of human sin, and in this letter he makes it plain that Jews and Gentiles have sinned. The Jews did so by disobedience to the law. The Gentiles did not have the law of Moses, but nevertheless they did

---

[49]This may sound tautological, but is not really so. "All Israel" is like "the full number of the Gentiles", the large number of those who will believe.

[50]On the whole issue see I. Howard Marshall, "The New Testament Does *Not* Teach Universal Salvation", in *Universal Salvation: The Contemporary Debate*, ed. Robin Parry and Christopher Partridge (Carlisle: Paternoster, 2003), pp. 55-76, and the other essays in the volume.

have knowledge of God's law in their hearts. And there was sin in the world even before the law was promulgated. Moreover, the law could not put people right with God if they had broken it. This statement might mean two things. It could mean that the law did not give people the capability of keeping it, and in practice they found themselves to be sold under sin. But also it might mean that the law did not provide for forgiveness for sins and transgressions already committed by those who were guilty of law breaking (Rom 3:19). Paul's gospel taught that what the law could not do God had done by sending his Son to deal with sin and by enabling people to live by the Spirit. He emphasized that justification takes place independently of the law but nonetheless the law is upheld.

So two points arise. The first is that justification does not depend upon doing what the law requires but upon faith that is related to what God has done in the death of Christ. Moreover, this is true for Jews and Gentiles. The important implication of this is that Jews need to be justified just as much as Gentiles. Therefore, their position as the people of God within the covenant is valid only if they believe in God rather than rest on their descent from Abraham or on their doing the requirements of the law.

The second point is that God's requirements are fulfilled by those who live by the Spirit. The law is thus fulfilled by them, whether Jews or Gentiles. Yet Paul can insist that the works of the law are not required any longer, certainly not for Gentiles and possibly not for Jews. Nevertheless, he insists that within the church Jews are free to keep the law and Gentiles are free from it, but each must respect the other's way of life and live in peace and harmony.

The term *work* is used by Paul in accordance with its usual meaning to refer to things that people do (requiring some effort on their part). A "task" may be laid upon a slave by a master (Mk 13:34). There are good works (Mk 14:6) and bad works (Jn 3:19). Not surprisingly, God's judgment is conducted on the basis of what people do, although how God balances the number and quality of good and bad works against each other is never discussed in general terms. However, within Judaism the works required by God were stated in the law (cf. Rom 2:15) and the principle is enunciated that whoever breaks one commandment is guilty of breaking them all, since the breaking of one commandment is indicative of rejection of the law as such (Jas 2:10). Paul claimed that nobody could be justified by the works of the law (Rom

3:20). Now, although Jews could claim to belong to the people of God (Israel) on the basis of their descent from Abraham and acknowledged this by accepting circumcision (in the case of males) and keeping the other requirements of the law, Paul was concerned with their real spiritual standing with God and the outcome of the final judgment, and he makes it clear that the conferral of righteousness does not take place on the basis of performance of the works required by the law (Rom 3:28). It depends entirely on the righteous action of Christ and is granted on the basis of faith; it is the believer to whom righteousness is credited by God. On the basis of this understanding of the work of Christ and the requirement of faith, Paul asserted that Gentiles were not required to accept the Jewish law.

*The Holy Spirit.* It is noteworthy that Paul refers to the Spirit especially in those contexts where he is making the contrast between Judaism and Christianity; the law and the Spirit stand over against one another (2 Cor 3; Gal). This is evident in Romans where there is a contrast between the inability of the law to deliver people from sin and the power of the Spirit to deliver them; if believers are no longer under the law, they live by the Spirit and are enabled to fulfill what the law requires (Rom 8:2-4). The flesh and the Spirit also stand over against one another, the former connoting human nature in its weakness, sinfulness and self-confidence, whereas the latter indicates the divine power that can transform human nature, bringing life and resurrection.

Despite this emphasis on the Spirit as a power that is effective in the life of believers, over against the power of sin,[51] there are hints of an understanding of the Spirit as an independent person who resides in believers (Rom 8:9) and who intercedes for them (Rom 8:26-27). The Spirit's power is also active in the task of the missionary (Rom 15:19). Christ and the Spirit are closely associated, so that the Spirit is called the Spirit of Christ (Rom 5:9) and the same effects can be attributed to Christ and the Spirit. Thus being raised to newness of life through union with Christ in his death and resurrection brings deliverance from the power of sin and the capacity to obey God (Rom 6), precisely what the Spirit conveys to believers in Romans 8. Paul can also speak of the gifts of the Spirit without using the term itself (Rom 12:6-8).

---

[51]Both the Spirit and sin can be personified as masters whom people must follow and obey (Rom 6:19-23; 8:14).

## Conclusion

Romans has been seen to live up to its reputation as the theological letter par excellence in the Pauline corpus. The need to expound his understanding of the gospel to a congregation that was not familiar with it gave Paul the opportunity to set out in detail his doctrines of justification by faith and the work of the Spirit in the believer in a more systematic form than in Galatians, where he treated the same issues.

## Bibliography

*New Testament Theologies:* (German) Hübner, 2:232-323.

Achtemeier, Paul J. *Romans.* Atlanta: John Knox Press, 1985.

Badenas, Robert. *Christ the End of the Law: Romans 10:4 in Pauline Perspective.* Sheffield: JSOT Press, 1985.

Barth, Marcus. *The People of God.* Sheffield: JSOT Press, 1983.

Campbell, William S. *Paul's Gospel in an Intercultural Context: Jew and Gentile in the Letter to the Romans.* Frankfurt: Peter Lang, 1991.

Chae, Daniel J.-S. *Paul as Apostle to the Gentiles: His Apostolic Self-Awareness and Its Influence on the Soteriological Argument in Romans.* Carlisle: Paternoster, 1997.

Cranfield, C. E. B. *A Critical and Exegetical Commentary on the Epistle to the Romans.* 2 vols. Edinburgh: T & T Clark, 1975, 1979.

Dunn, James D. G. *Romans.* 2 vols. Dallas: Word, 1988.

————. *The Theology of Paul the Apostle.* Grand Rapids, Mich.: Eerdmans, 1998.

Gathercole, Simon J. "A Law unto Themselves: The Gentiles in Romans 2.14-15 Revisited". *JSNT* 85 (2002): 27-49.

————. *Where Is Boasting? Early Jewish Soteriology and Paul's Response in Romans 1–5.* Grand Rapids, Mich.: Eerdmans, 2002.

Haacker, Klaus. *The Theology of Paul's Letter to the Romans.* Cambridge: Cambridge University Press, 2003.

Hay, David M., and E. Elizabeth Johnson, eds. *Pauline Theology 3: Romans.* Minneapolis: Fortress, 1995.

Longenecker, Bruce W. *Eschatology and the Covenant: A Comparison of 4 Ezra and Romans 1–11.* Sheffield: Sheffield Academic Press, 1991.

Marshall, I. Howard "For All, for All My Saviour Died". In *Semper Reformandum: Studies in Honour of Clark H. Pinnock.* Edited by Stanley E. Porter and Anthony R. Cross, pp. 322-46. Carlisle: Paternoster: 2003.

————. "The New Testament Does *Not* Teach Universal Salvation". In *Universal Sal-*

*vation: The Contemporary Debate.* Edited by Robin Parry and Christopher Partridge, pp. 55-76. Carlisle: Paternoster, 2003.

Moo, Douglas J. *The Epistle to the Romans.* Grand Rapids, Mich.: Eerdmans, 1996.

Morgan, Robert. *Romans.* Sheffield: Sheffield Academic Press, 1995.

Piper, John. *The Justification of God: An Exegetical and Theological Study of Romans 9:1-23.* Grand Rapids, Mich.: Baker, 1983.

Sanders, E. P. *Paul and Palestinian Judaism: A Comparison of Patterns of Religion.* London: SCM Press, 1977.

Sanders, John. *The God Who Risks: A Theology of Providence.* Downers Grove, Ill.: InterVarsity Press, 1998.

Soderlund, Sven K., and N. T. Wright, eds. *Romans and the People of God: Essays in Honor of Gordon D. Fee on the Occasion of His Sixty-fifth Birthday.* Grand Rapids, Mich.: Eerdmans, 1999.

Witherington, Ben, III, with Darlene Hyatt. *Paul's Letter to the Romans: A Socio-rhetorical Commentary.* Grand Rapids, Mich.: Eerdmans, 2004.

Wright, N. T. *The Climax of the Covenant: Christ and the Law in Pauline Theology.* Edinburgh: T & T Clark, 1991.

——— . "The Letter to the Romans: Introduction, Commentary and Reflection". In *The New Interpreter's Bible.* Edited by Leander E. Keck et al. Vol. 10, pp. 393-770. Nashville: Abingdon, 2002.

# 13

# THE LETTER TO
# THE PHILIPPIANS

⌒o⌒

Philippi was the first major town in ancient Macedonia to be visited by Paul and Silas when they crossed over into Europe from Asia (Acts 16:11-40), but Paul's letter to the church dates from a later stage when he was in prison, whether in Rome (cf. Acts 28:16-31) or less probably in some other location. The letter is essentially one expressive of the friendship or, better, fellowship between Paul, along with Timothy, and the congregation in Philippi, who were regarded with affection by him as sharers in the common task of Christian mission (Phil 1:5). The congregation had helped him by its prayers (Phil 1:19) and its giving (Phil 4:10-20).[1] Paul shares news about his situation as a prisoner with the aim of encouraging his readers (Phil 1:12-26) and writes about other contacts with the congregation through Timothy and Epaphroditus (Phil 2:19-30). At the same time there is a strong pastoral appeal in the letter to the congregation to avoid dissension and to cultivate unity so that they will not be weak and unable to resist the powerful temptation to give up their faith caused by active opposition (Phil 1:27—2:18; cf. Phil 4:2-9). There was also a danger to the church from a group of people (rival traveling preachers) who appear to have been encouraging Jewish ritual and legal practices as the path to spiritual perfection or maturity (Phil 3:1—4:1). We have, then, a letter that is shaped

---

[1]This element of friendship has been recognized as an important function of many ancient letters. Such letters contain the elements of friendly attitude, conveying the presence of the absent letter writer and promoting dialogue or conversation between writer and recipient. See John L. White, *Light from Ancient Letters* (Philadelphia: Fortress, 1986).

by the situation of Paul and that of his readers, and by the interplay between them. Paul's response to this situation in his letter is deeply theological and represents a typical use of his profound theology for pastoral purposes.

## The Theological Story

*Prayer report (Phil 1:1-11).* The letter opens with a prayer report in which Paul encourages the readers by telling them that he thanks God joyfully for their partnership in the work of the gospel, and he specifies more particularly that he is thinking of their ongoing spiritual progress and of their sharing in the task of mission. The former point is what we would have expected: Paul's concern is for the growth of his readers in such qualities as love, knowledge and righteousness, and he believes that his prayers to God will help to achieve this growth. The latter point is more surprising; it includes their support of Paul by their gifts, their prayers and their personal support through Epaphroditus, and, as seems likely, their witness to Christ despite the opposition that they were experiencing from people outside the congregation. Already in this section two key moods in the letter are highlighted, the joyfulness that Paul felt despite the difficulties faced by him and his readers, and the sense of partnership or fellowship that arose from their common experience of God's grace in their work for him.

*Paul's situation theologically examined (Phil 1:12-26).* In the main part of the letter that begins in Philippians 1:12 after the conclusion of the prayer report, Paul deals at length with his situation. This is appropriate since part of the occasion of the letter was to update his friends on a situation in which they were personally involved through Epaphroditus. At the same time, it is likely that Paul relates his experiences in such a way as to provide encouragement for the readers in their trying circumstances. There are two main factors in Paul's situation.

On the one hand, there is his imprisonment, which effectively impedes his freedom to be a traveling missionary. Nevertheless, it instantiates the principles that "in all things God works for the good of those who love him" (Rom 8:28) and that although the missionary may be "chained like a criminal. . . . But God's word is not chained" (2 Tim 2:9). The latter is Paul's chief concern. His imprisonment has led to knowledge of the gospel spreading among the people in the area, so that although he is limited in movement, he has been able to reach people who might otherwise not have been reached. At the same time, other believers have been encouraged and challenged to fearless witness.

On the other hand, there is the threat of further suffering and death that loomed over Paul. It seems more likely that this was execution related in some way to his activity as a missionary rather than the possibility of death by natural causes.[2] Either way, Paul had come to terms with this eventuality. He was able to recognize that death was a desirable experience in that it opens up the way to being with Christ. At the same time, he was prepared for continued work in this world despite all the harassment and pain that it entailed. And he had come to the conviction that for the time being this was his calling.[3] The belief that he would be reunited with his friends is dominant.

Imprisonment and the threat of death are thus relativized over against the hope of being with Christ and the progress of the gospel, but even the personal hope of the apostle is secondary to his concern for the good of the congregations that he had founded.

*Threats to the congregation (Phil 1:27—2:4).* Paul thus appears both as an example to the congregation at Philippi and as an encourager, and the focus of the letter now shifts to the way of life of the readers. Their Christian life individually and as a congregation is threatened in two ways.

First, there is the tension caused by threats from people characterized as opponents. From the beginning, the establishment of groups of believers in Jesus as Messiah and Lord has been opposed by the people among whom they hope to find converts. These are people who are on the road to destruction, since it is a firm element of Christian belief that those who reject Christ are destined for judgment. Therefore an obligation rests on believers to share their faith. But also they need to hold fast to their faith apart from which they too will suffer judgment. The Christian life, therefore, is one that involves whatever suffering may eventuate from the opposition outside the church.[4]

Second, there is the threat to the stability of the congregation due to the de-

---

[2] This is surely demanded by the reference to exalting Christ in his body in Phil 1:20, while not denying that the manner in which a person faces death from natural causes may also exalt Christ.

[3] How Paul knew this is not stated. It can hardly be simply a deduction from his belief that it was more necessary for the benefit of the congregation that he should remain alive to help them. Presumably it is a case of Paul's prophetic insight.

[4] It is worth reminding ourselves that, however indifferent many people in the Western and Northern world may be to Christians and their faith, to the extent that society is generally tolerant of different religions, it is not so in the world at large, and there has been more persecution of Christians in the twentieth century than at any earlier period in history.

velopment of tensions and disunity within it. If Christians do not love and tolerate one another and find unity in the gospel, then the congregation will not be able to withstand outside pressures and people will lack support and fall away from it. Internal dissension appears to have been a major problem at Philippi.[5]

Paul has two things to say to this situation. The first is to keep emphasizing that Christians must be prepared for hardship. They must realize that suffering for the sake of Christ is part of their calling as believers; it is integral to their Christian witness, just as it was for Paul. The second thing, developed rather more fully, is the need for internal unity and harmony in the congregation.

Such harmony could arise in two ways. One possibility is that there is considerable toleration of different points of view, so that people do not fight over differences of opinion on nonessential matters. The other possibility is that people are united because they are in agreement about how they should think and act. The former possibility is more concerned with such forms of behavior as cultural patterns. Elsewhere Paul insists that people are to receive one another, despite their cultural differences, as Christ received them, and not to dispute over what are ultimately things of no great importance (Rom 15:7). Here, however, he is concerned more with the second possibility, where disagreement arises through selfish aims and objectives, and his concern is that people should have a common goal in view of which they renounced selfish and conceited attitudes. They should be considering one another's needs rather than their own satisfaction. In short, the life of the congregation should be characterized by love for one another. Mutual love and a common set of purposes are linked together.

*The example of Jesus (Phil 2:5-11).* To reinforce this point Paul cites the example of Jesus, whose attitude should also be that of believers.[6] The careful language of Philippians 2:6-11 with its rhythmical prose is often taken to betray use of an earlier composition, a Christian hymn celebrating the career of Christ, which was then taken over into this letter to express Paul's sentiments. In my view the arguments against it being Paul's composition are not compel-

---

[5]On this see especially Davorin Peterlin, *Paul's Letter to the Philippians in the Light of Disunity in the Church* (Leiden: E. J. Brill, 1995); he may push his case too far but nevertheless correctly identifies a sad reality.

[6]This interpretation of a difficult phrase (TNIV) makes the best sense.

ling, and it is more plausible that this unit is the work of Paul.[7] The composition falls into two clear parts.

In the first there is described the way in which a being who had the nature of God renounced the privileges of that state and took on the form of a human servant of God, demonstrating an obedience to God that extended to willingness to die—and the most sordid of deaths at that.[8]

In the second part it is God who is the actor, and his action consists in exalting this being to the highest conceivable position alongside himself and requiring all creation to acknowledge him as Lord. The homage is that appropriate to God, as the echo of Isaiah 45:22-23 makes absolutely clear.

Two points appear to be implicit in this description. The first is that the attitude of self-denial shown by Jesus is the attitude that is to be cultivated by the readers. They are to deny themselves, even though their status is not that of Jesus. It is true that the self-denial of Jesus was in the interests of obedience to God rather than of service to other people, which is what we might have expected here. Nevertheless, since the call to serve other people is ultimately an expression of obedience to God, the difference is not significant. Certainly, although it is not stated here, the obedience of Jesus was in the interests of serving other people. The point, then, is primarily self-denial in order to achieve some other aim, and Jesus is the example of this.

The second point is that Jesus is declared to be the Lord before whom all must bow and confess him as Lord. The point is not explicitly pressed, but it would surely seem that this description functions as a summons to the readers to deny their selfish desires and obey Christ instead. Their unity will arise out of their common obedience to Christ and confession of him as Lord. While it is true elsewhere that believers are promised that they will reign or be glorified with Christ (Rom 8:30; 2 Thess 1:10), there is no indication that this motif is present here; on the contrary it is the exaltation of Christ over believers that is affirmed.

There is an imprecise fit between this statement about Christ and its context,

---

[7]For the former view see especially Ralph P. Martin, *Carmen Christi: Philippians 2:5-11 in Recent Interpretation and in the Setting of Early Christian Worship*, 2nd ed. (Grand Rapids, Mich.: Eerdmans, 1983); for the latter see Gordon D. Fee, *Paul's Letter to the Philippians* (Grand Rapids, Mich.: Eerdmans, 1995).

[8]The obedience was, of course, to God; to say that he was "obedient to death" as if death were the master is to misread the text.

in that Christ is obedient to God and serves him rather than other people, and his exaltation is not here a paradigm of what will happen to believers but rather constitutes the basis for their obedience to him. This constitutes the strongest ground for suspecting that the composition was originally intended to serve some other purpose than that to which it is put here, but it does not necessarily imply that Paul was not the author of it. Here we have a christological statement whose significance can appropriately be explored for its own sake rather than simply for its relevance to disunited believers.

*Application to the congregation (Phil 2:12-18).* Christian self-denial and obedience are rooted, then, in the story of Jesus Christ, and this theme is continued in the remainder of the section. The readers are specifically called to obedience and to the "working out" of their salvation. This phrase is ambiguous, but the most plausible view is that it refers to the expression in their lives of the fact that God is at work "in them". The "outward" life of the believer is guided and empowered by an "inward" divine influence. Although Paul does not refer to the Holy Spirit as the divine agent here, such a reference is probably implicit.

The practical expression of this obedience is a life that is free from selfish desires and is moving toward perfection and freedom from fault. And the achievement of this is a goal in which Paul hopes that he will be able to exult at the day of Christ (i.e., the day of judgment), when his work as a missionary will be vindicated. But the thought of exultation is not purely future. Even though Paul is presently expending his life, like the offering of wine that was poured out over a sacrifice, he can still rejoice over the congregation in Philippi, and he trusts that they too will rejoice over him despite his outward condition of imprisonment and the threat of death.

*Fellow workers (Phil 2:19-30).* At first sight the next section looks like a movement toward the conclusion of the letter as Paul intimates travel plans and possibilities for his colleagues and himself. Theologically, the section is notable for its stress on the overruling providence and goodness of God in relation to Epaphroditus, for the consequent confidence expressed regarding future plans, and for the way in which the Christian quality of Paul's helpers is described in terms of total commitment to Christ, to Paul and to the welfare of the congregation.

*The threat from Judaizers (Phil 3:1-21).* Instead of concluding at this point, however, the letter takes a sharp and somewhat unexpected turn. Or so it appears! In fact what we have is a command to "rejoice in the Lord" that is followed almost immediately by reference to exulting ("boast", NRSV and TNIV) in Christ Jesus. One of the threats to the spiritual progress of the Philippians was evidently that posed by a group of people who exulted and placed their confidence in what can broadly be called the flesh, that is, human credentials such as racial superiority or the performance of certain rituals such as circumcision or human zeal in carrying out religious duties that in themselves might be thoroughly commendable. These people not only did these things as born Jews or converts to Judaism but evidently believed that they constituted a basis for religious assurance of acceptance with God and hence of salvation, and they commended them to other people in the same way as we have already seen reflected in Galatians. Over against these sources of religious confidence Paul places Christ and encourages the readers to put their confidence solely in him. It is in the Lord that they are to rejoice and be confident and not in themselves.

Two motifs are contained here. First, Paul presents Christ as the source of true righteousness with God, that is, of a proper standing with him in which the problem of sin is dealt with. It is true that in the immediate context the word *sin* is not used; nevertheless, the whole thrust of a paragraph in which the aim is to attain righteousness clearly implies that people lack it because of their and need a new status.

Second, Paul insists that this new way of attaining righteousness cancels out the old way. The old way was by following the dictates of the Jewish law. This way does not work. It is an attempt at righteousness that is carried out by people ("a righteousness of my own") in accordance with what the law prescribes, but it is replaced by a righteousness that comes from God as his gift and is received not by our performance of the law but by faith, understood as the acceptance of what God does for us. So strong is the antithesis between these two ways of getting right with God that Paul can say that he now regards whatever he had inherited or achieved under the old way as a positive liability; he now regards it as so much rubbish to be discarded. This is perhaps the strongest language that Paul ever uses regarding status and achievements under the law as a means of getting right with God. It occurs in the context of the extremely violent language that he uses when he refers to circumcisers as "mutilators of the flesh" and even turns the Jewish vituperative epithet for Gentiles—"dogs"— back on the Jews (Phil 3:2). Elsewhere Paul can speak in more positive terms of the law (Rom 7:12), but here he has in mind the application of it to Gentiles as an integral ingredient of salvation. Christ and the law are incompatible as ways to salvation.

The thought, however, goes deeper. Paul is not concerned merely with gaining the righteousness that Christ provides. He sees this as part of a total experience of which the essence is that he "knows" Christ. The longing expressed in Philippians 1:21-23 thus returns to the center of focus. Paul wants to know Christ and to gain Christ. It is evident that the experience of justification cannot be separated off from the fundamental experience of whatever knowing Christ means. To some extent it is clarified in Philippians 3:10, where Paul speaks of sharing in the sufferings of Christ, becoming like him in his death on the cross (Phil 2:8!), experiencing the power of his resurrection and attaining to the resurrection from the dead. In this summary of the kind of thing said in Romans 6, Paul is saying that faith is an attitude in which people are so joined to Christ that they share in his death and resurrection and can expect to experience a final resurrection from the dead. The death is a complex experience of dying to sinful and selfish motives and the consequent actions, and the resurrection is to a new life of obedience to God empowered by the Spirit who raised Jesus from the dead, but above everything else there is the experience of knowing Christ, which appears here to be the central element in Paul's experiential religion.[9] This chimes in with other expressions of the nature of Christian experience in which it is evident that the decisive element is not so much a transformation of the individual or a blessing received but rather a relationship with God or Jesus Christ that is akin to knowledge and love of a human being. It is this relationship that results in the transformation and salvation of the believer.

The reference to attaining to the resurrection of the dead enables Paul to move from this intensely personal expression of the nature of Christian experience to the thought of the progress and development that takes place in the believer's relationship with God. He expresses this in terms of "perfection" or "maturity". The relationship with God is something that develops just as a human relationship will also do, as when we talk of "getting to know somebody better".

---

[9] The language of "knowing" Christ is admittedly rare in Paul, but it sums up his understanding of the central relationship in the life of the believer.

The imagery now changes as Paul expresses the same broad idea in terms of a runner getting closer to the goal. The manner in which Paul talks of the need for progress may well imply that there were other people around who did claim that they had "arrived". Certainly there were other people against whom he found it necessary to warn his readers. These were people who were enemies of the cross, and it makes best sense of the chapter if they are the same as the people who are described and implicitly condemned in such strong language at the beginning; they are opposed to the kind of religion that depends upon faith rather than upon works. The cross and people's attitude to it acts as a kind of litmus paper that brings out into the open the real nature of their relationship with God. It is not clear whether what is condemned here is their actual sinfulness in yielding to passion and desire or perhaps their glorying in the fulfillment of circumcision and the outward signs of Judaism.[10]

By contrast believers are people who are resident aliens in the world and therefore do not conform themselves to its ways but rather to the pattern of the kingdom to which they truly belong, the heavenly rule of Christ, who is already enthroned as the one to whom they must render their obedience (Phil 2:9-11). They look forward eagerly to the time when Christ will come and the kingdoms of the world will become the kingdom of God and the perishable will be transformed into the imperishable (as in I Cor 15).

*Joy, confidence and generosity (Phil 4:1-23)*. With this climax Paul reaches the end of the more doctrinally oriented section of the letter. In what remains he writes more on the practical and personal level. There is a repeated stress on the need for unity between believers in the congregation. They are encouraged to put their confidence in the Lord and, if they rejoice or exult in anything, to do so in him. They can be confident that when they pray to him God will provide for all their needs. They will be kept free from anxiety as the peace of God reigns in their lives.

Finally, Paul acknowledges the way in which the readers expressed their partnership in the gospel in a tangible way by sending him gifts through Epaphroditus, and he compares the gift to the offering of a sacrifice, in the sense of a gift made to God out of thankfulness to him rather than as an offering to deal with sin. The language of sacrifice is not unknown in the New Testament as a

---

[10]The term *flesh* could be used metaphorically or rather more literally.

way of categorizing service that is ultimately performed to God (Phil 2:17; Rom 15:16; Heb 13:15-16; I Pet 2:5).

### Theological Themes

From our survey of the theological story in the letter, it emerges that Paul is concerned with a number of issues relating to the Christian life of a congregation that was affected by the threat of opposition from outside the church and consequent suffering, the dangers of internal divisiveness, and the menace of some kind of Judaizing group. He was also concerned to reassure the congregation regarding his position, and he was able to use this part of the letter as a means of underpinning the paraenesis that he offered to them.

*Paul's relationship to Jesus.* Paul's central concern is with the advance of the gospel, that is, with the Christian message and the process of making it known, through which people come into an ongoing relationship with God through Jesus Christ and form a congregation (Phil 1:5, 12, 27). As in all his letters, Jesus Christ plays a crucial role in the argument. Paul refers to Jesus Christ at the beginning of the letter to define his own role as his servant and the Christian status of the readers (Phil 1:1); the latter are "saints in Christ Jesus". If the first part of this phrase picks up on Old Testament language to identify them as the people of God, set apart to belong to him as his distinctive people and to show this by various specific characteristics, the latter part of the phrase shows that they owe this status to their relationship to Jesus Christ. Similarly, when Paul prays for the divine blessings of grace and peace to be part of their experience in his opening greeting the Lord Jesus Christ is named alongside God the Father as the source of these gifts (Phil 1:2; cf. Phil 4:19).

One of the most important devices by which the significance of Christ for the readers is brought out in this letter, and indeed throughout Paul's letters, is through the use of the phrase "in Christ" or variants such as "in him". A brief survey of the usage in 1-2 Thessalonians was given earlier. The variety of usage here in Philippians is very similar. Sometimes it is the natural complement to a verb, such as to rejoice or be confident "in Christ", that is, on the basis of Jesus and who he is (Phil 2:19, 24; 3:1). At other times it expresses the way in which Christian conduct ought to be determined by the fact that Christ is the Lord of his people and requires a certain manner of behavior from them (Phil 2:29; 4:2). It is also used to indicate the person through whom God acts for the good of his people, calling them to salvation (Phil 3:14), protecting them (Phil 4:7) and generously meeting their needs (Phil 4:19). In several of these cases the phraseology indicates that the readers have a close relationship with Jesus through their faith in him (cf. Phil 3:9b), and this comes out even more strongly when they are simply said to be in Christ (as in Phil 1:1, 14; 3:9a; 4:21). Here the language suggests some kind of union with Christ, perhaps similar to the way in which Paul can speak of believers as parts of the body that belongs to Christ and of which he is the head, or again to the way in which John writes of believers being in Christ and Christ being in them.

This thought of close relationship to Christ emerges again when Paul writes about his desire to know Christ and the power of his resurrection and to participate in his sufferings (Phil 3:10). Plainly this is not simply knowledge about somebody but a personal experience in which Paul shares the experiences of Jesus. There is a great emphasis on the powerful effects of this union with Christ, in which the resurrection life of Christ is shared with Paul, now and after physical death. At the same time the experience involves Paul in sharing in the sufferings of Christ. The reference here is presumably to the pains and hardships associated with the Christian existence of all believers (Phil 1:29-30) and those of his missionary work (cf. 2 Cor 11:23-33), but at the same time we should surely see also some parallel to the way in which elsewhere Paul talks of being united with Christ in his death and resurrection as the experience of all believers (Rom 6:1-14; Col 2:20—3:4). There is, accordingly, an intense sense of personal relationship with Christ in this letter. For Paul Christian existence is not to be understood simply in terms of belief in a set of doctrines or as a way of life, although these are integral parts of it; it is also a spiritual experience of a relationship with God through Christ. It is one of the particular contributions of Philippians to a biblical theology that it lays such stress on this relationship.

In the light of this basic understanding of Christian experience we can now appreciate more fully what Paul has to say about his attitude to death in the first chapter. It is evident that he had been going through some situation in which the possibility of his own death was very real, whether through illness or through the threat of physical violence. In that situation he was brought up sharply against the question of what mattered most of all to him. He emphasizes that for him "life is Christ", that is, the opportunity to know Christ and experience his love (Phil 1:21). But if so, it follows that physical death is a better state, since it brings a believer into even closer union with Christ. This placed Paul in a dilemma, since he was aware that he was called to be a missionary during his life on earth and share the life of Christ with other people. Therefore, he accepted that he must be prepared to continue in the body for as long as God required of him rather than to be longing to go to be with Christ before God's time for him to do so (Phil 1:19-26).[11]

*Christ's humility and exaltation.* All this raises in the most pressing manner the question as to what kind of person Jesus could be for Paul to talk about him in this astonishing way. How can this person be the channel through whom God operates, a person with whom one can have this kind of spiritual relationship? The answer is provided within the letter by another passage. When Paul comes to deal with the problem of rivalry leading to disunity in the congregation, he uses various arguments (Phil 2:1-4), but the crowning one is to draw attention to the attitude of Christ Jesus. He is described as a person who existed in the form of God and did not regard his equality with God as something to be held on to or exploited (Phil 2:5-8).

This language appears to set Jesus on the same level of authority as God the Father (as he is called in Phil 2:11). It is true that some scholars have suggested that nothing more may be meant here than that Jesus in his earthly existence shared the same status as that with which Adam was created but chose not to take advantage of it.[12] However, the use of the verb *being* and the clear contrast between the original state of Jesus and the way in which he then took the nature of a servant and adopted a human likeness and appearance indicate fairly decisively that here Paul is describing what has come to be known as the preexistent

---

[11]This would seem to imply that the believer enters into this conscious, close fellowship with Christ from the moment of death, regardless of when Paul thought that the resurrection of the body would take place.

[12]James D. G. Dunn, *Christology in the Making* (London: SCM Press, 1980), pp. 114-21; more cautiously in James D. G. Dunn, *The Theology of Paul the Apostle* (Grand Rapids, Mich.: Eerdmans, 1998), pp. 281-88. There are two distinguishable issues here. The first is whether there are allusions to the Genesis story, so that we may justifiably speak of an "Adam christology" in which Christ is understood in terms of comparison and contrast with Adam. Against what is perhaps the consensus view see especially Peter T. O'Brien, *The Epistle to the Philippians: A Commentary on the Greek Text* (Grand Rapids, Mich.: Eerdmans; Carlisle: Paternoster, 1991), pp. 263-68. The second issue is whether the passage ascribes a preexistent status to Christ; some upholders of the Adam christology have tended to deny this, but, as Dunn agrees, this is not a necessary implication of that position.

state of Jesus, that is, the way in which he existed before God the Father sent him into the world to be born of a woman (Gal 4:4) and live a human life. This language is not surprising, given that Paul had earlier spoken of Jesus as the one Lord alongside the one God the Father who shared with him in the task of creation (1 Cor 8:6), and would repeat the description in all essentials elsewhere (Col 1:15-17). Paul's thinking may well have been influenced by the way in which Wisdom was personified as God's helper at creation and his messenger sent into the world in Jewish wisdom literature (Prov 8:22-31). For Paul, then, Jesus was a divine being, and, although strictly speaking the name Jesus was given to him at his birth, Paul was able to use it for the same person in this state of existence with God before his birth.

Paul's purpose in this description is not simply to discuss the status of Jesus before his human birth for its own sake. The whole point of the passage is to contrast the position of supreme authority enjoyed by him with the way in which he became a human being, and, even more to the point, a human being who plumbed the depths of self-negation and obedience to God by being prepared to die. In this connection Paul does not explain why Jesus had to die, or rather, why God required him to die.

Elsewhere in Paul's letters the character of his death as a means of salvation is often stated (e.g., Rom 3:25; 5:6-8, 9, 10), but here the point is the willingness of Jesus to "do nothing out of selfish ambition or vain conceit"—the very thing which was spoiling the life of the congregation in Philippi (Phil 2:3). It is then made clear that saying no to self is what God approves. Because Jesus was prepared to die, God subsequently exalted him to the highest place in the universe, that is, to where he was previously, but also (and this is the new thing) made him the object of universal worship by all people. They will recognize him as the Lord, and the language used here, which is obviously based on Isaiah 45:22-23, makes it absolutely certain that the term *Lord* here is the title of God the Father that he has bestowed on Jesus.[13] The immediate point of the passage is that the humble will be exalted, in other words, that God approves of the self-denying, self-negating spirit and will reward it. Yet this should not be misun-

---

[13]The term can be used elsewhere in the New Testament as a title of respect for a person as a human being, but there are passages, such as this one, where it carries this much fuller connotation of divine authority.

derstood to suggest that self-seeking people should be willing to forego selfish claims for a season in order to be finally and lastingly exalted by God; that would be to totally misunderstand what self-negation means. Moreover, the context makes it plain that there is no virtue in self-denial in the sense of asceticism for its own sake; what Jesus did was for the benefit of other people, offering an example to the readers of looking "to the interests of others" (Phil 2:4).

Demetrius K. Williams has drawn attention to the rhetorical significance (as he terms it) of the terminology of the *cross* in Paul's letters and specifically in Philippians, where Paul uses it in a situation of conflict to commend a way of life that is conformed to that of Christ and to warn against a life that is fundamentally opposed to it (Phil 2:8; 3:18).[14] He shows how the pattern of life of Christ (Phil 2:6-11) is intended to be repeated in the life of believers (Phil 3:1-21 contains numerous echoes of the earlier passage).

It is as a result of this V-shaped career (from God down to earth and back up again) that Jesus now has what has been called a "postexistence" in which, without losing his humanity, he is now an omnipotent (Phil 3:20), spiritual person, able to enter into relationships with those who believe in him. Consequently, he is able to act as the mediator of God's blessings to his people. To say that "the Lord is near" (Phil 4:5) is to acknowledge his availability to help his people in their needs. Such relationships will be fully realized when he returns in a glorious bodily form from heaven to earth to be the Savior of his people from their imperfect life in this corruptible world and to share his new existence with them (Phil 3:20-21).

*The Holy Spirit.* As the risen and exalted Lord, Jesus is the dispenser of the Holy Spirit (cf. Acts 2:33),[15] and the blessings bestowed by God on his people may be attributed both to him and to the Spirit. So when Paul refers to the way in which he is being sustained and delivered from danger by God in his present

---

[14]The table in Demetrius K. Williams, *Enemies of the Cross of Christ: The Terminology of the Cross and Conflict in Philippians* (Sheffield: Sheffield Academic Press, 2002), p. 26, shows how cross terminology is essentially confined to references in all the Gospels and in the Pauline corpus (plus Acts 2:23; Heb 6:6; 12:2). It appears to be distinctive of Paul's theological diction.

[15]This point is not made explicitly by Paul, who thinks of the Spirit as God's gift (Gal 4:6; 1 Thess 4:8; cf. 2 Tim 1:7; Tit 3:5). Nevertheless, the way in which the Spirit can be called the Spirit of Christ as well as the Spirit of God strongly suggests that he would not have dissented from this proposition.

sufferings he does so in terms of the help given by the Spirit of Jesus Christ, a phrase that demonstrates how closely the Spirit is associated with Jesus (Phil 1:19). The "one Spirit" in which believers should stand firm (Phil 1:27) is the Holy Spirit, who strengthens Christians (rather than being simply metaphorical).[16] In Philippians 2:1 "common sharing in the Spirit" is unambiguous in its reference to the way in which Christians together share in the blessings bestowed by the Spirit and are thus united with one another; it is striking how Paul uses very similar language to refer to participation in Jesus Christ (1 Cor 1:9). Christian worshipful service of God also takes place through the agency of the Spirit (Phil 3:3).

*God the Father.* The significant roles of Jesus Christ and of the Holy Spirit in Philippians should not be allowed to overshadow the place of God the Father in Paul's theology. While Jesus Christ is quite literally the beginning and end of the letter, and of the theology that it contains (Phil 1:1; 4:21-23), nevertheless the letter reaches its climax in a statement of the extraordinary generosity of the God who acts in Jesus and a doxology to him (Phil 4:19, 20; cf. Phil 2:11). This climax is in keeping with the role of God throughout the letter. Similar doxological language is used with reference to the ultimate purpose of the sanctification of believers (Phil 1:11) and the exaltation of Jesus (Phil 2:11). It is God who lies behind the action and who can also be said to be at work in believers (Phil 2:13; cf. Phil 3:15) and to protect and overrule in their lives (Phil 2:27). That is why it is to him that prayers of petition (Phil 4:6) and thanksgiving (Phil 1:3) are addressed.

*New life in Christ.* The nature of the new life in Christ has already been made clear. Two or three elements emerge with particular clarity.

First, it is a life of spiritual growth and progress. This emerges from the opening prayer report, which is entirely concerned with the development of the readers in love, knowledge, purity and righteousness that goes on right up to the day of Christ (Phil 1:9-11). Here, as especially also in 1 Corinthians 1:7-8 and 1 Thessalonians 5:23, great importance is attached to being blameless on the day when Christ comes.

Such statements raise the question whether there is some tension between the declarations about justification and reconciliation that appear to state that

---

[16]See especially Fee, *Philippians,* pp. 163-67 (contra O'Brien, *Philippians,* pp. 149-50).

believers have nothing to fear on that day (Rom 5:1-11) and these other texts in which growth in holiness is apparently a condition for blamelessness at that point. The tension disappears when we note that Paul appears to believe that God will achieve this blamelessness in the lives of his people; he is faithful, and he will do it (Phil 1:6).

Second, there is the way in which believers are exposed to the vicissitudes of mortal existence and would succumb to them, were it not for the mercy of God (Phil 2:27).[17] The afflictions of God's people, and especially perhaps of his missionaries, are seen here in the context of the work of mission. It might appear that God's decisions regarding what is best for them are made with reference to the needs of the congregations rather than in terms of personal concern for the people themselves (Phil 1:24). Yet this would be a mistaken impression, for the letter testifies as much and more to the concern of God for his people as people to whom he stands in a loving and caring relationship. They can pray to him with confidence regarding every aspect of their lives (Phil 4:6). On the human interpersonal level too it is manifest that the relationships between Paul and his converts are not simply on the level of coworkers for God but also on the level of genuine friendship and love; because they are all believers, however, these two levels merge into one.

This crucial element in the life of the church is summed up in the term *fellowship* (*koinōnia*), which functions significantly in this letter to indicate how believers participate in God's blessings and in the Holy Spirit (Phil 1:7; 2:1) and the work of the gospel (Phil 1:5), but in so doing they are brought into a relationship with one another and with Paul (Phil 4:14-15). Such a sharing includes participation in the sufferings of Christ (Phil 3:10), but this carries with it the hope of sharing in his resurrection.[18]

Third, possibly no other Pauline letter brings out so clearly the ongoing work of mission by the local church. Paul is especially concerned with his own

---

[17]The importance of suffering as a key theme in the letter is developed by L. Gregory Bloomquist, *The Function of Suffering in Philippians* (Sheffield: Sheffield Academic Press, 1993), but his study underplays the significance of the other themes in the letter and may leave readers with the mistaken impression that Philippians offers nothing more than a theology of suffering. I find the rhetorical analysis of the letter that Bloomquist offers in defense of his hypothesis quite unpersuasive.

[18]The primary element in the term *fellowship* is that of participation in some common blessing or task, usually by a plurality of people who are jointed to one another through this common participation.

role in mission, and we have seen how the task continues regardless of whether he is at liberty or in prison. What is especially noteworthy here is the role of the congregations that he founded in this work, in two ways. One is the support of Paul's work through a fellowship that involved tangible gifts of money and other resources, including the sending of colleagues to share with Paul in the work, but also the offering of prayers without which Paul believed that his work could not continue fruitfully. The other is that at the same time Paul fully expected the local congregation to be active in striving together for the faith of the gospel and in holding out the word of life (Phil 2:16).[19] Part of the purpose of his description of the situation surrounding his imprisonment with the gospel being preached by people from a variety of motives, but nevertheless being a means of making Christ known, is to stimulate the readers to their own witness by living blameless lives in the community and by their testimony to Christ.

### Conclusion

Like 2 Corinthians, Philippians shows the way in which Paul understood his circumstances theologically and in particular came to terms with the prospect of his death. A personal relationship of knowing Christ lies at the heart of Paul's religion, although it is not presented so explicitly elsewhere as it is here. Christ is seen not merely as the Savior but also as the pattern for Christian living. The threat of Judaizing leads to a succinct statement of the need to put one's confidence only in Christ for salvation and not in any human achievements; here the element of self-confidence involved in relying on the works of law comes especially into view. The Christian life must be conformed to Christ and his cross.

### Bibliography

*New Testament Theologies:* (German) Hübner, 2:324-37.

Bassler, Jouette M., ed. *Pauline Theology.* Vol. I. *Thessalonians, Philippians, Galatians, Philemon.* Minneapolis: Fortress, 1994, pp. 87-121 (articles by Pheme Perkins and Stanley Kent Stowers).

---

[19]This phrase is ambiguous, and it could refer to "holding fast" to the word, but on the whole a reference to witness to the surrounding world is probable, particularly in view of the immediately preceding phrase about shining out like lights in the world.

Bloomquist, L. Gregory. *The Function of Suffering in Philippians*. Sheffield: Sheffield Academic Press, 1993.

Bockmuehl, Markus. *The Epistle to the Philippians*. London: A & C Black; Peabody, Mass.: Hendrickson, 1997.

(Donfried, Karl P., and) I. Howard Marshall. *The Theology of the Shorter Pauline Letters*. Cambridge: Cambridge University Press, 1993.

Fee, Gordon D. *Paul's Letter to the Philippians*. Grand Rapids, Mich.: Eerdmans, 1995.

Hawthorne, Gerald F. *Word Biblical Themes: Philippians*. Waco, Tex.: Word, 1987.

Holloway, Paul A. *Consolation in Philippians: Philosophical Sources and Rhetorical Strategy*. Cambridge: Cambridge University Press, 2001.

Marshall, I. Howard. *The Epistle to the Philippians*. London: Epworth Press, 1991.

Martin, Ralph P. *Carmen Christi: Philippians 2:5-11 in Recent Interpretation and in the Setting of Early Christian Worship*. 2nd ed. Grand Rapids, Mich.: Eerdmans, 1983.

O'Brien, Peter T. *The Epistle to the Philippians: A Commentary on the Greek Text*. Grand Rapids, Mich.: Eerdmans; Carlisle: Paternoster, 1991.

Peterlin, Davorin. *Paul's Letter to the Philippians in the Light of Disunity in the Church*. Leiden: E. J. Brill, 1995.

Williams, Demetrius K. *Enemies of the Cross of Christ: The Terminology of the Cross and Conflict in Philippians*. Sheffield: Sheffield Academic Press, 2002.

Wright, N. T. "ἁρπαγμός and the Meaning of Philippians 2:5-11". *JTS* n.s. 37 (1986): 321-52.

# 14

# THE LETTER TO PHILEMON

⌇⌇

The shortest of Paul's letters may not seem to have much to offer to the student of New Testament theology, but it does have its own small contribution. The letter is a communal one, addressed to a congregation, but its real recipient is Philemon. Somehow his slave Onesimus had found his way to Paul in his prison and there became a Christian believer. Since he is described as "formerly . . . useless", the usual assumption is that he had done some wrong to his master and fled from the consequences. But now that he had become a believer, he was a changed person. Paul had developed an affection for him and wished to have him stay to help him on behalf of Philemon and the congregation in his missionary work. But he could not do so without first sending Philemon back to his lawful master and asking him to receive him back, forgive him and regard him now as his Christian brother; and he further expresses the hope that Onesimus might return to help him. Implicit in this request may be the further hope that Philemon would set Onesimus free.

The main theological significance of this letter lies in the fact that the whole of the appeal to Philemon is based upon the gospel and the fellowship that results from it. In the opening prayer report Paul thanks God for Philemon's faith and love toward Christ and God's people (cf. Col 1:4).[1] Then he prays that Philemon's "partnership with [Paul and Timothy] in the faith may be effective in deepening [his] understanding of every good thing we share for the sake of Christ" (TNIV); this has been paraphrased: "[May] the mutual participation

---

[1] It is probable that Colossians and Philemon were written about the same time and therefore verbal links between them are not surprising.

which is proper to the Christian faith have its full effect in the realization of every good thing that God wants to accomplish in us to lead us into the fullness of Christian fellowship, i.e., of Christ".[2] This suggests that it is as Philemon and other believers share their faith with one another that they all grow in a fuller knowledge of all the good things that God intends believers to have. Such an interpretation is strengthened by the mention in the next verse of how Philemon's love has led to encouragement for other believers.

On the basis of this common life in Christ, that is, in a situation in which writer and recipient are dominated by their relationship to Christ crucified and risen, Paul feels that he could have boldness to tell Philemon what it is appropriate to do. Nevertheless, he appeals for Onesimus rather on the basis of the love that exists among believers. He describes him as a child whom he has begotten, a metaphor that can only mean that Paul has brought Onesimus to Christian faith, so that there is a father-son relationship between them.[3] Although he would like Onesimus to stay with him, nevertheless he is sending him back. The temporary parting from Philemon could be the beginning of an eternal relationship in which Onesimus returns no longer as a slave but as more than a slave, as a beloved brother to Paul and to Philemon. Here we see the way in which the slave-master or slave-free relationship was to be transcended in the church by a higher relationship. This relationship should certainly be true "in the Lord", that is, so far as relationships between people as believers are concerned (cf. Col 3:11). But Paul also insists that it should be true *"in the flesh"*, that is, on the human level. The slave is to be treated as a brother—yes, as a beloved brother—and the master regarded as a brother. Commentators are not clear whether this should be interpreted as a request to set Onesimus free so that he would indeed be no longer a slave but a brother or is simply a request to recognize even a slave as a brother. What is clear in the light of nearly two thousand years of exegesis and application is that ultimately one cannot treat a brother as a slave and that slavery is incompatible with the Christian faith. The early church did not immediately reach this conclusion for slaves in general, and it may be that the most that Paul could have

---

[2] Josef Hainz, *KOINONIA: "Kirche" als Gemeinschaft bei Paulus* (Regensburg: Pustet, 1982), pp. 106-8. The sentence is far from easy to understand.

[3] It is quite possible that Paul was old enough to be his grandfather, but a few lines further down he also speaks of him as a brother.

had in mind was only the manumission of Onesimus for missionary service.

Yet the text is quite shattering. Philemon is to welcome Onesimus back as if he were Paul himself. And all this, although Onesimus has wronged him. Paul offers to repay whatever may be the cost, although in the next breath he seems to be saying that of course Philemon will not press him on the matter, because he is already spiritually in debt to Paul.

The whole appeal is made, then, on the basis of love. Yet at the same time Paul can express the hope that Philemon will "obey" him. The implications of this should not be overlooked. It does imply what we also find elsewhere, that Paul as an apostle could claim a remarkable authority over the congregations and over his fellow workers but that he did not always choose to exercise it and preferred to work by persuasion on the basis of love. Paul makes his appeal "in the Lord", and as an apostle he was a mediator of that authority and believed that he had the mind to know what the Lord required of people. But rather than simply issue commands, he tries to show how what is required should spring out of the faith and love that his fellow believers have.[4]

The letter is also important for the way in which the teaching about believers being all one in Christ is brought down to earth when Philemon is faced with the concrete problem of welcoming back and pardoning a slave who has wronged him, and of accepting him as a Christian brother with all that that could imply for their interpersonal relationships. The Christian church is still learning the same lesson with respect to people of different social classes, different income levels, different sexes, different races and different tribes.

Here, then, we have a theology of Christian action that shows how an appeal can be based on the gospel and the effect that it has in the lives of those who accept it.

### Bibliography

For commentaries on Philemon, see the bibliography on Colossians.

Barclay, John M. G. "Paul, Philemon and the Dilemma of Christian Slave-Ownership". *NTS* 37 (1991): 161-86.

(Donfried, Karl P., and) I. Howard Marshall. *The Theology of the Shorter Pauline Letters*. Cam-

---

[4]James D. G. Dunn, *The Epistles to the Colossians and to Philemon* (Grand Rapids, Mich.: Eerdmans; Carlisle: Paternoster, 1996), pp. 344-45, notes that *obedience* may be a softer term in Greek than in English, expressing something more like "compliance".

bridge: Cambridge University Press, 1993, pp. 175-91.

Harris, Murray J. *Slave of Christ: A New Testament Metaphor for Total Devotion to Christ.* Leicester: Apollos, 1999; Downers Grove, Ill.: InterVarsity Press, 2001.

Richardson, William J. "Principle and Context in the Ethics of the Epistle to Philemon". *Int* 22 (1968): 301-16.

# 15

# THE LETTER TO THE COLOSSIANS

ᨳᨠᨳ

Colossians, like Ephesians, is a letter whose Pauline origin is doubted by numerous critics who believe that its literary style and theology differ sufficiently from those of Paul, as known from his "main" letters, to demand the hypothesis of later authorship by a disciple or continuator of Paul. A mediating position between the traditional and the critical theories is occupied by those who propose that the letter may have been largely composed on behalf of Paul by Timothy, the named coauthor. On either the traditional or the mediating positions, the letter is a direct witness to Pauline theology, but to that theology at a later stage in its development and therefore with fresh emphases and nuances.[1] The letter is addressed to a congregation within Paul's mission field but not personally evangelized by him, and the occasion for it lies in the news received by Paul from Epaphras that indicated that the believers were in danger of being misled by what Paul calls a "philosophy". The nature of this subversive teaching is much debated, but it seems fairly clear that it combined Jewish elements together with other, syncretistic elements from the religions of Asia. It assigned great significance to spiritual powers that threatened human life. The way to ward off their influence lay in various ascetic practices, and the angels seem to have had some function in protecting people from them; Christ was assumed

---

[1]I shall refer to the author as Paul since the letter is written with a mixture of the first person plural and singular, like other Pauline letters, and since I accept a theory of authorship in which Paul is the direct author or the authority behind the letter.

to be no stronger than these other powers, and therefore he was insufficient to overcome their influence.[2]

The letter appears to have two main functions in the light of this. On the one hand, Paul makes a typical presentation of his theology with a fair amount of general teaching, first on doctrine and then on its implications for Christian behavior, set in the context of his situation as a missionary responsible for the welfare of the congregations in his field. On the other hand, this presentation is deliberately shaped so as to be a response to the misleading teaching that was threatening the congregation from outside, again as regards doctrine and behavior.

### The Theological Story

**Prayer report (Col 1:1-14).** After the usual greeting, Paul gives a typical prayer report in two parts. He expresses thanks to God for the spiritual progress of the congregation, using the familiar triad of faith in Christ, love for one another and hope to sum up the qualities of the believers. *Hope* is here used concretely of the object of hope that is already there in heaven, waiting for believers, namely, the glory already bestowed on Christ and that will be shared with his people (Col 1:27). It is thus the hope of future salvation that, in part at least, inspires the faith and love of the congregation. Their knowledge of it derived from the preaching of the gospel, which is likened to a plant that spreads and grows and bears fruit in the shape of Christian converts.

Since the love is inspired by the Spirit,[3] it is appropriate that Paul reports his intercession for the congregation as a prayer that God will continue to influence them, and he singles out "knowledge" as the primary quality that they need in order to live lives that are pleasing to God; in view of the threat posed by false teaching this emphasis is appropriate. But alongside knowledge believers also need strength and perseverance to live the Christian life. The need for

---

[2]See especially Clinton E. Arnold, *The Colossian Syncretism: The Interface Between Christianity and Folk Belief at Colosse* (Tübingen: Mohr Siebeck, 1995). His position is criticized by Allan R. Bevere, *Sharing in the Inheritance: Identity and the Moral Life in Colossians* (Sheffield: Sheffield Academic Press, 2003), who thinks that the problem was pressure to conform to Judaism from the local synagogue, but this does not adequately account for the references to the spiritual powers overcome by Christ.

[3]This is the only reference to the Spirit in this letter (Col 2:5 refers to Paul's spirit). Contrast the more frequent references in Ephesians.

power in the Christian life is not unheard of in the earlier letters, but it is particularly prominent in these later letters, and it may well have been called for in view of the teaching about other principalities and powers that was prevalent. The section concludes with a reminder of the need for them to give thanks for the gospel, which is briefly summarized as new life in the kingdom of Christ,[4] which is the realm of light, after rescue from the kingdom of darkness and forgiveness for the sins committed during their time in it.

*A celebration of Christ (Col 1:15-20).* The deliberate mention of Christ at this point enables Paul to slide over into a passage that celebrates Christ and his functions. As in Philippians 2:6-11 the style is an exalted prose,[5] and the passage has been suspected of being a preformed unit, whether by Paul, as I consider more probable, or by another writer. The passage falls into two parts, in the first of which Christ is seen in relation to the universe and in the second of which he is seen in relation to the church.

In the first part, Christ is the image of God, which means that he replicates God as a son replicates his father and mother; the reference to God as unseen may draw a deliberate contrast with the fact that Christ appeared on earth as a man and was visible. He is also "the firstborn of all creation" (NRSV). It is impossible that Paul thought of Christ as the first person to be created by God and as himself part of creation; the next verse states categorically that everything was created by him, and the sense is rather that Christ is therefore prior to creation and superior to it.[6] This priority enables Paul to assert the superiority of Christ over all the authoritative beings in the universe, whoever or whatever they may be.[7] As in I Corinthians 8:6, Christ is the creator and sustainer of the universe, but here his role in cosmology is developed and emphasized in an unparalleled manner.

---

[4]The kingdom is here the kingdom of Christ rather than of God. This corresponds with Paul's understanding elsewhere (I Cor 15:25; cf. 2 Tim 4:1) that it is Christ who is now reigning as God's agent until the point when he hands over the kingdom to God. However, Paul can also speak of the present kingdom as the kingdom of God (Rom 14:17; I Thess 2:12) or link the two names together (Eph 5:5).

[5]This phrase is more apt than the common description of the passage as poetic.

[6]If the concept of wisdom lies behind this understanding of Christ, then Prov 8:22-31 clearly states that wisdom existed prior to the created universe. No Christian would have affirmed less of Christ.

[7]Paul's listing here, as elsewhere, is probably not systematic and is simply a rhetorical way of saying "every powerful entity".

In a second, roughly parallel statement Paul then goes on to affirm that Christ is the head of the body, namely, the church.[8] This is the first time that Paul uses the metaphor of the body in such a way that the head is a separate entity and represents Christ; contrast I Corinthians 12, where the eye, the ear and the nose can be distinguished from the head and form part of the symbolism that is applied to the members of the church.[9] He is the beginning, and he is the first to rise from the dead so that he is supreme over all. The implication is that there are no other sources of authority in regard to believers over whom Christ is not supreme. There is nobody else who needs to be placated or obeyed in order to be saved. All the power of God resides in him; it is not distributed among other entities. And God chose him to be the means of reconciling the entire universe to him by making a peace offering through his death on the cross.

*The consequences of Christ's superior status (Col 1:21—2:7).* It is evident that this set piece about Christ has the twofold aim of insisting that Christ is superior to all the principalities and powers in the world and in the church, and that he alone is the means of reconciliation of the world to God. It is necessary to point out that reconciliation becomes effective only when the estranged parties make their peace with the God whose enemies they had become. Therefore Paul goes on to remind his readers how they had become reconciled to God through Christ. They had shared in the hostility of the world to God, but now they have been made God's friends through what Christ did by dying for them; since Christ has been presented as the Son of God, and therefore presumably immortal, it was necessary to mention that he died in his physical body. The aim of reconciliation is that God may have a people to whom no blemish or guilt attaches at the day of judgment.[10] This aim will be achieved provided that the readers remain steadfast in their faith. The implication is that their present

---

[8]It has been argued by many scholars that originally the whole of this composition was cosmological, that "the body" originally meant the universe and that Paul refashioned and restructured it by adding the explanation "the church"; see Ralph P. Martin, *Colossians: The Church's Lord and the Christian's Liberty* (Exeter: Paternoster, 1972), p. 47. Despite its popularity there are convincing arguments against this hypothesis; see the detailed investigation by Christian Stettler, *Der Kolosserhymnus* (Tübingen: Mohr Siebeck, 2000).

[9]The individual roles of the parts of the body fall into the background, although this aspect of the metaphor is by no means lost (Col 3:15; Eph 5:30).

[10]Cf. I Cor 1:8; 2 Cor 4:14; I Thess 3:13.

standing also rests on the faith that they put in Christ. Faith is the response to God's act of reconciliation in Christ through which there arises a new relationship in which each side is at peace with the other. They must persevere in their hope, which was based on the gospel (cf. Col 1:5-6), and again Paul comments that the gospel has been proclaimed worldwide. This is a rather sensational claim to make when the gospel had not yet reached westward of Rome; either it is rhetorical exaggeration, or it may refer to a universal proclamation to the universe at the time of Christ's exaltation.[11] Paul is a servant of this gospel; he does not say that he is the only servant of the gospel.

This gives him the opportunity to comment on his mission. Broadening the scope of his audience ("you" here in Col 1:24 is wider than just the congregations at Colosse and Laodicea), he refers to the fact that he has not only proclaimed the gospel but also suffers for the sake of the gospel and the church. The reference is presumably to his current imprisonment (Col 4:3) but also to the kind of experiences related in 2 Corinthians 11. Yet Paul's commission is a special one, in that he has been the recipient of God's plan kept secret for a long time but now revealed,[12] namely, that it is Christ who gives people the hope of future glory, and this hope is to be made known to the Gentiles because they are included, along with the Jews, in God's purpose. Accordingly, the secret has two aspects: Christ is the basis for hope in glory, and this hope is extended to the Gentiles and not just to the Jews.

Thus, alongside the earlier points emphasizing that Christ alone is supreme in the universe and the church, and he alone is the reconciler, we now have the further crucial point that the Gentiles are included in the reconciliation and must hear the gospel. The way has been prepared for an attack on any suggestion that the Gentiles are excluded or that they must follow some other route in order to be saved.

One other preliminary point needs to be made. Paul stresses how important it is for his readers to appreciate this secret that God has revealed through him. For all the knowledge that people need to have is to be found in Christ. Here is the basis for challenging whatever the philosophers may say about the need for further knowledge on the basis of the visions that they have received. Let

---

[11]Cf. 1 Tim 3:16.

[12]For the use of this motif earlier by Paul see 1 Cor 2:7-10. It is also found in Rom 16:25-27.

the readers continue in what they were originally taught by Epaphras and not be misled by high-sounding teachings that are actually human and do not come from Christ.[13]

*Response to the false teaching (Col 2:8-23).* At last Paul proceeds to engage with the syncretistic "philosophy" that was threatening the church. He begins by reminding the readers that as Christian believers they have received the fullness of God, since they have received Christ in whom there resides all of this fullness. This staggering statement goes beyond anything that Paul has said earlier, but it is the logical outcome of all that has been said about being united with Christ, putting on Christ, Christ living in Paul (Gal 2:20) and receiving the Spirit. What is new is the way in which Paul sees Christ as incorporating God in his body. But again it is the logical outcome of all that has been said earlier about Christ being the image of God, the Son of God and even being called God (Rom 9:5). It could be that it was the threat posed by the false teaching about the principalities and powers, perhaps with divine powers distributed among them, that led Paul to draw the logical conclusions from his earlier teaching and recognize that God was uniquely present in Christ, and, if so, that through Christ the divine power is conveyed to believers.[14]

Next he implies that believers do not need to be circumcised, because spiritually they have undergone the equivalent in their baptism.[15] Bodily circumcision was understood as an outward symbol of the cutting away of sin from the heart. But Christian baptism, as a symbol of cleansing from sin but also of union with Christ in his death and therefore of death to sin, was analogous. It would seem to follow that, since there has been a spiritual circumcision, there is no need for physical circumcision for Gentiles.

It is often said that Colossians goes beyond what Paul said in Romans 6 by

---

[13]This, to be sure, is assertion rather than argument. Paul pins his argument on his readers accepting the authenticity of the revelations and knowledge that he claims to have received from God.

[14]We might be tempted to think that this statement means that for Paul individual believers are "divinized", or made divine, and thus have a status similar to that of Christ. Elsewhere Paul claims that believers are being transformed into a glorious state (2 Cor 3:18), but the full realization of this is future (Col 1:27). Probably Paul means no more than that the divine power in all its fullness, that is, in more than sufficient measure to counterbalance the power of the hostile forces in the universe, is at the disposal of believers.

[15]Arnold, *The Colossian Syncretism*, pp. 296-97, doubts whether the "philosophers" were demanding circumcision of Paul's Gentile converts; against him see Bevere, *Sharing in the Inheritance*, pp. 65-73.

speaking here of Christians as having been raised with Christ, whereas there (it is argued) the resurrection is still future (Rom 6:5) and they merely live in newness of life (Rom 6:4). This is a misreading of Romans and of Colossians, since it is palpable that what Paul says in Romans in terms of newness of life (while still in this world) is the same as what he says here in terms of what can only be a spiritual resurrection. The difference is that in Romans Paul speaks of believers being baptized into the death of Christ and being buried with him through baptism, so that they may share new life with him, whereas in Colossians he says that they were buried with him in baptism and raised with him. This might be taken to imply that the new life is something subsequent to baptism in Romans but simultaneous with it in Colossians; but, whereas Paul is quite clear in Romans and elsewhere that physical resurrection is in the future, he equally clearly teaches that believers are already enjoying new life with Christ (Rom 6:11; Gal 2:20). The difference is verbal.

The basic point is repeated in greater detail. Some slight confusion is possible because Paul uses *death* to refer to two different experiences, the situation of people who are dead in sin and therefore dead so far as responding positively to God is concerned (Col 2:13), and then the situation of believers who die to the world (Col 2:20) and are "buried" (Col 2:12) through union with Christ in his death and become alive to God.

Two related facts are then introduced. The first is that this union with Christ in his resurrection was accompanied by forgiveness of sins (cf. Col 1:14). Paul imagines a list of sins committed against God that is taken and nailed to the cross on which Christ died, in accordance with the custom of placing a placard on a cross to indicate the offense for which the criminal was being punished (Mk 15:26). The implication is that Christ has suffered for sins and they no longer count against the offenders: there is forgiveness available for them.

The second fact is that on the cross Christ somehow triumphed over the principalities and powers. Whether this means that Christ disarmed these enemies or that he divested himself of them (NRSV mg.), he defeated them and then, like a Roman general celebrating with a triumphal procession he led them in chains to execution. They no longer have any power over against him.[16]

---

[16]Strictly speaking, the metaphor used here implies that they no longer exist; Paul may, however, mean no more than that they are powerless where the authority of Christ is recognized.

*Life as God's chosen people (Col 3:1—4:1).* Now at last comes the practical application; it falls into two parts.

First, if all this is true, there is no need for the readers to yield to suggestions that Jewish practices should be observed. Paul passes over circumcision and concentrates on foods and festivals, which would affect all believers, both circumcised Jews and uncircumcised Gentiles. These are no longer important because they pointed forward to Christ, but now that Christ has come these pointers are no longer needed. Equally, there is no need for "false humility"[17] or worship of angels, which were probably reckoned among the powers that needed to be honored.[18] The need for these things was apparently being taught on the basis of visions received by Paul's opponents. They had nothing to do with Christ, who is the true source of spiritual growth in the church. Their teaching was human and could be ignored.

This may seem to be a relatively minor conclusion after so much preliminary teaching. The point seems to be that the opponents were advocating Jewish practices and ascetic exercises that were associated with angelic worship, and these were not only forcing Gentile believers into Jewish practice but also above all threatening the position of Jesus as the one and only Savior. The menace, therefore, in Paul's eyes was extremely serious.

Once this problem had been dealt with, the way is open for the second stage in application, which is to urge the readers on to progress in their life in union with Christ. They were to seek after the way of living associated with the new life to which they had been raised by Christ. This life at present is hidden, in the sense that the future hope of glory is still a hope that has not yet been realized; nevertheless the death of believers to sin and their being raised to new life is a reality that must be expressed here and now in this world.

Negatively, believers who have died with Christ to the world must put their old way of life to death. This is the classic case of "become what you are". Believers are no longer to yield to the power of sin because they have been set free by Christ. Using a different picture, Paul insists that his readers have put off their old self and put on a new nature, like a person taking off dirty clothes and

---

[17] This may include fasting as a form of self-humiliation (Arnold, *The Colossian Syncretism*, pp. 210-14).

[18] It is debated whether "the worship of angels" refers to worshiping angels or to joining in worship by angels. Bevere, *Sharing in the Inheritance*, pp. 100-115, thinks that the two possible senses should not be made into an either-or.

putting on clean ones.[19] They are being made new[20] as regards their knowledge of God and how he wants people to live, by contrast with the sinful world, which does not know or chooses not to know what God requires.

Surprisingly, there is a concluding comment that repeats the statement found elsewhere in Paul that there is no distinction that counts any longer in the church between people of different races or between slaves and free people since Christ is in them all. The new self of the Christian believer really is new, and this has significant ethical implications.

Positively, the readers are called to put on the qualities of the new life. The theological motives are several. The readers are God's chosen people, called to be holy and loved by him. They have been forgiven by him and must show forgiveness to other people. They are members of one body, and so they must live at peace with one another. They must let the word of Christ[21] live in them; the teaching is not simply something that they learn and absorb into their minds but is perhaps also regarded as having a living force of its own. Whatever they do must be appropriate to being done "in the name of the Lord Jesus".

Specific teaching for the three main pairs of relationships within the household follows. What stands out here is the repeated reference to acting "in the Lord". This formula encapsulates the thought of living life in the new situation created by their acceptance of Christ as the Lord whose will should determine all that they do; it is a variant of "in Christ" that brings out more the nuance of obedience to him.[22] The behavior commended is what would have been recognized as good and fitting in the society of the time, but here it is baptized into Christian behavior, and it is to be done not simply because it will commend believers to other people but because it is an expression of obedience to the Lord (Col 3:22), who will reward it. This is particularly important in that it brings masters down to the same level as their slaves. Within the relationship (whose legitimacy is not questioned here) masters must be utterly just to their slaves.

---

[19]Cf. Gal 3:27. Note, however, that in Rom 13:12-14 the imperative is used.

[20]The present participle indicates an ongoing process. The aorist imperative is used in Rom 13:12, 14, and the indicative in Gal 3:27.

[21]Usually the reference is to the word of God, but cf. 1 Thess 1:8. The phrase could refer to teaching about Christ or emanating from him—or both at once.

[22]The distinction between "in Christ" as expressing more the benefits conveyed by life in him and "in the Lord" as expressing more the new authority in the lives of believers is not maintained consistently.

*Paul and his colleagues (Col 4:2-18)*. Finally, the importance of prayer, including prayer for Paul, is inculcated. No rationale is offered, but the implication is that opportunities for Paul to evangelize even while chained in prison will not arise without the prayers of God's people for him.

## Theological Themes

*Christology.* In all three prison letters (i.e., Philippians, Colossians and Ephesians) there is a rich christology that develops the ideas of Christ's preexistence and his present and future supremacy over all created entities, including what we might call extraterrestrial powers. In the case of Colossians and Ephesians there is a remarkable frequency of power language and a corresponding emphasis on the superior power of Christ over all that might stand in opposition to God and threaten the lives of believers. It is not just that the implications of the resurrection and exaltation of Christ are being expressed more fully and explicitly. Rather, the recognition that Christ's position and authority stretch back to eternity past is powerfully developed. A variety of models that could be drawn upon to provide the conceptuality and the language for expressing this were already present, in particular the role of wisdom as God's companion and helper in creation. But the references to principalities and powers form part of a developing angelology that recognized the existence of numerous, varied entities created by God with assorted powers and authority. The superiority of Christ to these is grounded in the fact that he is not a created entity but existed prior to them all. The question of his origin is not raised; he is simply there as the Son of God, reflecting in his own being the nature of God the Father.

But it is also of great importance in this letter that Christ incorporates the divine being in a bodily, human form (Col 2:9). Remarkably this statement is made in the present tense of Christ as he now is in his exalted state, as well as in the past tense with reference to his earthly existence. For Paul it is clear that the resurrection of Christ is a bodily resurrection; it was not the continuation in existence of a heavenly being who temporarily inhabited a human body and then left it behind. On the contrary, there is a man at the right hand of God who will come to judge the world (cf. Acts 17:31).

In this context the terms *fill* and *fullness* are important. Paul uses the verb quite naturally of the way in which believers are filled with various qualities and benefits in the earlier letters (Rom 15:13; Phil 1:11), and again it is natural to speak of people being filled with knowledge (Rom 15:14; Col 1:9). Here, however, there is a new development as the term is used of "the fullness" of God dwelling in Christ (Col 1:19; 2:9) and then of believers being filled in Christ, apparently with the same fullness. Similar language is used in Ephesians, where it is the goal that believers be filled with the fullness of God and of Christ (Eph 3:19; 4:13) and the church is said to be "the fullness of him of who fills everything in every way" (Eph 1:23). It is not necessary that the term should have the same reference each time it is used. The sense appears to be "the totality of the divine attributes",[23] and it may be that as applied to Christ the term indicates all the powers and qualities of God, whereas when applied to believers and the church the reference is more to the qualities of God. Nevertheless, in Colossians 2:10 the implication is that a power superior to that of the principalities and powers is present in Christ and is effective in believers so that they are not subject to these alien powers.

*Reconciliation.* In Colossians we have an understanding of humanity with two aspects.

On the one hand, we have the by now traditional picture of human beings as sinners (Col 2:13), alienated from God and at enmity toward him (Col 1:21); they belong to a world that is characterized by darkness (Col 1:13) from which they cannot deliver themselves. The coming of Christ is seen as a rescue operation, through which people are redeemed from their dire situation. Redemption is elucidated as "forgiveness of sins" (Col 1:14; 2:13). The earlier Paul rarely spoke of forgiveness (Rom 4:7, a citation from the LXX), preferring to use the term *justification*, although the language was common coin elsewhere in the New Testament, especially in the Synoptic Gospels. Here the traditional term makes its way in, so that redemption is explained in much the same way as in Romans 3:24-26. The same action of Christ is also described as reconciliation or making peace. The scope of reconciliation embraces "all things", in earth and in heaven; this might seem to allow the possibility of reconciliation for any rebellious powers, but this line of thought is never followed up, and the more significant implication may be that the sole mediatorship of Christ is be-

---

[23]In later Gnosticism the term *fullness (plērōma)* was used for the fullness of emanations from God that are in the universe. This usage does not seem to contribute materially to understanding Paul's usage. Cf. Hans Hübner, *EDNT,* 3:110-11.

ing emphasized. As elsewhere, the subjective experience of being forgiven and reconciled is also understood in terms of dying and rising with Christ, and this is fully developed for its ethical implications. Where Romans 6 develops more fully the theology of the experience, Colossians 3—4 explores in practical detail what it means to die to sin and to live to God. The purpose of God's action in Christ is thus that there may be created a holy people (Col 1:12) whose character befits them as the people of God.

On the other hand, as we have already noted, there is the understanding of the world as dominated by supraterrestrial beings, the principalities and powers. This is not a completely independent line of thought. Their position is somewhat ambiguous. It is difficult to avoid the impression that teaching was being spread in the church by people who believed that the powers had to be placated or obeyed. Since the law of Moses was given by angels (Gal 3:19), it could be that obedience to this law was part of the requirements on believers. At the same time these powers doubtless rule over the dark world of sin, and at least some of them are clearly opposed to God and Christ; otherwise, there would not be a description of their defeat. It could be that their status had not been fully thought out. Whatever the situation, the powers have been defeated by Christ and therefore believers are to let nobody condemn them or vote them down for not fulfilling the various commandments that were being imposed upon them in the name of the law.

It appears, then, that a form of Judaizing was being advanced in the church, but whereas previously the stress was more on obedience to the law of Moses as a means of justification,[24] here there seems to be the additional element of ascetic practice in order to appease the angels. For Paul the Christian life signifies deliverance from these demands because Christ has overcome the powers. Significantly the term *law* is not used in the letter;[25] this may be seen as an indication that the thought is somewhat distant from that of the earlier Paul or that the focus has shifted to the powers and to asceticism.

### Conclusion

The theology of Colossians shows some notable differences from that found

---

[24]Earlier, too, Paul's opposition was powerfully based on his refusal to admit that Gentiles should be required to keep the law in order to be justified. This element is in the background in Colossians.

[25]Note, however, the references to legal decrees in Col 2:14, 20 and to human commandments in Col 2:22.

in the earlier letters of Paul. There is a much more explicit understanding of the position of Christ as head over all things and as being filled with the fullness of the deity. He is now understood as the head of the church, which is clearly conceived as a cosmic entity. Believers are redeemed, forgiven and reconciled to God, and they have died and been raised with Christ, although their new life is hidden with Christ and is yet to be revealed. Nevertheless, the general pattern of the theology is the same as that of Paul, and I shall argue later that it is best understood as a development from that of the earlier Paul.

## Bibliography

New Testament Theologies: (English) Strecker, pp. 548-65. (German) Gnilka, pp. 326-49; Hahn, 1:343-66; Hübner, 2:348-62; Stuhlmacher, 2:1-53; C. Stettler, *Der Kolosse-rhymnus* (Tübingen: Mohr Siebeck, 2000).

Arnold, Clinton E. *The Colossian Syncretism: The Interface Between Christianity and Folk Belief at Colosse.* Tübingen: Mohr Siebeck, 1995.

Bevere, Allan R. *Sharing in the Inheritance: Identity and the Moral Life in Colossians.* Sheffield: Sheffield Academic Press, 2003.

Bruce, F. F. *The Epistles to the Colossians, to Philemon and to the Ephesians.* Grand Rapids, Mich.: Eerdmans, 1984.

Dunn, James D. G. *The Epistles to the Colossians and to Philemon.* Grand Rapids, Mich.: Eerdmans; Carlisle: Paternoster, 1996.

(Lincoln, Andrew T., and) A. J. M. Wedderburn. *The Theology of the Later Pauline Letters.* Cambridge: Cambridge University Press, 1993.

Lohse, Eduard. *Colossians and Philemon.* Philadelphia: Fortress, 1971.

O'Brien, Peter T. *Colossians, Philemon.* Waco, Tex.: Word, 1982.

Martin, Ralph P. *Colossians: The Church's Lord and the Christian's Liberty.* Exeter: Paternoster, 1972.

Sappington, Thomas J. *Revelation and Redemption at Colossae.* Sheffield: Sheffield Academic Press, 1991.

Wright, N. T. "Poetry and Theology in Colossians 1:15-20". *NTS* 36 (1990): 444-68.

# 16

# THE LETTER TO THE
# EPHESIANS

❧❀❧

The doubts about Pauline authorship that we noted in the case of Colossians are intensified when we come to Ephesians. There is a much stronger consensus of opinion that this composition is a post-Pauline expression of a Pauline theology that has been considerably developed in new ways by an unknown disciple.[1] Unlike other Pauline letters, this one does not seem to have a specific situation in view.[2] Nor is it clear what the purpose of the letter is. There is an extensive amount of material in common with Colossians, although it tends to be used with different nuances. Where Colossians could be said to center attention on Christ, Ephesians gives greater attention to the role of God the Father.[3] Where Colossians is dealing with a specific threat to the Christianity of the recipients, Ephesians is much more concerned with expounding the nature of Christian salvation with respect to the church composed of Jews and Gen-

---

[1]For the case against Pauline authorship see especially Ernest Best, *A Critical and Exegetical Commentary on Ephesians* (Edinburgh: T & T Clark, 1998), and Andrew T. Lincoln, *Ephesians* (Dallas: Word, 1990); for defenses of it (which I find the more persuasive) see Harold W. Hoehner, *Ephesians: An Exegetical Commentary* (Grand Rapids, Mich.: Baker, 2002), and Peter T. O'Brien, *The Letter to the Ephesians* (Leicester: Apollos; Grand Rapids, Mich.: Eerdmans, 1999). I shall refer to the author as Paul, since he is at the very least the implied author.

[2]We are not even sure of the destination of the letter since the crucial phrase "in Ephesus" is missing from the oldest manuscripts.

[3]Colossians uses "father" of God four times, compared with eight times in Ephesians. But beyond statistics, the action of God in salvation is central. Cf. Hahn, 1:356-59.

tiles, and then the character of the new life that flows from this. And where Colossians is generally argumentative and even polemical in tone, the style of Ephesians is much more that of prayer and meditation. The result is one of the most theological of the New Testament documents in which we see Pauline theology expressed in a fresh manner that almost defies analysis.[4]

## The Theological Story

**A berakah (Eph 1:1-14).** The broad shape of Ephesians with its clear division between doctrine and Christian behavior is the same as in Colossians and Romans. However, there are great differences in detail. This is obvious from the start, where the letter does not begin immediately with a prayer report about the recipients; this fits in with the fact that the letter is directed to believers generally, probably in Asia, and is not concerned with their specific situation past or future. Rather Paul uses the device of the *berakah*, an ascription of praise to God for what he has done and will do for his people before he goes on to a prayer for the readers that is also very general. But a specific concern emerges as we go through the material.

The *berakah* is an ascription of praise to God, who is identified as the father of Christ (as in 2 Cor 1:3; 1 Pet 1:3; cf. Rom 15:6; Col 1:3), and the various things that God has done are all associated with Christ as his agent; at the end of the ascription we also have a reference to the Spirit, whose presence in believers is like a stamp that confirms God's ownership of them. The structure is, however, not strictly trinitarian, with different aspects of salvation being assigned to different divine persons. On the contrary, God the Father and Christ are involved in them all, and the Spirit receives only passing mention at this point.

There is a three-part structure to the ascription in that each part ends with the phrase "to the praise of his glory" (Eph 1:6 [somewhat expanded], 12, 14). The first part begins with a broad statement that God has blessed his people in every way "in Christ" in the heavenly realms. Here we note that "in Christ" is used, as typically in this letter, to express the means or person through whom God accomplishes his purposes.[5]

---

[4]Characteristic of the letter are extremely long sentences in which the flow of thought is extraordinarily difficult to capture.

[5]This particular usage of the phrase is much more prominent in this letter than elsewhere, and correspondingly other types of use are less frequent.

The phrase "in the heavenly realms" (Eph 1:20; 2:6; 3:10; 6:12) is peculiar to this letter. The key verse here is Ephesians 2:6, which states that believers have been seated in the heavenly realms with Christ. Consequently in Ephesians 1:3 it makes sense that believers experience spiritual blessings in this heavenly sphere of existence. It seems that Paul envisages a spiritual resurrection of believers so that they now are alive to God and therefore in a spiritual sense are already in heaven, but this does not free them from attack by the powers of evil in the world and in heaven.[6] The heavenly realms are where the evil principalities and powers are to be found, although their influence extends to the world.

After this opening statement the rest of the first part of the ascription is essentially concerned with God's choice of his people. Salvation is rooted in the purpose and initiative of God. Before the world was even created he planned to have a holy people, and he further destined them to be his children.[7] Their adoption would take place through Christ, but also his choice of them took place "in Christ". Paul thus speaks on behalf of believers generally who are the recipients of this divine favor. And all of this redounds in Paul's eyes to the praise of the glory of God's grace; believers should be moved to praise God for the grace shown to them.

In the second part of the ascription the thought is rather of the way in which this plan has actually been realized through various actions of God through Christ. Primary among these is redemption and forgiveness, and here (in contrast to the parallel in Col 1:14, but cf. Col 1:20) the means of redemption is the blood of Christ, a point that will be elaborated in Ephesians 2. Noteworthy also is the stress throughout the letter on the abundance of the divine grace that motivated redemption. Grace is also at work in the way in which God conveys knowledge to his people (cf. 1 Cor 1:24, 30). The knowledge here is specifically of the plan of God that intends to bring together the whole universe in unity

---

[6]Something different is meant when Paul refers in 2 Cor 12 to being caught up to the third heaven in what was more of a visionary experience.

[7]I take the minority view that the passage does not actually say that God chose beforehand which specific individuals he would adopt as his children in this way to the exclusion of others whom he did not choose. Nothing is said here about individuals, but Paul simply says that God chose to have a holy people, consisting of adopted children. The explanation of why he says that God chose "us" is that he is writing from the standpoint of those who have experienced grace and adoption, that is, the people in whose case the divine plan has been effective. See on the one side Best, *Ephesians*, pp. 119-22 (but his suggestion that Ephesians may embrace universalism is unjustified), and on the other side, O'Brien, *Ephesians*, p. 99; Hoehner, *Ephesians*, p. 176.

in Christ. This presumably means that the divisions brought about by sin and rebellion and enmity between sinners and sinful powers will be brought to an end; it is the same cosmic reconciliation as in Colossians 1:20. This is God's plan for the fullness of time, that is, for the future, but already believers have become God's property (cf. NRSV mg.), so that their existence contributes to the praise that is due to God. And this is also true of the readers who have heard the gospel that brings salvation and have been marked as God's property with the Spirit, who is at the same time the first installment of their inheritance, until God fully redeems his people.

Throughout this section up to Ephesians 1:12 Paul has spoken in the first person and refers to those who have already put their hope in Christ. But in Ephesians 1:13 he switches to the second person "you", before returning to "us" in Ephesians 1:14. Thereafter he continues with the second person in Ephesians 1:15 to Ephesians 2:2 and then reverts again to the first person. The "you" are clearly identified as Gentiles in Ephesians 2:11, which implies that "we" are Jews. Probably Paul is thinking of himself as representing the Jewish Christians who were the first to believe in Christ and contrasting this group with the readers who were representative of the Gentiles.

*Prayer report (Eph 1:15-23)*. The relation of Jews and Gentiles will surface in Ephesians 2, but previous to this we now have a delayed prayer report by Paul, expressed in rather general terms, in which he comments on how he prays for the readers. As in Colossians, their lives are characterized by faith and love (Col 1:4), and Paul prays essentially for knowledge for them (Col 1:9), but, whereas in Colossians the knowledge is more concerned with how to live the Christian life, here it is a knowledge that is concerned with God's provision for his people and especially with the greatness of the power that he exercises for them. Even more so than in Colossians there is a remarkable number of words expressive of power in this letter, referring not only to the principalities and powers arrayed against God and his people but also to the power of God, which is far greater than that of the opposition. This power was especially displayed in the exaltation of Jesus to a place of authority over every conceivable other power.[8] Moreover, Christ has been made head over everything for the church, which

---

[8]Ephesians does not have the kind of statements about Christ's relationship to creation that occur in Col 1:15-17.

suggests that the point of this account is to make the readers aware that Christ's authority and power are exercised for their sake. Christ and the church are related as head and body, but also the church is "the fullness of him who fills everything in every way". The force of this ambiguous phrase seems to be that Christ who fills the universe with his power is also fully present in the church so that the church has the power to overcome any forces arrayed against it. The climax of the passage is thus an assertion of the important element in Christian salvation that the church through its Head is able to overcome all evil opposition. If the readers were people who lived in a world that was believed to be alien to God and themselves because it was under the control of evil powers and who therefore lived their lives in fear of the hostile universe, this knowledge would equip them for hope in the certainty of God's victory.

*Jews, Gentiles, salvation and reconciliation (Eph 2:1-21).* The thought of spiritual conflict now retreats from attention (it will recur powerfully in Eph 6:10-18). Paul reverts to the theme of Jew and Gentile that was quietly adumbrated in Ephesians 1 with his juxtaposition of "we" and "you". Ephesians 2 contains a description of the state of people, including the readers but also (Eph 2:3) including Paul and Jewish believers before their conversion. They were sinners whose life was governed by the world and its ruler, to which they conformed, and was therefore disobedient to God. They were dead as far as responding to God was concerned and destined to his wrath. Their conversion could be understood as an act of resurrection in which God raised them from their old life and brought them into a new "heavenly" existence in which they are alive to God. The thought is the same as in Colossians 2, but again the sheer grace and mercy of God are emphasized. Another agenda is now coming into play, namely, to emphasize that salvation is entirely due to God's gracious initiative and action through Christ[9] and does not depend upon any kind of works done by the recipients. Works done to gain salvation would give the doers occasion

---

[9]Elsewhere in the letter Paul affirms his understanding of Christ's work as motivated by love and expressing itself in a self-offering of himself to God whereby there is created a forgiven people whose destiny in the purpose of God is to be holy (Eph 4:32—5:2, 25-27; cf. Eph 1:7). The fact that this is expressed in terms of Christ's love for "us" and "the church" arises out of the situation where Paul is speaking on behalf of those who have experienced forgiveness and come to recognize that it is rooted in God's love; it does not mean that God's love is restricted solely to those who have received the gift.

for confidence in themselves and for boasting of their achievement. Rather, good works are the result of being saved, when people do what God has planned for them to do as part of the new life of a holy and blameless people.

This new agenda is obviously associated with the ongoing question of the relationship of Jews and Gentiles in the church and with the problem of whether people needed to fulfill the requirements of the Jewish law for salvation.[10] At the same time, Paul excludes works of any kind that might be thought to qualify a person to be saved and not simply the ritual works prescribed by the Jewish law. The rest of the chapter is devoted to an important aspect of this problem.

The point at issue may be the danger of Gentiles thinking that their salvation was independent of the Jews and that they formed a church apart from them. This problem could obviously arise in congregations where the number of Jewish Christians was few or none. So Paul reminds the readers that as Gentile unbelievers they had no part in the people of Israel but were uncircumcised and beyond the pale.[11] Only through Christ have those who were "far away" been brought near.[12] The operative force is again the death of Christ understood now in a new way as the place of reconciliation between Jews and Gentiles. The "dividing wall" may be a metaphor taken from the barricade in the temple that excluded the Gentiles from the Court of Israel, but it refers in fact to the law of Moses, observance and nonobservance of which formed the boundary between Jews and Gentiles. This has been broken down, and there is now one people of God, since through Christ Jews and Gentiles now have access to God the Father. The effect of this, then, is that the Gentiles are admitted to the people of God instead of being strangers outside it. Israel is enlarged to include believing Gentiles. There is thus continuity and yet there is also discontinuity in that the new house (or, better, household) of God is built upon a foundation that consists of the apostles and Christian prophets, which must mean upon their teaching, with Christ as the con-

---

[10]Here we can properly use the term *salvation* for what believers have received, since this is the vocabulary that Paul uses. In earlier letters Paul tends to reserve *salvation* for the deliverance of believers from God's wrath at the judgment, but he can also distinguish between people as "those who are perishing" and "those who are [being] saved" in 1 Cor 1:18. The language of Jesus, who said, "Your faith has saved you", would encourage the recognition that the decisive action in salvation took place at conversion.

[11]So it is not former Jewish proselytes who are addressed here.

[12]Although Ephesians quotes Scripture comparatively rarely (not at all in Eph 1—3), some of its language is formed by Scripture. Here Paul takes Is 57:19, which originally referred to Jews in Judea and the Diaspora, and reapplies it to Jews and Gentiles.

trolling stone. This building is a temple, that is, a place in which God is present, and the Gentiles form part of it.

*Apostleship to the Gentiles (Eph 3:1-13).* There is now a shift of theme in which Paul starts to announce his intention to pray for the readers in his capacity as an apostle for the sake of bringing the Gentiles into God's new people. But he interrupts himself, and before continuing his original line of thought he pauses to assure his readers of his authority for what he is saying and to reinforce what he is saying by reference to the revelation of God's previously hidden plan that has been made to the apostles. By God's grace Paul had been commissioned to serve the Gentiles, and to him there had been given a revelation whose content he has just briefly set out. This revelation was new in that it was not known to previous generations but had now been revealed to the apostles and prophets.[13] It affirmed that Gentiles and Jews together form one people of God, sharing the same divine promises.

Paul saw himself as particularly commissioned to bring this gospel to the Gentiles. The divine wisdom hidden from the ages is also to be made known to the principalities and powers through the witness of the church. Presumably they are being informed of the fact that God has acted to defeat them. Finally, Paul expresses the confidence that believers have in approaching God, doubtless in order to pray to him.

*Paul's prayer for the readers (Eph 3:14-21).* Having established the fact of his commission regarding the Gentiles all the more firmly, Paul at last moves into prayer. He addresses God as the Father from whom every family or his whole family or all fatherhood gets its name; the first of these possibilities, referring to every group of God's people on earth and in heaven, is perhaps the most likely.[14]

The prayer is for the spiritual strengthening of the readers, for Christ to live in them (Gal 2:20), and thus for them to grasp, that is, not just to understand but probably also to experience, the love of Christ in all its fullness.[15] The en-

---

[13]This denial is not inconsistent with the fact that Paul and other New Testament Christians believed that it had been foretold by the Old Testament prophets and cited them in support of it (e.g., Rom 15:9-12). Neither the prophets nor their hearers understood fully the import of the revelation to them.

[14]John Muddiman, *The Epistle to the Ephesians* (London: Continuum, 2001), pp. 166-67.

[15]Attempts have been made to identify specific elements corresponding to the four dimensions rather than to see the latter simply as a rhetorical expression. Height and depth also figure in Eph 4:8-10, so that the love of Christ encompasses heaven and earth. The breadth could be the extent of the earth horizontally, and the length might be interpreted temporally of the eternal extent of the love (so F. B. Watson in an unpublished paper).

suing doxology praises God for the anticipated fulfillment of the prayer. Once again the mention of God's power is significant.

*Unity and diversity in the church (Eph 4:1-16).* The opening verse of Ephesians 4 indicates the general theme of the second part of the letter in which conduct appropriate to the gospel set out in the first part is inculcated (cf. Colossians). The point that is immediately made follows on directly from what has preceded: the need to preserve unity in the church, since the church is one with one God and has one hope for the future.

This is not incompatible with the rich and diverse provision that God has given to the church in the form of different gifts for building it up. Whereas in I Corinthians and Romans Paul envisaged different spiritual gifts given to different individuals, here he speaks of people who have received grace (Eph 4:7) as themselves being God's gifts to the church (Eph 4:11). The earlier listing of many diverse spiritual gifts is now reduced in number to four groups: apostles or missionaries; prophets, who along with the apostles formed the foundation of the church with their revelations of God's mysteries and other teachings; evangelists, who shared in the missionary outreach; and pastors and teachers, linked together as a pair, and probably responsible for the two main tasks in the congregations of believers. It is notable that there is no use of the terminology of overseers and deacons (as used in Philippians and the Pastoral Epistles) or of elders, although it is not difficult to recognize that whatever the names and precise duties, the same functions would be carried out. The variety of ministries has the aim of enabling the church to grow as one body in a unity that is centered on Christ and to develop a maturity that will enable the believers to resist false teaching.[16] The church is thus seen as a body of parts working together and contributing to growth and to consolidating it in love.

*The old life and the new; family relationships (Eph 4:17—6:9).* The readers were converted Gentiles who would have had a very different way of life be-

---

[16]There is uncertainty regarding the interpretation of Eph 4:12a. Is the task of the various leaders "to equip God's people for works of service" (TNIV; cf. NRSV) or is it "to equip God's people, [and] to do the work of ministry": in other words, is the work of ministry something done by the congregation generally (for which the leaders prepare them) or is it the task of the leaders themselves? For the former view see O'Brien, *Ephesians,* pp. 301-3; for the latter view see Lincoln, *Ephesians,* pp. 253-55. Even on the latter view the letter still indicates that the members of the congregation have individual gifts and functions to perform (Eph 4:7, 16). The former view is on the whole the better supported.

fore their conversion, and therefore one important element in the growth of the church is the abandonment of their former sinful way of life and the putting on of a new pattern of behavior. The details of this behavior do not concern us here; what matters is the theological motivation that keeps recurring. Paul traces unchristian, immoral conduct to the ignorance of the Gentiles whose hearts were hardened, that is, impervious, to divine teaching; by contrast, Christian believers learn Christ, which must surely include instruction about his character (cf. 2 Cor 10:1) and teaching.[17] Paul develops his point by using the contrast between the old nature and the new, the former being shed like dirty clothes and the latter being put on instead. He warns against conduct that causes grief to the Holy Spirit (Eph 4:30; cf. Is 63:10),[18] a casual remark that indicates that the Spirit was understood as a personal being rather than an impersonal power.

Paul roots his call for mutual forgiveness in the way that God in Christ forgave believers; here the basis is not simply that God has provided an example of how to act but rather that divine forgiveness entails human forgiveness, as Jesus had taught. Similarly, love for one another is rooted in the love that Christ demonstrated in giving himself as an offering and sacrifice to God. Here we have an important statement about how Christians understood the death of Jesus in sacrificial terms made almost casually in an ethical instruction (cf. the later example in Eph 5:25-27); this shows how Christian teaching on behavior was continually buttressed by central theological statements.

The contrast between the old and the new lives is important. People who practice sinful behavior characteristic of the world have no place in the kingdom of God, with the implication that persisting in such conduct will lead to loss of their position and to facing the wrath of God. Those who once had a character befitting the darkness in which they lived must now live as befits the

---

[17]Although there is surprisingly little direct quotation of the teaching of Jesus in the New Testament letters, there is a lot of instruction that echoes that teaching, particularly in James and I Peter, but also in Paul's writings. For a judicious study of one area see Michael B. Thompson, *Clothed with Christ: The Example and Teaching of Jesus in Romans 12:1—15:13* (Sheffield: Sheffield Academic Press, 1991).

[18]Note how Ephesians makes significant use of Old Testament material, particularly in the second part of the letter for more doctrinal purposes (Eph 4:8) and as a source of precepts in the ethical teaching (Eph 4:25, 26). In this respect Ephesians is markedly different from Colossians. See Thorsten A. Moritz, *A Profound Mystery: The Use of the Old Testament in Ephesians* (Leiden: E. J. Brill, 1996).

light. For living in the light shows up sin for what it is. Intoxication is contrasted with the joy and thanksgiving expressed in songs of praise that goes along with being filled with the Spirit.

Believers are to subject themselves to one another. This is not a one-sided submission, as might be assumed from the one-sided submission of wives, children and slaves in the following verses. The parallels in Galatians 5:13 and Philippians 2:3 indicate that a genuine two-sidedness is indicated by "one another". Nevertheless, out of this principle there come reminders to these three classes of people to be submissive to their counterparts in accordance with a mixture of natural and cultural reasons. In the case of wives and husbands the teaching is developed at some length. The submission of the wife to the husband and her respect for him (Eph 5:33) is related to the submission of the church to its Head and Savior, Christ.[19] There is an analogy between Christ as the Savior on whom the church depends and the husband as the person on whom his wife depends for care and support. The matter is put into some perspective by the way in which the husband for his part is counseled at much greater length to love his wife, and as example and motivation Paul cites the way in which Christ loved the church and gave himself for it, so that the church might be pure and holy. This goes beyond anything that a husband can do for his wife,[20] and the application is simply that the husband must do everything possible in love for the welfare of his wife, just as Christ does for his body, the church. Finally, Genesis 2:24 is cited as scriptural authority for the husband to hold fast to his wife in love, but Paul goes even further and sees in the biblical text a picture of Christ leaving his Father to take the church as his bride.

The teaching to children is based on Old Testament principles and is balanced by instruction to the fathers, as in Colossians.[21] The same is true of slaves and their masters. The obverse of the fact that Christian slaves and masters are brothers with the same heavenly Father is that both have the same heavenly

---

[19]The idea that the husband is head of the wife has not been found before its occurrence in I Cor 11 and appears to have been first stated by Paul.

[20]It may be that the analogy between the purity of the church and the purity that should characterize a bride (cf. 2 Cor 11:2) is an implicit exhortation to the wife.

[21]However, in the New Testament world the submission of sons to their fathers may have been expected to continue into adulthood in a way that is different from that in Western society today.

Master or Lord who administers justice impartially, by which Paul means that he treats slaves and their masters alike.[22]

*Spiritual battle (Eph 6:10-24).* In the last section of the letter Paul sums up by calling his readers to prepare themselves for what he sees as not so much a moral struggle but rather a spiritual battle against the evil forces that hold people in captivity. The implication is that believers are not immune from being attacked and may succumb if they do not take precautions. The essential preparation is the putting on of Christ (Rom 13:14), but this basic thought is developed here (cf. 1 Thess 5:8) by using the traditional picture of a suit of armor, each part of which represents a Christian quality (faith) or a spiritual gift (truth, righteousness, salvation, the word of God). There is no obvious way in which these spiritual qualities fit the particular pieces of armor with which they are equated; the presentation seems to be a vivid teaching aid and nothing more. Singled out separately from these is the need to pray and to be watchful at all times.

## Theological Themes

What stands out from this reading of the letter is the emphasis on the love and the power of God, both of which are described in superlative terms, and the stress on the unity of Gentiles with Jews in the people of God. Ephesians has been well described as "pastoral rather than polemical", and it is of special interest in giving a theological discourse that is not shaped by the need for polemic. Nor is it shaped by the need to respond in detail to a particular local situation. Rather it appears to represent what could be said to churches largely composed of Gentiles after some years of development.

*Prayer and worship.* Ephesians is a letter in which a very significant amount of space is devoted to what we may call worship, the directing of thanksgiving and petition toward God for his grace toward believers in the church. These prayers are unusual in their style and are imbued with a deeply theological content. However, it should be observed that similar lengthy sentences with ideas strung on to one another in a manner that almost defies analysis are also recorded in

---

[22]Contrast the justice system of the Roman world in which a person's superior or inferior position was an important factor in assessing their guilt or innocence; see Brian Rapske, *Paul in Roman Custody* (Carlisle: Paternoster; Grand Rapids, Mich.: Eerdmans, 1994), pp. 46-62.

other letters of Paul, and this indicates that the peculiar style found here may have been characteristic of prayer in the early church. These prayer reports, although they refer primarily to Paul's prayers, must surely be an indication of the important place occupied by prayer in the lives of individual believers and Christian congregations; we have noted elsewhere the frequency with which Paul asks the congregations to pray for him.[23]

What does distinguish this letter is more the remarkably strong way in which the grace and power of God are celebrated. The nearest neighbor to Ephesians in this respect is to be found in the songs of worship in Revelation and the picture of the enthronement there. It would seem that an emphasis on the greatness of God has as its inevitable concomitant a mood of worship and praise. In this connection we may recall again the significant analysis of New Testament theology by Ethelbert Stauffer, who traced three main elements, which he called doxological, antagonistic and soteriological.[24] Stauffer saw these exemplified in the relationships of Jesus to God, the devil and the world. Ephesians is a prime example of these motifs in relation to the church. It formulates the language for glorifying God the Father for his greatness demonstrated in his blessings bestowed on his people. It brings out dramatically the nature of the spiritual warfare in which believers are engaged. And it describes the way in which God acts for the salvation of his people.

*Jews and Gentiles in the church.* A central concern of the letter is the relationship between Gentiles and Jews in the church. The lively polemic of Galatians and Romans against Judaizers is toned down. There is no trace of the curious teaching that was threatening the church at Colosse, but the issue has not gone away, and the description of the conversion of the readers stresses the theme of grace and not works that is fundamental to Paul's gospel for the Gentiles. The dominant theme is more the way in which Jews and Gentiles have been reconciled by the death of Jesus and form one people and one temple for God to dwell in. The mood seems to be one of reassuring the readers that this is really true, based as it is on divine revelation given to the apostles and prophets with Paul as the apostle specially commissioned to take this message to the Gentiles.

---

[23]See David G. Peterson, "Prayer in Paul's Writings", in *Teach Us to Pray: Prayer in the Bible and the World*, ed. D. A. Carson (Exeter: Paternoster; Grand Rapids, Mich.: Baker, 1990), pp. 84-101. Other essays in the book cover other areas of the Bible.

[24]See pp. 36-37.

There is nothing of the agonized struggle with the problem of Jewish unbelief that we found in Romans 9—11.

Rather there is a practical emphasis on the maintenance of this unity in the manifold life and ministry of the church. Here the concern has broadened out from the issue of Jews and Gentiles to the unity of all believers with one another in love and the development of spiritual maturity.

The concept of the church in Ephesians is particularly significant. In the earlier letters of Paul the term *church* (Gk. *ekklēsia*) is used in the singular for an individual congregation, or perhaps more precisely I should say for the totality of believers in a given geographical area. Sometimes the reference may be to a smaller group meeting in somebody's house (Rom 16:5; I Cor 16:19; Philem 2). A number of churches in different places are naturally referred to as "the churches". Only rarely is the term used in the singular for the totality of believers (I Cor 10:32; 12:28; 15:9; Gal 1:13; Phil 3:6). Although some of these references may be debatable, there is probably sufficient evidence to show that although Paul used the term overwhelmingly to mean a local group of believers, nevertheless he could think of "the church" as an entity that existed across time and comprised the whole of the new people of God at any particular moment. So when Paul comments that he persecuted "the church of God" (I Cor 15:9; Gal 1:13; cf. Phil 3:6), it is most likely that he is thinking of Christians generally and not just one specific congregation.

When we come to Colossians and Ephesians, the picture changes. Two occurrences of *ekklēsia* in Colossians (Col 4:15, 16) refer to local congregations; the remaining two refer to "the body" of Christ, which is identified with "the church". In Ephesians the term is used nine times, and in every case it refers to the church as a whole and not to an individual congregation,[25] although obviously what Paul says about the whole could be said of an individual congregation insofar as it is a part of the whole.[26] This development is perfectly natural. It corresponds to the way in which believers increasingly came to recognize themselves as belonging to one people and understood themselves to be the people of God or the new Israel as a corporate entity; it is a moot point but

---

[25] Andrew C. Perriman (unpublished article) thinks that the temple in Eph 2:21 refers to a local congregation.

[26] Parallels have often been drawn with the way in which we may talk about "the bank" or "the post office", meaning the institution as a whole or the individual branch of it.

probably in I Corinthians 12:28 Paul is thinking of the ministers in the church at large and not just locally at Corinth. The church as a whole is accordingly the object of Christ's love (Eph 5:25, 29). He is the Head over it all, and it can therefore be thought of as his body (Eph 1:22; 5:23). It is this sense of the church as a kind of cosmic entity that is characteristic of Colossians and Ephesians. And it is at this point that these letters go further than the earlier letters.

Most scholars assume that this cosmic entity, as I have termed it, is the totality of local congregations and believers throughout the world, and since it extends through time we can think of it as an entity with a history and a particular composition at any given time; by extension we may speak of "the church in earth and heaven" to mean the totality of believers over the centuries. However, a different view has been developed by some Australian scholars, of whom Peter T. O'Brien is representative. They propose that the reference is to "a heavenly gathering centered on Christ", and not to the church on earth; however, this heavenly gathering does consist of the living believers who according to Ephesians have already been raised up to the heavenly places. Local churches are earthly manifestations of this heavenly gathering. To make this concept work, O'Brien has to admit that in some references the term *church* has a twofold nuance to both the local earthly church and the heavenly gathering.[27] There are other weaknesses as well in this interpretation.

Ephesians appears to preserve the distinction found earlier in Paul's writings between those church leaders who form the foundation of the church and are responsible for its mission (apostles, prophets and evangelists) and those who are active in local congregations (pastors and teachers). Implicitly this would recognize that there was a mission or, more accurately, missions that went on alongside and in conjunction with local congregations but were separately organized to plant new congregations. Nevertheless, Ephesians gives no support to the idea of a universal, world institution such as the church was later to become.

Ephesians emphasizes more than any other part of the New Testament (except possibly Jn 17) the need for unity in the church. This goes beyond the exhortation that people should have the same mind and purpose in the local congregation that we find in Philippians 2:1-4 to the insistence that Christians

---

[27]See briefly O'Brien, *Ephesians*, pp. 25-29; cf. idem, *DPL*, pp. 123-31. For a critique see Kevin Giles, *What on Earth Is the Church? A Biblical and Theological Enquiry* (London: SPCK, 1995), pp. 125-51.

have one God (Spirit, Lord and Father—implicitly trinitarian) and one way of
salvation through faith and baptism, and one hope. In the light of Ephesians 2
this is probably meant to stress that Jewish and Gentile believers have these
common possessions (cf. the stress on one God and one Mediator for all, i.e.,
for Jews and Gentiles in 1 Tim 2:5). There are thus common goals for them all
to fulfill. Yet it is also affirmed that there is variety in the church in the different
gifts of grace given by Christ to different individuals to build up the body of
Christ. All these varied gifts are seen as contributing to the one aim of building
up the body of Christ. Paul uses the plural form for the various leaders, an indication that he is thinking of the church as a whole and not just one local congregation.

   *Principalities and powers; the lordship of Christ.* The other central theme is the
problem of the principalities and powers that dominate the world of darkness
and threaten believers. Though they have been disarmed and defeated according
to Colossians 2:15, this point is not made in Ephesians. Rather, the stress is
more on Christ's supremacy over them from his throne beside God. Nevertheless, they are still active, and believers must oppose them.

   It is important to take note of this point because the impression is sometimes given that the author of Ephesians has raised believers to the heavens and
made them perfect. It is claimed that there is an overrealized eschatology in
which the blessings of the future age are already fully enjoyed by believers.[28]
This view of the letter is patently false.

   To some extent we can agree with the suggestion that the eschatology is not
so much futurist as rather vertical. That is to say, instead of the hope of Christians being oriented toward the future and the end of the world when Christ
returns, it is directed upward to the heavens, where Christ now sits enthroned
and from where he empowers his people. It is true that the second coming is
not directly mentioned in the letter and the future consummation is not
strongly thematized, but the belief in a future consummation that is not yet realized is certainly there (Eph 1:10), and the notion of future ages is present.

   It is important to realize that elsewhere in Paul's writings we have the same
upward look; the center of gravity of Paul's theology in his undisputed letters
lies in the past (the death and resurrection of Jesus) and the present (the exist-

---

[28]Cf. the similar point raised concerning the resurrection of believers in Col 3:1.

ence of believers "in Christ") rather than in the future.

The present lordship of Christ is of vital importance. It is part of the general picture of Christ that fits in with what we have found elsewhere in Paul. In particular there is the important little christological statement tucked away in Ephesians 4:9-10 that affirms the descent and ascent of Jesus. This is best understood in terms of the V-shaped trajectory that we also found in Philippians 2:6-11, the "lower, earthly regions" (TNIV) referring to the earth rather than the underworld (NRSV). The significant points here are, first, that in connection with his ascent Christ bestowed these gifts of grace, that is, the gifts of the Spirit, on his people (cf. Acts 2:33), and second, he is now said to fill everything. This statement goes beyond earlier statements in Colossians that Christ is filled with the fullness of God. Now Christ is said to "fill" everything. Similarly, in Ephesians 1:23 Paul states that the church is "the fullness of him who fills everything in every way". These statements indicate that the divine characteristic of being everywhere present is now shared with Christ. Probably the emphasis is on the fact that Christ is present in this way in the church, but the point in Ephesians 4:10 seems to be rather to emphasize the exaltation and omnipotence of Christ. What is said in Philippians 2:9-11 in terms of lordship is here stated in terms of omnipresent rule and authority and influence.

At the same time, it is notable that Paul also prays that believers will be filled with all the fullness of God (Eph 3:19). This statement may explain the emphasis on the power of Christ. The church is engaged in a struggle with the opposing powers, and for this task nothing less than the power of God is adequate. That power was seen in Christ and continues to be present in him, and through him it is conveyed to his church and to the individuals who compose the church.

*The Holy Spirit.* In a document that lays such strong emphasis on Christ and the way in which he fills the church and individual believers there might seem to be no place for the Holy Spirit. Nevertheless, the Spirit occupies a central position in this letter that contrasts sharply with the paucity of mention in Colossians. The revelation of God's mystery to the apostles and prophets took place through the Spirit (Eph 3:5). The Spirit is the seal placed by God upon his people (Eph 1:13), and it is through the Spirit's influence that believers are strengthened with divine power (Eph 3:16); they are to seek to be filled with the Spirit (Eph 5:18), and they are equipped for their battle with the powers by the Spirit in the Word of God.[29] The Spirit is active in the church in producing oneness, since all Christians share in one and the same Spirit (Eph 2:18; 4:3-4), even if the Spirit works in them in different ways. The Spirit is also associated with wisdom and knowledge (Eph 1:17). In short, the Spirit is the divine agent through whom God acts at every point in the lives of believers, including their approach to God in prayer (Eph 2:18) and the gifting of the church, and in the battle against evil powers.

## Conclusion

The theology of Ephesians and, to a lesser but still significant degree, Colossians is dominated by the cosmic scope of the powers arrayed against God and his people and by the immense stress on the superior power of God and Christ that is made available to believers. At the same time, the more traditional understanding of the nature of sin and redemption and life in Christ is fully present. There is also a stress on the place of knowledge of God's purpose and his love. Thus, alongside the understanding of the work of Christ in terms of forgiveness of sins and raising up believers to new life in the power of the Spirit, there is also a conception of Christ as the omnipresent, supreme manifestation of the power of God through which the forces hostile to God will be overcome. Although there is not the development of a distinctive vocabulary such as we have in the case of justification, redemption and reconciliation, nevertheless there is a definite concept of the victory of Christ as an indispensable part of the understanding of his death and resurrection.

We have here a powerful development of the doxological motif in which the attitude of worship and praise dominates the presentation. The first part of the letter is essentially a celebration of God's mighty work of redemption in a lofty style. It is entirely in keeping with this that in the second part of the letter the characteristic activity of people filled with the Spirit is that they speak "to one another with psalms, hymns and songs from the Spirit" (Eph 5:19); the first part is a demonstration of what this might mean. Something similar can be seen from time to time in Paul's earlier writings, specifically in Romans (Rom 8:31-39; 11:33-36; 15:1-13). It is easy to overlook this element in the exposition of

---

[29]The Word of God, here as elsewhere, is the gospel message with all the power that is inherent in it and not the written Scriptures.

New Testament theology and to attempt to reduce everything to cold, systematic, propositional form. Ephesians reminds us that for the New Testament writers theology was expressed in worship.

## Bibliography

*New Testament Theologies:* (English) Strecker, pp. 565-76. (German) Gnilka, pp. 325-49; Hahn, 1:343-66; Hübner, 2:363-75; Stuhlmacher, 2:1-53.

Arnold, Clinton E. *Ephesians: Power and Magic: The Concept of Power in Ephesians in Light of Its Historical Setting.* Cambridge: Cambridge University Press, 1989.

Best, Ernest. *A Critical and Exegetical Commentary on Ephesians.* Edinburgh: T & T Clark, 1998.

————. *Ephesians.* Sheffield: JSOT Press, 1993.

————. *Essays on Ephesians.* Edinburgh: T & T Clark, 1997.

Giles, Kevin. *What on Earth Is the Church? A Biblical and Theological Enquiry.* London: SPCK, 1995.

Hoehner, Harold W. *Ephesians: An Exegetical Commentary.* Grand Rapids, Mich.: Baker, 2002.

Kreitzer, Larry. *The Epistle to the Ephesians.* London: Epworth Press, 1997.

Lincoln, Andrew T. *Ephesians.* Dallas: Word, 1990.

Lincoln, Andrew T., (and A. J. M. Wedderburn). *The Theology of the Later Pauline Letters.* Cambridge: Cambridge University Press, 1993.

Moritz, Thorsten. *A Profound Mystery: The Use of the Old Testament in Ephesians.* Leiden: E. J. Brill, 1996.

Muddiman, John. *The Epistle to the Ephesians.* London: Continuum, 2001.

O'Brien, Peter T. *The Letter to the Ephesians.* Leicester: Apollos; Grand Rapids, Mich.: Eerdmans, 1999.

Turner, Max. "Ephesians". In *New Bible Commentary: Twenty-first-Century Edition.* Edited by D. A. Carson et al. Leicester: Inter-Varsity Press, 1994.

# 17

# THE PASTORAL EPISTLES

❧

The letter addressed to Titus and the two addressed to Timothy clearly belong together by virtue of their common style and theological character, although they are individual compositions, each with their own peculiar characteristics and contribution to the theology of the New Testament. Although it could be interesting to discuss them separately, the constraints of space require that they should be considered together.[1] The likeness between them extends further in that each of them is ostensibly concerned with the life and work of a church leader and colleague of Paul in a situation where he is absent. This feature is adequate to explain the fact that they are written to individuals rather than to congregations, as is the case with the other Pauline letters.[2] The difference in addressees, however, is not by itself a sufficient explanation of the fact that the letters are written in a different linguistic and theological idiom from the acknowledged letters of Paul.

Explanations of this fact fall into three categories. First, there is the possibility, strongly favored by a number of scholars, that the individuality of these letters is due to their being written to their purported addressees by a colleague

---

[1] Although attempts have been made by some scholars to detect differences of authorship and of theological outlook between the letters, I remain persuaded that they come from one author or circle and that any differences between them are due to addressing different situations. Cf. Rüdiger Fuchs, *Unerwartete Unterschiede: Mussen wir unsere Ansichten über die Pastoralbriefe revidieren?* (Wuppertal: Brockhaus, 2003), who argues that there are significant differences in the theologizing in the three letters but that these are contingent on the different situations addressed; he assigns the letters to Paul's lifetime with Luke as the amanuensis.

[2] Therefore it is not the case that the congregation has ceased to matter and the leaders alone are significant in the spiritual formation of the congregation.

of Paul acting as a secretary or amanuensis with a degree of freedom unknown in the earlier letters.[3] Second, there is the majority view that the letters are pseudonymous compositions, dating from a time considerably later than that of Paul when it was necessary to invoke his authority for teaching intended to help local church leaders to prevent their congregations from sliding into heresy. Third, there is the minority view that the letters are allonymous. That is, that they contain Pauline materials that have been adapted within a Pauline circle after his death in order to make his teaching available in a form adapted to the needs of the congregations at the time when there was the danger of succumbing to a heresy compounded of Jewish and ascetic elements and some misrepresentation of Paul's teaching. The matter continues to be debated, but the third option will be adopted for the purpose of this chapter; the Pastoral Epistles represent the kind of teaching that Paul gave to his missionary colleagues. It is presented here with no intention to deceive the readers by a skillful follower of Paul who did his best to be faithful to the Pauline tradition while expressing it newly for a developing situation.[4]

## The Letter to Titus: The Theological Story

The situation addressed in Titus appears to be less developed ecclesiastically than in I Timothy, and the treatment is simpler and covers a narrower range of topics; therefore, whatever the order of their composition,[5] Titus is a good introduction to the Pastoral Epistles.

*Greeting (Tit 1:1-4).* Titus begins with a lengthy greeting, the longest in the Pauline corpus after Romans, that spells out three things.

First, it describes the role of Paul, who was appointed an apostle in order that through his preaching he might help people to grow in faith and knowl-

---

[3]The distinctiveness of the letters over against the acknowledged letters of Paul is generally admitted. A minority of scholars think that the degree of distinctiveness is not sufficient as to require any other hand than that of Paul in their composition.

[4]For detailed justification of this position see I. Howard Marshall, in collaboration with Philip H. Towner, *A Critical and Exegetical Commentary on the Pastoral Epistles* (Edinburgh: T & T Clark, 1999), introduction. I use the term *pseudonymous* to refer to documents that were intended to deceive their recipients into thinking that somebody other than the real author wrote them, and the term *allonymous* to refer to documents composed by somebody other than the purported author (in this case Paul) but in a way that was transparent and not intended to deceive the readers.

[5]It may well be that the stimulus to the composition of the letters was an authentic letter of Paul that has formed the basis for 2 Tim.

edge of the truth that leads to godliness. Here are the two stages in the Christian life, the moment of conversion and the growth in godly living. As a missionary, an apostle is concerned with both of these, with developing faith and knowledge and with helping believers to become godly.

Second, the gospel that lies behind this process of conversion and growth is briefly characterized. It is analyzed here by using a pattern of promise and fulfillment, expressed in terms of God's premundane promise of eternal life and of the realization of that promise through the apostolic proclamation of the gospel. Instead of contrasting the promise of the coming of a Savior or of an act of redemption with its fulfillment in the Christ event, the letter contrasts the hope of eternal life promised by God and the revelation of his word in the gospel that is preached by Paul. Thus a lot of stress rests upon the Word of God and its proclamation.

Third, the letter is addressed to Titus, who is Paul's true son and who therefore may be presumed to continue the apostolic task that has just been defined, although neither he nor Timothy is given the designation of apostle.

At the outset, therefore, the letter is concerned with the central themes of Christian salvation in a remarkably succinct and comprehensive manner. This greeting, therefore, puts all that follows into a spiritual context. The practical and ethical instructions that follow must be understood in its light, and the author continually reminds us of this.

*The appointment of elders (Tit 1:5-16).* The task of Titus is defined broadly as that of completing an unfinished task in Crete—presumably unfinished by Paul—and in particular of appointing church leaders in the several churches (Tit 1:5-16). The broader statement (Tit 1:5a) can stand as a general description of all that follows in the letter—the continuation of a work of establishing congregations that has been begun. The narrower statement (Tit 1:5b) specifies a crucial element in this task. The stress is laid on the character of these leaders in terms of Christian behavior and sound belief, although the ability to lead and to teach is implicit in the description. The kind of character that is sought is positively seen in an orderly and seemly way of life, free from any grounds for moral censure in terms of sexual morality, greed and violent behavior. The reason for appointing leaders of this kind is closely related to the presence of people who oppose the message and teach other things for sordid reasons. They are to be silenced. They can corrupt the believers, and they themselves are corrupt.

The opposition is thus taken very seriously, and its evil character is depicted with remarkably strong language. It is pernicious and its effect is spreading. Titus, therefore, is to appoint godly leaders and to rebuke those who promulgate and those who are deceived into accepting false teaching.

*The teaching that Titus is to give (Tit 2:1—3:11).* By contrast Titus is to teach the truth. The instructions on what he is to say and how he should do so form the major theme of the letter (Tit 2:1—3:11). The section falls into two parts.

In the first subsection (Tit 2:1-15) the teaching is detailed in terms of what he is to say to older men and to older women, who in their turn will teach the younger women, and to younger men and slaves. The instructions to the different groups are concerned broadly with the particular temptations and characteristics of the groups, but the qualities inculcated are sufficiently general to apply to everybody. The term that stands out in the description is self-control in whatever manner is appropriate to the group mentioned. The teaching is given backing by a doctrinal statement that gives a basis for abandoning sinful behavior and living godly lives. Believers live between the first appearing of God's grace and the future glorious revelation of Christ; they are redeemed from sin and live in hope. The effect of the coming of salvation and of the hope of its consummation should be that it teaches people to eschew wickedness and live lives dedicated to God and filled with good. The subsection ends with a summary (Tit 2:15) that recapitulates Titus 2:1.

In the second subsection (Tit 3:1-11) there is some general teaching for everybody about submissive and good behavior in society. This teaching is backed up by a further doctrinal basis that details the nature of salvation and in particular contrasts the preconversion life of the believers with their new situation. It brings out strongly the nature of conversion as a divine act that powerfully renews people by the bestowal of the Holy Spirit. Those who have experienced divine grace in this way should show a character that is very different from what they were like before being saved. The subsection concludes with a warning to Titus not to enter into debate with his opponents because this will be unprofitable. At most he must warn divisive people and then ignore them. The implication is that he should concentrate on positive teaching rather than on debate.

*Concluding notes (Tit 3:12-15).* The letter closes with some more personal notes, concerned principally with the progress of Paul's mission through his colleagues. It brings out the important fact that Titus's mission is a limited one;

other duties elsewhere lie ahead of him. He is, therefore, not a permanent local leader but more of a troubleshooter with a limited remit.

From this brief summary of the letter we note that although the major part of the content is apparently nontheological, the practical instruction is backed up by three significant passages of doctrinal teaching (Tit 1:1-4; 2:11-14; 3:3-8; but note also Tit 1:7, 9; 2:1, 5, 10). The main concerns of the letter are the appointment of godly leaders, teaching the members of the church what is involved in Christian living, and encouraging people to concentrate on serious Christian living instead of futile arguments. This practical instruction is based throughout on the gospel, and the letter effectively reminds the reader(s) of the main features of the gospel. Further, the situation that gives rise to the letter is the activity of heretical teachers in the churches who are promoting error and ungodliness. The letter has a limited purpose, and it will not cover the whole of Christian life and experience. It is slanted in a particular direction to deal with particular problems, and therefore we are not to expect a full exposition of Christian theology from it. The two main positive motifs of the letter are right belief and godliness of character, and these are closely related to each other. It would seem that the problem caused by the letter's opponents lay more in the area of ethical slackness than in doctrinal error, and that the doctrinal teaching is not intended so much to refute error as to be a reminder of the basis for ethical living and to show how necessarily it arises out of the gospel.

### The First Letter to Timothy: The Theological Story

The first letter to Timothy shares the same general characteristics as Titus in that it too is concerned with church life threatened by the activity of opponents (cf. especially 1 Tim 1:3-7, 18-20; 4:1-3; 6:3-10, 20-21).

*Timothy's commission (1 Tim 1:1-20).* After a much briefer opening greeting (1 Tim 1:1-2) the rest of 1 Timothy 1 has the character of an introduction to a letter in which the recipient is to be given a number of instructions concerning what he is to do in the church and how he is to live personally. The introduction is concerned with the renewal or reinforcement of a commission that has previously been entrusted to Timothy by Paul (cf. Tit 1:5). Timothy is to continue to use his authority as a church leader in Ephesus to restrain the efforts of opponents of Paul who are teaching doctrines that cause controversy and which appear to be foolish and futile. They are based on a misuse and misunderstanding of the law, that is, the Old Testament Scriptures. This law properly understood and used has its place in the context of the gospel. Paul then develops the thought of his commission to be God's servant in the gospel, which took place despite his previous sin as a result of divine grace and mercy displayed toward sinners. Timothy, for his part, is to "fight the battle well" as he holds on to faith and keeps his conscience pure, unlike some who have gone astray. The task of serving the Lord is difficult because of the opposition that it faces.

*Prayer in the congregation (1 Tim 2:1-15).* The introduction is followed by a first series of instructions to Timothy that are concerned with what he is to encourage in the church (1 Tim 2—3). Attention is directed away from the controversies that are spoiling the life of the congregation to the positive activity that needs to be commended, namely, intercessory prayer for all people and specifically for peaceful conditions in which they may hear the gospel. The instruction is backed up by a doctrinal statement that emphasizes that God wants all people to be saved and Christ gave himself as a ransom for all, and that there is a testimony to this for which Paul was appointed as a messenger. There then follows a section that starts off with the conditions for effective prayer, first in the case of men, and then in the case of women.[6] The women are to pray with a proper demeanor, which is expressed in their outward appearance. In an addendum, which is clearly important in its own right, it is laid down that the women must not teach men, although they are allowed to learn, and that they will "be saved" through childbearing.[7] The connection between these instructions and the problem of the opposition in 1 Timothy 1 may not be immediately apparent. It is probable that congregational prayer was suffering because of dissension in the meetings and that some of the women were affected by the teaching of the opposition to Paul and needed to be restrained.

---

[6] I regard 1 Tim 2:9-10 as parallel to 1 Tim 2:8: both prescribe the appropriate requirements for people at prayer, and then the writer develops a further, associated theme concerned with the role of women in the teaching aspect of the congregational meeting.

[7] This probably meant that even though women were not allowed to teach, this would not put them at any disadvantage and they would still be able to persevere in their Christian lives to final salvation through fulfilling their other Christian duties, including (for most women) motherhood. The whole passage is difficult of interpretation, and I take the view that the restriction here on women teaching was necessary because of specific circumstances and is not a timeless principle; see Marshall, *Pastoral Epistles*, pp. 436-71.

*The appointment of leaders (1 Tim 3:1-16)*. First Timothy 3 moves to the key element in dealing with the opposition already seen in Titus 1. This is the character and ability of people who should serve as church leaders in three types of position, traditionally bishops, male deacons and female deacons. The description reads like a set of qualifications for people who are to be appointed to do these tasks, but it is surely also intended to present the ideal for those who are already doing them. The section is bracketed by comments that suggest that people were slow to take up responsibility in the church. These comments are in effect encouragements to the right people. At the same time, it is made clear that not everybody is spiritually and otherwise qualified for the tasks. The qualities are much the same for all three categories; they repeat in different words and elaborate on what we have already found in Titus 1.

Again, the connection between this set of instructions and 1 Timothy 1 is not made explicit; it is only perhaps because we have already read Titus that we recognize that the purpose of appointing bishops and deacons is to counteract the work of the opponents. Curiously, the importance of sound doctrine emerges only incidentally in 1 Timothy 3:9.

However, a stronger basis for the teaching may lie in what immediately follows (1 Tim 3:14-16). These instructions are said to be for the time being and cannot wait to be communicated to Timothy until the uncertain time of Paul's coming to see him. They are concerned with life in a congregation that is meant to be the buttress that upholds the truth, and, just as in 1 Timothy 1:15-17 and 1 Timothy 2:3-5, we have a brief statement of the truth that is to be upheld. The doctrinal statement here is concerned with the wonder of what took place in the bodily appearing and subsequent glorification of Jesus. This is the great "mystery" committed to the safekeeping and proclamation of the church. How important, then, it is that the church fulfill its role—that is, by faithfully upholding and presenting the truth and by withstanding heresy.

*How the church leader is to behave and teach (1 Tim 4:1—6:21)*. Following on from this we have a fresh start to the instructions. First Timothy 4 begins with a prophecy of false teaching and practice that, it can be assumed, is already coming true, and a rebuttal of one aspect of the heresy concerning marriage and asceticism. This merges into a direct instruction to Timothy to act in a godly way in the midst of this false teaching, paying heed to the truth, avoiding error and teaching the truth (1 Tim 4:1-16). Again, there is a reminder of the doctrine that is at stake. Then some practical instruction is given to Timothy on carrying out his tasks, the stress being on diligence and confidence.

This is followed by a series of instructions on how Timothy is to treat specific groups of people who may cause problems. Old and young men, and older and younger women are briefly mentioned. There is a remarkably lengthy discussion of the principles for caring for widows in the church (1 Tim 5:1-16). They receive more detailed comment than any other group in the letter.

Next, there is comment about elders, both the congregation's tangible responsibility toward them and matters of discipline. The final part of the chapter seems to be directed more toward Timothy as he deals with these two groups of people who might well cause difficulties. And then, to round off this section of the letter, there is some instruction about how slaves should behave toward their masters, and again this is presented as teaching that Timothy should be giving (1 Tim 5:17—6:2).

Finally, there is a lengthy section that deals with the character of the opponents and identifies them as people who are motivated in part at least by love of money. The dangers into which this can lead are described. Then by contrast instruction is given to Timothy personally regarding his stance amid these temptations, and he is told to stand fast in his life and in his church duties. The point is backed up by reminders about God and Jesus. The section concludes with how believers should use their wealth rightly, if they have any (1 Tim 6:3-19).

The closing part of the letter is a further reminder to Timothy to be faithful to his charge and to resist the false teachings (1 Tim 6:20-21).

There is not a lot of direct teaching in 1 Timothy about the content of the gospel, less proportionately than there is in Titus. The greeting is much briefer. The main doctrinal material comes in the description of Paul's conversion, in the basis for prayer in God's universal saving purpose, and in the statement of the truth that is upheld by the church. Again, as in Titus, the letter is dominated by the fact of opposition to Paul.[8] Attention is also devoted to things that are generally wrong in the church without being tied too tightly to a specific heresy, such as the sensuality attributed to some of the women and the money grubbing of the rich and the would-be rich.

---

[8]The description of the opponents and their teaching is fuller than in Titus, but it is broadly similar, and I can see no basic differences.

The letter, then, is mainly concerned with things to be done in the church or by Timothy. But there is a general pattern in the Pastoral Epistles of giving instructions that are then backed up by warrants. The practical teaching is backed up by various arguments: reminders about Paul's own position and status as an apostle, statements about the content of the gospel, putting the opposition in the context of prophecy, putting Timothy under the judgment of God, reminding Timothy of his conversion and commission. Thus doctrinal material is used to provide the basis for the life of the congregations and their leaders.

### The Second Letter to Timothy: The Theological Story

Second Timothy stands apart from Titus and I Timothy in that the whole letter is concerned with Timothy as Paul's colleague and with his personal behavior in a time of increasing godlessness.

*Encouragement to a church leader (2 Tim 1:1—2:13).* The letter begins with a long section (about a third of the whole) that is headed "Encouragement to Be Faithful" in the NIV.[9] This is a fair description. Timothy is depicted as a person who needs encouragement because of timidity and the temptation to weakness in the face of possible suffering. Paul gives thanks for him and especially for his faith, to which needs to be added boldness. This is the gift of the Spirit. Equipped with it Timothy is called to fearless presentation of the gospel, which is briefly summarized, and again we hear of Paul's role as a herald. Timothy is to preserve and teach the apostolic deposit faithfully. He is reminded of the desperate situation of desertion of Paul in Asia and the contrast provided by Onesiphorus. Not only is he to be strong himself; he must also entrust the message to faithful people who will continue the task. He is to be single-minded and diligent and prepared for suffering, like Paul. Again the injunctions are backed up with a doctrinal argument that refers in turn to Jesus and his resurrection, God's purpose for his people, and the promises given to those who are prepared to be identified with Jesus.

*Practical advice (2 Tim 2:14-26).* The second major section is a series of more practical injunctions to avoid useless controversy, to be aware of the spread of evil, which, however, will not triumph, and to act wisely. The main emphasis is

---

[9]TNIV has adopted different section headings.

on Timothy's conduct, but there is some reference to passing on the same injunctions to other people and to the danger of heresy and the possibility of reclaiming the opponents for the truth.

*Opposition and steadfastness (2 Tim 3:1—4:8).* Then, as in 1 Timothy, we have a reminder of the dangers that are afflicting the church in the last days (2 Tim 3:1-9). The picture is bleak, but again the danger is limited. Although the description is that of ungodly people, it is probably meant to be a picture of apostasy in the church.

Over against this Timothy is again reminded of Paul's example of patience and suffering, and of the need to hold fast to what he has learned from the Scriptures, provided they are rightly understood! Practical advice is given, mixed again with warnings about heresy and buttressed by the example of Paul (2 Tim 3:10—4:8). It is the strength of the opposition that appears to be the greatest threat to Timothy, and it is counterbalanced by reference to what he has learned from Scripture and by Paul's example of steadfastness.

*Paul the missionary in prison (2 Tim 4:9-22).* Finally, there is a section of personal news and instructions that is concerned with how Timothy is to help Paul in his mission and in his situation in prison (2 Tim 4:9-22). The position of the missionary with colleagues and opponents, with discouraging situations and divine help, and with a concern for the ongoing work of the gospel, emerges vividly.

Summing up the letter, we find the constant repetition of a number of themes that are meant to encourage and commission Timothy for his work. He is assured of the help of the Spirit, he is reminded of the examples of Christ and Paul, he is told to expect opposition, persecution and suffering, he is urged to stand firm, to avoid evil, to preach the gospel, to rebuke heresy and to hope that some heretics may repent. He is to guard the truth and pass it on to future teachers, but this note is not dominant. The work of Paul goes on despite his imprisonment and the other difficulties.

What is lacking from 2 Timothy in comparison with 1 Timothy and Titus is teaching on church order, with the exception of 2 Timothy 2:2. There is rather less material on false teaching and more emphasis on the sheer fact of opposition. In contrast, there is much more on the example of Paul. There is a lot on Timothy personally, but his personal Christian life and his work as a leader are closely intertwined.

## Theological Themes

*Traditional features.* It is a feature of the Pastoral Epistles that in view of their purpose they tend to give practical teaching and exhortation that is backed up by doctrinal teaching. Large sections of Titus, for example, are primarily concerned with ecclesiastical instructions and moral teaching to be passed on to the congregations (Tit 1:5-16; 2:1-10, 15; 3:1-2, 9-15), but they are either built upon a theological introduction (Tit 1:1-4) or are backed up by theology (Tit 2:11-14; 3:4-8), and there is little theology in the practical sections. The same is true of 1 Timothy, but there is more of an interweaving of doctrine and exhortation in 2 Timothy, where the element of personal exhortation addressed to Timothy is more marked.

At various points there is appeal to "trustworthy" sayings (1 Tim 1:15; 3:1; 4:9; 2 Tim 2:11; Tit 3:8). This rubric, which may be used to introduce or to follow the text to which it refers, appears to be primarily a statement of the trustworthiness of the material in question rather than, as used to be thought, an indication that some kind of authoritative, traditional material is being cited.

Nevertheless, at least some of these sayings may rest on tradition, and this possibility introduces us to the question of the nature of the theology in the Pastoral Epistles. There is no doubt that the writer continually appeals to an accepted body of teaching and picks up earlier formulations of it (e.g., 1 Tim 2:6; Tit 2:14). There is particular stress on the gospel in its Pauline form. Some scholars have detected echoes of the earlier Pauline letters, but it is disputed whether there is literary dependence. In any case, the verdict of Joachim Jeremias still stands: "nowhere in the whole of the non-Pauline literature does Pauline teaching appear so clearly as in the Pastoral Epistles".[10] Whether or not the author knew the Pauline Epistles or even composed them, the fact remains that the Pastoral Epistles are confessedly a statement of Pauline teaching and are basically in harmony with his theology.

They faithfully present Paul's doctrine of justification by grace through faith without any works (Tit 3:5; 2 Tim 1:9); they echo his concept of Christian sal-

---

[10]Joachim Jeremias, *Die Briefe an Timotheus und Titus*, 8th ed. (Göttingen: Vandenhoeck und Ruprecht, 1963), p. 8. Jeremias accepted the authenticity of the ten other letters ascribed to Paul, and his statement was intended to be an argument for the Pastoral Epistles being the work of Paul through a secretary.

vation as mediated in Christ (I Tim 1:14; 3:13; 2 Tim 1:9, 13; 2:1, 10; 3:12, 15), and his understanding of the Christian life as one of identification with Christ in his death and new life (2 Tim 2:11-13). They insist on the universality of the provision of salvation for all people (I Tim 2:6; 4:10; Tit 2:11), with special emphasis on the inclusion of the Gentiles (I Tim 2:7; 3:16; 2 Tim 4:17). They draw attention to the gift of the Spirit as the agent in new birth (Tit 3:5), the source of power for Christian living (2 Tim 1:7, 14) and the source of charismatic gifts for ministry (I Tim 4:14; 2 Tim 1:6). They reflect the Pauline understanding of the Christian life as characterized by strength in weakness and of the life of the missionary in particular as one of suffering and imprisonment and even death, although the triumph of the gospel is assured. They thus share the paradox of the tension between the "now" and the "not yet" of salvation. There is, then, no doubt that an authentically Pauline spirit breathes through these letters.

Yet it remains hard, if not impossible, to separate out what is traditional in formulation from the author's own contribution, in the way in which it is possible to do so in the earlier letters of Paul himself where tradition can often be recognized by linguistic and other peculiarities. The unique style constitutes a fairly seamless robe that gives the letters a uniform appearance.[11] It is difficult to avoid the impression that the author has used his traditional materials in a creative way, carefully expressing them in his own characteristic idiom. This idiom pervades the letters and indicates that we are dealing with a writer who has his own distinct contribution to make.

Alongside the traditional material, then, we have other ways in which the writer expresses what he wants to say in a manner that is not found in the acknowledged letters of Paul. This comes out in three specific areas.

*Jesus and God.* First, there is christology. This is expressed primarily in terms of "epiphany" or "appearing". This term is used by Paul in 2 Thessalonians 2:8 with reference to the parousia of the Lord Jesus, and this usage is repeated here (Tit 2:13; 2 Tim 4:1, 8), but it is also used to refer to the earthly life of Jesus (2 Tim 1:10). The term was used elsewhere of theophanies that were in

---

[11]This is not to deny that there is some concentration of unusual vocabulary in particular passages. The individual distinctives in thought and expression in the letters are set out carefully by Fuchs (see p. 397 n. 1), but they are not sufficient in my opinion to call in question the existence of a basic common theology in them.

some way visible and brought the saving intervention of God to his people. Here the coming of Jesus is envisaged as such a visible, saving action of God. The language suggests that the One who appears is a heavenly being who is made manifest on earth. This is particularly evident in the succinct and cryptic statement in I Timothy 3:16 that speaks of the One who appeared[12] in flesh and was vindicated "in spirit" (NRSV; "by the Spirit", TNIV). His coming into the world (I Tim 1:15) carries resonances of similar incarnation language in John and is best understood in the same way. This is perhaps further confirmed by the insistence in I Timothy 2:5 that Christ Jesus was human, a point that there was no need to emphasize if he was not already thought of as divine. And there is also the difficult statement in 2 Timothy 1:9-10 that speaks of the grace "given us in Christ Jesus before the beginning of time"; again this is best understood by appeal to the concept of preexistence.[13]

It is important now to observe that the thought of epiphany is extended to include the whole of the saving action of God in and through Christ. This emerges in Titus 2:11, where it is the grace of God that has appeared, and similarly in Titus 3:4 "the kindness and love of God our Savior appeared". The recognition elsewhere in the New Testament that the saving event comprises not only the coming of Christ but also the associated events, such as the pouring out of the Spirit and the apostolic testimony to the significance of Jesus, comes to expression here. We find something similar in I Timothy 2:5-6, where the self-giving of Christ and the testimony to it are closely linked, just as in 2 Corinthians 5:18-21 the reconciling action of God in Christ and the message of reconciliation are tightly bound to each other.

Intermingled with this new presentation of the coming of Christ as epiphany is traditional material that interprets his death as self-giving in order to redeem sinners (Tit 2:14). There is a lack of emphasis, however, on the resurrection of Jesus in connection with the act of salvation, although it is stressed in connection with the resurrection of believers (2 Tim 2:8) and clearly implied in a reference to Jesus as the destroyer of death (2 Tim 1:10). The messiahship of Jesus is mentioned almost in passing in what is probably a traditional for-

---

[12] A different verb *(phaneroō)* is used here; cf. 2 Tim 1:10; Tit 1:3.

[13] These statements are made in full recognition that some scholars have denied the existence of an incarnational type of christology in the Pastoral Epistles. See I. Howard Marshall, "The Christology of the Pastoral Epistles", *SNT (SU)* 13 (1988): 157-77.

mulation (2 Tim 2:8) and not developed in any significant way. And, as we have seen, there is certainly stress on the future coming of Jesus as Judge and Savior (2 Tim 4:1).

This last term is possibly the most apt for summing up the person of Jesus in these letters. It is significant not only because it emphasizes the fundamentally salvific character of their theology but also because it is a description shared by Jesus (Tit 1:4; 2:13; 3:6; 2 Tim 1:10) with God (Tit 1:3; 2:10; 3:4; 1 Tim 1:1; 2:3; 4:10). Jesus and God are tied together closely through this shared function. The closeness of the link is even more evident in the reference to the character of the Christian hope—"the appearing of the glory of our great God and Savior, Jesus Christ" (Tit 2:13). Attempts to understand this phrase as a reference to "the glorious appearing of our great God *and* [our] Savior Jesus Christ" fall foul of the syntax (the absence of the article with "Savior"), the use elsewhere of "God and Savior" as a well-attested formula, and the Christian background of an increasing tendency to apply the title of God to Jesus. There is thus a functional equivalence between Christ and God; the Old Testament concept of the coming of Yahweh is here interpreted in terms of the coming of Christ in the same way as the title of God ("Lord") is also transferred to him.

The distinctive element in this christology is the concept of epiphany to apply to the incarnation. This language was very much at home in Hellenism, and its use has given rise to the view that the Pastoral Epistles represent a Hellenization of Christian theology. There is truth and error in this statement. It is inexact in that the concept of theophany and the use of epiphany language were already to be found in Greek-speaking Judaism in the canonical books of the Old Testament and in later writings, and there was even reference to the Messiah being revealed in the future (4 Ezra 7:28). There is no need to look for an external source for the language or to regard it as the intrusion of an alien category. But it is also the case that the language was familiar in the Hellenistic religious environment, and therefore its choice here would enable the writer to speak the language of the Greco-Roman world. It may be understood as part of an attempt, conscious or unconscious, to use new language to express the gospel in a way that would be intelligible and contemporary in the surrounding world of Ephesus and Crete, and more generally.

The concept of God that stands alongside this picture of Christ has sometimes been thought to be somewhat remote and lofty in view of the descriptions found in I Timothy 1:17 and I Timothy 6:15-16. Certainly these passages do emphasize the majesty and transcendence of God, although it is questionable whether they really go beyond what can be found in Judaism and other Christian writings of the time. Perhaps more surprising is the absence of the term *Father* with reference to God, whether in his relationship to Christ or to believers, except in the stereotyped language of the epistolary greetings (I Tim 1:2; 2 Tim 1:2; Tit 1:4). Correspondingly the terms *son* and *child* are not employed for relationships with God. This absence could reinforce the impression of separation and majesty. It is, however, offset by the use of the term *Savior*, which, as we have seen, ranges God and Christ closely alongside each other. There is also the language of "kindness and love" (Tit 3:4), which reflects the Pauline use of "grace" and "mercy". The vocabulary here is that used of gods and rulers in the Hellenistic world.

*The life of believers.* The second main area to be considered is that of the nature of the Christian life. Here again we have a basically traditional understanding. A person becomes a member of God's people (I am tempted to say "becomes a Christian" but recognize that this is a form of words marginal to the New Testament) through the action of God as Savior (I Tim 1:15; 2:4; 4:16; 2 Tim 1:9; Tit 3:5; cf. I Tim 2:15; 2 Tim 4:18).

This action presupposes that human beings are sinners whose lives are characterized by wickedness, ungodliness and futility (Tit 2:11, 14; 3:3). Salvation is deliverance from such a way of life to a better one. It is described in familiar terms as life or eternal life (I Tim 1:16; 6:12, 19; 2 Tim 1:1, 10; Tit 1:2; 3:7); the reference here is generally to endless life in God's heavenly kingdom (2 Tim 4:18), but it is also to a new quality of life here and now (cf. I Tim 4:8). Although little is said directly about it, the references to the day of judgment (I Tim 5:24) and to mercy being shown on that occasion (2 Tim 1:18; 4:8) clearly imply that unless they have been saved sinners face condemnation and loss; yielding to temptation entails ruin and destruction (I Tim 6:9) which are not necessarily confined to the future.

The experience of being saved is expressed as deliverance or redemption, using the concept of ransom that can ultimately be traced back to the saying of Jesus in Mark 10:45 (I Tim 2:5; Tit 2:14); this deliverance is from the whole sinful way of life and its consequences. It can also be spoken of in Pauline terms as justification (Tit 3:7). We also have the language of rebirth and renewal (Tit 3:5), which expresses the idea of a fundamental change or transformation in the person who is being saved through the working of the Holy Spirit.[14] The observation has been made that references to the Holy Spirit are sparse in the Pastoral Epistles; admittedly they may be few, but they are powerful in their depiction of the lavish outpouring of the Spirit on believers (Tit 3:6) who creates power, love and self-discipline (2 Tim 1:7) and provides help to believers in their custody of the gospel (2 Tim 1:14). These last two references do raise the question whether the thought is particularly of Spirit endowment for church leaders, particularly since there is mention in the context of the laying on of hands. However, it must be insisted that Titus 3:6 is quite clearly about the gift of the Spirit to all believers, and that the statement in 2 Timothy 1:7 is about qualities that are common to all believers and not just to leaders (cf. Rom 8:15). The author may be thinking especially about the equipping of Timothy for his work, but he does so by referring to what would be true of all believers.

The new life that results from this saving act will find its appropriate consummation in being finally brought into the heavenly kingdom of God (2 Tim 4:18; cf. 2:10; 1 Tim 4:8; 6:19). Meanwhile, there is a life to be lived. It is a life of identification with Christ (2 Tim 2:11-13) in which the believer shares in the death of Christ. The past tense used here suggests that the moment of conversion is regarded as a metaphorical death to the old life that entails the readiness even for martyrdom as the extreme possibility that faces believers; the ongoing nature of this life is seen in the need for readiness for endurance and faithfulness despite the temptations to apostasy and unfaithfulness. But the new life is empowered by the grace that is in Christ (2 Tim 2:1). This is doubtless another way of describing the help given by the Spirit; compare the way in which the gifts of the Spirit and the divine empowerments are paralleled in 1 Corinthians 12:4.

On the human side, so to speak, the inner basis of the Christian life resides in "a pure heart and a good conscience and a sincere faith" (1 Tim 1:5). There is a mixture here of what might be regarded as parts of the human personality that have been renewed by God's power and the activity of the human person in faith. The heart is the seat of motives and is to be pure, single-minded in de-

---

[14]The concept of rebirth is not explicit in the earlier letters of Paul.

votion to God (I Tim 1:5; 2 Tim 2:22). The word *conscience* is used in much the same way of the organ that adjudges conduct or planned conduct. It can be described as "good" (I Tim 1:5, 19) or "clear" (I Tim 3:9; 2 Tim 1:3). The contrasting condition is when the conscience is seared or corrupted (I Tim 4:2; Tit 1:15). In the latter condition the conscience is not working properly, giving false judgments or no judgment rather than condemning wrong conduct. It follows that the ideal is a conscience that is in good working order, in that it warns against what is bad conduct by God's standards and nevertheless finds nothing to condemn; it is both "good" and "clear".

Alongside these aspects of personality is placed faith, which is the most conspicuous theological term in the Pastoral Epistles. Faith is thus the most characteristic attribute of the Christian, and the use of the word in the Pastoral Epistles embraces the typical nuances found in Paul. There are some special emphases that are worthy of note. First, faith is closely linked with knowledge (Tit 1:1) as constituting the two qualities that define Christian existence. This element of knowledge corresponds with the very great stress in the letters on the place of sound teaching in the church. The presence of erroneous teaching is doubtless the occasion that gave rise to this stress. Consequently, the notion of faith itself broadens to include "the faith" as the objective expression of what Christians should believe and as the act of acceptance of this creed (I Tim 3:9; 6:21; 2 Tim 2:18). There is nothing new about this nuance, which is firmly established in earlier usage (cf. I Cor 15:1-2), but it is more central in the Pastoral Epistles. At the same time there is the conspicuous concept of faith as trust in God or Christ and commitment to him (I Tim 1:16; 3:16; 2 Tim 1:12; Tit 3:8). Although faith is directly associated with the moment of conversion (I Tim 1:14; 5:12; 2 Tim 1:5; 3:15), it is of course an ongoing attitude, and thus the nuance of faithfulness and perseverance is naturally accommodated within the concept (I Tim 2:15; Tit 3:15). It is not surprising, then, that the standard term for Christians is "believers/faithful" (I Tim 4:3, 10, 12; 5:16; Tit 1:6) and that the phrase "in [the] faith" is used to express the new situation brought about by acceptance of the gospel (I Tim 1:2; Tit 1:4). In view of this preponderance of evidence there is no significance in the lack of mention of faith in the statement about justification by grace in Titus 3:7 (note how faith is mentioned in the very next verse!).

Lists of vices and virtues are typical of the Pastoral Epistles, and faith figures in the latter with great regularity. It has been suspected that the effect of such listings is to make faith merely one of a number of Christian qualities, no more significant than the others. But this suggestion breaks down on the sheer prominence of faith in the Pastoral Epistles as a whole and also on the fact that elsewhere in the New Testament faith can occupy a subsidiary role in such lists (Gal 5:22; it is not even mentioned in 2 Cor 6:4-10).

Faith is most frequently linked with love in such lists or enumerations of Christian qualities (1 Tim 1:5, 14; 2:15; 4:12; 6:11; 2 Tim 1:13; 2:22; 3:10-11; Tit 2:2). What is in effect the content of love is fleshed out in the numerous references in the Pastoral Epistles to works or deeds. These deeds are qualified as "good" or "beautiful" (Gk. *kalos*). They are the positive outcome of Christian conversion, a life of usefulness and profit expressed in love to other people (cf. Tit 2:14; 3:8, 14).

There is another aspect to the Christian life that finds expression in a characteristic vocabulary embracing ideas of sobriety, moderation, dignity and self-control. Believers are to live orderly lives that will win respect in the community at large. The general concept covering this area of behavior is summed up in "piety" (Gk. *eusebeia*), a term that was current in Hellenistic Judaism and in the Hellenistic world more generally to signify the type of life that was determined by a right attitude to God or the gods. The content of piety was determined by the specific religion in question, and within Judaism the term was tantamount to the "fear of the Lord" and combined reverent knowledge of God based on his self-revelation and conduct in the light of that knowledge. It was thus a comprehensive term for religion in all its aspects. In the Pastoral Epistles godliness is naturally shaped by Christ, so that the "mystery" of our religion is identified with Christ (1 Tim 3:16), and piety is shaped within the context of a life "in Christ" (2 Tim 3:12). It is closely linked to faith and to knowledge of the truth revealed in the gospel.

Without developing the ethical outworkings of this concept further, we can note how in this second area (alongside christology) there is a use of terminology and concepts that were at home in the wider world and helped to express the Christian faith in a way that would have been widely intelligible to both Hellenistic Jews and Gentiles.

*The church.* The Pastoral Epistles are the New Testament documents that are most deeply concerned with the polity of the church. They come from a situation where two important tendencies were at work. First, although certainty is not attainable, the setting of the letters is the period during which the congregations founded by the Pauline mission were no longer under his direct supervision and were developing alternative forms of leadership. Second, the opposition to Paul and the growth of forms of teaching in conflict with his understanding of the gospel, which were already rampant during his lifetime, were increasing in influence. The confluence of these two movements explains the strong stress on eccesiology in the letter. The practical measures taken by the Pauline circle included, first, a stress on the importance of teaching that was in conformity with the gospel of Paul; the deposit handed down from Paul was to be preserved carefully by his successors and passed on to other people who would make it the basis of their teaching (1 Tim 6:20; 2 Tim 1:13-14; 2:2). Second, it was necessary to appoint local church leaders who would hold fast to the gospel as well as being fit in terms of character and gifts of leadership to guide the congregations (1 Tim 3:1-12; Tit 1:5-9). Third, time-wasting debates with opponents were to be avoided, and disciplinary action was to be taken with the recalcitrant (Tit 3:9-11; 2 Tim 2:23), although this did not exclude the possibility of discussion and instruction that could lead them back to a knowledge of the truth (2 Tim 2:25-26).

The emphasis in the Pastoral Epistles lies on the development of an orderly and recognized leadership and ministry in the congregations, within which these activities would be carried on. Little is said about the exercise of gifts of ministry in the congregations other than by those who were appointed to positions of leadership. It can be presumed that such ministry did exist: the activity of the opponents strongly suggests that it was not confined simply to the leaders, and the fact that Titus is portrayed as introducing elders where there formerly had not been any points in the same direction. Nevertheless, it has been thought that the Pastoral Epistles testify to the transition from a charismatically inspired form of congregational life to one that is dominated by appointed officers to whom alone the gifts of the Spirit are conveyed by the formal laying on of hands. Stated in such absolute terms, the contrast is clearly false. In the earlier Pauline epistles there is a combination of charismatic ministries and appointed leaders with a fluid boundary between the two. At Corinth ministry was open to all the congregation according to the gifts given to each, but at the same time there were recognized

leaders, both the apostles and their colleagues, who exercised superinten-
dence from outside, and the local elders or overseers and deacons (as attested
in Phil 1:1). In the Pastoral Epistles we see local congregations that are under
the care of Paul's colleagues, Timothy and Titus, but their task is to facilitate
the development of local leadership, and they are not regarded as being permanently on hand. Apostolic delegates come and go. The structure of the local leadership is still in process of evolution; it is significant that it is not possible to gain an absolutely clear picture of what was going on—why are the
terms *elder* and *overseer* apparently used for the same groups of people,[15] and
why do deacons figure in 1 Timothy but not in Titus?

Underlying these practical measures there is a developing concept of the nature of the church. The dominant motif is that of the church as a household (1
Tim 3:14). This stands in some contrast with the earlier Pauline picture of the
congregation as the body of Christ, in which all the members have their respec-
tive functions (Rom 12; 1 Cor 12). Nevertheless, the images are not as different as some have thought. Fatherhood (i.e., householder) language is used earlier by Paul of his own role in the congregations (1 Cor 4:14-15; 1 Thess 2:11).
Within the body metaphor it is certainly true that all members are important
and have a function, but at the same time there is a recognition that some parts
seem to be weaker and lacking in honor (1 Cor 12:21-24). And when Paul lists
the different parts of the church in 1 Corinthians 12:28, he does put them in
order with "first of all apostles, second prophets, third teachers" and then the
others. It may also be significant that, although in these earlier letters the body
exists "in Christ" (Rom 12:5; cf. 1 Cor 12:12), the metaphor is not developed
in terms of leadership or headship, the need to do so evidently arose and is reflected in Ephesians and Colossians, where Christ is the head on whom the
body is dependent. The picture of the household (i.e., a building with a family
living in it) brings out more this concept of rule and direction; in Hebrews
Moses and then Christ are envisaged as the faithful stewards in charge of God's
house, and in Hebrews the congregational leaders are seen similarly. A person
must be competent to direct his own household affairs if he is to be chosen as

---

[15]It is most probable that this was the case, but it is not absolutely impossible that the overseers were
a subgroup of the elders, although on this hypothesis it is very difficult to see why the qualifications
for elders and overseers are juxtaposed in Tit 1:6, 7-9. If the structure had been more rigid, we would
not have expected the material to be so difficult to interpret.

God's steward. The metaphor may also convey the thought that the different people have assigned roles and positions within the household with corresponding duties, just as in an ordinary household there were various roles for the wife, children, slaves and other members (cf. Tit 2:2-10; I Tim 6:1-2). However, it must be recognized that the picture of the church as household is not explicitly developed in this manner. What we do have certainly is teaching about the need for younger people to treat older people with respect and for appropriate respect between the sexes (I Tim 5:1-2). The concept of the church as household thus fits in with the general stress on orderliness in the letters.

A second, closely related picture sees the church as the pillar and bulwark of the truth (I Tim 3:15). There is probably a combination of ideas here in that the church is to be a guardian or firm basis for the truth and also a freestanding pillar (such as stood outside the Solomonic temple, I Kings 7:15-22) that bears testimony to the truth.[16] Thus the church is assigned a central role in the preservation and proclamation of the gospel.

Third, the church is identified as the church of the living God (I Tim 3:15). The description of God as "living" probably conveys the thought of God as powerfully present in the church, and the whole phrase echoes the description of Israel as the "assembly of Yahweh". Without using the word *temple* the author identifies the congregation as the group of people who belong to God (cf. Tit 2:14), within whose assembly he is present, and who form his "house". This is a much more dynamic concept of the church than might have been expected. The church is far from being a static institution.

### Conclusion

The surface intention of the Pastoral Epistles is to call back the congregations to the Pauline model of belief and life in the face of an opposition that represented a reversion to a peculiar type of Jewish Christianity that was in danger of losing itself in speculation and a corresponding asceticism. The insights of Pauline theology and ecclesiology had to be adapted to deal with this new situation, and this in part explains why the letters present Pauline material in a new way: there is a powerful stress on the need for teaching that is in accordance with the deposit handed down from Paul and on the need for a church polity

---

[16]This, of course, assumes that the church is founded on the truth and is continually submissive to it.

that will ensure that this takes place. Controls and curbs needed to be introduced to replace the personal authority of Paul. It is not that Paul superintended congregations that were free from problems; he too had to impose discipline.

This process is sometimes labeled as the institutionalization of the church and its theology.[17] But this description oversimplifies the situation and does not do justice to the parallel process that was going on, namely, the restatement of the gospel and of Christian behavior in a new vocabulary and conceptuality that retained the essential Pauline notes but is recognizably in a somewhat different idiom. This should come as no surprise when we recollect the number of different idioms that coexist in the other New Testament writings and that were in no way a stumbling block to the process of canonization. They show that the circle in which the Pastoral Epistles were put together did not interpret its task as the wooden reproduction of tradition in a way that stifled creative thinking.

The difficulty may be, of course, that the Pastoral Epistles, while not themselves succumbing to the temptation to make the church a static repository of fixed teaching administered by a select group of leaders, nevertheless set a direction that inevitably led to this result. Are they early catholic in that sense? Their problem is that they were dealing with very real threats to the future of the faith, and therefore they do emphasize the elements of orthodoxy and order that were essential in that situation. Those who criticize them may well be asked to consider what else could have been done if the truth of the gospel and the commission to evangelize were to be maintained and revitalized in the church. The fact is that there is a very difficult balancing act to perform between veering into the rigidly orthodox institutionalization that produces a dead, introspective orthodoxy and slipping into the enthusiastic freedom in thought and behavior that can lose anything recognizably Christian. It is worth considering whether what happened was that the later church tended to follow the rules and order in the Pastoral Epistles to the neglect of those elements that call for a lively discipleship under the shadow of the cross.

---

[17]Cf. Margaret Y. MacDonald, *The Pauline Churches: A Socio-historical Study of Institutionalization in the Pauline and Deutero-Pauline Writings* (Cambridge: Cambridge University Press, 1988).

## Bibliography

*New Testament Theologies:* (English) Strecker, pp. 576-94. (German) Gnilka, pp. 350-68; Hübner, 2:378-79; Stuhlmacher, 2:1-53.

Campbell, R. Alastair *The Elders: Seniority Within Earliest Christianity.* Edinburgh: T & T Clark, 1994.

Collins, Raymond F. *1 and 2 Timothy and Titus: A Commentary.* Louisville, Ky.: Westminster John Knox, 2002.

Davies, Margaret. *The Pastoral Epistles.* Sheffield: Sheffield Academic Press, 1996.

Johnson, Luke Timothy. *Letters to Paul's Delegates: 1 Timothy, 2 Timothy, Titus.* Valley Forge, Pa.: Trinity Press International, 1996.

Knight, George W., III. *The Pastoral Epistles.* Grand Rapids, Mich.: Eerdmans; Carlisle: Paternoster, 1992.

Lau, Andrew Y. *Manifest in Flesh: The Epiphany Christology of the Pastoral Epistles.* Tübingen: J. C. B. Mohr [Paul Siebeck], 1996.

MacDonald, Margaret Y. *The Pauline Churches: A Socio-historical Study of Institutionalization in the Pauline and Deutero-Pauline Writings.* Cambridge: Cambridge University Press, 1988.

Marshall, I. Howard, with Philip H. Towner. *A Critical and Exegetical Commentary on the Pastoral Epistles.* Edinburgh: T & T Clark, 1999.

Mounce, William D. *The Pastoral Epistles.* Dallas: Word, 2000.

Quinn, Jerome D. *The Letter to Titus.* New York: Doubleday, 1990.

Towner, Philip H. *1-2 Timothy and Titus.* Downers Grove, Ill.: InterVarsity Press, 1994.

————. *The Goal of Our Instruction.* Sheffield: Sheffield Academic Press, 1989.

Verner, David C. *The Household of God: The Social World of the Pastoral Epistles.* Chico, Calif.: Scholars Press, 1983.

Young, Frances M. *The Theology of the Pastoral Letters.* Cambridge: Cambridge University Press, 1994.

# 18

# THE THEOLOGY OF THE
# PAULINE LETTERS

⮰⚬⮲

Now that we have examined individually the thirteen letters in the Pauline corpus we have the task of attempting some kind of synthesis of their theology. Since the question whether they are all directly from Paul or some are later compositions, is a matter of dispute, it will make good sense to tackle our task in a way that recognizes the existence of this unsettled debate. The problem is to some extent eased by the fact that the letters about which there is dispute are generally dated, if authentic, to the later part of Paul's career, and therefore a distinction between the earlier and later letters corresponds approximately to one between the authentic and the secondary letters.[1] On the whole, a treatment that recognizes the chronological difference between the earlier and the later letters, whether authentic or post-Pauline, will enable us to do justice to the problems. I shall note where the later letters corroborate the earlier ones and where they introduce new ideas. We must bear in mind that the letters were written to different concrete situations and addressed different specific audiences and their problems, factors that may have shaped the agenda and the way in which the writer responded to it.

---

[1]The only doubtful letter that if authentic would belong to the earlier period is 2 Thessalonians. Colossians and Ephesians, if authentic, belong to Paul's captivity in Rome. If authentic, 2 Timothy is generally thought to be Paul's last extant letter; if authentic, Titus and I Timothy could be exceptions to this dating, since some defenders of them think that they are best dated during the third missionary campaign (Acts 19).

## The Framework and Background of Paul's Theology

By "framework and background of Paul's theology" I am referring to the framework of thought, the given set of basic presuppositions about the nature of reality, within which Paul did his theology. As is the case with the other New Testament authors, the framework of Paul's theology is constituted by Judaism. Three elements in this are significant.

The first is the Old Testament. Although formal citations are largely confined to Romans, 1-2 Corinthians and Galatians, there are allusions throughout the corpus, and it is clear that the Old Testament has decisively helped to shape Paul's thought. Attention to Scripture was in any event inevitable for Paul, since he had to develop and defend his theology over against other views that claimed to be based on it.[2]

The second element is the manner in which Scripture is used; here Paul shows similarities to the kind of exegesis found in the Judaism of his time, as attested especially in the Dead Sea Scrolls and reflected in the later rabbinic literature.

The third element is Paul's acceptance of the kind of outlook that can be broadly termed apocalyptic. That is to say, he is less concerned with the kind of religion found in the rabbinic literature that was largely concerned with the exposition of the law and is much more at home in the sort of theology that is centered on God's intervention in history through the Messiah and the life of the world to come. This framework establishes what we might call the shape of the theology; it does not establish the content that is developed within these categories. There can be enormous differences in the scenarios developed by apocalyptic writers.

To insist on the fundamentally Jewish character of Paul's theology is not to deny the presence of influences and concepts drawn from other sources. There were already Hellenistic elements in the Judaism that Paul knew. Hence, for example, there is some interaction in Romans with the kind of thinking found in the Hellenistic Jewish book of Wisdom.[3]

Second, we must not underestimate the significant role played by Paul's Christian experience and by his thinking about its significance. Paul's conver-

---

[2]See D. Moody Smith, "The Pauline Literature", in *It Is Written: Scripture Citing Scripture: Essays in Honour of Barnabas Lindars*, ed. D. A. Carson and H. G. M. Williamson (Cambridge: Cambridge University Press, 1988), pp. 265-91.

[3]Hellenistic in the sense that it was originally composed in Greek.

sion experience played a decisive part in the development of his theology.[4] He also refers on occasion to prophetic experiences that he had in which he received visions and messages from the Lord.

Third, Paul's thought was also shaped decisively by that of the earliest Christians who were his contemporaries. Paul did not do his missionary work and theology in a vacuum but learned from those who were Christians alongside him and developing their theological understanding of the gospel simultaneously. References to Cephas (Peter), James, John, Barnabas and Silas in his letters indicate something of the close personal contacts that he had with other missionaries and leaders associated with Jerusalem and Antioch. There are quotations from traditions handed down within early Christian circles. And included in these traditions were things said and done by Jesus.

No attempt has been made in this book to reconstruct the theology of this early period. The task of extracting pre-Pauline material from the various sources is speculative, although in my opinion the presentation by Luke in Acts should be given much more credence than it often receives. In the discussion above of the Synoptic Gospels and Acts I have set forth the view that the theology of the early Christians as portrayed in Acts is very much what we would expect to have developed among the followers of the earthly Jesus in the light of their experiences of the resurrection and the outpouring of the Spirit, and under the constraint of their commission to continue the work of mission to which he had called them. Further, it is vital to remember that Paul was converted within a very short period after Easter, and therefore we cannot posit a lengthy period of development at the end of which he came upon the scene.

### The Central Theme of Paul's Theology

There has been much controversy as to whether it makes sense to identify a central theme or core in Paul's theology, and if so what that core might be. Paul was primarily a preacher and teacher, and therefore the problem is essentially settled by his summary of what he proclaimed in 1 Corinthians 15:2-8: "the gospel I preached to you. . . . By this gospel you are saved, if you hold firmly to the word I preached to you. Otherwise, you have believed in vain. For what I

---

[4]Richard N. Longenecker, ed., *The Road from Damascus: The Impact of Paul's Conversion on His Life, Thought and Ministry* (Grand Rapids, Mich.: Eerdmans, 1997), explores this topic comprehensively.

received I passed on to you as of first importance: that Christ died for our sins according to the Scriptures, that he was buried, that he was raised on the third day according to the Scriptures, and that he appeared to Cephas, and then to the Twelve. . . . And last of all he appeared to me also". But this statement is about the gospel as it is made known to unbelievers. What it does not bring out is that the content of this salvation is that God calls believers into the church, the company of people who receive the Holy Spirit, to live a new life in union with the crucified and risen Christ that expresses itself in holiness and love, and to look forward to the parousia of Christ and the resurrection of the dead.

In identifying this whole complex of motifs as the heart of Paul's theology we are recognizing that he was essentially a missionary and that therefore a theological statement of the gospel that he preached takes us to the central theme of his Christian thinking. We have expressed this central theme in the form of a doctrinal statement, and we have the excellent justification for so doing in that the first part of it is a straight quotation from such a statement by Paul. Another possibility might be to follow one of the fashions of the present time and say that Paul tells a story or narrative whose plot can be recounted. The concept of a narrative is a helpful one in that the Scriptures do tell the story of the ongoing interrelationship between God and humankind from the creation of the world and Adam and Eve right up to Paul's time. It makes sense to see what was happening in Paul's experience as the continuation of that story and to recognize further that to some extent the future development of the story can be foreseen. Early Christians such as Paul did take over the story contained in the Scriptures, understanding it in a new way in the light of their history, and they did see their experience as the next stage in that story. Paul, however, does not so much tell a story in his letters as rather comment on the story and its implications for his readers. It is important that the story be told correctly and not given a different kind of spin, as was happening in the Jewish understanding of it that led on a trajectory to a rabbinic Judaism that denied that the Messiah had come.[5]

### Specific Elements in Paul's Theology

*God—the Father.* The brief summary of Paul's theology above very nearly missed

---

[5]See Bruce W. Longenecker, ed., *Narrative Dynamics in Paul: A Critical Assessment* (Louisville, Ky.: Westminster John Knox, 2002).

out the word *God*. To some extent one can understand why Rudolf Bultmann structured his theology of Paul around his anthropology rather than his theology (in the narrow sense), since it could be argued that Paul is more concerned to tell his readers about themselves than about God. In the same way our survey of the individual letters has shown how Paul spends little space on Jesus Christ as a person and far more on his significance for the readers. This superficial impression is misleading, since God the Father is the initiator of the story for Paul, as he is for all the New Testament writers: the gospel is the gospel of God (Rom 1:1). God the Father is the creator of the universe (1 Cor 8:6), and human beings are made in his image (1 Cor 11:7). He expects their worship and their willing obedience to his way of life for them (cf. Rom 1:21). He is living and active, by contrast with the idols worshiped by the Gentiles (1 Thess 1:9). He will judge the world for its sinfulness (Rom 2:5); his wrath is already being revealed in the way in which human sin leads to human misery (Rom 1:18). He has been active in the story of Israel, the nation called to be his people, who turned out to be generally rebellious against him (Rom 9—11). And now he is active in initiating and effecting salvation. He is faithful to the people whom he has called and who have responded to his call (1 Cor 1:9; 1 Thess 5:24; cf. Phil 1:6).

Already in this summary it has been necessary to speak more precisely of "God the Father" in order to distinguish him from Jesus Christ. Paul uses "Father" in various ways and contexts. Epistolary opening greetings, specifically the "grace and peace" wish but also the surrounding material, regularly refer to God as "our Father", that is, the father of the correspondent and his addressees, or simply in later letters as "the Father" (1 Tit; 2 Tim; Tit).[6] Some epistolary endings also use this language (Eph 6:23; cf. Phil 4:20). Elsewhere, however, the form "our Father" is rare (Phil 4:20; 1 Thess 3:11, 13; 2 Thess 2:16). The indications are that the term was liturgical[7] and strengthened the expression of God's fatherly care for his people (cf. Eph 5:20; Col 1:12; 3:17). God is also

---

[6]First Thessalonians has a shorter greeting but still mentions the Father in 1 Thess 1:1, 3; the text in 2 Thess 1:2 is uncertain, but 2 Thess 1:1 includes "our Father".

[7]By this slippery and perhaps anachronistic term I refer to words, phrases and longer statements that were used orally in set phraseology in Christian meetings without necessarily implying that these existed in written form or that they dominated in the informal setting of early Christian congregational meetings.

spoken of as "the Father of our Lord Jesus Christ", and this expression is likewise used in liturgical contexts (Rom 15:6; 2 Cor 1:3; 11:31; cf. Eph 1:3; 3:14; Col 1:3); calling on God as *"Abba,* Father" (Rom 8:15; Gal 4:6) falls into the same category of usage (cf. also 2 Cor 1:3b, "the Father of compassion"). Otherwise, the term does not figure much in Paul's writings, apart from the crucial confession of "one God, the Father" (I Cor 8:6; cf. Eph 4:6; see also Rom 6:4; I Cor 15:24) and the citation from 2 Samuel 7:14 in 2 Corinthians 6:18, which gives scriptural backing for the usage. We see from this survey that "Father" occurs predominantly in the context of prayer, blessing and doxology but otherwise is comparatively rare. The frequent use of "our" conveys a sense that God is the Father of believers inasmuch as they have become his people.

God is not the only superhuman being. There are angels who act as his servants (Gal 3:19; cf. 4:14),[8] and there are his opponents, Satan (the devil) and the various evil powers who threaten the peace and well-being of the universe (Rom 8:38-39; I Cor 2:8; 15:24; cf. Eph 1:21; 6:12; Col 1:16; 2:15).

*God—the Son.* God has a Son, identified as the human figure Jesus. This extraordinary statement (for a Jew) is made quite naturally by Paul and does not seem to have been a matter of surprise or controversy to his readers. Paul, as we have noted, does not explain this relationship. When he does comment on the relationship of God's Son to God, it is more to express the paradox of this figure becoming human and surrendering his sovereign position to become a slave; that is the mystery rather than the fact that God could have a Son. The term *Son* is not all that frequent in Paul.[9] It occurs only once in I Thessalonians (I Thess 1:10), where the Son is the one whom God raised from the dead and is awaited by believers from heaven. In Galatians it is associated with the sonship of believers (Gal 4:5-6) but also with the personal experience of Paul, whose conversion entailed the revelation of God's Son to him (Gal 1:16) and whose life is one of faith in the Son of God who loved him and gave himself for him (Gal 2:20). The inclusion of believers in God's family as his children leads to the usage in Romans 8:19 (cf. I Cor 1:9). Paul uses the term when bringing out the greatness of God's self-sacrifice in giving Jesus up to death (Rom 8:32).

---

[8]It has to be said, however, that although angels are part of Paul's theological cast, they are more background figures and an audience for what happens (I Cor 4:9) than significant actors in the story.

[9]As a christological term *son* is absent from Philippians, 2 Thessalonians, Philemon and the Pastoral Epistles.

In Romans 1:3 the content of the gospel is said to be the Son of God. Paul expands on this by referring to the fact of Jesus Christ's human descent and to his appointment as Son of God with power at the resurrection. By this statement Paul does justice to the Davidic sonship of Jesus, which qualifies him to be the Messiah, and to his status after the resurrection in which he exercises the function of Son of God with a power that was not evident previously. Whether or not this statement is a reworking of a tradition or an ad hoc creation by Paul, it is highly appropriate in emphasizing the centrality of Jesus in the gospel, his unimpeachable status as Messiah (of crucial importance for debates with Jews) and his divinely confirmed status as Son of God, which includes and transcends messiahship. The form of words implies that he was Son of God throughout his career (Gal 4:4) but became the enthroned Son of God after the resurrection.[10] Thereafter Paul uses the term *Son* to express the greatness of the gift made by God in sending Jesus to die for sinners (Rom 5:10; 8:3, 32).

The closely related idea of Jesus as the image of God is found in 2 Corinthians 4:4 and Colossians 1:15, and in both cases the concept of believers being transformed to bear the same image is not far distant (2 Cor 3:18; Col 3:10; see also Rom 8:29; 1 Cor 15:49).

Jesus Christ[11] is distinguished terminologically from God not only as the Son from the Father but also by the way in which Paul uses the term *Lord* to refer to him. It is likely that several influences have contributed to the usage of this term, stretching back to the consciousness of Jesus as the master and teacher of the disciples during his earthly life and taking into account the parabolic teaching about the master of the servants who will return to judge them on their conduct during his absence. But it is also the case that here Paul is tak-

---

[10]There is no suggestion of two stages in the career of Jesus with messiahship during his earthly life being followed by "adoption" or "enthronement" as God's Son from the resurrection onward, or with messiahship as a preliminary but inferior status. For Paul Jesus was the Son of God also during his earthly life; the resurrection was exaltation and vindication of that status and hence "with power". This does not rule out the position of Christ alongside God the Father before his incarnation that Paul assumes in 2 Cor 8:9 and Phil 2:5.

[11]Paul uses the forms "Jesus Christ" and "Christ Jesus" indifferently. Attempts to find different nuances in the change of order are inconclusive. Probably the two forms arose from the two statements "Jesus is the Christ" and "The Christ is Jesus" depending on whether the underlying question is "Who is Jesus?" or "Who is the Christ?" It is not clear whether "Christ" figures more as a simple name or identifier, or whether it is more a title equivalent to "Messiah" in Paul's usage. My impression is that the titular force is weakening and often it has become more of a name.

ing over a term that connoted God in the Scriptures and generally reserving it for Jesus Christ.[12]

The naming of Jesus alongside God as the source of spiritual blessings is found in the epistolary greetings. Implicitly this assigns to him the same role as that of God, and this is further seen in the way in which he can be named in other blessing statements, in particular the "grace" benedictions that typically conclude Paul's letters. Equally significant is the contrast that Paul makes in Galatians 1:11-12 when he insists that he did not receive his gospel from a human source, literally, "from a man", but from a revelation of Jesus Christ. A further important passage is 1 Corinthians 8:6, where God and the Lord Jesus Christ are named alongside each other as the source of all things. Here Paul takes the Jewish confession that there is one God and places alongside it the affirmation that there is also one Lord, namely, Jesus Christ. This same close relationship with God may be implicitly present in Romans 14:9-12; what is said here about appearing before God's judgment seat and bowing before him and confessing him is said elsewhere with explicit reference to the role of Christ as Lord and judge (2 Cor 5:10; Phil 2:10-11). As elsewhere in the New Testament, the exaltation of Jesus as Lord is of central importance; it is precisely faith that this is so that constitutes saving faith (Rom 10:9). Consequently, Paul can identify Jesus and God as the objects of faith (Rom 4:24; 10:11).

Side by side with this understanding of Jesus in relation to God is the stress on him as a human being; if Romans 5:1-11 presents him as the Lord and Son of God, Romans 5:12-21 emphasizes that he is the "one man" whose righteous act undid the effects of that other man, Adam (Rom 5:15; cf. 1 Cor 15:21, 47).

Despite the high place given to Jesus, God the Father remains the supreme being in the universe, so that ultimate worship and obedience is given to him, even by Jesus, who shares his authoritative position over against the universe (1 Cor 15:28; Phil 2:9-11).

All of this material that indicates the role and status of Jesus is in the nature of incidental information. It is not something that Paul is teaching his readers

---

[12]On the whole, Paul uses the term *Lord* for God the Father when he is writing in a context influenced by the Old Testament, and especially in quotations, but he uses it for Jesus the rest of the time. Here also he can take it from Old Testament texts and assume that the reference is to Jesus rather than to God the Father without attempting to justify his interpretation. For a helpful summary see Joseph A. Fitzmyer, *EDNT,* 2:328-31.

but uncontroversial material that he can assume is accepted already by them. It is rare for him to do something that is more like specific teaching about him. Thus even the statement of Jesus' self-humbling in becoming poor in 2 Corinthians 8:9 is introduced by "you know". The fullest passage about Jesus is in Philippians 2:6-11, where his career is adduced in order to reinforce an appeal for the kind of self-humbling that enables believers to think of one another's interests rather than just their own. The development here is in terms of the self-emptying and self-humbling of Jesus; these are motifs not found elsewhere—Paul more normally talking of the self-giving of Jesus for the sake of humanity (Gal 1:4; 2:20; cf. Eph 5:2, 25; 1 Tim 2:6; Tit 2:14) or of his being given by God (Rom 4:25; 1 Cor 11:23)—and their occurrence rather strengthens the view that the story of Jesus given here has been deliberately framed for its context in the letter.

The other detailed presentation of Jesus is in Colossians 1:15-20, which brings together the concepts of divine sonship (Col 1:13) and the divine image, the latter being a motif associated not only with sonship but also with the figure of wisdom. The association of the Son with creation (cf. Heb 1:2-3 for the same combination of sonship, wisdom and creation) is developed here in the interests of emphasizing his supremacy over all that has been created. The supremacy of Christ is already present in the references to his exaltation to the right hand of God (Rom 8:34; cf. Eph 1:20; Col 3:1) and his reign (1 Cor 15:25), but it is developed in Colossians, where Christ is filled by God (Col 2:9).

Against this background it is not surprising if Christ is actually referred to as "God", and this is almost certainly the case in Romans 9:5 (cf. Tit 2:13, where it is virtually certain). Here we have what appears to be the beginning of a balanced statement about Jesus according to the flesh and then according to the spirit (cf. Rom 1:3-4), but in the second half he is actually stated to be "God over all, forever praised". The uniqueness of this direct appellation raises the question whether we should repunctuate the sentence to give a separate doxology concerning God the Father (TNIV mg.; NRSV mg.) rather than a description of Jesus, but this rendering is intrinsically less probable. We have the same kind of thinking as in John 1, where the Word can be God and yet distinguishable from God the Father.

It is now crucial to remember the point made at the beginning of this section, that God's Son is identified with the human figure Jesus.[13] Here three points are significant.

First, the existence of the human figure Jesus as a human figure was not in any dispute. There were, we may presume, plenty of people who could testify to the life and death of this human being, just as they could testify to his resurrection. Nor does there appear to have been any dispute about the reality of the manhood (cf. I Tim 2:5). The ancient world knew well enough the possibility of supernatural beings, the gods of the Greeks and Romans or angelic messengers in Judaism, being transformed into a human form for a temporary period, but that is not the impression that we get from Paul, who refers quite unequivocally to Jesus as a man. This is confirmed by the way in which he understands Jesus as the heavenly man (I Cor 15:45-49) and conceives of him as having a body (Phil 3:21; cf. I Cor 15:44).

Second, the direction of Paul's thinking is summed up in Galatians 4:4, where God sent his Son, born of a woman. It is not that a human being ascended to heaven and became a heavenly being, but that a heavenly being became human. It is true that Galatians 4:4 is the only place where Paul speaks of God sending Jesus, a motif strongly attested in John, but his other references to incarnation (2 Cor 8:9; Phil 2:6-8) are clear enough.

Third, the human character of Jesus is theologically significant for Paul because it enables him to make his comparisons with Adam in Romans 5 and I Corinthians 15 as well as to characterize Jesus as one who was born and lived under the law and therefore was able to come under the curse of the law in order to deliver humanity from it (Gal 3:13).

---

[13]Dunn has proposed that the decisive mark of Christian faith was what he expresses as "the centrality and primacy of the exalted Lord, and the identity of the crucified Jesus with the exalted Son of God" (James D. G. Dunn, *Unity and Diversity in the New Testament* [London: SCM Press, 1977], p. 307). The second part of this formulation may lead to some unintended misinterpretation. It could be taken to imply that there was certainty about belief in the exalted Lord worshiped by the early Christians but that there was a possible question as to whether this Lord was to be identified with the earthly Jesus, as if one could have the former without the latter. Now it is certainly the case that Christians had to defend their belief that the earthly Jesus had been raised from the dead and exalted, an event that confirmed for them that he was the Lord and the Son of God. But there does not seem to be any indication that there was any Christian belief in the risen Lord that was not a belief that Jesus was this Lord. It is the word *identity* that is the source of the possible confusion. There may have been Christians who majored on the resurrection and tried to ignore the death of Jesus and the need to live a cruciform life, but that is a different issue.

*God—the Holy Spirit.* Paul's theology assigns a central place also to the Holy Spirit. The Spirit is at the very least an enhanced form of divine power that operates in individual believers and congregations to bring about God's purposes for them. But the evidence that Paul is well on the way to understanding the Spirit in personal terms is incontrovertible, and this conclusion is not surprising, given the existing belief in Judaism in other personal beings (angels) associated with God. The Spirit intercedes for believers with the Father (Rom 8:26-27) and can be grieved by the sin of believers (Eph 4:30). When Paul links together the Lord Jesus Christ, God and the Holy Spirit—in that order!—in a benediction (2 Cor 13:13), and we compare that statement with the other cases where the juxtaposition of God our Father and the Lord Jesus Christ undoubtedly indicates their closeness to one another and their joint function as the source of blessing for believers, it is clear that a very special position is also being given to the Spirit.[14] One could also compare the ways in which the same effects in the lives of believers are attributed to Christ and the Spirit (cf. 1 Cor 12:4-6, where God is also brought in alongside the Lord [Christ] and the Spirit).[15] And, finally, Paul is able to identify "the Lord" in Exodus 34:34 as the Spirit (2 Cor 3:18) in the same way as he can interpret other Old Testament occurrences of "the Lord" as references to Christ. And again what is significant is the way in which Paul is not trying to teach people about the nature of the Spirit. It all comes out by the way as he teaches them about other matters.

*God—as communicator.* Paul was heir to a religion in which the action of God in the world was an accepted fact. He possessed the Jewish Scriptures which, whatever their precise extent, certainly began for him with the creation of the world by God (Rom 1:20), the stories of the first man (Rom 5:14; 1 Cor 15:45) and woman (2 Cor 11:3; cf. 1 Tim 2:13-14), Abraham (Rom 4; Gal 3:6-9; 4:21-31) and the patriarchs (Rom 9:6-13), and so on. People had religious experiences, like Abraham who believed in God, and God made himself

---

[14]Although it is more probable that in the benediction "the fellowship of the Holy Spirit" means participation in the Spirit (objective genitive) rather than a fellowship created by the Spirit (despite the fact that God and Christ are here the authors of love and grace [subjective genitives]), nothing suggests that this reduces the Spirit to some kind of impersonal power in which believers share. The parallel in 1 Cor 1:9, where believers are called into fellowship with or participation in the Son, is decisive.

[15]See Max Turner, " 'Trinitarian Pneumatology' in the New Testament?—Toward an Explanation of the Worship of Jesus", *Asbury Theological Journal* 57.2/58.1 (2002-2003): 167-86.

known to them in a variety of ways. The lasting monuments of this activity were the Scriptures, understood to be *divine oracles enshrining what God had said to Moses and the prophets* (Rom 3:2).

There was thus a story or, better, history of God's dealings with humanity and especially with the line that began with Abraham and unfolded into Israel, the people of God to whom he gave his law. The climax in this lengthy history was the sending of God's Son as the Messiah to the Jewish people (Rom 9:5). Paul says little about Jesus' life and teaching, and his attention is concentrated on Jesus' resurrection and exaltation and subsequent activity. He knows that Jesus had followers, twelve in number, who were included in a wider body of apostles, to which Paul belonged (1 Cor 15:5-8). These apostles had experienced appearances of the risen Jesus and been commissioned by him to act as missionaries, a task that involved preaching the gospel, making converts, planting congregations and caring for and teaching their members. It was thus a role that made them stewards or trustees of divine revelation and assigned appropriate authority to them (1 Cor 4:1). They could have a prophetic role in that they became conscious of what God wanted them to say to people, and Paul refers to "divine secrets" *(mystēria)* that had been revealed to him personally (Rom 11:25; 1 Cor 4:1; 15:51; cf. Eph 3:3-4).

The boundaries between apostles and other people were somewhat hazy. Thus their functions were in some ways similar to those of prophets, who also received divine messages. There is a reasonable case that in some circles there developed evangelists who carried out similar missionary tasks without the same basis in a personal commission from the risen Christ (Eph 4:11; 2 Tim 4:5). Also we find the term *apostles* used of "apostles of the churches" who seem to have been people commissioned for specific tasks by local congregations, but the similarity in terminology may have caused some confusion (2 Cor 8:23). And Paul refers to "false apostles" (2 Cor 11:13), by which he means people who evidently had not received the kind of commission that he had received and were spreading teaching that he did not regard as coming from God. It might be thought that the requirement of a commission from the risen Christ was a qualification that could not be easily counterfeited, since people would know who belonged to the earliest company of followers of Jesus, but if Paul could claim such a revelation at a later date than the Twelve ("last of all . . . as to one abnormally born", 1 Cor 15:8), presumably other people could falsely or mistakenly make similar claims.

In any case, for Paul this self-understanding was crucial, and he resisted any challenges to it.

*The gospel—the need for salvation.* The main theme of Paul's apostolic preaching is undoubtedly the gospel, good news for humankind. He was called to the service of the gospel (Rom 1:1, 9; 15:16; 1 Cor 1:17; Gal 1:16; cf. Eph 3:8). However, this basic assertion needs to be qualified in two ways.

On the one hand, it might be thought that this calling indicates that Paul's message and the underlying theology were primarily concerned with the welfare of humankind. But there are various indications that the decisive concern is to bring glory to God (cf. Eph 1:6, 12, 14). *Glory* is a term with a range of meaning and reference. It can refer to the praise and worship that people offer to another person, supremely to God. It can then refer to the exalted state of God or some other person that is increased by having large numbers of people offering praise. And more broadly it can refer to the visible expression of that state, seen in being seated on a throne and shining with radiant light that can prevent people from looking directly at God or coming near to him. For Paul the ultimate purpose and effect of all human endeavor must be to glorify God, expressed vocally in the form of a doxology (Rom 11:36; 16:27; Gal 1:5; Phil 4:20; cf. Eph 3:21; 1 Tim 1:17) and more generally by obedience to God, who is seen to be glorious in that people acknowledge him as Lord and do his bidding (1 Cor 10:31). So it is that even his Son, Jesus Christ, brings glory to God, even when he himself is being glorified (Phil 2:9-11). And the effect of preaching the gospel and bringing salvation to people is that they offer praise to God (Rom 15:9; Gal 1:24). Although ultimately God alone is to be glorified, nevertheless he shares his glory with his people (1 Thess 2:12; 2 Thess 2:14; Rom 8:30). But since this obligation to glorify God was not being fulfilled, there was need to recall humanity to its duty (Rom 1:21).

On the other hand, the message of Paul was not entirely good news for humanity. Good news presupposes that there is some kind of lack in the human situation for which it provides a welcome remedy. Advertisements for an antidote to hay fever are irrelevant in a region where the ailment is unknown. So the presupposition of the good news is that people need what is being offered to them. If they are unaware of their need, then their position needs to be made clear to them.

Consequently, the message of Paul begins with the announcement of the wrath of God (Rom 1:18). The term conveys the sense of a negative reaction by God that finds concrete expression against those who incur his wrath. Specifically it is linked to a future time or "day" when God will judge humanity and express his anger against sinners who disobey him (Rom 2:5; 5:9; cf. Eph 5:6). We therefore need to explore what it is that arouses this wrath and how it is experienced. Attempts to turn the wrath of God into an impersonal principle at work in human history and to see it simply as something that happens rather than also as a personal reaction of God have not been successful.

The concept is not as widespread in Paul's writings as is sometimes assumed. But it is significantly present when Paul sums up the nature of salvation as the action of Jesus Christ in delivering people from the wrath to come (1 Thess 1:10; 5:9) and the fact that he begins his systematic exposition of the gospel in Romans by asserting that God's wrath is revealed against all sin is significant. The picture broadens out when we take into account the fact that this "wrath to come" is associated with judgment (Rom 2:2-3, 16; 2 Thess 2:12). We should not be misled by the fact that in a culture such as ours judges are supposed to be disinterested and not to let their personal feelings affect their judgment; here what is being emphasized is impartiality and freedom from arbitrary sentencing. However, it is quite normal for a judge to express the righteous reaction of the community against cruelty and violence, and this is what is meant by the wrath of God. God is impartial (Rom 2:11; cf. Eph 6:9; Col 3:25). The content of judgment is variously detailed as death (Rom 5:12-21; 6:23) and destruction, in other words, separation from God and his kingdom (2 Thess 1:9). It follows that salvation is essentially deliverance from wrath and judgment.

From judgment we are led back to the situation that causes this reaction, which is sin. It may cause some astonishment that although this word group is overwhelmingly present in Romans, it is comparatively sparse in Paul's other letters, even in Galatians. Roughly two-thirds of all the occurrences in the Pauline corpus are in Romans. Whereas other New Testament authors tend to use the plural form (and less frequently the singular) to refer to individual sinful acts, these forms are conspicuously rare in Paul,[16] and he uses the term pre-

---

[16]Rom 3:25; 4:7 (LXX); 7:5; 11:27 (LXX); 1 Cor 6:18; 15:3 (tradition), 17; Gal 1:4; Eph 2:1; Col 1:14; 1 Tim 5:22, 24; 2 Tim 3:6. Note that he uses "transgression" *(paraptōma)* in the plural for sinful acts (Rom 5:15-20; 2 Cor 5:19).

ponderantly to refer to sin as a kind of force or power that enters and overcomes human beings (Rom 7:17, 20) or the state of sinfulness that results from it (Rom 6:1). Humanity in general is under the control of sin (Rom 3:9; Gal 3:22);[17] it is a baleful influence that made its entry into the world through Adam (Rom 5:12). There is no escape from its control (Rom 7:14). And it is like a terminal disease, leading inexorably to death (Rom 5:12; 7:13; 8:2; I Cor 15:56). Paul can write as though the sentence of death has already been executed (Rom 7:11; Rom 8:10). Already in Romans the motif that sinners are "dead" in sin is present (Rom 8:12), and this way of putting the situation emerges the more strongly in the later letters (Col 2:13; Eph 2:1, 5; cf. Eph 5:14) where the motif of being unresponsive to the call of God until he brings to life is developed.

Closely connected with Paul's understanding of sin are his assumptions about human nature. The word *flesh*, literally the characteristic stuff of which human beings are made (Rom 2:28; 2 Cor 4:11), is used to refer to them in their weakness and mortality. It expresses humanity as opposed to "spirit", which tends to express the divine. Although in itself the term could be neutral, the fact that human beings have succumbed to sin allows Paul to regard the flesh as more or less "fallen flesh", human nature that is inevitably sinful and opposed to God. So when Paul talks about the desires or works of the flesh, he is thinking of humanity following its own desires in rebellion against the commands of the Creator and the guidance of the Spirit (Rom 8:4; Gal 5:17). This antithesis between flesh and the Spirit entails that salvation issues in the setting free of the sinner from the power of the flesh to be led by the Spirit (Rom 8:1-13; Gal 5:16-26). As the space occupied by sin, the flesh is incapable of redemption; rather the sinner is delivered from its domination. In this respect there is a crucial difference between the flesh and the body despite the fact that both terms are used to refer to the material, visible aspect of the human person. The body is also spoken of as being subjected to the hostile power of sin (Rom 6:6; 7:24), but can be redeemed and transformed (Rom 8:23; I Cor 15:44, 51).

---

[17]While Paul's use of "all" has in mind the fact that Jews and Gentiles alike are under sin, it would be unjustifiable casuistry to suggest that he was thinking purely of human groups and not of all the individuals who compose them.

The Jewish people had received from God a gift that might be thought to provide the answer to sin. The law given by Moses expressed the will of God for them, and it could well be thought that obedience to its commandments would lead them to life (Rom 10:5; Gal 3:12). But Paul saw it differently. He agreed that the possession of the law made clear to people just which forms of conduct were sinful (Rom 7:7). But he argued that such knowledge has the effect of bringing sin to light. The sinful impulses that are already there in a person come to life and issue in sinful desires and actions (Rom 7:7-11). This does not mean that the law is the cause of sin and therefore evil, but rather it functions as the indicator that registers the presence of sin. But there is nothing in the law that can give a person the power to overcome sin and cease to sin.[18]

*The gospel—the means of salvation.* Paul's gospel is the announcement of what God has done to save humanity from its plight. The caricature that Paul portrays an act of mediation by Christ between sinners and a hostile God who needs to be persuaded to forgive them is a travesty of his teaching. The same should be said of portrayals of a God whose wrath and love are in tension with each other. This is proved by the persistent stress on the love, grace and mercy of God toward sinners. Paul does not use the ordinary verb *phileō* for the love shown by God, but his use of the more characteristically biblical words, the noun *agapē* and the verb *agapaō*, is reasonably frequent (Rom 5:5, 8; 8:35, 37, 39; 2 Cor 5:14; 13:11; Gal 2:20; 1 Thess 1:4; 2 Thess 2:13, 16; cf. Eph 2:4; 3:19; 5:2, 25; Col 3:12). When used of God, the term expresses a love that is concerned with the good of those who are loved rather than the satisfaction felt by the lover.[19] Grace appears to be the most characteristic term for this attitude in Paul's vocabulary. The usual epistolary greeting (shared with 1 Pet; 2 Pet; 2 Jn; Rev) associates God with grace, a term that expresses the underlying motive and the effective action of God in his relationships with people. It conveys the fact that God shows this attitude to those who do not deserve it and have done nothing to merit it. The term *mercy* is much less frequent with reference

---

[18]Paul does not take up the question of whether the law could deal with the penalty that rested upon sinners through their offering of the sacrifices that it prescribed. It looks as though he was more concerned with the deeper problem of how people might be delivered from sinning.

[19]That is to say, it is not essentially a self-regarding feeling in which people love what brings them personal satisfaction but an other-regarding love in which the decisive element is the desire to confer some benefit on the object of the love.

to God.[20] It suggests compassion for those who are suffering as a result of sin. Both words appear to express the feelings and action of God with respect to people who are in a dreadful plight from which they cannot deliver themselves and who have no specific claims to favor, no "saving graces" as the cliché puts it. Grace is operative in the initial saving action of God but also throughout the subsequent lives of God's people and in the work of missionaries (Rom 1:7; 15:15; Gal 2:9). It becomes thematic when Paul is discussing the contrast with justification by works of the law, and he uses this term to show how justification is the gift of a God who gives and does not impose human works as the condition for being justified (Rom 4:4).

*The saving event.* The central event in the gospel is the death and resurrection of Jesus. These two actions belong closely together (Rom 4:25; 8:34; I Cor 15:3-5; 2 Cor 5:15; Phil 3:10; I Thess 4:14), but the weight lies on the former.[21] How it is to be understood is more difficult. It is basic that the death of Jesus was concerned with sin (I Cor 15:3; Gal 1:4; cf. Rom 8:3; 2 Cor 5:19-21) and that it was for all people (2 Cor 5:14-15; cf. I Tim 2:6), specifically as sinners (Rom 5:6). Again and again the reference is expressed confessionally with regard to "us", those who have benefited from the death (Rom 5:8; 8:32; 14:15; 2 Cor 5:21; Gal 2:20; 3:13; cf. Eph 5:2, 25; I Thess 5:10; Tit 2:14).

How does Paul understand the death of Jesus? The phrase "for all" or "for us" might simply mean that he died for our benefit without implying that he did something so that other people would not have do it, specifically that he died in order to save them from having to die. Certainly that is part of the meaning. But when Paul says that Christ delivered us from the curse of the law imposed upon those who do not observe it by himself becoming a curse for us in his death (Gal 3:10-14), this can only mean that Christ bore the curse instead of us. Paul is saying that Christ died the death that is due to sinners because of their sin.[22]

---

[20] Rom 9:15-18, 23; 11:30-32; 15:9; I Cor 7:25; 2 Cor 4:1; Gal 6:16; Eph 2:4; Phil 2:27; 2 Tim 1:13, 16, 18; Tit 3:5 and the greetings in I Tim 1:2; 2 Tim 1:2.

[21] It is not surprising that there are far more, and far more detailed, books on the significance on the death of Christ than there are on his resurrection.

[22] Bradley H. McLean, *The Cursed Christ: Mediterranean Expulsion Ritual and Pauline Soteriology* (Sheffield: Sheffield Academic Press, 1996), pp. 105-45, who denies that Paul thought in sacrificial terms, explains the rationale of this passage in terms of the scapegoat as the victim who takes upon himself the curse that threatens the people and lets its force be expended upon himself.

In 2 Corinthians 5:18-21, having written about Christ dying for all, Paul goes on to say that the good news of reconciliation rests on the fact that "God was reconciling the world to himself in Christ, not counting people's sins against them. . . . God made him who had no sin to be sin for us, so that in him we might become the righteousness of God". Here the sinless Christ[23] becomes "sin" so that sinners might become "righteousness". As we saw, this means in effect that Christ became a sinner so that sinners might become righteous. But how did Christ's becoming a sinner produce this effect? The context demands that it was through his death; in some way this takes away sin so that there is no barrier to reconciliation with God. Had Christ not died, reconciliation would not have been possible. Again, the implication is that Christ becomes the representative of sinners and dies on their behalf (2 Cor 5:14) so that they may be delivered from their sins and have the status of righteous people.

A further type of explanation comes in Romans 3:25, where people are put in the right with God because he "presented Christ as a sacrifice of atonement, through the shedding of his blood".[24] The reference to Christ's death suggests that he died as a sacrificial victim, but one provided by God rather than by human beings, and just as the offering of the appropriate kind of sacrifices cancelled out sin under the old covenant, so the offering of Christ cancels out sin. Romans 8:3 may also refer to Jesus as a sin offering (TNIV text) The motif of sacrifice reappears in 1 Corinthians 5:6-8, where the death of Jesus is compared with that of a Passover offering, and in Ephesians 5:2.[25]

*The nature of salvation.* Having considered the death of Jesus, we must now look at the ways in which Paul sees it as affecting human beings. There are four principal images.

First, there is *salvation* itself. This term carried a variety of nuances in the ancient world, being used literally of healing from illness, including life-threatening illness, and of rescue from life-threatening danger, but also more positively of the benefits brought to a people by a ruler ("Savior" was a title for kings and

---

[23]This motif is repeated across the New Testament and appears to have been unquestioned.

[24]Cf. Rom 5:9; 1 Cor 10:16; 11:25, 27; Eph 1:7; 2:13; Col 1:20 for other references to the blood of Christ as a way of referring to his death.

[25]McLean, *Cursed*, pp. 22-64, denies that Paul compared the death of Jesus to an atoning sacrifice, insisting that the language used in the various passages is either nonsacrificial or refers to nonatoning sacrifices. His objections vary in strength but are not compelling.

emperors). Paul uses "salvation" as a general term for the benefits brought by the gospel (Rom 1:16; cf. Eph 1:13), but it is used particularly for the concept of being delivered from the effects of God's wrath at the final judgment (Rom 5:9; 13:11; 1 Cor 5:5). This has suggested to some scholars that it is essentially a future concept, so that Paul cannot speak of people being already saved.[26] Certainly there are texts that can be interpreted as referring to salvation as something yet to be received, a future hope (Phil 1:28; 1 Thess 5:8, 9). However, to interpret it exclusively in this sense is not justified, and a number of texts are much more plausibly understood as containing a present reference (1 Cor 15:2; 2 Cor 1:6; 6:2), and Romans 8:24 is unequivocally in the past tense. What is at issue is not whether God's transforming grace and power are being experienced now by believers; that is clearly attested. Rather it is whether the particular term *salvation* refers specifically and only to a future experience; the evidence does not permit such a narrow interpretation. The use of the present participle "the saved" (1 Cor 1:18; 2 Cor 2:15; cf. Acts 2:47) suggests the subjects of an ongoing life-giving operation.

Second, the English term *redemption* covers two related Pauline metaphors. One is the deliverance of captives from bondage, often by the payment of a ransom (Is 43:1-4; 52:3) or simply by the exercise of superior military power (so of God in Deut 7:8). We find this metaphor taken up in Galatians 3:13 and Galatians 4:5, where God is said to deliver those who were under the law and its curse. Redemption is also the key term in the explanation of justification in Romans 3:25. In Titus 2:14 deliverance from wickedness is presumably from both its power and its consequences. The nuance in this usage is the concept of freedom. However, Paul can also refer to the buying of people so that they belong to God; here the thought is more of a change of master with the obligation to serve God (1 Cor 6:20; 7:23). The purchase involves a price, and this is most naturally understood of God giving his Son.

Already by this point we can see that Paul's different forms of imagery for understanding the death of Jesus and its effects are used alongside one another and mutually condition one another. No one picture, it seems, is adequate on its own to explain the cross.

This is equally true of the third main imagery, that of *justification.* Justification

---

[26]On this view Eph 2:5, 8 is un-Pauline language.

is concerned with righteousness. The best starting point is the verb that in the Septuagint has a legal setting and refers to the action of the judge in dealing with accused people. His duty is to acquit, or justify, the innocent who are wrongly charged with some crime or wrong and to condemn the guilty, and he is unrighteous if he does otherwise. Paul uses the verb almost exclusively in the passive when it has human beings as the subject, and he uses the active of God.[27] Justification is something that happens to human beings, and it is concerned with their relationship to God. One theoretical way to be in the right with God is through the law, and Paul makes the point that it is not simply possessing or hearing the law that counts but actually doing it, something that can be done even by Gentiles who have not heard the law of Moses but have a knowledge of God's requirements from some other source (Rom 2:13-16). Paul contrasts two ways of being justified, either by (Gk. *ek* or *en*) works of the law (Rom 3:20; 4:2; Gal 2:16; 3:11) or by faith (Rom 3:26, 28, 30; 5:1; Gal 2:16; 3:8, 24). But behind this contrast lies the fact that God confers justification by Christ (Gal 2:17: contrast "by law", Gal 5:4) or by his name (1 Cor 6:11) or by his blood (Rom 5:9). It is thus to be seen as a gift (Rom 3:24), God acting by grace (Rom 3:24; cf. Tit 3:7). All of this adds up to saying that justification takes place through the grace of God and is tied in some way to the death of Christ. The connection is brought out in Romans 3:24, where it takes place through the redemption that is "in Christ", the Christ who died sacrificially. The implication is that Christ's death takes away the sin that human beings have committed, so that God is righteous in justifying them and not like a judge who acquits the guilty. Consequently, justification is bestowed in the manner of a gift and not as something that God is obliged to give, like an employer paying a wage to somebody who has done satisfactory work.

In our discussion of Galatians we picked up three clues as to how justification becomes effective. First, it is received by faith, a faith that was clearly in God in the case of Paul's star witness, Abraham (Rom 4:3) and that is naturally understood to be in the same God in the case of Paul and his readers (Rom 4:25). But there is more to it than that in Paul's understanding. In quite a number of cases no object is supplied, and the point being made is that faith as such is contrasted with working as the means of justification (Rom 3:28; Gal 3:5).

---

[27] The verb can also be used of God when seen as righteous and fair in what he does (Rom 3:4).

Sometimes he refers to faith in Christ (Gal 2:16), which is not surprising since he is clearly the agent through whom justification takes place. But there is also the phrase "the faith of Jesus Christ", which is thought by some to mean "the faith[fulness] shown by Jesus Christ" (Rom 3:22, cf. Rom 3:26; Gal 2:16, 20; 3:22). This would yield the sense that the basis for justification was the attitude of Jesus, who trusted in God and was obedient right through to the point of death (cf. Phil 2:8). True though this statement is, it is hotly debated whether the actual phrase does not rather mean "faith in Jesus Christ".[28]

Second, justification is closely tied to the believers' relationship to Jesus in that Paul proceeds to develop his understanding of their being joined to Christ in his death and resurrection. Justification could be regarded as delivering people who are sentenced to death and giving them life. It has a negative and a positive aspect in that it sets them free from sin and brings them into a new relationship with God, so that elsewhere Paul can speak of the effect as being like a new creation (2 Cor 5:17). We can see that justification thus takes place as the believer shares in Christ's death and resurrection; the cryptic and laconic statement that Christ "was delivered over to death for our sins and was raised to life for our justification" (Rom 4:25) demonstrates that justification includes the conferring of new life. The clear implication is that this new life cannot be conferred until something had been done about sin.

The third element to be noted is the tie-up with the phrase "in Christ", which expresses some kind of personal relationship between believers and Christ. Being "justified in Christ" (Gal 2:17) might simply mean "by Christ" (in contrast with "by the law", Gal 3:11; 5:4), but there may well be a deeper nuance. Justification exists when a person is so united with Christ by their faith that they share in his new life.[29]

The importance of these elements is that together they demonstrate that justification is not a mere declaration of pardon that could be bestowed without any real change taking place in the sinner. Although the term refers to a change of status from sinner to righteous, justification is inextricably linked to the change in character that comes about through being united with Christ.

Before we explore the results further, we need to take in the fourth main im-

---

[28]See p. 225 n. 36.

[29]See p. 312 n. 10, on whether they have the righteousness of Christ imputed to them.

age used by Paul, *reconciliation*. This is a motif that has sometimes been regarded as the central or unifying theme in Paul's theology, even though he does not develop it explicitly at great length.[30] Certainly, as the use of a metaphor based on human relationships, specifically diplomacy, it might well be thought to be more personal than language drawn from law courts, slave markets and even rescue operations, but the exigencies of debate with Judaizing opponents led Paul to major on justification at least in Galatians and Romans.

Reconciliation is the establishment of peace between two opposing or warring groups or individuals, and it may be achieved either by one party taking the initiative or by a third party intervening as a mediator to bring about peace. The latter possibility might be present where the term *mediator* is used of Christ (1 Tim 2:5; cf. Heb 8:6; 9:15; 12:24), but is open to the misunderstanding that an outsider had to intervene to bring God and humanity together. Since Paul stresses that God in his grace sent Jesus his Son, it follows that Jesus is to be seen as the envoy of God bringing the offer of peace to his enemies rather than as somebody who has to persuade God and humanity to come together. When Paul first uses the imagery in 2 Corinthians 5, he could not make it plainer that it was God who was acting in and through Christ, offering peace to sinners and not holding their sins against them (2 Cor 5:18, 19, 20, 21). But it is not that God could simply overlook the sins. The statement that God made Christ to be sin for us so that we might become righteousness through him shows that God was prepared to treat sinners as righteous, but that this was possibly only as the result of his making Christ to be sin for them, to be the bearer of their sins.[31]

Reconciliation is closely linked with justification as another way of making essentially the same point. This is clear from Romans 5:9-11, where Paul wants to emphasize the security of believers. If they have been justified by the blood of Christ, they will be saved from God's wrath at the final judgment through him; that follows from the fact that if God justified sinners by Christ, how much more will he deliver those who now count as righteous in his sight. Then he repeats the point: If God's enemies were reconciled by God giving his Son

---

[30]See Ralph P. Martin, *Reconciliation* (London: Marshall, 1981).

[31]See McLean, *Cursed*, pp. 108-12, who sees Christ here as the substitute for sinners, bearing their sin and dying because of it. Cf. the discussion of reconciliation in chap. 11 (pp. 294-96).

to die, how much more will God deliver his friends who put their confidence in him. Furthermore, the outcome of justification here and now is peace with God (Rom 5:1). This motif is picked up again in Colossians 1:20-21, where God makes peace through the blood shed on the cross and thus reconciles all things to himself, including specifically the readers who had been enemies of God but have now been reconciled through the death of Christ. The same motifs recur in Ephesians 2:16-18.

These passages show that reconciliation is initiated by God and is directed toward those who are his enemies, primarily in the sense that they are hostile to him and disobedient. Whether or not he sees himself as hostile to them, he cannot offer peace to them apart from Christ and his death, and there is nothing to justify reducing the purpose of that death to being simply a costly demonstration of love and willingness to receive them. It is the death that makes peace and turns sinners into righteous.

*Election and calling.* In the previous section we have essentially been surveying the way in which Paul explains the saving event of the death and resurrection of Jesus Christ. Now we must consider how the salvation that is offered becomes a reality for human beings.

In a few passages Paul refers to those who are saved as "the elect" (Rom 8:33; 16:13; cf. Col 3:12; 2 Tim 2:10; Tit 1:1). In all of these cases the term refers to those who are actually among the saved people.[32] The choice of term indicates that there was a prior act of choice by God, but the context shows that the call of God was met with a positive response of faith. There was, then, a purpose of God to create a people for himself and to deliver them from their sin. This purpose found its realization in the calling of Abraham and subsequently of his offspring, although Paul emphasizes that it was carried out irrespective of any specific qualities by those who were chosen or not chosen.

We should be careful not to draw out from the use of the language more than Paul intends. The point that he appears to be making is twofold. On the one hand, the making of a relationship between God and human beings rests entirely on the initiative of God and his creation of the possibility. On the other hand, it does not depend on the display of any particular qualities by people

---

[32]I. Howard Marshall, "Election and Calling to Salvation in 1 and 2 Thessalonians", in *The Thessalonian Correspondence*, ed. R. F. Collins (Louvain: Louvain University Press, 1990), pp. 259-76.

that might be thought to entitle them to God's favor or make him prefer one person against another (cf. 1 Cor 1:26). Rather, it rests on his mercy to the undeserving. He issues his call and the appropriate response by those to whom it is made is faith. It depends not on works but on the God who calls (Rom 9:12). Consequently it can be said that the whole process depends on God and not on the recipients (Eph 2:5).

The extent of this calling in Paul's time encompassed both Jews and Gentiles (Rom 9:24). There is debate as to whether God's purpose should be seen corporately or individually, that is to say, whether God's choice was that he would have a people, for whom he had further particular purposes (cf. Eph 1:4-5, 11), or whether his choice was that he would have specific individuals (Gal 1:15). To some extent this is a false antithesis, since there is evidence for both aspects. What is not said is that God's calling is independent of the human response or makes it inevitable, or that this calling implies the passing over of other people whom God has decided not to save.[33]

In any case, the process by which people become God's people takes place as God makes his calling known to them, and they can confess that God has graciously called them (Rom 9:24; 1 Cor 1:9; Gal 1:6; 1 Thess 2:12; 4:7; 5:24; 2 Thess 2:14; cf. Eph 4:1, 4; 1 Tim 6:12; 2 Tim 1:9). The calling is a summons to be a people who reflect the holy character of their God (1 Thess 2:12; 4:7; cf. Eph 4:1; 2 Tim 1:9).

Therefore, a vital part of the process is the proclamation of the gospel. The verbal activity of preaching is of key importance (Rom 10:8, 14-15; 1 Cor 1:23; 2 Cor 1:19; 4:5; Gal 2:2; Phil 1:15; 1 Thess 2:9; cf. Col 1:23; 1 Tim 3:16). Paul would have repudiated the idea that the church's responsibility is fully carried out in manifesting a silent Christian presence in a non-Christian society without verbalizing God's act of redemption in the death and resurrection of Christ. Such verbal proclamation is effective because the power of the Holy Spirit is at work in it (1 Thess 1:5), and it originates not from the human beings who proclaim it but from the God who gave them his word (1 Thess 2:13).

---

[33]For some interpreters the logic of election and predestination requires a doctrine of so-called double predestination whereby God also decides not to elect some individuals; to affirm this is, in my opinion, to go beyond what Paul says and to raise serious questions about the justice of God.

*The human response—faith, not the works of the law.* The appropriate human response to this word is faith (I Cor 15:2; I Thess 1:8), a concept that includes acceptance that the message is true (Rom 10:9) and commitment to the God who speaks. For Paul faith includes belief that God raised Jesus from the dead and confession of Jesus as Lord (Rom 10:9-10). This stress on the person's attitude to Jesus Christ was necessary because it was this that was the distinctive feature of the message of the Christians.

Understood in this way, faith is primarily the expression of a dependence upon God for salvation and not upon one's qualities or position. This, however, is not to the exclusion of other facets. For Paul faith comprises a new way of living that is appropriate to the people of God. Sometimes this is expressed more in terms of holiness, a term that is perhaps used to bring out the fact that Gentiles, who were formerly counted as unholy by Jews, now are part of God's people and are no longer unclean. Or perhaps we should say that this is the ideal that they are to show in their lives, since Paul was sufficient of a realist to know that it was not accomplished in a moment. At other times, the emphasis lies more on love as the characteristic expression of new life. It is, therefore, possible for Paul to speak of the work of faith (I Thess 1:3; 2 Thess 1:11).

At the same time, Paul places faith and works in sharp contrast. He rejects any suggestion that justification is on the basis of performance of the works of the law. He may have had more specifically in mind the outward observances commanded in the law of Moses that were characteristic of Judaism; there is debate as to whether "works of the law" refers specifically to these or should be understood more widely. These were not required of Gentiles who became believers, as if faith in Christ was not a sufficient response to God's calling. Paul feared that people could put their confidence in what they themselves were doing rather than exclusively in what God had done in Christ (I Cor 1:29-31; cf. Eph 2:9).[34] But equally he held that the works of the law were not required of Jews. Paul believed that many Jews, but by no means all of them, were putting their confidence and trust in their fulfillment of the requirements of the law and so thinking to be in the right with God on the basis of their own achieve-

---

[34]By the time we get to Ephesians and the Pastoral Epistles there is a tendency to include any kind of human endeavors to win God's favor and not just obedience to the Mosaic law (Eph 2:9; 2 Tim 1:9; Tit 3:5). See I. Howard Marshall, "Salvation, Grace and Works in the Later Writings in the Pauline Corpus", *NTS* 42 (1996): 339-58.

ments. He had once done so himself, but now he realized that his confidence must be wholly in what God had done in Christ (Phil 3:1-11).

At this point we need to consider what has come to be known as the "new perspective" on Judaism and Paul's view of it. In earlier discussions of the matter it was generally said that Paul was here rejecting the Judaism of his time, in which it was necessary to do the works of the law in order to be accepted by God. Acceptance by him was based on merit, the worthiness of the person in his sight. (One might go so far as to think of a pile of merits outweighing a pile of sins.) The Jewish religion was understood to be legalistic, not just in the sense that it made much of the fact that God had revealed his commandments to people to show how they must live, but rather in the sense that acceptance by God depended upon human performance of these legal requirements. It could then be suggested that this religion depended upon human works rather than divine grace and it could be contrasted unfavorably with Christianity.

There has been a strong reaction by some contemporary scholars against this understanding of Judaism. It has been demonstrated that according to much of the literature of Judaism the Jews believed that they were accepted as the people of God on the basis of his gracious initiative in setting up his covenant with them and that the keeping of his laws was the response to grace and not the meritorious grounds for initial acceptance.[35] Keeping the law and doing good works were what the Jews did in order to remain within God's favor rather than to gain it. They fulfilled the law as a sign of their belonging and not as a condition of entry, a set of "works" that entitled them to God's favor. The works of the law were not a way of gaining merit and so being accepted by God. Such an understanding could be widely traced in the literature of Judaism.

Such works were required of Gentile proselytes not because they were meritorious but because they were the signs that they were now within the people of Israel and also because they were essential if former Gentiles were to be able to have table fellowship with practicing Jews. A refinement of the position proposed that the "works of the law" were those specific things that marked Jews out publicly and acted as boundary markers from the Gentiles (circumcision,

---

[35]E. P. Sanders, *Paul, the Law and the Jewish People* (Philadelphia: Fortress, 1983).

food laws, festivals), and these were more like identity markers or badges that people wore rather than things that were constitutive of their position.[36]

Advocates of this understanding of Judaism have then to account for what Paul was teaching over against it. One possibility would be that Paul misunderstood it and mistakenly saw Judaism as a legalistic religion based on merit. Another is to argue that he opposed the works of the law because they were being forced upon Gentiles: they had to assimilate to Judaism and adopt its markers if they were to be truly part of the people of God. (There was also the problem of fellowship at church meals between those who kept the Jewish food laws and the Gentiles who did not do so.) Yet another suggestion is that Paul's criticism of Judaism arose from his discovery of Christ and that essentially what was wrong with Judaism was that it was not Christianity.[37]

How are we to assess this interpretation? The new perspective has rightly reinstated the place of grace within Judaism. It is also right in what it asserts about Paul, namely, that at least one of the reasons why he was attacking the works of the law was because they were being imposed upon Gentile believers, but it is wrong in what it denies.

It seems clear enough that in the eyes of Paul Judaism could be a religion in which grace and works were compatible. Paul makes two clear distinctions. One is between works and faith, excluding any suggestion that faith is also a work, but the right kind of work. The other, more basic and important, one is an antithesis between grace and works, and not simply between faith and works (Rom 11:6). The Judaism of the new perspective could combine God's initial act of grace with reliance on the works of the law to stay in the covenant. But Paul makes a contrast between faith and the law (Rom 4:14) that can only mean that these are two contrasting ways to righteousness, the latter of which is not in fact a way. Paul describes the exclusion of many Israelites from favor with God because they followed the law rather than faith; this demonstrates further that in his eyes they were relying on the works of the law to gain righteousness. Thus the observances of the law were being treated not just as identity markers but also as the basis of misplaced confidence.

---

[36]James D. G. Dunn, *The Theology of Paul the Apostle* (Grand Rapids, Mich.: Eerdmans, 1998), pp. 354-59.
[37]Sanders, *Paul*, p. 552.

When Paul discusses faith and works, it is in the context of justification, and the question is: on what does justification depend? In what do the justified sinners place their confidence ("boast"), in Christ or in the works of the law? The language of boasting indicates unequivocally that the question concerns that on which a person depends for a right relationship with God, on what they themselves do or on what Christ has done for them. Consequently the element of achievement ("merit") cannot be eliminated. This emerges clearly enough from the contrast between the obligation created by good works and the free gift given to believers in Romans 4:4-5. Paul's point is that works entitle a person to a wage that the employer is obliged to give. He then argues that Abraham was put right with God before he had carried out circumcision and purely on the grounds of his faith. Similarly, Paul talks about the Jewish attempt to have "a righteousness of my own that comes from the law" contrasted with that which is by faith in Christ (Phil 3:9) and the way in which people could put their confidence in such factors. Belonging to Israel and being zealous for the Jewish religion and striving to keep the law perfectly were things in which Paul himself had previously trusted for his righteous standing with God; these were human possessions and achievements, and here he clearly regards them as things on which people relied rather than on grace.

Justification is for Paul not a matter of reward or payment for deeds done but of gracious gift (Rom 4:1-8; cf. Rom 6:23); righteousness is attained not by doing what the law requires but through faith in Christ (Phil 3:9). This is further expressed with all desirable clarity in Ephesians 2:8, 2 Timothy 1:9 and Titus 3:5, where the antithesis between grace and works is decisive; whether these texts stem from Paul or represent the earliest interpretations of his teaching by his followers, they indicate unequivocally how the material in Romans and Galatians should be understood. Christ is thus the end of the law (Rom 10:4).[38] When Paul discusses the works of the law, he does not dwell on the relationship between Jews and Gentiles and the function of the works as markers but on what needs to be done for people to be justified in the sight of God—do they have to achieve their own righteousness by the works of the law and put their confidence in them or do they merely have to put their faith in God and Christ on the basis of Christ's death and resurrec-

---

[38]Whether this means goal or termination is immaterial.

tion? The issue is the theological one of the grounds for justification. The traditional understanding is accordingly essentially right and the "new perspective" must be regarded as flawed.[39]

What, then, was the law all about? The issue emerges particularly in Romans and Galatians.[40] Paul's teaching is not easy to systematize, and there are some loose ends. There might appear to be some tension between the statement that people who keep the law will live and another statement that the law was never intended to give life (Gal 3:12, 21). But the fact that these statements come almost side by side indicates that Paul did not see them as being in tension. The law of Moses gave concrete expression to the way in which God wanted people to live, and specifically the Jews; there was recognition that some elements of the law were also meant for Gentiles. In the situation of the people called by God to be his people in pre-Christian times, it makes sense to see the law as prescribing the way of life for them with the implication that obedience is rewarded and disobedience leads to death. But in fact nobody ever kept the law fully—Paul could have pointed to an outstanding figure like David for an example—and Paul seems to have deduced that consequently the law was not given as the means by which people could gain and maintain life. On the contrary, the law was meant to expose the sinfulness of their hearts by bringing it out into the open in specific actions and to make people aware of their need for forgiveness. It was a kind of guide to lead people to their need for justification by Christ. Did Paul see the provision for atonement in the law as fulfilling this function, as Hebrews does? He does not specifically say so, but it would fit his thinking nicely. Then, once Christ has come, the supervision of the law is no longer needed.

This leaves two questions. First, has the law a continuing function? Second, what is the place of works in the life of the believer?

---

[39]The whole topic has generated an immense literature and requires much more extensive discussion than can be provided here. In particular, the nature of first-century Judaism needs a fuller treatment. See, for example, D. A. Carson, Peter T. O'Brien and Mark A. Seifrid, eds., *Justification and Variegated Nomism*, vol. I, *The Complexities of Second Temple Judaism* (Tübingen: Mohr Siebeck; Grand Rapids, Mich.: Baker, 2001); Frank Thielman, *The Law and the New Testament: The Question of Continuity* (New York: Crossroad, 1999).

[40]See also I Cor 9:8-9, 20; 15:56; Phil 3:5-9. The issue also emerges in I Tim 1:8-9. It would seem that Paul has an understanding of the law that developed through his conflicts with opponents and comes to the surface primarily when he is dealing with these opponents.

Believers are no longer under the law, but under grace (Rom 6:15). Believers have died to the law (Rom 7:4-6). Their relationship with God is dependent on his grace, not on their fulfillment of the law. That need not mean that Christian Jews should abandon the whole way of life that was based on the law. The teaching of the law was "holy, righteous and good" (Rom 7:12). In practice, however, some of the law had become obsolete for believers. Paul does not discuss the issue, but it would surely be the case that the Jewish sacrificial system was obsolete now that Christ had died. This is certainly the argument in Hebrews, but it does not arise in Paul. The fact that Paul never mentions the temple and its ritual shows that it had no significant role for him. Once Paul had argued that spiritual circumcision is what matters, the outward ritual became unimportant (Rom 2:25-29). And the coexistence of Jews and Gentiles in the same congregations must have led to some indifference regarding food laws, although Paul insisted on mutual respect for people with different practices (Rom 14—15).

Yet this did not prevent Paul from making positive reference to the law and expressing obvious approval of some of its commandments. He speaks positively of love as the fulfillment of the law and exhorts Christians to love (Rom 13:8-10). His ethical thought is often shaped by scriptural teaching. Over against the law he places the Spirit. If the law could not engender obedience in its hearers, the Spirit can do just that. Believers are to live by the Spirit, and in this way they will do what the law requires and not be led into conduct that is contrary to the law (Gal 5:16, 18, 23). Paul is not particularly clear here, but appears to believe that somehow the Spirit guides believers as to how they are to live and gives them the power to do so (Rom 8:1-13).

The second question concerns the nature of judgment. Here again there are tensions. On the one hand, Paul is emphatic that those who are justified have peace with God, and there is no longer any condemnation for them (Rom 5:1; 8:1). They are confident in their hope of sharing in the glory of God (Rom 5:2) and will be delivered from his wrath (Rom 5:9). On the other hand, Paul insists that everybody must appear before the judgment seat and give account of themselves to God or to Christ (Rom 14:10; 2 Cor 5:10).

How is the dilemma to be resolved? We may note in passing that Paul recognizes the possibility of judgments here in this life upon those who sin, perhaps even the infliction of illness and death, whose aim is to bring about repentance here and now, so that people may enter into a restored relationship with

God before it is too late (1 Cor 11:29-32; cf. 1 Cor 5:5). He also refers to some kind of judgments after death that fall short of exclusion from salvation; is that what Paul means when he talks about those who are saved like somebody escaping through a fire (1 Cor 3:10-15) if they have failed to produce the right kind of work in their lifetime or done evil? Paul also holds open the possibility that even a person who has preached the gospel to others might end up excluded from the prize because of lack of self-control (1 Cor 9:24-27), and he can liken the Christian life to a race with a prize at the end of it (Phil 3:14).[41] Paul needs to hold out some kind of inducements and warnings to believers since they are now called to a life of faith working by love and to good works. Clearly good works can be seen as the evidence of justification, but he has the problem of ensuring that people do not trust in them but in the One who justifies them. Paul can see his missionary work as what Christ has accomplished through him, and therefore he has grounds for confidence in Christ (Rom 15:17-18). The confidence of believers at the judgment would then rest on the indications that Christ had been working through them, and this would be the evidence of their justification. And this ties in with the promises that God who has started a good work in believers will accomplish it in the day of Christ (Phil 1:6; cf. 1 Cor 1:8-9). Thus it seems that Paul recognizes the danger of people being judged for sins and failures after justification, but he would regard good works after justification as evidence that God was at work in their lives and not as their own achievements in which they could trust.

*The ongoing work of God in the believer.* The life of believers, individually and corporately, is manifestly at the center of Paul's theological expression in his letters since the letters are addressed to believers and are fundamentally concerned with them as believers.

As we have seen, God the Father stands at the heart of Paul's thinking, since it is ultimately his purpose that is being carried out and it is to bring glory to him that believers live and act (1 Cor 10:31; Phil 1:11; cf. the rhetorical effect in Eph 1:6, 12, 14). It is God who is at work in the lives of believers (1 Cor 1:8-9; Phil 1:6; 2:13).

But when we enquire more closely as to how God works, we find that Paul

---

[41]The question whether Paul and other New Testament writers believed that it was possible to fall away from a state of salvation is variously answered. See pp. 618-19.

refers time and again to Christ and to the Holy Spirit. Believers live a life that is "in Christ" or "in the Lord". They live in a new situation that is determined by the fact of Christ, crucified and risen. Paul claims to be strengthened by Christ (Phil 4:13). Therefore, the teaching and exhortation that he gives as to how to live is given "in the Lord" (Phil 2:29; I Thess 4:1), that is, in a way that is conditioned by the pattern of Christ and has its authority in Christ as Lord. Sometimes it rests on the actual words of Jesus; at other times Paul may be expressing prophetic insight (I Thess 4:15). But the same phrase also expresses the way in which God conveys blessings to believers through the agency of Christ (Rom 6:11; Gal 2:4, 17), and this applies not only to Christ's action in dying for them and being raised but also to his continuing relationship with them and his future role at the judgment. With this kind of usage we come closer to an understanding of the phrase as an expression of some sort of close bond between the believer and Christ (Rom 8:1; Phil 1:1). This sort of understanding would seem to be required by the way in which Paul describes believers as having died with Christ, been buried with him and raised to new life with the hope of future resurrection of the body (Rom 6.1-11; Gal 2:20; 6:14; Phil 3:10; cf. Col 2:12; Eph 2:5-6; 2 Tim 2:11). This could simply be exuberant rhetoric: "when Christ died for you on the cross, it is as though you were present with him so that his death was your death". But since we are dealing with the spiritual reality of Christ, it can and must be more than rhetoric and express a real relationship, so that as believers are joined to Christ by faith they participate in his death and resurrection.

Paul's other way of describing the agency of God is by reference to the Holy Spirit. The Spirit is certainly to be understood as a divine power that can affect human beings and enter into their personalities (Rom 5:5; 2 Cor 1:22; Gal 4:6). The Spirit is a gift received by believers (I Cor 2:12; Gal 3:2, 14; 4:6; I Thess 4:8). All this suggests a continuous, lasting endowment rather than a momentary inspiration for a specific purpose, as when Christian missionaries stand up to speak in Acts (Acts 2:4; 4:8, 31; 13:9). Certainly the gift is associated with initiation into the people of God; through the Spirit people are adopted as God's children (Rom 8:14-15; Gal 4:6) and have God's seal upon them (2 Cor 1:22; cf. Eph 1:13-14). Above all the Spirit creates in believers the qualities and virtues and experiences of the people of God: they are subjectively aware of God's love for them (Rom 5:5; cf. Rom 8:16), and they have the basis for an assurance that what they have received is only the beginning of God's blessing upon them (Rom 8:23). They experience joy (Rom 14:17; Gal 5:22). They also acquire qualities of character, such as self-control and gentleness, and at the same time they are able to withstand temptations to show sinful qualities. These two types of characteristic, what we might call experiences of divine favor and the resultant expressions of emotion, on the one hand, and what we can understand as moral and spiritual virtues expressed in appropriate behavior, on the other, are not sharply differentiated from one another, as the lists in Romans 14:17 and Galatians 5:22-23 clearly show.

Paul does not deal with the theoretical side of the problem as to how it is that those who are in Christ, have the Spirit and are living under grace still yield to temptation and commit sin. He was well aware of the problem, and all his letters deal with sin in believers. Some scholars have argued that Paul's theology effectively excluded the possibility of sin by believers and that the occurrences of it must have taken Paul by surprise; he expected sinless perfection and was puzzled when it did not happen. But in fact there is no evidence that he was surprised by it (Gal 1:6 is rhetorical). Rather he simply warns people against the consequences and urges them to right behavior.

*The communities of believers.* All of the Pauline letters presume that believers live their lives in local communities, and therefore nearly all of what Paul has to say is addressed in the plural to them collectively; the major exceptions are the three letters to leaders, which by implication contain material for communities.[42]

For Paul the church is a complex reality that can be mapped in two dimensions, geographical and temporal.[43] The geographical dimension is that in which the local communities of believers are seen to belong together as "the church". The one word *ekklēsia* has to do duty for both entities. It can refer to believers generally as well as to specific groups.[44] Paul tends to use the term

---

[42]This can lead to unjustified conclusions as when it is said that Paul never refers to saints in the singular but always in the plural, implying that there is something essentially corporate in saintliness. The conclusion may be true in itself, but the logic is faulty. The plural is used simply because Paul is addressing a plurality of saints in each case.

[43]Or synchronic and diachronic.

[44]I have adopted the practice of generally using the term *congregations* for local communities to avoid the misleading later associations of "church" (denominations; buildings). The problem is complicated by the fact that the Christians in a given locality may have belonged to more than one house group.

more for local groups than for the totality of believers. The exceptions are in Colossians and Ephesians, particularly the latter, where the relationship of Christ to his people is expressed cosmically and therefore a reference to his relationship to all believers is a natural development. But this usage is already latent in the earlier letters. Thus "the church that meets at their house" (Rom 16:5) could refer to "those members of the whole church who meet in this particular locality". When Paul says that he persecuted the church of God (Gal 1:13; I Cor 15:9; Phil 3:6) the reference might be simply to the Christians in one locality (Jerusalem), but the story in Acts implies a wider activity, and therefore the term may encompass the Christians in a number of places.[45] And when Paul thinks of the church as the body of Christ (I Cor 12:27), while he may well be thinking primarily of the problems within the one congregation at Corinth, it is highly unlikely that he thinks of Christ having numerous bodies.[46]

This body imagery is dominant in Colossians and Ephesians. The local usage persists (Col 4:15-16), but the church is essentially one entity. Christ loved the church and gave himself for it, and the church becomes the means through which God works to reveal his wisdom and the sphere within which he is glorified (Eph 3:10, 21; 5:23-32). The "body" language is fused with bridal imagery, which again assumes that there is one entity and not a whole host of separate congregations. But the bridal language also goes back into the earlier period (2 Cor 11:2), and although the thought is primarily of the one congregation at Corinth, nevertheless the imagery is strained if Christ is thought of as having several different brides.

There is also the temporal dimension in which the church is understood as standing in continuity with Israel, the people of God descended from Jacob. Collectively believers are known as "saints", a term that implicitly identifies them as standing in continuity with the people of God in the Scriptures, Israel, although the latter term is generally used by Paul for the Jewish people.[47] Nevertheless, Paul was aware of a distinction between the physically defined people and the "true" people within them (Rom 9:6).[48] When he is addressing his

---

[45]Other references are debated: cf. I Cor 10:32; 12:28.

[46]Paul refers once to the churches of Christ (Rom 16:16; cf. Gal 1:22); otherwise he refers to the church(es) of God.

[47]The probable exception is Gal 6:16, which is more likely to refer to the church. See p. 227 n. 37.

[48]I Cor 10:18 may also point in the same direction.

readers as Christians, the usual address is "brothers", which was a common term for co-religionists.[49]

The nature of this relationship is easily misunderstood as implying that the covenant of God with Israel has been replaced by something else (super-sessionism). For Paul it is clear that throughout the historical period de-scribed in the Old Testament a distinction could be made between those who physically belonged to the descendants of Jacob and the smaller group within this larger number who showed faith and obedience to God; the Scriptures indicate plainly enough the repeated backsliding of numerous Is-raelites into idolatry and disobedience to the commandments, and the growth of the idea that they could be in the right with God by their perfor-mance of the law.[50] Paul thus has a remnant theology in which the true peo-ple of God are, and indeed always were, a smaller number within the phys-ical unit. The coming of Christ led to two crucial changes. First, since Jesus was understood to be the Messiah, the deliverer sent from God, expected by the Jews on the basis of prophecies in the Old Testament, it followed that the way to be in the right with God was by acceptance of the Messiah in faith. Thus the faith in God that characterized the true people of God from Abraham onward was now redefined in terms of faith in the Messiah. So there continued to be a remnant of Jews who were truly God's people. And, second, the believing remnant was opened up to include Gentiles who shared the same faith. This remnant was thus now embodied in the church. If unbelieving Jews were not included in the church as the people of God, this was no different from what had always been the case, namely, that phys-ical descent was in itself inadequate and a right relationship to God was all-important. Hence *supersessionism* is not the right term. God's promise to the

---

[49]The Greek word *adelphoi* can refer in different contexts to brothers or to a mixed group of brothers and sisters; in the latter case the focus may be primarily on the brothers but not to the exclusion of sisters. The decisive consideration is that Paul deliberately recognizes both men and women as mem-bers of God's family by referring to them as sons and daughters of God (2 Cor 6:18, where the LXX cited has only "son"). The fact that he refers to specific individual female believers as "sisters" makes it is unlikely that they were excluded when the term *brothers* was being used to address a congregation. Contemporary translations rightly tend to render the Greek term *adelphoi* as "brothers and sisters", unless it is clear that only males are intended.

[50]There is some tension here between the disobedience of the people (Rom 10:21) and their trust in their own works as a means of getting right with God. But for Paul one aspect of their disobedience was precisely their attempt to get right with God on their own terms instead of on his.

descendants of Jacob that they would be his people has not been revoked, but it is now made clear that it is not a matter simply of physical descent but rather of faith that recognizes that God has sent the promised Messiah, and the promise is enlarged to include non-Jews.[51]

The nature of the church as the people of God is further seen in the way in which in Colossians believers are said to have been circumcised through their baptism (Col 2:11). Here the concept of a spiritual circumcision, already familiar from the Old Testament, is taken up and applied to the baptized. Needless to say, this is not the replacement of one outward, physical rite by another, but a statement that what happens spiritually in baptism corresponds to what should happen spiritually in circumcision, namely, the cutting away of sinful tendencies.

Baptism was the outward rite of initiation into the believing community. Those who were baptized were admitted into one body and shared in the gift of the one Spirit, even if the gifts given to them by the Spirit were diverse (1 Cor 12:12-13; cf. Tit 3:5-6). The imagery of washing was associated with baptism and may well be alluded to by Paul (1 Cor 6:11, cf. Tit 3:5); it would naturally be thought of as symbolizing cleansing from sin (cf. Acts 22:16). But specific to Paul is the notion that baptism into Christ symbolizes sharing in his death and burial so as to share in his resurrection (Rom 6:3-5; cf. Col 2:12). Paul was probably influenced here by his understanding of faith as joining the believer to the Christ who had died and been raised, and the symbolism of the water could well be understood as signifying death, temporary burial and resurrection.[52]

Similarly, the church is seen as the place where God is present. In the Old Testament his presence was specifically associated with the temple, but now there is a twofold development, in that the temple is replaced by the church, and the church is understood not as a material building but as the company of God's people (1 Cor 3:16-17; 2 Cor 6:16; cf. Eph 2:21).[53] God's presence is

---

[51]Maybe we could call the principle "spiritual inclusivism".

[52]This symbolism is most readily apparent if candidates were immersed, but it is also possible with affusion, and the latter method is probably reflected in the analogy of plants being watered that lies behind the imagery in 1 Cor 12:13. Probably both methods of baptism were practiced; cf. the liberty permitted in *Didache* 7.

[53]A similar development took place in Judaism after the destruction of the temple with the recognition that God was present with his people when they read the Torah.

also understood to be with individual believers, whose bodies are the temples of the Holy Spirit (I Cor 6:19).[54]

From these considerations we can understand the functions that Paul ascribes to the congregations.

First, if the congregation is the place of God's presence, then God is active in it. Here Paul develops his idea of the spiritual gifts or charismata that are manifested in the congregation through the various activities of the Spirit in different individuals. Although these activities are primarily ascribed to the power of the Spirit, they are also said to have their source in God and to be exercised in the service of the Lord (Jesus) (I Cor 12:4-6). The purpose of these activities is so that the members of the congregation may work for their common good and thus promote the edification of the church, that is, the maturing of its members in their faith, love and hope. The congregation thus becomes the kind of community that God wishes his people to be, characterized by having the same aims and mutual concern for one another, since they seek to please God and their brothers and sisters rather than selfishly pleasing themselves.

Second, as the place where God is present and active, the congregation acts as a witness to the world of the divine reality (cf. I Cor 14:22-25).

Third, the congregation is the place where prayer and praise are made to God. Although these activities are scarcely mentioned in Paul's descriptions of congregational practices, nevertheless the calls to pray in his letters indicate that this was a significant aspect of the meeting. The prayer reports in the letters show that praise, thanksgiving, petition and intercession were aspects of prayer.[55] Prayer was addressed to God (Rom 1:8; 2 Cor 1:3; cf. Eph 1:3, 17; 3:14) but was directed through Jesus Christ and took place in the Spirit (I Cor 14:16; cf. Eph 6:18). This involvement of Christ and the Spirit is to be linked with the role of Christ and the Spirit as intercessors (Rom 8:26-27, 34).

---

[54] Again we have what appears to be a tension between statements about the presence of God with his people as individuals and as a group. In this case the tension is relieved by the fact that we are dealing with spiritual realities so that it is not contradictory to think of two modes of divine presence. Compare the similar problem of language that arises when distinguishing between the universal presence of God throughout the universe and his presence with his people.

[55] For the significant place of worship in the early church and its importance for the development of theology see Larry W. Hurtado, *Lord Jesus Christ: Devotion to Jesus in Earliest Christianity* (Grand Rapids, Mich.: Eerdmans, 2003).

Fourth, the congregational meeting was held in a domestic setting in which the sharing of a meal was natural. From I Corinthians we learn that the meal was intended to be stamped by the fact that at its heart was a sharing of bread and a cup that symbolized the dying of Christ for his people and his sacrificial inauguration of the new covenant. Nothing is said in this context about the resurrection of Jesus, but the fact that the death of Jesus was to be proclaimed "until he comes" shows that his resurrection and exaltation were implicit in the occasion. Nor, similarly, is anything said explicitly about Jesus being the host, a motif that might perhaps be thought to sit uneasily with the symbolism of his death; nevertheless, for Paul it is the Lord's table around which they gather, and the contrast he draws with having fellowship with demons (I Cor 10:20) indicates that believers have communion with the Lord. The sharing together symbolized the fact that all believers belong to the one body and thus was a means of expressing the unity of believers with one another, no matter what their racial and social backgrounds. Significantly, precisely the same role is attached to baptism (I Cor 12:13; Gal 3:28; cf. Eph 4:5), although the practice did not always measure up to the symbolism (1 Cor 11:18-22).

In this context it is unnecessary to go into details about the organization of the congregations. We have seen that for Paul the Spirit is active in the different ministries performed by the members and that in principle each and every believer can contribute in this way and indeed is under obligation to exercise the gifts and functions conferred by the Spirit. Further, these activities included such gifts as prophecy, through which divine messages were given to the congregations, and the tasks of apostleship, which involved responsibility for the planting of congregations and oversight over them. In the earlier letters of Paul there is a recognition that there are individuals who have particular responsibility for teaching (Gal 6:6) and for leadership, which appears to have included what we would call pastoral care and discipline, and therefore involved some measure of authority (I Cor 16:15-16; I Thess 5:12). Appropriate respect was to be shown to all who ministered. It is impossible to evade the existence of this element of authoritative leadership, sometimes exercised by individuals and at other times evidently by the collective decision of the congregation over individuals who had to be disciplined (I Cor 5). The precise form that local leadership took as it developed is not clear; only once does Paul refer to specific leaders as overseers and deacons (Phil 1:1; note also Rom

16:1), and in the earlier letters the term *elders* does not occur.

In the later letters there is more prominence given to leadership. In Ephesians there is a careful listing of the gifts of God to the church for the purpose of building up the people of God, and these are apostles, prophets, evangelists, pastors and teachers (Eph 4:11-13). Arguably, the first three of these are more the church planters and those who bring revelation from God, whereas the latter two are the local leaders responsible for care and teaching of the faith as it was already given by revelation.

These same elements are visible in 1 Timothy and Titus, where there is more developed instruction about overseers and deacons as leaders in the congregations. Scarcely anything is said about their tasks directly, but throughout the letters there is considerable emphasis on the need for teaching based on the truth as it has come to be known particularly through Paul and on oversight and direction for the congregations, particularly so as to counter the false teaching and the false behavior that was associated with it. Paul, Timothy and Titus are seen as exercising general oversight over the congregations, but at the same time they function as role models for the local leaders.

*Theology and behavior.* Throughout the Pauline writings there is a close connection between the gospel and behavior. The gospel contains binding implications for how believers are to live. This is particularly evident in the shape of Romans and later in Ephesians and Colossians, where the first parts of the letters lay theological foundations for practical teaching in the second parts, but elsewhere practical teaching can be backed up by doctrinal statements (cf. 1 Tim; 2 Tim; Tit) or the two can be closely interwoven (1 Cor). The connections can be made in several ways.

Believers are to live lives worthy of the God who has called them and made them his people (1 Thess 2:2; 4:7; cf. Eph 4:1; 2 Tim 1:9). The children are to be worthy of their father and to live in a way that brings credit to him (1 Cor 10:31). They are also reminded that God is their judge and that they will be assessed by what they have done with their lives. The function of judgment is also associated with Christ, and his coming acts as a stimulus to holy living (Rom 13:11-14; 1 Thess 5:1-11).

The fact that believers are "in Christ" or "in the Lord" is of decisive importance. There is a present shaping of their lives in between their calling and their final judgment (Rom 16:2, 8, 11-13; Phil 2:29; 1 Thess 4:1; cf. Eph 6:1; Col

3:18). Although the thought is not developed with any concrete particulars Paul thinks of believers as being under the law of Christ (1 Cor 9:21). Probably Paul saw this law as being summed up in the command to love. Christ's commands are given through the apostles, including Paul. Even if they are not under the law of Moses, they are not free from commandments and patterns to be imitated and followed (cf. 1 Cor 11:1).

This kind of living is most profoundly expressed as one in which believers take on the cruciform shape of the character of Jesus through sharing in his death and burial and resurrection, dying to sin and rising to newness of life. Colossians presents most sharply the way in which this involves putting off the characteristics of the old, sinful life, and putting on the character of the new person who has been raised to life with Christ. But 2 Corinthians is the most profound expression of the way in which the life of believers (and especially missionaries) here and now is one in which they are being changed from glory to glory (2 Cor 3:18) while at the same time they are living in weakness and death is at work in them (2 Cor 4).

Such a life is one of freedom, understood as deliverance from the power of sin that prevents people from being what God wants them to be, and so as having the capacity to do what God requires not out of the constraint of keeping commandments in order to be put in the right with God but rather as the expression of love and gratitude to him.

***The future of God and his people.*** It is evident that the heart of Paul's theology is concerned with the present existence of God's people and is based on the past act of redemption proclaimed in the gospel. At the same time we have been constantly aware of the future dimension. God is not yet "all in all" (1 Cor 15:28), while rebellion against him continues, while the creation is subject to bondage and decay, and while death continues to reign over humanity. Consequently, there is a forward look to the time when the final victory will be won. The present time is one of conflict between Christ and his enemies in which they are being defeated; ultimately Christ will return to this world and his return will involve the raising of the dead, the judgment of all people and the transformation of God's people as they receive the inheritance that has been promised to them.

The key elements thus include, first, the defeat of the forces opposed to God. Here, as elsewhere in Paul's theology, his thinking has a characteristic "already . . . not yet" pattern, in that the defeat of the evil powers has already taken place in the death and resurrection of Christ, but nevertheless the victory is not finally consummated. On the basis of what has been done Paul is sure of the final victory. The metaphor of mopping up forces already defeated in battle is not one that he uses but it is probably a fair statement of the position. All the powers in the universe come to the point of accepting that Christ is Lord (Phil 2:9-11).

Second, the hostile forces are not only defeated but also destroyed. Death is singled out for particular mention (1 Cor 15:26).

Third, there is a transformation of the universe as it is set free from the powers of death and destruction (Rom 8:21).

Fourth, the people of God are transformed as they put on spiritual bodies that are like that of Christ in his risen state, incorruptible and immortal (1 Cor 15; 2 Cor 5:1-10; Phil 3:21). Paul's vision is evidently of a new universe that shares the eternal character of the heavenly world where God is. At the present time believers, and perhaps especially the missionaries, live a precarious, dying existence, "always being given over to death for Jesus' sake, so that his life may also be revealed in our mortal body" (2 Cor 4:11). This verse sums up Paul's deeply realistic understanding of the situation of believers in what is his most profound meditation on it (2 Cor 4:7—5:10).

Paul does not go into any detail concerning this process of transformation, and what he does say is extremely difficult to interpret. How he conceptualized it we do not know. He is making use of the worldview of his time with its distinction between the material, corruptible universe and the heavenly world in which God dwells, and he sees this distinction melting away. But our inability to envisage what is meant is not ultimately significant. For it is clear that for Paul the important thing was the full realization of the life of God's people with him. Already in 1 Thessalonians the heart of the hope lies in being with the Lord forever (1 Thess 4:17; 5:10; Phil 1:23).

### The Later Letters

The exposition of Paul's theology above has turned out to be based to a considerable extent on Romans, where numerous themes are treated in a fuller way than they are elsewhere; there is the danger that this may lead to overemphasis on material there. Nevertheless, a picture has emerged that may fairly be said to be much the same as that evidenced by 1-2 Corinthians, Galatians and Philippians. Philemon fits in with it but is too short to permit firm conclusions. There is a unified theological outlook in these letters, although we have detected paradoxes and tensions within it.

The contents of 1-2 Thessalonians are also intelligible within this framework, although several characteristic features of Paul's theology are absent or understressed. The much more prominent role given to the parousia and associated matters in these two letters is due in part at least to the specific problems of the readership, but it could also be urged that the parousia occupied a more dominant role in Paul's theology and preaching than in the other letters. Yet this insistence could be mistaken. The fullest treatment of the problematic of the resurrection of believers, which is closely related to the parousia, is to be found in 1 Corinthians 15, and it must be borne in mind that here also the treatment arose directly from questions raised in the congregation; had the questions not been raised, we might never have had this lengthy discussion of the matter and would have formed a false estimate of its importance for Paul. In fact, 1 Thessalonians displays considerable contacts with 1 Corinthians. On the other side, it can be urged that the prominence of the parousia in 1 Thessalonians must reflect the place that it had in the preaching and instruction given by Paul and suggests that it was greater than the later letters might suggest. The problem with 1 Thessalonians is not so much the positive links that it has with the other letters as rather the things that are missing from it. We learn little about the death and resurrection of Jesus beyond the bare fact that he died for us and that he died and rose so that we might be saved from the wrath of God and receive salvation and life. But that is the same solid core that we find expanded in detail in Romans. Again, we read little about the Holy Spirit, but what Paul writes here ties in well with fuller treatments elsewhere: the Holy Spirit is active in the proclamation of the gospel (1 Thess 1:5; 1 Cor 2:4), inspires joy in those who respond to it (1 Thess 1:6; Rom 14:17; Gal 5:22; cf. Rom 5:5), is God's gift to believers and by implication guides them to holy living (1 Thess 4:8; 1 Cor 6:19), and is active in the congregation, probably in the distribution of charismata, including prophecy (1 Thess 5:19; 1 Cor 12:7).

At the other end of the spectrum from 1-2 Thessalonians we have Colossians and Ephesians on the one hand and the Pastoral Epistles on the other.

*Colossians.* Colossians shows a number of developments when compared with the earlier letters of Paul.

The christology, particularly as expressed in Colossians 1:15-20, contains new features. The discussion of the relationship of Christ to creation is a theme that is presented in a new way with its naming of him as the firstborn and the emphasis on him as the head over all powers and as the goal of the creation. The statement that all the fullness of the Deity is present in Christ (Col 2:9) goes beyond anything we have come across in the earlier letters.

Typically Pauline teaching on the law and righteousness is absent, even though the teaching that is opposed in the letter contains elements of Judaizing. Whereas Paul relates the death of Christ to sin, the law and death, here it is related to victory over the principalities and powers.

Believers are said to have been already raised with Christ and to have a life that is hidden with him in God. The teaching about the life of believers centers on this statement of dying and rising with Christ, and the Holy Spirit, who occupies an important role in the life of the believer and the congregation in the earlier letters of Paul, is not mentioned.

Likewise, Christ's position as head of the church is new, and the church is universal in scope rather than being the local congregation.

The position of Paul as the key figure in the revelation that the gospel is also for the Gentiles is emphasized.[56]

These differences should not be exaggerated into contradictions or inconsistencies. The thematization of Christ's status and role over against creation, though considerably developed and thematized, is in basic harmony with 1 Corinthians 8:5-6, and the particular form of development here arises from the need to deal with the problem raised by the understanding of the supernatural powers that was troubling the congregation. These powers were already mentioned in Romans 8:38 and 1 Corinthians 15:24, where Christ's future victory over them is stated.

The relationship of Christ to God is also prepared for in the earlier letters. To say that Christ is the firstborn is part of the field of ideas expressed in the understanding of him as the Son and image of God, and the actual term is al-

---

[56]This listing of points largely follows (Andrew T. Lincoln and) A. J. M. Wedderburn, *The Theology of the Later Pauline Letters* (Cambridge: Cambridge University Press, 1993), pp. 58-61.

ready used in Romans 8:29 and recurs in Revelation 1:5, suggesting that the phrase "firstborn from among the dead" is traditional. The new concept is that the fullness of Deity is bodily present in him.[57] Here the language moves from relationship and role to something more like substance and ontology.[58]

The understanding of Christ's death and its effects includes the Pauline concepts of redemption and reconciliation; forgiveness is a near synonym for justification (Rom 4:6-8; cf. Acts 13:38-39).[59] The raising of believers with Christ is already taught in Romans 6, where the difference between spiritual life now and physical resurrection still to come is recognized. The new element here is the description of believers as being already in the heavenly sphere, but the author is quite clear that this is not the same experience as glorification with Christ, which still lies in the future.[60] There is also the understanding of believers as those who have died with Christ and now have been raised with him. What we have here is similar to what we find in Revelation, where the concept of heaven appears to encompass the visible sky, the invisible spiritual realm and the realm where God is enthroned; the boundaries between these three conceptually distinguishable spheres are fluid, and it would be mistaken to look for absolute consistency in understanding them. The idea of an invisible spiritual sphere in which the presence and power of God are experienced by people living in the world but not entered by those who are dead in sin comes to expression here.

The position of Christ as head of the church seems to have developed from

---

[57]The concept that the risen Christ has a body is already present in 1 Cor 15, since Christ is there depicted as a man and as the paradigm for the resurrection of believers.

[58]There is no contradiction or tension with Phil 2:5-8, where the earthly Jesus divests himself of the authority that he possesses by virtue of his equality with God to act independently for his own advantage and becomes a servant to carry out his purposes. The belief that Jesus was led and empowered by the Holy Spirit naturally comes to be understood in terms of a total and unique presence of the power of God with him and finds expression in statements like this one in Colossians.

[59]Forgiveness *(aphesis, aphiēmi)* is a concept that is much more at home in the Synoptic Gospels (and Jn 20:23); the usage continues into Acts (Acts 2:38; 5:31; 10:43; 13:38; 26:18). Otherwise, it is rare (Heb 9:22; 10:18; Jas 5:15; 1 Jn 1:9; 2:12). If there is an oddity, it lies not so much in the use of forgiveness in Colossians (and Eph 1:7) as rather in the absence of the terminology of justification and righteousness. The verb *charizomai* is also used (Col 2:13; 3:13; Eph 4:32); elsewhere in Paul it is used of God's gracious giving (e.g., Rom 8:32) but also of human forgiveness (2 Cor 2:7, 10; 12:13; cf. Lk 7:42-43).

[60](Lincoln and) Wedderburn, *Theology*, p. 63, sees this statement as a dangerous experiment, but it seems to me to be in harmony with Rom 6.

the thought of him as head or supreme over the universe, and the fact that the church was seen as a body led naturally enough to the understanding of his relationship to it as being like that of a head to a body. This is a new idea compared with the picture in Romans and I Corinthians, but there is nothing strange about such a development as a new way of expressing the relationship of Christ to what Paul already called the body of Christ.

The statements about Paul reflect the consciousness of the significance of his role as the apostle to the Gentiles (Gal 1:16; 2:7) and thematize it in a way that is entirely natural with the passage of time and the development of a sense of what was historically significant in the spread of the mission.

It can fairly be maintained that what we have in Colossians is a Pauline theology that has developed in depth of understanding as the result of controversy and mature reflection. The conspicuous feature is the development of the concept of the power and superiority of Christ over supernatural forces and his being filled with the fullness of divinity. What we have here is a theology that builds upon theological motifs that are already present in the earlier letters. The new features appear to me to be developments that legitimately follow on from the earlier material rather than shifts in direction or contradictions of what went before.

*Ephesians.* The similarities between Ephesians and Colossians are immediately obvious and manifest themselves at the level of a considerable amount of parallel phraseology, although the similar wording does not necessarily express exactly the same thoughts. The theological motifs that make Colossians stand out compared with the earlier letters of Paul are to be found here also.

Ephesians has in common with Colossians the understanding of Christ as being superior to all conceivable powers in the universe, a position that makes him the mediator or agent through whom God accomplishes all his purposes. This position is related to his being raised from the dead and exalted by God to his right hand. Where Colossians draws attention to the role of Christ in creation, Ephesians ignores this theme. Both letters use the vocabulary of filling. In Colossians it is Christ who is filled with all the fullness of God, but those who are in Christ are also filled. In Ephesians there is specific reference to the church as "the fullness of him who fills everything in every way". The understanding of God, and especially of his Spirit, as everywhere present and effective is applied to Christ, who similarly is present in all believers and thus conveys to them the fullness of God. This thought comes to its climax in Ephesians 3:14-21, where Father, Son and Spirit alike are active in believers, and it becomes clear that the power of God and the love of God are very closely related in the subjective experience of believers. Similar thoughts are present in the earlier letters of Paul (Gal 2:20), but there is a dramatic escalation in the way that they are presented here. There is no thought of believers being made divine; the point is rather to assure believers that they have the power to resist the evil powers in the universe.

Ephesians has the same basic understanding of the process of salvation as in Colossians and the earlier letters. Like Colossians it develops the idea of human beings being dead in their sins and being awakened by the call of God. It sees salvation as consisting in being raised from the dead in union with Christ. It does not refer to dying with Christ and being buried with him, but this is implicit in the calls to put off the old self and put on the new. The imagery of moving out of darkness into light is also used (Eph 5:8). The traditional imagery of redemption, forgiveness and reconciliation is used, and Christ's death is understood as sacrificial. The experience of reconciliation is seen to involve the coming together of Jews and Gentiles in one people, emphasizing that the Gentiles are part of the people of God; this motif is implicit in Colossians (Col 1:27; 3:11), but is not thematized.

Although the Holy Spirit does not figure in the theology of Colossians, this agent of God is active in every aspect of the mediation of salvation in Ephesians.

The church plays a much greater role in the theology of Ephesians than in Colossians. In Colossians 1:18, 24 the body of Christ is given further definition as the church, and it is not otherwise mentioned (Col 4:15-16 refers to local groups of believers); by contrast it has a rather central position in Ephesians, and this is particularly evident in Ephesians 5:22-33, where the love of Christ for the church as the church is expounded; here it is the church which is given further definition as the body of Christ. The understanding of the church includes more traditional elements. These have become more formalized than earlier with the development of specific functionaries, but the Spirit-enabled ministry of the congregation as a whole is maintained, and there is perhaps a greater stress on the need for teaching in the faith that will come to even fuller expression in the Pastoral Epistles. The place of Paul as a crucial figure in the revelation of God's plan and purposes is conspicuous, but he is firmly placed in the midst of the apostles and prophets and not regarded as the one and only apostle. There is nothing static about the understanding of the church. It is seen as a body that grows, a temple that is in process of building, a company of believers who are progressing toward maturity, a company of soldiers who are engaged in defensive battle against the powers of evil, a people who pray for the effective working of their evangelists.

In all this there is a distinctive expression of the Pauline gospel that in various respects goes beyond the earlier letters and adopts new ways of conceptualizing.

*The Pastoral Epistles.* The Pastoral Epistles are primarily concerned with the problem of opponents with false teaching and practice who are hindering the church from its proper work of mission. They differ from the other letters in that they are addressed primarily to fellow missionaries, although they are to be overheard by the local congregations under their charge and their leaders. They deal with the problems of the time in very different ways from Colossians and Ephesians. First, they are concerned with practical measures to deal with false teaching by the appointment of local leaders who will be sound in the faith and appropriate role models for the congregation. Second, they include various disciplinary measures to quiet the false teachers. Third, they give teaching about the way of life that should be followed by the congregations and particular groups within them. And fourth, they give instruction to the missionaries about their own way of life.[61] In doing so, the accent falls upon practice and ethics rather than doctrine, but the practice arises out of the gospel and is buttressed by appeals to it. The letters recall the readers to Paul's teaching and the traditions current in the church, but at the same time the doctrine and the practice are developed with the aid of concepts that were either new or not strongly present in Paul's earlier writings. The result is that there is a very considerable stress on the need for teaching based on the apostolic message, and there is little of the sort of development of doctrine to meet fresh challenges that we find in the other letters. The general character of the theologizing is thus somewhat different from that in the earlier letters, but this does not necessarily mean that

---

[61]This is most obvious in 2 Timothy and least obvious in Titus, but even there it is not wholly absent (Tit 2:7-8, 15).

the theology is different. For whatever reason, there is much more stress on the need to be based on the tradition, but this means the kind of teaching given by Paul.

Although God has been thought to be somewhat remote in the Pastoral Epistles by reason of the lack of use of *Father* and the language used in I Timothy 1:17 and I Timothy 6:15-16, he is characterized as the Savior who acts in grace and love. Such phraseology could be used of ancient rulers and stresses God's benevolence without taking away from the element of worship and respect that is appropriate to him. God acts through Jesus Christ, who is ranked alongside God the Father and shares his titles of God and Savior. The coming of Jesus into the world as a man to give himself in death is seen as a revelation of the saving will of God. His mediatorial role is seen in his giving himself as a ransom to deliver humanity. Through it salvation is bestowed on sinners, with Paul as a paradigm, and they receive eternal life, which is understood as both present and future in God's heavenly kingdom. Salvation is received entirely by faith and not by human works, so that there is no distinction between Jews and Gentiles. It includes the lavish pouring out of the Holy Spirit and leads into a life where there is the familiar tension between being kept by the faithful God and having to resist temptations that could prove fatal.

More weight attaches, perhaps, to the way in which the church is understood in terms of the household rather than the body, with a tendency to concentrate on the ministry of the appointed leaders rather than that of the members. The differences from the earlier understanding can be exaggerated, since elements of the later forms can be found in Paul's earlier letters, and the developments brought about by the withdrawal of Paul from the scene and the threats caused by heretical teaching made some kind of more disciplined and structured congregational life virtually inevitable. Much has been made of the replacement of a "body of Christ" understanding of the church with a "household of God" understanding. But the use of the household analogy and its emphasis on the role of leaders who display the qualities of householders (as husbands, fathers and masters) is already anticipated by the way in which Paul uses the imagery of fatherhood to describe his relationship to his congregations (I Cor 4:15; I Thess 2:11). In all this, there is no real difference from the understanding of the gospel that we find in Paul's earlier letters. The differences are differences within the same basic understanding.

## Conclusion

In considering the variations from Pauline teaching in the later letters that may or may not be directly from him, I have not been attempting to demonstrate one way or the other whether they stem from Paul or to show that their theology is expressed in the same way, which it clearly is not. Rather, I have adopted the more limited purpose of asking whether there is a basic harmony between them. Put it this way. Suppose that these letters were not written by Paul. Is their teaching and underlying theology of such a kind that, if Paul were to read them, he would be saying, "No, I can't agree with that"? Would he have reacted negatively to them as he did to the teaching that was prevalent in the Galatian congregations? Would he have been less tolerant than he was to the preachers of the gospel whom he mentions in Philippians 1? Would he have found issues of principle where he would have felt compelled to speak out against them? Or would he have allowed that there was room for putting things differently from the way that he did in the earlier letters and that these expressions of the gospel and Christian practice fell within the acceptable limits of freedom of understanding? That is the question, and I cannot see that Paul would have had any real difficulties with these ways of teaching the congregations.

## Bibliography

Beker, J. Christiaan. *Paul the Apostle: The Triumph of God in Life and Thought.* Philadelphia: Fortress; Edinburgh: T & T Clark, 1980.

Davies, W. D. *Paul and Rabbinic Judaism: Some Rabbinic Elements in Pauline Theology.* 2nd ed., London: SPCK, 1955; 4th ed., Philadelphia: Fortress, 1990.

Dunn, James D. G. *The Theology of Paul the Apostle.* Grand Rapids, Mich.: Eerdmans, 1998.

Fitzmyer, Joseph A. *Paul and His Theology: A Brief Sketch.* 2nd ed. Englewood Cliffs, N.J.: Prentice Hall, 1989.

Hooker, Morna D. *Paul: A Short Introduction.* Oxford: Oneworld, 2003.

Kim, Seyoon. *The Origin of Paul's Gospel.* Grand Rapids, Mich.: Eerdmans, 1981; 2nd ed., Tübingen: Mohr, 1984.

Lincoln, Andrew T., and A. J. M. Wedderburn. *The Theology of the Later Pauline Letters.* Cambridge: Cambridge University Press, 1993.

Longenecker, Bruce W., ed. *Narrative Dynamics in Paul: A Critical Assessment.* Louisville, Ky.: Westminster John Knox, 2002.

Longenecker, Richard N. *Paul, Apostle of Liberty: The Origin and Nature of Paul's Christianity.* Grand Rapids, Mich.: Baker, 1964.

————, ed. *The Road from Damascus: The Impact of Paul's Conversion on His Life, Thought and Ministry.* Grand Rapids, Mich.: Eerdmans, 1997.

McLean, Bradley H. *The Cursed Christ: Mediterranean Expulsion Ritual and Pauline Soteriology.* Sheffield: Sheffield Academic Press, 1996.

Marshall, I. Howard. "Salvation, Grace and Works in the Later Writings in the Pauline Corpus". *NTS* 42 (1996): 339-58.

Martin, Ralph P. *Reconciliation.* London: Marshall, 1981.

Munck, Johannes. *Paul and the Salvation of Mankind.* London: SCM Press, 1959.

Ridderbos, Herman. *Paul: An Outline of His Theology.* Grand Rapids, Mich.: Eerdmans, 1974; London: SPCK, 1977.

Sanders, E. P. *Paul and Palestinian Judaism: A Comparison of Patterns of Religion.* London: SCM Press, 1977.

————. *Paul, the Law and the Jewish People.* Philadelphia: Fortress, 1983.

Schreiner, Thomas R. *Paul, Apostle of God's Glory in Christ.* Downers Grove, Ill.: InterVarsity Press, 2001.

Smith, D. Moody. "The Pauline Literature". In *It Is Written: Scripture Citing Scripture: Essays in Honour of Barnabas Lindars.* Edited by D. A. Carson and H. G. M. Williamson, pp. 265-91. Cambridge: Cambridge University Press, 1988.

Turner, Max. *The Holy Spirit and Spiritual Gifts Then and Now.* Carlisle: Paternoster, 1996; Peabody, Mass.: Hendrickson, 1999.

————. " 'Trinitarian Pneumatology' in the New Testament?—Towards an Explanation of the Worship of Jesus". *Asbury Theological Journal* 57.2/58.1 (2002-2003): 167-86.

Wenham, David. *Paul: Follower of Jesus or Founder of Christianity?* Grand Rapids, Mich.: Eerdmans, 1995.

Whiteley, D. E. H. *The Theology of St. Paul.* Cambridge: Blackwell, 1964.

Wiles, Virginia. *Making Sense of Paul: A Basic Introduction to Pauline Theology.* Peabody, Mass.: Hendrickson, 2000.

Witherington, Ben, III. *Paul's Narrative Thought World: The Tapestry of Tragedy and Triumph.* Louisville, Ky.: Westminster John Knox, 1994.

Ziesler, J. A. *Pauline Christianity.* 2nd ed. Oxford: Oxford University Press, 1990.

# 19

# PAUL, THE SYNOPTIC GOSPELS AND ACTS

~~∘~~

$A$t the conclusion of our discussion of the work of the three Evangelists, Mark, Matthew and Luke, I attempted to draw together the results of our study by comparing their Gospels with one another and with Acts. Bearing in mind that the Gospels were written after Easter and were inevitably influenced by that perspective, I concluded cautiously that the picture of the theology of the early church that can be derived from Acts was what might have been expected to arise as the followers of Jesus continued his mission. Now that we have examined the theology associated with the figure of Paul, whose mission and sufferings are the major theme in the second half of Acts, it is appropriate to make some comparisons between them in order to see whether they are diverse to the point of real difference or stand in some more harmonious kind of relationship.

## The Framework

We can see immediately that Paul works within the same Jewish frame of reference as Jesus and the Evangelists. They share the same basic understanding of God as he is revealed in the Old Testament, as the Creator of the universe and in particular the God who has acted in history as the God of Israel. His will is revealed in Scripture, and he carries out his plans despite opposition from Satan and sinners. They also share the same understanding of human nature with their recognition of human sinfulness. Paul, however, displays a much more detailed anthropology, and he wrestles at a deeper level with the nature of sin.

## The Central Thrust

In the Synoptic Gospels the major theme of the mission and teaching of Jesus is the announcement of the kingdom of God, leading to the announcements of divine judgment upon human sinfulness, to the call to repentance and disciple-ship, and to the teaching regarding the blessings associated with the kingdom and the way of life required of those who enter it. At the same time the mission raises the question of the identity of Jesus and leads to the recognition by some that he is the Messiah and to his teaching that the Messiah must be put to death and be raised from the dead, so that despite his death he is confirmed as the Messiah by God. In Acts the teaching of the missionaries centers on this second area: the missionary sermons confirm that Jesus is the Messiah on the basis of the conformity of what has happened to Jesus with Scripture, the confirmation of his status by the resurrection and the pouring out of the Spirit, and the tes-timony of his followers to what has happened, and especially to the resurrec-tion. Thus Jesus is identified as the exalted Messiah and now also as Lord, and he is in a position to offer forgiveness and the gift of the Spirit. In this way the blessings of the kingdom are now available to all, including the Gentiles. The bringer of the kingdom is proclaimed rather than the kingdom itself; implicitly it is realized that Jesus is the kingdom.

The Pauline letters may be said to assume all this. Paul is a missionary called to bring the good news of Jesus to the Gentiles in particular, and he shares the same gospel as other early Christians (1 Cor 15:3-5). But his gospel is shaped by the fact that he is addressing Gentiles and Jews of the Dispersion, and there-fore he has to relate it to their situation and background, such as the polythe-istic idolatry of the Gentiles. Further, his letters are without exception directed to Christian congregations, and therefore they move on beyond evangelistic preaching to instruction for Christians regarding their relationship to Christ and their life together as congregations. Such matters as his ongoing mission and the place of the Holy Spirit in Christian experience come to the fore.

## Specific Elements

*God—the Father.* Paul can assume the understanding of God as Father that we find in the Gospels. The most convincing explanation of the dominance of this title in the New Testament generally as compared with Judaism is that it reflects the characteristic speech of Jesus when talking to his disciples. Paul even retains the Aramaic *Abba* that is so far unknown elsewhere as a form of address to God in prayer. The concept of God as the Father of Jesus Christ is a title based on the traditions about Jesus' self-understanding. And the understanding of God as the sovereign ruler who is carrying out his purpose through the mission of his people and specifically those called to be witnesses and apostles is common to both.

*God—the Son.* The fact that Jesus was a human being is taken for granted by Paul and is theologically important for him since it identifies him as a representative of the human race, a Jew subject to the law, but also as the man from heaven through whom believers receive justification and new life. Here Paul draws conclusions that go beyond the Synoptic Gospels and Acts.

The messiahship of Jesus is important for Paul, particularly in relation to the Jews: the Messiah came from Israel and fulfills God's promise of a deliverer for the Jews. He is the crucified Messiah.

As in Acts, Jesus is the Lord, shown to be such by his resurrection and exaltation, and this title is used to indicate his divine status but without confusing him with God the Father. He is the Son of the Father, reflecting his image, and for Paul the Son preexisted the creation of the world and became incarnate in Jesus. In the later letters the language used is even more expressive of sovereignty and of the fullness of God being present in Christ and flowing through him to the church.

The way in which all this is expressed goes some distance beyond what we have in the Synoptic Gospels and Acts. It is clear that the Pauline theology can assimilate the christology in the Gospels and Acts without difficulty, but that it might be said to include implications and developments that go beyond anything envisaged in the latter. We know that there were other Christians, whose views are not represented in the New Testament writings, who held to so-called Ebionite views of Jesus as simply a human messiah. Such views were seen at the time as contrary to mainline Christianity and could not be harmonized with the theology of Paul. In Acts, however, the understanding of Jesus as the exalted Lord and Son of God is essentially the same as that of the christology developed in Paul and in John and Hebrews.

*God—the Holy Spirit.* The significant element in Paul's understanding of the Spirit is the development of recognition of the Spirit as personal, leading to the way in which the Spirit can be placed alongside the Father and the Son in what may be called an incipient trinitarianism, that is, an understanding of Father, Son and Spirit each as personal and sharing similar functions in such a way that the later church recognized them as equally divine and sought for a way of expressing their interrelatedness that did justice to their unity as well as their individuality. This personal character of the Spirit is not so apparent in the Synoptic Gospels and Acts, where the Spirit is more a source of insight (like Wisdom) and power. Yet the Spirit gives guidance and apparently speaks in the same way as the Lord or angels (Acts 1:16; 5:32; 8:29; 10:19; 11:12; 13:2; 15:28; 16:6-7; 20:23; 21:11; 23:9; 28:25).[1] and this suggests that a clearer articulation of the personal nature of the Spirit was a natural development.

*God—as communicator.* Under this heading we noted the place of the Scriptures as the means whereby God expressed his will and his pattern for history in the Pauline writings. The use of this motif in the Synoptic Gospels and Acts is essentially the same as in Paul. For all the writers the Scriptures tell the story of God's dealings with Israel in time past and they see the contemporary events as foretold in Scripture or following a pattern laid down there.[2] They also see there commandments given by God for the life of his people. These fundamental points are common to the Evangelists and to Paul.[3]

God continues to speak in New Testament times through apostles and prophets, and it is probable that Luke thought of himself, though neither an apostle nor a prophet, as continuing the task of writing Scripture. A distinction between the Old and New Covenants was developing, and once Paul saw himself and other missionaries as servants of the latter, the recognition of new covenant revelation by the Spirit alongside the Scriptures of the Old Covenant was a natural development.

There is a well-known problem in that Acts is often thought to limit the apostles to the reconstituted Twelve, whereas for Paul the apostles, including himself, form a wider group than the Twelve. For Luke the apostles figure as the Twelve appointed by Jesus with a special role in relation to Israel, but for Paul the number includes also the missionaries to the Gentiles. Luke is certainly

---

[1] Evil spirits can also speak or inspire human speaking (Acts 19:15).
[2] Cf. the title of Darrell. L. Bock's study of Luke's use of the Old Testament, *Proclamation from Prophecy and Pattern: Lucan Old Testament Christology* (Sheffield: Sheffield Academic Press, 1987).
[3] See p. 475 on the problem of the law.

aware of this calling to the Gentiles and makes much of Paul's special commission. In fact, Luke does refer to Paul and Barnabas as apostles in Acts 14:4, 14, and it is plausible that he recognized their role, but when he refers to the leaders of the essentially Jewish Christian church in Jerusalem, he uses the term for them along with the elders. The problem, if there really is one, is a matter of terminology rather than of substance.

*The gospel—the need for salvation.* There is no doubt that all the New Testament writers regard humanity as sinful and in need of deliverance from their sin. We have seen how the Evangelists show Jesus as bringing deliverance and healing to the victims of evil but also as condemning the sins of the Jewish religious leaders and humanity generally, although there is not a lot of stress on sin in general. Nevertheless, the mission of Jesus presupposes that people are outside the kingdom of God unless they respond positively to it. In Acts the Jews are assumed to be implicated in the sin of their rulers in crucifying Jesus unless they repent and accept forgiveness; the Gentiles likewise are seen to be in need of the gospel because of their sin and failure to recognize the one God.[4] Judgment faces all alike, conceived of as condemnation at the last day, and failure to acknowledge Jesus leads to rejection by the Son of Man.

The Pauline picture is the same. In Romans Paul teaches that all people have sinned and stand under God's judgment. That he means all individuals and not just that there are some Jewish sinners as well as Gentile sinners is beyond question. This is particularly evident from the teaching about the relation of the whole human race to Adam in Romans 5. We noted that there is less material on this topic in the other letters than might have been expected, but the all-pervasiveness of this concept is necessary to explain the Pauline proclamation of the gospel. It is the exposition of Paul's anthropology that goes beyond anything elsewhere in the New Testament with its understanding of the flesh being under the control of evil impulses and the sinners being in some sense dead in their sin. This radical language is not found in the Synoptic Gospels and Acts, although the wickedness of the human heart is already recognized in the Gospels (Mk 7:6, 21) and hardness of heart, that is, imperviousness to the voice of

---

[4]We saw earlier that Luke has been accused of a shallow view of sin in Acts, presenting a picture of Gentiles who merely need to be helped rather than saved; this interpretation does not do justice to the evidence.

God, is a concept taken over from Isaiah 6:10 by the Evangelists if not by Jesus himself (Mt 13:15; Acts 28:27; cf. Mk 8:17).

Prominent in Paul is the claim that human beings can do nothing to put themselves right with God. This arises particularly in the context of discussion about the role of the law of Moses. Paul attacks the view that people may do so by what he calls "the works of the law." This phrase signifies obedience to the precepts of the Mosaic law, circumcision, observance of festivals and food laws being the aspects that are to the fore. Paul attacks these observances as works in which people may put their confidence ("boast") and rejects them as being unable to fulfill this function. To adopt them is to misconceive the Mosaic law as a means of justification. This was not the intended purpose of the law. Paul's opposition was related to the way in which some people were requiring that Gentile Christians should do these works of the law in order to be justified and in order that there could be fellowship between them and Jewish Christian believers who continued to regard Gentiles who did not keep the law as unclean and their foods as unclean.

This same issue does arise in Acts, though not in the Gospels where the Jew-Gentile problem would have been an anachronism. But the issue of whether Gentiles are required to keep the law is settled by a recognition that circumcision is not required of Gentiles, and the requirements that are laid down concern foods offered to idols, sexual immorality and blood in meat. The first two of these requirements correspond with Paul's teaching, while the latter may be simply a requirement not to offer unacceptable foods to Jewish Christians in shared meals. There is no conflict with Paul at this point.[5] Moreover, Acts confirms that Gentiles were saved and received the Spirit without having to keep the law (Acts 15:8; cf. Gal 3:1-4). As for Jewish Christians, Paul recognizes that they may continue to keep the law (Rom 14), and Acts presents him as doing the same, despite accusations brought against him (Acts 21:20-26).

*The gospel—the means of salvation.* For Paul the way in which people come into contact with the means of salvation is through the gospel, that is, the spoken

---

[5]This is admittedly a controversial view. Many scholars hold that Paul's account of the meeting at Jerusalem in Gal 2:1-10 rules out that anything was added to Paul's gospel by the Jewish Christians and that this means that the requirements in Acts 15:20, 29 could not have been accepted by Paul.

message that is proclaimed by the missionaries and may be accompanied by powerful manifestations of the Holy Spirit. The gospel is a given, handed down to Paul by other Christians, and there is no evidence of any dispute with the leaders in Jerusalem over its essential contents.

The content of the gospel is, then, centered on the death and resurrection of Jesus, understood as the means through which people can be delivered from their sins and God's judgment upon them. The death of Jesus is variously seen as the bearing of sin and the curse (scapegoat imagery) and as a sin offering that atones for sin. It is an act of deliverance or redemption that sets sinners free from their sin. Essentially it is an act of Christ for the benefit of and on behalf of sinners and is concerned with their sin.

This understanding can be traced back to the teaching of Jesus as recorded in the Synoptic Gospels, where his death is understood as a ransom for many and as having a sacrificial character (Mk 10:45; 14:24).[6] But there is a major difference between Acts and Paul in that the preaching in Acts assigns no particular saving significance to the death of Jesus, seeing it rather as the act of sinful opponents (though not outside the purpose of God) that was undone by the resurrection. In our discussion earlier I raised the possibility that the earliest stage in Christian preaching may have concentrated on this theme for apologetic purposes. Sacrificial redemption language is not completely absent (Acts 20:28), and the identification of Jesus with the suffering Servant is used by Luke (Lk 22:37; Acts 8:32-33); these points were capable of exposition in a Pauline direction, but Luke has not done so. What we can say is that Paul's understanding of the death of Jesus as sacrificial and redemptive is dependent on material that he has received from early Christian tradition; in other words, it is the silence of Luke that requires explanation rather than the expressed theology of Paul.

The importance of the resurrection for Acts and Paul is self-evident. It is the exaltation of Jesus as Lord and Christ.

*The nature of salvation.* We noted that Paul has four key motifs for understanding the nature of the effects of the death and resurrection of Jesus, namely, salvation, redemption, justification and reconciliation. Salvation language is char-

---

[6]Here the sacrifice is that which inaugurates the covenant, as described in Ex 24, even if its precise significance there is not clear.

acteristic of Luke and is also found in Matthew and Mark. It is pervasive throughout the New Testament and forms an important bond of theological unity.[7] Redemption is a less common concept. It does occur in Luke-Acts but refers in a rather general kind of way to God's action in delivering his people from their enemies and from their sins. Justification is very much a Pauline motif, and it is found on Paul's lips in Acts 13:38-39 (cf. Lk 18:14). Reconciliation likewise is a Pauline word not found in the Gospels and Acts, but what is the parable of the prodigal son about if it is not about forgiveness and reconciliation? We should not be deceived by the absence of the word. Here, then, we can see the development of a theological vocabulary of salvation in the broad sense by Paul that is in harmony with the Gospels and Acts but is much more articulate than they are.

*The reception of salvation.* In Paul's theology the reception of salvation depends upon God's prior action in making known the gospel to those who do not yet believe. This action depends in turn upon his saving purpose. Here there is some controversy over whether there is a particular purpose of God directed only at some people and excluding others from the possibility of salvation. The same general point arises in the Synoptic Gospels and Acts. However we account for it theologically, there was an inevitable selectivity in the mission of Jesus in that he could not be everywhere and had to leave one place in order to visit others (Mk 1:35-39); to some extent he compensated for this by enrolling the Twelve and the seventy-two as his helpers. The comment in Matthew 22:14 that many are called but few are chosen has sometimes been thought to mean that, although the gospel may be heard by many, in fact only a few are actually chosen to be saved by it; this interpretation is unlikely, and the thought is rather that although many hear, in fact not all respond and become numbered among God's people. Compare how Jesus encourages people to let nothing stand in the way of their entry into the kingdom because it is a matter of observation that few travel the narrow way (Mt 7:13-14). In Acts there is the indication that it is those who are appointed for eternal life who believe (Acts 13:48; cf. 18:10) and that God opens hearts so that people respond to the preaching (Acts 16:14). Such comments are isolated but demonstrate that God can and does bring people to faith (otherwise there would be no point in interceding for un-

---

[7]The only books not to use the vocabulary of salvation are Galatians, Colossians and Philemon.

believers), but more should not be taken out of them than they actually say. They underline that God wants to save people and that he takes the initiative without which they could not be saved.

At the same time there is an unambiguous agreement between Paul and Acts on the necessity and sufficiency of faith as the human response to the gospel (e.g., Acts 10:43; 11:17; 16:31; 26:18). The object of faith is normally the Lord or Jesus in Acts (occasionally God, Acts 16:34), but Paul tends to refer more to faith in God or to use the term without an expressed object. There is no great difference here; note how Acts 16:34 is closely linked to Acts 16:31. Repentance is the flip side of faith in Luke-Acts, but it is generally not part of the vocabulary of conversion in Paul (though see Rom 2:4; 2 Tim 2:25); occasionally he mentions it in relation to backsliding believers (2 Cor 7:9-10; 12:21). The contrast between faith and works, which is central to Paul's understanding of faith, is not found in Acts. But although the statement that anybody who fears God and does (lit., "works") righteousness is acceptable to him (Acts 10:35) might be thought to contradict Paul's view, the gift of the Spirit is in fact conferred on Cornelius at the point when he hears the good news of Jesus and believes (cf. Acts 11:14-17; 15:7-9). Luke knows that justification is not possible under the law of Moses but only through Jesus (Acts 13:38-39).

*The ongoing work of God in the believer.* A major element in Paul's theology is the continuing work of God in believers, expressed in a variety of ways. This stands in sharp contrast with Acts, where the speeches that contain most of the theological teaching are addressed primarily to nonbelievers and thus have a different focus. Paul's language of being in Christ is absent. The concept of believers being united with Christ in his death and resurrection is likewise missing. Although Acts has much to say about the Holy Spirit, there is very little reference to the work of the Spirit in the development of Christian character. If Acts does not know the works of the flesh (though it is well aware of human sin!), neither does it know the fruit of the Spirit. Nevertheless, Acts shares with Paul the belief that the Spirit is given to all believers and is an essential element in their experience. Acts 2:38 cannot be understood in any other way. The Spirit in Acts is primarily associated with the guiding and empowering of individuals and the church for witness and mission. But despite this emphasis there are a few indications that the presence of the Spirit is to be seen as a sign of the reality of salvation and hence as the means of Christian assurance (Acts 2:38;

9:17) and reassurance (Acts 4:31); the Spirit is associated with encouragement (Acts 9:31) and joy (Acts 13:52). The gift of tongues is an evidence of conversion, and this was for the benefit of the recipients, since it moved them to praise God, as well as a testimony to other people (Acts 10:44-46; 19:6). There is no difficulty in seeing the Spirit-inspired phenomena of 1 Corinthians 12 in the context of Luke's record in Acts. Further, Luke recognizes the importance of Christian character, expressed in the goodness of Barnabas (Acts 11:24) and the good works of Tabitha (Acts 9:36), even if it surfaces only occasionally. Unfortunately, even when we have a speech directed toward those who are already believers, it is focused on the leaders and not on the members as a whole (Acts 20:17-35), and we never learn what a Lukan character might have said to edify the believers. Luke's interest is concentrated on the mission of the church to Jews and Gentiles and in the missionaries.

*The community of believers.* The place and importance of the church in Paul and Acts is obvious. For both writers the church consists of Jewish and Gentile believers and stands in continuity with the Israel of the old covenant. A major theme of Acts is the way in which the church, originally composed of Jewish believers, realizes that it is called by God to be open to Gentile believers who share equally with Jewish believers in forgiveness, the gift of the Spirit and membership of the people of God without the requirement of circumcision. Although another point of view existed among early Christians, requiring Gentile believers to accept the Jewish law and customs, the Pauline understanding is the one that prevailed in the church at Jerusalem according to Luke and Paul.

Like Paul, Luke uses the term *ekklēsia* initially for the church in Jerusalem and then for local groups of Christians and corporately for Christians in different places (Acts 9:31). The original church in Jerusalem spreads, and it becomes possible to speak of the churches (plural; Acts 16:5). Again like Paul, he refers occasionally to the saints (Acts 9:13, 32, 41; 26:10) and frequently to "the brothers". In both Acts and Paul the language used makes it evident that the church is seen as the continuation of the historical people of God. In Acts as in Paul, however, the term *Israel* is employed for the Jews as the historic people of God rather than for the church.

Paul develops the thought of the church as the body of Christ. There is some analogy with the usage in Matthew where Jesus speaks of "my church" (Mt 16:18). In Acts, however, the term *church* is used absolutely. There is no development of imagery for the church comparable with that in Paul; the rich understanding of the church in Colossians and Ephesians goes well beyond anything in Acts.

Paul and Acts reflect the practice of the early church generally in their recognition of baptism as the rite of initiation into the church. In Acts baptism is associated with forgiveness, expressed in the metaphor of washing away of sin (Acts 22:16) and with the reception of the Holy Spirit. Both of these aspects of baptism are found in Paul (I Cor 6:11; 12:13; cf. Tit 3:5). Paul states explicitly that baptism brings believers into the body of Christ, the church (I Cor 12:13), and this is implicit in Acts. Where Paul goes beyond the rest of the early church is in his understanding of baptism as being into the death of Christ so as to share in his resurrection life here and now, and his physical resurrection in the future. A further difference is that in Acts baptism is done in or into the name of Jesus, but in Paul it is done into Christ (Rom 6:3; Gal 3:27). In these ways the personal relationship with the risen Jesus that we have seen to be much less conspicuous in Acts is brought out in Paul.

The activities of the congregation when it gathered together included prayer and praise to God, the functions of prophets and others gifted by the Spirit, and the celebration of the Lord's Supper, and these things happened in a domestic setting. Not surprisingly, these same activities are attested for the early church in Acts. We learn more from Paul about the details since his letters are focused on the internal life of congregations. Questions have been raised about possible differences between the breaking of bread in Acts and the Lord's Supper in Paul. It has been suggested that the events in Acts were more in the nature of meetings with the risen Lord whereas in Paul they were more a means of remembering the death of the Lord.[8] Certainly the accounts in Acts must be read in the light of the Emmaus story in Luke 24, and the significance of this should not be missed: the meals in Acts are the occasion of fellowship with the risen but unseen Lord. In this way Luke implicitly recognizes the element of personal communion with the risen Lord that otherwise is passed over in comparative silence in Acts. This element is present in Paul (I Cor 10:14-22). As for remembrance of the death of Jesus, from I Corinthians 11 it appears that this

---

[8]The theory that historically there were two different types of meal, perhaps associated with Galilee and Jerusalem, has not found lasting favor.

element was in danger of being overlooked in practice. Again it may be necessary to remind ourselves that Acts should be read in the light of the Gospel, where the link with the death of Jesus emerges in the Last Supper.[9] Here, as elsewhere, it is essential to remember that Luke has a limited purpose in Acts, which is to relate the story of the Christian mission rather than to describe what congregations of believers believed and practiced. We must be careful to distinguish between matters that he has chosen not to elaborate on because they fell outside his purpose and other matters where the narrative explicitly or implicitly suggests that he or the early church held particular views about them.

In the light of this consideration we should not draw wrong inferences about the lack of material regarding the internal organization of congregations in Acts. Paul and Luke have in common the recognition of the existence of the Twelve and other apostles. For Luke, the Twelve, headed by Peter, are concerned with mission to the Jews, whereas Paul with his companions are called to go to the Gentiles (though neither group goes exclusively to the one constituency), and Paul recognizes the separate callings of Peter and himself to the Jews and Gentiles respectively. Both writers view mission as the work of traveling missionaries, with Paul working alongside one or more companions. In Acts it is the way in which the leaders function as evangelists that stands out: Peter, Stephen, Philip and Paul and his companions are missionaries, even if, as in the case of Stephen and Philip, they were appointed to other tasks. Both writers envisage leaders being appointed in new congregations, using such terms as *elders* and *overseers* to refer to them. Inevitably there is more about this in Paul and particularly in the later letters as some institutionalization takes place.

*Theology and behavior.* For Paul it is self-evident that conversion leads to new patterns and standards of behavior. We have seen how his letters base the practice of Christian life as individuals and as community on the Gospel. The instruction is sometimes given "in the Lord", acknowledging his authority to direct the life of his people. Occasionally teaching of the earthly Jesus is given, referring to him in this context as "the Lord". The Mosaic law is no longer to be kept as the means of justification, but it finds its fulfillment in the law of

---

[9]The tradition followed by Luke here (Lk 22:19-20) differs from Mark and is shared with Paul (1 Cor 11:23-25). On the uncertainty about the text in Luke (with some authorities omitting most of Lk 22:19-20) see p. 139 n. 18. Even if the shorter text were to be adopted, the links between the meal and the forthcoming death of Jesus are still palpable.

love and through the work of the Spirit producing the fruit of Christian character. There are stern warnings against sin in the lives of believers.

All of this is in implicit agreement with the Gospels, where the same law of love is taught by Jesus. A life lived "in the Lord", as Paul calls it, is one in which the teaching of Jesus is accepted as providing the pattern for life. We see Paul taking up this teaching and applying it to a new situation in his discussion of marriage and divorce. Strong measures against blatant sin are found in Acts 5 and I Corinthians 5.

What is lacking in the Gospels and Acts is the developed teaching of Paul about the direction and enabling of the Holy Spirit for believers in their personal lives.

*The future of God and his people.* The Evangelists share with Paul the belief in the future coming of Christ and both depict something of the course of future events. The place of Christ as judge is recognized, as is his gathering together of his people to be with him. The resurrection of the dead is a belief shared by the Jews (other than the Sadducees) and Christians but mocked by Greeks. Neither in Acts nor in Paul is there much emphasis on the kind of matters treated in the apocalyptic passages in the Gospels. Acts is primarily concerned with the need for people to repent and accept the salvation offered by the risen Lord here and now lest they come under his judgment. It recognizes the fact of ongoing persecution of believers, but it does not put this into the context of signs of the end that we find in the Gospels, and it is silent on the judgment of Jerusalem, despite the clear references to this in Luke 21.[10] The kind of warnings given by Jesus regarding the coming judgment on Jerusalem find no place in the preaching of the apostles. Similarly, the apocalyptic manner of presentation of the future is largely absent from Paul. Where it is found in I Thessalonians 4—5 and in I Corinthians 15, it arises out of problems relating to the destiny of deceased believers, and in 2 Thessalonians it functions to give a different understanding of the events surrounding the end from that held by the readers. The material used by Paul is certainly related to the traditions utilized in the Gospels, and it is clear that there was a place for such teaching in his instruction of believers, but it was not central to the gospel as he under-

---

[10]Whether as a result of use of variant traditions or of Lukan editing to bring out the point, Luke 21 identifies the impending judgment upon Jerusalem far more clearly than in Mk 13 or Mt 24.

stood it. Paul's understanding of the transformation of believers at the parousia and their close relationship to Christ is of decisive importance, but here he is once again developing theological motifs in an individual manner compared with the Synoptic Gospels and Acts.

## Conclusion

We have now been through the main aspects of Paul's theology, following the headings used in our earlier summary of it, and compared them with the picture of the beliefs of other early Christians as given by Luke in Acts and with the teaching in the Synoptic Gospels insofar as comparisons are possible. We have discovered a fair measure of agreement on the basic theology that comes to expression in both sets of writings. There is an entity that may fairly be called Paulinism, attested by the acknowledged writings of Paul and supplemented in the varied contributions of the later letters wherein the hand of Paul himself or of his followers may be seen. Equally there is an entity that we have discovered consisting of teaching inspired by the mission of Jesus and continued in the mission of his followers in the early church. Our comparison has shown that there are differences between them. They are not identical, but they are recognizably the same. The Paul who rejoiced in the preaching of other believers, even if their motives were questionable in his eyes (Phil 1:15-18), would have rejoiced all the more in the gospel reflected in the Synoptic Gospels and Acts (cf. I Cor 15:3-11, where he affirms that he and the first followers of Jesus preached one and the same gospel).

This broad conclusion could certainly be attacked from various angles.

First, there is the fact that the picture of the teaching of Jesus given by the Evangelists was created after Easter by people like Paul, and it is arguable that they painted the picture (unconsciously, no doubt) in the light of their situation and religion. The degree of similarity between the teaching of Jesus and that of the early church may well have been enhanced, and historically they may have been much less similar to one another.

To this objection various replies may be made. The first is that for our purpose, which is to outline the theology of the New Testament writers, the historical question is not of first importance. It is sufficient to be able to show that there is a harmony between the different writers, and this we have been able to do. Second, the Gospels are based on the traditions about Jesus that were circulating in the early church. They show the influence of Jesus, as he was remembered. There is an essential homogeneity and coherence between the different elements, drawn from numerous different traditions, in the Gospels that indicate that the Gospels faithfully reproduce the traditions.[11] We have been at pains to bring out the characteristic differences between the Gospels, and in a more detailed treatment it would be possible to distinguish between tradition and redaction, but nevertheless it is possible to speak of a common theology shared by the Evangelists despite their individual nuancing of it. They are all singing from the same hymnbook, although they may be singing different parts.

Second, we have the problem of identifying the theology of the earliest Christians as compared with the depiction given by Luke. Throughout this chapter I have been making a comparison between Paul and Luke as the author of Acts. The puzzled reader may well be perplexed as to whether the comparison that was being made was between Paul and the early church or Paul and the author of Acts.

On the one side, it is argued by some that the author of Acts has painted a more biased and inaccurate picture of the early church than the Evangelists did of Jesus. The latter were guided by traditions that were handed down with some faithfulness because of the respect in which Jesus was held, whereas there is less likelihood that the activities of the early church were the subject of a tradition-forming process in the same kind of way. Luke, it is often held, had little to guide him for his account of the earliest Christian mission and its preaching, and what we have reflects the flawed memory of a later Christian reconstructing the story as best he could but inevitably attributing his own theology to Peter and the others.

On the other side, there is the specific problem of Luke's presentation of Paul's teaching. No doubt Luke thought of himself as essentially a Paulinist,

---

[11]We could use the principle of multiple attestation here for a different purpose than that for which it is normally used. In his pioneering book, C. H. Dodd, *History and the Gospel* (London: Nisbet, 1938), pp. 84-103, showed how various key motifs in the teaching and mission of Jesus could be seen to be present not only in different form-critical categories of tradition (pronouncement stories, miracle stories, parables, wisdom sayings and the like) but also in different sources (material preserved by Mark; traditions in Q; traditions preserved solely by Matthew [M] or Luke [L]—and, I could add, by John). The existence of multiple independent forms and sources is a strong factor in favor of the historicity of the material reliably reflecting the teaching and activity of Jesus. But one might also observe that the continuity between the different sources demonstrates their fundamental agreement in their presentation of Jesus, even though they each have their own characteristic nuances and emphases.

concerned to uphold the theology of Paul and to defend Paul against his attackers. Clearly Paul is one of the two heroes of the book, and the theology of Luke demonstrates some Pauline features, if only because Luke spends so much space on Paul and his mission. However, much of Paul's characteristic theology is not present. But, it is claimed, Luke was not a close follower of Paul, as is evident from the ways in which he misunderstands and misrepresents his theology. A major element that is absent is Paul's theology of the union of the believer with Christ, expressed in such phrases as being "in Christ".[12] A well-known discussion by Philipp Vielhauer accuses Luke of fundamental misunderstanding of Paul in at least four areas: christology, natural theology, the law and eschatology. Luke did not understand Paul's theology and presented a theology that was both less developed and in contradiction to Paul's, and they are so unlike that the modern reader must make a choice between them.

So, it can be argued, Luke has smoothed out the differences between the other early Christians and Paul by writing an account that unhistorically assimilates the preaching and outlook of Paul to that of Peter by attributing to both a theology of his own that was not typical of either of them.

In response to these arguments we may reply, first, that the picture of the theology of the early church that we get in the first half of Acts is at the very least historically appropriate. That is to say, it agrees broadly with what we may deduce about the preaching and practice of the first Christians from evidence elsewhere in the New Testament, and it also makes sense historically that followers of the earthly Jesus who had experienced his resurrection and the commission to evangelize that was bound up with it and the gift of the Holy Spirit would have acted and preached in the kind of way that Luke describes.

Second, to some extent the differences between the Paul of Acts and the Paul of the letters arise because Luke is telling a story rather than writing letters. He is narrating an evangelistic mission rather than dealing with the upbuilding of congregations. It is not surprising that Luke is closest to Paul when he recounts Paul's talk to the congregational elders in Acts 20.

---

[12]See, for example, Eric Franklin, *Luke: Interpreter of Paul, Critic of Matthew* (Sheffield: JSOT Press, 1994), pp. 274-78.

Third, the differences between the two pictures of Paul must not be exaggerated. Vielhauer's arguments have been frequently discussed, and in my view there are telling objections to them.[13] At the very least it is surely blindingly obvious that Luke uses the theological language of Peter and Paul rather than of John or Hebrews.

Fourth, we have to recognize that Luke did not have the depth of theological insight possessed by Paul. There is no point at which he contradicts Paul, but equally he does not share Paul's profundity.

The crucial question, then, is whether the two theologies, those of Acts and of Paul, have essentially the same structure and content. Granted that there may be similarities between them, may it not be that the structures in which they are set differ from one another? Compare how it might be possible to draw up a list of common beliefs held by Roman Catholics and Protestants despite the fact that the two forms of Christianity are significantly different as a result of their overall structures and emphases being so different. Thus the understanding of the ministry and the sacraments is so different that the nature of the churches is fundamentally different. The concept of one man being the vicar of Christ on earth simply does not fit within a Protestant framework, and the place given to Mary and the saints, especially in the practice of the religion, is also violently at odds with the ethos of Protestantism. May there not be differences in structure and ethos between the two types of theology investigated in this chapter that have not surfaced in the comparison of individual theological themes?

Let us remind ourselves that in both cases we have a theology that is expressed in categories drawn from the Old Testament and making considerable use of scriptural citation and allusion. It presupposes the sinfulness of all people, Jews and Gentiles. It offers salvation from sin and judgment through the man Jesus Christ, who died and has been raised from the dead, thus confirming his status as Lord and Savior. The gift of salvation includes the gift of the Holy Spirit, who is the active agent both in personal Christian experience and in the charismatic enablement and guidance of the mission and ministry of the church. Salvation (justification) is by, and only by, faith in God and Jesus

---

[13]See F. F. Bruce, "Is the Paul of Acts the Real Paul?" *BJRL* 58 (1976): 282-305; Stanley E. Porter, *The Paul of Acts* (Tübingen: Mohr Siebeck, 1999).

Christ, and such faith is expressed in baptism, which incorporates believers in the fellowship of the people of God. This people of God is one with the historical people of God, Israel, and now consists of all who believe, whether circumcised Jews or uncircumcised Gentiles; in the past it was faith in God that was determinative (and not just belonging to the physical people of Israel), but now that God has sent the Messiah, it is a faith that acknowledges Jesus as the Messiah and risen Lord. This risen Lord is active in the church through the Spirit and is known to his people in a personal relationship, epitomized in the breaking of bread (Lord's Supper) and expressed in prayer. To the followers of Jesus is committed the task of evangelism to all peoples, Jews and Gentiles, and this is carried out especially, but not exclusively, by those specifically called out to be missionaries with the active support of the congregations. Their task and indeed their existence as believers is met by opposition, so that the believers generally must suffer as Jesus did, even to the point of martyrdom. Their way of life is determined by the teaching of Jesus and the guidance of the Spirit. They look forward to the resurrection of the dead of believers to everlasting life with Christ, and of unbelievers to judgment and loss.

This outline of Christian theology is common to Acts and to Paul. It is greatly elaborated by Paul, specifically in reference to the concept of sin and the flesh, the significance of the incarnation of the Son of God; the detailed understanding of the significance of his death, the whole understanding of the new relationship with him through faith, the ongoing transformation of the believer through the work of the Spirit in union with Christ, the nature of Christian existence as dying and living with Christ; the church as the body of Christ; final resurrection; the issues relating to Israel, the Gentiles and the law. There is a vast theological achievement here, but it is recognizably the same kind and shape of theology. Paul's theology is a statement of the same theology at a different level, but it is the same theology, just as a high Anglican liturgical service with its elaborate ritual and use of centuries of Christian language and music may have the same shape and content as a simple nonliturgical service that expresses an identical faith and experience in a different mode.

There are, then, distinct differences in emphasis and content, but there is a basic identity. In every case it makes sense of the evidence to see the theology of Paul as going further than and developing the theology in Acts. This simple observation makes it plausible that Luke has portrayed a theology that is less complex and developed than that of Paul. This is true even where Luke is describing Paul.[14]

## Bibliography

Barrett, C. K. "The Theology of Acts". In *Acts*. 2 vols. Edinburgh: T & T Clark, 1998, 2:lxxxii-cx.

Bock, Darrell L. *Proclamation from Prophecy and Pattern: Lucan Old Testament Christology*. Sheffield: JSOT Press, 1994.

Bruce, F. F. "Is the Paul of Acts the Real Paul?" *BJRL* 58 (1976): 282-305.

Dodd, C. H. *History and the Gospel*. London: Nisbet, 1938.

Franklin, Eric. *Luke: Interpreter of Paul, Critic of Matthew*. Sheffield: JSOT Press, 1994.

Marshall, I. Howard. "Luke's View of Paul". *Southwestern Journal of Theology* 33 (1990): 41-51.

Porter, Stanley E. *The Paul of Acts*. Tübingen: Mohr Siebeck, 1999, pp. 199-206.

Vielhauer, Philipp. "On the 'Paulinism' of Acts". In *Studies in Luke-Acts: Essays in Honor of Paul Schubert*. Edited by Leander E. Keck and J. Louis Martyn, pp. 33-50. Nashville: Abingdon; Philadelphia: Fortress, 1980.

---

[14]With one exception, the speeches of Paul in Acts are directed toward non-Christians. We should not be surprised if they do not display the kind of theology that Paul could share with believers.

# PART 4

## THE JOHANNINE
## LITERATURE

# 20

# THE GOSPEL OF JOHN

❧

John's Gospel stands apart from the first three in that it narrates a different set of events and teachings of Jesus from them. Although some of the events are the same and others are of a basically similar character, the general way in which they are discussed and the character of the theological argumentation are very different. This raises important and difficult questions about the relationship of the Jesus depicted by John to the picture that we gain from the first three Gospels and also about the way in which John has developed in such an independent and distinctive manner. At one extreme we have the view that Jesus was a multifaceted character who behaved and taught at times in what we might call a Synoptic manner and at times in a Johannine manner, so that what we have are two pictures which are equally closely based on the historical Jesus. At the opposite extreme is the view that John's picture is heavily fictional, Jesus being used as a vehicle for the author's theology, whose roots lie largely elsewhere.[1] Somewhere in between is the view that John has taken the historical traditions regarding Jesus and given them a novel transformation and development. What we have is the Jesus of the Synoptic Gospels translated into a different idiom.[2]

Our first task is to see what the author of the Gospel is saying theologically,

---

[1]This view is presented most extremely by Maurice Casey, *Is John's Gospel True?* (London: Routledge, 1996), who argues that John's Gospel is untrue, historically and theologically.

[2]For a critique of Casey see Craig L. Blomberg, *The Historical Reliability of John's Gospel* (Leicester: Apollos, 2001).

and as with the other New Testament books we begin by trying to trace the theological story.[3]

### The Prologue (Jn 1:1-18): The Theological Story

Beginnings are important. John begins his Gospel with a prologue (Jn 1:1-18) that more than those in the other Gospels combines theological explanation and events.

One event is the coming of John the Baptist, who acted as a witness to the light (Jn 1:6-7) and his identification of Jesus as the one to whom he had borne testimony that one would come after him who surpassed him (Jn 1:15). Sandwiched in the middle of these statements is a further event that takes place in history, namely, the Word becoming a human being and being seen by a group within which the author of the Gospel places himself (Jn 1:14). But these events are placed in the context of a theological statement by the author, whose principal points are:

First, in the beginning (which seems to mean "as far back as we can go in thought") there was a being with God called the Word who was God. This paradox is stated without explanation.

Second, this being was responsible for the creation of the universe.[4] He himself was the source of life and light for the universe, which would otherwise be a place of darkness. How the universe created by the Word should come to be in darkness is not explained. This is the mystery of evil.

Third, the light shines in the darkness, evidently bringing salvation and life to people. One way in which the light was manifested was through the testimony of John. He bore witness to the light that was to come into the world.

Fourth, the light was not generally recognized in the world, not even by his own people. This must be a reference to the Jewish people. But there were some who did recognize and accept the light, and they became God's children.[5] This

---

[3]Inevitably there will be some repetition here of material from I. Howard Marshall, "Johannine Theology", in Geoffrey W. Bromiley, ed., *The International Standard Bible Encyclopedia* (Grand Rapids: Eerdmans, 1982), 2:1081-91.

[4]Since God was the Creator in the thought of the time, it may be assumed that the Word acted as his agent. But the main thought may be that this activity placed the Word on a par with God.

[5]There is the clear implication that apart from this acceptance of the light, people are not God's children, even though they are created by the Word and even though they are Jews.

took place through a process akin to birth, which it is not in human power to bring about but depends upon a divine action.

At this point we have another paradox in that some people do believe and so become children of God, but this birth is brought about by God. One way of understanding this is to say that God responds to human faith by conferring the new birth on believers. This explanation does not explain why these particular people respond whereas others do not. Another way of understanding it is to say that God causes certain people to believe and so to come to new birth. This explanation does not explain why God causes certain people to believe and not others. The text clearly favors the former type of understanding rather than the other.

Fifth, the particular way in which the Word entered the world was by becoming "flesh", which in context means that he took on the form of a human being.

What is not immediately clear is whether this is a recapitulation and hence a making more precise of what has just been said about the Word being in the world or whether it is a new stage, with a spiritual presence of the Word in the world in John 1:10-13, followed by a physical presence in John 1:14. The decision is not easy, but on the whole the former interpretation makes better sense. John 1:10-13 reads much more like an interpretation of Christian response to Jesus than of anything that occurred in the pre-Christian era.[6]

Sixth, the author identifies himself and his community as the group who recognized him. Although he was a human being, nevertheless they saw beyond the mere humanity to a person who embodied the glory of God. At this point God is identified as the Father, and the Word is identified as his Son.

Seventh, the fullness of the blessings mediated through the Word is emphasized. It is not denied that God's grace was active in and through Moses as the giver of the law; but grace and truth are fully revealed in Jesus, to such an extent that Jesus as the only One, himself God, reveals God.[7]

What is the function of this prologue in relation to the Gospel? On a basic level it has introduced very many of the terms that the author uses to express his theology: *Word, God, life, light, darkness, testimony, believe, name, children/sons, birth,*

---

[6]This is confirmed by the probable futurity of Jn 1:9 and the contrast between the two eras inaugurated by Moses and Jesus Christ in Jn 1:17.

[7]It is only at this point that it becomes explicit that the Word became a human being as Jesus Christ. Up until this verse the author has been speaking about "the Word".

*flesh, glory, Father, grace,*[8] *truth, law, seeing.*[9] More significantly, it has set out the basic
story of salvation in brief fashion, anchoring what happens on the historical
plane in a metanarrative that sees things in terms of divine activity transcending
the universe and before its creation. Above all it is concerned with who Jesus is
and what he does, but it achieves this by a kind of inversion in which it takes
another figure, the Word, and explains Jesus as the incarnation of the Word.

An important question is why the term *Word* should be chosen for this purpose. The other Gospels begin rather with the identification of Jesus as the
Messiah, God's human agent who comes to establish God's kingdom on earth
and to announce its future consummation and calls people to repentance and
faith and discipleship. Yet at the outset they too are conscious that this figure
is more than a human being; he is the Son of God, and the change involved
in becoming disciples can be described as becoming like little children. John,
however, begins with the identification of Jesus as a divine being from outside
the world who comes to share his heavenly status and nature with human beings. But as the story develops he too has to deal with the inevitable question
from a Jewish perspective of whether Jesus is the Messiah, and with the call
of Jesus to discipleship. The ingredients are the same, but the blend is rather
different.

After the prologue Jesus is no longer referred to as "the Word". Yet he continues to fulfill the functions of the Word in that he reveals and communicates
life, light and glory, and makes the Father known, and he does this primarily
through his words.[10] Just as Jesus dispenses the bread of life and is that bread,
so too he speaks the words of God and thereby functions as the Word of God.

The prologue says nothing about the events that form the climax of the
story, the death and resurrection of Jesus. It may be that the death is in view in
John 1:5 where the darkness did not understand and rejected the light, but
nothing is said at this stage about the supreme function of the death and resurrection in bringing life to the world. But the prologue is a prologue, not a

---

[8]This term is not actually used outside the prologue (Jn 1:14, 16-17) but is in effect replaced by
"love".

[9]Some crucial terms are absent: *love* (included in grace); *Spirit/Paraclete; sin.* Jesus is not called "Son"
(except perhaps in Jn 1:18 according to one version of the text adopted by NRSV text; TNIV mg.),
but "only" by itself in Jn 1:14, 18 is equivalent to "only son".

[10]Robert H. Gundry, *Jesus the Word According to John the Sectarian* (Grand Rapids, Mich.: Eerdmans, 2002).

preview or précis of the whole story. What the rest of the story does is to describe more fully and with added detail what has been stated briefly in the prologue. From the beginning the reader knows the interpretation of the story, and the ongoing story will provide evidence that can only confirm that the interpretation that John has provided is the right interpretation. We may compare how in the Synoptic Gospels something very similar takes place.

### *Jesus and the Jews (Jn 1:19—12:50): The Theological Story*

*John's testimony to Jesus (Jn 1:19-51).* There is a sense in which the prologue is not a prologue. It is not separated from the rest of the story but flows straight into it. John the Baptist already appears as a character in it, and the focus on him in the first part of John 1:19-51 is simply a case of zooming in on him and developing more fully what he said in John1:15. Already at this point we face the tantalizing problem that John can move from what is said by a character in the story to his own further theological development without any clear signposts to indicate this to the reader.[11]

John 1:19-28 confirms that John the Baptist is not any recognizably messianic figure—which is the way in which Jews of the time would have posed the question. Whereas in the Synoptic Gospels it is God who at his baptism acknowledges Jesus as his Son with a mission to fulfill, in this Gospel it is the Baptist who points out Jesus as the one who fulfills his own prophecy on the basis of what happened when God acknowledged Jesus at his baptism. Thus the revelation of sonship is fundamental in all the Gospels. But, as we have seen, whereas the Synoptic Gospels develop this more in terms of the messianic mission of Jesus, in John the tendency is to develop it more in terms of the divine status of Jesus as the one who reveals light and life from God.

Even this statement, however, is in danger of overstressing the point, because here the significant way in which John testifies to Jesus is that he is the Lamb of God who takes away the sin of the world (Jn 1:29, 36). This is unexpected

---

[11]Jn 1:15/16-18 is a particularly clear example of such a transition, where the latter part can only be intended as Johannine comment, and this encourages us to recognize the same sort of silent transition elsewhere, although it may be hard to know where the break comes. Cf. the uncertainty of NRSV and TNIV as to whether the speech of Jesus starting at Jn 3:10 terminates at Jn 3:15 or Jn 3:21, and whether the speech of John starting at John 3:27 terminates at Jn 3:30 or Jn 3:36; in both cases the former option is preferred.

and yet it occupies center stage. "Lamb of God" is probably a messianic term, and "taking away sin" indicates that in some way Jesus takes away the guilt and penalty that await sinners.[12]

A second element in the mission of Jesus is that he will baptize with the Holy Spirit (Jn 1:33). Here is another element that was not present in the prologue, and as with the reference to the Lamb of God it comes unexpectedly and without elucidation. What baptism does is not explained, but clearly what John achieved by a rite involving a symbolic cleansing with water will be paralleled and achieved on a higher level by an action carried out with the Holy Spirit. If baptism signifies cleansing from sin, then Jesus will carry out the spiritual side of that which John's baptism with water only symbolized and will deliver people from sin. Thus the activities of Jesus as the Lamb and as the baptizer with the Spirit are complementary.

We should not overlook the note that Jesus was to be revealed in particular to Israel, that is, to "his own [people]" (Jn 1:11), although the universalistic note of taking away the sin of the world is also sounded. Israel, that is, the Jewish people, needs a Messiah.

The effect of John's testimony is that people do follow his pointer to Jesus. If they find that Jesus knows who they are and what they can become, equally they confess who he is, the Messiah, the coming one prophesied in Scripture, the Son of God, and the king of Israel. Again, somewhat surprisingly, the climax to the revelation is that Jesus is the One through whom communication with the heavenly world is established in his role as Son of Man (Jn 1:51). This is a new facet of the Son of Man, expressed in terms of the typology of Jacob's ladder.

*The old and the new (Jn 2:1-25).* In swift chronological succession (Jn 2:1) John gives the account of a wedding at which Jesus takes six stone jars filled with water for Jewish rites of purification and the contents are turned into wine in a manner to which the attendant servants and the disciples were privy but not apparently anybody else. This was the first of a series of signs, actions by Jesus that accomplished what is normally impossible to human beings, and as such they were indicators that God was working through him in the kind of

---

[12]The phrase may refer to the offering of a sacrifice that cancels out the effects of sin or to bearing the penalty of sin on behalf of others.

way associated with outstanding servants of God in past history. At the same time, the actions are all capable of bearing symbolical significance as they point to what God can accomplish on a spiritual level. Wine was the symbol of joyous celebration and its abundant provision points to the image of the kingdom of God as a banquet in which God's people eat and drink in his presence. A traditional symbol of salvation is thus employed to bring out the significance of what Jesus will achieve. There is the implication also that the old ways of Israel are being superseded. The disciples get at least part of the message, and the key word *believe* is used of their nascent attitude to Jesus.

Whereas the so-called cleansing of the temple takes place toward the end of the story in the Synoptic Gospels and acts as one of the main triggers of the hostile response of the authorities to Jesus, here it takes place at the outset. The incident is related in similar terms and constitutes a condemnation of the misuse of the temple for trade instead of its being a place where God the Father might be met. However, in a typical Johannine fashion the incident here leads on to a declaration by Jesus that if the temple were destroyed, he would rebuild it in three days. Again typically the audience misunderstand Jesus to be talking literally about physical destruction and miraculous reconstruction. John's comment is that Jesus was referring to his own body, and the significance of the remark was seen only in the light of the resurrection on the third day. The implication, which is not spelled out, is that Jesus will replace the temple as the place where the Father is revealed (cf. Jn 1:18), and it may not be going too far to see a further reference to the group of his disciples as the new temple in which this revelation through Jesus takes place.

One of the subplots running through the Gospel is concerned with faith or belief, and the final note in the chapter is that some people believed in him because of the miraculous signs that he did.[13] Such faith, however, was not sufficiently deep for Jesus to commit himself to them. We are at the beginning of the tension between the performance of signs, which are necessary in order to reveal the glory of God and which can nevertheless be the means of awakening a less than adequate response that is more that of amazement than of real conversion of the heart.

---

[13]These are not reported individually. Presumably John's readers were familiar with the broad outline of the story of Jesus and did not need to be told.

*The new birth and eternal life (Jn 3:1-36).* It is against the background of this comment that we have the story of Nicodemus, who makes such a response and is told that it is inadequate if there is not a birth from above. Again the goal is expressed in Jewish terms as entry into or seeing the kingdom of God, although this is soon transposed into experiencing eternal life (another traditionally Jewish category; cf. Mk 10:17/23). The misunderstanding of Nicodemus is the cue for Jesus to enlarge upon the nature of this new birth as a life-giving action that can be conferred only in a spiritual manner, that is, by the Holy Spirit, and cannot be manufactured in this world. Here we have the fundamental dualism between the world and the divine sphere (heaven), the sphere of darkness and that of light, the world of death and the world of life, the realm of evil and the realm of righteousness. Entry into the kingdom of God is the same as coming to life, so that a person while continuing to exist in this evil world is nevertheless now alive spiritually. An analogy might be a world in which people are physically blind and are conscious only of those things that they can perceive with their other senses, but some people gain physical sight and can now perceive and experience a whole host of wonderful things while still living in the same world.

Nicodemus is unable to comprehend what Jesus is driving at. The matter is therefore re-presented in a different manner. Instead of using the picture of new birth, Jesus speaks of the divine messenger who came down from heaven and who was "lifted up" to die so that those who believe in him might have eternal life. An enormous amount is packed into this statement, and it is difficult to see how a Nicodemus could have appreciated it all on the spot. The analogy of the snake recalls the Old Testament story of Moses erecting a brass serpent on a pole, and Israelites afflicted by a punitive plague were healed when they looked at it; it was thus a symbol for divine healing and removal of the deadly plague. Readers who knew that Jesus was crucified would spot the intended analogy and in view of other statements in the Gospel would know that somehow his being put to death had a healing effect spiritually in delivering them from death and giving them life, provided that they looked to Jesus and put their faith in him. The point is emphasized by repetition in John 3:16, giving a statement that sums up the gospel memorably. What follows makes it clear that the people who perish do so because they are committed to evil and therefore hate the light; it follows that although Jesus came as the light of the world, to save people, one effect of his coming is to condemn those whose evil nature is revealed in their refusal to believe in him.[14]

The remainder of the chapter clarifies the relation between John the Baptist and Jesus and indicates that the proper course for disciples of John is to believe in the One to whom John bore testimony. The superiority of Jesus lies in the fact that he came from heaven as the Son of God bearing the authoritative words of God and conferring life on believers (Jn 3:22-36).

*The Savior of the world (Jn 4:1-54).* The meeting of Jesus with a Samaritan woman serves a number of theological functions (Jn 4:1-42). First, it again presents Jesus as the giver of life, symbolized in this case by water. The contrast between ordinary water and spiritual water and between what the past can offer (Jacob) and what Jesus can give drives the conversation. Second, although Jesus recognizes the superiority of Judaism to Samaritanism, both are superseded in a new way of approaching God that takes place in the realm of the spirit and rests upon the new, true revelation of God in Jesus. Jesus is indeed the promised Messiah of Judaism and Samaritanism, but he transcends these religions and is in fact the Savior of all people.

The story of the healing of the royal official's son (Jn 4:43-54) is an example of the miraculous signs done by Jesus that he performs even though he is skeptical of a faith based purely upon such signs; it is clear that Jesus responds to human need despite this danger.

*The Father and the Son (Jn 5:1-47).* In the next story Jesus takes the initiative in healing a paralyzed man whom nobody else could help or had helped (Jn 5). The story combines two motifs: first, that the man's illness may have been related to his sinfulness, and the cure of the illness was not a cure for his sin; and, second, that the cure involved the breaking of the Jewish understanding of the sabbath commandment. This latter point becomes the occasion for the theological disquisition that ensues in which Jesus claims that he is doing only what his Father, God, does on the sabbath. The sabbath issue is soon forgotten, and the relationship of Jesus to God is thematized. Jesus claims to have the divine prerogatives of judging and conferring life, and these have been passed exclusively to him, so that even the dead may be raised by his voice (cf. Lazarus). But

---

[14]The function of the light is thus similar to that of the law in Paul's theology when it brings the sin that is in people's nature to expression in rebellious deeds (Rom 5:20).

his prerogatives do not go beyond what the Father permits; obedience characterizes the Son. In saying these things Jesus is in effect testifying to himself, but he insists that what really counts is the testimony of others, including John the Baptist, the Scriptures and God and the work that he has given Jesus to do.[15]

*The bread of life (Jn 6:1-71)*. Jesus continues to respond to people who have seen his mighty works by feeding a multitude of them in a miraculous way, so that the people concluded that he was the expected Prophet.[16] John also relates the story of Jesus walking on the sea but does not explicitly develop its significance. Rather he goes on to a lengthy dialogue in which the feeding miracle is made into a symbol or sign of spiritual food, contrasted with the manna that merely supported physical life although it was of divine origin. This spiritual bread is identified with Jesus; the gift of salvation is equated with the giver, since ultimately salvation is a personal relationship with the giver of life rather than something that can be handed over by him and then he withdraws, his task completed. It is given by the Father, and a distinction is made between the Father "giving" people to the Son and the Son welcoming them and conferring life upon them. At first sight this appears to suggest that a predestination is at work whose effects are seen in those who respond positively to Jesus, with the implication that those who do not respond or reject Jesus are those whom the Father did not give to him. That is to say, the mystery of why some respond and others do not is ascribed to a drawing action by the Father, an "effectual calling" to use the language of later theology. The point of the statement appears to be, first, to recognize that people can come to Jesus and yet not believe despite seeing the signs and hearing his words; second, to emphasize that if anybody comes to Jesus and seeks salvation, he or she is welcome because the Father and the Son are united in loving purpose; third, to make it clear that salvation results from God's initiative and deed and not from anything that people do; and fourth, to stress that believers can be certain that at the last day they will experience resurrection. The statement must be read in the context of the love of God for the world in John 3:16 and the statement in the present passage that "they will all be taught by God" (Jn 6:45), which would seem to forbid

---

[15]Presumably the "successful" performance of the mighty works and the conferring of life on believers are the testimony of the "work".

[16]Since they wanted to make him king, a prophet who functions as the Messiah must be meant.

the view that God's love is selective and reaches only to some people while passing by others. There is thus a tension in this passage and in the Gospel as a whole (cf. Jn 1:12) that must not be resolved one-sidedly.

In the final part of the chapter there is a development in the conversation as Jesus insists that for people to have life they must eat his flesh and drink his blood. It is impossible for readers of the Gospel not to see here an allusion to the symbolism of the Lord's Supper. Since Jesus rejects the flesh as counting for nothing and emphasizes that it is the Spirit who gives life, it follows that there may well be a warning against assuming that eating the bread and drinking the cup confer life, and a reminder that what Jesus is talking about is once again the relationship of belief to him, but this time using the imagery of eating and drinking. This would, of course, correspond with the use made of the imagery of drinking water in John 4.

*Who is Jesus (Jn 7:1—8:59)?* The use of water imagery continues in the next scene, at the Feast of Tabernacles. The earlier part of this scene is again concerned with the relation of Jesus to God and with his identity. As is typical of the Gospel, the discourse of Jesus moves rapidly from topic to topic and does not follow the sort of logic that some of us might expect to see. Thus Jesus deals again with the origin of his teaching (it comes from God and it glorifies God, not himself), the murderous intent of his opponents springing from Jesus' apparent breaking of the sabbath law, and his identity as the Messiah, which was disputable because people thought they knew his origin. (This is not clarified until we reach Jn 7:40-44.) What we learn now is that this opposition is going to take action against him but cannot do so yet because Jesus' "time" has not yet come. (There is thus a divine timetable that is being followed, and people are powerless to vary it.) This leads to the Johannine equivalent of a passion and resurrection prediction (Jn 7:33-36), but couched so obscurely that people cannot understand it. (There is an ironic interpretation that Jesus will leave Judea and go to be among the Greeks, which of course is also true spiritually.)

Then comes the promise of water given by Jesus, with the significant interpretation that this water is the Spirit who would be given to believers, but not at this point; it would have to wait for the glorification of Jesus. Here, then, we discover that eternal life = Jesus = the Holy Spirit.

If we omit, as we must, John 7:53—8:11, the conversation continues without a significant break in John 8. As in the earlier part, the logic of the discourse is not easy to follow, and all that can be done here is to pick up a number of themes that are fresh and/or significant. First, there is the express statement that Jesus is the light of the world (cf. Jn 1:9). This is the second of the statements in which Jesus declares that he is himself one of the symbols that express the giver of salvation or salvation itself. Common objects, which have a history as spiritual symbols, are used to express a spiritual claim that is exclusive to Jesus. They constitute an invitation to believe.

The affirmation is not directly followed up, and second, we have teaching that is somewhat repetitious of what has gone before. Again we have a dialogue about Jesus and the nature of the testimony that confirms who he is. It emerges that the questioners do not know the Father and belong to this world. Nevertheless, some of them do come to belief and accept the teaching of Jesus. Through their knowledge of this teaching, which is truth, they will become truly free (a key term that figures only in this brief section, Jn 8:32-36); the implication is that other people are slaves to sin and therefore will be excluded from the family of God, where only sons and daughters are permanent members. Being a Jew is thus not in itself an adequate qualification for eternal life; Abraham's children by descent are not Abraham's children in terms of family likeness. On the contrary, they are children of the devil who do not accept the truth but prefer lies, as is demonstrated by their rejection of Jesus. By contrast Abraham is said to have rejoiced at the thought of seeing the day of Jesus. From this statement it is deduced conversely that Jesus claims to have been a contemporary of Abraham, and he states that before Abraham was born "I am". This statement need mean no more(!) than that Jesus was in existence before Abraham (cf. Jn 1:15, 30; 12:41). However, here and elsewhere it may echo the self-identification of God, "I am (he)" (Deut 32:39; Is 41:4; 43:10, 13) and may be a claim to parity with God.

*Spiritual blindness (Jn 9:1-41).* This long scene is succeeded by the self-contained story of the healing of a blind man (Jn 9). It is emphasized that his blindness was not a punishment for sin by either the man or his parents; it is simply there and offers an occasion for display of God's power through Jesus. Although the sign might have been made the basis for a discussion of Jesus as the spiritual light of the world (Jn 9:4), this theme has already been adequately expounded, and the story continues with the way in which the healed man gradually comes to a recognition of Jesus as a man of God, a prophet and the Son of Man, whereas the Jewish authorities are obsessed with the fact that the healing was done on the sabbath and therefore constituted a sin. In the ejection of the man by the Pharisees we see foreshadowed the rejection of Jesus and his disciples. Spiritually the Pharisees are blind to what God is doing in Jesus and they are said to be guilty. This is because they should have been able to see but failed to do so.

*True and false shepherds (Jn 10:1-42).* We can regard John 10 as providing something of a commentary on what has just preceded, although it picks up a fresh set of images drawn from sheep and shepherding. On the one hand, Jesus is presented in a rather complex way as being the shepherd who truly cares for the sheep and who is also the gate by which they enter the sheepfold that typifies salvation and life. On the other hand, there are the "thieves and robbers" who destroy the sheep; it is clear that Jesus has in mind those who have failed in their duty to shepherd God's flock and specifically people like the Pharisees who have just been accused of blindness and inability to lead God's people. But the positive side of the imagery leads further. The sheepfold and the sheep stand loosely for the Jews, but Jesus speaks about other sheep who will come in and join the one flock; these must be the Gentiles. Jesus also affirms that the good shepherd lays down his life for the sheep in free obedience to the Father's will. How this benefits the sheep is not explained, but the thought at the very least is that he goes to the uttermost in self-sacrifice to care for the sheep and to give them life.

After the break in the middle of the chapter (Jn 10:21/22) there is a continuation of the conversation. The first point made is that the mighty works done by Jesus should make it plain that he is the Christ, but the people do not believe because they are not his sheep. In passing, the crucial point is made that those who are his sheep cannot be snatched out of the Father's hand; in its context this may be a promise to the disciples that, no matter how fierce the persecution against them (cf. Jn 12:10; 15:18—16:4), it is powerless to deprive them of their salvation. The second point is that Jesus tacitly accepts the accusation that he claims to be God ("the Word was God") but corrects it by stating that what he actually said that might be regarded as blasphemous was that he is God's Son, closely united with the Father. Finally, we hear of many people[17]

---

[17]As in the other Gospels, we are told that Jesus' signs and words affected many people positively. The mission should not be regarded as a failure.

across the Jordan who accept John's testimony, though it was not backed up with signs, and believe in Jesus.

*The raising of the dead (Jn 11:1-57).* The catalog of signs reaches its climax with an event that exceeds all the others in that it brings back to life a man who was indisputably dead and so brings glory to God through whom the man is raised from death. This event points clearly to the spiritual counterpart of raising people from spiritual death to eternal life, which necessarily includes their ultimate and permanent resurrection, unlike Lazarus, whose physical death was merely postponed for a time. The motif finds expression in the assertion that Jesus is the resurrection and the life, and this is understood correctly by Martha as part of what it means for Jesus to be the Christ, the Son of God.

The incident also forms the climax of the story so far in another sense, namely, that it is the event that finally leads the growing unbelief and hostility of the Jewish authorities into action against Jesus by resolving to put him to death. The reason given for doing so is self-seeking and mundane. If Jesus gains lots of followers, there will be an uprising that the Romans will put down by force, and the present Jewish rulers will be put out of office for having failed to prevent it. This could be interpreted as sensible politics (wise politicians know from experience that an uprising is the last thing the country needs since the Roman response will be overwhelming and cruel), but it is presented ironically here since if Jesus were truly from God, then presumably he could overcome any opposition. Be that as it may, the high priest suggests that it is cheaper for one man to be put out of the way by execution for the sake of the people than for the whole nation to suffer. Therein John sees an unintended prophecy that Jesus would die for the people, but not in the sense that Caiaphas imagined. This would indeed be the death of the shepherd for the sheep, both near and far.

*The end of the witness to the Jews (Jn 12:1-50).* The writing is on the wall, and one further chapter remains in which the curtain comes down on the evangelistic work of Jesus. It includes the story of the procession of Jesus into Jerusalem, accompanied by such a crowd that the leaders commented that "the whole world has gone after him" (Jn 12:19). Again the saying says more than the speakers intended, in that those seeking Jesus include some Greeks.

The motif is not taken further. Instead Jesus states that the hour appointed by the Father has now come. He must die, but his death will be like that of a seed that leads to new life. Similarly, his followers must be prepared to die in order to live. He explains his death by stating that it will have the twofold result of bringing about judgment upon the ruler of this world (i.e., the devil) and of drawing people to himself.

Then Jesus in effect closes his evangelism, and John comments on the unbelief of those who were unmoved by the signs and were blinded by God. It is evidently possible for people to go so far in rejection of the light that eventually God judges them by making it impossible for them to respond to it. And yet John again notes that even among the leaders there were the exceptions who did come to some kind of belief.

### Jesus and His Disciples (Jn 13—17): The Theological Story

*The Last Supper (Jn 13:1-30).* The attention of Jesus now shifts from the crowds and the Jewish leaders to those who were his own sheep, the small group of close disciples who represent the broader body of disciples and believers. At his last meal with them the central incident is the action of Jesus in washing their feet.[18] This is interpreted not only as a symbol of Jesus serving the disciples but as an example of how they are to serve one another in humility. The washing is purely of the feet and not of the whole body, which must suggest that those who have been washed in baptism still need (and only need) a minor washing to deal with the ongoing blemishes and sins that affect them. It is the Johannine equivalent of "forgive us our sins" in the daily repetition of the Lord's Prayer.

A second incident at the meal is the identification of the disciple who would betray Jesus, despite sharing with him in the fellowship of the meal and having shared in the foot washing. John would no doubt remind us that the flesh profits nothing; it is the Spirit that conveys life. The mystery of how Judas is the victim of Satan and how this relates to God's purpose is not taken up here (but note Jn 17:12).

*Farewell teaching (Jn 13:31—17:26).* Jesus turns immediately to the fact of his death and speaks of it in terms of the Son of Man being glorified (Jn 13:31-32; cf. Jn 12:23). For John the crucifixion is part of the glorification; it is not a case of suffering followed by glorification, death followed by resurrection, but of the Son of Man being "lifted up" and glorified in the cross, and thereby glorifying God.

---

[18]The symbolism with the bread and the cup that is central in the Synoptic accounts is conspicuously omitted. John has already given an equivalent to it in the sayings of Jesus in Jn 6.

So Jesus will no longer be with the disciples, a statement that opens up a new part of the Gospel, in which Jesus deals with the time when he will no longer be physically with his disciples.

Remarkably briefly the disciples are told that they must from now onward love one another, and this will be their distinguishing mark in the world. The point is, however, repeated in John 15:9-17, where obedience to this command is the condition for remaining in the love of Jesus. The disciples are Jesus' friends insofar as they obey his commands, including principally this one. This may seem to clash with the spontaneity and undeservedness of the divine love for humanity.[19] However, Jesus assumes that this obedience arises out of love, just as his love for the Father issues in obedience (Jn 14:31). The point is emphasized by repetition (Jn 14:15, 21, 23-24).

But the main theme is the departure of Jesus (Jn 14:1-31). Various themes intermingle as Jesus deals with the new situation. In a sense the departure of Jesus is necessary because he is going ahead of the disciples to prepare their future abode. (In what way he prepares it is not discussed.) If so, his work would be incomplete if he did not return to take them there. (The doctrine of the parousia or second coming of Jesus is thus justified.) At the same time, it can be said that the disciples already know the way to the place where Jesus is going. That place is with the Father, and he is the way, in that to know him is to know the Father. The thoughts of knowing and being with the Father spiritually here and now through Jesus and of going to be with the Father in heaven intermingle. Jesus can now speak even more plainly to the disciples about his closeness to the Father, and the language of mutual dwelling or being in each other is all the more prominent. The disciples are presented as still needing to learn, even though they have faith, and asking questions to which Jesus thinks that they ought already to have the answers. But these are enquiring rather than hostile questions, and they act as pegs on which Jesus' teaching can hang. So there is repetition of earlier material, but there is also new teaching. Thus statements about belief on the basis of the works[20] done by Jesus move forward into statements that the disciples will do even greater works than these because the Fa-

---

[19]There is a similar tension in Paul between justification by faith and yet the need for the justified to fulfill the law of Christ.

[20]In Jn 14:11 and Jn 15:24 NIV has "miracles" for Gk. *erga;* this is corrected to "works" in TNIV.

ther will answer the prayers of the disciples offered in the name of Jesus.

A fresh element is the promise of "another Paraclete" to be with the disciples. The promise of the coming of the Holy Spirit has already been made, and we have learned that the Spirit is intimately involved in the communication of salvation to believers, so much so that the Spirit can be said to be the gift of salvation. What is new here is the role of the Spirit, who takes on the task of Jesus as "another" Paraclete. This term is used of Jesus in 1 John 2:1, where it describes his role in relation to the Father on behalf of believers. Here, however, the sense is more of help to the believers and the term *Counselor* may convey this. He appears to act as guide and companion to the disciples (Jn 14:16-17). The immediately following statement is that Jesus will not leave the disciples but will come to them. The implication appears to be that it is through the agency of the Paraclete that Jesus makes himself present. Again, when the disciples no longer have Jesus to teach them, it is the Paraclete who teaches them and reminds them of the teaching of Jesus (Jn 14:25-26). A third passage indicates that the Paraclete will testify about Jesus, and the disciples who have been with Jesus from the beginning must also testify. Probably the Paraclete is envisaged as testifying through the disciples, just as was promised with regard to the Spirit in the Synoptic Gospels (Jn 15:26-27). This is confirmed in the fourth passage (Jn 16:7-11), where the Paraclete comes to the disciples, and then his task is described as convicting the world about sin, righteousness and judgment, which means that through the disciples the Spirit tries to get the world to understand the truth about sin (the world is guilty of sin because it rejects Jesus), about righteousness (the way of Jesus is vindicated and shown to be righteous by his going to the Father who accepts him), and about judgment (judgment is a reality because in the cross and resurrection of Jesus the ruler of this world has been shown to be powerless and stands condemned). It follows, fifth, that in all this the Spirit glorifies Jesus by continuing his work and pointing people to him (Jn 16:13-15).

A further factor in the scene is the hostility of the world to the disciples (Jn 15:18—16:15). Not only are they alone in that Jesus is no longer physically with them, but also they are alone in the world in the midst of enemies. They are hated, just as Jesus was. This can be interpreted positively as a sign that they do not belong to the world. All this happens because the world did not recognize Jesus or know the One who sent him, despite the words and works of

Jesus.[21] And if the world sought to kill Jesus, the disciples can expect the same treatment.

Over against this hostility the disciples are encouraged to remain in close union with Jesus (Jn 15:1-17). In the last of the symbolic sayings Jesus likens himself to a vine supplying nourishment to its branches so that they will bear fruit, the sign of life.[22] But again there is a conditional element, in that branches that do not remain in union with the vine itself will be cut off and burned.[23] Jesus then expounds what remaining in the vine means in terms of obedience to his commandments out of love for him.

Finally, the disciples revert to the actual departure of Jesus and specifically to the fact that it will be for "a little while" (Jn 16:16-18). When we first read about Jesus going away and coming back (Jn 14:1-3) it was natural to think in terms of the parousia. Now, however, there is a shift, and the present theme seems to be the return of Jesus after his resurrection. The whole of John 16:19-24 refers to the situation of the disciples once Jesus has left them. The difficulty arises because Jesus does not make plain that after his return he will again depart.

The lengthy discourse ends with encouragement as Jesus contemplates the victory that he has in effect already won over the world and its hostility. Then Jesus moves over into the longest prayer in the New Testament (Jn 17), in which again a fascinating interplay of themes occurs. Part of the prayer is concerned with Jesus and his imminent glorification, but much the major part of it is about the disciples. The purpose of Jesus' coming was to give eternal life, which consists in knowledge of God and Jesus. This work is now complete in his mind's eye, Jesus having taught the disciples what they need to know. He therefore prays primarily for them as they have to continue in the hostility of the world that God will protect them from it and that they will be sanctified by the

---

[21]Jn 15:24 appears to suggest that people who have not seen or heard Jesus are not guilty of sin. The sin must be that of rejecting Jesus; it cannot be meant that they were sinless in other respects.

[22]Probably the reference in the metaphor of fruit is a quite general one to the expression of the divine life in the disciples rather than being specific to converts won by their witness, but not excluding the latter.

[23]This stands in apparent tension with the saying that nobody will snatch the sheep out of the Shepherd's care. There seems to be a contrast between assuring the disciples who want to enjoy eternal life that nobody can come in and deprive them of it and warning disciples who disobey Christ that they may cut themselves off from him.

truth contained in the words they are taught. *Sanctified* suggests that they are set apart to serve God, but also that they are kept pure from the sins of the world. By the disciples' living a life like that of Jesus and loving one another, the world may come to believe that Jesus is indeed God's agent. Here at last we have in unambiguous terms the commission of the disciples to be missionaries in the world, with the result that some will believe through their message.

### The Death and Resurrection of Jesus (Jn 18—21): The Theological Story

*Trial and crucifixion (Jn 18:1—19:42).* The interlude between the decision of the Sanhedrin to do away with Jesus and its accomplishment is now over, and the rest of the story describes the arrest, trials and death of Jesus. The arrest scene is notable for taking up the Synoptic language of Jesus' fate as the "cup" that the Father has given him (Jn 18:11); from its Old Testament background the cup signifies suffering of the kind God laid upon sinful peoples as a judgment upon their sin (cf. Mk 10:38). In the light of the guideline established by John the Baptist's saying, the thought that Jesus suffers death on behalf of the sinful world is appropriate here.

Paradoxically in the same context we again have the ambiguous formula used by Jesus, "I am (he)", which emphasizes that he is not only the principal agent of God but also in some way himself to be identified with God. It is in this role that Jesus, the obedient Son, takes the cup.

The trial before Pilate occupies the principal place in the Johannine story, and it centers on the two themes of kingship and truth. Kingship of the Jews is a messianic category, but it is quickly transmuted on to a higher level as Jesus speaks not in terms of politics but of truth. Pilate represents a world that does not understand what truth is or is perhaps unconcerned about it. Nor of course does he understand that he really has no power over Jesus unless God allows it to him. Nor, again, do he and the other participants realize that it is they who are implicitly on trial.[24]

The account of the actual execution of Jesus emphasizes that what happens is not simply what human beings wanted to do with Jesus. The decision that Jesus suffers as "the king of the Jews" is taken out of the hands of the Jewish

---

[24] Andrew T. Lincoln, *Truth on Trial: The Lawsuit Motif in the Fourth Gospel* (Peabody, Mass.: Hendrickson, 2000).

leaders. The distribution of the clothes of Jesus, the cry of Jesus, "I am thirsty" and the piercing of the side of Jesus all take place in fulfillment of Scripture.[25] The Scriptures cited are also important in that like the others earlier in the Gospel, they show how Jesus fulfills patterns and prophecies concerning the Messiah.[26]

*Empty tomb and resurrection appearances (Jn 20—21).* But it is not the end of the story. There is no public glorification of Jesus after his death and burial, but there is an empty tomb discovered by the disciples, out of which the body has vanished, and then there is a series of appearances that would repay more attention than can be given to them here. Suffice it to make the following comments. First, the fact of the resurrection is hard to accept, and there is doubt and lack of recognition, but the disciples do believe. Second, the promise of "peace" given by Jesus (Jn 14:27; 16:33) is fulfilled. Third, the disciples are granted the Holy Spirit and the commission to forgive sins, with the comment that if they do not forgive sins, they are not forgiven (Jn 20:22-23).[27] It is significant that we are again reminded of John the Baptist's programmatic statement. Ultimately this Gospel, like the rest of the New Testament, is concerned with sin, sacrifice on behalf of others and forgiveness of sins. It is the Johannine equivalent of the Great Commission. It has to be read in the light of the Paraclete sayings. Fourth, the comment to Thomas should not be misunderstood. Jesus is not disparaging those who have seen him and believed. He is drawing a contrast between the time of his earthly mission and the time when he is physically absent, when it will be in a sense more difficult for people to believe.

The last chapter looks like an addition after the climactic statement in John 20:30-31, which establishes that the aim of the Gospel is to bring people to a faith in Jesus that will confer eternal life on them.[28] It reinforces the fact that

---

[25]The participants are like unskillful chess players who may not realize that the moves that they think of as being the result of their own decision are in fact forced upon them by their opponents who have put then in a situation where they cannot do anything else.

[26]This is something of an oversimplification, but it is the direction in which John is pointing.

[27]Can this mean that if the disciples fail to proclaim forgiveness, there is no other source of it?

[28]The manuscripts of this saying vary between "may believe" (aorist aspect) and "may believe" (present aspect), which may make a contrast between "starting to believe" and "going on believing"; John's purpose is then either evangelistic directed toward unbelievers or edificatory directed to existing believers, depending on which reading is adopted. This tendency to adopt one interpretation of the purpose of the Gospel or the other is to be resisted; the Gospel is plainly intended to fulfill both purposes and contains material intended for both groups of people. It could not be otherwise.

the disciples have a commission from Jesus. Note how throughout the postresurrection story he is now known as "the Lord" (cf. Jn 13:12-17). There is a three-line whip on Peter to make sure that he gets the message: sheep must be taken care of, and you must do it. Nor does it matter what happens to the disciples. Not only excommunication from society had been prophesied, but also murder. Even though that may be their fate, they are still to remain disciples and glorify God by their death, as by their life.

### Theological Themes

From the analysis of the theological story it is evident that the theology of John, although expressed with a remarkably simple vocabulary and with considerable repetition of the basic motifs, is nonetheless highly complex and weaves together many strands of thought.

*The framework of thought.* Throughout the Gospel there is a palpable background in the Old Testament and Judaism, where most of the ideas expressed are at home or can be seen as providing the source of the thought. Yet, although the framework of thought appears to be fundamentally Jewish, the Gospel would also have been comprehensible to people of a more Hellenistic outlook.

The basic Jewish contrast between the two ages, this age and the age to come, is taken over, but it tends to be eclipsed by a dualism of the world and God. In Jewish thought the present world is thought of as evil and the world to come is the realm of righteousness that will succeed it, but there was always some recognition that God was already active in this world. Hence the distinction between present and future was not a sharp boundary. Since God was recognized as eternally present in heaven, there was a further impetus to recognizing the distinction as being not only between present and future but also between below and above.

This type of understanding was developed even further in second-century Gnosticism according to which the present world was not the creation of God but was fundamentally evil, although some traces of God's working were present in it. The dualism is accordingly one of evil-goodness. A light-darkness dualism appropriately conveys the character of the two realms. Even more fundamental is the dualism between death and life. All this constitutes a situation in which human beings need redemption. John, however, does not reflect Gnosticism: for him the world is the creation of God and the Word. One can accept dualism of this kind without becoming a Gnostic.

*The main theme.* The main theme of the theology in the Gospel is undoubt-edly the presentation of Jesus as the Messiah and Son of God who came into the world to bear witness to the truth and to give his life so that all people might have the opportunity of receiving eternal life through faith in him.

*Jesus, his role and status.* The Gospel is primarily concerned with the interac-tion between Jesus and Judaism, particularly as represented by the Jewish lead-ers, the priests and the Pharisees.[29] The main interest lies in Jesus and his role and status.

Two concepts describe his role in general terms. First, he is the agent of God on earth. The verb *send* expresses the fundamental relationship between God and Jesus in the world. The Jewish concept of the *shaliach* who has the authority of the sender comes into play, to emphasize that Jesus is the authorized agent of God, to whom significant functions are delegated (Jn 3:17; 4:34; 5:23-24, 36; 6:29, 38-39; 10:36; 11:42; 17:3). Similarly, the Holy Spirit is sent by the Father and Jesus (Jn 14:26; 15:26). The same motif of being sent also forms the pattern for the relationship of the disciples to Jesus (Jn 9:4; 13:20; 17:18; 20:21).[30]

Implicit in this theology of sending is the concept of God as the one whose will and purpose is to save the world. As elsewhere in the New Testament, the will of God that is carried out by Jesus (Jn 4:34; 5:30; 6:38-40) has already been established in the Scriptures, which testify to it (Jn 6:45; 7:38, 42; 12:14-16; 20:9).

Thus the Gospel is about a mission and a missionary who is sent by God into the world with a task to fulfill. That task is to act as the light and to offer people eternal life. So, second, Jesus can also be understood as the founder of salvation. He is not to be understood primarily as the Revealer (so Rudolf Bultmann) or as a mythological divine figure (so Ernst Käsemann)[31] but rather as the counterpart to Moses (cf. Jn 1:17) who establishes the new com-

---

[29]When John refers, as he frequently does, to "the Jews" collectively, he appears to have the leaders mainly in mind. He is not guilty of an anti-Semitism (better "anti-Judaism"), which condemns the Jewish people out of hand as if they had collectively rejected Jesus; on the contrary the story shows that Jesus was accepted positively by many of the people, including some of the leaders.

[30]John the Baptist is also sent by God (Jn 1:33). See especially Andreas J. Köstenberger, *The Missions of Jesus and the Disciples According to the Fourth Gospel* (Grand Rapids, Mich.: Eerdmans, 1998).

[31]Ernst Käsemann, *The Testament of Jesus: A Study of the Gospel of John in the Light of Chapter 17* (Philadelphia: Fortress; London: SCM Press, 1968).

munity, bestows salvation on its members and gives it its rule for life.[32]

These rather general descriptions of the role of Jesus are made more precise in terms of messiahship, according to which Jesus is the prophet and king who will bring about God's salvation for his people. John is the only book in the New Testament to use the Semitic term *messiah* (Jn 1:41), which it straightway translates as "Christ", and then uses the latter consistently (except in Jn 4:25). The question whether Jesus is the Christ arises in John 4:29 and continues to be a matter of controversy in discussions among the people and with Jesus (Jn 7:25-44; cf. Jn 10:24). The purpose of the Gospel is that people may come to believe with Martha (Jn 11:27) that Jesus is the Christ (Jn 20:31; cf. Jn 17:3). The question whether Jesus is the Christ thus becomes a matter for open discussion with the people in this Gospel by contrast with the secrecy surrounding it in the other Gospels until it becomes an issue at his trial.

Side by side with this is the role of Jesus as prophet.[33] On a comparatively lowly level Jesus is a person with supernatural knowledge (Jn 4:19) and power (Jn 9:17), but at a higher level he is seen as the final prophet (cf. Jn 1:21) who was expected to come to the world (Jn 6:14; 7:40). When he is recognized as such by the people, they want to make him king (Jn 6:15). Jesus refuses to be that kind of king, but his status as king is recognized by Nathanael (Jn 1:49) and the welcome to him as king on his entry to Jerusalem is endorsed by the narrator (Jn 12:13-15). It becomes a major theme in the trial before Pilate, where Jesus' kingship is distinguished from human kingship and put on a higher plane. Nevertheless, despite the earlier willingness to make him king, the crucifixion marks the rejection of Jesus as king.

The concept of the shepherd is very closely related to this, since the role of the king was understood to be the shepherd of his people. It is confined to the parabolic material in John 10 but is also presupposed in the references to the role of Peter after the departure of Jesus (Jn 21:15-17).

The term "Son of Man" also belongs to this circle of ideas shared with

---

[32]This phrase (Ger. *Stifter*) was taken up by Klaus Haacker, *Die Stiftung des Heils: Untersuchungen zur Struktur der johanneischen Theologie* (Stuttgart: Calver, 1972), to epitomize the role of Jesus.

[33]The terms "chosen one" (Jn 1:34) and "holy one" (Jn 6:69) also belong here.

the Synoptic Gospels, but the Johannine use goes beyond it. In John the Son of Man is a figure who must be "lifted up" in crucifixion (Jn 3:14; 12:34) but who will also take part in judgment (Jn 5:27). But beyond this he is a figure who has come down from heaven (to which he will return) and who is the agent of revelation (Jn 1:51; 3:13; 6:62). He is the giver of salvation (Jn 6:27) and is identified with salvation (Jn 6:53) in that he is the dispenser of the bread of life and people must eat his flesh in order to have life. The once-blind man is urged to believe in the Son of Man (Jn 9:35).[34] What is note-worthy here is the wider use of the term and the way in which salvation is particularly associated with the Son of Man (as in Lk 19:10). Finally, the term "lifted up" seems to encompass resurrection and exaltation as well as crucifixion, and the events of the passion constitute a glorification of the Son of Man (Jn 3:14; 12:23, 34; 13:31). These statements about the Son of Man go beyond what is said about the Messiah and raise the question as to the precise significance of the term itself as a designation of Jesus. Clearly the designation is taken over from tradition, in which the term was used not only for the role of Jesus as future judge and king but also for his earthly role. But its usage in John suggests that it has come to stand for God's representative and messenger who brings salvation.

Many of the things said about Jesus as Son of Man—his coming from heaven and his return thither—could equally well, or perhaps even more aptly, be said about him as the Son of God. We have seen that already in the Synoptic Gospels Jesus has a unique relationship to God, expressed in his repeated references to God as his Father and in his use of the imagery of sonship. This relationship goes beyond the metaphor found in the Old Testament, where God cares for the king as a father does for his son, and is much more expressive of a personal relationship with God into which Jesus also initiates his disciples. In John this relationship comes to the fore, and the implications for the status or nature of Jesus and for the under-standing of God are brought into the open. Whereas in the other Gospels, Acts and Paul, the term *God* occurs proportionately more often than the term *Father*, in John the proportion is decisively reversed, and the major term for God is *Father*, which is used very frequently of the relationship of God

---

[34]It is not surprising that scribes altered this to "Son of God".

to Jesus.[35] (But 1—3 John follow the usual pattern elsewhere in the New Testament.) The usage is almost exclusively on the lips of Jesus, who speaks of "the Father" and "my Father"; once he speaks to his disciples of "your Father" (Jn 20:17)[36] but never of "our Father". The trend that may be seen in Matthew is here carried very much further. Since Jesus speaks frequently about his relationship to *God*, the frequent usage of *Father* is readily explained. By contrast, the narrator and other actors in the story tend to refer to *God*. The result is that the imagery of fatherhood is powerfully stamped upon the relationship of God to Jesus and to the disciples.

"Son of God" is a confessional term, and it is the purpose of the Gospel to bring readers to share in that confession (Jn 1:49; 20:31), which is a matter of faith and commitment (Jn 3:18, 36; 6:40; 11:27) and honor (Jn 5:23). The Son was in the bosom of the Father (Jn 1:18).[37] He was sent by the Father to the world (Jn 3:17). He describes himself as being loved by the Father (Jn 5:20), and he has authority conferred by the Father to exercise judgment and to give life. Yet this does not make him independent of the Father, and at all times he follows and obeys the Father's will (Jn 5:19). Although he is the judge (Jn 5:22; cf. Jn 9:39), nevertheless he came to save the world and to confer life (Jn 3:17; 5:21, 26). Those who believe in him receive life (Jn 6:40).

As Son of God, Jesus can be regarded as "God" (Jn 20:28), intimate with God's plans and as close to him as almost a second self, so much so that to see and hear Jesus is tantamount to seeing and hearing the Father (Jn 14:9). Yet this does not mean that there are two gods; Jesus refers to the Father as the only true God (Jn 17:3; cf. Jn 5:44).

There is no place for any other being occupying such a position in relation to the Father. The adjective *only* (Jn 1:14, 18; 3:16, 18) emphasizes this and stresses his role as the only Revealer and Savior. Nevertheless, the Son opens up

---

[35]The statistics are impressive. "God" and "Father" are used as follows:

|  | Mt | Mk | Lk | Acts | Jn | 1-3 Jn | Paul |
|---|---|---|---|---|---|---|---|
| God | 51 | 48 | 122 | 166 | 83 | 67 | 548 |
| Father (of God) | 44 | 4 | 17 | 3 | 127 | 15 | 43 |

[36]But Jn 8:42 denies that the speakers are really children of the Father.

[37]It is preferable to take this phrase of the situation from which the Son came, but it is also possible to take it metaphorically of the Son being in close contact with the Father while on earth so that he always knows the mind of the Father.

to human beings the possibility of becoming children of God (Jn 1:12), and the language of mutual indwelling that is used of the relation of Father and Son is extended to believers in relation to God the Father and Jesus.

The use of the concept of the *Word* as the key term that introduces the Gospel may seem less happy to modern readers than the more personal term *Son*, but it has the important advantage that, whereas the term *Son* in itself need imply nothing more than the relationship of Jesus to the Father, *Word* expresses his role as the means of divine communication with the world. The Gospel is fundamentally concerned with the role of Jesus as the light through whom the invisible God and his grace are made known (Jn 1:18; cf. Jn 5:37; 6:46). What God says is his Word, and this Word in the last analysis is Jesus. Although, therefore, the term *Word* is not used of Jesus after the prologue, nevertheless, he acts as the Word throughout the remainder of the Gospel. But more than this, John directly identifies the Word as God (Jn 1:1), and this statement is confirmed by the testimony of Thomas (Jn 20:28).

In a number of statements Jesus uses the phrase "I am [he]" (Jn 4:26; 6:20; 8:24, 28, 58; 13:19; 18:5-6). By itself this may be nothing more than a self-identification ("Who's there?" "It's me", where the characteristic voice may be sufficient of an identification of the speaker's identity). But the phrase is used in the Old Testament by God to identify himself as God, and some of the usages in John seem to require that Jesus is echoing this way of speaking and thereby speaking in the place of God (Jn 8:24, 28; 13:19; 18:5-6). On one occasion Jesus declares that he existed before Abraham (Jn 8:58). Statements about his coming down from heaven (Jn 3:13, 31-32) and having seen the Father (Jn 6:46) similarly testify to his existence before coming into this world and to a knowledge of the Father gained before he came into the world.

There is less stress on the fact that the person of whom all this is said is at the same time a human being. Even so, John contains one of the clearest New Testament statements of incarnation: the Word became "flesh", that is, human (Jn 1:14). To some interpreters Jesus has seemed to be simply a divine, heavenly figure in human guise, like a Greek god or goddess metamorphosing into a human form in outward appearance but not really becoming a human being. Yet, for John this is manifestly not the case with Jesus, who has human experiences, including death. One needs to ask, however, whether it is theologically significant for John that Jesus is human, or whether he simply takes over—certainly, without question—that Jesus was a human being. The statement of Pilate, "Here is the man" (Jn 19:5), may suggest that John did see significance in the humanity of Jesus.

*Humanity in its need.* Jesus is, then, the prophet who speaks on behalf of God to the Jewish people, who should already have been prepared for his coming by the Scriptures and the temple. Simply belonging to the Jewish people is not a means of salvation if that does not lead to acceptance of the Messiah (Jn 8:31-41). The people should have recognized Jesus, thanks to the witness borne to him by the Scriptures (Jn 5:39), by John the Baptist (Jn 1:6-8, 19-36; 3:26-30; 5:33), by other people (Jn 4:39; 12:17; 19:35; cf. Jn 21:24) and by his own mighty works (Jn 5:36; 10:25),[38] but nevertheless for the most part they failed to do so.[39] A central theme, therefore, is the refusal of the people, especially their leaders, to recognize Jesus as the messenger of God. Other themes also play a role in their attitude, such as their preservation of a rigid attitude toward what is permissible on the sabbath: Jesus does not behave as a godly person is expected to do according to their ideas (Jn 9:16).

The attitude of the Jewish people by and large is placed in a larger context as their conduct is portrayed as typical of that of the world and as being shaped by it. Although John recognizes the special position of the Jews in the purpose of God and the fact that the mission of Jesus was focused upon them, nevertheless the basic concern is with the world as a whole. The world is essentially the arena of human life and the people in it, with the emphasis falling sometimes on the one aspect and sometimes on the other. It is the creation of God, but it is nevertheless characterized by sin, falsehood, bondage and darkness (Jn 1:5; 3:19; 8:34; 12:46). It is ruled by a "prince" who is fundamentally opposed to God (Jn 12:31; 14:30). There is a dualism expressed in various pairs of contrasts, including some that are cosmological ("above" and "below", Jn 8:23; cf. Jn 3:31; 19:11), but others that are moral and spiritual (light and darkness, Jn 1:4-5; 3:19-21; 8:12; 9:4-5; 11:9-10; 12:35-36, 46), truth and falsehood (Jn 8:44; cf. Jn 4:6), freedom and slavery (Jn 8:31-36), and life and death (Jn 5:24). The world is a place or community of ignorance where people do not know God (Jn

---

[38]The witness of the Father (Jn 5:37; 8:18) may be the Father's working through these various means rather than some independent event.

[39]After the departure of Jesus the task of witness is continued by the Spirit of truth and the disciples (Jn 15:26-27).

1:10; 16:3; 17:25) and reject the light (Jn 3:19). They stand self-condemned (Jn 3:17-19; 8:15; 12:47-48), under judgment from God. The judgment is in the future (Jn 5:24, 29; 12:48), but it can also be regarded as having taken place already (Jn 3:18; 16:11); it places the world under God's wrath (Jn 3:36), and the sentence pronounced is death (Jn 8:24).

Another way of putting this human situation is by reference to the concept of glory. This word combines the nuances of praise and worship offered to God, and the splendor manifested by God in virtue of his greatness in power and in love, and of his being the recipient of such worship. The sin and failure of human beings lies in the fact that they seek praise from one another instead of from God (Jn 5:44; 12:43), by contrast with Jesus who does not seek praise and honor for himself but speaks and works so as to bring honor to God (Jn 7:18; 8:50, 54). Jesus is glorified in that his self-sacrifice on the cross is the kind of action that demonstrates his character and that is recognized and approved by God (Jn 7:39; 12:16, 23; 13:31), and at the same time it brings honor to God (Jn 17:1). So the raising of Lazarus leads to the glorification of Jesus in that people recognize the power of God working through him to bring life and praise God for it (Jn 11:4), and similarly God is glorified when the disciples bear fruit (Jn 15:8) or offer themselves in sacrifice (Jn 21:19). Thus, although glory can refer to the splendor enjoyed by the Son with God before the creation of the world (Jn 17:5), the more usual reference is to the recognition of character and conduct that leads people to praise God for it. It is the failure of human beings to recognize the goodness of God and to acknowledge him that constitutes their sin. It is all part of loving darkness rather than light (Jn 3:19).

Nevertheless, the light of God shines in the darkness bringing knowledge of him and salvation (Jn 1:1-9). Already in the Scriptures the way to life was revealed (Jn 5:39), but this life comes through Jesus, whose function is to bring light and who can therefore be identified as the light (Jn 9:5; 12:46). The world is the scene of the Son's mission, and he comes to bring light to those in darkness (Jn 8:12), life to the dead, and salvation to the perishing. The effect of his coming is twofold. To those who respond to him he gives salvation (Jn 8:12). But there are others who reject the revelation (Jn 3:19-21), and they are guilty and come under judgment because the coming of the light has exposed and brought to expression their fundamental rejection of God (Jn 12:37-50).

*The Savior.* For John Jesus functions in two related ways.

First, he is the Word of God, communicating the message of God to the world. His task is revelation. The content of the revelation is truth, a term that links together concepts of trustworthiness and reliability (Jn 3:33) but also of ultimate reality (Jn 6:55; 17:3). The world into which Jesus came was characterized by error and untruth (Jn 8:44), but whatever Jesus says is true (Jn 8:40), so that he can be said to be the truth (Jn 14:6) and to bear witness to the truth (Jn 18:37). Similarly, the Spirit is the Spirit of truth who guides people into the truth (Jn 16:13). Thus the message can be identified simply as the truth (Jn 17:17) because it is the expression of what is real and true. Truth is closely linked to grace (Jn 1:14) and to righteousness (Jn 3:21).

At the same time, various statements by Jesus (Jn 10:11-18) and by others (John the Baptist, Caiaphas) convey that he was also to die for the world (Jn 1:29, 36; 11:50-2). The purpose of Jesus is expressed in traditional terms as the removal of the sin of the world (Jn 1:29). The language of sacrifice is used in that Jesus is seen as the Lamb of God and his actual death is also understood as like the death of an animal sacrifice (Jn 19:36) and the drinking of the cup given by God (Jn 18:11). More broadly, his death is seen as being for the benefit of others, and he sees his flesh which he gives for the life of the world as symbolized by bread (Jn 6:51-58). Still more broadly his lifting up on the cross becomes the means whereby he overcomes Satan (Jn 12:31) and draws all people to himself (Jn 12:32).[40]

Although the terminology is not used by John, the concept of reconciliation is thus highly apt for describing what Jesus does.[41] Nevertheless, it has often been argued that it is the revelatory function of Jesus as the Word that is the key concept for John, so that Jesus saves people by bringing them the light of the knowledge of God, and the redemptive or sacrificial language is not much more than a vestige of tradition that John has incorporated in his theology without it being of decisive significance. However, the strong emphasis in the Gospel upon sin as something of which people are guilty, particularly when they sin against the light, rules out this either-or type of interpretation of the

---

[40]There have been repeated attempts to deny the central and sacrificial character of the death of Jesus in this Gospel, but they can be confidently rejected; see Max Turner, "Atonement and the Death of Jesus in John: Some Questions to Bultmann and Forestell", *EQ* 62 (1990): 99-122.

[41]Although the term *peace* is used, it conveys the sense of freedom from anxiety and not of the removal of hostility (Jn 14:27; 16:33; 20:19, 21, 26).

Gospel. Moreover, the sacrificial interpretation of his death is front-loaded in the Gospel and sets the context for the interpretation of the remainder.

Jesus, then, does function to bring light (Jn 8:12), but the light is a revelation that has a content (truth, Jn 14:6). The view of Bultmann that in effect Jesus reveals nothing more than that he is the revealer is superficially plausible but breaks down on closer inspection.[42] For Jesus is not simply the Revealer; he is also the Messiah, with a role that was well understood by the Jews from their traditions and their Scriptures. And again, he is not simply the Revealer; he is also the one who conveys eternal life to those who believe in him. A Savior (Jn 4:42) is more than a prophet or revealer.

*Salvation.* The nature of salvation naturally corresponds with the description of human need. The most comprehensive term in John for what Jesus gives to people is *life* or *eternal life,* which is to be understood as sharing in the life of God (Jn 1:4). It is eternal, in that those who receive it shall never perish (Jn 3:16; 6:27; 10:28). The metaphor of birth from God (Jn 1:13) or being born again (Jn 3:3, 5) conveys the fact that people are without life until they receive the divine gift. Such life is defined as knowing God and Jesus Christ (Jn 17:3), language that suggests something akin to a personal relationship. At its deepest it is thus life in relationship with God, in which the love that God has for the world becomes a reality in human experience, and there is a response of love to him. It follows that this is a fuller life than the world can offer (Jn 10:10).

It is also an incorporation into the life of God. God the Father (Jn 14:23; 17:21), Jesus (Jn 14:20, 23; 17:21, 23, 26) and the Holy Spirit (Jn 7:39; 14:17) are all said to come into believers and reciprocal language is used, so that believers are in God. The imagery of eating bread and drinking water is used to express the spiritual satisfaction of human desires that comes about through this union with Jesus. This life is everlasting and not broken by physical death (Jn 5:21-29; 6:40, 51, 54, 58). Thus there is an anticipation of the future resurrection in the present new life of believers. Whereas in Judaism eternal life tended to be thought of as a future, otherworldly experience, here it is regarded as a present possession (Jn 3:36; 5:24; 6:47; 11:25-26). It is sustained by Jesus, who is said to offer the life-giving water (Jn 4:10-14; cf. Jn 7:38) and himself

---

[42]Bultmann, 2:66.

to be the bread of life (Jn 6:27-36).

How is salvation received? There are two aspects to this, divine and human.

Salvation is entirely due to God's initiative. This is seen not only in the sending of the Savior but also in the drawing of people to him so that they may believe. Although Jesus has come into the world as the giver of eternal life, nevertheless nobody can come to him except the Father draws them (Jn 6:44; cf. Jn 6:37, 65; 8:47; 10:29; 15:16, 19; 17:2, 6). The purpose of these statements is to indicate that from start to finish salvation is the gift of God. How the Father draws people to Jesus is not explained. It might be thought that this takes place through the agency of the Spirit, in which case it could be proposed that the birth from the Spirit (Jn 3:1-8) is the process through which faith is engendered in people. But John does not make that connection. In any case, it is clear that people are not intended to sit and do nothing and wait until they feel constrained to come to Jesus. On the contrary, Jesus appeals to people to come to him, and the offer of salvation is to all (Jn 3:16-17; 6:45; 12:32; cf. 1 Jn 2:2). And it is to those who believe that God gives the right to become his children (Jn 1:12-13), so that the new birth appears to be dependent upon faith (so also in Jn 7:38-39). To be sure, when people hear the offer and respond to it, this is the evidence that the new birth has taken place.

Alongside God's calling, then, there is the need for the human response to the gospel. The basic relationship with Jesus is belief, or faith (Jn 3:16-18), which involves total commitment to him. There is a contrast drawn between believing what Jesus says (Jn 6:69; 8:24; 11:26-27, 42) and making a commitment on the basis of his word (Jn 1:12; 2:11, 23; 3:16, 18, 36). John's usage makes it clear that faith is not only the intellectual acceptance of the message but also a total commitment of the person to Jesus and to God (faith is usually linked to Jesus but also to God, Jn 5:24; 14:1). Similarly, phrases like "coming to Jesus" and "following Jesus" can be used to express the same reality (Jn 6:35; 8:12). Such an attitude is receptive of what Jesus has done; the denial that people can do certain things in order to be saved is less of an issue than it is in Paul, but the point is made (Jn 6:28-29). It appears to be possible for there to be a level of faith that is no more than accepting that Jesus has come from God and falls short of commitment to him (Jn 2:23-25; 12:42-43). Manifestly, faith is more than a single act but becomes a continuing relationship. To express this attitude John uses the term *remain* (Jn 6:56;

15:4-10) to refer to an active holding on to Jesus and his teaching (Jn 8:31). But he also uses the same term for the way in which he and his teaching remain in believers (Jn 5:38; 15:4-7); the Spirit also remains in them (Jn 14:17). The same thought is expressed simply by using the preposition *in*. Just as the Father is in the Son (Jn 14:11; 17:21, 23) so the Son is in the Father (Jn 14:11, 20; 17:21); and this sets the pattern for believers. They are in the Son (Jn 14:20; 17:21), and he is in them (Jn 14:20, 23; 17:23, 26); equally they are in the Father (Jn 17:21), and he is in them (Jn 14:23). There is the danger that believers may fall away under persecution (Jn 16:1), but there is also the repeated promise that Jesus will preserve his people and raise them up at the last day (Jn 6:39-40, 44, 54; 10:28-29; 17:11-12).

*The relationships of believers.* Believers are drawn into a relationship with God that is similar to that between the Father and the Son. The Father and the Son know each other (Jn 10:15), and so believers know the Father (Jn 8:19; 14:7; 17:3) and the Son (Jn 10:14b) and are known by the Son (Jn 10:14a); in fact, eternal life can be defined as knowing the Father and the Son (Jn 17:3).

Similarly, believers know the Spirit (Jn 14:17). In John the Holy Spirit plays a much greater role in the lives of believers than in the Synoptic Gospels, so that John reflects much more fully the actual place of experience of the Spirit in the early church. Thus the gift of eternal life, symbolized by living water, is identified with the Spirit given to those who believe in Jesus (Jn 7:37-38). The use of the term *Paraclete* is unique to John (Jn 14:16, 26; 15:26; 16:7); as a personal term it brings out more clearly the personal nature of the Spirit by comparison with some of the usage elsewhere, which may suggest that the Spirit is little more than a divine force or influence. John provides a solid basis for the understanding of God as a Trinity of divine persons in communion with one another and all related to believers; nevertheless the personhood of the Spirit is much more inferential than is the case with the Father and the Son, whose names primarily express the existence of relationships. Yet since God is spirit in nature, there is no obstacle to understanding the Spirit in personal terms.

Love is a much-used concept in John to describe the relationships between God and Jesus (Jn 3:35; 5:20; 17:23-26), and between God and Jesus and believers (Jn 13:1, 34; 14:21; 15:9; 21:15-17), and between believers and one another (Jn 13:34-35; 15:12, 17). As a mutual relationship it clearly does not apply to the relationship of believers to unbelievers; nevertheless there can be the one-sided relationship in which God loves the sinful world (Jn 3:16), and Jesus and his followers are sent out in mission to the world (Jn 20:21-23). Love for Jesus is expressed in keeping his commandments (Jn 14:15, 21; 15:10). The precept of Jesus for his disciples after he has departed from them is that they should love one another, and this will be the sign to the world that they are disciples (Jn 13:34-35; 15:12-13). They have a mission to the world, just as Jesus did (Jn 20:21), and their task is to bear fruit, which is a metaphor that probably includes the winning of converts. Jesus prays for those who will believe through their activity (Jn 17:9, 20).

Although John does not use the word *church*, the concept of mutual love is indicative of an organic unity binding believers to God and to one another. Further, the believers are thought of as members of the flock of God under the good Shepherd, imagery that indicates not merely that they belong together but that they belong to the Israel of God, even though they are not Jews by birth (Jn 10:16; 11:52; 12:20-22). Similarly, they are branches of the vine, which is also a symbol for Israel (Jn 15:1-8). As God's people they are sanctified, a term that refers to being set apart and dedicated to God's service (cf. Jn 10:36; 17:19 of Jesus) but also includes moral transformation even while they remain in the sinful world in which the evil one is operative (Jn 17:15-19).

Pastoral care, doubtless including teaching, is indicated in the command to Peter to feed the flock (Jn 21:15-17). The outward practices of baptism and the Lord's Supper are implied. Jesus is said to have baptized with water, as John did (Jn 4:1-2), and baptismal imagery is used in John 13:1-17. Although the Lord's Supper is not described, eucharistic language is employed in John 6:51-58 in a way that most probably indicates the spiritual significance of what happened in the church meeting. The true worship of God that Jesus looks forward to (Jn 4:21-24) is not confined to the traditional holy places of the Jews and the Samaritans but is possible anywhere.

*History and eschatology.* John is aware of the past history of Israel, with Abraham and Moses both figuring in his story. He knows that the Jews claim to be the people of God, who have the Scriptures, and the dialogue of Jesus is conducted primarily and almost exclusively with them. Jesus and salvation are seen as the fulfillment of the Old Testament promises (Jn 1:46; 5:39, 46-47; 6:45). The rejection of Jesus and the events associated with his passion and crucifixion are seen as fulfillment of prophecy (Jn 2:17, 22; 12:14-16, 37-41; 13:18; 15:25; 17:12; 19:24, 28, 36-37; 20:9). There is thus a concentration of allusion to Scripture in the latter part of the Gospel.

Like Matthew and Mark, John has written a Gospel, and nothing that corresponds to Acts. Yet like them he writes from the perspective of a time that has seen the rise of the church and the creation of Christian communities. The history of the church is expressed through the teaching of Jesus, which looks forward to the mission of the disciples and the opposition of the Jewish authorities. Human life will end in physical death, sometimes as the result of this opposition, but it is transcended by the belief in resurrection. The belief that there will be a coming of Jesus remains as a horizon to human history. He will come to take his people to himself (Jn 14:3; cf. Jn 17:24), and there will be a last day with a resurrection of all to face judgment, issuing in life for believers and condemnation for others (Jn 5:25-29; 6:39-40, 44, 54; 11:24; 12:48). But, just as in the rest of the New Testament, this future hope is not the content of salvation to the exclusion of present experience. Jesus already comes to his disciples through the Holy Spirit (Jn 14:18, 23). For John the emphasis is on the present experience of eternal life in communion with God, a life that will find its consummation in the heavenly world; the formula "the hour is coming and now is" brings out the "already-not yet" tension that is characteristic of New Testament Christianity (Jn 4:23; 5:25; 16:32).

It has been argued that the eschatology in John is unique in the New Testament in that salvation is fully realized in the present time rather than being a limited anticipation of what is to come in the future or being held in balance with the future expectation. Rather, that which is to come but not yet manifested is fully realized in the here and now for believers.[43] This representation of John's teaching does not fit the facts; disciples live in this world, exposed to the dangers of persecution and death and needing to be preserved from succumbing to temptation; the world and its desires will indeed pass away (cf. 1 Jn 2:17), but they have not yet done so.

---

[43]Hahn, 1:702-16. It is not surprising that while Hahn holds on firmly to the future dimension in John's theology, nevertheless he has to follow Bultmann in regarding some phrases as later glosses on the text.

## Conclusion

If we attempt to sum up the theology of this Gospel in the same kind of way as we did earlier for the individual Synoptic Gospels, we can offer the following observations.

The framework of thought is shaped by the Old Testament and Jewish background that we found in the other Gospels but also by a sharper dualism between God and the world, light and darkness, and truth and error, righteousness and sin.

The main theme of the Gospel is to present Jesus as the Messiah and Son of God who came into the world to reveal the truth and to die so that all people might have the opportunity to receive life through believing in him.

Significant themes developed in detail include

1. The situation of the world, including the Jewish people, is characterized by darkness and the absence of eternal life despite the fact that the Scriptures bear witness to the Messiah as the source of life.

2. Jesus came to reveal the truth by knowledge of which people are set free from bondage to sin. Even more than in the other Gospels he depicted the character of God as Father.

3. Jesus is presented unequivocally as the incarnate Word, through whom God created the world and communicates with it, and more personally as his Son who was with the Father before he came into the world and will return to him. His place within the divine identity is clearly depicted. This christology is also expressed in terms of his being Messiah and Son of Man. Jesus acts as God's messenger and his mission establishes the possibility of salvation. In so doing he brings glory to God.

4. Jesus gathered disciples, but the language of believing in him is used more than in the other Gospels. Various symbolical sayings that identify Jesus as the bread of life and so on indicate that he is the giver of salvation and the gift itself; in other words, eternal life is not so much an abstract thing as a living relationship with Jesus. There is consequently a much richer development of what the relationship will be between believers and himself when he is no longer physically present; this is expressed as a mutual indwelling, similar to that be-

tween the Father and the Son and between the Father and believers. The Holy Spirit, whose role is described in terms of a Paraclete, is instrumental in the creation and sustaining of the disciples. The new community thus created will be characterized by mutual love,

5. The Gospel looks forward to the bringing in of other sheep, typified by the response of the Samaritan converts and some Greeks. Jesus is the one way to life.

6. There is great stress on the new commandment of love and the need for believers to live together in love so that the world may believe. Although love for people in the world by the disciples is not stressed, the fact that God loved the world is doubtless intended to be exemplary to them.

7. Although this Gospel makes more of the way in which the whole life of Jesus reveals God and knowledge of the truth brings freedom, nevertheless the death of Jesus who takes away the sin of the world is clearly identified as the key element in his career, and far more is said about faith than about knowledge as the way to eternal life. Knowledge of God is the content of eternal life rather than the way to it.

8. While the Gospel is mainly concerned with the eternal life experienced by believers here and now, the fact of future judgment carried out by the Son of Man sets the need to respond to the gospel and receive eternal life in its ultimate context.

Our survey of the Gospel has shown us an account of Jesus that brings out the kind of spiritual significance that he has for the Evangelist's contemporaries within the horizon of his earthly life. This emerges through the teaching given by the writer but also in the teaching given by Jesus in which he speaks of the relationships between himself and believers in a mixture of the present and the future tense. The experience of following Jesus is recounted in terms of belief in the exalted Lord. And, however the earthly Jesus may have spoken of himself and understood himself, in this Gospel he speaks as one who is fully conscious of his relationship with the Father stretching back before his entry into the world. He also speaks much more openly about his relationship with God and about the Holy Spirit than was the case in the other Gospels. All of this raises questions regarding the nature of the Evangelist's theology in comparison with that of the Synoptic Evangelists and of other early Christian writers to which we must return after we have surveyed the rest of the Johannine literature.

## Bibliography

*New Testament Theologies:* (English) Bultmann, 2:1-92; Conzelmann, pp. 321-90; Ladd, pp. 247-344; Goppelt, 2:289-305; Morris, pp. 223-86; Strecker, pp. 455-515. (German) Gnilka, pp. 226-324; Hübner, 3:152-205; Stuhlmacher, 2:199-286.

Ashton, John. *Understanding the Fourth Gospel.* Oxford: Oxford University Press, 1991.

Barrett, C. K. *The Gospel According to St. John.* 2nd ed. London: SPCK, 1978.

Beasley-Murray, George Raymond. *Gospel of Life: Theology in the Fourth Gospel.* Peabody, Mass.: Hendrickson, 1991.

Blomberg, Craig L. *The Historical Reliability of John's Gospel.* Leicester: Apollos, 2001.

Brown, Raymond E. *The Gospel According to John.* 2 vols. Garden City, N.Y.: Doubleday, 1966, 1970.

Burge, Gary M. *The Anointed Community: The Holy Spirit in the Johannine Tradition.* Grand Rapids, Mich.: Eerdmans, 1987.

————. *Interpreting the Gospel of John.* Grand Rapids, Mich.: Baker, 1992.

Carson, D. A. *Divine Sovereignty and Human Responsibility: Biblical Perspectives in Tension.* Atlanta: John Knox; London: Marshall, Morgan & Scott, 1981.

————. *The Gospel According to John.* Leicester: Inter-Varsity Press; Grand Rapids, Mich.: Eerdmans, 1981.

Casey, Maurice. *Is John's Gospel True?* London: Routledge, 1996.

Dodd, C. H. *The Interpretation of the Fourth Gospel.* Cambridge: Cambridge University Press, 1954.

Forestell, J. Terence. *The Word of the Cross: Salvation as Revelation in the Fourth Gospel.* London: Pontifical Biblical Institute, 1974.

Gundry, Robert H. *Jesus the Word According to John the Sectarian.* Grand Rapids, Mich.: Eerdmans, 2002.

Köstenberger, Andreas J. *The Missions of Jesus and the Disciples According to the Fourth Gospel.* Grand Rapids, Mich.: Eerdmans, 1998.

Lincoln, Andrew T. *Truth on Trial: The Lawsuit Motif in the Fourth Gospel.* Peabody, Mass.: Hendrickson, 2000.

Lindars, Barnabas *John.* Sheffield: Sheffield Academic Press, 1990. Reprinted in Culpepper, R. A., et al., *The Johannine Literature,* Sheffield: Sheffield Academic Press, 2000.

Motyer, Stephen. *Your Father the Devil? A New Approach to John and "the Jews".* Carlisle: Paternoster, 1997.

Painter, John. *John: Witness and Theologian.* London: SPCK, 1975.

Pryor, John W. *John: Evangelist of the Covenant People.* Downers Grove, Ill.: InterVarsity Press, 1992.

Schnackenburg, Rudolf. *The Gospel According to St. John.* 4 vols. London: Burns Oates, 1968-1982.

Smalley, Stephen S. *John: Evangelist and Interpreter.* 2nd ed. Carlisle: Paternoster, 1998.

Smith, D. Moody. *The Theology of the Gospel of John.* Cambridge: Cambridge University Press, 1995.

Turner, Max. "Atonement and the Death of Jesus in John: Some Questions to Bultmann and Forestell". *EQ* 62 (1990): 99-122.

# 21

# THE LETTERS OF JOHN

⌒∘⌒

The New Testament contains two very short letters sent by a writer who does not reveal his name but refers to himself simply as "the elder" (2-3 Jn) and a third, longer document (1 Jn) whose style and content indicate that it is most probably by the same author.[1]

## Third John

The letter known as 3 John is one of the few New Testament letters addressed to an individual Christian rather than to a community.[2] The specific occasion for the letter is apparently twofold.

First, the letter is probably conveyed by visitors to the elder who brought news about his friend Gaius. These visitors were traveling teachers and evangelists who did not want to claim hospitality from non-Christians. Gaius was singled out for special praise because of his generous hospitality to these people, although some of them at least were strangers to him.

Second, a certain Diotrephes is pictured as attempting to secure or maintain

---

[1]The common authorship of the three letters is sometimes disputed, but in any case they belong so closely together as to form a unity for the present discussion. Whether or not these documents are by the same author as the Gospel of John, with which they have a close affinity, is a much more disputed point. Although the current tendency is to deny common authorship, the case for one author is stronger in my view; cf. Martin Hengel, *The Johannine Question* (London: SCM Press; Philadelphia: Trinity Press International, 1989), pp. 176-77.

[2]The writer, presumably an older man, speaks of Gaius as a beloved friend and implicitly as his "child", which may be no more than a term of affection but probably also implies some kind of spiritual care for him. When Paul uses the term, he is probably thinking of people whose spiritual father he was in that he brought them to Christian faith.

a position of leadership in the church and being animated by rivalry against the elder and traveling Christians who belonged to his group. He is presented as a bad example and contrasted with Demetrius, who is universally respected.

Within this simple framework the basic elements in the theology of the writer come to expression.

He is very concerned about "the truth" (3 Jn 1, 3, 4, 8, 12). The truth is evidently the Christian message, as it is understood by the elder, with its implications for belief and behavior. Christians are to be faithful to the truth and to live (lit., "walk") by it. It is almost personified when Christians are encouraged to be fellow workers with it, and when it is said to testify to the goodness of Demetrius.

The elder is also concerned about love (3 Jn 6), which is clearly the practical expression of living by the truth. This love is to be shown to fellow Christians, and the showing of it is a form of conduct that is appropriate for and therefore demanded of those who serve God.

A sharp distinction is drawn between those who do good and those who do evil; the former belong to God and the latter do not. The latter are said not to have seen God.

Finally, Christian missionaries are said to travel "for the sake of the Name", which must be the name of Christ, although Christ is not named anywhere in this brief letter.

It emerges from this survey that the elder wants Christians to persevere in loyalty to the truth contained in the gospel and in the practice of love to one another, and he makes a sharp distinction between those who do so and those who do not. There is also a distinction between those who are believers and the people to whom they go as evangelists. What is important, then, is the way in which the content of Christianity is referred to simply as "the truth"; this expresses a self-consciousness on the part of the elder that his version of the faith is authentic over against other versions that may be corrupt in one way or another.

### Second John

In his other short letter, 2 John, these same accents reappear and in some ways become more specific. The occasion of the letter again appears to be the movements of Christian travelers who visit the elder, and he employs them to send a letter of general pastoral concern to the group to which they belong.[3]

Again there is the emphasis on the truth (2 Jn 1, 2, 3, 4). The personification is continued as it is said to remain in Christians. They for their part live in it. The elder refers to people who are deceivers and thus do not hold to the truth in that they do not confess that Jesus Christ is coming in the flesh, and they are condemned in the strongest terms as deceivers and being "antichrists". They are not to be received into the Christian fellowship. The readers may be enticed by their teaching and are warned not to listen to them in case they themselves fail to remain in the teaching of Christ. Only those who hold to this teaching have God and also have Jesus, that is, have a positive relationship with them. To reject Christ, as he is perceived by the elder, is to lose one's relationship with God.

Alongside the stress on truth we also find the same emphasis on love between those who know the truth. From the beginning God's command has been one of mutual love, and therefore there is nothing novel about insisting on it. The elder appears to distinguish between God's command (singular), which is to love (2 Jn 5, 6b; cf. 1 Jn 2:7-8; 3:23; 4:21), and his commands (plural), obedience to which is the substance of loving (2 Jn 6a; cf. 1 Jn 2:3-4; 3:22, 24). In brief, God's command is to love, and loving is carrying out his commands, which are presumably the specific commands of God understood as different facets of the showing of love.

This detail fills out the basic structure of truth and love that we found in 3 John. The significant new item is the identification of the error that indicates that people are not in a right relationship with God, namely, the refusal to acknowledge Jesus Christ as coming in the flesh. It is unfortunate that so important a belief is expressed in a rather unclear manner.[4] The problem is the tense. A perfect or aorist participle would probably give a reference to the earthly, human life of Jesus as having really taken place. But the participle is imperfect.[5] It could be in effect future ("who is going to come in the flesh"); if so, we would

---

[3]It is a moot point whether the "lady" who is addressed with her children is an actual person (an older view that is again enjoying some popularity) or is a metaphor for a Christian congregation with its members. Either way, the letter is addressed to a group of Christian believers, but it would be pleasant to think that at least one New Testament writing was addressed to a specifically female recipient.

[4]Presumably it was clear enough to the original readers.

[5]I use this term rather than "present" to emphasize that the participle conveys aspect and not tense.

then have a reference to a future human coming of Jesus that is not paralleled elsewhere in the New Testament; the future coming *(parousia)* of Jesus is firmly enough attested, but there is not the present stress on his coming in the flesh; indeed according to Paul he will have a spiritual body. So this can hardly be the meaning.[6] From the evidence of 1 John we can only conclude that despite the puzzle of the participle, the elder is referring to the life of the earthly Jesus. He lays such stress on this that he must be reacting against some other view that was being promulgated. But is he concerned simply with what we might call orthodoxy, the holding of some particular form of words that enshrines a doctrinal truth that is thought to be vital? Or is his concern not rather that in some way those who deny it are in fact denying that Jesus is in a meaningful sense the person through whom people can have a positive relationship with God that leads in the end to life with him?

### First John: The Theological Story

The two short letters by themselves do not take us to a well-grounded answer to these questions, and to go further we must now turn to the so-called first letter.[7]

If ever a document in the New Testament defied analysis to yield a clear structure, it is probably this letter, which appears to go over the same ground repeatedly with interesting variations and to consist of short sections that are intelligible in themselves but are loosely connected to one another. We can summarize the theological argument as follows.

The opening paragraph (1 Jn 1:1-4) announces the purpose of the letter in very general terms. The writer claims that he and his colleagues have had personal experience of the Word that conveys eternal life; the very concrete

---

[6]Nevertheless, it is taken up and defended by Georg Strecker, *Theology of the New Testament* (Berlin: de Gruyter; Louisville, Ky.: Westminster John Knox, 2000), pp. 425-28, who thinks that the elder shares a belief found elsewhere in a temporary messianic kingdom inaugurated by the second coming of Christ in the flesh.

[7]This document is anonymous in that it does not name its author within the text. There is nothing strange about this—we know the identity of most authors from statements outside the actual text (such as a title page or preface) or sometimes from knowing who the person was who delivered the speech that we now have in written form. The original hearers of what may have been a sermon or the recipients of a tract knew who was the author. Nor are the recipients named, but this probably means that it was to be read by any Christian believers into whose hands it came. It can be assumed that originally it was meant for readers in specific congregations or a specific area.

language used suggests that he is thinking of the way in which the original followers of Jesus experienced a concrete manifestation of the Word in him. This implicit identification of Jesus as the incarnate Word is presented all the more clearly in John 1:1-18.[8] The writer's aim is to proclaim this life so that the readers may have "fellowship" with "us" and thus share in their fellowship with God the Father and with the Son. This would appear at first sight to be an evangelistic aim, the sharing of the message that offers life with those who are not yet in a positive relationship with God. Nevertheless, the letter seems to be addressed more to those who are already Christian believers with the aim of helping them to persist in their faith, to develop further in it and to avoid being led astray by people with wrong teachings and a sub-Christian way of life.[9]

The letter begins with a declaration that God is light and there is no darkness in him. Light is symbolic of truth, purity, goodness and revelation, whereas darkness is suggestive of ignorance and evil. This basic distinction runs through the letter. People who do evil—the writer uses the traditional term *sin*—are in the darkness, no matter whether they claim to be in the light and in a positive relationship, here called fellowship, with God. Then in a paradoxical way we learn that all of us are sinners (therefore in the darkness) but by confession of sin, admitting that we are doing or have done wrong, we can be forgiven by God and be purified and so come into the realm of light. The paradox is that we are

---

[8]There is ambiguity in the present passage between "that which was from the beginning" (a neuter pronoun in Gk.), "the Word of life" and "the life" that appeared. The writer is struggling with the difficult task of talking about Jesus, who is the Word and the life, and also about the proclaimed word, with which in a sense he is identical.

[9]The existence of a group of people, at least some of whom had left the congregation(s) addressed, who fell short of John's understanding of Christianity in belief and behavior is a fixed point in interpretation of 1 John and 2 John. Greater precision is difficult to achieve. The author writes to encourage his readers not to be disheartened by the opposition (cf. 1 Jn 4:4-6) and to keep them on the right road. Attempts to explain the nature of the opposition in detail, for example by suggesting that misinterpretation of the previously written Fourth Gospel (Raymond E. Brown, *The Epistles of John* [Garden City, N.Y.: Doubleday, 1982]) lay at the root of the problem, or that there were two different parties in the church (Stephen S. Smalley, *1, 2, 3 John* [Waco, Tex.: Word, 1984]), have not commanded wide support. In my view it is most probable that we have to do with some people who were unable to believe that Jesus was truly the Messiah and Son of God come in human form, who attached considerable importance to Spirit-inspired utterances in the congregational meetings, and whose standard of Christian love within the community was low; it may be that these three characteristics were found in one and the same group of people, but this is not certain.

living in the light, although apparently we go on sinning and are continually in need of cleansing. The writer's purpose is to help to bring it about that his readers do not sin. But even if he does not succeed, there is forgiveness for the sins they do commit. And this forgiveness is through "the blood of Jesus", an expression that encapsulates his death and its effects. Put otherwise, Jesus in his death is a means of canceling sins without limit, and so he can be further represented as an advocate or counsel for the defense who pleads with God to forgive on the basis that sin has been dealt with by his act of sacrifice (1 Jn 1:5—2:2).

In a second stage, instead of writing about having fellowship with God the author writes about knowing God (1 Jn 2:3-11). People who know God keep his commands or his word, and to do so is to live in the same way as Jesus did. At this point in the letter the writer is thinking principally of the command to love and its subcommands. Since the content of the commands is love, obedience to them means that God's love is expressed perfectly in obedient people. In a sense this is a new event, since although the command is an old one, it is now being fulfilled in a new way, so that the darkness is being more and more dissipated through the shining of the light. The light must somehow be tantamount here to the fresh revelation of God's word through Jesus, and people who live in the light are those who receive this revelation and live by it.[10] As in 2 John the love is to be shown to fellow believers.

A short interlude sums up some of this teaching by describing Christian believers as those who know God and have overcome the evil one (so the darkness has a personal character to it, expressed by using the language of the devil or Satan), and they have the Word of God in them. This conveys something more than knowledge and is a power of some kind that helps them to conquer evil, although it obviously does not exclude the need for their own effort (1 Jn 2:12-14).

The need for effort emerges in the next section, which warns against loving the world, which is here the state of people who live in darkness, instead of God. There is a stark choice between a way of life that leads ultimately to destruction and one that leads to everlasting life with God (1 Jn 2:15-17).

---

[10]Evidently knowing the revelation and living by it are or should be inseparable; only those who live in love have really received the revelation.

Part of the problem for the readers is that in the period leading up to the end of the world evil is particularly rampant, and out of the church have proceeded many people who are opposed to Christ and the truth. Now we move focus from love to truth. Sharp lines are drawn between the readers who know the truth because they have been anointed by God and the liars who deny that Jesus is the Christ and the Son of God and thereby deny God also. The writer's assumption is that only those who accept Jesus as the Christ and hence as the agent of forgiveness can have a positive relationship with God. He is worried lest his readers succumb to the temptation to deny Jesus, but this should not happen because they have the result of their anointing in them. Whether the writer is thinking of the Word of God or of the Spirit of God or of the truth being "in them", they have the spiritual resources to enable them to resist this temptation, although again we note that this is not apparently an automatic guarantee of success (I Jn 2:18-27).[11]

In what looks like a fresh start the readers are positively encouraged to stay "in him" (I Jn 2:28—3:3). There does not seem to be any significant difference between spiritual powers being present in the readers and their being in God or Christ. They can look forward to standing before him without fear at his future coming. And they are again reminded of the need to do what is righteous. When he appears, they will resemble him in their righteousness. All of this causes the writer to burst out into praise of the greatness of God's love that has given the readers such a hope.

The theme of the need for righteousness is continued with a further explanation that sin is "lawlessness" (better understood as "rebellion"), and the statement that people who remain "in him" do not sin (I Jn 3:4-10). This could simply be a way of claiming that saying that you are in him and yet continuing to sin are incompatible (cf. I Jn 2:4). But the writer seems to be going further than this and saying that if we remain in him, then we will not sin, particularly as he also states the inverse, namely, that if anybody sins, they have not seen or known him. In fact, he goes on to say that people who are born of God and have God's seed in them cannot sin.

---

[11]It may well be that this anointing is the source of the true "spirits", that is, the genuine "Spirit-inspired" utterances that were received in the congregation, as opposed to those attributed to the spirit of antichrist (I Jn 4:1-3).

In the next section (I Jn 3:11-24), the writer reverts to the topic of love and hatred, which are the practical expressions of doing righteousness and unrighteousness respectively, and he reemphasizes the need for love between Christians—love that is genuine and shown in action, and that is demonstrated paradigmatically in the death of Jesus for the readers. Again there is a summing up of the main thoughts, tied on this occasion to a statement about the confidence that the readers can have when they pray to God.

We then have a section that deals with the question of spiritual messages, which purport to be revelations delivered by prophets (I Jn 4:1-6). These may be true or false, and the test is whether they express the true doctrine about Jesus Christ or not. It is true that the readers have the Spirit of God and recognize the truth, whereas false prophets draw their inspiration from the world and the spirit of falsehood; nevertheless the readers need to be warned against them.

Yet again the writer emphasizes the need for love as the outward expression and evidence of a positive relationship with God, and repeating that the paradigm of love is God's own love (I Jn 4:7—5:5). The God who is light is also love. To live in love is the way to have confidence before God. To fail to love one's Christian brothers and sisters is an indication of an imperfect love for God, since loving God entails keeping his command(s) to love his children. His commands are in principle fulfillable because we have been born of God and have faith in him.

But once more it is emphasized that this faith must incorporate right belief about Jesus who "came by water and blood" (I Jn 5:6-12). The Spirit of God testifies to the truth about him, and we should accept that testimony.

Finally, we come to some practicalities and summarizing conclusions (I Jn 5:13-21). The writer's aim is to build up his readers' confidence that they have eternal life and can be sure that God will answer their prayers. He encourages them to pray for their Christian brothers and sisters when they see them sinning. And he repeats the assurances: true believers do not sin because Christ keeps them. True believers are separated from the world, which is under the control of the evil one. True believers have received revelation from the Son of God, and are in him. Finally, and surprisingly, they are told to keep themselves from idols. The point of this statement is that "idols" are whatever people turn to when they turn away from the true God (I Jn 5:19), so that this command reinforces negatively the implicit injunction to hold fast to Jesus as the true God.[12]

## Theological Themes

From this summary we can try to identify the lineaments of the writer's theology. The central theme is encouragement to the readers to persist in truth and love on the basis of their spiritual union with God. Such persistence will be expressed in freedom from sin, although the writer is scared about actual claims to be free from sin. The letter has in effect filled out the picture we got from 2-3 John where we saw how important truth and love were for him. This is not surprising, given the much greater length of I John compared with the two very brief letters.

The framework for the writer's discussion is characterized by a dualism that expresses itself in antithetical statements. There is a dualism or polarity of darkness and light, of true and false spirits.

*Truth.* Again, then, we have the strong emphasis on truth. The term can be used in a fairly nontechnical way to signify the opposite of lies and deceit (1 Jn 1:6), but it also refers quite concretely to the divine reality that finds expression in the Christian message and the pattern of conduct that it requires. When the writer talks about the truth being in people, he is not just saying that their behavior is in accordance with what is true, but that there is a divine entity that exercises control over them, just as he can speak of God's love or even God or Christ or the Spirit being in them. When he says that believers "belong to the truth" (lit., "are from the truth"), again the idea that they somehow owe their origin and being to the truth is present. The truth then is tantamount to an expression for God, as ultimate reality, but also for what is correct as opposed to what is false; true is a positive, commendatory word. We can now appreciate how easy it was for the elder to personify truth in 3 John.

It is not surprising that there is a considerable emphasis on light in 1 John 1—2 but not thereafter. Light can express the pure character of God, stressing his unapproachability and his condemnation of darkness, but it also conveys the idea of the revelation of truth that dissipates the darkness of ignorance.

---

[12]Terry Griffith, *Keep Yourselves from Idols: A New Look at 1 John* (London: Sheffield Academic Press, 2002), pp. 1-89.

God is light; the light shines in the darkness, and people live in the light and
behave in appropriate ways. We thus have a dualistic view of things according
to which the dark world is illuminated from outside by the light that shines
from God, so that in a way a new space or area is constituted, like the area on
which a spotlight is shining. The author's way of putting things does not allow
for the existence of a penumbra, half light and half darkness, a gray area. He
uses absolute terms.

The other side of the picture, therefore, is the darkness of the world, a darkness that signifies its evil character, a world in which hate and bloodshed are
characteristic, and its lack of divine revelation to bring life and goodness. But
the metaphor is not pressed to suggest that people are forced to live either in
the darkness or light, depending on where they happen to be spiritually. There
appears to be an element of choice in that people can move out of darkness into
light and vice versa. So we are really thinking of two conditions that people can
be in rather than simply two spheres to which they may belong.

A further characteristic of the sphere/condition of light is obviously righteousness, used in its traditional sense of just and fair behavior that is in accordance with God's commands. Righteousness is seen to perfection in Jesus, and
those who live in the light are accordingly to be like him. The term *righteous* is to
be given only to people who actually practice righteousness; it is thus a term that
arises out of behavior. It follows logically, in the way in which the writer develops
his logic, that if people are not righteous, they are not from God (1 Jn 3:10).

Still in the area of truth and righteousness is the stress on commandments.
This term occurs with surprising frequency. As we have noted already, there is
a basic command to believe and to love one another, but a plurality of commands also given by God. The content of these is never stated; it is the fact of
obedience to whatever God may command that is the real concern.

*Love.* But it is the concept of love that stands out in the author's vocabulary.
The word group signifying love (i.e., *agapē* and cognates) occurs 62 times in
the three letters out of 310 occurrences in the New Testament, that is, one fifth
of the total is concentrated in these few pages.[13] It follows that love is thema-

---

[13]If we include the verb *phileō* and the noun *philia*, which are not used in 1-3 Jn but 26 times elsewhere, and the noun *philos*, "friend", which occurs 29 times, then the proportion is roughly 62 to
365, which is still one sixth of the total.

tized in a way that is unparalleled elsewhere in the New Testament; even in John's Gospel the total number of occurrences is only 63! The frequency may be due to John's peculiar style of writing with its frequent repetition of phrases and themes. Nevertheless it remains significant. The indications are that for all the emphasis on right doctrine, the author's main concern is with the Christian behavior of his readers. He encourages them not to love the world or the things in it, and he contrasts that kind of love with love for God (1 Jn 2.15). His teaching can be summed up in a few basic statements.

1. Love has its beginning in God who is so loving that it can be said that he is love. God's love is shown to humankind in the death of Jesus his Son, which is a sacrifice for sins carried out for their benefit. If we want to know what love is, we shall see it supremely in this action.

2. It is in response to God's love for us that we should love him. Human love for God is implicitly gratitude.

3. Those who love thereby demonstrate that they are born of God. The implication is that a divine action of begetting has taken place through which the life of God is implanted in people, and this life then expresses itself in love.

4. This love for God must be expressed in obedience to his commandment, which is that we are to love one another. This point is repeated and emphasized in all kinds of ways. The basic argument is: If God so loved us, we ought to love one another. We may want to ask what the basis is for the logic here: why does the fact that God loved us entail that we should love other people? The answer to the question is probably that God sets an example that those who are born of him and are thereby his children must follow.

5. It is possible to *say* that one loves in the way that we are commanded to do and yet to fail to *do* so. This happens when love is merely a matter of words and is not expressed in loving action.

6. So integral is love for one another to having a right relationship with God that John can argue from its presence to our belonging to God. At times he states this so absolutely that it might seem that anybody who loves is born of God, but of course John would also insist on right belief as well as right behavior. It is also made clear that the absence of love for one's fellow believers is

a reliable indication that the person does not love God, since the latter includes the former. For John there is only black and white: you either love your fellow believers, or you hate them.[14]

Two points arising out of this need further attention.

*The importance of right belief about Jesus.* We have seen that John is concerned with the message about the Word of life. Although this phrase might refer simply to the Christian message, there is more to it. It was "the life" itself that appeared; it was originally with God, but the writer and his friends have seen and heard it. Therefore, it must be identical with Jesus, the Son of God, as in John 1:1-18. It is further important that Jesus laid down his life for us and shed his blood in a way that made him an atoning sacrifice for sins. And he will reappear in accordance with what by now was a firm and living Christian hope. It will be noted in passing that the resurrection of Jesus is not mentioned anywhere, although it is assumed that he is a continuing spiritual reality in the experience of believers.

It follows from all this that the crucial mark of the readers is that they believe in Jesus and are thereby drawn into a spiritual relationship with him. Put otherwise, they have been born with God as their father and have become his children.

And it is in this context that the question of right belief becomes so important for the author. He evidently holds that Christian salvation is jeopardized if there is false belief about Jesus. As we have already seen, the crucial factor is belief that Jesus is the Christ and the Son of God. To deny this is to deny that there is a Savior, and it is also to deny that a relationship with God is possible. The point is made in stark terms, as we have seen.

Not much, if anything, is said about people who are on the wrong side coming back to the right side. There is the possibility of prayer for sinners to be saved, but not if theirs is a sin that leads to death. While this statement is a needed reminder that Christians should be praying for those who sin, the negative implications may seem difficult. Certainly John's statement is ambiguous: "I am not saying [commanding] that you should pray about that" may mean

---

[14]This clearly applies to specific people within your circle, to whom you must form an attitude. Manifestly it doesn't apply to people outside our orbit where relationships don't exist; yet presumably John would say that in principle we must love all our fellow believers, known and unknown.

no more than that prayer is not commanded in such circumstances (but you can pray if you want to), but then one would have thought that such circumstances made prayer all the more necessary. And did the readers know what John was referring to, even if we cannot be sure? On the whole, it is most likely that the sin referred to is that of deliberate and persistent apostasy, the rejection of Christ as Savior that may go so far as to put a person virtually beyond the reach of prayer.

The two things that are not clear are what exactly was being said by the people who are opposed here, and how the author came to this belief. It is understandable that people outside the church would deny that Jesus was the Messiah; unbelieving Jews would have done so. But how was this possible for people in the church? In 1 John 5:6-8 we have John's comment that Jesus Christ did not come "by water only, but by water and blood", and this cryptic statement presumably holds the answer to the question. The traditional explanation of it is that there were people who held that the heavenly Christ descended on Jesus at his baptism—so that one could say that Jesus Christ came by water—but held that this Christ departed from him before his crucifixion—so that Jesus Christ did not come by blood. We know that there were teachers in the church who held to this bizarre view, arguing that there was not a real and lasting incarnation of the Son of God in Jesus, possibly because of an assumption that the divine being could not have suffered crucifixion and death. Therefore they held that the divine being came upon Jesus at his baptism and departed before his crucifixion, so that it was merely the human being who suffered. Irenaeus tells us about Cerinthus, who believed that "after his baptism Christ descended upon him in the form of a dove, from the power that is over all things, and then he proclaimed the unknown Father and accomplished miracles. But at the end Christ separated again from Jesus, and Jesus suffered and was raised again, but Christ remained impassible, since he was pneumatic" (Irenaeus *Adversus Haereses* 1.26.1). Such a Jesus Christ could be said to have come through and in water (his baptism) but not through and in blood (by dying on the cross).[15]

Nearer in time than Irenaeus is Ignatius, who stresses the facts that Jesus

---

[15]However, there were other strange views held by Cerinthus, which are not mentioned or opposed by 1 John, and this makes some scholars doubt whether he was in John's sights here.

was "truly of the race of David according to the flesh, but Son of God by the divine will, . . . truly born of a virgin and baptized by John, . . . truly nailed up in the flesh . . . as also he raised himself up truly; not as certain unbelievers say, that he suffered in semblance" (Ignatius *Letter to the Smyrneans* 1-3).

It is noteworthy that Ignatius also attacked his opponents for their lack of love; they "have no care for love, none for the widow, none for the orphan, none for the afflicted, none for the prisoner, none for the hungry or thirsty" (Ignatius *Letter to the Smyrneans* 6:2). Such a description would correspond to the lack of love that is castigated in I John 3:17. And it was the presence of love that was for John one of the signs of truly belonging to God (I Jn 2:5-6).

Terry Griffith argues that references to "coming in the flesh" do not necessarily refer to incarnation but simply to existing in this world; "in the flesh" is concerned with the fact of the incarnation, not with its specific mode. The "water and blood" saying is not concerned with a specific christological heresy but stresses the importance of the atoning death of Jesus. Rather the concern is with those who deny that Jesus is the Jewish Messiah, otherwise called the Son of God. The problem is not christological heresy within the church but the secession of Jewish Christians back to the synagogue and a denial of their previous belief that Jesus was the Messiah. Consequently, the basis for postulating a christological controversy in the church is removed.[16]

Other recent scholars, such as Judith M. Lieu and Ruth B. Edwards, tend to be agnostic about the identification of the opposing views and insist that John's statements are too opaque for us to be able to draw firm conclusions from them. This is not a very satisfactory state of affairs. The evidence of Ignatius and Irenaeus indicates that docetic views of Jesus were developing, although they are admittedly writing in the early second century rather than the first, and Irenaeus thought that John was opposing Cerinthus (Irenaeus *Adversus Haereses* 3.3.4). It remains possible that over against such views John is affirming not that the Christ came on Jesus at his baptism and then remained on him right through the crucifixion and beyond, but rather that

---

[16]Hence the idolatry that is condemned is a return to Judaism, the language used by Jews against pagans being turned against them by Christians.

Jesus, who was already and remained the Christ, was baptized with water and died with the shedding of blood.[17]

Positively, then, the important fact for John is that Jesus Christ comes in the flesh, in a real incarnation. It is evidently important that there is a real incarnation so that Jesus is the Christ, the Son of God, in the flesh. And his cryptic statement in I John 5:6-8 must be an affirmation of this.

We are then left with the problem of the three witnesses to him, the Spirit, the water and the blood. The best explanation remains that the Spirit witnesses through the baptism or the birth of Jesus and through his death, although some interpreters want to see a reference to Christian baptism and the Lord's Supper as continuing testimonies to Jesus.

We should not be too surprised that people with such strange views of Jesus were to be found in the early church. Heresies, as they came to be called, were movements that happened in the church, and the variety of views that can be held in churches today shows that they can and do arise. It is not too difficult to believe that some people had problems with the idea of a divine being living a human life and dying a human death and therefore tried to find ways around these problems.

But another factor was probably also present. Such people may have majored on their experiences of the Spirit and developed a form of Christianity in which the significance of Jesus was played down and the importance of charismatic activities was played up. This suspicion is confirmed by the way in which John has to deal with the need to "discern the spirits". It is patent that spiritually inspired messages were being delivered in church meetings. As in I Corinthians the congregation needed to "test the spirits", since the mode of their delivery was no guarantee of their origin. John proposes the test of orthodox belief regarding Jesus on the part of those who delivered such messages. But what if the prophets claimed that their understanding of Jesus was confirmed by their messages? How were people to know that John's christology was right and his opponents' was wrong? For answer John would probably have appealed to the test of antiquity and personal testimony to the reality of the appearance of the

---

[17]An alternative view is that the "water" refers to the physical birth of Jesus, and John is stressing the reality of the birth of Jesus as the Christ (Ben Witherington III, "The Waters of Birth: John 3:5 and I John 5:6-8", *NTS* 35 [1989]: 155-60). Adoption of this view does not affect the main point at issue.

Word of life. John believed that the Spirit would give believers in what he regarded as the truth an inward conviction that it really was the truth.

*The problem of sinlessness.* This association of belief and behavior forms the bridge for us to the other major problem in I John. This is the question of sinlessness. Here John speaks in two ways. On the one hand, he insists that believers are not free from sin and therefore need to confess their sins and be forgiven. He encourages them not to sin, and this makes sense only if they do sin (I Jn 2:I). On the other hand, he insists that people who remain in Christ do not sin; no one who lives in him sins; those who are born of God cannot sin because they have been born of God (I Jn 3:4-10). This second set of statements is problematic. The problem is not simply that it may seem to represent an impossible ideal; after all, there are some people who do claim Christian perfection in their lives and proclaim it as a goal to other believers. The problem is rather that it apparently contradicts the first set of statements. The first set of statements could well be directed against people who uttered the second set of statements and claimed that they were free from sin. And certainly it is possible for people to make just that claim even though other observers may detect sin in them. It is also notorious that people can seek after, or even claim, spiritual perfection while neglecting to show love to the needy. The great stress on the need for love within the community in I John demands that this was a problem. Yet the second set of statements seems to play right into the laps of those who claimed to be perfect.

Various ways of avoiding the apparent thrust of John's statements have been tried. Suggestions include the possibility that here John was referring to a limited group of "super Christians" or that he was referring to freedom from one specific variety of sin. For example, the specific sin here could be apostasy, and this would then be the sin that leads to death (I Jn 5:16-17). The TNIV boldly translates by the present continuous forms "keeps on sinning" and "continues to sin", although I am not aware that it follows this procedure anywhere else. Others suggest that the ideal rather than the reality is being described or that the statements really function as exhortations and imperatives; probably the best suggestion along these lines is that John is describing what will be true in the new age but is not yet complete in the time between the ages. This is not dissimilar to the view that what is described is the ideal, but it brings out more strongly the fact that the ideal is something that is truly being increasingly realized in practice. We may think of the way in which a head teacher could say, "Pupils in this school do not tell lies", stating an ideal that ought to have been actual in the school, but the fact that it needed to be said shows that it was not being followed by everybody all the time.[18] The difference is that the Spirit of God, God's seed, is in the believer, and therefore there is genuine potential for the actualization of God's ideal here and now. Consequently John is not speaking simply about an ideal that the church ought to pursue and expressing it as if it were already a fact, but he is speaking about the character of the new life that is already being increasingly realized in the lives of believers.

No more than any other New Testament writer does John explore the relationship between the fact of this divine life and the way in which they must live in the strength of it, or the way in which despite this divine enabling they can continue to sin and fall short of God's purpose for their lives. The crucial fact is simply that believers have been brought into a spiritual relationship with God that makes their religion more than a matter of knowledge or behavior but rather a personal relationship with God and the experience of a transforming divine power.

## Conclusion

The antithetical manner of presentation is very characteristic of these letters, especially the simple polarization with no gray areas. It is based on sharp disjunctions between darkness and light, good and evil, love and hatred, and life and death. People are sharply divided into two groups, the true believers and those who are "antichrists". This has raised the question whether the author is on the road that led to Gnosticism with its sharp dualism between God and the world, light and darkness, and even two types of people, those possessing the divine spark and therefore capable of salvation and those lacking it. It is not likely. Although Gnosticism proper was developing in the late first century and probably arose out of Christianity, nevertheless in this letter its characteristic feature of an evil world created by some being other than the supreme God and its emphasis on salvation by means of knowledge rather than by faith are lacking. For John salvation is potentially available for the whole world (1 Jn 2:2), and it is conferred on those who believe (1 Jn 3:23; 5:1, 5, 13, 20).

---

[18]Cf. J. L. Houlden, *A Commentary on the Johannine Epistles* (London: A & C Black, 1973), p. 94.

John's main aim is to encourage the believers, and the whole mood is one of positive encouragement. They are not to be dismayed by the fact of many "antichrists", since this is only to be expected in the last days, the time when it was commonly believed that things would get worse as evil mounted its last and greatest offensive against God.

Despite all the emphasis on what believers must do, there is the underlying fact that they have been born of God, remain in him, and he (or his truth, or anointing) remain in them. They thus share in the divine life and have the spiritual resources that they need to live this life.

We may summarize the significant elements in 1-3 John as follows.

1. The ideal of a sinless life as the only appropriate way of life for God's children who claim to be in the light. Yet this truth is expressed paradoxically. On the one hand, believers do sin and can be forgiven and purified by confessing their sins. On the other hand, it is categorically stated that people who live in God do not sin.

2. The reality of a spiritual union with God, expressed in terms of living "in God" and of God's word or anointing being in believers.

3. The need for love of God to be expressed in love for one another within the community of faith, and for this love to be a matter of action and not simply of words.

4. The need to avoid false belief, especially about Jesus having come in the flesh, and therefore the need to test the statements of people who claim the inspiration of the Spirit for their prophecies.

5. The possibility of confident prayer that God will answer.

6. The paradox that believers are kept from harm by Christ and yet must ensure that they remain "in him".

### Bibliography

*New Testament Theologies:* (English) Childs, pp. 477-87; Ladd, pp. 657-65; Morris, pp. 287-91; Strecker, pp. 423-55. (German) Berger, pp. 236-248; Gnilka, pp. 226-324 (passim); Hahn, 1:585-732 (*passim*).

Bogart, John. *Orthodox and Heretical Perfectionism in the Johannine Community.* Missoula,

Mont.: Scholars Press, 1977.

Brown, Raymond E. *The Community of the Beloved Disciple.* New York: Paulist Press, 1979.

——— . *The Epistles of John.* Garden City, N.Y.: Doubleday, 1982.

Edwards, Ruth B. *The Johannine Epistles.* Sheffield Academic Press, 1996.

Griffith, Terry. *Keep Yourselves from Idols: A New Look at 1 John.* London: Sheffield Academic Press, 2002.

——— . "A Non-polemical Reading of 1 John: Sin, Christology and the Limits of Johannine Christianity". *TynB* 49.2 (1998): 253-76.

Hengel, Martin. *The Johannine Question.* London: SCM Press; Philadelphia: Trinity Press International, 1989.

Houlden, J. L. *A Commentary on the Johannine Epistles.* London: A & C Black, 1973.

Lieu, Judith M. *The Second and Third Epistles of John: History and Background.* Edinburgh: T & T Clark, 1986.

——— . *The Theology of the Johannine Epistles.* Cambridge: Cambridge University Press, 1991.

Marshall, I. Howard. *The Epistles of John.* Grand Rapids, Mich.: Eerdmans, 1978.

Painter, John. "The 'Opponents' in 1 John". *NTS* 32 (1986): 48-71.

Smalley, Stephen S. *1, 2, 3 John.* Waco, Tex.: Word, 1984.

# 22

# THE REVELATION OF JOHN

❧◦❧

Revelation poses a different sort of challenge to the New Testament theologian from the documents examined previously in that it is an apocalypse, that is, an account of a visionary experience by a writer in which he was permitted to see inside heaven and to be given a prophecy of what would happen in the future expressed in symbolic manner. The visionary nature of the account makes the interpretation all the more difficult. An important consideration that may help us to avoid error is that the purpose of the book is not primarily to satisfy curiosity about the detailed course of future events but rather to prepare and encourage a group of churches that were on the whole ill-equipped spiritually to face a future in which faith would be tried to the limit.

From the beginning we have a theological presupposition that governs the thought of the book. This is that it is possible to foretell what is going to happen by the will of God and also how people will respond to it. Many scholars down the centuries have gone further and assumed that the book is giving a detailed forecast of events, so that, if one knew the code (e.g., the identity of the beast and the false prophet), one could correlate the story in the book with history so far and see what still remains to be fulfilled. Although in one form or another this approach persists at a more popular level, the growing tendency among scholars is to recognize that what John presents is a highly symbolical account of the ongoing conflict between God and the evil forces opposed to him. Moreover, rather than presenting one story in chronological order John takes us over the same ground several times, looking at the conflict from several different angles. If this is the case, then we do not have a continuous, coded account of human history whose course we can plot. Nevertheless, the situation remains much the same in principle, that God knows what his enemies are capable of doing and that he will act in such a way as to ensure their final defeat. The situation may be not very different from that of a strong nation fighting a war against a weaker one, in which it knows the range of responses open to the enemy but is nevertheless able to devise and develop strategies that will lead to victory, just as Grand Masters can normally win at chess and know that they will win no matter what an unskilled opponent may try to do.

Revelation appears to have been composed in a situation where the church was facing severe persecution, or believed that such persecution was imminent and likely to be extremely severe, involving the martyrdom of many of its number. The situation was envisaged as one of unparalleled opposition to God and his people from a totalitarian society in which the church could scarcely hope to survive. The encouraging message of the book is that God will not be defeated and that he will bring judgment to bear upon the godless society and its rulers; from one angle the judgments are meant to be warnings of worse to come unless people repent, and from another they are indeed judgments upon them for their failure to do so. At the same time, John is aware that the congregations with which he is familiar are not strong enough to cope with the hostility that they will face, and the book is meant to prepare them to meet the challenge.

The book as a whole is heavily dependent upon the Old Testament for much of its language and content, although the use is allusive and there are no formal quotations. It also uses the idiom of the so-called apocalyptic literature. In this literature there is abundant use of symbolism and of the imagery of cosmic events that may refer to judgments in history rather than in nature.

### The Theological Story

*Prologue and greeting; Jesus and his message (Rev 1)*. The opening of the book shows that it combines the genres of apocalypse, prophecy and letter in a unique manner. There is accordingly a prologue that establishes that what we have is the account of a revelation given by Jesus Christ to the author, concerned with what was soon to happen.[1] The content of the book is thus given the highest author-

---

[1] John would have expected the events foretold to take place in the immediate future rather than over many centuries.

ity, and this is confirmed by the severe warning at the end of the book (Rev 22:18-19). But the revelation has the function of a prophecy in that it contains commands and promises for the readers to receive and act upon. It is an account of the future that is intended to prepare them for what is to happen and to encourage them by assuring them of God's victory and of the ultimate peace in which they will live with God.

After the prologue there is the kind of greeting that we expect in a New Testament letter (Rev 1:4-5a). It conveys blessings from God, first from God the Father, who is characterized as eternal, that is, eternally the same.

Second, blessings come from the seven spirits before his throne. This is a startling phrase, coming as it does from a late book of the New Testament, by the time when the doctrine of the Holy Spirit was well developed. Nothing is said to explain the significance of this phrase, which reappears in Revelation 3:1 alongside references to seven stars in God's hand (Rev 1:16). Whatever its origin, it would seem to refer to the varied functions and powers of the Spirit (cf. TNIV mg.), perhaps in relation to the seven congregations that are specifically addressed in the book.

Third, blessings come from Jesus Christ, and the build-up in the description indicates that he has immense significance in the accomplishment of God's purposes for the world and for his people, but always under God.

A very full christology is indicated in a succinct set of phrases (Rev 1:5a). Jesus is first and foremost the faithful witness (Gk. *martys*) and therefore the pattern and inspiration for his followers in the church. He is the first to rise from the dead, and while this phrase may indicate sovereignty over the dead, it may also hint at the fact that those who are faithful to death will also be raised from the dead. He is the ruler of the kings of the earth, not in the sense that they presently obey him, but that one day they will have to do so.

This description is followed by a doxology addressed to Christ (not the Father!) that gives as the reason for praising him the fact that he loved the readers and set them free from their sins by his blood (Rev 1:5b-6). This is the language of redemption or liberation, and it presupposes the by now familiar understanding of the death of Jesus as the means of redemption. The effect of redemption is to give believers a new status as a kingdom and as priests to God. The latter phrase indicates that they are now God's servants with the privilege of access to him. The whole phrase is based on Exodus 19:6, where the people are made "kings" rather than a kingdom; here, then, the thought may be not so much that they have been made God's subjects but that they shall reign (as Rev 22:5 clearly states).

Finally, there is the promise of the future coming of Jesus described in language that echoes Daniel 7:13 and Zechariah 12:10, so that Jesus is understood as the judge before whom his opponents will appear (Rev 1:7). Whether the mourning is that of repentance (leading to conversion) or remorse in face of inevitable judgment is not clear at this point. The certainty of fulfillment of that for which John longs ("So shall it be. Amen" contains his response) is confirmed by a powerful statement of the omnipotence of God, whose rule extends from eternity past to eternity future.

John now appears again and describes how he was "in the spirit" on the Lord's day[2] and received a message for the churches from Christ (Rev 1:9-20). The description of Jesus combines elements of the Son of Man (Dan 7), possibly the high priest, and God.[3] It becomes symbolical when we read of his having a sword proceeding from his mouth; biblical symbolism indicates that this refers to his powerful words. But the description is nevertheless that of a super-human figure like a superman in science fiction. Some critics have felt that this kind of description is a long way from the loving Savior and great high priest who sympathizes with his people in their weaknesses. It is true that the picture of Jesus and of God is of gigantic size and power, but this stands over against the more-than-human character of the principal opponents. We are dealing with apocalyptic symbolism, and in this context the readers need a symbolical picture of God and of Christ that indicates superior power. John is told not to be afraid:[4] the power will be used against his adversaries.

The main point here, however, is to underline the authority and authenticity of what is to follow. The authority of Jesus as the one who lives forever and has the keys of death and hades signifies that he is ultimately in control, no matter how great the powers arrayed against him may seem to be. The message that he gives is concerned with past and present as well as with the future. It will be

---

[2]This is usually understood to be the first day of the week, but it has also been suggested that he means the final day of the Lord.

[3]The description is based on that of the Ancient of Days in Dan 7.

[4]This is the standard response of God to his fearful people, but it is not to be taken other than seriously. It is spoken by the Creator of the universe, who is by definition greater than it.

mostly about the future, but much depends on what has happened in the past (especially the death and resurrection of Jesus) and what is going on in the present (the preparation of the church to face the future).

*Seven congregations (Rev 2—3).* There are individual messages to the seven congregations. These have much the same basic structure, and with obvious individual nuances and differences they convey much the same message. The congregations are closely linked to Christ by their "angels". They are in a situation where there is opposition from outside, in some cases from the state with its emperor worship, but also from groups of Jews who are opposed to them. There is also internal weakness and dissension, sometimes caused by groups with sinful tendencies. In some cases there are elements of witness and love that are to be commended, but the general picture is one of spiritual and moral weakness, a declension from earlier zeal, and the congregations are in a poor state to cope with the hard times ahead. There is, therefore, a general call to recognize the voice of Christ calling them to repentance, and to do so before it is too late. There is also a repeated call to individual believers to conquer, that is, to stand firm in the battle against temptation and persecution, and the future reward of those who stand firm to the end (Rev 2:26) is described with a rich variety of imagery. The tree of life, deliverance from the second death, the crown of life, sharing the authority of Christ, having one's name eternally in the book of life, becoming pillars in the temple of God, and sitting alongside Christ on his throne—these are varied ways of expressing eternal salvation. It follows that these are not special rewards for first-class Christians but the promised reward for every believer, and that therefore all believers are called to be faithful even when faced by the threat of martyrdom. This may seem to put the onus on the believer to persevere in faith and faithfulness, but at the same time we shall see that there are promises of divine protection and preservation.

*The scene in heaven (Rev 4—5).* We have seen the situation on earth. But Revelation is concerned with a spiritual conflict that takes place in both heaven and earth, in which the supernatural or superhuman powers of good and evil are involved. The next stage, accordingly, is to give the readers a fuller picture of the heavenly scene, of which they have had glimpses in the first chapter. So John describes how he was taken up into heaven and saw what was there. Presumably what he is describing is strictly indescribable, and it is significant that he does not describe God in any concrete sort of way. The picture is one of glory and power, expressed by using various kinds of imagery that would convey this impression.

The activity that goes on is perpetual worship by a symbolical group of beings who surround the central element, the throne and its occupant. God is adored first of all for his eternal being in holiness, and here holiness is expressive of his transcendence, rooted in his perfection. Then he is praised for his creation of everything by those whom he has created. The appropriate attitude before God is accordingly one of worship in which his greatness is acknowledged. Nothing else happens, or at least is thought worthy of record.

But there is some action! God holds a scroll bound up with seals that nobody is able to open, because nobody is worthy to do so. Only one such person is found. He is the Messiah of the Jews, described in language taken from the Old Testament, and he is able to act because he has triumphed. This refers to his willingness to die rather than to his resurrection in which he conquered death (cf. Rev 3:21). It was his death that entitled him to be raised to the right hand of God. Here, however, he is not pictured as sitting with God, but he stands in the center of the picture, and he is portrayed as a lamb bearing the marks of slaughter; his death, therefore, is interpreted as a sacrifice. He also has the symbols of strength in his seven horns, and he is depicted as the one who sends out the seven Spirits of God into the world. We are accordingly in the time after the death and resurrection of Jesus and his sending out of the Spirit at Pentecost. This is confirmed by the words of the chorus that celebrate the fact that the scroll can be opened and God's future purposes come to fulfillment because the Lamb has redeemed the people of God from the peoples of the world with the ultimate aim that they will be kings and priests for God. Praise to the Lamb from the inhabitants of heaven and everybody else in the whole universe follows.[5]

*Series of judgments (Rev 6).* Thus far the story has not been too difficult to follow. From this point onward it becomes much more difficult.

The vision begins with the opening of the seals of the book rather than reading the contents of the book. Four riders emerge to cause mayhem, limited in

---

[5]This may seem strange in view of the rebelliousness that characterizes so much of the creation. It is hardly a proleptic vision of the final state after evil has been defeated (contrast Rev 7:9-17). Presumably we are to take it for granted that rebellious beings, supernatural and human, are not included.

scope but nonetheless terribly severe, upon the world. The limited nature of the judgments suggests that they are in the nature of warnings to make people aware that the wrath of God is about to fall completely on the world (cf. Rev 6:16) and to encourage them to repentance (cf. Rev 9:20-21; 16:9). The fifth seal is different: it reveals a group of martyrs for the gospel and for their witness to Christ; they call out to God to judge their opponents, that is, presumably to hasten the time of his final judgment, but they are told that this will not happen until the full number of martyrs is complete. So the seals indicate that the warning judgments are falling upon a world system that is opposed to God and to his people. The sixth seal describes cosmic disasters that are fantastic and are seen by the people of the world as indications that the day of the Lord's wrath has come and judgment is about to strike. Nevertheless, there is no indication of readiness to repent. The language used here (which is repeated later) strongly suggests that at this point the last day is on the point of dawning.[6] But instead of proceeding to the dénouement the writer launches into further sets of visions that appear to give parallel accounts of the future from different aspects.

*Sealing, prayer and further judgments (Rev 7—10).* There is accordingly an interlude at this point as the sequence is interrupted. Before a judgment upon the world can take place, God places a seal on his people to make it clear that they belong to him and so to preserve them from the effect of judgments to come (Rev 9:4).[7] The description is of them as people who belong to the twelve tribes of Israel. However, this cannot be meant literally, since the tribe of Dan is omitted and the tribe of Manasseh (Rev 7:6) was a subgroup of the tribe of Joseph (Rev 7:8).[8] It follows that the numbers and tribes must be symbolical. This interpretation is confirmed by the fact that the immediately following vision (a glimpse into heaven) is of an innumerable crowd from every people of the world who have come out of the great tribulation and are now in the presence of God. This must be a proleptic vision of the future reward of the people of

---

[6]Compare the description of the seventh trumpet in Rev 10:7; 11:15-19.

[7]It has also been suggested that they are preserved in this way from natural disasters so that they can be the victims of their enemies as martyrs at a later stage. This probably goes beyond what the text implies.

[8]The lists in Scripture vary considerably in order and contents. Joseph's two sons, Ephraim and Manasseh, were reckoned as two separate tribes in the division of the land among the twelve tribes, the number being kept at twelve because Levi was excluded from the division. In the present list Joseph appears to replace Ephraim, and Dan is omitted.

God, placed here to encourage those on earth who must undergo tribulation. They are not actually said to have been martyrs, although they may well have been, and they owe their position to the salvation bestowed by God and the Lamb through the death of the Lamb. There is general agreement that the symbolical 144,000 in the first vision and the great multitude in the second vision are the same people before and after their deaths. The purpose of the chapter is thus to assure God's people that he has set his mark on them as his, and therefore, as those who have been redeemed by Christ, they will receive their reward, no matter what the opposition arrayed against them. If the great tribulation is understood as a tyranny from which nobody can escape, then the implication may be that they came out of it by martyrdom.

The main plot with its series of opened seals then resumes, with God's action stimulated by the prayers of his people. The final seal does not bring about the end, as we might have expected, but rather opens up (like a box containing a fresh set of boxes to open) to reveal a further set of judgments heralded by trumpets. Enormous natural disasters take place, which it is appropriate to regard as judgments on the persecutors of God's people. Supernatural plagues supervene. But again these are partial in their effects, and it emerges that one purpose of these plagues is to warn people that these judgments have come upon them for their sin and so to urge them to repent, presumably lest worse befall them (Rev 9:20-21).

*The two witnesses (Rev 11).* Another lengthy set of interludes follows before the next series of seven judgments commences in Revelation 15. First, there is an announcement that there will be no further delay in the execution of God's plans (Rev 10:7). This is presumably meant to encourage the people on earth who, like the souls under the altar (Rev 6:10), ask "How long?"[9] Further reve-

---

[9]The problem caused by the long period during which people go on waiting for a divine intervention that never happens is present throughout the New Testament. Some interpreters argue that the earliest Christians expected that God's intervention would take place very soon indeed and underwent considerable strain when their hopes were disappointed. They had to shift the emphasis in their theology and find ways to account for the ongoing delay. There is reason to doubt whether the parousia was thought to be as imminent as this theory claims; nevertheless, with the passage of time the question of when God was going to act must have raised doubts as to whether he was going to act at all, and this problem is reflected in the later books of the New Testament (2 Pet 3:3-9). The problem became all the more acute with the Jewish war with Rome and the fall of Jerusalem; it was natural to think that this "great tribulation" for the Jewish people was a sign of the end.

lations and visions will make clear what is to happen.

Then there comes a very different set of scenes. First, we have a vision of two witnesses who have divine protection until they complete their act of testimony. For a time they even have the power to destroy their enemies. But their period of immunity is limited, and they will be slain by God's archenemy from the abyss (cf. Rev 9:11). After three and a half days they are resurrected and are visibly caught up to heaven. The imagery is based on the figures of Moses and Elijah and also of Jesus, and the witnesses symbolize the church in its witness. This is a further means of indicating that God's people will be protected during the period allotted for their witness, and although there may be martyrdoms at the end of it, yet they are assured of resurrection. The vision takes it for granted that the nature of the church is to bear witness during this period. The period of witness (a symbolical period of time) coincides with the trampling of the holy city by the Gentiles (see Lk 21:24).

The interrupted sequence of trumpet judgments then comes to a conclusion with an account of the seventh trumpet, which announces the final victory of God: the time has come for judgment and reward. This can only be a vision of the end event, and it confirms that what we have in this book is a series of more or less parallel accounts, each of which takes us up to the end.

*The woman and child; the dragon; three angels (Rev 12—14)*. So it is not surprising that yet another parallel account follows in Revelation 12, where we have a new set of images of a woman who brings forth a child clearly identified as Christ. There is opposition from a dragon who is unable to harm the child, who is caught up to God. This is presumably a reference to the death of Jesus, understood as the attempt of evil powers to destroy him.[10] The dragon is defeated (Lk 10:18; Jn 12:31) and cast down to the world, where he attacks the woman and the rest of her offspring. The woman appears to personify Israel, at first the old Israel from which came the Messiah and then the new Israel consisting of the followers of Jesus. This apparent shift in reference is explicable if the woman represents the faithful, pious remnant in Israel under the old covenant (the kind of godly people depicted in Luke 1—2 out of whom came John the Baptist and Jesus) and then in continuity with them God's faithful people under the new covenant.

---

[10]If 1 Cor 2:8 refers to supernatural powers rather than to earthly rulers, it would give a parallel to the thought here, but the interpretation is insecure.

It is perhaps difficult to understand how the casting down of the dragon can be interpreted as the coming of God's salvation and kingdom, but the point is that the accuser of God's people has been cast out of heaven and can no longer prosecute them there. True, there is a price to be paid for the victory. For the vision proceeds with an account of how the dragon's agents on earth take over and impose a totalitarian regime in which the followers of the Lamb are attacked and overcome, while everybody else follows and worships the anti-Christian beast. Just as we have had imagery of God as a superhuman being, so here the opposition to him is described in superhuman terms, only this time in terms of horrendous, fantastic animals rather than human beings.[11] The implication is that the increase in suffering and persecution on earth is due to this satanic invasion.

Since what is to happen is so fearsome for believers, another vision of the 144,000 is given, this time showing that they have safely arrived in heaven. This confirms our understanding of the 144,000 as being identical with the great multitude in heaven in Revelation 7:9-17.

We are also given a foretaste of what is to come in three angelic messages. The first makes clear that there is still opportunity for people to hear the gospel and to repent; nevertheless, when the seven last plagues come, there will be a melancholy refrain that people did not repent (Rev 16:9, 11). The offer is accompanied by warnings of judgment on Babylon and by the threat of eternal judgment.[12] There is a separate vision of the actual gathering together of people for the judgment by the Son of Man;[13] this again appears to be a vision of the ultimate end.

*Seven final plagues; Babylon and its fate (Rev 15—18).* Seven final plagues to be poured out from bowls are intimated. Meanwhile, those believers who have not yielded to temptation to apostasy are gathered in heaven and praise God for his

---

[11] Compare how the evil forces in Dan 7 are represented by fearsome animals, whereas the people of God are represented by "one like a human being".

[12] The picture of torment here is drawn from the practice of oriental potentates who had their enemies tortured in public and presumably gloated over their sufferings. John uses the language of the worst pain that he knows and magnifies it to infinity by saying that it is "forever". In a book where there is so much symbolism, it is inconceivable that this language is to be taken literally. The problem is rather to consider what it means when it is taken seriously.

[13] This contrasts with the picture in Mk 13:27, where it is only the elect who are gathered together by the Son of Man; however, he judges his enemies in Dan 7.

great and righteous deeds. These deeds are understood to be the judgments that
a righteous God will carry out (cf. Rev 16:5-7). The judgments this time are
much more severe than in the previous series; nevertheless, they are not to be
identified as the final judgment but rather as further warnings. Yet, although
they are intended to lead people to repentance, they fail to do so. They culminate in fact in the gathering of the surviving people to war against God for the
last time at Armageddon. A final judgment falls upon the great city here named
as Babylon, which seems to symbolize both Jerusalem and Rome and indeed
the whole earth.

Two chapters are devoted to a description of this archenemy of God, em-
ploying the imagery of a prostitute to express the temptation and lure exercised
by the world on people to lead them into sin. It is this city and the people affected by it who have practiced every kind of oppression and evil, including the
murder of the people of God. There could hardly be a more powerful indication
that the world is seen as totally given over to sin and godlessness.

*The victory of God (Rev 19—20).* Revelation 19 celebrates the victory of God
over this evil system and the reward of God's people in terms of their taking
part in a banquet where the guests also figure as the bride of the Lamb.

The judgment is described as a conflict between the divine Leader and all
the people who have followed the beast and his minions. Total defeat results.
Yet no battle is described, and all that we hear is the announcement of victory
and defeat, and the death of all the participants with the lurid imagery of the
defeated foes forming carrion for the birds to eat.

Revelation 20 remains enigmatic. As it stands, it appears to describe a temporary imprisonment of the dragon (Satan) to prevent him from deceiving the
nations for a thousand years (but did they not all die in Rev 19?). Meanwhile,
the martyrs come to life and reign with Christ for what is presumably a simultaneous period. Then Satan is released and deceives the nations again—but how
is this possible, since everybody has died and only God's people have been resurrected with Christ? A further battle takes place that ends with the judgment
of the opponents of God and of all people, including those who had died and
who are now resurrected to face the final judgment.

A more or less literal interpretation of this millennium seems to be ruled out
because of the problems of determining where the nations come from and because a temporary kingdom of Christ seems utterly pointless. We also know

that there is a good deal of parallelism in Revelation. Therefore we seem to be shut up to one of two solutions. The traditional one is that here John takes us back again to the beginning: the binding of Satan is one aspect of the death and exaltation of Christ, the millennium is the present age, and then there is a final fling of evil leading to its defeat, so that the battle in Revelation 19 and the destruction of evil in Revelation 20:9-10 are the same event. An alternative solution is that the millennium is a proleptic or parallel image for the new earth that will be described in remarkably similar terms in Revelation 21—22.[14] Neither of these solutions is free from problems, but it seems to me that the hypothesis of the temporary millennial kingdom is rather more problematic and should probably be dropped from the discussion.[15]

*The new Jerusalem (Rev 21—22).* The remainder of the book is given over principally to a description of the new Jerusalem (which replaces the old one) where God dwells with his people. The city is apparently equated with the bride of the Lamb, and we have something like the imagery elsewhere where the church can be a female person and its members her children. Here the geographical and architectural imagery takes precedence to describe the conditions under which the people of God live. They do not need a physical temple, because God is with them. They do not need physical light, because God is their light. Only those written in the book of life gain entrance.

In Revelation 22:14-15 it seems that there are still sinful people outside the city. This could be another image for exclusion from God's new world (a much milder image than the fires of hell; cf. Rev 21:8), but maybe it is simply a contrast between the saints and sinners now on earth, as part of the appeal for people to come and receive the water of life and so to qualify for entrance to the heavenly city.[16]

The book closes with a further stress on the imminence of the coming of Christ. Although there are terrible things ahead, the coming of Christ to deliver

---

[14]See discussion of this hypothesis in I. Howard Marshall, "The Christian Millennium", *EQ* 72 (July 2000): 217-35.

[15]The question as to whether any other New Testament authors believed in a millennium continues to be debated; see Seth Turner, "The Interim, Earthly Messianic Kingdom in Paul", *JSNT* 25 (2003): 323-42.

[16]This is justified by the fact that the water of life (Rev 22:1) is already available here and now (Rev 22:17).

his people will not be long in happening. Meanwhile, the book urges people to come and receive the gift of eternal life.

### Theological Themes

There is a wealth of theological detail in this book, together with a host of difficult questions. Here, more than anywhere else in the New Testament, difficult problems are raised for the modern reader as we attempt to reconcile the kind of pictures of God's working in the world with what we learn from elsewhere in the New Testament.

*Framework: The geography of Revelation.* The writer operates with a three-level universe in which God is in heaven surrounded by his servants who worship him. In heaven God decides what is to happen upon the earth. The earth is the arena of conflict between the followers of Jesus and the world. Supernatural powers of evil can come down or be cast down from heaven to deceive and deprave them. Underneath the earth is the abyss, which is a place of captivity and punishment for these powers and those who yield to them.

This is the standard representation in the literature of the time, but it is more prominent in Revelation than elsewhere in the New Testament. For John the close relationship between heaven and earth is of particular importance.[17]

*Main theme.* The purpose of the book of Revelation is to prepare God's people for the difficult future that lies ahead of them and to issue an evangelistic appeal to those who have not yet responded to their witness. There were shortcomings in the readers' Christian life and witness that needed to be cured if they were to be able to stand up to the hard times caused by persecution and opposition from the sinful world around them and its state religion. The writer's main way of encouraging them was to use the resources of apocalyptic writing in order to present them with a series of visions that would give them an insight into the way in which God would work in the world. The purpose was to assure them that although there would be martyrdoms, nevertheless God would vindicate his people by judging their opponents both in such a way as to warn them to repent before it was too late and also as a final judgment upon

---

[17]See Paul S. Minear, "The Cosmology of the Apocalypse", in *Current Issues in New Testament Interpretation: Essays in Honor of Otto A. Piper,* ed. William Klassen and Graydon F. Snyder (London: SCM Press, 1962), pp. 23-37.

their opposition to him. At the same time there was the promise that their future was bound up with Christ, who would bring his people to the heavenly city and take them to himself, as a bridegroom takes a bride. The book is thus a powerful statement of hope based upon the sovereignty of the God who has revealed himself in Jesus.

*God and his power.* Turning to the detailed outworking of the theme, we begin by observing that the picture of God is of a powerful creator and potentate whose throne dominates the heavenly scene. We have already noted how the picture of God and of Christ is of tremendously powerful, superhuman figures, but this is matched by the pictures of the opposing forces. Although, therefore, it can be argued that John has a macho God and that the gracious, even humble, aspects found elsewhere in the New Testament are absent, it would seem that this is rather part of the apocalyptic imagery that is intended to bring out the cosmic nature of the struggle. In the passages using this imagery God may appear to be distant and removed from his people, but nevertheless he is to them "our God" (Rev 7:12). The picture of him with his people is of a God who wipes away tears from eyes, like a caring mother or nurse (Rev 21:4); it is matched by the picture of the Lamb acting as a caring shepherd for his people (Rev 7:17). However, in the context of the oppression experienced and feared by the church the stress on his omnipotence and his ultimate control of history is natural and essential.

The appropriate response to such a God and to the Lamb is worship; what takes place continually in his presence in heaven is to be understood as a paradigm for believers on earth over against the temptation to worship the rulers of this world.

*Jesus Christ, Messiah and witness.* Equally central alongside God is Christ, depicted in various roles taken from Old Testament messianology as the Messiah, Son of Man, Lion of Judah, but also and preeminently as a Lamb that has been slain; astonishingly the title is used twenty-six times of him in this book. The metaphor of the Lamb may be drawn also from messianic imagery, but here the fact that the Lamb has been slain (Rev 5:6, 12; 13:8; cf. Rev 12:11) evokes a powerful image of sacrifice. As elsewhere in the New Testament, Jesus has been raised from the dead and exalted, but he still bears the marks of death, a symbol that the efficacy of his sacrifice persists eternally. Language used of God is also used of him; like God he is the first and the last. So not only is he the highest being under God, the only one qualified to open the scroll that sets God's future plan into operation, but he is also on a level with God, to whom he refers as "my Father" (Rev 2:27; 3:5, 21; cf. Rev 1:6; 14:1). He is praised and worshiped in the same way as God; they share the same throne (Rev 22:1, 3), and often the two of them are bracketed together (Rev 5:13; cf. Rev 12:10). The christology of Revelation is thus second to none in the New Testament in the status assigned to Jesus.

Jesus is also described as the faithful witness, a phrase that is used of Antipas the martyr. He has set the example of faithfulness to death. Where literal language is used of Jesus, he appears as a victim of violence, and he does not practice it. Warlike imagery is used of him (Rev 19:11-16), but there is no account of him engaging in conflict. It is strange that whereas God can be said to inflict horrendous natural disasters on people, he does not fight against them.

*The Holy Spirit; the angels.* The role of the Spirit is much less central. We have already noted the unusual character of the reference to the seven spirits (Rev 1:4; 3:1; 4:5; 5:6) who appear to have the same function as the one Spirit of God has elsewhere. They are around the throne of God, but they are also sent out into the world. It would seem that the imagery of the angels who surround God and go out to do his bidding has been transferred to the Spirit. The Spirit is prominent in the early part of the book as the one who speaks to the seven congregations and conveys the promises of God to them (Rev 2:7; cf. Rev 14:13; 22:17),[18] but otherwise the Spirit plays no part in the action of the book.[19]

Angels, however, are very important. No other book of the New Testament contains so many references to them.[20] They dominate the book, acting as messengers conveying revelation to human beings, as heralds and agents of the successive series of judgments, and in other capacities as God's agents.

A particular role is served by the seven angels of the congregations who are the recipients of the messages to the churches. They are usually said to be heavenly doubles of the congregations, but their role in the communication of the messages, which are couched in the second person singular (and therefore could

---

[18]Here should be included references to the Spirit in relation to prophecy (Rev 19:10; 22:6).

[19]Other usages of the term refer to evil spirits or to John being "in [the] spirit", that is, able to enter heaven and see what is going on there.

[20]Sixty-seven of the 175 uses of the term in the New Testament are in Revelation.

be addressed to the angel or to the congregation as a whole) is obscure. It is significant that the messages all culminate in statements addressed directly to the members of the congregations.

*The forces of evil.* Over against God and his agents we have the forces of evil. What we might call the beastology of Revelation is as complicated as the angelology. The principal evil force is the dragon, alias the devil and Satan (Rev 12:9; 20:2 make the equation) who is the instigator of action against God. He does not make his appearance until the vision of the woman with the child (Rev 12:3). He is involved in conflict in heaven with Michael, is defeated and is hurled down to earth, so that he ceases to accuse the people of God before God but is now able to persecute the church on earth. His allies are described as two wild animals or "beasts" that are satanically inspired to mimic the power of Christ and (in the case of the second wild animal) the role of his prophets, and between them to exercise totalitarian power over the world. Like God they have impressive supernatural agents at their command. Yet they remain under God's control; frequently the verb "it was given" is used to express the permission given to them by God (e.g., Rev 6:2, 4, 8, 11).[21] The world that they create is one that is opposed to God and his witnesses and therefore is characterized by its role as persecutor. At the same time, however, it is strongly condemned for its way of life described in Revelation 18, where the world is characterized like ancient Babylon as a city that grew wealthy not only on its trade but also on its violence and godlessness and especially its attacks on God's people. It would not be difficult to see the Rome of the Caesars in this way.

*The church.* In this situation we have human beings sharply divided into two groups, those who follow the Lamb and those who yield to the enticements and temptations of the satanic forces. These are not two groups whose members are fixed by divine fiat. There are calls to the ungodly to repent, and there is no indication that these calls are other than genuine. There is also the fear that people in the congregations may succumb to apostasy: the book hardly needed to be written if the danger was not a real one. At the same time, the followers of the Lamb are those who are sealed by God before the judgments take place. Their names are written in the book of life (Rev 13:8; 17:8) from the founda-

---

[21]Grant R. Osborne, *Revelation* (Grand Rapids, Mich.: Baker, 2002), p. 32.

tion of the world.[22] However, the reference in Revelation 3:5 to names not being blotted out of the book of life suggests that some names could be blotted out. We have the familiar New Testament tension between calls to persevere and assurances of divine protection that should not be smoothed out in favor of guaranteed perseverance or timid uncertainty.

Consequently, the all-important thing is that believers should conquer or prevail, in the sense that they stand up to temptation and persecution and successfully resist it. For John it is necessary not only to be a believer but also to overcome the temptations to unbelief. The verb "to believe" is missing from Revelation, but the adjective *faithful* is used of Jesus (Rev 1:5; 3:14; 19:11) and of believers (Rev 2:10, 13; 17:14).

This suggests that the Christians thought of themselves as a ghetto surrounded by hostile forces, perhaps seeing this as an almost inevitable fate, like the experience of Jews in Nazi Germany and its satellites. It is a world in which there can be no compromise with the ways of sin and ungodliness.

John envisages congregations in different localities.[23] Their primary task appears to be to witness to Jesus, and the content of their message is "the word of God testified to by Jesus Christ" (Rev 1:3). The church has thus a missionary task. Within the congregations prophets are active, John being the outstanding example (Rev 1:3; cf. Rev 22:9), but there can be false prophets alongside the true (Rev 2:20). No prophets apart from "Jezebel" are named in the seven messages, but the prophetic character of the church's witness is clear enough later on (Rev 11:18; 16:6; 18:24). There is also reference to "apostles" (false ones in Rev 2:2), who are linked with the saints and prophets in Revelation 18:20. These should be differentiated from the twelve apostles (Rev 21:14). There are echoes of the language of baptism and the Lord's Supper but no direct references (Rev 3:20; 7:14; 22:14).

*The action.* Now that we have considered the principal actors, we can ask what they do. We have a picture of a godless world going about its own business with no thought of God, rejecting the witness of believers to the gospel and putting them to death. Even the Jews or some of them can be characterized as a syna-

---

[22]In Rev 13:8 it is not clear whether this phrase refers to the slaying of the Lamb or the writing of the names in the book; in Rev 17:8 it has to be the latter.

[23]The number of seven must stand symbolically for an indeterminate number of congregations.

gogue of Satan. This world is open to evil influences, and it is taken over by them. But the major action is that of God, who brings various judgments upon the world for its evil. The body of the book describes several series of awful disasters that take place in the world, some of them more easily conceivable than others to modern minds, others of them described in ways that defy imagination. There are strong elements of the supernatural throughout the book, and the boundary between what is meant literally and what can only be symbolical is hard to draw. These disasters seem to be in the nature of premonitory warnings to people of the final judgment and are intended to awaken people to the awful plight that will be theirs if they do not repent. However, we hear little, if anything, of them being successful.[24] The book culminates in a final judgment in which the forces of evil and those who succumbed to them are destroyed.

The nature of the final judgment is portrayed with various different kinds of imagery. Mostly the imagery is of destruction and death; at one point there is a lake of fire in which the devil and his accomplices are tormented day and night forever (Rev 20:10), and those whose names are not in the book of life are also thrown in there (Rev 20:15). Although it is not explicitly said that the latter are tormented in this way, it is a fair inference that this also applies to them. The question, therefore, is whether this is the dominating image, or whether, as seems more probable, the images of death and destruction control the discourse.[25]

Equally, the final destination of God's people is described with varied imagery. People are invited to the marriage banquet of the Lamb, but the bride and the guests are the same people. There is a holy city, which is likened to a bride and appears to be identified with the bride (Rev 21:2, 9-10). The city is on a new earth rather than in heaven, and since God and the Lamb are in the city, it would seem that earth and heaven merge. The description of the city is heavily symbolic, picking up motifs from Scripture. Within it is the tree of life that the original inhabitants of the Garden of Eden did not eat but whose fruit is now there for the picking. With the image of the city, it is possible for John to speak

---

[24]It is debated whether or not the possibility of repentance is really envisaged. See the discussion, concluding in favor of true repentance in Rev 11:13, in Osborne, *Revelation*, pp. 433-35. But this does not mean that every individual is envisaged as repenting, as Richard J. Bauckham, *The Theology of the Book of Revelation* (Cambridge: Cambridge University Press, 1993), pp. 139-40, clearly notes.

[25]Literally eternal torment and death/destruction are incompatible with one another.

of the area outside it where saints and sinners are: the former may enter, but the latter are excluded. This imagery comports ill with the image of the sinners in the lake of fire. The possibilities would seem to be either that these are two different images for the crucial reality of judgment, or possibly that the difference between outside and inside is not geographical but temporal, between the "now" when people outside may respond to the gospel and the "then" when those who respond actually enter the city.

For John this action is to take place soon (Rev 1:1; 4:10). The final words of the book emphasize that Jesus is coming soon (Rev 22:20). The book thus shares the general New Testament belief that the end is not far distant. What was certainly not far distant is the kind of human society described in the book, in whose history may be seen sin and its judgments, the witness of the church and the attacks upon it, the failures of the church and attempts to reform it. But the time of the end remains unknown.

## Bibliography

New Testament Theologies: (English) Ladd, pp. 669-83; Morris, pp. 292-97; Strecker, pp. 515-45; Zuck, pp. 167-242 (passim). (German) Gnilka, pp. 398-420; Hahn, 1:448-75; Hübner, 3:206-15; Stuhlmacher, 2:199-286 (passim).

Aune, David E. Revelation. Vol. 1, Dallas: Word, 1997; vols. 2 and 3, Nashville: Nelson, 1998.

Bauckham, Richard J. The Theology of the Book of Revelation. Cambridge: Cambridge University Press, 1993.

Beale, G. K. The Book of Revelation. Grand Rapids, Mich.: Eerdmans; Carlisle: Paternoster, 1999.

Beasley-Murray, George R. The Book of Revelation. London: Oliphants, 1974.

McKelvey, R. J. The Millennium and the Book of Revelation. Cambridge: Lutterworth, 1999.

Minear, Paul S. "The Cosmology of the Apocalypse". In Current Issues in New Testament Interpretation: Essays in Honor of Otto A. Piper. Edited by W. Klassen and G. F. Snyder, pp. 23-37. London: SCM Press, 1962.

Osborne, Grant R. Revelation. Grand Rapids, Mich.: Baker, 2002.

Smalley, Stephen S. Thunder and Love: John's Revelation and John's Community. Milton Keynes: Nelson Word, 1994.

# 23

# THE GOSPEL, LETTERS AND
# REVELATION OF JOHN

❧⚬❧

The major witness to what is generally called Johannine theology is the Gospel itself. Its closest links are with the letters of John, and nobody doubts that these documents are closely related. A problem is posed by the book of Revelation. It stands apart by reason of its genre and is sui generis. Before we can proceed to place the Johannine theology in relationship to the rest of the New Testament, we need to discuss briefly the theological relationships of its possible components.

## The Gospel and the Letters of John

As we have noted, the current tendency is to ascribe the Gospel and the letters to different authors, often to the accompaniment of hypotheses regarding the development of a Johannine community that passed through various phases. Even if different authors were at work, there is nevertheless a real identity of theology between John and 1-3 John, provided that we bear in mind the different purposes and genres of the writings. They share a common theological vocabulary and idiom.

The Gospel is richer in its theology than 1 John, not merely because of its greater length but also because of the wealth of imagery that it uses and the breadth of the issues that are discussed. First John has a much narrower focus; it is largely concerned with things that can go wrong in the church, and so it concentrates essentially on the issues of denial of Christ, claims to sinlessness, lack of brotherly love and dubious spiritual revelations. But arising from these concerns it sets out a positive theology and way of life for its readers. It can certainly be seen as applying the kind of theology found in the Gospel to specific problems and developing it accordingly.

The letter begins with a christological statement that echoes the prologue to the Gospel establishing the reality of the revelation of the Word of life, which is implicitly identified with Jesus. As yet, there is no suggestion of any problems in this area. This is followed by a section dealing with the importance of not falling into sin and with the danger of denying that one's behavior is sinful. The Christian life is understood as a life of fellowship with God and with Christ, characterized positively by obedience to Christ's commands. The tone is one of encouragement not to sin, coupled with the positive promise that sin in the lives of believers is forgiven by God in response to the intercession of Christ. This picture coheres with that in the Gospel, where the Christian life is spelled out in terms of a spiritual relationship of mutual indwelling and where disciples are expected to follow the commands of Jesus (Jn 13:34; 14:15, 21; 15:10-12). But the danger of falling into sin receives more attention here than in the Gospel.

The specific command at issue is that of love for other believers, and this is simply a development of the basic command to love one another. The teaching about the world ties in with the Gospel, where the world is the sphere of human life characterized by darkness and sin but still the object of God's loving concern. We find essentially the same kind of dualistic idiom in the Gospel and the letters.

One new feature is the warning about antichrists (1 Jn 2:18), which is not prepared for in the Gospel; the Gospel and the first letter are familiar with the activity of the devil as the ruler of this world, but only the latter has the concepts of antichrists who deny Christ. We may also mention here the concept of a sin that leads to death, generally equated with apostasy; those who deny the Savior manifestly cannot be saved. The close link between such sin and belonging to the world is seen in 1 John 5:18-19.

Then comes the major point of christology. As we saw, there is debate whether John is countering simply a Jewish denial that Jesus is the Messiah or a denial that the Son of God truly became incarnate. We encounter the warning that those who reject Jesus as the Son of God are thereby rejecting the Father as well (as in Jn 5:23). If we accept that in the Gospel the identity of Jesus as Messiah is closely tied to an interpretation of messiahship in terms of divine sonship (cf. Jn 1:49; 10:24/36; 11:27; 20:31), we can see that the kind of denial found in I John could be essentially the same repudiation of Jesus. The Gospel and the first letter are prepared to use the designation *God* of Jesus (Jn 1:1; 20:28; I Jn 5:20).

The understanding of the death of Christ in I John has been thought to differ from that in the Gospel, but this view rests on a misrepresentation of the teaching in the Gospel. The first letter does lay more stress on the sacrificial character of the death of Jesus (I Jn 2:2; 4:10), but it does so in the context of the same teaching as the Gospel that the death of Jesus is an expression of divine love (I Jn 4:10), that Jesus bears sin (I Jn 3:5) and that he laid down his life on behalf of us (I Jn 3:16). In both writings the blood of Jesus is significant, although the motif is developed in different ways.

First John does not mention the resurrection of Jesus, although it assumes that he is in heaven and has access to the Father (I Jn 2:1) and that believers can have a spiritual relationship with him.

Statements about anointing with the Spirit express the Gospel teaching about the Spirit being given to believers (Jn 7:39; 20:22) using a new metaphor (I Jn 2:20, 27).[1]

The motif of the sanctification of believers (Jn 17:17; I Jn 3:3) is not developed in the Gospel or the letter, but whereas the Gospel has no discussion of sin on the part of the followers of Jesus, the letter is concerned with this problem. This is a clear case of development to deal with a contingent situation. The future hope that believers will be like Christ is also new, but it could be deduced from statements in John 17, where Jesus speaks of the disciples being with him, seeing his glory and receiving the glory that the Father has given him (Jn 17:20-24).

The fact that God keeps and protects believers is common to both writings (Jn 10:28-29; I Jn 5:18).

In all this the writer of the letter maintains the theological idiom of the Gospel. I cannot see any major point at which the Evangelist would want to dis-

---

[1] It is used elsewhere of believers in 2 Cor 1:21.

agree violently with him and say, "No, that's not right". Within the framework of thought assumed by the Gospel, the letter develops an appropriately contingent application of the same basic theology.

Thus what is being urged here is that the differences between the Gospel and the letter are only such as one might expect to arise within a theological framework that is essentially defined by the Gospel.[2] We can, therefore, make use of the Gospel and the letters in a comparison of Johannine theology with that of other parts of the New Testament.

## The Revelation of John

*Revelation and the Johannine Literature.* The relation of Revelation to the Gospel and Letters of John is problematic. It is not impossible that one and the same author could express himself in different ways as occasion required,[3] but the very considerable differences in ways of thinking would seem to rule out this possibility.[4] The question is rather whether there is a deeper affinity that places Revelation closer to the Gospel and Letters of John than to other New Testament writings. At the deepest level, of course, there is a Christian understanding of reality that is shared by all the New Testament writers and is constituted by their understanding of Jesus as being one with God the Father and the Savior of believers from sin and the source of the hope of resurrection and new life. That binds the varied books of the New Testament together so that they all reflect a common set of core beliefs. But within that unity of diverse theological expressions the question arises of the closer links: is Revelation closer to the Johannine writings than to any other? Where does it find its place on a theological map?

The major problem is the apocalyptic genre and content of Revelation,

---

[2]Here, as elsewhere in these theological comparisons, it is important to stress that we are not denying the existence of more subtle differences in expression and content between the documents, and these would require treatment in a fuller treatment of the topic. We are simply affirming that there is an essential theological identity between them that is not, in our opinion, called in question by any such differences.

[3]So Grant R. Osborne, *Revelation* (Grand Rapids, Mich.: Baker, 2002), pp. 2-6.

[4]See Stephen S. Smalley, *1, 2, 3 John* (Waco, Tex.: Word, 1984), pp. 35-73 (cf. Stephen S. Smalley, *Thunder and Love: John's Revelation and John's Community* [Milton Keynes: Nelson Word, 1994]), who argues for composition of the Revelation by John the apostle and of the Gospel and Letters by a follower of his.

which sharply distinguish it from the Gospel and Letters. This character links the book closely to the traditions that are found in the apocalyptic sections of the Synoptic Gospels and in 2 Thessalonians and elsewhere. These were clearly important in areas of the early church in the critical times of the Jewish war and the growth of persecution later in the first century. The development of these themes appears to be dominant in the book. Nevertheless, it is perfectly conceivable that such a way of thinking could coexist with other ways, perhaps at different points over a period of time depending on the intensity of outside pressures.

A specific illustration of this is provided by Wilbert Francis Howard, who juxtaposed two hymns that typify two types of Christian outlook. The first is what he called "Christian mysticism":

> Open, Lord, my inward ear,
> And bid my heart rejoice;
> Bid my quiet spirit hear
> Thy comfortable voice;
> Never in the whirlwind found,
> Or where earthquakes rock the place,
> Still and silent is the sound,
> The whisper of Thy grace.

The second is "undiluted Jewish apocalyptic":

> Come, Thou Conqueror of the nations,
> Now on Thy white horse appear;
> Earthquakes, dearths and desolations
> Signify Thy kingdom near;
> True and faithful!
> 'Stablish Thy dominion here.

The point of the quotations derives from the fact that they are works by the same writer, Charles Wesley, dated in 1742 and 1759 respectively.[5] Howard used the example to argue that in the same way Jesus could combine mysticism and eschatology in his teaching. We can use it to argue that the same combination could be found in the outlook of a single New Testament author or within

---

[5]Wilbert Francis Howard, *Christianity According to St. John* (London: Duckworth, 1943), pp. 201-4.

a single school of Christian theology.[6] It is, therefore, not impossible that Revelation may be accommodated within the broad range of Johannine Christianity. Alongside the main stream of Johannine theology, seen in the Gospel and letters, we may have a further tributary through which apocalyptic thinking was fed in.

Is it, then, justified to claim that Revelation is at home within Johannine Christianity rather than anywhere else? The alternative would be to argue that Revelation belongs elsewhere for its main inspiration but has also been influenced secondarily by Johannine ideas.[7]

A number of common features may be noted. First, the designation of Christ as the Lamb of God that dominates Revelation is echoed in John 1:29, 36 (cf. Acts 8:32; 1 Pet 1:19). In both cases the imagery is that of a sacrificial animal. But it has to be admitted that there the similarity ends. Two different Greek words are used, *amnos* in John and *arnion* in Revelation (also used of Christ's flock in Jn 21:15), the former of which means a young animal whereas the latter can be used of an adult animal (Rev 13:11). Further, in the two references in John the phrase is "the lamb of God", whereas in Revelation the term is used absolutely: "a/the lamb". Finally, the term is marginal to the christology in the Gospel, although it is used to make a significant theological point about the death of Jesus. Other terms are more significant, whereas in Revelation it is a central category. The importance and significance of the term in Revelation are thus quite distinctive.

A further link lies in the use of the name "the Word of God" for Christ in Revelation 19:13, raising echoes of the use of "Word" in John 1:1-14 and 1 John 1:1-4. This designation for Christ is not used elsewhere in the New Testament. But again there are significant differences. In John and 1 John the term is set prominently at the beginning. In John it is used absolutely, whereas in Revelation it is qualified, "the Word of God" (cf. 1 Jn 1:1, "the Word of life").

---

[6]One could also compare the coexistence of these two types of thinking that is traditional within the theology and preaching of such a contemporary group as the Christian Brethren with their combination of intense spirituality centered on the death of Christ in their service for the breaking of bread and their dispensationalism. They see no incongruity between the two, since they find both in Scripture.

[7]Compare how Hanna Stettler, *Die Christologie der Pastoralbriefe* (Tübingen: Mohr Siebeck, 1998), pp. 325-28, found influence from Johannine traditions in the Pastoral Letters.

It is not clear whether the rich background that is needed to understand the usage in John 1 is required in Revelation 19.

Another important link is the use of "I am" sayings (Rev 1:17; 2:23; 21:6; 22:13, 16), but the predicates in Revelation are different from those in the Gospel. However, it should be noted that the use of "I am [he]" that appears to be a divine self-affirmation in the Gospel is paralleled in Revelation with the use of "I am the Alpha and the Omega, the First and the Last, the Beginning and the End", which is language used by God (Rev 1:8).

Fourth, the language used to connote salvation also has links with Johannine usage. The term *life* is widely used in both books but is too well attested throughout the New Testament to be regarded as distinctive. The metaphorical use of "water" for salvation is found in John and Revelation, thematically in the former (Jn 4; 7:38) and occasionally in the latter (Rev 7:17; 21:6; 22:1, 17), but is not found elsewhere; the related metaphorical term *thirst* is common to both books (Jn 4:13-15; 6:35; 7:37; Rev 7:16; 21:6; 22:17). Revelation does not use *bread*, but it does have the imagery of manna (Rev 2:17; cf. Jn 6:31, 49). Both books are conspicuous for their use of a range of imagery to describe salvation and the blessings given to God's people, but they go their own ways in doing so. The imagery of Christ coming in through the door and having table fellowship with the believer (Rev 3:20) is not unlike the imagery of indwelling used in John (Jn 14:23).

But there are also differences. Although the use of *Father* to refer to God is of central importance in John, the term is used only five times in Revelation and then always qualified as the Father of Christ (Rev 1:6; 2:28; 3:5, 21; 14:1). The combination "Lord God" is common in Revelation but is not found in John (see, however, Jn 20:28), and the adjective *almighty (pantokratōr)* is characteristic (nine times; elsewhere in the New Testament only in 2 Cor 6:18 ). The overwhelming picture of God is of a mighty potentate seated on his throne (another characteristic concept), a picture that is determined by the visionary nature of the book and by the need to stress the sovereignty of God over the forces of evil.

The Holy Spirit acts primarily as the conveyor of divine messages in Revelation (Rev 2:7; 14:13; 22:17), and there is also the unusual reference to "the seven spirits" (Rev 1:4; 3:1; 4:5; 5:6), which are held by Christ (Rev 3:1). The Spirit evidently conveys messages to John as to a prophet, and this corresponds with the picture elsewhere in the New Testament.

In both the Gospel and Revelation there is the consciousness of the threat to the church from persecution that could lead to death (Jn 15:18—16:4), but the theme is almost incidental in the Gospel as compared with the centrality in Revelation. The term *world* plays no significant role as a theological entity in Revelation, and the detailed development of God's judgments upon rebellious and unbelieving society has no parallel in the Gospel, which speaks simply of judgment. The Gospel does not have the apocalyptic descriptions of what is to happen in the future; this also distinguishes it from the Synoptic Gospels.

These points are sufficient to show that there are features of the underlying Johannine theology in Revelation, but they are used in a book that has a very differently expressed set of interests. However, there is also the significant point that the author of Revelation is called John, and the best explanation of this feature in the context of early traditions about the Johannine writings is that there is some association between Revelation and the Gospel and Letters.[8]

We should probably be cautious about attempting to create a meaningful synthesis of the material in Revelation with that in the Gospel and Letters to produce a "Johannine theology" in the sense of an identifiable, coherent subgroup within the theology of the early Christians generally. We just do not know how far the outlook expressed in Revelation was shared by the author(s) of the Gospel and the Letters and vice versa. What we propose to do, therefore, is to make a brief comparison of Revelation with the rest of the New Testament at this point, and to leave it on one side in our subsequent comparison of Johannine theology with that of the Synoptic Gospels and Acts and Paul.

*Revelation and the rest of the New Testament.* How do we account for the theology of Revelation and see its relationship to the rest of the New Testament? The most conspicuous feature of the book is its use of the apparatus of apocalyptic. The situation of the congregations is understood in terms of a clash with the satanically inspired forces of the world engaged in persecution of the followers of the Lamb; the forces arrayed against the church are worldwide and cosmic, and there is no human hope of survival. The threat of suffering and martyrdom looms large and fills the horizon. So part of the message of the

---

[8]The question arises whether Revelation has closer theological links with any other parts of the New Testament. I find no clear indicators of any.

book is to warn against the temptation to apostasy and to encourage steadfastness to the point of death by assuring the threatened believers that God is on
their side, and they are assured of a heavenly reward provided that they continue
to be faithful. At the same time it is made clear that the forces arrayed against
them will be judged by God and ultimately totally destroyed. The judgment of
the oppressors is something that is a necessary part of God's victory and vindication of his people. Great stress is laid on the recalcitrance of the oppressors
who refuse to repent despite every painful warning. The implication is that God
is more powerful than the oppressors and therefore the believers can be assured
of ultimate victory.

The understanding of the contemporary situation in apocalyptic categories
may have been the only viable option for a church that felt overwhelmed and
threatened. Whether there was actually serious persecution (especially from the
state) at this time is still debated, but it seems clear that the older former picture of worldwide persecution to the death cannot be substantiated. Yet there
was clearly a sense of separation from the surrounding society with its godless
values and a related feeling of rejection and opposition that placed their life under threat.

Is the response different from that of other early Christian authors who find
routes other than the apocalyptic one? The apocalyptic line is seen in the Synoptic Gospels with their awareness of the Jewish war with Rome, and the effects
of that fearful time must not be underestimated. It emerges elsewhere, if only
briefly (1-2 Thess; 1 Cor 15; 2 Pet; Jude).

How, then, does Revelation stand in relation to the apocalyptic teaching
elsewhere in the New Testament? Putting together the material in the Synoptic
Gospels, particularly in Mark 13 and Q, we have an account that starts with
the threatened destruction of the temple and its relationship to the fulfillment
of all that has been prophesied, that is, the end of the world. The picture unfolded is one of worldwide anarchy and disorder. Paradoxically perhaps there is
also the picture in the Q material (Lk 17; Mt 24) of the people of the world
going about their ordinary daily lives as if there was nothing the matter and no
God to whom they are answerable. There will be attacks on Christians, despite
which they have to continue to preach the gospel. There is the danger of them
being deceived by false claimants to be prophets and messiahs. They are counseled to stand firm. There are specific warnings about getting away from Jeru-

salem when it is attacked. Finally, the Son of Man will come and gather together his elect, and they must remain spiritually vigilant in anticipation of that event. A final judgment involving the Son of Man will separate people depending on their attitude to him and his brothers and sisters.

In Revelation we can see most of these features, but there are shifts in emphasis. The city imagery speaks of Rome as well as of Jerusalem and has become symbolical of the unbelieving world as a whole. Much of the war and suffering is seen as a series of judgments upon the world inflicted by God. The motif of martyrdom is strongly developed. The danger of deceit and forcing believers to conform to false worship is strong, but the concept of divine protection for God's people is also emphasized. The notion of a final conflict is developed. Above all, the concept of the devil and his allies in an evil trinity comes to the fore. There are visions of the action in heaven and the new heaven and earth that are unparalleled in the Gospels.

It is clear that Revelation fits into this general framework of apocalyptic presentation, and there is a similar scenario of events, but at the same time there is much, much more. Elsewhere in the New Testament, particularly in 2 Thessalonians 2, we have evidence of other attempts to provide a scenario of future events that also includes God's ultimate opponent. In these cases the apocalyptic material is inserted in the context of mainline Pauline Christian teaching without any appearance of incongruity caused by the change of genre. We shall have to explore the possibility that Revelation occupies a similar kind of slot within the broader family of Johannine Christianity.

When we look at the theological motifs that are expressed within this framework, we find that the picture of God concentrates in a vivid way on the sheer power of God. Although his sovereignty and power are taken for granted elsewhere in the New Testament, Revelation makes much of them, partly because the author is adopting the style of apocalyptic with its striking imagery and partly because he saw the immensity of the threats to the church and needed to reassure his readers that God was in ultimate control.

The picture of Jesus is a combination of typical messianic features and of an exalted figure who is closely related to God and shares his status. The specific concentration on the imagery of the Lamb is unusual and again may be due to the apocalyptic background; it aids the author in presenting a crucified Messiah and indicating the sacrificial character of his death. The understanding of his death as redemptive fits in with the use of this motif elsewhere.

Revelation is unique in its portrayal of the seven spirits of God as divine messengers and in the prominent place given to angels as divine agents. There is certainly a plasticity in the depiction of heavenly and supernatural agents, good and evil, in the New Testament, and the language used may well be rhetorical rather than realistic. Revelation offers a much more individualistic presentation here that again fits in with its apocalyptic genre. The same is true of the descriptions of the sinful world and the evil forces that control it. Here we have a pictorial, imaginative presentation of what is expressed in more sober and abstract terms elsewhere.

The phrasing of the call to sinners and opponents of God to repent, rather than to believe, is not surprising in view of the way in which their sin is seen as rebellion and enmity. It is also entirely fitting that the call to God's people is to avoid contamination with sin and to resist like an army fighting a battle and making every effort to win. Elsewhere we can readily find appeals to separation from sin and to perseverance in resisting temptation (especially the temptation to yield to persecution) that say the same thing in less vivid ways.

Where Revelation goes beyond the other New Testament writings is in its rather detailed account of the new Jerusalem. Here there is a rich variety of scriptural allusions and pictorial imagery that create an attractive prospect. The point to be noted and stressed is that this imagery does not detract from the fact that the central feature of the age to come is the presence of God and of the Lamb with his people so that their chief delight is in him; the description of the attendant features does not divert readers from this primary experience but rather serves to enhance it.

From this summary account we can see that the theology expressed in Revelation is essentially similar to that found elsewhere in the New Testament but is richly colored by the use of apocalyptic imagery and is developed in the context of a concentration on the situation of the church in a world that is resisting God and stands under divine judgment. The question would then be whether this concentration has in any way skewed the theology. For example, there is a lack of interest in the spiritual relationships of believers with Christ and the Holy Spirit, and there might be the danger of underemphasizing these elements that are so important in Paul and John. Again, we might wonder whether adoption of the apocalyptic framework has led to a more pessimistic and gloomy understanding of the situation of the church in the world than was justified. Even so, however, it would still be the case that in some situations, such as the darkest days of the Holocaust, persecuted and threatened people will find more help in a book like Revelation, which takes the depths of evil seriously than in other parts of the New Testament written in more peaceful circumstances.

Revelation may thus to some extent be a book on its own in the New Testament, but its theology does not differ significantly in its broad features from that of the other books.

### Bibliography

Osborne, Grant R. *Revelation.* Grand Rapids, Mich.: Baker, 2002.

Smalley, Stephen S. *1, 2, 3 John.* Waco, Tex.: Word, 1984.

————. *Thunder and Love: John's Revelation and John's Community.* Milton Keynes: Nelson Word, 1994.

# 24

# JOHN, THE SYNOPTIC GOSPELS
# AND ACTS, AND PAUL

❧✦❧

W e now face the question of the character of the theology of John in comparison to that of the Synoptic Evangelists and to that of Paul.

### The Gospel of John and the Synoptic Gospels

We have no means of knowing what personal links there may have been between the different authors of the books of the New Testament. Here we are
almost completely in the dark. It can be taken for granted that early Christians
did communicate with one another, although some modern scholars tend to
write as if the various New Testament authors lived on separate islands with no
contact with other known figures; personal communication is ignored, and
there are vague references to traditions and influences. But Galatians 1—2
places it beyond any doubt that James, John, Paul and Peter knew each other
and talked together, and in the immortal phrase of C. H. Dodd, "we may presume they did not spend all the time talking about the weather".[1] I see no reason to deny the well-founded belief that this John, the son of Zebedee, had
something to do with the origins of this Gospel.

Further, there is increasing support for the view that although John was not
writing with another Gospel before his eyes, in the manner in which Matthew
and Luke are generally thought to have used Mark, nevertheless he could well
have had some contact with earlier Gospels, specifically Mark and Luke. At the

---

[1]C. H. Dodd, *The Apostolic Preaching and Its Developments* (London: Hodder & Stoughton, 1944), p. 16.

very least he had knowledge of the traditions that lay behind them or at least with traditions of a very similar character. There is thus some continuity traceable with the kind of material recorded in the other Gospels.[2]

All this might be regarded as making the problem more acute. How did John then come to write so different a Gospel? Why did he write the kind of Gospel that he did write, knowing that those who had done so previously had written in a different style from that which he adopted? And how do we explain the differences between Pauline and Johannine theology? I have no fresh solution to offer for these puzzles. What I shall attempt to do is to look at the prior question of the nature of the differences and the similarities between them in order to answer the specific question whether there is a basic unity between them.

A further limitation to our enquiry must be mentioned. Our concern is primarily with the theologies of the Evangelists and not with their different depictions of the teaching of Jesus. There are considerable differences in style and content between the kind of statements attributed to Jesus in the Synoptic Gospels and in John, but our concern is not primarily the historical one of how it comes about that there are two different presentations of the teaching of Jesus. It is a comparison of the theologies of the Synoptic Evangelists and John to see whether there is some kind of unity and harmony between them rather than a discussion of how the Johannine understanding arose in relation to the Synoptic picture and to Jesus.

*The kingdom of God.* We saw that in the Synoptic Gospels the main theme of the teaching of Jesus was the announcement of the coming of the kingdom of God with all the consequences that this had for the lives of those who heard it. Although the phrase clearly indicates the importance of God reigning, this must be qualified or unfolded in various ways.

First, the reign of God is associated with the agent through whom it is proclaimed but also through whom it comes into being. The reign of God is proclaimed by Jesus, but the proclamation itself, both in word and accompanying deed, is the manifestation of the reign, the means by which it is brought about.

---

[2]Opinions differ whether John knew the Synoptic Gospels and developed themes from them or was dependent upon other, closely related traditions. Either way, there are close links to the historical Jesus.

Therefore, the question of the identity of Jesus as God's agent is a central issue. Even if Jesus was reticent about himself, nevertheless it is clearly a concern of the Evangelists, so much so that in the case of Mark it is possible to understand his Gospel as falling into two parts, concerned with whether Jesus is the Messiah and then with what kind of Messiah he is.

Second, the reign of God brings the blessings of God's rule to human beings, spelled out most directly by Luke in his unfolding of the concept in terms of salvation, both now and in the form of entry into God's heavenly kingdom in the future.

Third, the proclamation of the kingdom challenges the hearers to respond positively to the message, and this involves discipleship of Jesus and total commitment to him.

Fourth, the reign of God imposes a way of life upon those who enter the kingdom, with Matthew especially systematizing the teaching of Jesus on how people should live.

In John the language of the kingdom of God has all but disappeared (Jn 3:3, 5; 18:36), although it is important to note that the concept of Jesus as king and therefore the ruler of a kingdom (Jn 18:36) is powerfully present. As has often been observed, in effect it is replaced by the concept of eternal life. This should not be misunderstood to mean that one set of terms has been replaced by another that has the same function, in the way that the metaphor of bread could be replaced by that of water. Rather, there is a shift in expression, comparable with that in Luke where the concept of salvation is introduced to explain the effects for human beings personally of the coming of the kingdom. This has two immediate results. The one is that the crucial issue in the Synoptic Gospels of whether the proclamation of the coming of the kingdom has to do with a new state of affairs that has already come about (or at least been initiated) or that is imminent and expected to come soon moves away and is no longer present in this form. The other effect is that the question of the identity of Jesus becomes a question that is openly discussed. This does not mean that the so-called messianic secret ceases to play any role; on the contrary, Jesus is reticent about revealing who he is to those who are set on unbelief. But it does mean that the proclamation about the coming of the kingdom is replaced by the question of Jesus himself. Perhaps a third point should be added here. Although John foresees the onset of persecution directed against the disciples after his departure, it is placed within a Jewish context (Jn 16:2), and there is no detailed description of future events in apocalyptic language. Yet within the total context of what may be broadly called Johannine Christianity we might reckon that the Revelation is the Johannine equivalent to the apocalyptic sections in the Synoptic Gospels; there are certainly sufficient similarities between them to indicate a common inspiration behind them.

*The identity of Jesus.* In the Synoptic Gospels the essential question about Jesus is whether he is the Messiah of Jewish expectation and how his suffering and death fit in with this. The same question of messiahship figures in John, and we have the same combination of christological designations. But the accent has shifted. In the Synoptic Gospels the designation "Son [of God]" is used of Jesus and is clearly important for the Evangelists; indeed, it plays a rather larger role in the actual story than is sometimes realized. Even in Mark it figures in exorcism stories (Mk 3:11; 5:7) and in the transfiguration (Mk 9:7); it appears occasionally in the teaching of Jesus (Mk 12:6 is parabolic but surely understood of Jesus himself by the Evangelist), and it becomes a key issue at the trial of Jesus (Mk 14:61) and is affirmed at the cross (Mk 15:39). It is no less prominent in the other Gospels. But it does not become the object of teaching by Jesus and controversy with his opponents. It is only rarely linked to teaching about a close personal relationship between Jesus and his Father and about preexistence in the way that it is in John (Mt 11:25-27; Lk 10:21-22).

It is a moot point whether the picture of Jesus given by the Synoptic Evangelists includes the concept of his preexistence.[3] For some scholars the birth traditions in Matthew and Luke rule out the idea. Jesus comes into being through the operation of the Holy Spirit on Mary rather than through (let us say) the preexistent Word or Son of God coming to reside in her womb and coming to birth as a divine-human being.

Such a judgment may be premature. The birth stories, it may be said, are more concerned with the twin facts of the birth of Jesus as the Jewish Messiah (cf. the genealogies) and as the Son of God. In both stories the Holy Spirit is the agent through whom God acts (Mt 1:20; Lk 1:35). If—at least for Paul—it is the Spirit of God by whose agency Jesus is raised from the dead, rather than

---

[3]The question, long ignored, is now firmly back on the scholarly agenda.

by his own power, it is not inappropriate that it is by the agency of the same Spirit that he enters into human life. That is to say, for a theologian who accepts the concept of the preexistence of the Son of God, there need be no tension with the birth stories; there has to be some means by which the preexistent Son comes into the human world, and Spirit conception and the virgin birth can be the means. If we start from the birth stories, these in themselves do not necessarily imply preexistence. However, elsewhere in the Synoptic Gospels there is a certain amount of material about Jesus coming from or being sent by God that may point in this direction. The problem is that such statements may be nothing more than expressions of what a person feels to be their calling in life or their commissioning by God (cf. the self-consciousness of the prophets) rather than a statement of origin. The possibility that the Son of Man was understood to be a preexistent figure who comes from God should also be mentioned.

By contrast, in John the evidence, as we saw, is clearly in favor of a belief in preexistence. At the same time, the fact that Jesus had a human mother, Mary, and human brothers is taken for granted; there may be ironical implications in John 6:42. So, whether or not John believed in the virgin birth, he certainly accepted that Jesus was a human being with a human birth.

The difference, therefore, lies more in the way in which the preexistence of the Logos or Son of God is thematic and central in John. The Synoptic Gospels come from a time when the preexistence of Jesus as the Son of God was accepted by at least some Christian theologians, and therefore there would be nothing unusual or problematic about them believing in it. But their reporting of the teaching and debates of Jesus reflects more what was actually said in his lifetime, whereas John is bringing out rather the issues that emerged with the passage of time and fuller and deeper reflection on the identity of Jesus.

As far as the role of Jesus is concerned, messiahship is understood in much the same way in the Synoptic Gospels and John. The concept is one that developed and changed in the light of the actual performance of the role by Jesus. This is conspicuous in John 4, where the initial suggestion to the inhabitants of Sychar that Jesus is the Messiah leads eventually to their confession that he is the Savior of the world (Jn 4:29/42). The role of the Messiah consists in bringing benefits to people and delivering them from their present plight.

The recognition of Jesus as a prophet is common to all the Gospels. The concept of Jesus as *the* prophet emerges much more clearly in John (Jn 1:21; 6:14; 7:40) and chimes in with the presentation of Jesus in Acts 3:22-23, where the prophet is equated with the Messiah. And, as we have seen, the concept of Jesus as the king of the Jews is common to all the Gospels but is rather more prominent in the trial scenes in John.

The usage of "Son of Man" goes far beyond what we found in the Synoptic Gospels. The close link between the Son of Man and the passion and resurrection of Jesus persists, but the Son of Man is also identified as having come down from heaven and being the agent of revelation and salvation. "Coming down from heaven" is a phrase also used with reference to Jesus as the bread that comes down from heaven and is linked to his identity as the Son (Jn 6:33, 51), the language being based on the description of the manna. The role of the Son of Man as the judge or counsel[4] at the last judgment is mentioned in John 5:27 but otherwise has retreated into the background.

In comparison with the Synoptic Gospels, then, the figure of the Son or Son of God is much more prominent in John and is used in discussion with the crowds and Jesus' opponents in an open way. He is God's agent sent into the world to bring salvation and has full authority to act on behalf of God. The term *Logos* is used in much the same way. This concept is peculiar to John. Even if the concept of Wisdom is used as a christological category in the Synoptic Gospels, nevertheless the motifs of preexistence and agency in creation do not figure in this context. The term *Logos* is deeply significant because the Evangelist uses it to introduce the Gospel, and it profoundly and succinctly expresses the totality of his christology.

It is apparent that, although this christology is rooted in the kind of utterances that we find in the Synoptic Gospels and that can be traced back to Jesus, nevertheless the picture of Jesus is one in which the earthly Jesus is portrayed in the light of the understanding of him as the risen Lord.

*Response to the message.* In John there are the two lines of thought: that God's love extends to the whole world and salvation is offered to all who believe and that only those who are drawn by the Father can come to the Son and believe and will be raised up at the last day. The Synoptic Gospels do not contain any significant theologizing along these lines. The universality of the offer of salva-

---

[4]Either role is used to indicate that the Son of Man has the decisive role at the judgment.

tion emerges explicitly occasionally (Mt 11:28-30), but is always implicit: a call such as that in Mark 1:14-15 is manifestly intended for all who hear it.[5] Some of the pericopes on discipleship are so framed that the initiative lies with Jesus, who calls people to be his disciples (Mk 1:16-20; 2:13-17), although cases of people coming to Jesus are also recorded (Lk 9:57-62). Matthew 22:14 comments that many are invited but few are chosen, but in its context this saying functions to warn people against abusing the invitation.

The motif of faith/belief as the essential response of people to the Christian message and the means of appropriating salvation comes to the fore in John. Somewhat surprisingly the noun *faith* is absent from John (except in 1 Jn 5:4), although it is found in the Synoptic Gospels mainly in connection with the performance of mighty works (though see Lk 18:8; 22:32, where the nuance of persistent faith emerges). It is the verb that is dominant. In the Synoptic Gospels it is also used of faith as the condition for mighty works, but the thought of acceptance of Jesus as the Messiah is also present. Now in John faith becomes the crucial mark of the followers of Jesus.[6] Three elements come together in it. First, there is the sense of believing what a person says to be true and accepting their statements (e.g., Jn 6:69; 8:24; 11:26-27, 42; 14:10; 16:27; 20:31). Second, it refers to self-commitment to the person whose teaching has been accepted intellectually (e.g., Jn 1:12; 2:11, 23; 3:16; 6:29; 7:31).[7] And, third, there is the element of faithfulness expressed in a continuing relationship, which is expressed in Johannine vocabulary by the term *remain* (Gk *menō*) Jn 6:56; 8:31; 15:4-10). This is a usage that is peculiar to the Johannine literature.

This understanding of response to the message of Jesus corresponds fairly closely with that in the Synoptic Gospels. There the essential element of commitment to Jesus is expressed in terms of following him, and there are demands for self-denial. This element persists in John (Jn 12:25-26); moreover, just as the call to self-denial and bearing the cross comes in the context of references to Jesus' way to the cross in the Synoptic Gospels (Mk 8:31-38), so also here

---

[5]Clearly at this point the audience is Jewish, but the problem of Jews and Gentiles does not affect the basic issue.

[6]As in the other Gospels, the term *disciple* is used frequently to designate the followers of Jesus, both in a narrow sense of his continual companions and in a broader sense of his adherents, and it has some theological significance (Jn 8:31; 13:35; 15:8).

[7]This kind of faith is often expressed by the use of *pisteuō eis*.

(Jn 12:23-24). Similarly, the opposition that disciples will face is associated with the fate of Jesus (Jn 15:20-21). The thought of continuing faithfulness to him is expressed in the Synoptic Gospels by the imagery of bearing the cross.

*Salvation and eternal life.* We have seen how the proclamation of Jesus regarding the kingdom of God tends to be understood in terms of salvation in Luke, although the language is not entirely absent from Mark (Mk 10:26, 52) and Matthew (Mt 1:21; 19:25). This tendency is carried further in John. The motif of the kingdom of God plays an important role in the trial and crucifixion narrative (Jn 18:33-39; 19:3-21), where the question whether Jesus is a king assumes central importance. But this messianic theme has already emerged in John 1:49; 6:15; 12—15, and entry into salvation is understood as entry into the kingdom of God in the conversation with Nicodemus (Jn 3:3, 5), but this is the only place where the full phrase is used. By contrast the purpose of Jesus is expressed as saving the world (Jn 3:17; 4:42; 12:47) and so of saving the individuals who compose it and who believe (Jn 5:34; 10:9). The total number of references, however, is not great.

Much more importance attaches to the theme of life or eternal life. Again the concept is used in the Synoptic Gospels for the life of the world to come (Mk 9:43, 45; 10:17, 30; Mt 7:14; 18:8-9; 19:16, 17, 29; 25:46; Lk 10:25; 18:18, 30), and there is some tendency perhaps toward using the word to refer to a present experience of life (the combination of "be healed/saved and live" in Mk 5:23; Mt 9:18; life dependent on the words of God, Mt 4:4 par. Lk 4:4; cf. Lk 10:28; 15:24, 32). By contrast the usage of "life" and "live" assumes massive proportions in John. The full phrase *eternal life* occurs no fewer than sixteen times, and the synonymous use of the simple *life* (cf. Jn 3:36a/36b) occurs a further twenty times. The verb is less frequently used but nonetheless significantly. The usage thus indicates that this is a major category in Johannine thought. The gift of life is said to reside in Jesus (Jn 1:4; cf. Jn 6:35, 48; 11:25; 14:6) or even to be identified with him, and his teaching leads to life (Jn 6:68). Such life is closely associated with resurrection (Jn 5:29; 11:25) and also with the Spirit as the life-giving force (Jn 6:63). But it is equally understood as a present experience (Jn 3:36; 5:24; 6:47), so that physical death does not interrupt it. It is God's gift to those who believe in him or in Jesus (Jn 3:16, 36; 5:24), but it is fundamental for John that the Father has authorized Jesus to give life to believers. Thus the life of the world to come becomes a reality here and now for believers.

All of this is expressed in the present tense for those who hear Jesus speaking. The language is clearly appropriate for the period after Easter in that it is common in the early church for the here and now experience of believers. For John it also describes the experience of those who believed in Jesus in his lifetime; he interprets the experience of those who respond to the message of Jesus and become disciples as being essentially the same as that of believers after Easter (though see Jn 7:37-39).

We may compare the way in which in Matthew 18:20 Jesus says, "Where two or three come together in my name, there am I with them". It can be safely assumed that Jesus here is describing something that will happen after his resurrection rather than suggesting that people meet in his name and enjoy his spiritual presence while he is physically somewhere else during his earthly lifetime.[8]

*Union with Christ.* There is much stress in John on faith in Jesus, and he is spoken of as a spiritual figure who is in the disciples and they are in him, just as they are in the Father and the Father is in them. The concern here appears to be with the relationship of the disciples to the risen Jesus, but this is expressed through the words of the earthly Jesus. So there is a considerable amount of teaching in which Jesus looks forward to the situation after the resurrection. This is clearly evident in John 14—16, where Jesus speaks in the future tense of what will happen after he has gone: the Father will send the Counselor; you will do greater works; they will persecute you. But tied in with these future statements are statements in the present tense about Jesus as the vine and the disciples remaining in him. It seems that Jesus uses the present tense here and elsewhere to describe spiritual relationships that exist after his resurrection, but he speaks as if these relationships are already possible during his earthly life, as indeed in some sense they were. Thus, for example, he offers living water to the Samaritan woman there and then, and he tells the crowds that they must eat his flesh and drink his blood and that if they do so they will remain in him and he in them (Jn 6:53-57).

---

[8]Admittedly this text stands on its own. Nevertheless, we may cite Mt 10:40; Mk 9:37; Jn 13:20, where acceptance of the messenger is tantamount to acceptance of the sender. It is easy to see how this could be understood in terms of representation during Jesus' earthly life but in terms of a spiritual coming of the sender to those who accept the human messengers in the period after the resurrection of Jesus.

It is tempting to suggest that the roots of this language lie in the Last Supper and the sayings of Jesus there in which he identifies the bread with his body (or flesh) and the wine with his blood and invites them to eat and drink. The primary significance is that the elements represent his body and blood given in death, so that the action at the Lord's Supper is a visible proclamation of his death. But side by side with this there is the symbolism of somehow feeding on Christ and receiving the benefits of his death, and this is understood in terms of a spiritual relationship between the believer and Christ. We could say, therefore, that the fuller implications of the words and action at the Last Supper here come to expression. At the same time other imagery—drinking water, grafting into the vine—conveys the same point. The more personal imagery of the good Shepherd likewise expresses a personal relationship between the believer and Christ, but not the thought of mystical union.

The motif of spiritual union with Christ is shared with Paul, who speaks of Christ living in him (Gal 2:20; Col 1:27), of being "in Christ" and of knowing Christ (Phil 3:10), and of dying and rising with Christ. It is absent from Acts. Yet it is adumbrated in Luke, where the risen Christ is with the disciples at the breaking of bread. John is thus expressing a central motif of postresurrection Christianity with a root in the tradition of the Last Supper.

In this way the theme of the spiritual relationship between believers and the risen Jesus that is not raised in the Synoptic Gospels, except briefly in Matthew, comes to the fore in John. The same is true of the teaching about the coming of the Holy Spirit. Teaching about spiritual relationships with the risen Christ and the Holy Spirit that is elementary in the Synoptic Gospels is taken much further. Even in Acts this kind of experience is not to the fore, and the divine is experienced more in the manner of visions and messages. John's teaching is much more akin to the Pauline understanding than to the Synoptic with his understanding of the Spirit as the inward source of eternal life and spiritual guidance.

*The way of life.* The way of life expected of disciples in the kingdom of God as it is presented in the Synoptic Gospels can be summed up very briefly as follows.

1. Negatively, there are warnings against following the practices and teachings of other people. The disciples are warned against the hypocrisy of the

Pharisees, which includes self-seeking and outward observance of certain aspects of the law while ignoring the core values of righteousness and mercy. By contrast Jesus gives teaching about the right attitude in giving alms, praying and fasting. There are warnings against false prophets and even false messiahs.

2. Positively, there are the commandments to love God and one's neighbor, stretched to include love of enemies.

3. There is specific instruction regarding marriage and divorce.

4. Jesus teaches his disciples about the hard times that will come in the future before the coming of the Son of Man and urges them to be watchful and ready.

5. Jesus warns against the dangers associated with wealth and calls at least some disciples to give away their wealth.

6. Jesus inculcates trust in God to provide for their needs and bases this on the character of God as Father. He also promises the help of the Holy Spirit in times of special need.

7. Jesus instructs his disciples in how to pray and encourages them to pray.

8. Some disciples are sent out on mission, with specific instructions regarding their conduct particularly in terms of material conditions.

9. There is some teaching that relates to the establishment of a community of disciples and how they are to live together.

Let us now compare what we find in John.

1. Warnings against the Pharisaic way of life are largely absent; the questions that arise in discussion with the Pharisees have more to do with christology. They are castigated for their love of human praise, and this may well reflect the same criticism as we find in the Synoptic Gospels, but here the accusation is made more because they refuse to believe in Christ (Jn 12:42-43).[9]

---

[9]Strictly speaking, the accusation is against the Jewish leaders who feared the Pharisees, but the point still stands.

2. The centrality of love in John is self-evident, although the radical element of love for enemies is missing.

3. The issue of marriage and divorce does not arise (except in Jn 4:16-18).

4. There are specific warnings against persecution, but there are no detailed apocalyptic forecasts.

5. The issue of wealth does not arise (except indirectly in Jn 12:6).

6. Trust in God and the promise of help from the Spirit are expounded at length. The role of the Spirit is considerably enlarged.

7. There is strong encouragement to "ask" (i.e., pray) in the name of Jesus.[10]

8. The mission of the disciples is a conspicuous feature (Jn 4:38; 17:18; 20:21).

9. The disciples are addressed as if they are a community through the use of such imagery as that of the flock and the vine.

These points indicate a basic agreement between the Synoptic Gospels and John on the nature of the way of life of disciples.

*The future and believers.* Although the Synoptic Gospels are primarily concerned with the new situation brought about by the proclamation and activity of Jesus, they also contain teaching about the future. They all are written from a post-Easter standpoint and know that the Christian church continues to exist, committed to the mission entrusted to it by Jesus. They have an understanding of history in which the outlook is bleak. On the one hand, there is every reason to believe that the negative reaction of the Jewish authorities to Jesus will continue, directed now against his followers; Jesus had foreseen that this would happen. On the other hand, the Evangelists were conscious of indications that the kind of cosmic and human events associated with the coming of the end of the world were already happening. Specifically, they knew of the prophecies of judgment made by Jesus against Jerusalem and the temple, and they saw signs of them being fulfilled, along with the broader evidences of wars and natural

---

[10]The words *pray* and *prayer* (*proseuchomai, proseuchē*) are conspicuous by their total absence; a different set of prayer words and phrases is used.

disasters. Most scholars would accept that the war between the Jews and the Romans in A.D. 66-70 forms the backdrop to the writing of the Gospels, whether as something seen to be increasingly inevitable and near or as an event that had already taken place.

It is not surprising that a significant amount of attention is given to these events. A further factor in the situation was the belief that imposters would appear, claiming to be the Messiah or Jesus, with the danger that followers of Jesus would be misled. Therefore there are detailed warnings to prepare the readers for these events accompanied by assurances that despite the dreadful things that were going to happen, the Son of Man would intervene to rescue his people and bring about the final judgment. All the Synoptic Gospels devote major sections to these matters and use cosmic imagery, typical of apocalyptic writings, to describe what will happen. We should bear in mind that any attempt to prophesy what will happen at the end of the world was bound to describe events that fall outside the borders of normal human experience, but also that the boundaries between describing appalling human events (the ancient equivalents to the Holocaust and great natural disasters) and cataclysmic divine interventions are inevitably fuzzy.

In John's Gospel account is similarly taken of the future of the disciples and the world. To the so-called apocalyptic discourses in the Synoptic Gospels there correspond two sections in the Johannine literature. The one is the main storyline in Revelation, which likewise traces the course of future events. Although there are similarities in the basic account of what will happen, Revelation goes well beyond the Synoptic material in extent and content. The differences are, first, whereas the Gospels deal almost entirely with events in this world, Revelation also describes the concurrent events in heaven from which the judgments come. Second, Revelation describes at some length the actual judgment and the new world that follows it. Third, Revelation goes into much detail about the temporal judgments of God on the sinful world. In all of this the aim of the book appears to be to prepare the church to face up to the persecution that lies ahead by issuing a call for preparedness for martyrdom and by assuring believers of the ultimate triumph of God and of the new world into which they will be resurrected.

Within the Gospel we have the lengthy section comprising John 14—17 in which Jesus deals at length with the situation of believers after his departure.

The dangers arising from opposition and persecution are made clear; there is a warning against the possibility that believers may fall away. The disciples are promised the help of the Spirit in a much broader way than is found in the Synoptic Gospels, and they are allowed to overhear the prayer of Jesus in which he seeks divine resources for them to protect them. But otherwise there is little resemblance. The shadow of the Jewish war is not evident. The coming of Jesus for his disciples is muted (Jn 14:3).[11] The end of the world is scarcely in view.

It seems to be the case that the core teaching can be presented in two different idioms. John 14—17 prepares the disciples for the future without the physical presence of Jesus by forewarning them of hostility and persecution, and urges them to stand firm, relying on the help of the Holy Spirit. The Gospel implicitly rather than explicitly indicates that the time of trial is a limited one, since Jesus will return, and as he returned to the Father after being sent into the world to bear witness, so they too will be with Jesus in the end. Elsewhere in the Gospel there are promises that disciples will be raised at the last day (Jn 6:39-52; cf. Jn 11:24; 21:22), and the hope of being with Christ when he comes is repeated in I John 2:28 and I John 3:2.[12] What is said here in a mood of didactic encouragement is in essence what is said much more graphically in the Synoptic Gospels. But there the teaching about the help of the Spirit is much less developed, and the material is interwoven with the other theme of the fall of Jerusalem and the temple, coupled with the danger of misreading this event as a sign of the imminence of the last day.

*Conclusion.* What has not come out so far in this comparison of motifs is the framework of thought within which John operates. This is his dualism in which there is a clear distinction between the spheres symbolized by light and darkness. The world is in darkness, but the light can shine in it, and there can be people who belong to the light within it (Jn 12:35-36). The language is not so very different from that in Matthew 4:16 (Is 9:2) and Matthew 5:14-16, but it is used to express a basic structure of John's thought. However, we have observed the great differences in emphasis between the Synoptic Gospels and John, so that (for example) the proclamation of the kingdom of God

---

[11]Jn 14:8 would seem to refer more naturally to the spiritual coming of Jesus to the disciples through the Spirit.

[12]I see no reason to accept the view that these references to the last day are glosses added to the text by a later reviser.

has all but disappeared. The way of expressing the theology is thus significantly other.

Nevertheless, despite all the differences between them we can now see that the essential structure and content of the theologies of the Synoptic Gospels and of John are very much the same. The Synoptic Gospels are probably much closer to the *ipsissima verba* of Jesus and to his teaching about the future, whereas the Johannine literature evidences a much more developed theology that reflects more fully the insights of early Christians in the period after the resurrection. Let it be repeated: it is emphatically not the aim or intention of this present discussion to iron out the differences between John and the Synoptic Gospels or to trivialize them. Nor is it possible in this context to attempt a historical explanation of how they have arisen. The aim is much more modest: to ask whether there is sufficient agreement in substance between them to allow us to conclude that they are different expressions of the same underlying theological apprehension. In my view this is in fact the case.

### John and Paul

Our next task must be to compare the Johannine theology with what we know of the postresurrection theology of the early church from its principal witness, the Pauline literature.

The theology of Paul is constituted in part by the debate with Judaizers and with proponents of a way of thinking that was more indebted to Hellenistic ways of thinking that emphasized wisdom, knowledge and human status. In the later writings there is a strong consciousness of the threat of supernatural powers that was worrying to believers. Throughout the letters there is much engagement with the general problems and issues that arise within the congregations as they struggle with the growing pains of learning to live as Christians in fellowship. These matters are much less to the fore in the Gospel of John, where the dispute is much more with the synagogue and its rejection of Jesus as the Messiah and where the more specific issues of life within the church are not a primary concern; however inner-church issues are to the fore in the letters of John. We shall therefore expect that the general shape and manner of expression may be rather different.

**God and Jesus Christ.** Clearly the understanding of God is the same for both writers. For Paul, as for John, there is one God whose character is summed up in the title of Father. He is the God of Israel, active throughout the history of that people.

Jesus Christ is for Paul the one Lord who is regularly placed alongside God the Father in regard not only to creation but also to the spiritual blessings given to believers. He is preexistent, associated with God in creation. He is the Son of God, sent from God to the world to redeem humanity. In so doing, he laid aside his equality with God and took the role of a servant in becoming human. He was raised from the dead and exalted to sit at the right hand of God, where he presently reigns, and he will return at the end of history to gather together his people, to raise the dead and to execute judgment.

John presents the same picture. He identifies Jesus as the eternal Word who was with God in the beginning and shared in the task of creation. The Word became flesh and shared human life. The humanity of Jesus is real in John. Incarnation means nothing less. Pilate's comment "Here is the man" (Jn 19:5) has doubtless a deeper meaning, but there is no trace of any Adam typology.[13] John develops massively the concept of Jesus as the Son of God and his sending by God into the world. Originally sharing a glorious state with the Father, he came into the world, where his glory was visible to his disciples, although in a different form, and he returns to God and to the glorious state that he formerly had. Where Paul stresses more his exaltation to the right hand of God (cf. Ps 110), John emphasizes his close relation to God as Son. Where Paul makes some limited use of the concept of wisdom, John's prologue makes full use of the concept of the Word, which is closely linked to wisdom.

*The Holy Spirit.* For Paul the Holy Spirit is beginning to be understood as a personal being who can be named along with the Father and the Son, and in John this understanding is taken further with the identification of the Spirit as the Paraclete who acts as a person and is not simply a form of divine power.

*The Scriptures.* Paul and John accept the authority of the Scriptures as divine revelation (Rom 1:2; cf. 2 Tim 3:16; Jn 7:19; 8:17; 10:34), although they differ in the ways in which they make use of them. The Scripture is authoritative in its teaching. It bears testimony to an ongoing history of God's dealings with his

---

[13]Interestingly Jn 1:30 is the only instance of *anēr* (rather than the usual *anthrōpos*) being used of Jesus in the New Testament. It is natural for other people to refer to Jesus as a man (Jn 4:29; 7:46; 10:33).

people in judging and saving them. Moses and the prophets bear witness to the coming of the Messiah and to the way of salvation through him (Rom 3:21; Jn 1:45). Paul has a lot to say about the law of Moses because it was an issue with the Judaizers. This was evidently not the case for John; his reference to the law in John 1:17 is not pejorative. Similarly, the issue of works of the law is marginal in John (Jn 6:28-29), presumably because the matter of Gentiles being required to keep the law was not a problem for his readers.

*Humanity and its need.* For both writers the main story is concerned with the fact of human sin and the divine response. Paul paints a picture of humanity in which the concepts of sin and the flesh are central tools for his exposition. Sin is the alien power that overcomes human beings and renders them liable to death. The flesh is human nature, captivated by sin and incapable of doing what is good and right. John works with the same concept of sin but does not have the same concept of the flesh; instead he operates with various expressions of a dualism in which the world of human beings is in darkness, conceived as a sphere in which evil reigns, a realm below and distinct from the divine realm. Either way, human beings are in the grip of sin and under the threat of death. They stand under divine judgment. Where Paul can speak of God's wrath already being revealed from heaven (Rom 1:18), John talks of a divine judgment that people have already brought upon themselves (Jn 3:18); for both authors the future judgment is a recognition of the existing state of humanity, and the issue is death (cf. 1 Jn 5:16-17).

*Jesus and his role.* For John Jesus appears much more in the role of a teacher simply because he has expressed his theology in the form of a Gospel. Nevertheless, this earthly role becomes one of revelation that is ongoing after the departure of Jesus through the Spirit. The question arises whether the story of Jesus is understood from the cross as its focal point or from the incarnation. Hahn suggests that "whereas for Paul the incarnation is the essential presupposition for the death of Jesus, the Johannine theology is conceived from the incarnation, so that the death of Jesus is the final consequence of the incarnation".[14] He insists that this is a difference in emphasis. Certainly the human life of Jesus plays an almost negligible role in Paul; it is important that he was a man, born of a woman and born under the law, and there is the very occasional

---

[14]Hahn, 1:612.

reference to his authoritative teaching. One could say that, like the creed, Paul moves straight from the incarnation to the cross, and the cross-resurrection is the saving event. For John the life and teaching of Jesus constitute the heart of the story, but in his letters it disappears almost completely from view in the same way as in Paul. Nevertheless, the role of Jesus as the Lamb of God is stressed at the outset of the Gospel. Moreover, the way in which this Gospel devotes an even greater proportion of its space than the Synoptic Gospels do to the final visit of Jesus to Jerusalem shows that "his hour" is indeed the climax of the story, for which the rest is preparation.

In Paul the death of Jesus is understood as his becoming one with sinners in order that through him they may become righteous. The concept of justification is the most fully developed of the images used by Paul, and even though this development may have been catalyzed by the need to interact with Judaizers, it is still of key importance to him. This language is unknown to John. But he knows that Jesus takes away sins, that he dies on behalf of human beings and that the cross and resurrection constitute the point where Satan is driven out. And in I John the same understanding of the cross as an atoning sacrifice for the sins of the world as in Paul is clearly present. Even without the evidence of I John the testimony of the Gospel, where the role of the Lamb is either as a sacrificial victim or as a scapegoat, is quite sufficient to make the point.

*God's initiative in salvation.* Paul and John display a tension between universality and particularism. The purpose of God is the salvation of humankind, and both authors make statements that indicate unequivocally that his sending of Jesus Christ is to provide a means of salvation from sin for all people. In the case of Paul, this is particularly directed to stressing that this purpose includes Gentiles alongside Jews. This point is equally firmly made in John (Jn 12:20-33; cf. Jn 10:16). Such statements do not carry anything to indicate that this offer of salvation is in reality intended only for certain Jews and Gentiles, namely, those foreordained to salvation by God, and the gospel is presented in such a way that whoever believes the message may have salvation.

However, we also have statements in both authors that might appear to teach some kind of limited election. In Paul we find that it is those whom God foreknew who are predestined to be conformed to the likeness of his Son (Rom 8:29-30). In Romans 9 it appears that God has the freedom to choose some and pass over others or even harden their hearts so that they cannot believe, although Paul shrinks back from actually saying that God has so acted except in judgment on those who have sinned. Similarly, in John 6 it is said that those whom the Father gives to Christ will come to him, and he will accept whoever comes to him in this way. There is the statement that some of Jesus' audience do not believe because they are not his sheep (Jn 10:26), with the apparent implication that people who have been chosen to be sheep are able to believe, but others are not able to believe; yet even in this context Jesus still urges his audience to believe (Jn 10:37-38). Again it seems possible that those who are not Jesus' sheep are those who have refused to believe and consequently stand under judgment. If people are not saved but remain under condemnation, it is because they have refused the good news, and not because God did not give them the opportunity to be saved. Both writers hold that in the case of some people their continuing refusal to believe is because of a divine hardening of their hearts, apparently as a judgment upon them for an earlier refusal to believe. The question of those who never have the opportunity to hear the gospel is not raised. Paul appears to believe that all Israelites have heard (or will hear) the message through the messengers whom God sends, and he urges the importance of evangelists taking the good news into the world (Rom 10.14-21).

The existence of these tensions in the two writers is striking. Both Paul and John teach the universality of the offer of salvation and the sufficiency of the work of Christ for all humanity. Both affirm that God and Christ are entirely at one in their will to save (Rom 8:31-35; Jn 6:37). Both recognize that not everybody who hears responds to the offer with faith. Equally, both authors indicate that salvation results entirely from the initiative of God in sending Christ and in sending out his followers to proclaim the good news; human beings can contribute nothing to their own salvation, and the only work that is required of them is not a work but is faith.

Paul and John give different explanations for unbelief. Paul states that some Jews have chosen to follow the path of salvation by works and rejected the path of faith, and they are held to be culpable for doing so. John says that some people do not openly believe out of fear of excommunication and because they love human glory more than divine glory (Jn 12:42-43), and he warns those who refuse to believe that they stand condemned.

**New life in union with Christ.** The fundamental theologoumenon that brings Paul and John together is probably the way in which they each have a profound

understanding of the spiritual relationship between Christ and believers, corporately and individually. In Paul this is primarily conveyed by the "in Christ"
phraseology that establishes the way in which the lives of believers are determined by their relationship to Christ. The reciprocal thought that Christ is in
believers is extremely rare by comparison (Gal 2:20; cf. Eph 3:17; Col 1:27).
The same closeness of relationship to God is expressed by the way in which the
Holy Spirit is closely linked to believers. Corporately, the church is the body
and bride of Christ, and in the later letters this is expressed in terms of a divine
fullness that flows from Christ to the church. Through the relationship with
Christ believers are understood to have died with Christ and to have been raised
to newness of life that will culminate in their being raised with spiritual bodies
or being taken to be with Christ.

In John we find language of mutual indwelling between Christ and believers
and the Father and believers, and this is closely linked to the thought of the Spirit
coming or being given to believers, but reciprocal language is lacking at this
point. John does not have the concept of dying and rising with Christ (but he
comes close to dying with Christ in Jn 12:24-26). John develops the imagery of
the vine and its branches to describe the relationship of believers collectively to
Christ, and Paul has something similar in his brief allusion to the olive tree and
its branches (Rom 11:16-24). And John develops the thought of the essential
content of eternal life being to know God and Christ (Jn 17:3), a thought that
surfaces briefly in Paul (Phil 3:8; cf. Eph 3:19). In both sets of writings there is
frequent reference to prayer as the natural expression of the relationship between
believers and God. Both writers thus have highly developed understandings of
the new life in Christ, although they develop the same idea in different ways.

*Life in community.* John's Gospel has an implicit understanding of the disciples of Jesus as forming a community. The images of the flock and the vine
bring out this fact that disciples are not isolated individuals but belong together. It might be objected that in both cases the links are between the individual disciples and Jesus rather than between the disciples themselves. This objection is overruled by two considerations. The one is the way in which Jesus
recognizes a distinction between the sheep belonging to "this sheep pen", evidently the Jews, and his "other sheep", presumably the Gentiles, and goes on
to state that they will be brought together to constitute one flock cared for by
the one shepherd (Jn 10:14-16). There is thus a union between different

groups of disciples. The other factor is the way in which the imagery of the vine is immediately followed by Jesus' teaching about love and specifically that the disciples are to love one another as he has loved them (Jn 15:1-17). This teaching is then reinforced in 1 John, where the recipients are related to one another as brothers and sisters and must love one another in action and not just in words (1 Jn 3:11-18, 23; 4:11-12, 20—5:2; 2 Jn 5), and also pray for one another (1 Jn 5:16).

This understanding of the church is shared by Paul. It emerges all the more sharply because he is writing to congregations about their life, and therefore the mutual relationships of believers are continually under discussion. Consequently there is far more development and detail in Paul on fairly practical levels of what happens when believers come together. The exercise of the gifts of the Spirit is prominent, not just in 1 Corinthians 12 and Romans 12 but also briefly in 2 Corinthians 12:12, Galatians 3:5 and 1 Thessalonians 5:19-21 (cf. Eph 4:7-13). Comparison of the lists in this set of passages demonstrates the variety of gifts and erases any impression that there is one fixed list of gifts.

With that point made, we can then observe that the Spirit is also active in gifting the disciples for mission in John 20:21-23. John accordingly is aware of the activity of the Spirit in the work of the disciples. Indeed, the Spirit's activity in witnessing to the world about sin, righteousness and judgment (Jn 16:7-11) is, as we noted earlier, an activity carried out through the disciples. There is also the activity of the Spirit in teaching within the Christian group (Jn 14:25-26; 16:12-15), which should not be understood simply as the guidance of individual believers but as the gift of teaching for the benefit of the disciples generally. In 1 John the readers are said to have received an anointing that conveys teaching to them. It is recognized that the existence of prophets in the congregation necessitates some kind of testing of them to see whether they are truly inspired by the Spirit since unfortunately in every age there is the danger of false prophets leading God's people astray (1 Jn 2:26-27; 4:1-6). Here we have a remarkably close parallel to Paul's teaching about the need for the testing of prophecies (1 Thess 5:21). From 2-3 John we learn of the existence of traveling teachers and the development of local leadership (not without some problems reflected in 3 John) in a way that is not dissimilar from what we find in Paul. Otherwise, there is little to pick up from John about what happened when Christians met together. We must beware of assuming that practices were the same everywhere;

what we are concerned to demonstrate is the charismatic nature of congregational life coupled with the development of local leadership across early Christianity.

*Mission.* The missionary nature of the church is immediately apparent in Paul's letters. He introduces himself as an apostle or missionary writing to the congregations that he has founded and planted. There is an ongoing mission to which he is obligated, and there is a sense of geographical goals to be reached. Although he says surprisingly little about the responsibility of congregations to engage in mission where they are, he expects them to participate in the mission that has been entrusted to his colleagues and himself by their support in prayer and by the provision of helpers; he is somewhat ambivalent about monetary support but nevertheless did receive gifts.

The concept of mission in John is presented in terms of Jesus as being sent on a mission whose goal is to save the world, and he entrusts his mission to his followers (Jn 4:38; 17:18; 20:21). The catch of 153 fish after the resurrection appears to be symbolical of the harvest to be gathered. The disciples are to confer forgiveness or to withhold it, presumably from people who refuse to believe, and they are given the Spirit to enable them for their task. The Pauline and Johannine pictures agree on the fundamental fact that the followers of Christ are called to a mission that brings salvation to those who accept their message.

*The coming of Christ and the resurrection.* Paul's teaching about the ultimate future ("eschatology" for shorthand) centers on the coming of Christ and the resurrection of the dead. History moves to a climax during which the effective dominion of Christ is extended over all things, and he returns as a glorious figure to gather together his people who are still alive, raise up those who have died, and transform them to be like himself for their future life with him. The rest of the dead are raised up, but not transformed, to face the wrath of God at the judgment, which is carried out by Christ. Paul knows of a final outbreak of evil in power before the coming of the end.

For John there is the same hope of eternal life for those who belong to Christ. The story of Lazarus offers an acted parable of resurrection from the dead. But John also teaches that all the dead will hear the voice of the Son of Man and be raised to life or to condemnation and wrath (Jn 5:28-29). As in Paul, it is Christ to whom the task of judgment is delegated. The hope of the return of Christ is still there, but there is less stress on it in the Gospel. The basic structure of expectation that we have in Paul is thus also present in John, but the accents are differently placed, with rather more stress on eternal life. This would not be surprising for an author writing somewhat later at a point when far more believers had already died. But we must not omit to note that the Johannine literature includes the full-scale drama concerning the activity of evil in the last days and the judgment upon all people in Revelation and also the recognition of the activities of antichrists here and now wherever the coming of Jesus as the Christ is denied (1 Jn 2:22; 2 Jn 7).

*Conclusion.* This comparison shows that in Paul and John we have two presentations of early Christian theology that have essentially the same basic structures and agree to a very considerable extent in their detailed content; at the same time, they do differ in their conceptuality and style. We have two different artists or schools of artists who see the same subject in different ways, but it is the same subject, and we need both sets of pictures to bring out the richness of the common theme.

# PART 5

# HEBREWS, JAMES, 1-2 PETER AND JUDE

# 25

# THE LETTER TO THE
# HEBREWS

❦

The letter to the Hebrews begins majestically like a speech and ends personally like a letter. It presumably incorporates a written form of a sermon on a single theme that the writer sent to a congregation for which he had a particular concern. The most plausible account of their situation is still that a group of Christians were being tempted to fall away from their Christian faith as a result of a combination of external pressure and internal weakness. An older view was that their precise temptation was to relapse into the Judaism from which they had turned to Christianity.[1] Whether this be so or not, the author wrote to demonstrate to them the impossibility of salvation apart from Christ on the basis of their shared acceptance of the Old Testament Scriptures and to call them to be prepared for the long haul of faith and the tribulations associated with it.

The author's identity is unknown, but he was a man, not a woman,[2] and he was familiar with the thought world of Hellenistic Judaism. The identity of the readers is likewise unknown, but Hebrews 13:24 probably implies that

---

[1]Barnabas Lindars, *The Theology of the Letter to the Hebrews* (Cambridge: Cambridge University Press, 1991), pp. 12-15, suggests that the readers had a consciousness of sin but had lost faith in the power of Christ's sacrifice to deal with their guilt and were turning to Jewish rites to give them the peace that they lacked.

[2]The masculine gender of the participle in Heb 11:32 is decisive.

they were in Italy. The date of the letter is disputed, but I favor a date before A.D. 70.

The structure of the argument has been a matter of intense detailed discussion, but we may safely adopt the following analysis or something like it.

Hebrews 1:1—2:18 The revelation of God through his Son
Hebrews 3:1—5:10 The Son as high priest
Hebrews 5:11—10:39 The high priestly office of the Son
Hebrews 11:1—12:13 The need for faith and endurance
Hebrews 12:14—13:25 The Christian life in a hostile world

Within this broad framework there is an alternation of sections that are more doctrinal and more paraenetical; the latter are found in Hebrews 2:1-4; 3:1—4:14; 5:11—6:12; 10:19-39; 12:1-13; 12:14—13:25.[3] It is thus characteristic of this writer that he weaves together instruction and exhortation.

### The Theological Story

The writer's theological style is a mixture of assertion and of exposition of Scripture. No other New Testament writer makes such full and explicit use of Scripture as the foundation of his argument.

*The revelation of God through his Son (Heb 1:1—2:18).* In his opening section (Heb 1:1-14) the writer plunges straight into a statement of the high position of Jesus, whose message is superior to that of the prophets in virtue of his role in relation to the universe and of his status as the one who shares the being of God and is enthroned beside him. This makes him superior even to the angels, a theme developed in the rest of Hebrews 1 by a series of scriptural quotations that show how God addresses Jesus in a way that he never addressed the angels and makes assertions about him that are superior to anything that is ever said about angels.[4] No arguments are advanced for the way in which the writer can regard certain Old Testament texts as being about Jesus; he must have been able to assume that his readers

---

[3]This analysis is based on William L. Lane, *Hebrews* (Dallas: Word, 1991), 1:cii-ciii.

[4]Hübner, 3:61-62, draws particular attention to the way in which God speaks to the Son (and addresses him as God!) and the Son speaks to the Father (Heb 10:5-7), thereby demonstrating their complete unity in the work of redemption. The Holy Spirit also speaks to the people on behalf of God (Heb 10:15-17).

shared his method of understanding the Old Testament.[5]

The practical corollary (Heb 2:1-4) is that it is all the more culpable to neglect the salvation provided by Jesus if the lesser message spoken by angels incurred penalties for disobedience. The reference is to the giving of the law through the mediation of angels. The description of the announcement of salvation is of particular interest for its close congruence with the way in which Luke describes the preaching of the gospel with accompanying signs and the gifts of the Spirit in Acts.

In the second installment of this first part of the letter (Heb 2:5-18) the writer next proceeds to accommodate the suffering and death of Jesus, which might appear to be an argument against his superiority to the angels. By using Psalm 8 he is able to show how Jesus was made lower than the angels only for a short time so that he might be one with his human kindred and suffer death for the twofold purpose of defeating the devil and making atonement for the sins of humanity. With this comment the writer introduces the dominant theme of Jesus as high priest that will occupy him for most of the rest of the letter.

*The Son as high priest (Heb 3:1—5:10).* However, the writer begins his exposition a little distance away from this in a practical section (Heb 3:1—4:13) by first of all comparing Jesus with Moses and establishing his superiority as that of the Son as compared with the servant, even though Moses was the principal servant. But as with the message given by the angels, so the Israelites were persistently unbelieving and rebellious over against Moses, and there is the continuing danger that those who have heard the gospel may equally fail to believe and so be excluded from the "rest" spoken of in Psalm 95. This concept of rest is tantamount to salvation, and the writer explains that although originally it signified entry to the Promised Land, the promise is not exhausted by that;

---

[5]The quotations are from Ps 2:7; 2 Sam 7:14; Deut 32:43; Ps 104:4; Ps 45:6-7; Ps 102:25-27; Ps 110:1. Ps 104 is about the angels and causes no difficulties. The messianic interpretation of Ps 2, 2 Sam 7 and Ps 110 is shared with other New Testament writers. The interpretation of Ps 45 as messianic was natural, since this was also a psalm about the Lord's anointed. The use of the other passages is more problematic. Deut 32:43 in the form cited here was part of the Odes attached to the Psalter (cf. also Ps 96:7), and the reference to the making of atonement may have been sufficient to justify seeing in it a reference to Christ rather than to the Father. In the LXX Ps 102:25-27 was understood as a statement by God rather than an address to him (as in the MT). See Stephen Motyer, "The Psalm Quotations of Hebrews I: A Hermeneutic-Free Zone?" *TynB* 50.1 (1999): 3-22.

there is still an experience of salvation available for believers. The implicit exhortation to persevere in belief is buttressed negatively by a warning that the state of the human heart is visible to God and positively by an intimation that with Jesus as their high priest the readers can come with confidence before this God and expect to find mercy.

With the theme of the high priest now clearly intimated, the way appears to be open for a more detailed exposition, and the writer begins to give this (Heb 5:1-10) with a general statement of the need for a high priest to be a sympathetic representative of humanity and to be appointed by God to his office. Both of these requirements are fulfilled in the case of Jesus, particularly through his suffering, which perfected him for his role as Savior.

*The high priestly office of the Son (Heb 5:11—10:39).* The next step in the argument should be to develop the exposition of the task of Jesus as high priest, but before being launched into it we again have a practical section (Heb 5:11—6:20). The writer warns his readers that they are in danger of spiritual unpreparedness for the teaching that he is about to give. Ironically he suggests that they need a simple diet of teaching, but nevertheless he proposes to continue as if they were ready for more advanced teaching, providing that they are prepared to receive it. There is the danger that people may turn their backs on salvation and so on the Savior, in which case there is no hope for them. But although the danger is real, he is not persuaded that it is the case with them, and when he bears in mind the signs of salvation that he has observed in the readers he is encouraged to press on with his teaching. They for their part must continue in faith and they will inherit what God has promised. For God's promise, confirmed to Abraham with an oath, is utterly reliable. Believers, therefore, have a hope on which they can rely. Beyond what they can see is the heavenly sanctuary within which Jesus is present as their high priest.

So he begins his major teaching section, which is concerned with the role of Jesus as high priest (Heb 7:1—10:18). The right of Jesus to be high priest, although he belonged to the tribe of Judah and not to the priestly tribe of Levi, is justified by comparison with the intriguing figure of Melchizedek, who functioned as an independent priest of God in the time of Abraham, long before the levitical priesthood came into being. So too Jesus owes his position to his indestructible life and to his appointment by God, confirmed by God's oath. Thus Jesus is able to continue in office, uninterrupted by death, by contrast with the earthly levitical priests. He has made a once-for-all sacrifice, and he is able to exercise an uninterrupted ministry of intercession.

An elaborate comparison is now developed to assert the superiority of Jesus' priesthood. Two contrasts are drawn. The first is between the earthly character of the levitical priesthood, serving in the tabernacle built by Moses, and the heavenly character of the priesthood of Jesus, serving in the heavenly tabernacle of which the earthly was merely a copy. Here the writer takes up the story of the heavenly drawing used by Moses (Ex 25:40) and concludes from it that there is a heavenly tabernacle to which the earthly one corresponds as a shadowy outline of the real thing.[6] The second contrast is between the first or old covenant made with Moses and the promise of a new covenant made to Jeremiah. It is an easy step for the writer to assert that the second covenant must be superior to the first, since otherwise God would not have made it, and to identify it with the new state of affairs mediated by Christ. Here he is building on the already current belief of early Christians that Jesus had inaugurated the new covenant by his death.

With this parallelism established, it is possible for the writer to draw out the correspondences and contrasts between the two systems. It would be fair to say that the two systems have the same general structure of a tabernacle with an altar and a system of offerings of sacrifices whose blood cleanses from sin. The contrast is that the heavenly tabernacle is not material, that Christ has offered himself and not an animal, that Christ has made one offering of himself once for all by contrast with the repeated sacrifices of the levitical priests, and that there is no need for repetition of the one offering. When Christ returns, it will not be to act again as a sacrificial victim but to bring salvation to those who are waiting for him.

But the point is taken further. The contrast is not between two efficacious ways of dealing with sin, the first being the one that worked in the past until it was superseded by the second, namely, the sacrifice of Christ. In fact the levitical sacrifices could not of themselves take away sin: how could the blood of animals possibly do so? Even though the law required them, they were not in fact what God wanted. These sacrifices, therefore, were simply shadows or reflections of the real thing. The sacrifice of Christ achieves its end perfectly and

---

[6]The writer's thought is sometimes thought to be based on the well-known Platonic contrast between the "ideas" in heaven and the copies of them on earth. Against this view see especially L. D. Hurst, *The Epistle to the Hebrews: Its Background of Thought* (Cambridge: Cambridge University Press, 1990), pp. 13-17.

once and for all, and thus it inaugurates a new covenant under which people can be truly cleansed from sin.

The practical lesson emerges at once (Heb 10:19-39). Christian believers can confidently approach God in prayer free from the guilt of sin. With such a privilege in mind they should continue in faith and the activities that faith inspires. They must remember that if they go on sinning, there is no other way of forgiveness; the particular sin in mind is the rejection of Christ as Savior. But again the writer is warning against a possible danger rather than one that has overcome his readers—or at least he writes in these terms in order to encourage them not to proceed further on the downward track away from belief. Let them persist in their faith, for it cannot be that long until Jesus returns.

*The need for faith and endurance (Heb 11:1—12:13).* The carefully contrived mention of faith creates the bridge for the final teaching section of the letter, which develops the notion of a faith that trusts in God where it cannot see and that persists in belief despite every disincentive to do so. The parallel between the old and the new covenants continues in that the faithful believers under the old covenant persisted in faith although they could not yet see the realization of the promises of God and walked by faith rather than by sight. They recognized that the world that they could see was not the world to which they really belonged, and they believed that God could triumph over death. So too it is with those who live under the new covenant; they are equally strangers and pilgrims, gripped by the firm hope that God will fulfill his promises.

Again the practical relevance is pressed home to Christians who are under pressure to give up their faith. There is every encouragement from the believers of the past and Jesus to persist and persevere. Let them see the pressures to abandon faith positively as tests to strengthen faith; God is using this painful means of discipline to make them stronger. And (a repeated thought in the letter) let there be mutual encouragement as the strong help the weak.

*The Christian life in a hostile world (Heb 12:14—13:25).* The final section of the letter deals on an even more practical level with life in the hostile world.[7] There are warnings against sexual immorality and material greed. There is en-

---

[7]Heb 13:22-25 is the typical conclusion of a letter, turning what precedes (if it was originally a sermon) into the body of a letter. This process was aided by the fact that the final main section of the document is very similar to the closing sections of other New Testament letters in its coverage of miscellaneous practicalities.

couragement built on a contrast between the fearsomeness of Mount Sinai, where the law was given, and Mount Zion, where there is a vast company to welcome the readers; but with the encouragement there is a repeated warning not to treat the God of Zion with contempt and incur his wrath. The Christian situation is seen as one of privilege over against the emptiness of what Judaism has to offer but also of disgrace in terms of the social exclusion that Christians may have to endure. In the end, Christians depend upon their prayers for one another and upon the inward working of the power of God (Heb 13:21) to provide them with the spiritual resources that they need for their pilgrimage.

## Theological Themes

*The old and the new.* As the summary of the argument has shown, the conceptuality of the letter is provided in large measure by the category of priesthood and sacrifice that is developed in this document in a way unparalleled elsewhere in the New Testament. The writer's concern is primarily with the work of Christ, and everything that he says about the status of Christ is preparatory to the discussion of his work and is designed to establish that he is indeed fit to be the high priest under the new covenant. The aim is to show clearly that the work of Christ was to bring salvation in a unique way, so that the readers would realize that there was salvation nowhere else but through Christian faith.

The development of this argument is structured in terms of a basic general contrast between "the past" and "these last days", intimated at the beginning of the letter, and this governs the thought of the writer. The point of the contrast is not to condemn the set-up in the past as though it were invalid but rather to establish the following points.

First, "in the past" God interacted with his people through prophets who were genuinely his messengers, through the agency of Moses who ranked highly as the servant in charge of God's house, through the angels by whose agency the law was given, through the law as the revelation of God's ways for his people, through the promises of God which were real, and specifically through the sacrificial system laid down in the law, by means of which the succession of priests made atonement for the people, and through the faith of God's people by which they gained genuine blessings.

Second, this set-up is contrasted with that of the present time as being no longer valid, however much it once was. The old covenant has been succeeded by the new, which indeed it had foretold; the priesthood of Christ has replaced that of Aaron; his single sacrifice has replaced the many offerings of the ancient priests; a heavenly offering has replaced the earthly offerings at the tabernacle. Nevertheless the way of faith is still the same.

Third, the old set-up provided the pattern for interpreting what is going on now. Thus the present age can be understood as that of the new covenant, but we learn what a covenant is from the old covenant. Equally the whole enterprise of understanding the work of Jesus as sacrificial depends upon drawing analogies from the Old Testament system to the work of Jesus. This analogy requires that there is a real, structural similarity between the two. It is important to show that Jesus was appointed as a priest so that his work can be understood in terms of the Old Testament priesthood.

However, it is vital to observe that although the writer argues from the Jewish system, with which his readers were familiar, to the work of Christ, as if the former provided the categories for interpreting the latter, nevertheless he recognizes that the ontological order is the reverse. In fact what Christ did in the heavenly sanctuary is the pattern that was followed by the old system of tabernacle and sacrifices, so that the latter can be regarded as shadows of the real thing (Heb 8:5; 9:23-24).

Fourth, although the law laid down God's requirements that had to be carried out (Heb 10:8), the writer emphasizes that the old set-up could not take away sins and was thus not efficacious (Heb 9:9; 10:11). Its effects were purely external (Heb 9:13). It could not produce perfection (Heb 7:11, 19; 10:1). The old covenant had something wrong with it, or else it would not have needed to be replaced (Heb 8:7).

To be sure, this fundamental criticism of the sacrificial system creates the same problem as we find in Paul, where the question of how people got right with God before the coming of Christ also arises. The system was a shadow or reflection of the true system (Heb 10:1). It might be possible to assert that by reason of this it was efficacious in taking away sin, but the writer does not go so far as to say so. He limits its efficacy to an external cleansing and its time span to the period before the new order was introduced (Heb 9:10). Nevertheless it was there by divine command. Moreover, we are not told that it was impossible to be in a right relationship with God before the coming of Christ. There is a significant statement that people who sinned under the first covenant are granted redemption through the death of Jesus (Heb 9:15). This may be a hint that the sacrifices under the old system achieved an outward cleansing that was symbolical of the spiritual cleansing achieved by the sacrifice of Christ to which they pointed. However, the point is not made clear, since the writer's main concern is to demonstrate that, now that Christ has come, there is no longer any need for the old.[8]

Here we must introduce yet another concept which is fundamental to the letter, that of perfecting God's people. This language is used of Jesus and of his people. It is brought into the discussion of the sacrifices, which were not able to perfect the worshipers so far as their consciences were concerned, but only to cleanse them externally (Heb 9:9) and temporally (Heb 10:1). Here, then, the term refers to the sacrifices accomplishing that which ideally they should have been able to do, namely, to cleanse people completely from their sins. But the ordinances of the law could not do this (Heb 7:19); they were weak and imperfect. By contrast Christ is able to make perfect those who are being made holy (Heb 10:14). The implication is that he does fully and effectively what the law could not achieve, to cleanse people inwardly and permanently from their sins and so make them fit to enter into the presence of God without fear (Heb 12:23). And this prospect is held out as a reality for people of faith under the old covenant as well as the new (Heb 11:40).

Accordingly, the relationship between the old and the new systems is not simply one of contrast. There is also a strong element of continuity. This is provided by the concept of faith. Whether or not Paul thought that the era of faith did not come until Christ (Gal 3:23-25), the writer of Hebrews is quite clear that faith was characteristic of the true people of God right through the Old Testament period (Heb 11). He refers on occasion to the people's lack of faith (Heb 3:19; 4:2; in terms of disobedience, Heb 4:11), and the implication would appear to be that faith was a genuine possibility for them, but some of them did not grasp it rather than that they lived in an era when faith was not a possibility.

*The Christian life as a journey.* Alongside the use of the concept of sacrifice

---

[8]If the letter comes from after A.D. 70, then it may be, as is suggested by Marie E. Isaacs (*Sacred Space: An Approach to the Theology of the Epistle to the Hebrews* [Sheffield: Sheffield Academic Press, 1992], p. 67), that one of its purposes or effects was to reassure people who felt acutely the cessation of the sacrificial system that the death of Christ had made the temple redundant in any case.

and priesthood, a further important structural element in the thinking of Hebrews lies in the concept of the journey in space and time. Here there is not the same developed, systematic conceptuality and terminology; nevertheless, the reality forms a significant subtheme in the development of the author's appeal to his readers.

The key illustration here is that of Abraham, who left his own country to go wherever God would direct him. His hoped for goal was a city, a place of security built by God (Heb 11:16). But he spent his life in a tent, waiting for the fulfillment of the promise. Evidently the city is heavenly, and there is no sense in which Abraham already arrived there. Nevertheless, to some extent the Promised Land of Canaan may be seen as a shadow or foretaste of the ultimate goal and destination that is depicted as a heavenly Jerusalem (Heb 12:22; 13:14; cf. Gal 4:26). Thus there develops the idea of God's people as strangers and aliens in this world looking forward to a better country, a heavenly one.[9] At the same time the writer can tell his readers that they have come to the heavenly city, so that there is the characteristic Christian blend of the "already" and the "not yet". Already Christians by faith have access to the unseen God and his city, and one day they will see the reality of that which they firmly believe at present (cf. 2 Cor 5:7). For the writer this would seem to be a difference between those believers under the old covenant who merely looked forward and new covenant believers who already enjoy that to which they look forward.

A related contrast is that between the two mountains to which people may come. The first generation of Israelites in the desert literally came to Sinai, which was a fearsome place. But the readers have come to Mount Zion, understood spiritually as the city of God and populated by angels, other believers, God and Jesus, and to a sacrifice that is efficacious. But in what sense have they come? Again this is the goal of their journey, but at the same time it is the place with which they are in spiritual contact through their faith. Perhaps there is a parallel between Mount Sinai at the beginning of the journey to the Promised Land and Mount Zion as the spiritual equivalent at conversion; in both cases the experience marks the nature of the God with whom they have to do. The

---

[9]This raises the question whether there is a depreciation of the material world as opposed to a heavenly spiritual one. See Hurst, *Epistle*, p. 73, for a denial that the outlook is dualistic and the suggestion that it is more future-orientated.

purpose, as in the earlier chapters, is to draw the contrast between the inferiority and the superiority of the two situations and then to stress that, if failure to listen to the God of Sinai carried such serious consequences, how much more will failure to listen to the God of the new covenant. However, the point that immediately concerns us is that the nature of the eschatological goal, which is real and present in heaven, determines the nature of the present relationship with God and speaks of privileges already enjoyed by faith.

The same pattern is established with the concept of rest. One reading of the biblical texts is that the rest promised by God was the goal of the journey through the wilderness to Canaan; the angry response of God to the rebellion of Israel in the desert was to condemn them to forty years of wanderings so that they would all die and not enter into rest (Heb 3:7-11, citing Ps 95:7-11). This literal understanding is pressed throughout Hebrews 3:12-19 in the interests of establishing that it was unbelief that leads to exclusion from God's blessings. But then the writer asserts that the promise of entering into rest is still there as an offer to his readers, since the purpose of Psalm 95 is not simply to record what happened in the past but to challenge the readers not to behave like the wilderness generation and so cut themselves off from God's rest. That rest is still a goal set before the new generation of readers; the offer made by David, as the author of the psalm, still stands.

A further image used by the writer is that of the race, in which the readers are moving toward a goal where Jesus stands to inspire them with his example. The imagery of the race enables the writer to develop the thoughts of the need to keep going to the end and to bear with the tough demands of the course (Heb 12:1-3). Here the metaphor of the race tends to merge into that of the struggle against enemies, perhaps like a visiting football team having to contend also with the mass of spectators shouting for the home team and discouraging the visitors.

It may be noted, finally, that the use of journey language was not seen by the author as incompatible with the hope of the appearing of Christ at the end of the age to bring salvation to those who are waiting for him (Heb 9:28). Travelers can also be people living in hope of a taxi drawing up alongside them to take them the rest of the way!

***The nature of faith.*** It is now appropriate to consider this key characteristic of God's people under both covenants, faith. Faith in this letter is "being sure of what we hope for and certain of what we do not see" (Heb 11:1). In this phrase are the two elements of futurity and invisibility. There is a realm that we cannot at present see nor enter, but one day we shall see the unseen and enter the inaccessible. So faith is concerned with belief in the invisible God (e.g., Heb 11:6) and with conviction that what is prophesied for the future will happen (e.g., Heb 11:7). It was characteristic of the old covenant as well as of the new. Thus Abel could by faith offer a sacrifice to God that was acceptable to him and be commended for his righteousness (Heb 11:4). The same could presumably be said about Abraham's willingness to offer Isaac in sacrifice (Heb 11:17). The Passover sacrifice carried out by Moses was efficacious (Heb 11:28). Clearly such faith, especially as illustrated by the cases of Abraham and Moses, involves commitment, in that a life is lived on this basis, preferring the future reward to the present, tangible "treasures of Egypt". It must also involve trust in God that he will fulfill his promises. And it certainly involves perseverance in the face of opposition and every temptation to fall back into a more comfortable, less risky way of living. Thus it requires the believer to recognize that unpleasant experiences may still be within the purpose of God inasmuch as they constitute part of the training or discipline that he uses for our own good (Heb 12:4-13).

Nevertheless, the key question remains whether this kind of faith with its strong emphasis on perseverance and hope for the future is essentially a personal relationship with God and Christ and leads to the kind of spiritual union with God that is characteristic of Paul and John. Has the concept of faith in these writers been replaced by something that is more "early catholic"? Has faith acquired more the sense of faithfulness and perseverance?[10]

Part of the answer to this question is that we may be dealing simply with a changed emphasis, with nothing more than a shift of focus to bring out the need for persistence in faith in a situation where this was the quality chiefly needed in the readers. For Hebrews the church is a body of Christians who should be moving forward and not backward (Heb 2:1), and so the elements of

---

[10]On this point see especially Graham Hughes, *Hebrews and Hermeneutics: The Epistle to the Hebrews as an Example of Biblical Interpretation* (Cambridge: Cambridge University Press, 1979), pp. 137-42, with its careful refutation of the view of Erich Grässer that faith in Hebrews has become faithfulness rather than a personal relationship with Christ. See further Victor (Sung-Yul) Rhee, *Faith in Hebrews: Analysis within the Context of Christology, Eschatology and Ethics* (New York: Peter Lang, 2001).

belief in the promises and persistence despite opposition are of cardinal importance.

But having accounted for the distinctive character of faith in Hebrews in the light of the situation that is addressed, the question still remains whether the author has a somewhat different understanding of faith from elsewhere in the New Testament. This ties up with the question of the nature of salvation and to what extent it is a present possession.

*Salvation, future and present.* The writer of the letter is addressing a group of people who had received a message concerning salvation that had been powerfully attested to them in various ways (Heb 2:1-4). Our problem is whether the message concerned a salvation that they could experience and receive there and then or something that still lay in the future but of whose future possession they could be confident because of the trustworthiness of the divine promises.

The accent is probably on the future in Hebrews 5:9, where Christ is the source of eternal salvation for all who obey him, and also in Hebrews 9:28, where Christ will appear the second time to bring salvation to those who are waiting for him. In Hebrews 1:14 the writer speaks about the angels serving those who are to inherit salvation, that is, come into the possession of what has been promised to them. This looks like a reference to aid given to believers in the course of their pilgrimage on the way to inheriting salvation.

Further, the writer has a clear concept of a heavenly sphere into which believers will one day enter, and has a terminology to describe it. "Mount Zion, the city of the living God, the heavenly Jerusalem" (Heb 12:22) is the heavenly destination. Where the author of Revelation appears to locate believers on the new earth and the Jerusalem that has descended from heaven, the author of Hebrews is less precise about the locale. The essential feature that the future dwelling of believers is with God is common to both authors.

On the one hand, then, the temptation is to regard the present life of believers as one in which they do not yet have salvation but live in a hostile world, experiencing pain and hardship, falling far short of God's purpose for their lives, not yet mature, always liable to fall away, and to think of salvation as the perfected life of heaven to be reached after a long and arduous journey.

On the other hand, consider these elements of their position. In Hebrews 2:1-4 it is significant that the contrast is between the law that was spoken by angels, that is, a proclamation from God, and salvation announced by the Lord.

It is a contrast between breaking the law and ignoring an announced salvation rather than an announcement of salvation. It is impossible to avoid the conclusion that salvation itself rather than simply a message about future salvation was brought to the readers. As Werner Foerster puts it, "salvation takes place with being spoken about".[11] The readers have been freed from the fear of death (Heb 2:15), a clear description of a present experience in this life. They are already described as God's sons and daughters who are destined for glory, and this description is tightly linked to a mention of Jesus as the author of their salvation (Heb 2:10; cf. Heb 5:9). They already form part of God's household (Heb 3:6). Above all, they share in Christ (Heb 3:14). They can enter into rest—which may combine elements of the present and the future (Heb 4:1-11). They receive mercy and grace to help them in their time of need: here mercy and grace are understood as divine power, motivated by love, that strengthens believers facing temptation and hostility (Heb 4:16). They are able to come to God in prayer, even though they cannot see him (Heb 4:16). There is the powerful description of the state from which people may fall away, which includes enlightenment, participation in the heavenly gift, sharing in the Holy Spirit, tasting the goodness of the Word of God and experiencing the powers of the coming age (Heb 6:4-5). The writer goes on to describe his readers as people who experience or manifest the things that accompany salvation (Heb 6:9). Christ is able to save completely and for all time[12] those who come to God through him (Heb 7:25). The promise of the new covenant is fulfilled, according to which God's laws are written in the hearts of his people; they are his people, and they know the Lord; their sins are forgiven (Heb 8:10-12). Their consciences have been cleansed from sin so that they can serve the living God (Heb 9:14), and they have been made holy (Heb 10:10). Having been thus cleansed, they have confidence to enter the Holy Place and draw near to God with full assurance.

In view of this accumulation of evidence, there can be no doubt that for this writer believers look forward to a salvation yet to be revealed (cf. 1 Pet 1:5), but at the same time they experience a real and comprehensive set of divine blessings, including entry into the presence of God with complete confidence (cf.

---

[11]Werner Foerster, *TDNT*, 7:996.
[12]Lane, *Hebrews*, 1:176.

Rom 5:1). It would be playing with words to suggest that this was anything less than a genuine experience of salvation.

Perhaps what leads to the writer's stress on salvation as a future experience is his concern over the possibility that people may experience all these divine gifts and yet fall away from their faith. So perseverance or patience is an essential ingredient in faith, and because the writer knows of the theoretical possibility of falling away and wrote because the possibility was in danger of becoming a reality, he recognizes that in a sense nobody can be said to be saved until they have safely entered into the unseen world.

*Falling away.* This last thought directs us to a further characteristic of Hebrews. The letter is, as we have seen, written to a community that was in some danger of drawing back from its faith and ignoring the salvation that it had received. In a number of passages (Heb 2:1-4; 3:7—4:13; 5:11—6:20; 10:19-39; 12:12—13:19) there are warnings against the danger of falling away from one's Christian profession coupled with encouragements to remain faithful to the end. These passages seem to allow that a person who has been a believer and enjoyed the blessings of salvation may lapse into a state of unbelief. But, more than that, it is also stated that if this happens to people, it is impossible to bring them back to repentance and all that awaits them is judgment; even though Esau sought the blessing with tears, he could bring about no change of mind. Thus to the possibility of falling away there is added the impossibility of restoration to faith and salvation.

It should be noted, first, that when Hebrews speaks of the impossibility of apostate people coming back to salvation, it appears to be suggesting that people who reject the way of salvation and the Savior cannot be saved so long as they do so. There is no other sacrifice for sins, no other way for them to be saved. The strong language in Hebrews 10:26-31 is meant to be a warning to those who are tempted to reject Christ and to persist in doing so. The statement in Hebrews 6:4-6 may also be somewhat hyperbolical in presenting a worst-case type of scenario, and the point may simply be that so long as people continue to reject Christ they cannot be brought back to repentance and salvation. Alternatively, the wording may be deadly serious and indicate that there is a point known only to God at which repentance becomes impossible, and the writer faces his readers with this awful possibility in order to make them fully aware of the dangerous end result of yielding to the temptation to apostasy.

Second, it must be insisted that while the tone is indeed one of warning

against a possible danger, it is coupled with strong statements of encouragement—"we are confident of better things in your case". Nobody is unequivocally identified here as having crossed over the fatal line.

Third, all attempts to evacuate the statements here of their significance fail
to convince. The writer is dealing with a real, if remote, possibility. Therefore,
consideration must be given to whether the rest of the New Testament in fact
excludes the possibility.[13]

*God as judge and Father.* It is now appropriate to examine what sort of picture
of God emerges from the letter. Much of the traditional or typical Christian
understanding of God can be illustrated from the letter. God is the Creator of
the universe, who completed his work in six days and rested on the seventh day.
He lives in a heaven that is pictured in spatial terms. He is the glorious and omnipotent ruler of the universe but also the God who speaks through the prophets and his Son. In various ways the exalted position of God gets perhaps more
emphasis than in some other parts of the New Testament. He established a
household with Moses as his housekeeper and the people of Israel as its members, and he made his covenant with them. He is active in the inauguration of
salvation, which is due to his purpose (Heb 2:10). He is aware of all that goes
on in the whole of his creation, which means that human motives and actions
are laid bare before him (Heb 4:13). He is presented in powerful terms as the
Judge (Heb 12:23) who acts to punish those who transgress the commands
given through Moses and reject the salvation offered through his Son. The language used in this context is extremely powerful, summed up in the conception
of him as a consuming fire (Heb 12:29).

The other side of the picture is that God is presented as a Father to the children
who constitute his family (Heb 2:10; 12:5-8). In relation to believers the term is
used only in one passage where the point is the discipline of the Father, which may
seem harsh but is intended for the good of the children (Heb 12:4-11). In the context, however, the point is to reinterpret the hardships through which the readers are
passing by means of the analogy with human parents who discipline their children
in a manner that was presumably fully acceptable to the readers since otherwise the
analogy could not have been used as a persuasive argument. Moreover, it is shown

---

[13]See I. Howard Marshall, *Kept by the Power of God: A Study of Perseverance and Falling Away,* 3rd ed. (Carlisle:
Paternoster, 1995).

how Jesus as God's Son went through the same kind of experience (Heb 5:8). Believers have access to God through the efficacy of Christ's sacrifice (Heb 10:19-22) and are able to serve God like priests (Heb 9:14; 12:28). The writer appears to suggest that this privilege takes them into heaven (Heb 10:19), identified further as the heavenly Jerusalem, the city of the living God (Heb 12:22-24).

*Son and high priest.* The christology of the letter is detailed. As we have already seen, it is developed in terms of the sonship of Jesus, which forms the basis for his high priesthood, and it emphasizes his genuine humanity and his divine sonship. The writer makes use of the familiar terms *Christ* and *Lord.* The former of these is virtually a name for Jesus but may on occasion carry the connotation of "Messiah" (Heb 6:1; 11:26). The term *Lord* is used only four times for Jesus, twice with reference to his earthly career (Heb 2:3; 7:14) and twice of his exalted position (Heb 1:10; 13:20).

It is more striking that the simple term *Jesus* is found no fewer than ten times. There may be nothing significant in this. But if this term does not allude to the humanity of Christ, there is sufficient other evidence that the real human experience of Christ, which made him in all respects like his human brothers and sisters (Heb 2:17), to the point of learning obedience to God and of suffering a human death (Heb 2:14-18; 5:7-9), was a matter of great importance to the writer. He saw this kinship and sympathy with humankind as the indispensable qualification for acting as a high priest in his intercession for them and in his dying for them.

In this connection we should note that the writer uses the same term (*perfecting*) with reference to Jesus as he uses for believers. Describing Jesus as the author or originator of salvation, he insists that in this capacity Jesus had to be made perfect through suffering (Heb 2:10; cf. Heb 5:9; 7:28). The term *to perfect* derives its meaning partly from its context; it means to make a thing perfect in whatever it is supposed to be or do. Here it refers to the vocation of Jesus as Savior, and the thought is that he could achieve his purpose only through "a whole sequence of events: his proving in suffering, his redemptive death to fulfil the divine requirements for the perfect expiation of sins and his exaltation to glory and honour".[14] It is important for the writer that the high priest who of-

---

[14]David Peterson, *Hebrews and Perfection: An Examination of the Concept of Perfection in the "Epistle to the Hebrews"* (Cambridge: Cambridge University Press, 1982), p. 73. Other writers stress more the idea of his consecration as a priest (e.g., Lane, *Hebrews,* 1:57).

fers himself in sacrifice has a human face. It is not just a case of making a costly self-sacrifice but of being a person who has fully entered into the situation of humanity and is able to sympathize with them. His sacrifice is made by one who knows and understands the suffering of humankind and thereby constitutes a genuine appeal by one representative of them to God. Perhaps more clearly than anywhere else in the New Testament, Hebrews makes it clear why the Savior had to be truly human.

On the other side, there is the exalted status of Jesus. This is brought out at the beginning of the letter with the description of the Son in terms used elsewhere of Wisdom as sharing in the glorious image of God and being his close companion and helper (Heb 1:1-4; cf. Wis 7:25-26). This language is generally taken to imply a belief in the preexistence of the Son, that is, that the Son literally existed before creation and shared in the task of creation. However, this understanding has been challenged by James D. G. Dunn, who has argued that "Christ alone so embodies God's Wisdom, that is, God's creative, revelatory and redemptive action, that what can be said of Wisdom can be said of Christ without remainder. The thought of pre-existence is present, but in terms of Wisdom christology it is the act and power of God which properly speaking is what pre-exists. Christ is not so much the pre-existent act and power of God as its eschatological embodiment".[15] This interpretation of the language is not persuasive. The critical point is the claim that the creative and redemptive action of God, given literary personification in the figure of Wisdom, is somehow embodied in Christ. It breaks down on the language of Hebrews 1:2, which does not say that God made the world by means of his creative power or wisdom but by means of his Son. Further, there is no good reason for saying that creation is excluded from the activity of the Son but the upholding of the universe and the making of purification for sin are included. Furthermore, the concept of Christ embodying the impersonal power of God is very different from the New Testament way of speaking of his status in relational and personal terms as that of a Son to the Father.

The most unusual feature in the christology is probably the introduction of the figure of Melchizedek. The writer uses Melchizedek to demonstrate how there can be a priesthood distinct from that of the tribe of Levi but yet perfectly

---

[15]James D. G. Dunn, *Christology in the Making* (London: SCM Press, 1980), p. 209.

legitimate in its function and in a sense superior to that of Levi. The priesthood of Christ, who came from Judah and not Levi, can be seen as falling into the same category. The inspiration for this move could have come simply from the writer's use of Psalm 110:1, which he understood christologically (Heb 1:13). It was easy to read further in the psalm and find a motif that could then be developed in the light of Genesis 14 and its picture of a priest whose origin was unknown and who therefore had, so far as Scripture is concerned, no genealogical qualifications for his task. Further, the biblical language about being "a priest forever in the order of Melchizedek" could be taken to imply that Melchizedek, whose death is not reported in Scripture, held an eternal priesthood. At the same time speculation about Melchizedek was in the air and could have had some influence. For Philo, Melchizedek was an embodiment of the Logos, and in a Qumran text he is an angelic type of figure.[16] However, nothing suggests that Melchizedek was seen in this way in Hebrews,[17] and certainly Christ is not identified with him but merely seen as being in the succession of Melchizedek.

The task of Christ needs to be understood in terms of its goals, which are variously described. The ultimate aim is, as we have seen, summed up in the concept of salvation (Heb 2:3; 7:25), but this is a rather formal concept that needs to be fleshed out.

One aim is to bring God's people to their future destination and condition, described as glory (Heb 2:10). This is understood to be God's original aim for humanity (Ps 8), which at present is fulfilled only in the case of Jesus. Another description of it is as rest; it may not be fanciful to see an implied contrast in Hebrews 4:8 between the Joshua who did not give rest and the new Joshua who can do so.[18]

A second aim is to deliver people from the fear of death (Heb 2:15). This is achieved at least in part by rendering the devil powerless since he has the power of death. Surprisingly, this thought is not developed at any length here or elsewhere in the New Testament.[19] It would be possible to argue that the

---

[16] 11QMelch. See Fred L. Horton Jr., *The Melchizedek Tradition: A Critical Examination of the Sources to the Fifth Century A.D. and in the Epistle to the Hebrews* (Cambridge: Cambridge University Press, 1976).

[17] See the discussion in Lane, *Hebrews*, 1:155-72.

[18] The Greek word for Joshua (*Iēsous*) is the same as for Jesus.

[19] The concept of *Christus Victor* became more prominent in the patristic period, but in the New Testament it is a matter of hint and allusion rather than of a systematically worked out motif.

devil loses his power as the inflictor of death in that if people have been cleansed from their sins they no longer come within his sphere of power, and this is what was achieved by the death of Jesus. But it is also possible to argue that the death of Jesus, followed by his resurrection, broke the power of death and was a victory won on behalf of his brothers and sisters by Jesus.

A third aim is to make people holy (Heb 2:11) or to cleanse them (Heb 9:14). This is manifestly the principal theme of the letter. The work of Christ is understood as the offering of a sacrifice and the provision of forgiveness (Heb 8:12). The Old Testament sacrificial system provides the categories used by the writer, although, as we have noted, properly speaking this is because they are shadows and copies of the real thing.

The writer uses more than one aspect of the sacrificial system, but the principal one is the annual Day of Atonement, on which the high priest entered the innermost part of the tabernacle carrying the blood of a sacrificed animal with which he smeared the cover of the ark of the covenant. The blood was the indication that a sacrifice had been made, and the offering of it sufficed to expiate the sins of the people.[20] For the writer the death of Jesus on the cross constituted the sacrifice. His exaltation to heaven and entry into the presence of God constituted the offering to God that he made once and for all. The writer is quite emphatic on this point, which contrasts the action of Jesus with that of the levitical priests (Heb 7:27; 9:12, 26, 28; 10:10, 14; cf. 1 Pet 3:18); he made his offering once and for all, and then he sat down (Heb 10:12). It is the basis for the traditional phrase "the finished work of Christ". His intercession for sinners continues (Heb 7:25), a motif that could lead to the misunderstanding that God the judge has to be persuaded to forgive sinners, whereas in fact it is God himself whose grace led to the whole action of salvation (Heb 2:10). It is at this point that the use of the imagery of intercession and mediation by a high priest shows up the limitations of any human attempts to comprehend the reality of God and his action within human analogies.

The writer also uses the language of sacrifice in a different way when he brings in the fact that alongside the offering of the sacrifice to God there was

---

[20]Strictly speaking, it covered only unintentional sins as opposed to deliberate acts of disobedience to God; it is the difference between accidentally driving down a one-way street in the wrong direction and deliberately breaking a known speed limit. In practice, it was probably interpreted rather elastically.

the sprinkling with blood of the sinful worshipers in various rites (Heb 9:13, 19; cf. the metaphorical application in Heb 10:22). Here the symbolism associated particularly with the inauguration of the old covenant is brought into play, the sprinkling of the blood signifying the cleansing and the consecration of the people to God.

The effect of sacrifice is that people can come into the presence of God without fear (Heb 10:19). Here again the point is made by contrast with the old covenant, under which only the high priest could enter right into the innermost part of the tabernacle, which symbolized the presence of God. But Christian believers now have a positive relationship with God that can be described in terms of coming into his presence—a present anticipation of the future consummation.

*The people of God.* The letter to the Hebrews offers little explicit teaching on the common life of Christian believers, although it assumes that they meet together as a congregation and warns against slipping away from the church meetings—and so from Christian profession (Heb 10:25). It encourages believers to express their faith in praise to God and doing good to others; these activities provide the opportunity for something equivalent to sacrifice in the Christian life (Heb 13:15-16). There is a fairly certain allusion to baptism in Hebrews 10:22, where it is a symbol of spiritual cleansing. Some interpreters understand Hebrews 13:9-10, which refers to an altar from which those who minister in the tabernacle have no right to eat, as an allusion to the Lord's Supper. But it is inconceivable that the author thought of the Lord's table in the church as an altar, since the only altar that he knows is in heaven. He is referring to the spiritual benefits that come from the death of Christ, using the imagery of the worshipers under the old covenant eating the portions of the sacrifices that were reserved for them.

## Conclusion

The framework of the theology of Hebrews is set by the way in which the writer uses the continuity and contrasts between the old and new covenants to shape his exposition of the superiority of the latter in its own time. Linked to this contrast is that between the earthly tabernacle and the heavenly temple. A typological understanding of the Old Testament is developed.

The main theme is the obsolescence of the old covenant and its replacement by the new, which makes it inconceivable that Christians should want to abandon their pilgrimage of faith.

Significant elements in the theology are

1. The understanding of Jesus as the Son of God, who is superior to all other figures, including Moses, as the mediator of the new covenant.

2. The centrality of the concept of priesthood. Jesus Christ is the high priest, qualified for his role not only by being the Son of God but also by his incarnation and human experience.

3. The self-sacrifice of Jesus in his death followed by his entry into the heavenly temple to make a once-for-all offering for sin. Despite the importance of this heavenly offering, the resurrection of Jesus plays no significant role in the theology.[21]

4. The impossibility of forgiveness other than by the offering of Christ and the impossibility of forgiveness for those who turn away from Christ.

5. The understanding of the Christian life as a pilgrimage or journey in faith.

## Bibliography

*New Testament Theologies:* (English) Goppelt, 2:237-66; Ladd, pp. 617-33; Morris, pp. 301-11; Strecker, pp. 605-20. (German) Gnilka, pp. 368-92; Hahn, 1: 424-47; Hübner, 3:15-63; Stuhlmacher, 2:84-105.

Bruce, F. F. *The Epistle to the Hebrews.* Grand Rapids, Mich.: Eerdmans, 1990.

——— . "The Kerygma of Hebrews". *Int* 23 (1969): 3-19.

Dunnill, John. *Covenant and Sacrifice in the Letter to the Hebrews.* Cambridge: Cambridge University Press, 1992.

Ellingworth, Paul. *The Epistle to the Hebrews.* Grand Rapids, Mich.: Eerdmans; Carlisle: Paternoster, 1993.

Horton, Fred L., Jr. *The Melchizedek Tradition: A Critical Examination of the Sources to the Fifth Century A.D. and in the Epistle to the Hebrews.* Cambridge: Cambridge University Press, 1976.

Hughes, Graham. *Hebrews and Hermeneutics: The Epistle to the Hebrews as an Example of Biblical*

---

[21]The resurrection of Jesus is not mentioned explicitly until Heb 13:20, although it is implicit much earlier in references to his entry into heaven and exaltation.

*Interpretation.* Cambridge: Cambridge University Press, 1979.

Hurst, L. D. *The Epistle to the Hebrews: Its Background of Thought.* Cambridge: Cambridge University Press, 1990.

Isaacs, Marie E. *Sacred Space: An Approach to the Theology of the Epistle to the Hebrews.* Sheffield: Sheffield Academic Press, 1992.

Käsemann, Ernst. *The Wandering People of God.* Minneapolis; Augsburg, 1984.

Lane, William L. "Hebrews". In *DLNTD,* pp. 443-58.

————. *Hebrews.* 2 vols. Dallas: Word, 1991.

Lindars, Barnabas. *The Theology of the Letter to the Hebrews.* Cambridge: Cambridge University Press, 1991.

Marshall, I. Howard. *Kept by the Power of God: A Study of Perseverance and Falling Away.* 3rd ed. Carlisle: Paternoster, 1995.

Motyer, Stephen. "The Psalm Quotations of Hebrews 1: A Hermeneutic-Free Zone?" *TynB* 50.1 (1999): 3-22.

Peterson, David. *Hebrews and Perfection: An Examination of the Concept of Perfection in the "Epistle to the Hebrews".* Cambridge: Cambridge University Press, 1982.

Pursiful, Darrell J. *The Cultic Motif in the Spirituality of the Book of Hebrews.* Lewiston, N.Y.: Edwin Mellen, 1993.

Rhee, Victor (Sung-Yul). *Faith in Hebrews: Analysis Within the Context of Christology, Eschatology and Ethics.* New York: Peter Lang, 2001.

Scholer, John M. *Proleptic Priests: Priesthood in the Epistle to the Hebrews.* Sheffield: Sheffield Academic Press, 1991.

Tasker, R. V. G. *The Gospel in the Epistle to the Hebrews.* London: Tyndale Press, 1950.

# 26

# THE LETTER OF JAMES

～⌒∽

Of all the books of the New Testament the letter of James is the one that may appear at first sight to be least theological. But it at least mentions Jesus, which is more than can be said for 3 John! Whatever may have been the theological beliefs of the author, he has chosen to write a letter that is concerned largely with the moral and practical behavior of his readers, although their spiritual life is not forgotten. The letter contains plenty of what we might call good advice for people who may be subjected to different temptations. It has been described as a "witness to a form of life which is formulated almost entirely in Old Testament terminology without an explicit christology".[1] Our task will be to find out what the implicit theology of the letter is.

## The Situation

The letter is addressed by James, the brother of Jesus and the leader of the church in Jerusalem,[2] to "the twelve tribes scattered among the nations". The writer here takes up the tradition of Jewish leaders writing to Jewish people living in exile from their homeland and exposed to the difficulties and trials of this situation (cf. the letters in 2 Macc 1:1-9; 1:10—2:18). However, this is a Christian letter to Christian believers, and it is addressed in this way to Christians wherever they may happen to be, and implicitly it identifies them as the new Israel, just as we find in other New Testament writings. The writer addresses his readers as the diaspora, or dispersion (the name used for Jews living

---

[1]Brevard S. Childs, *The New Testament as Canon: An Introduction* (London: SCM Press, 1984), p. 444.
[2]The attribution of the letter to this James rather than to a pseudonymous author is well grounded; see, for example, Richard J. Bauckham, *James* (London: Routledge, 1998), pp. 11-28.

outside Judea), but there is no agreement as to whether the diaspora is to be taken literally of Christians living outside Judea or metaphorically of their sojourn in this world away from their heavenly home. Their situation is one of testing and oppression, and James's aim is primarily to strengthen and encourage them but equally to exhort them to Christian behavior as they progress toward maturity of faith. The readers are manifestly people with a Jewish heritage and may be presumed to be Jewish Christians. Although the subject of faith and works is discussed, there is no reference to any of the problems regarding relationships between Jews and Gentiles in the church such as we find in Acts and Paul. Nevertheless, this certainly does not exclude the possibility that the envisaged audience could include Gentile Christians in their number.

### The Theological Story

James confronts two perennial problems in his letter.

The one is the threat to the attainment of Christian maturity through pressure from outside, apparently from rich people who oppress the poor Christians and attack their religion (Jas 2:7). There is some debate over whether the rich people who are addressed in the letter were inside the church or outside it, but certainly there was opposition from outside the church, from rich people who dragged some of the Christians off to court (Jas 2:6).

The other is the threat to the unity of the congregations through internal bickering and slander (Jas 4:11). We hear of envy and ambition, of fights and quarrels (Jas 3:16; 4:1).

We thus have the paradox that the writer appears to be writing to a very broad audience, the Christians scattered among the nations, and yet seems to have a very specific congregation or congregations in view. Evidently, he assumes that what is true of the Christians he knows is also true fairly widely and that what he has to say to this kind of situation can be heard with advantage by his wider audience. Paul wrote similarly to the church in Corinth and meant his letter to be read throughout Achaia, and in the same way the letters to Colosse and Hierapolis were to be exchanged by the churches.

There is no reference to false theological teaching as a danger in the church.[3]

---

[3]The view that people could be justified by faith without deeds is more a matter of a wrong emphasis regarding practice than of doctrinal error.

We do not have the problems with Judaizers that we find in Paul, and if there was christological heresy, such as we find attacked in I John, the writer has nothing to say about it. It follows that the primary purpose of this letter is not evangelistic, doctrinal or polemical but rather pastoral, as the writer displays his pastoral concern for the readers and exhorts them to show spiritual care and love for one another (Jas 5:13-20; cf. Jas 2:14-17)

A first glance may suggest that the letter treats one theme after another with no discernible order. While it is possible to detect a structure in the letter which makes it more than a collocation of teachings on unrelated paraenetic topics,[4] it may be more helpful for us in our survey of it to follow a very simple— indeed oversimplified—analysis of the letter in terms of five recurring main themes that have been interwoven.[5]

These themes are temptation and maturity, wealth and poverty, faith and actions, sins of speech, and patience and prayer.

*Temptation and maturity (Jas 1:2-8, 12-18).* The readers are seen as people who are constantly subjected to temptations. These can be seen from two perspectives, either as circumstances in which God is testing and so developing their faith as they learn to resist evil impulses, or as situations in which they are being enticed to do what is evil and get trapped into a process that culminates in death (cf. Jas 5:20). In particular, there is the continual temptation to follow

---

[4]This view of James was powerfully presented in the influential commentary by Martin Dibelius and Heinrich Greeven, *James* (Philadelphia: Fortress, 1975), but is convincingly rejected in more recent work, particularly by Peter H. Davids, *The Epistle of James: A Commentary on the Greek Text* (Exeter: Paternoster Press, 1982). Davids's analysis is complex and open to refinement, but in essence it is on the right lines. A simplified version of it is as follows:

Jas 1:1          Greeting
Jas 1:2-27       Opening statement on trials and temptations, which deals in turn with testing
                 (Jas 1:2-4, 12-18), prayer and wisdom (Jas 1:5-8), poverty and riches (Jas 1:9-11),
                 speech (Jas 1:19-21), obedience and generosity (Jas 1:22-27)
Jas 2:1-26       Poverty and riches; faith and deeds
Jas 3:1-4:12     Wisdom and the tongue
Jas 4:13-5:6     Testing and wealth
Jas 5:7-20       Closing statement: patience and prayer

The essence of this analysis is the recognition that various themes are adumbrated in the opening statement and then discussed in turn more fully in the central part of the letter.

[5]This analysis goes back to J. A. Findlay, as reported in A. M. Hunter, *Introducing the New Testament* (London: SCM Press, 1945), p. 97; he thought that five short sermons or homilies had been broken up and stitched together. Without sharing this theory of compilation we may nevertheless find his analysis useful for highlighting the main topics in the letter.

the so-called wisdom of the surrounding world (Jas 4:4) with its emphasis on success and consequent boasting (Jas 3:14). The Christian life is thus understood as a process of testing. In the concluding exhortations the theme is taken up again with a calling to be patient and to persevere in the face of suffering (Jas 5:7-11).

However, more important than the process of testing is the goal of maturity or perfection, which is reached by a path that includes testing. This notion of perfection is particularly significant for James.[6] The aim of the Christian life is to be perfect and lacking in nothing (Jas 1:4). Its environment is created by the heavenly Father whose gifts are perfect and whose law is perfect (Jas 1:17, 25; 2:8). Believers must move forward to a faith that is perfect, and this perfection is achieved when faith works in harmony with deeds (Jas 2:22). Perfection in the Christian life is to be seen in the absence of sins committed by the tongue, since the people who can control their tongues are a fortiori able to control the rest of their sinful impulses (Jas 3:2).

Temptation has to do with the contrast between the two ways, the path that leads to the crown of life awarded by God and the path that leads to death. James thus assumes the normal Christian understanding of life as following either the way of righteousness that leads to the kingdom of God or the way of sin that leads to death. He is aware of the possibility of believers falling into temptation and coming into danger of death, and the very last word of the letter emphasizes the importance of pastoral care for those in the church who are liable to fall away into sin and death (Jas 5:19-20).

*Wealth and poverty (Jas 1:9-11; 2:1-13; 4:8-10, 13-16; 5:1-6).* The church evidently contains a range of people from the rich to the poor, with the main body falling between the two extremes, and there is a temptation for those in the middle to show partiality toward the rich out of self-interest and to discriminate against the poor. At the same time there is a temptation on the part of the rich toward complacency and to oppression of the poor in order to maintain their own lifestyle. The difficulties encountered by the church are apparently not due, as is more common elsewhere in the New Testament, to persecution of Christians as Christians but rather to the oppression of the poor by the rich. The author very much sides with the oppressed poor who trust in God

---

[6]Cf. Robert W. Wall, "James, Letter of", in *DLNTD,* pp. 545-61 (p. 553).

and points out to them the judgments that await the people who are rich and immoral.

*Faith and actions (Jas 1:19-25; 2:14-26; 3:13-18; 4:1-7, 17).* There is the temptation to assume that faith is the sufficient mark of a Christian regardless of the need to demonstrate the reality of faith through appropriate action. Certainly faith is extremely important; it is the typical quality of the Christian, and the readers can be described as "rich in faith" (Jas 2:5). However, faith is not everything. The author's slogan is "faith and actions working together". The specific context of the teaching here is the existence of bad relationships within the congregations; alongside the partiality shown to the rich there is a lack of concern for the needy and a strong tendency to quarrelsomeness and to arrogance. From the amount of space given to this theme it looks as if it is the most important one in the letter, or at least the one that requires the most attention.[7]

*Sins of speech (Jas 1:26-27; 3:1-12; 4:11-12; 5:12).* There is a considerable body of traditional teaching on the sins of speech; the tongue can be an uncontrollable source of evil, especially in the slanderous and angry things it says about other people, particularly fellow believers. Here the author chimes in with a long tradition in the ancient world of teaching regarding speech.[8]

*Patience and prayer (Jas 5:7-11, 13-20).* The closing section of the letter stresses the importance of patience and of intercessory prayer for the members of the church.

### Theological Themes

It may be as difficult for us to see the rationale for this collection of topics as it is in the case of Jewish wisdom books like Proverbs, where the themes jostle somewhat untidily against one another. And it would be unwise to do too much mirror reading and attempt to identify the readers and their situation on the basis of the sins that are being condemned, especially as James names his readers in very broad terms. One can easily imagine many a Christian congregation or

---

[7]If we ignore the greeting, there are 108 verses in James, and 34 of them, that is, a third, are devoted to this topic.

[8]See the detailed survey by William R. Baker, *Personal Speech Ethics in the Epistle of James* (Tübingen: J. C. B. Mohr [Paul Siebeck], 1995).

congregations for which any of these topics would be appropriate subjects of exhortation.

What is surprising is the gathering of them together with so little of the kind of theological backing that is typical of the rest of the New Testament; the contrast with I Peter, with which James has some significant contacts, is very marked. In fact, however, the essentially practical focus of the letter can cause readers to overlook the fact that the topics discussed all have theological roots and significance. What is lacking in James is the explicit use of christological and soteriological material to form a basis for following exhortations, such as we find in some of the Pauline letters, or the use of doctrine to form the theological backup for preceding exhortations, such as we find on occasion in Titus and in I Peter. Nevertheless, a doctrinal basis is present. Note for example, how respect for other people is built upon a doctrine of the image of God (Jas 3:9). Even more significantly, James is explicitly concerned with the crucial questions of how people are saved (Jas 1:21; 2:14; 4:12) and justified (Jas 2:21-25). What is happening is that to a considerable extent James emphasizes elements in New Testament theology and ethics that tended to be ignored or marginalized elsewhere, and he has an important corrective to offer to some mistaken practical consequences that were being drawn from mainline Pauline theology.

*Jesus Christ.* There is no explicit christology in the letter, but only hints that show that the writer had such a doctrine but expressed himself without recourse to it here. Jesus appears to be mentioned or alluded to only four times apart from the reference in the opening greeting (Jas 1:1).

In James 5:7-8 the readers are instructed to be patient until the Lord's coming. In view of the unified expectation of the coming of Jesus rather than of God in the New Testament, this is best taken as a reference to the parousia of Jesus.[9] The reference to the future coming of the Lord is thus pregnant with meaning in that here the same shift has taken place as elsewhere in the New Testament, where the future coming of God on the Day of the Lord has been replaced by the coming of the Lord Jesus as judge, with all the implications that

---

[9]There are six clear uses of *Lord* for Jesus (Jas 1:1; 2:15; 5:7, 8, 14, 15). Elsewhere in the letter the term *Lord* refers to God the Father (Jas 1:7; 3:9; 4:10, 15; 5:4, 10, 11). As elsewhere in the New Testament, it is not always absolutely certain whether God or Christ is the referent. See William R. Baker, "Christology in the Epistle of James", *EQ* 74 (2002): 47-57.

this has for the Christian estimate of Jesus as being God's supreme agent and entitled to the same honor.[10] Although God is the only judge (Jas 4:12), here this function is assigned to Jesus.

This exalted understanding of Jesus is confirmed by the description of him in James 2:1 as "our glorious Lord Jesus Christ".[11] For James Jesus is not simply a human teacher or a human Messiah; he is the Lord of glory, the status assumed by Jesus as a result of his resurrection and exaltation. His character is seen in the way in which an appeal to faith in the Lord is used to back up a condemnation of favoritism or partiality.

It is not surprising, then, that in a third passage those who are ill are to be anointed in the name of the Lord and the Lord will forgive any sins that they have committed (Jas 5:14-15).[12]

And, finally, when James mentions "the noble name of him to whom you belong" (Jas 2:7), this is surely a reference to baptism in the name of Jesus, again with all that this implies for the position of Jesus as Lord and Savior.[13]

What must not be forgotten, however, is that this letter includes numerous echoes of the teaching of Jesus, largely drawn from the Sermon on the Mount.[14] The influence of the teaching of Jesus is pervasive, and indeed for its size James shows proportionately more such influence than any of the other letters.

*God as giver and judge.* James takes up two possible misconceptions about God. One was that people were lacking in faith in the goodness of God and his willingness to answer prayer; they thought that God does not bestow good gifts on those who ask. The other misconception was that God is the author of temptation and that he is trying to pull people down.

Against such misconceptions James wants to reassure his readers that God is

---

[10]This expectation of the parousia is a lively one, and it is clearly still within the horizon of the readers and not something shifted into the distant future (Jas 5:3, 9).

[11]One possibility here is that we should translate "the Lord Jesus Christ, [who is] the glory [sc. of God]" (cf. Sophie Laws, *A Commentary on the Epistle of James* [London: A & C Black, 1980], pp. 94-97), but many commentators prefer to see "glory" as a descriptive genitive.

[12]In Jas 5:10 the name is presumably that of God.

[13]There is only one possible reference to the Spirit in the obscurity of Jas 4:5 (cf. the variants in TNIV), but here it is more probable that the reference is to a human spirit, namely, the evil *yetser* which inclines to envy; see Joel Marcus, "The Evil Inclination in the Epistle of James", *CBQ* 44 (1982): 621.

[14]See the table in Wiard Popkes, *Adressaten, Situation und Form des Jakobusbriefes* (Stuttgart: Katholische Bibelwerk, 1986), pp. 156-57.

gracious (Jas 4:6; 5:11) and generous (Jas 1:5). All good gifts come from him (Jas 1:17). He is ready to answer prayer.

The picture of God is developed positively in such a way as to emphasize his role as lawgiver and judge and his lack of partiality. God desires a righteous life on the part of his people (Jas 1:20). The sort of life that God wishes to see is characterized by concern for the needy and by freedom from succumbing to the sins of the surrounding world. The basic commandments found in the Old Testament are held up as God's continuing will (Jas 1:25).

There is a strong stress on God as the judge before whom all will eventually stand (Jas 2:12-13; 4:12). James does not mince his words about the fearsomeness of the judgment that is in store for the wicked and unjust (Jas 5:1, 3, 6, 9, 12).

God is further described as choosing the poor for his kingdom (Jas 2:5). Here, if anywhere in the New Testament, there would seem to be a bias to the poor on the part of God, which his church should imitate. James would justify it by pointing to the oppressive character of rich people, especially as this was experienced by his readers, and he condemns the favoritism that fails to give the poor their rights. He insists that God is concerned for the people who are oppressed by the rich (Jas 5:4).

Already we can see two main influences from the Old Testament shaping the thought of James. The first of these is that James stands in the tradition of wisdom teaching, which in its turn was carried on in some of the teaching of Jesus.[15] Here we may remind ourselves that the teaching in the Old Testament falls into three main categories. First, there is the category of law, in which God's instructions to his people have a characteristically legal character and are expressed in terms of commandments that have to be obeyed under pain of penalties. Leonhard Goppelt has argued that the "royal law" (Jas 2:8) is more than the Old Testament; it is "the claim of God that stood behind the Old Testament commandments".[16] Second, there is the category of prophecy, in which God speaks to his people more in terms of exhortation backed up by promises

---

[15]It is interesting that the form-critical analysis of the sayings of Jesus in the Synoptic Gospels has found that many of them fit into the patterns of legal sayings, prophetic sayings and wisdom sayings, thus corresponding to all three main divisions of the Hebrew Bible—the law, the prophets and the writings.

[16]Goppelt, 2:206.

and warnings of what will happen to them according to whether they accept or reject the prophetic message. And, third, there is the category of wisdom, in which God's instruction is given largely in short, independent, pithy sayings that are often self-evidently true or are based on profound observation of what happens in life. Proverbs and Ecclesiastes are the outstanding examples of the form, but it is also found in some of the psalms, like Psalm 1 and Psalm 49. Now the teaching in James is generally of this character, although elements of law and prophecy can also be found.[17] This applies to its form, but it also applies to its content; there is explicit reference to the importance of wisdom.

The other is that James picks up the theme of the righteous sufferer found in the Psalms and elsewhere, especially the book of Wisdom. The meaning of this term is obvious enough; it refers to the kind of person who is upright and honest in behavior and trusts implicitly in the power and love of God. Nevertheless, such people can be the objects of attack and persecution by other people who take advantage of them, and in that situation they commit themselves afresh to the care of God, and they have his promise that in the end he will vindicate them. James believes that God will ultimately uphold the poor, not necessarily the poor in general but the poor who believe in God and commit themselves to him (Jas 1:12; 5:10-11). The motif of the righteous sufferer is thus used to say something significant about the character of the God in whom the sufferers put their trust.

In both of these cases James is carrying further motifs found in the Gospels. Jesus is presented as the prime example of the righteous sufferer who commits himself into the care of God and is vindicated for this faith and obedience. And Jesus spoke as an envoy of wisdom and used the forms of the wisdom literature.

*The life of the believer.* James has a powerful sense of the reality of sin. He is well aware that temptation works by the stimulation of evil desires that are part of a person's nature. Here the Jewish background of James is particularly evident in that his writing probably reflects the Jewish doctrine of the good impulse and the evil impulse that are present in human nature, and our behavior depends on which has the upper hand; what James says about evil desire is very

---

[17]For the former see Jas 1:25; 2:8-13; for the latter see Jas 4:13—5:6, which has the marks of a prophetic denunciation of the sins of the rich.

like Jewish teaching about the evil impulse or *yetzer*.[18] There can therefore be no excuse for sin by claiming that it was the result of an overpowering outside impulse (Jas 1:13-15).

James identifies his readers as people who have been given birth through the word of truth (Jas 1:18). This statement brings James remarkably close to Peter (1 Pet 1:23), and it strongly suggests that there is more to the theology that is held by James than what surfaces in this particular writing. His theology of conversion is thus expressed in two standard ways. First, in terms of God's action, Christians are people who have experienced a new birth, but, second, in terms of human action they are also people who profess faith in Jesus Christ (Jas 2:1). James is thus writing to people who are identified as believers, and his concern is with their life of faith, the temptations to give it up, the ways in which they may live inconsistently and the path to maturity.

James also describes them as being under the law of liberty (Jas 1:25). The law is described as "perfect" and "royal" (Jas 1:25; 2:8), powerful adjectives that emphasize its preeminent place in the theology of James. In a paradoxical way the law sets people free because it is part of the word, that is, the gospel, through which they receive new birth.[19] It is important for James that there is an element of law in Christian teaching. The law found in Scripture (i.e., the Old Testament) is part of the "word" that Christians hear, for the "word" is not simply gospel but also teaching about behavior (Jas 1:22-23). Is there here a difference from Paul? Hardly, for Paul is equally concerned that believers fulfill the law and cites the same supreme command (Rom 13:8-10). It is true that different New Testament writers give different degrees of emphasis to the place of the Old Testament law in the lives of believers. Paul was quite emphatic that believers are no longer under the law and that people cannot be justified by the works of the law, but this does not seem to have meant for him that the moral and spiritual teaching of the law was no longer relevant for them.

It is noteworthy that James makes no mention of the Holy Spirit in relation to the life of the believer. One possible explanation is that wisdom in James is

---

[18]There are links here with the Jewish understanding of the two impulses, good and evil, within human beings *(yetser)*. For a full survey of the background see Marcus, "Evil Inclination".

[19]See Goppelt, 2:204-5.

equivalent to the Holy Spirit in other parts of the New Testament.[20] Wisdom is a gift given by God (Jas 1:5; 3:15) that leads to humility (Jas 3:13); in James 3:17-18 it produces qualities in believers that are remarkably similar to the fruit of the Spirit in Galatians 5:22-23; even the word *fruit* is common to both passages (cf. 2 Pet 1:5-8). Does James, then, in effect use the term *wisdom* with reference to those aspects of the Christian life that other writers refer to by means of language about the Spirit? This is an attractive hypothesis particularly when we remember the close connection between wisdom and the Spirit in some of the background material (Is 11:2; cf. Eph 1:17).[21] However we answer this question, it emerges that James does have a concept of a divine power at work in the lives of believers without which their path to perfection would be impossible.[22]

**Faith and actions.** James is particularly insistent on the need for faith to be expressed in actions (e.g., Jas 2:1-4) and the uselessness of a faith without actions (Jas 2:14-26). We should carefully distinguish three related motifs here. First, listening to the Word must be accompanied by obedience to what it says (Jas 1:22). Second, words without deeds are useless when people need to express both (Jas 2:15-16). Third, and equally, faith not accompanied by works is dead (Jas 2:14, 17).[23] James builds up an argument for action that is not based simply upon logic but is defended by appeal to biblical examples, Abraham and Rahab. He can pick up the Old Testament example of Abraham and demonstrate from it the need for deeds to make faith complete.

Here James is talking about faith and works in relation to salvation (Jas 2:14) and to justification, God's declaration that a person is righteous and stands in a good relationship to him (Jas 2:21, 23-25). Now it was Paul who developed the doctrine of justification and insisted that it was by faith and not by works. This has naturally raised the question whether James has got Paul or followers of Paul in his sights and is handing out a corrective. This may well be

---

[20] Compare how the exorcisms of Jesus are attributed to the Spirit of God in Mt 12:28 but to the finger of God in Lk 11:20.

[21] The case is strongly argued by J. A. Kirk, "The Meaning of Wisdom in James: Examination of a Hypothesis", *NTS* 16 (1969-1970): 24-38.

[22] Note that there is no suggestion of the sort of perfectionism in James that would divide believers into two categories, the ordinary believers and the "perfect". Perfection is always seen as a goal rather than as an achievement.

[23] Note how "words without deeds" is used as an analogy to argue against "faith without works".

so, and we must discuss the point later. James is attacking a false view of faith that sees it as little more than orthodox belief that does not change a person's lifestyle. He is quite clear that the Christian life can be summed up in terms of faith (Jas 1:3; 2:1, 5) and that faith is essential to our ongoing relationship with God expressed in prayer (Jas 1:6; 5:15). There is, then, a genuine kind of faith, but there is also a faulty kind of faith that is no faith.

Further, it is important to observe that what James does throughout is to insist on faith *and* works. What James defends is the view that faith is demonstrated to be real by issuing in actions that express it, like being prepared to offer one's son to God (Jas 2:21) or welcoming spies and protecting them from capture (Jas 2:25). Although the illustration in James 2:15-16 is concerned with the contrast between words and deeds of love as a parallel to the contrast between faith without deeds and faith with deeds, it is a highly apposite illustration in that James undoubtedly saw loving deeds as opposed to ritual requirements as one of the necessary expressions of true faith.

*The life of the congregation.* The fact that Christians meet together comes out almost incidentally in James 2:1-4, where their gathering is called by the Jewish name of synagogue. They form a group led by elders (Jas 5:14) whose pastoral care extends to visits to the sick to anoint them and pray for them. There is no mention of overseers/bishops or of deacons, and we may perhaps presume that the elders fulfilled the functions of these leaders. The activity of teaching is evidently important, and it was not confined to the elders, but rather it would seem that there was a wider circle of people who gave teaching or had a recognized role as teachers. Teaching was regarded as a desirable occupation even by people who were not well suited to it (Jas 3:1-2).

The teaching is described in traditional Christian fashion as "the word" (Jas 1:22-25), and it can include the "perfect law" as well as specifically Christian instruction. Wiard Popkes characterizes the church of James as a church of the Word—and of words![24] It is the emplanted word that is able to save people, and they are brought to the new birth through the Word of truth (Jas 1:18); their role as a congregation is to receive the word.

The life of the congregation includes prayer and singing of praise (Jas 3:9) as well as mutual confession of sins (this seems to mean confession of faults

---

[24]Popkes, *Adressaten*, p. 103.

committed against the other person) and prayers for healing (Jas 5:13-18). Nothing is said explicitly of baptism or the Lord's Supper, but these can fairly be assumed to have taken place, and the "name" in James 2:7 has been plausibly connected with baptism. There is thus a framework of Christian meetings at which people praise, pray and are taught as the background to all that the letter is concerned with. Here James is simply assuming the common pattern of congregational meetings that was to be found, with minor variations, throughout the early Christian world. The only oddity is the use of the term *synagogue* for the Christian meeting; this word is not found elsewhere in the New Testament in a Christian sense, but it is attested later in Ignatius and Hermas. Clearly a Jewish background is present.

Moreover, the way in which James addresses his readers as belonging to the Dispersion probably indicates that they regarded themselves as the true successors of the Old Testament people of God. Their present existence is similar to that described in I Peter as "strangers and pilgrims", people living in the midst of an environment that was at best uninterested and at worst inimical to their faith. The way in which Abraham is claimed as their father (Jas 2:21) is a further indication of this takeover of a Jewish heritage.

### Conclusion

The framework of James is provided by the Jewish wisdom tradition that molds the form and the content of his thought.

The main theme is the development of Christian perfection, seen in a life of active faith that successfully copes with the temptations arising from the love of money and the abuse of the tongue.

The significant elements James stresses are

1. Human answerability to the judgment of God through Christ, whose coming is near.

2. The provision of God's word and divine wisdom to enable believers to develop maturity.

3. The need for faith to be expressed in action.

4. Life lived according to the law of God to love one's neighbor; this forbids partiality.

5. Life lived in dependence on God through prayer.

James thus makes a rather distinctive theological contribution to the New Testament.

## Bibliography

*New Testament Theologies:* (English) Childs, pp. 431-45; Goppelt, 2:199-211; Ladd, pp.
634-39; Morris, pp. 312-5; Strecker, pp. 654-82. (German) Berger, pp. 165-73;
Gnilka, pp. 444-53; Hahn, 1:395-407; Hübner, 2:380-86; Stuhlmacher, 2:59-69.
See also Ulrich Luck, "Die Theologie des Jakobusbriefes", *Zeitschrift für Theologie und
Kirche* 81 (1984): 1-30; Wiard Popkes, *Adressaten, Situation und Form des Jakobusbriefes*
(Stuttgart: Katholisches Bibelwerk, 1986).

Adamson, James B. *James: The Man and His Message.* Grand Rapids, Mich.: Eerdmans,
1989.

Baker, William R. *Personal Speech Ethics in the Epistle of James.* Tübingen: J. C. B. Mohr [Paul
Siebeck], 1995.

Bauckham, Richard J. *James.* London: Routledge, 1998.

Cargal, Timothy B. *Restoring the Diaspora: Discursive Structure and Purpose in the Epistle of James.*
Atlanta: Scholars Press, 1993.

Chester, Andrew, and (Ralph P. Martin). *The Theology of the Letters of James, Peter and Jude.*
Cambridge: Cambridge University Press, 1994, pp. 1-62.

Davids, Peter H. *The Epistle of James. A Commentary on the Greek Text.* Exeter: Paternoster,
1982.

———. "The Epistle of James in Modern Discussion". *ANRW* 2.25.5 (1988): 3621-
45.

Dibelius, Martin, and Heinrich Greeven. *James.* Philadelphia: Fortress, 1975.

Kirk, J. A. "The Meaning of Wisdom in James: Examination of a Hypothesis". *NTS*
16 (1969-1970): 24-38.

Laws, Sophie. *A Commentary on the Epistle of James.* London: A & C Black, 1980.

Marcus, Joel. "The Evil Inclination in the Epistle of James". *CBQ* 44 (1982): 606-21.

Martin, Ralph P. *James.* Waco, Tex.: Word, 1988.

Penner, Todd C. *The Epistle of James and Eschatology: Rereading an Ancient Christian Letter.* Sheffield: Sheffield Academic Press, 1996.

Wall, Robert W. "James, Letter of". In *DLNTD*, pp. 545-61.

# 27

# THE FIRST LETTER
# OF PETER

⌒o⌒

T he so-called first letter of Peter has the familiar form of a real letter that we know from the writings of Paul. It is addressed to Christians in a specific, though wide, area of the ancient world.[1] It takes account of a broad situation that may be presumed to be generally true of the readers without evidencing a specific occasion of the kind that we find in, say, the Corinthian correspondence. The concrete circumstances that are reflected are the attacks on Christians that constitute painful trials (I Pet 4:12); the short letter uses the verb *suffer* about twelve times, more than any other book in the New Testament. These sufferings are evidently happening rather than being merely a threat on the horizon, but they are for the most part insults and harsh treatment from other people, such as slaves might receive from unsympathetic masters (I Pet 2:18-20) rather than any kind of official state action. nevertheless, since the possibility of suffering is compared with what may happen to murderers or thieves (I Pet 4:15), it may be that prosecution was a possibility.

The people addressed form Christian congregations that are led by elders (I Pet 5:1), but the tasks of ministry are carried out by any members of the congregation who are appropriately gifted by God (I Pet 4:10-11). We get the impression of a church that has had sufficient time to spread throughout the world (I Pet 5:9), but at the same time the character of the teaching suggests

---

[1]For a slightly fuller defense of the critical and exegetical positions adopted in this section see I. Howard Marshall, *1 Peter* (Downers Grove, Ill.: InterVarsity Press, 1991).

that the readers included people who had just become believers; healthy established congregations would naturally include new believers.

Perhaps a majority of contemporary scholars hold that the letter is later than Peter but comes out of a group who evidently held that what they had to say could fitly be associated with him. But there is nothing in the letter that demands allonymity,[2] and we may well have here a valuable testimony to the thinking of Peter himself.

The aim of Peter is to give a general letter of encouragement and teaching to his readers, much in the way in which many a modern sermon does not deal with one specific set of circumstances among the hearers but gives them a general exhortation that is concerned with the Christian life as a whole but may be slanted in some particular direction. The major theme, then, is the way in which Christian believers are to live in the world despite the hostility that they experience from some of its members.

As with so many Christian writings, it is not easy to discern the detailed logic of the discourse. There are some clear breaks, but there are also some lengthy threads where the author moves from one topic to another with a logic that is not ours; in particular, he has the artifice of tagging on a phrase to the end of one sentence and then making it the theme of the next one (e.g., I Pet 1:9/10). Nevertheless, there is an integrated structure of theology and exhortation in which "the theological statement gives the basis for the exhortation, and then the exhortation refers back to the statement about salvation".[3]

The letter begins with an opening greeting and thanksgiving (I Pet 1:1-12) and has a closing greeting (I Pet 5:12-14). In between we can distinguish three main sections that are concerned with the basic characteristics of Christian living (I Pet 1:13—2:10), social conduct (I Pet 2:11—3:12) and the Christian attitude toward hostility (I Pet 3:13—5:11).

## The Theological Story

*Greeting and* **berakah** *(1 Pet 1:1-12)*. The opening greeting employs the same concept of the Christian dispersion as we find in James. The readers are further

---

[2]I use this term in preference to pseudonymity to refer to composition by an unknown person or persons using the name of somebody else without the intention of deceiving the readers on the matter. See page 398 n. 4.

[3]Hübner, 2:392.

described as being God's elect people. They are such through the foreknowledge of God, which is a way of saying that he took the initiative in bringing the church into being; through the sanctification wrought by the Spirit, which molds their character to be appropriate for God's people; and with the purpose that they might be obedient and sprinkled with the blood of Jesus, these being the signs that they are now in covenant with God (like the Israelites in Ex 24).

Since the Christian way is not easy and involves suffering, a good part of the letter is devoted to rehearsing the nature of Christian salvation in such a way as to encourage the readers. The mood of the letter is accordingly one of praise to God for the gift of salvation (1 Pet 1:3). The opening section of the letter takes the form of an extended expression of praise to God[4] and serves to remind the readers of the nature of this gift (1 Pet 1:3-12). Peter emphasizes that although the readers may be suffering now in all kinds of ways, they can look forward confidently to a future in heaven, and therefore while suffering they enjoy a confident hope of what God has promised to them. There is accordingly a contrast between present suffering and future blessing.

One purpose of putting the matter like this is to indicate that there is a sense in which the present trials of the readers are allowed by God as a means of testing and strengthening their faith. For the moment they live by faith rather than by sight of Jesus Christ.

All this might make us think that Peter is working with a simple contrast between present suffering, sustained by hope, and future realization of that hope. This would be a serious misunderstanding of the letter. There is also a strong element of present salvation in the letter. The revelation of Christ has taken place "in these last times" (1 Pet 1:20). The coming of Jesus is the beginning of the end and so brings a new era in world history. The readers have already experienced a new birth (1 Pet 1:3, 23). Already the prospect of the future causes the readers to experience great joy. So, although they look forward to the coming of Christ (1 Pet 1:7; 5:4), here and now they know what it is to love him and believe in him, and this experience causes intense emotions of joy (1 Pet 1:8). When Peter says that they are receiving the goal of their faith, the salvation of their souls (1 Pet 1:9), the present tense should be taken seriously and not softened into a future. Already they have tasted that the Lord is good;

---

[4]Cf. 2 Corinthians and Ephesians for the use of the *berakah* form of thanksgiving to God.

they have had evidence of his care for them (I Pet 2:3).

It emerges, then, that Peter uses this now-then contrast in order to stress the need for godly living during the period that leads up to the final revelation of salvation. He is concerned with how believers live in this interim period, and he motivates them by the hope of what is to come. He uses the hope to encourage them in that he stresses the certainty of its being fulfilled. This is accomplished by rooting the hope in the resurrection of Jesus as an event that the readers would have taken for granted as historical fact (I Pet 1:3). It is also achieved by the claim that the sufferings of Christ and the glories to follow were the theme of prophecy and that the prophets were told by God that their message was for the benefit of the future generation to which the readers belong (I Pet 1:10-12). Thus the readers can be sure that they are the people for whom the blessings are prepared.

*The basic characteristics of Christian living (1 Pet 1:13—2:10).* In the light of this statement of their status as the objects of God's grace, Peter can move into exhortation. Despite their present trials, the readers are to set their sights on the future. The element of future hope, already stressed in I Peter 1:3, reappears in I Peter 1:13. Throughout this period of confident waiting the readers are to seek to be holy, like their God (Lev 11:44-45). There is an element of the fear of the Lord. God is their Father, but a Father can also be a judge,[5] and God is the impartial judge of his people (I Pet 1:17; cf. I Pet 2:23; 4:5).[6] So there is an incentive to live in way that will earn his approval.

But Peter does not linger long on that theme before giving further encouragement to the readers by referring to the way in which they have been delivered from their old, futile way of life and its consequences by the shedding of the blood of Jesus, who is the counterpart of the sacrificial victims in the Old Testament. Here redemption is not simply from the consequences of sin but from their sinful way of life. But the appeal is based not simply on the fact of deliverance but on the great cost with which it was achieved. So precious a gift is not to be treated lightly by continuing to live useless lives. The outcome is a new life in which their faith and hope rest in a God whom they can fully trust. If this statement is meant to

---

[5] This combination would not have sounded strange to Peter's readers, although it may do so to modern readers.

[6] First Pet 4:6, however, refers to the mistaken judgment of human beings on the believers whom God will vindicate at his judgment.

assure them of the certainty of their salvation, it is also meant to fill them with a powerful motive of gratitude to sustain them in their pilgrimage.

The exhortation continues with an appeal for sincere love within the Christian community (1 Pet 1:22), but this is not developed in any detail. Instead there is a further statement of their new status, this time using the metaphor of rebirth through the Word of God to eternal life. This new picture allows Peter to briefly develop the thought of spiritual sustenance by the milk that is appropriate for newly born children.

Then the imagery shifts yet again, and Peter now develops a more extended metaphor of the believers as a spiritual building, with Christ as the cornerstone. The building is specifically a temple whose purpose is to offer spiritual sacrifices to God, and the readers appear to be understood simultaneously as the stones of which the building is made and also as the priests who function within it. The imagery serves as yet another source of encouragement, since the texts about the stone refer to the safe position of those who believe in the cornerstone contrasted with those who do not believe and so are rejected.

This leads to a summary statement in which the readers are understood to be the new Israel, a priestly nation whose task is to praise God. Language used of Israel in the Old Testament is here directly applied to the company of believers.

*The social conduct of believers (1 Pet 2:11—3:12).* The appeal for Christian conduct now becomes more concrete as Peter develops the need for the readers to live in a way that will be recognized as good by the world around them. Conduct that would be generally accepted as good is here motivated and taken to a higher level by theological backing.

All believers are to be submissive to the rulers and to honor people in general for the Lord's sake. Obedience to God entails obedience and respect to the authorities that he has set up in the world.

Slaves are to obey their masters no matter whether the latter is good or faulty. Here Peter develops the thought that suffering that is undeserved brings credit with God, and he backs it up by reference to the example of Jesus, here described in terms of the suffering Servant (Is 53). But the example merges into a reminder of the way in which as the suffering Servant Jesus bore the sins of the readers and healed them; picking up another metaphor from the same context, the readers are to be seen as wayward sheep that are now obedient to their shepherd.

Wives are also to be submissive to their husbands, an attitude that was expected in the culture of the time and one that would help to commend the gospel to non-Christian partners. Husbands for their part are to show due consideration for their wives and not to act selfishly toward them. Their equality as inheritors of God's salvation is emphasized.

All of this climaxes in a call to mutual love and to refraining from answering evil with evil, based on Psalm 34.

*The attitude of believers to hostility (1 Pet 3:13—5:11)*. The remainder of the letter is concerned with the situation of believers in a hostile world, of which we have already had several hints in the earlier part of the letter. This now becomes a theme in its own right. Believers are encouraged that the suffering that will inevitably come their way cannot really harm them. Therefore, they should not be frightened of the opposition but prepared to bear witness to their faith. Peter repeats his point that it is no credit to anybody to put up with punishment because it is deserved, but if a person suffers innocently, that is, for being a good person or a believer, then this is creditworthy. Again the example of Jesus as the innocent sufferer is invoked. This time, however, the thought is elaborated in a different direction by referring to the way in which he was brought back to life and preached to the spirits in prison who had been disobedient in the time of Noah. At that time God was acting to save Noah and his family, and he is now acting to save believers through "baptism", which corresponds to the "salvation" of the people in the ark through water. There seems to be an implicit parallelism between Noah, who was a preacher of righteousness (2 Pet 2:5), and Christian believers as witnesses in a hostile world. But God raised Jesus from the dead and the opposing powers have been subjected to him. God saved Noah, and God saves believers. The victory of Jesus thus encourages believers in their witness; they know that the forces arrayed against them are ultimately powerless.

So the believers can be encouraged to see that their sufferings will turn out for their good. They are not to fall back into their old way of life, in which they were free from persecution because their life was like that of the world around them. Instead they are to live lives that are different, knowing that even if they are abused for it, they will ultimately be vindicated in that their opponents will be judged by God.

Over against the sinful life that they once practiced is placed the Christian alternative, a life of sobriety, prayer, mutual love and mutual service, in which they use the gifts that God gives them for ministry to one another that, like their evangelism (1 Pet 2:9), will bring glory to God.

Yet again the readers are warned to expect opposition, but it is to be seen as a form of testing and as a path that will lead to sharing in the glory of Christ. Persecution can be understood as a means that God uses to purify the church by separating out the faithful from the unfaithful. Sufferings can thus be regarded as a kind of judgment by God (1 Pet 4:17) through which his people are purged of sin.

In this situation, the church needs leaders who will care for the flock and members who are prepared to be humble in their attitudes to one another. They are also to be humble over against God, submitting to his way for their lives. The situation can be summed up in terms of the church being under attack worldwide from the devil seeking to destroy it, but its members are in the care of God, who will strengthen them to withstand attack and bring them to glory, just as he exalted Christ after his sufferings.

### Theological Themes

*The general character of the theology.* The dominant theme of the letter is one of encouragement to the readers to live steadfastly and positively as Christian believers in the world, despite the sufferings and opposition they encounter. Peter encourages them by dwelling on the future hope that is guaranteed to them, the way in which Christ has redeemed them, and the various ways in which they experience God's grace and strength here and now, and by encouraging their communal life as the people of God. Theology thus serves to motivate Christian living.

First Peter illustrates well the structure of Christian belief and experience in terms of the three categories: doxological, antagonistic and soteriological. The Christian life is expressed in praise, worship and thanksgiving to God; it is lived in opposition to Satan and evil; and it derives its strength from the salvation bestowed by God in Christ and through the Holy Spirit.

We have seen how the dominant note at the outset of the letter is praise to God. The theological teaching is couched in the form of praise to God because of what he has done. The effect of rehearsing the great deeds of God is to bring about spontaneous expressions of thanksgiving to God.[7] Behind this thanksgiving there lie the two elements of God's working in the world.

There is his victory over the forces of evil leading to their defeat. At the heart of the letter is the enigmatic passage about the two stages in the victorious journey of Christ after his death: first, his triumphant message to the spirits in prison and, second, his enthronement alongside God as supreme over angels, authorities and powers (1 Pet 3:19, 22). Believers in their own way are immersed in the fight against the evil passions that make war upon them (1 Pet 2:11), but Peter assures them that they are fighting against a defeated foe.

There is also Christ's deliverance of believers from sin to bring them to God and the promise of their future inheritance. The language of redemption is used to describe how believers have been delivered from their past way of life by the death of Christ (1 Pet 1:18-19).

*The influence of the Old Testament.* Considerable importance is attached to the written and spoken Word of God as the means whereby God saves and strengthens his people (1 Pet 1:23-25; 3:1); here we have the major statement in the New Testament regarding the prophetic character and continuing relevance of the Old Testament (1 Pet 1:10-12). The letter is remarkable for the extensive use of citations from and allusions to the Old Testament. This takes place used in several ways.

First, the Old Testament is used to explain who Jesus is and what he does. We have here the fullest use of Isaiah 53 by any New Testament author; Jesus is preeminently the Suffering Servant who is not merely an example of how to respond to persecution, but above all the One who bore the sins of humanity in order that they might die to sin and live to righteousness (1 Pet 2:21-25). He is also likened to a sacrificial lamb whose blood was shed to redeem or deliver people from their old, sinful way of life and its consequences.[8] The allusion appears to be primarily to the Passover lamb, but since the descriptions of

---

[7]Cf. how Geoffrey Wainwright, *Doxology* (London, Epworth Press, 1980), has emphasized the element of doxology as the mood of Christian theology.

[8]Arland J. Hultgren, *Christ and His Benefits: Christology and Redemption in the New Testament* (Philadelphia: Fortress, 1988), p. 115, makes the point that Peter is less concerned with the problem of consciences disturbed by guilt and more with "the disturbed consciousness of living as exiles in a world of abuse". This is true up to a point, but Peter is concerned that his readers are delivered from a sinful way of life and the judgment that will befall the rest of the world.

the various sacrifices in the Old Testament are not dissimilar, we should not tie down the reference too tightly; we may compare, for example, the description of the burned offering in Lev 22:17-25. This language is part of a general application of the idea of a new exodus and of an understanding of the requirements of the Christian life as a counterpart to the teaching on the holiness of God's people in Leviticus.

Second, then, at the beginning of the letter, in the theological definition of the readers that forms part of the greeting, they are described as God's chosen people, made holy by his Spirit and destined for obedience to God and being sprinkled with the blood of Christ (1 Pet 1:2). This last phrase in particular is lifted from the description of the covenant ceremony in Exodus 24 and shows how Peter regards the church as the counterpart of Israel at Sinai; it stands in continuity with the people of God in the Old Testament and is now that people. This Old Testament teaching about the people of God can be used to shape the exposition on the ground that the readers are the people of God and therefore the promises and the exhortations in the Old Testament both apply to them. Consequently, the immediate goal of Christian living can be described in terms of holiness (1 Pet 1:15-16), using language inspired by Leviticus 11:44-45, Leviticus 19:2 and Leviticus 20:7. It is noteworthy that the question of the status of Jews who had not become part of the Christian church is not discussed. The place of the church as the successor of Israel in the Old Testament is taken for granted.

Third, it has been suggested that some sections of the letter use parts of the Old Testament to provide the guiding thread.[9] This is evident in the sustained use of Isaiah 53, but also there is the use of Psalm 34 in 1 Peter 3 and of Leviticus in 1 Peter 1—2. Some of the material, such as the quotations in 1 Peter 2:6-8, is also used independently by other New Testament authors, probably drawing on a common stock of Christianly interpreted texts, but there is also material that is peculiar to this letter. In any case, the understanding of the exodus from Egypt and the associated setting up of the covenant with its accompanying teaching on how God's people are to live has been understood as the prototype of Christian redemption; Peter, in other words, uses typology as a

---

[9]See especially William L. Schutter, *Hermeneutic and Composition in 1 Peter* (Tübingen: J. C. B. Mohr [Paul Siebeck], 1989).

means of utilizing the Old Testament revelation.

*The significance of Jesus Christ.* The person of Jesus is of central importance, particularly in his role as the Suffering Servant who died to redeem the readers, but also as the resurrected and exalted Lord who is to be revealed in glory.[10] First Peter also, like James, contains a significant number of echoes of the teaching of Jesus, introduced without specific identification of their source. The more ethical teaching of Jesus fits in comfortably alongside the Old Testament as a basis for how believers should live. Whatever theological struggles there may have been over the observance of the Torah as the way to be right with God, in practice Christians accepted the Old Testament as a guide to God's will for holy living.[11]

Obviously the main interest of Peter is in the death and resurrection of Christ and specifically in their significance for the lives of the readers,[12] but he goes beyond this in three ways.

First, he speaks of Jesus as the one who was chosen by God before the creation of the world but who was revealed in these last times for the sake of the readers (1 Pet 1:20). Here there is the familiar New Testament contrast between what God planned before creation and what he did to carry his plan into effect later, between what was at first hidden and secret and afterward was revealed to human beings. This emphasizes that God took the initiative in salvation and carried out his plan in due course. He chose Jesus before creation to be the Savior and then brought him into the world to carry out his task. While the language might mean nothing more than that God carried out a preconceived plan, it is more likely that Peter is thinking of a preexistent being whom God appointed for his task even before creation and then revealed him to the world. However, Peter does not develop the relationship of Jesus Christ to God his Father (1 Pet 1:3) in any way; he simply takes it for granted.

---

[10]Attempts have been made to identify specific traditions utilized in the three christologically rich passages 1 Pet 1:18-21, 1 Pet 2:22-24 and 1 Pet 3:18-22, but, while traditional phraseology is doubtless being used, the formulation is most probably the author's own.

[11]The question of the law and the works of the law is not raised in this letter. Peter is able to take over ethical teaching from the law without being troubled by the problems that are reflected in some of the Pauline letters.

[12]Peter normally refers to him as "Christ" (thirteen times), "Jesus Christ" (eight times) and "Lord Jesus Christ" (once). The name *Christ* predominates in references to the suffering and death of Jesus, reflecting early Christian usage. Peter does not use the term *Son* with reference to Jesus. He uses *Lord* in agreement with the Old Testament (1 Pet 1:25; 2:3; 3:12, 15), and also independently in 1 Pet 2:13.

Second, Peter develops the story of what happened after the death of Jesus. He was put to death "in flesh" but brought to life "in spirit". This compressed phraseology is hard to elucidate, but it appears to mean that on the human level, as regards the physical sphere of existence, Christ died; his body physically died. But on the divine level, as regards the spiritual sphere of existence, he was made alive in a life that is not physical or not simply physical but spiritual, and therefore eternal and not bound by the constraints of the physical. When Christians today affirm belief in the physical resurrection of Jesus and consider it important to do so, what they are denying is that the physical body of Jesus simply perished in the grave and only some kind of spiritual entity was brought to life. What they are affirming is that the physical body of Jesus died but came to life in a new way in the spiritual realm as a spiritual body. In this way the importance of the physical is preserved; it is not merely a shell for the spiritual that can be cast away when it is no longer needed but is an essential part of the whole person.

Peter goes further, however, and tells his readers that in this spiritual mode of existence Christ made a journey to the prison where the spirits are and preached to them. The spirits are best understood as the evil, supernatural powers that are kept imprisoned by God until the day of judgment (2 Pet 2:4; Jude 6). The main alternative is that they are the spirits or souls of dead people, separated from their bodies, but this is a very unusual use of the term. Some commentators strengthen this interpretation by arguing that the reference in I Peter 4:6 is to the same beings, but it is more likely that this verse refers to the way in which the gospel was preached to believers who have subsequently died and are destined for life with God.

The prison is generally thought to be the underworld, but in some writings the opponents of God are kept in subjection in a lower part of heaven (cf. Rev 12:7 of the devil). The term *preached* in itself does not tell us what Christ's message was; normally the verb is used of proclaiming the gospel, but in the present context the proclamation is more likely to be of the victory of Christ.

The whole passage is intended to make two points. The first is that the evil powers are identified with the evil beings whose sin and rebellion led to the flood. Just as God saved Noah and his friends then despite the flood—almost, one might say, through the flood on which Noah's boat could float safely—so now too God saves the people who submit to the water of baptism from perishing with his opponents. The second thing is that these powers that threaten believers have been vanquished and Christ is supreme over them. The purpose of the passage, therefore, is to encourage believers facing hostility by reassuring them of their salvation and the defeat of their enemies. Peter assures the readers of the continuing care of Christ for them by referring to him as the Shepherd who cares for his sheep (1 Pet 2:25; 5:4).

Finally, as in the writings of Paul, Christ is the source of all the blessings of salvation, and this is expressed by the use of the characteristically Pauline phrase "in Christ". God addresses his call to people, as we would say, "in and through Christ"; he is the channel of God's communication (1 Pet 5:10). The closing benediction is addressed to all those who are "in Christ" (1 Pet 5:14): the thought is that they are joined to him so closely by their faith that he determines their way of life. Hence the good way of life of Christians is described as being "in Christ" (1 Pet 3:16); it is determined in every way by Christ, through his example and as the result of the believers' trust and obedience to him. Peter does not actually speak of "dying and rising with Christ" in the manner of Paul, but he comes close to it with his teaching on dying to sins and living to righteousness (1 Pet 2:24).

*The Holy Spirit.* There is no particular emphasis on the Holy Spirit. There is debate whether in 1 Peter 3:18 Jesus is made alive "in the Spirit" (TNIV) or (more probably in my view) "in the spirit[ual realm]" (cf. NRSV). When Peter refers to the gifts that enable believers for ministry, it is not clear whether the word which he uses (*charisma*, 1 Pet 4:10) would automatically arouse associations with the Spirit or not, although 1 Corinthians 12 does make the link quite explicitly.

Other references are quite unambiguous. The Spirit is referred to as the inspirer of the prophets and Christian preachers (1 Pet 1:11-12), as the agent in the sanctifying of believers (1 Pet 1:2), and most interestingly as the Spirit of glory and of God who rests on believers when they are persecuted (1 Pet 4:14). Here we have a powerful restatement of the motif that the Spirit will aid believers when they face hostile questioning in court (Mk 13:11).

*The church as the people of God.* The experience of present salvation provides the ground and motivation for the new behavior of believers. It also draws them together as the people of God. Peter takes for granted the fact that believers corporately form the people of God, although he never uses the term *church (ekklēsia)*. Instead, he uses a whole lot of phrases that, as we have seen, indicate that he saw Christian believers as now forming the people of God. They are God's flock (1 Pet 5:2). This phrase picks up the imagery of Jeremiah and Ezekiel in particular regarding Israel in relation to God. Peter's understanding of Christian leadership is of people acting as subshepherds under the chief Shepherd. They should not only care unselfishly for the flock but should also—rather breaking the parameters of the metaphor—be examples to those for whom they care (1 Pet 5:2-4).

The believers also form the *house* of God (1 Pet 4:17); this word can refer either to a "household" (so TNIV) or, as is much more likely here, to the place where God is present, his temple. This fits in with the same image in 1 Peter 2:4-5 and with the passage that probably inspired the thought here (Ezek 9:6; cf. Mal 3).

In 1 Peter 2:1-10 we have one of the most powerful statements in the New Testament identifying the company of believers as the people of God; language used to describe the privileged position of the Jews as the people of God in the Old Testament is now deliberately applied to the readers so that they are identified as this people. They are God's household and God's people. The identification is even more focused in that the Christian congregation is declared to be both temple and priesthood with the task of offering the spiritual counterpart of sacrifices to God. These sacrifices are evidently the praise of God by words and by the living of lives that honor him in the world and so increase his glory (1 Pet 2:4-10).

On the practical level believers form a community and love one another. They show this love by giving hospitality to one another. Prayer is also a part of their life; the implication is that it is a communal activity as well as a private one (1 Pet 3:7; 4:7). It is also assumed that they will share Christian teaching with one another and serve one another. They don't have to be told to do these things but rather are encouraged to do them better, and they can do so because God's grace gives them the insight and the strength that they need. Here we have an important parallel to what Paul says in Romans 12 and 1 Corinthians 12 on spiritual gifts of ministry. Like Paul, Peter assumes that any and every member of the congregations may be equipped to serve in this way, and it is taken for granted that ministry of this kind was practiced, although there were people recognized as elders in the congregations. Further, the possession of a spiritual gift entails a responsibility to use it.

The outward mark of entry to the church is baptism (I Pet 3:21), which is said to save the readers. This bold language is justified in that baptism was probably taken with great seriousness as the sign of acceptance into the church and above all either as a pledge to live a new life or a prayer to God to enable this to happen.[13] The older view that the letter as a whole reflects what was said at a baptismal service is no longer seriously held, but the hypothesis is significant as demonstrating the way in which much of the letter does reflect the theology of conversion. There is no mention in the letter of the Lord's Supper.

*The characteristics of believers.* In the description of Christians we have observed a powerful element of hope (I Pet 1:3, 13, 21; 3:5, 15), although this has not displaced faith (I Pet 1:5, 7, 8, 9, 21; 2:6-7; 5:9, 12; cf. I Pet 4:19). These two qualities are the appropriate ones in this letter for people who are thought of as "strangers and exiles". They are living in the world as temporary residents and do not really belong to it. Indeed the world thinks them very strange people because its pleasures are not their pleasures, even though they once enjoyed them (I Pet 4:1-4). The thought is different from that of Hebrews, which is more concerned with the journey or the race that constitutes the Christian life. Nevertheless, the forward look is important, as well as the sense of trusting in the unseen Creator (I Pet 4:19) and Christ (I Pet 1:8). And the strong stress on their being the people of God gives them a status and a self-respect that contrasts strongly with their situation vis-à-vis the world.

Alongside faith and hope, however, love for God and Christ (I Pet 1:8) and for one another (I Pet 1:22; 2:17; 4:8-9; 5:14) and holiness (I Pet 1:2, 15-16; 2:5, 9; 3:5) stand together as the qualities or characteristics that Christians must show, mirroring the life of God. Rather than referring to the love of God, however, Peter speaks repeatedly of his grace, using this term to sum up the entire series of events and spiritual gifts through which life was brought to the world (I Pet 1:2, 10, 13; 3:7; 4:10; 5:5, 10, 12; cf. the use of "mercy", I Pet 1:3).

*Life in the world.* The major theme of the letter is the way in which Christian believers are to live in the world despite the hostility that they experience from some of its members.

---

[13]The meaning of *eperōtēma* is debatable, and both possibilities listed above are defensible.

Peter makes use of a pattern of teaching found elsewhere in the letters, especially in Titus, in which believers are told how to behave in relation to other people and institutions in society. Such teaching was found in non-Christian sources also and was concerned with relationships within the ancient household and toward the state. We find it in the New Testament mainly in Ephesians, Colossians and Titus.

In Peter's development of this pattern there are two key words. The one is *do good* (1 Pet 2:15, 20; 3:6, 17). This term is particularly important in making it clear that Peter is concerned to commend an outgoing, positive attitude toward life in society, however much the Christians may have been the objects of hostility. The other significant term is *submit* (1 Pet 2:13, 18; 3:1; 5:5), and this expresses the appropriate attitude toward people who in one way or another are placed over the readers—the governing authorities, the masters of slaves, the husbands of wives and the elders of the church (1 Pet 2:13-17, 18-25; 3:1-7; 5:5). There is nothing surprising in this given the existing framework of ancient society, which took these relationships for granted. In the first three instances Peter is thinking particularly of situations where the superior party was not necessarily Christian, and he is insisting that in these circumstances Christians show the effects of their obedience to the Lord by living according to the norms of ordered society.

At the same time he does have something to say to the people on the other side. He insists that Christian husbands must show consideration to their wives, and he regards them as joint heirs of the gift of life (1 Pet 3:7); he also requires the elders to avoid the characteristic faults of leaders and calls all the members of the church to show humility toward one another (1 Pet 5:5b; cf. 1 Pet 3:8-12). The concept of mutual responsibilities was known in the ancient world, but Peter perhaps goes further in emphasizing this mutuality in a direction that leads to a recognition that believers are fundamentally equal in the Lord. Nothing is said about the duties of governors to their subjects or of masters toward their slaves; at least in the former case it can be assumed that these are non-Christians who would not be accessible through a Christian letter. In any case, since Peter is addressing himself particularly to people who suffer, teaching for governors and masters of slaves would be less appropriate here.

Peter's audience clearly includes people, probably especially Gentiles, who had undergone a profound conversion in becoming Christians; the language of new birth is used at the outset of the letter to convey the newness of the existence of Christians (I Pet 1:3, 23). He recognizes that his readers will include people who once lived like the rest of pagan society, and he expects that they will now live sober lives (I Pet 4:3). For this and other reasons Christians may expect abuse from other people, but they can reflect that there is no credit in suffering punishment or abuse for doing wrong, but if they are doing what is right and suffer for it, this is praiseworthy in God's eyes (I Pet 2:20; 4:15-16).

Refusal to take part in a sinful way of life does not mean the same thing as withdrawal from the world. Rather, Christians are to do good in the world and in the particular social settings in which they are placed (I Pet 2:15). There is thus a thoroughly positive attitude to the opportunities given by living in the world. There is probably also an eye to Christian mission here in that the hope is that through their good deeds Christians will lead non-Christians to glorify God (I Pet 2:12); this ties in with the way in which Christians are also to be prepared to respond to people who question them about their faith (I Pet 3:15-16).

From these instructions we can see that Peter presupposes that the human authorities in the world owe their positions to God and therefore they and the sociopolitical order that they embody are to be respected and obeyed. In developing his rationale for Christian behavior in this situation Peter's thought is dominated by the role of Christ. The behavior of believers is to be determined by their loyalty to Christ as their Lord (I Pet 2:13). Moreover, when it comes to suffering, Christ functions as the exemplar of innocent suffering endured in the confidence that God will vindicate his faithful people. When Christians suffer as a result of their faith, they are participating in the sufferings of Christ (I Pet 4:13).

### Conclusion

First Peter is a letter in which the theology is explicit and is used constantly to encourage the readers and to back up the practical instruction. The density of the theology of I Peter is quite remarkable; it is a rich source for understanding the nature of the Christian life in a hostile world. Compared with James it is more a letter of encouragement than of practical instruction.

The letter is distinguished by not engaging in any polemic with the readers or with groups among them who are expressing false doctrines and false understandings of Christian behavior. There are warnings against failure to live up to Christian standards and encouragements for those whose hopes are weak, but there is no trace of false views that need to be corrected. New Testament theology is not always conducted in an arena of debate.

The framework of thought in the letter appears to be broadly that of the other New Testament letters.

The main theme in the theology is the nature of the Christian life in a time of testing; believers, called to a living hope, are to live holy lives in the fear of God and mutual love, respecting the society in which they are placed but avoiding its temptations and standing firm in the face of persecution.

Significant themes worthy of note are

1. The way in which the theology is expressed in strong dependence upon the Old Testament and in the consciousness that believers now form the people of God.

2. The accent on the hopeful aspect of faith as belief in the God who raises the dead and guards his people.

3. The understanding of Jesus Christ in terms of stone and servant imagery.

4. The unique reference to Christ's preaching to the spirits in prison.

5. The recognition of persecution as an opportunity for witness and the positive attitude toward living out the Christian life in the world despite its sinfulness and opposition.

In summary, Peter has a very positive attitude throughout the letter to what God is going to do in and for the readers; his promises will be fulfilled, and the life of the readers in the world will have a positive influence. Suffering is real but is relativized by the promises of God, which are fulfilled now and in the future. The designation "epistle of hope" is thoroughly appropriate for this letter.

## Bibliography

*New Testament Theologies:* (English) Bultmann, 2:180-83; Childs, pp. 446-62; Goppelt, 2:161-78; Ladd, pp. 641-48; Morris, pp. 316-321; Strecker, pp. 620-40. (German) Gnilka, pp. 422-37; Hübner, 2:387-95; Stuhlmacher, 2:70-84.

Achtemeier, Paul J. *1 Peter.* Minneapolis: Fortress, 1996.

(Chester, Andrew), and Ralph P. Martin. *The Theology of the Letters of James, Peter and Jude.* Cambridge: Cambridge University Press, 1994, pp. 87-133.

Elliott, John Hall. *A Home for the Homeless: A Sociological Exegesis of 1 Peter, Its Situation and Strategy.* Philadelphia: Fortress, 1981.

Goppelt, Leonhard. *A Commentary on 1 Peter.* Grand Rapids, Mich.: Eerdmans, 1993.

Green, Gene L. *Theology and Ethics in 1 Peter.* Ph.D. thesis, Aberdeen, 1980.

Marshall, I. Howard. *1 Peter.* Downers Grove, Ill.: InterVarsity Press, 1991.

Martin, Troy W. *Metaphor and Composition in 1 Peter.* Atlanta: Scholars Press, 1992.

Schutter, William L. *Hermeneutic and Composition in 1 Peter.* Tübingen: J. C. B. Mohr (Paul Siebeck), 1989.

Selwyn, Edward Gordon. *The First Epistle of St. Peter.* 2nd ed. London: Macmillan, 1947, pp. 64-115.

Thurén, Lauri. *Argument and Theology in 1 Peter: The Origins of Christian Paraenesis.* Sheffield: Sheffield Academic Press, 1995.

———. *The Rhetorical Strategy of 1 Peter with Special Regard to Ambiguous Expressions.* Abo: Academy Press, 1990.

# 28

# THE LETTER OF JUDE

❧

I f somebody writes an article on the most neglected book of the New Testament, it does not need much reflection to conclude that the reference will be
to the letter of Jude.[1] Opinions vary greatly over the origin of this brief letter,
but it remains likely that it is the work of the implied author, Jude, here identified as the brother of James, the leader of the Jerusalem church, and the relative of Jesus.[2] The author wrote in order to deal with the problem caused by
the intrusion of godless people into the church and to remind his readers to
hold fast to the apostolic gospel. The purpose of the letter is thus not primarily polemical in the sense that the author attacks and denounces opponents;
it is rather pastoral in that he warns the readers against the danger caused by
the infiltrators into the congregation, exhorts them to remain faithful and encourages them to win back the people who are in the grip of error or in danger
of succumbing to it.

Thus, as various commentators have noted, the real heart of the letter is Jude
20-23; the theme is summed up in Jude 3, where the readers are encouraged to
contend for the faith, and the danger is spelled out in Jude 4-19, where the false
teaching is unmasked and characterized. The readers are assured that God will
bring it to naught and judge it, as he has done with previous examples of the

---

[1] It merits less than one full page in George Eldon Ladd, *A Theology of the New Testament.*
[2] The date of the letter is uncertain, since there are no specific references within it. It need not be late,
since there are no signs of early catholicism and the opponents are not Gnostics; cf. Jonathan Knight,
*2 Peter and Jude* (Sheffield: Sheffield Academic Press, 1995), pp. 81-83.

same thing.[3] The missionary concern of New Testament theology is thus not to the forefront in this letter, concerned as it is more with the spiritual well-being of those who faith is endangered; the existence of error in the church means that attention is directed to the perseverance of God's people and the reclamation of those in danger of falling away.

## The Theological Story

*Opening greeting and closing doxology (Jude 1-2, 24-25).* The opening greeting emphasizes the way in which the readers are the objects of God's love and so dwell in him and are "kept for Jesus Christ" (i.e., probably for his final coming; Jude 1). The closing doxology forms an *inclusio* with its emphasis on this thought, that God is able to keep them from falling and to bring them into his presence (Jude 24). Nevertheless, this reassurance does not do away with the need for the readers to keep themselves in the love of God (Jude 21) and to guard against the effects of the godless people who are now in the church. Although the readers already know what the writer is going to say, nevertheless it is important for him to repeat it for their benefit.

We thus encounter in this letter the tension between the keeping love and power of God, and the need for human effort not only by church leaders in instruction and pastoral care but by believers in preserving themselves from error and sin, that we find to be a constant factor in New Testament theology.

*The danger caused by false teaching (Jude 3-16).* The situation is that various people have in some way or other become part of the Christian congregations although they do not share the apostolic gospel and way of life. The use of the term *shepherding* (Jude 12) and the reference to flattering other people "for their own advantage" (Jude 16) may suggest that they held positions of leadership in the congregation; in any event they were able to give teaching that encouraged their particular way of life. They may have been wandering prophets of a type whose activity is amply attested elsewhere in early Christian literature and whose numbers included teachers both orthodox and unorthodox according to the standpoint of mainstream Christianity.[4] The language used accuses them of

---

[3] I have followed the accepted division of the letter, but it should be noted that Jude 17-19 constitutes something of a bridge between the two sections, and some commentators place the division at Jude 16/17.

[4] Cf. Knight, *2 Peter*, pp. 29, 78-81.

gross sins, which according to some scholars is simply a means of denigrating opponents without actually being true.

Jude describes their sin (Jude 4). They have turned grace into license for immorality. This would appear to mean that they think that because they are saved by grace, they are therefore free to indulge in sin without fear of any consequences. They also deny Jesus Christ as Lord (the less usual word *despotēs* is here linked with *kyrios*). This is again probably a matter of behavior, a refusal to obey the commands of Jesus.

Further (Jude 8), they are described as dreamers, which may suggest that they laid claim to visions (cf. the condemnation of such in Deut 13). The description of them as lacking the Holy Spirit may perhaps imply that they claimed to be Spirit-inspired in their teaching but fell under the kind of censure found in I John 4:1. Their pollution of their bodies probably refers to sexual sins, and this is confirmed by other references to animal-like behavior (Jude 10). They are said to reject authority and slander celestial beings.[5] This is unusual and implies a greater role for angels in early Christianity than we would otherwise have guessed. Were the angels regarded as guardians of the law, and was it taken as still valid?

They are attacked as selfish and unproductive, as grumblers and faultfinders, boasters and flatterers. This suggests nothing more than a generally low level of behavior.

The total picture is thus one of broadly immoral and boorish behavior that is incompatible with the way of Christ. It is coupled with a lack of respect for Christ or any other spiritual authority. It is not surprising that they are categorized as people who do not have the Spirit (Jude 19), which can only mean that their teaching was not inspired by the Spirit because they did not possess the Spirit and so were not truly Christian believers despite whatever profession they made. Nevertheless, this behavior was being practiced by people in the church who were able to reconcile this way of life with the desire to be part of the church and to enter into its fellowship. The effect was a split in the church, and presumably the danger of orthodox Christians joining the immoral group.

*Responding to the false teachers (Jude 17-19, 22-23).* Jude holds that the church

---

[5]On the details of the heresy see especially (Andrew Chester and) Ralph P. Martin, *The Theology of the Letters of James, Peter and Jude* (Cambridge: Cambridge University Press, 1994), pp. 68-75.

should not be surprised by what was happening since it was already prophesied. In particular, the apostles had foretold what would happen (Jude 17-18). Not only so, but such sins have been common throughout the span of Old Testament history. From the time of Cain onward there have been sinners who have behaved similarly. It is not clear to what extent the contemporary sinners behaved in precisely the same ways as their various forebears.

Jude emphasizes that such people will not escape divine judgment. He does this by first pointing to the way in which similar people and communities had been punished—the disobedient Israelites at the time of the exodus, the fallen angels (Gen 6), Sodom and Gomorrah and the sons of Korah. Second, he refers to the prophecy of judgment that he found in I Enoch 1:9 and that was based ultimately on Zechariah 14:5.

Nevertheless, Jude has great concern for those who have succumbed to such sins or who may be in danger of doing so. Unfortunately his precise recipe for dealing with this situation is shrouded in the uncertainties of the text of Jude 22-23.[6] There is probably a distinction between believers who are being enticed by the false teachers and who must be urgently rescued before they come under judgment and the false teachers themselves, to whom mercy must be extended but in the fear of God (who will judge such people if they don't repent) and taking care not to be infected by their sin.[7] Even the false teachers are not beyond redemption.

***Persevering in the faith (Jude 20-21).*** From this material we can see that Jude is primarily concerned to unmask these sinners for what they are, to show that they belong with earlier sinners and to emphasize that they will not escape divine judgment. What, then, are the faithful to do, and what is the danger to them?

The matter was evidently so urgent that Jude claimed to have abandoned his intention to write in more general terms about salvation and to have concentrated on the need for his readers to contend for the faith that was handed down

---

[6]It is not clear whether the original text referred to two or to three groups of people; remarkably there is a split between commentators, who adopt the former view (e.g., Richard J. Bauckham, *Jude, 2 Peter* [Waco, Tex.: Word, 1983], pp. 108-11, and various textual scholars), and recent translations, which adopt the latter (so the Nestle-Aland Greek text and REB; TNIV; NRSV).

[7]This may imply that contact should be kept to the minimum so as to prevent the teachers exercising their bad influence.

to them, that is, to proclaim this message and to uphold it over against any attempts to promote an understanding of the faith that gave license to sin (Jude 3-4).

He urged the readers to four personal activities: building themselves up on the basis of their faith; praying in (i.e., as they are led by) the Holy Spirit;[8] keeping themselves in the love that God has for them; and awaiting the mercy of Christ (at his future advent) that leads to eternal life (Jude 20-21). These are the characteristics of healthy Christian living. It is notable that nothing is said here about avoidance of sin and cultivation of Christian qualities. The stress is rather upon the personal relationship to God (note the implicit trinitarianism), the spiritual activity of prayer and the attitude of hope. It therefore appears that Jude did not contemplate too great a degree of spiritual danger for the readers through succumbing to the heretical way of life.[9]

### Theological Themes

*God as loving and merciful.* Jude varies the opening greeting that is common to many New Testament letters but nevertheless retains a reference to God as the Father and to Jesus Christ, who are named in parallel as the spiritual agents through whom believers are loved and guarded. When he writes of the blessing of "mercy, peace and love", it can be assumed that these gifts come from God and Christ, just as in other New Testament letters. Thus the love and mercy of God are paramount. Although grace is not mentioned in this variation of the greeting formula, the term is used for the all-encompassing quality of God in Jude 4. At the end of the letter this same picture of God recurs with a reference to the love of God and to the mercy of Christ. All this is summed up in the closing doxology, which characterizes God as Savior.

In common with other writers Jude describes the "glory, majesty, power and authority" of God in the kind of language that we find in some of the later New Testament writings where Christian worship is expressed in the language of ascription, stating that these qualities or attributes belong to God. The style of the doxology has some similarities to that of a benediction, but whereas in the

---

[8]This may include, but is certainly not confined to, prayer in tongues.

[9]On the question of whether Jude envisages believers as capable of falling into apostasy and being restored to faith see I. Howard Marshall, *Kept by the Power of God: A Study of Perseverance and Falling Away,* 3rd ed. (Carlisle: Paternoster, 1995), pp. 162-68.

latter there is an implicit or explicit prayer to God to bestow his grace and peace or whatever upon believers, in the former the believers acknowledge that glory belongs to God. In this case the effect is to enhance the glory of God by swelling the number of persons who bestow praise on him and occasions when this happens.

But God is also the stern judge who destroyed those who did not believe and who is to be feared (Jude 23). Whether "the Lord" in Jude 5 refers to God or Christ,[10] it can be assumed that whatever is said about the one would be considered to be equally true of the other, since Christ is always understood as the agent of his Father, carrying out his will. Jude sees no tension between these two sides of God's activity, as judge and as savior.

*Jesus Christ as Lord.* The descriptions of God the Father and of Christ are almost interchangeable. As we have seen, they are named together in the manner familiar from elsewhere in the New Testament that indicates that they belong closely together. If it is God who keeps believers in Jude 24, it is Christ who does so in Jude 1. If it is God who loves believers in Jude 1, 21, it is Christ who shows mercy to them (Jude 21). If God is the one to whom power and authority belong (Jude 25), it is Christ who is given the title of Lord, both *despotēs* and *kyrios* being used of him. If it is God who is Savior (Jude 25), it is Christ whose mercy brings the readers to eternal life (Jude 21). If it is God who judges (Jude 5; but see above), it is Christ who will come in judgment, according to Jude's likely interpretation of Enoch's prophecy.

Jesus Christ is thus described in a way that puts him on an equal footing with God. Nevertheless, it is to God that the closing doxology is addressed, and the glory is ascribed to him "through Jesus Christ", just as elsewhere in the New Testament prayer is offered to God through Jesus.

*Possession of the Holy Spirit.* It is characteristic of believers that they "have" the Spirit (Jude 19) and of the sinners that they do not. The latter are characterized as people "who follow mere natural instincts" (Gk. *psychikoi*), a term that is used here of people devoid of the Spirit and living life on a purely natural level. By contrast believers are able to pray "in the Spirit".

---

[10]Some manuscripts have "Jesus". Bauckham, *Jude, 2 Peter,* pp. 49-50, holds that Christ is meant. Cf. Jarl Fossum, "Kyrios Jesus as the Angel of the Lord in Jude 5-7", *NTS* 33 (1987): 226-43, for the view that Christ is here understood to be preexistent as the Angel of the Lord.

*Sin and judgment.* Jude has a sharp division of people into sinners (Jude 15, citation) and saints (Jude 4). The sinners are further characterized as ungodly (Jude 4, 15). They stand condemned by God for their evil ways. What happened to Sodom and Gomorrah, which were destroyed by fire, is taken as a vivid picture of what will happen to the sinners. This judgment is associated with a final day; meantime the angels who fell into sin are kept in painful confinement until that day. When Jude speaks of rescuing sinners from the fire (Jude 23), the meaning is that they are to be rescued from the impending judgment rather than that they are in the fire already. The language of fire is traditional for destruction, and it need not convey the sense of an unending torment.

But although there is such a strong stress on judgment, it is significant that the last word of the letter before the doxology is one of pastoral care for sinners. Whatever the solution to the textual problem, some distinction is made between different types of people affected to greater or less degree by the beliefs and behavior that had infiltrated the church, but the important point is that in all cases the attempt is to be made to rescue such people from their danger by showing mercy to them. They are seen as victims to be pitied, but nevertheless as responsible persons who need to repent.

*Salvation.* The readers are described as "the called [ones]". Jude regards the essential possession of the saints as being salvation (Jude 3; cf. Jude 25), and the rescuing of the sinners in the church from their sinful ways and the consequent threat of judgment is "saving" them (Jude 23). The characteristic quality of the saints is, again as elsewhere, faith. This term can be used as summing up of the Christian religion, which is seen as a body of saving truth handed over to God's people once and for all. Here Jude is emphasizing the authority of the tradition of what God has spoken to the first Christians and implying that any later alterations to it are ipso facto lacking in divine authority. Faith can be described as "most holy", an adjective that serves to stress its great value (Jude 20). The emphasis here is thus on the content of the Christian message that is to be believed rather than on faith as the activity of belief and commitment, but the use of the word *faith* for the gospel demonstrates that the activity of believing is integral to Christianity. There is the danger that Christians may be pulled into sin by the sinners in the church. Traditional Jewish language is used of the need to avoid being contaminated by them; but although this language was originally understood literally of physical contamination by contact with sinners, here the reference is clearly to the spiritual danger of being induced into sin through relationships with sinners, even when attempting to rescue them.

The goal of believers is to stand before God without any such stains, an experience that produces intense joy (Jude 24). Although the coming of the Lord is described in terms of judgment upon sinners, this is not its character for believers. This future hope, which will bring vindication for God's faithful people, remains living and real. For Jude, the readers are already living in the last days, and prophecy is being fulfilled (Jude 18).

*Scripture and other sources.* Jude rests his thought partly on what has been prophesied in the past and therefore is sure to happen. When he writes about the sinners in the church "whose condemnation was written about long ago", his language could perhaps be taken to mean that the condemnation of these specific people was already the subject of prophecy; however, this is unlikely, since no such prophecies are known. It is therefore more probable that he is referring simply to those prophecies that state that God will certainly condemn and punish any people who are godless and unrepentant. Such prophecies include the one by Enoch, which is found outside Scripture in 1 Enoch 1:9. Opinions differ whether this means that Jude regarded 1 Enoch as part of Scripture and indeed that he ascribed the prophecy to a literal seventh-generation descendant from Adam. He need be doing no more than citing what was generally believed, and the dividing line between Scripture and what were presumably believed to be antique writings by inspired prophets was a fluid one at this time. (The question may even be anachronistic, since the concept of a closed canon of Scripture was still in process of formation.) Earlier in the letter Jude also describes the contention between Michael and the devil over the body of Moses, which is allegedly from the pseudepigraphical *Assumption of Moses.* Various scholars have drawn attention to Jude's use of exegetical procedures akin to the pesharim found at Qumran in which scriptural texts are made the basis for a commentary that applies them to the contemporary situation.

*The congregation and its life.* Jude maintains the practice of writing to the congregation(s) rather than to Christian leaders. The Pastoral Epistles constitute the only exception, and they are presented as letters to fellow missionaries rather than as letters to the actual local church leaders. The congregation as a whole remains responsible for dealing with the problem caused by the troublemakers in its midst, and its members are the people who stand in danger as a result of their activities. The activity of restoring the sinners is carried out by the congregation as a whole. It is not surprising that when Jude looks for examples of similar problems, he turns to the history of God's people within the Old Testament and Judaism. Evidently the church stands in succession to this people of God; continuity is assumed. We hear in passing that the congregation meets together for what is here called a love feast (Jude 12). At this early stage this must be identical with the church meal at which the Lord's Supper was celebrated, but nothing is said about the specifically eucharistic aspects of the meal; the origin of the term needs investigation.

### Conclusion

The framework of the theology is that of Jewish Christianity with particular use of the Jewish apocalyptic tradition.

The main theme is the call for Christians to persevere in the faith under the protection of God despite the existence among them of false teachers who will be judged by God just like the notorious sinners of the past.

Significant elements include

1. The correlation of God's judgment upon immoral sinners and his mercy for those who repent.

2. The juxtaposition of God and Christ in judgment and salvation.

3. The use made of the apocalyptic strand in Judaism.

4. The role of the congregation in pastoral care for sinners and those in danger of being led astray by them.

There is naturally much left unsaid in this short letter. In particular, there is nothing about the death and resurrection of Jesus. Yet it is remarkable how much theology we have been able to draw out of it when it is borne in mind that a good deal of it is taken up with describing the faults of the sinners in the church and citing the examples of previous sinners and what happened to them.

### Bibliography

*New Testament Theologies:* (English) Ladd, pp. 655-56; Strecker, pp. 641-53. (German)

Gnilka, pp. 437-43; Hahn, 1:743-45; Hübner, 2:396-98; Stuhlmacher, 2:105-14.

Bauckham, Richard J. *Jude and the Relatives of Jesus in the Early Church.* Edinburgh: T & T Clark, 1990.

————. *Jude, 2 Peter.* Waco, Tex.: Word, 1983.

(Chester, Andrew, and) Ralph P. Martin. *The Theology of the Letters of James, Peter and Jude.* Cambridge: Cambridge University Press, 1994, pp. 65-86.

Ericson, Norman R. "Jude, Theology of". In *EDBT,* pp. 432-34.

Fossum, Jarl. "Kyrios Jesus as the Angel of the Lord in Jude 5-7". *NTS* 33 (1987): 226-43.

Gerdmar, Anders. *Rethinking the Judaism-Hellenism Dichotomy: A Historiographical Case Study of Second Peter and Jude.* Stockholm: Almqvist and Wiksell, 2001.

Knight, Jonathan. *2 Peter and Jude.* Sheffield: Sheffield Academic Press, 1995.

Webb, Robert L. "Jude". In *DLNTD,* pp. 611-21.

# 29

# THE SECOND LETTER
# OF PETER

⤳০⤔

The second letter ascribed to Peter is generally thought to be so different in style from 1 Peter that it can scarcely be by the same author. Although some would give a considerable share in the composition of 1 Peter to Silvanus, this would not make it much easier to assign 2 Peter to Peter himself (whom I regard as the author of 1 Peter), since the way in which the thought is expressed is also very different. Until fresh arguments are brought forward, it therefore seems wisest to admit that we do not know who wrote this letter but to recognize that it claims to stand in the tradition associated with Peter.[1] This means that for practical purposes we have yet another, semi-independent voice in the chorus of New Testament theology. The letter displays very considerable similarities with the letter of Jude that have led most scholars to conclude that it has taken over and rewritten much of Jude or perhaps that both writers each used in their own way a common earlier document whose wording is reproduced much more closely by Jude.

Whereas the main concern in Jude is with the need for the readers not to be attracted to false teachers who do not appreciate that the gospel is intended to lead to moral behavior and to stand firm on the basis of the gospel, there are two differences in 2 Peter. The first is that the material about the false teachers

---

[1]Michael J. Kruger, "The Authenticity of 2 Peter", *JETS* 42 (1999): 645-71, argues that the case for inauthenticity falls short of proof.

in this letter is incorporated in a much broader set of instructions and exhortations. The second is that while much of the polemic appears to be directed to the same situation as in Jude, we also learn that there was great skepticism regarding the promises of the future coming of Jesus since with the passage of time it looked as if they were not going to be fulfilled.[2] This raises the question whether the false teachers attacked in Jude also questioned the parousia. Although Jude stresses the future hope of believers, there is no hint that his opponents denied it.

## The Theological Argument

**The spiritual progress of the readers (2 Pet 1:1-11).** Second Peter begins with a greeting that describes the readers as people who have "received" a faith of equal value with that of "us" (the writer and his circle) in (i.e., through) "the righteousness of our God and Savior Jesus Christ". Here faith is thought of as a gift that one can receive, and it is precious, doubtless because of the salvation that it brings. The actual greeting is also unusual in linking the growth in grace and peace of the readers with their knowledge of God and Christ.

The letter moves straight into a statement of the spiritual resources provided for the readers and again made accessible through knowledge of God (2 Pet 1:3 11). Through the gifts promised to them believers may obtain the twofold goal of escaping from the corruption that is in the world and participating in the nature of God. The thought here may be particularly of incorruptibility and immortality, such as Paul associates with the new spiritual bodies prepared for believers.

With this incentive before them, believers are urged to develop a set of qualities that are closely akin to the fruit of the Spirit. They are presented in a rhetorical form that leads from faith to love through various steps, but the arrangement is probably purely rhetorical and does not represent a fixed order or series of upward steps. Those who pursue this road will find that they increase in knowledge of God. In this way they will confirm that God has called them and

---

[2]Although the heresy has been thought to be an expression of Gnosticism, there is nothing specifically Gnostic about it. Since on other grounds a first-century dating for the letter is plausible (Richard J. Bauckham, *Jude, 2 Peter* [Waco, Tex.: Word, 1983], pp. 157-58), second-century Gnosticism is in any case an unlikely part of the context. But the fact that there are no obvious Gnostic traits in the false teaching fits in with and confirms the earlier dating.

made them part of his people and will enter his eternal kingdom.

Peter's main concern is to rehabilitate the expectation of the future coming (parousia) of Jesus. He achieves this in three stages. First, he stresses the truth of the apostolic testimony confirmed by eyewitness experience of the transfiguration of Jesus and supported by the voice of prophecy. Second, he states that the coming of false teachers is nothing new, that they are destined to certain judgment and that God can deliver his people from their enticements. And third, he engages directly with the arguments of the false teachers and rebuts them.

*Apostolic testimony and the voice of prophecy (2 Pet 1:12-21).* In the first stage Peter emphasizes the importance and the reliability of the teaching that he is giving. Like Paul in I Thessalonians he is conscious of encouraging his readers to do what they are already doing. Even after he is gone, Peter will ensure that they are still able to remember what he has said, presumably by having it in written form.[3]

He commences his refutation of attacks on the promise that Christ would return by reference to the transfiguration of Jesus, which was witnessed by himself and his companions and gave confirmation of the glorious status of Jesus.[4] What he says about the power and the future coming of Jesus is not an invented story, since he himself had heard the divine voice that confirmed the status of Jesus at the transfiguration. Like people in darkness who rely on a lantern until the day dawns, so in the darkness of this world believers should hold on to the words spoken by the prophets until the full light is revealed. The coming of Christ has confirmed what the prophets said. But it is important to remember that they spoke as they were moved by the Holy Spirit, and therefore (it is implied) their words are not open to any arbitrary interpretation.[5]

Then in the next paragraph he comments on the sure testimony of the prophets, who prophesied the coming of the Lord or of the Son of Man. Here

---

[3]This is generally taken as a reference to 2 Peter itself, but the hypothesis that the reference is to the Gospel of Mark has some support.

[4]It should be noted that the purpose of this paragraph is not to provide verisimilitude for the identity of the author but primarily to refer to the confirmation of the position of Jesus as God's glorious Son, which was attested by the apostles as was presumably known to the readers from the Gospel tradition. Consequently, even if the letter is allonymous, the argument loses none of its force.

[5]This has surely some negative implications for the contemporary, postmodern view that readers are free to interpret texts as they please.

the reference is to the appropriate passages in the Old Testament, whose reliability rests on the fact that they were not written by persons following their own ideas but by people who were inspired by the Spirit to a correct understanding of what God was saying to them.

*Condemnation of false teachers (2 Pet 2:1-22)*. This appeal to the prophets rightly understood is important because there will be false teachers with teaching that leads to destruction, associated as it is with immoral ways of living. Practically it denies the lordship of Christ. Such people stand under divine condemnation, which is sure to come upon them in the same way as judgment came upon the sinners in the Old Testament. Peter then lists some of the same examples as in Jude: the fallen angels and the people of Sodom and Gomorrah. But a new note, as compared with Jude, is introduced in that Peter also notes how God was able to rescue godly people from the midst of the sinners who were tempting and persecuting them and from the judgment that fell upon them. So, introducing a new example, Peter relates how God saved Noah and his family from the flood, and then Lot.

He proceeds to characterize the false teachers for their lack of respect for authority and their sensual, animal nature, in much the same way as Jude did. He develops the picture of their immorality, their tempting of others to sin and their greed, and fills out the brief reference to Balaam in Jude. Here are people who once escaped from the corruption of the world through their knowledge of Christ, but now they have fallen away and are in a worse position than previously, presumably in that, if their former sins might be regarded as sins of ignorance, their present sins are deliberate and witting.[6]

*Rebuttal of the false teaching (2 Pet 3:1-18)*. There is now a new beginning, in which Peter reminds his readers of a further antidote to the false teaching in the words of the prophets and of the apostles (2 Pet 3:1-11). Echoing teaching by Jesus and Paul, Peter prophesies the coming of such people in the last days. But a fresh element enters in that these people deny that there will be a future coming. Life appears to go on unchanged. They have forgotten the story of the flood! The God who created the world and separated the waters to do so was able to bring

---

[6]There is nothing in this lengthy section about the views of the false teachers on the parousia. This may be because Peter is here using material taken over from Jude that was concerned more with the moral failure of the teachers. He homes in on the false teaching itself in 2 Pet 3.

about the destruction of the world by water. Similarly, God will keep his promise to destroy the universe by fire. If things seem to go on unchanged, this is because God's timescale is not ours, and he is giving people every chance to repent before it is too late. Then there will be total destruction of the universe. But not quite! For God will create a heaven and a new earth characterized by righteousness, and those who are holy and godly will live in that home.

This is the hope that the readers should have, and it should spur them on to live righteous lives (2 Pet 3:11-16). In what is almost an aside Peter comments that the same things have been said by Paul, although some people give his teaching an interpretation that he regards as twisted.

In short, the letter concludes, the readers must beware of being led astray by false teaching that issues in immoral behavior and must rather continue to grow in grace and knowledge (2 Pet 3:17-18).

### Theological Themes

There is more theology than might have been expected in this short letter, sometimes expressed in ways that may seem surprising when compared with the manner of expression that we have found in the main stream of New Testament writing.

*Jesus as Savior.* Puzzles face the reader in the first verse. Peter describes his readers as those who have received faith by (or in) the righteousness of our God and Savior Jesus Christ. Is Peter here referring to two persons "Our God and Savior Jesus Christ" or to one figure, Jesus Christ, who is said to be both God and Savior? In the epistolary greeting in the next verse the rather similar sounding wording clearly refers to two persons. Elsewhere in the letter Peter uses *God* to refer simply and unequivocally to the Creator (2 Pet 3:4), the ultimate source of prophecy (2 Pet 1:21) and Judge (2 Pet 2:4; cf. 2 Pet 3:12) and once appropriately to him as the Father in relation to his Son Jesus (2 Pet 1:17). Nevertheless, taken by itself the phrase in 2 Peter 1:1 would most naturally refer to one person.[7] The reference, therefore, is probably to Jesus as God. Elsewhere in

---

[7]The combination "God and Savior" is a stock phrase in which the two words refer to the same person; the shape of the phrase is identical with "our Lord and Savior Jesus Christ" (2 Pet 1:11; 2:20; 3:18; cf. 2 Pet 3:2). The use of similar language elsewhere in the New Testament strengthens the case for our interpretation here. See Murray J. Harris, *Jesus as God: The New Testament Use of Theos in Reference to Jesus* (Grand Rapids, Mich.: Baker, 1992), pp. 229-38.

the letter Jesus is commonly referred to as "our Lord Jesus", and the term Savior is applied to him (2 Pet 1:11; 2:20; 3:18).

But how does Jesus function as Savior? In the opening greeting Peter refers to the "righteousness" of Jesus Christ through which people receive the gift of faith. This use of "righteousness" *(dikaiosyn)* is unusual. It may well refer to the act of Christ, which brings about justification; the language is close to that of Paul when he mentions the *righteous act (dikaiōma)* of Christ through which people receive justification that leads to life (Rom 5:18).[8]

Jesus is also referred to as the Lord who bought his people; this verb is used very similarly in I Corinthians 6:20, I Corinthians 7:23, Revelation 5:9 and Revelation 14:3-4 with reference to the redemptive action of Jesus. In these passages, with the exception of the last listed, there is specific mention of the price that was paid or of the blood of Christ. Now the use of the term *buy* would inevitably carry with it some understanding of when and how the purchase took place, and the other passages clearly spell out what this understanding was; it can be assumed that it was tacitly present in the present passage. There is, therefore, an implicit reference to the death of Jesus in these two passages, and this adequately counterbalances the fact that there is no explicit reference to it.

As in the case of James, which also lacked any reference to the resurrection of Jesus, the supreme status given to Jesus as Savior, Lord and God, indicates that he is regarded as the exalted Lord. The christological moment that is related is, somewhat surprisingly, the transfiguration. This incident is related because it was a conferral of honor and glory by the Father, and it gives credence to the prophecy of the future coming in power of Jesus. Whereas in Acts 1:11 the ascension is seen as a pledge of the return of Jesus in the same way as he departed, the establishment of his majesty at the transfiguration is here seen as confirmation of his exalted status.

*Faith.* At the outset of the letter Peter speaks of being given faith (2 Pet 1:1). This language is reminiscent of Ephesians 2:8, where the event of being saved by grace through faith is said to be the gift of God. It may be surprising that

---

[8] Bauckham, *Jude, 2 Peter,* p. 168, takes it of the justice of God that grants salvation to people without favoritism or partiality. Hübner, 2:403-4, draws attention to Christ as our righteousness in I Cor 1:30 and suggests that here he is seen as the righteousness of God.

faith is mentioned only here and in 2 Peter 1:5 in a list of Christian characteristics. However, it is highlighted as the foundation to which believers are to add
goodness and other qualities. The structure of the list is rhetorical, and it is not
meant to suggest that one acquires the characteristics in the order given. Although the qualities also feature in non-Christian ethical teaching of the time,
a comparison with other New Testament passages shows that this list is in no
way idiosyncratic.[9]

There are close links with Galatians 5, and significantly we are told that the
people who cultivate these qualities will not be fruitless.[10] The fact that the
readers are told to make every effort to gain these qualities may seem to stand
in tension with teaching elsewhere that suggests that they are the fruit of the
Spirit (Gal 5:22-23), but the same tension can be found in Paul (Gal 5:25).

As in Jude, the antidote to the false teaching that threatens the church is thus
spiritual growth. More pointedly than in Jude the emphasis is on spiritual
progress, both in knowledge of Christ and in the qualities characteristic of
Christian community life. The list is a combination of qualities that are personal and social.

*Knowledge.* When Peter tells his readers that they are to add to their faith various qualities, "knowledge" *(gnōsis)* comes second in the list (2 Pet 1:5-6).
Growth in these qualities means that their knowledge of Jesus Christ is being
fruitful (2 Pet 1:8).

The noun *epignōsis* is used four times (2 Pet 1:2, 3, 8; 2:20), the noun *gnōsis*
three times (2 Pet 1:5, 6; 3:18) and the verb *epiginōskō* twice (2 Pet 2:21a,
21b).[11] Knowledge is the means by which salvation is gained (2 Pet 2:20). Such
knowledge is of the way of righteousness, which no doubt involves obedience

---

| [9]Faith | Gal 5:22 | | | I Tim 6:11 | |
|---|---|---|---|---|---|
| Goodness | | | Phil 4:8 | | |
| Knowledge | | 2 Cor 6:6 | | | |
| Self-control | Gal 5:23 | (Tit 1:8) | | | |
| Perseverance | (Gal 5:22) | 2 Cor 6:4 | | | |
| Godliness | | | | I Tim 6:11 | |
| Mutual affection | | | Rom 12:10 | | I Pet 1:22 |
| Love | Gal 5:22 | 2 Cor 6:6 | | I Tim 6:11 | |

[10]The qualities are also found in non-Christian lists of virtues in the Hellenistic world. This was in-
    evitable. The point that is being made above is simply that the spirit of the list here, both the actual
    Christian qualities listed and the idea of incorporating them in a list, can be traced back to Paul.
[11]The verb *ginōskō* is used in a nontheological sense in 2 Pet 1:20; 3:3.

to the "holy command" mentioned in the same context (2 Pet 2:21). The continuing experience of God's grace and peace comes about through knowledge of God and Jesus our Lord (2 Pet 1:2). All that we need for life and godliness comes through out knowledge of him (2 Pet 1:3). The distinction between the two terms for knowledge is not clear, particularly since in 2 Peter 3:18 *gnōsis* is used of a personal relationship with the Lord. However, it may well be that in 2 Peter 1:5-6 the thought is more intellectual.

*Partaking of the divine nature.* It is in this context that we should consider the phrase "participate in the divine nature" (2 Pet 1:4). This is the clearest statement in the New Testament about believers somehow being given a divine nature, and it has aroused considerable criticism because of its more or less unique, explicit use of the concept of divinization. However, something similar is implied by Pauline statements that give believers a share in divine glory and Johannine statements that envisage believers being joined to God or Christ in a way that is similar to that in which God and Christ are joined to each other. It must be remembered that Peter is here talking about the divine promises, and this confirms that he is thinking of something that is to be conferred in the future, doubtless when believers appear before God and Christ, and are found blameless and at peace before him.

The negative side of conversion is escaping from the corruption that is in the world caused by evil desires (2 Pet 1:4). *Corruption* is another key word of the letter. The false teachers are likened to mere animals that are caught and destroyed in that they too will be destroyed; although they offer freedom to their converts, they themselves are held captive by destruction (2 Pet 2:12, 19). Behind this statement lies the general understanding that the people in the world who follow their own desires instead of obeying the will of God are in fact captives to them and will end up in destruction meted out by God as the judgment on their sin. Believers are people who have been enabled to escape from this inevitable sequence of cause and effect. No language is too strong to characterize this network of evil, which is regarded as foul and unclean. Moreover, the judgment is certain, as is attested by the various accounts in Scripture of what happened to the evil angels and people of past days. The judgment is a combination of physical destruction and death and of the fate that follows a final day of judgment. Even the time before the judgment is one of punishment for the angels preserved in gloomy dungeons until that time. It seems probable that Peter

envisages the destruction of the world by fire as coinciding with the destruction
of the evil at the judgment.

*Salvation.* Salvation is manifestly the work of God through Christ, particularly if we are correct in the interpretation of 2 Peter 1:1. It involves cleansing,
in which we may perhaps detect an allusion to the symbolism of baptism (2 Pet
1:9);[12] cleansing is an important picture for salvation in view of the great stress
on the defiling character of sin. Salvation further depends upon the call and
choice of God (2 Pet 1:10), which are effective only insofar as they are confirmed by the response of people to them. Those who do so attain a position
of stability (2 Pet 1:10, 12; cf. 2 Pet 2:9), but they need to be continually reminded of the truth lest they stumble through, for example, the influence of the
unstable false teachers (2 Pet 3:16) and their deceptive promises (2 Pet 2:14;
3:17). The Christian life thus calls for effort (2 Pet 3:14) and watchfulness (2
Pet 3:17). There is perhaps more stress on the need for effort and less on the
keeping power of God than there is in Jude, but the basic pattern of thought is
the same. Although Peter does not speak of the influence of the Holy Spirit in
the lives of believers, the reality is present when he mentions the divine power
that equips believers for the Christian life (2 Pet 1:3) and refers to growth in
grace (2 Pet 3:18).

Salvation also includes the hope of a future life in a new heaven and a new
earth that will be characterized by righteousness. This state is also described as
the eternal kingdom of our Lord and Savior Jesus Christ (2 Pet 1:11). Those
who enter this new state must obviously themselves be pure and blameless. This
dimension of hope thus imparts an urgency to the effort to be holy and blameless when the Lord comes. In the Pauline writings there is an unresolved tension
between the injunctions to believers to grow in faith and love and the references
to the way in which God will cause believers to be blameless and mature when
the Lord comes. This same tension is probably reflected here.

It is at this point that the function of the letter as a theodicy is to be seen.
Jerome H. Neyrey in particular has produced evidence that the false teachers
reflect the kind of things said by Epicurean thinkers in their practical atheism
and denial of future retribution, and that Peter makes use of similar arguments
to those found both in non-Christian philosophers, specifically Plutarch, and

---

[12]As in Jude 12, there is a probable reference to the church's communal meals in 2 Pet 2:13.

in Judaism to refute such claims. It is because of this theological focus of the letter that the writer does not need to discuss christology and soteriology at any length.

## Conclusion

As with Jude, the framework of the theology is Christian Judaism with an apocalyptic accent, but not so marked as in Jude.[13] If Neyrey is right, the author has used material from the philosophical tradition that had already found a home in Hellenistic Judaism.

The main theme of the theological message is the perseverance and spiritual growth of the readers in their faith in Christ, avoiding the dangers of false teaching that led to immorality and skepticism about the Christian hope of the parousia.

Significant elements include

1. The unusual stress on the transfiguration of Jesus as a pointer to his exaltation as Savior, Lord and God.

2. The linking of faith with a personal knowledge of Christ

3. The sharing of believers in the divine nature.

4. The negative verdict on the perishable world and its replacement by a new heaven and earth.

5. The importance attached to holding fast to the apostolic tradition and to the correct understanding of it.

## Bibliography

New Testament Theologies: (English) Childs, pp. 463-76; Ladd, pp. 649-55; Strecker, pp. 641-53. (German) Gnilka, pp. 437-43; Hahn, 1:743-44, 746-49; Hübner, 2:399-410; Stuhlmacher, 2:105-14.

Bauckham, Richard J. *Jude, 2 Peter.* Waco, Tex.: Word, 1983.

————. "2 Peter". In *DLNTD,* pp. 923-27.

(Chester, Andrew, and) Ralph P. Martin. *The Theology of the Letters of James, Peter and Jude.*

---

[13]See Anders Gerdmar, *Rethinking the Judaism-Hellenism Dichotomy: A Historiographical Case Study of Second Peter and Jude* (Stockholm: Almqvist and Wiksell, 2001), for a detailed exploration.

Cambridge: Cambridge University Press, 1994, pp. 65-86.

Ericson, N. R. "Peter, Second, Theology of". In *EDBT*, pp. 606-7.

Fornberg, Tord. *An Early Church in a Pluralistic Society: A Study of 2 Peter.* Lund: Gleerup, 1977.

Gerdmar, Anders. *Rethinking the Judaism-Hellenism Dichotomy: A Historiographical Case Study of Second Peter and Jude.* Stockholm: Almqvist and Wiksell, 2001.

Harvey, A. E. "The Testament of Simeon Peter". In *A Tribute to Geza Vermes: Essays on Jewish and Christian Literature and History.* Edited by P. R. Davies and R. T. White, pp. 339-54. Sheffield: JSOT Press, 1990.

Käsemann, Ernst "An Apologia for Primitive Christian Eschatology". In *Essays on New Testament Themes.* London: SCM Press, 1964, pp. 69-95.

Knight, Jonathan. *2 Peter and Jude.* Sheffield: Sheffield Academic Press, 1995.

Neyrey, Jerome H. "The Form and Background of the Polemic in 2 Peter". *JBL* 99 (1980): 407-31.

Wolters, Albert. "Partners of the Deity: A Covenantal Reading of 2 Peter 1:4". *CTJ* 25 (1990): 28-44.

# 30

# HEBREWS, JAMES,
# 1-2 PETER
# AND JUDE
# IN THE NEW TESTAMENT

∽⚬∾

W̲e have been able to identify three main sets of writings in the New Testament: the Synoptic Gospels and Acts; the Pauline letters, including those that are later compositions by Paul or are the work of his followers; and the Johannine literature, comprising the Gospel and Epistles with the Revelation sitting somewhat uneasily on the fringe. This leaves us with a collection composed of the remaining books—Hebrews, James, 1-2 Peter and Jude. "Collection" implies that the books belong together in some meaningful kind of way, and so they do in the broad sense of being early Christian compositions included in the canon, but in the narrow sense they obviously do not constitute a collection in the same kind of way as the three collections already mentioned. There are certainly some links between individual members of the group. Jude and 2 Peter clearly belong together. There are links between James and 1 Peter in their common and extensive use of Jesus traditions and other overlaps. But that is about all, and therefore our question here is whether these basically independent documents broadly testify to the same underlying theology and fit in with the three major collections.

## The Letter to the Hebrews

The weightiest and most distinctive of this group of writings is the letter to the Hebrews. The theology of the letter is distinctive in many ways, but it nevertheless rests firmly upon the basic beliefs of early Christianity. Although C. H. Dodd did not follow up the "developments" in Hebrews to any extent in his study of the apostolic preaching and the way in which it controlled the growth of New Testament theology,[1] the indebtedness of Hebrews to the pattern of early Christian thought has been demonstrated by other scholars.[2] We have, then, a distinctive development of the common Christian message, rather than something of a different character. The letter is primarily concerned with the danger that faced the readers of abandoning their faith in Christ, and the author deals with this problem by developing a theological approach that combined two elements.

*Covenant and journey.* On the one hand, he develops the contrast between the two covenants, the old and the new, to show how the Christian faith can be understood as the fulfillment of the Jewish religion. He presents an account of Christianity using the categories provided by the Old Testament, specifically by its sacrificial system, and proceeds to argue that the new covenant has replaced the old, so that it does not make sense to go back to the old.

On the other hand, he recognizes the difficulties that surround Christians and develops the concept of the Christian life as a journey like that of the Israelites through the wilderness, in which they must maintain a steadfast faith in God; already they are experiencing the life of the world to come, but they must press on until they reach perfection. They are the traveling people of God.

This understanding of the Christian life in terms of a journey is an important part of his encouragement to his readers. The choice of the imagery is called forth by the particular problem facing him, that of reinvigorating believers who are in danger of abandoning their faith through weariness in withstand-

---

[1]C. H. Dodd, *The Apostolic Preaching and Its Developments* (London: Hodder & Stoughton, 1936, 1944 [2nd ed.]).

[2]See especially R. V. G. Tasker, *The Gospel in the Epistle to the Hebrews* (London: Tyndale Press, 1950); F. F. Bruce, "The Kerygma of Hebrews", *Int* 23 (1969): 3-19. The discussion of the point by Robert H. Mounce, *The Essential Nature of New Testament Preaching* (Grand Rapids, Mich.: Eerdmans, 1960), pp. 142-45, is unfortunately quite brief, but he notes how the author of Hebrews sees access to God as the essence of true religion and is prepared to use philosophical terminology to present Christian truth.

ing the pressures upon them. So the journey and the race images are brought together to give a fuller understanding of the need for Christians to persevere in their faith.

The effect of this situation is that greater emphasis is given to the element of continuation in faith that is expressed in the cognate English term *faithfulness*. This is not a different understanding of faith from that elsewhere in the New Testament, but the accentuation of the element in faith that was most needed in this situation. We might contrast how the element of knowledge and acceptance of the truths contained in the gospel was necessary in the situation faced in the Pastoral Epistles.

In both cases, the writer is latching on to existing motifs in the early church. The motif of the new covenant is not all that widespread, but it is certainly there. The cup saying at the Last Supper indicates that the death of Jesus is to be understood as the sacrifice that inaugurates the new covenant, and this is also reflected in 1 Peter 1:2. The concept of the new covenant is then taken up by Paul in Galatians 4:24 and 2 Corinthians 3.

Nowhere, however, is the motif so fully and distinctively developed as it is in Hebrews in the service of his particular pastoral encouragement to his readers. The contrast between the old and new covenants is developed in such a way as to show that the old covenant has now been renewed and in that sense superseded. It would be instructive to make a detailed comparison here with Paul's approach to the same topic in 2 Corinthians 3.[3] Use of the term *supersession* sets alarm bells ringing for some theologians, so let it be said that we are talking of one covenant in two phases rather than the replacement of one covenant by another and different one.[4] God has not rejected the Jewish people and turned instead to the Gentiles, but he has revealed himself through the Messiah and declared him to be the one mediator through whom all people can come to him.

The notion of the Christian life as a journey through the wilderness is also part of early Christian paraenesis, but again it is more fully developed here than

---

[3] Devisers of essay topics for your graduate students take note!

[4] We are dealing with two stages in the history of the same entity, like the development of Nota Bene for Windows (with the excellent aid of which this book was composed by its author) from Nota Bene for DOS, rather than two different entities, like Nota Bene and MS Word. Nota Bene for DOS did a fine job in its time, but who would want to go back to it now?

elsewhere in the New Testament. The journey motif is used by Luke with reference to the life of Jesus but also to the Christian movement. Peter again provides a parallel with his understanding of believers as strangers in this world, although Peter's motif is more that of believers living in a world to which they do not belong rather than of travelers making their way through it (1 Pet 2:11). The metaphor of the Christian life as a race to be run in Philippians 3 is not dissimilar.

*Priesthood and sacrifice.* It is in this context that the writer makes his detailed comparison in which he shows how Jesus is the counterpart to Moses and Aaron, so that his role is to be understood by analogy with theirs. This is the New Testament document that makes the most far-reaching employment of typology, whereby God is seen to act in such a way in certain people and institutions in Old Testament times that they embody the patterns according to which he acts later in a superlative and final matter. Jesus is the new Moses and the new Aaron, or you might say that in their different roles Moses and Aaron were the old Jesus. The author's aim is not so much to use the typology to provide the categories for understanding Jesus but rather to show that because this is the role of Jesus, therefore the former embodiments of these roles have now run their course and gone into retirement. So the sacrifices prescribed in the Old Testament had a limited effectiveness in their time because the blood of bulls and goats could not really take away sin, and the cleansing produced was external. They are now replaced by the fully effective sacrifice of Christ, which is able to bring perfection to the worshipers.

In expounding this theme, the author goes into considerable detail to show how the sacrifice on the Day of Atonement is the model for understanding the sacrifice of Christ. He takes up the pattern of slaying the animal on the altar and then taking its blood into the innermost part of the tabernacle to make atonement for sin. He compares the way in which Christ could be said to shed his blood on the cross and then to go into heaven to offer his sacrifice to God to make full and final atonement for human sin. Here we have an important example of the way in which he takes his understanding further than that of other New Testament writers who do not tackle this question. He provides us with the rationale of how the sacrifice made on the cross takes effect and indicates how the exaltation of Christ, or rather his entry to heaven, is an essential part of the saving event.

Priestly language is used elsewhere of Jesus to a limited extent, it being more normal to think of him as the sacrifice. We find the rudiments of it in the statements that he gave himself up for us, and then in the statement that he gave himself for us as an offering and sacrifice to God (Eph 5:2). But the theme is more widespread. The understanding of the death of Jesus as sacrificial is an underlying motif that surfaces regularly without being thematized at length. Paul sees the death of Jesus in terms of the Passover sacrifice and the sin offering, alongside his possible understanding of his role as scapegoat.[5] Sacrificial ideas are also present in John, 1 John, 1 Peter and Revelation.

*The problem of falling away.* We have seen how the letter warns against the danger of believers falling away from Christ and coming under divine judgment. However, it is commonly thought that elsewhere in the New Testament the nature of salvation is such that, once a person has become a Christian believer, there is no possibility of their falling away and losing their salvation. Believers are people who were chosen by God for salvation in an act of choice that is held to have preceded even the creation of the world. They have been called by God and drawn to Christ in faith through God's action. They have been born or regenerated by the Spirit of God and have an indelible status and character conferred upon them. And they are promised that they will be kept by the power of God, that they are the sheep whom nobody can or will pluck out of the Shepherd's hand. The God who called them is faithful and will not abandon them. They have been justified by his grace, and this justification is full and final, so that, no matter how much they may sin thereafter, this cannot alter their status with God. Nothing can separate them from the love of God. This combination of statements drawn principally from Paul and John appears to forge a cast-iron case for the eternal security of believers. True, they may sin grievously, but their sins will never be great enough to cause God to reject them, for he will so work in their lives as to preserve them from falling away. This does not mean that they may presume on their security and sin to their heart's content. In some cases, the presence of this tendency would be an indication that they were not truly saved after all. In other cases, true believers who fall into sin

---

[5]Cf. p. 438 n. 22. There I was sympathetic to the suggestion of Bradley H. McLean that Paul sees Christ in terms of the scapegoat on the Day of Atonement but denied his claim that Paul did not also see him as a sacrifice for sin.

will suffer other penalties or chastisements short of final separation from God.[6]

Conspicuously the letter to the Hebrews appears to go against this impressive consensus. The problem can be resolved in various ways. First, one may simply admit a contradiction between two different understandings of salvation. Second, it may be denied that Hebrews teaches what it appears to teach. This route is followed by scholars who try to show that the description of those in danger of falling away is of people who were never truly believers and had no real or full Christian experience. Alternatively, it is argued that the cases described are hypothetical in the sense that *if* these people were to fall away, they would suffer this fate, but the if clause is an impossible possibility, for God will always intervene to prevent people reaching the point of danger and apostatizing. A variant of this view is that the warnings are there as God's way of ensuring that his people do persevere: the exhortations are there "to secure the obedience of faith, not to imply possible failure of faith".[7] The third possibility is that Hebrews does teach what it appears to teach and that this teaching is not incompatible with that of the other New Testament authors.

In my earlier discussion of the letter I have argued that the warnings appear to be genuine and not hypothetical; they point to a real if remote danger. The question then is whether the teaching elsewhere in the New Testament can accommodate this emphasis in Hebrews. Elsewhere I have developed a case that the New Testament writers lay stress on the faithfulness of God in caring for his people and preserving them from falling (Jude 24) while at the same time encouraging them to continue in faith in this God and not to fall away from him. Their security rests on the faithful love of God. Nevertheless, alongside this motif there are the warnings against the danger of falling away that are not to be emptied of their force. They urge people to put their faith in the Lord and to accept his promises. There is a paradox here akin to that of the relationship between divine empowering and human effort in achieving holiness. The warnings would lose their effectiveness in preventing believers from falling if they knew that there was in fact no danger of falling. The believer is called to

---

[6]These have to be temporal penalties in this world or some deprivation of rewards that they would otherwise have received in heaven (cf. 1 Cor 3:10-15). For Protestant Christians, who are the usual defenders of this position, the thought of purgatory would be anathema!

[7]Thomas R. Schreiner and Ardel B. Caneday, *The Race Set Before Us: A Biblical Theology of Perseverance and Assurance* (Downers Grove, Ill.: InterVarsity Press, 2001), p. 163.

live by faith in the faithfulness of God rather than by faith in a theological dogma (cf. Heb 6:16-20).[8]

*The nature of the Christian life.* So far, then, it makes good sense to see the Writer as taking further motifs found in Paul and elsewhere and doing so in a way that can certainly be seen as legitimate extension of the thought. However, there is a comparative silence or at least muting on some other aspects of early Christian theology. Certainly, as we urged above, the activity of the Holy Spirit in the letter can easily be overlooked. The Spirit not only bears witness to Christ and to the good news (Heb 2:4; 3:7; 9:8; 10:15) but is also active in the life of Christ (Heb 9:14) and is closely related to the lives of believers (Heb 6:4; cf. 10:29). The power of God is also present in believers to enable them to do God's will (Heb 13:21; cf. Phil 2:12-13). The lack of fuller mention of these motifs might be compared with the way in which some modern Christians will express the nature of their spiritual life in terms of their personal relationship with Christ and neglect to mention the Spirit in this connection.

But it is not clear that this explanation will work for Hebrews, where, it can be argued, there is also very little of the language of spiritual union with God and Christ that is so characteristic of Paul and John. The use of the language derived from the sacrificial system under the old covenant has tended to restrict the range of the writer's coverage of Christian experience. God is inevitably pictured as a more distant figure who is always approached through Jesus Christ— but who can be approached in the same kind of way as Paul describes in Romans 5:1. There is less emphasis on the spiritual resources that people need for the long haul of faith; they are upheld by hope, but this hope, it must be emphasized, is likened to an anchor rope that holds them absolutely firmly. Inverting the metaphor, we might perhaps think of a lifeline connecting a diver to his ship and conveying the life-giving oxygen. In this respect, Hebrews may be thought to be more akin to Acts, where there is certainly spiritual succor for believers in various kinds of ways, but the concept of a personal relationship with Christ and the inward working of the Spirit other than in empowering for mission is considerably muted.

But we should probably see this apparent omission being compensated for

---

[8]See I. Howard Marshall, *Kept by the Power of God: A Study of Perseverance and Falling Away*, 3rd ed. (Carlisle: Paternoster, 1995).

by the presence of another theological motif, namely, the way in which believers have access through prayer to God in his heavenly dwelling, thanks to the priestly mediation of Christ, and thus participate in the life of heaven. Here we have an expression of the nature of the new spiritual life to which believers are admitted that bears some resemblance to the concepts of the Jerusalem above (Gal 4:26) and of the heavenly places in which believers now exist (Eph 1:3) and the realm above to which they have been raised with Christ (Col 3:1). There is thus a spiritual life for believers in which they are in the heavenly presence of God, while still on earth. Hebrews has a vertically realized eschatology in which believers are already now raised to be with God and are able to approach him with confidence (cf. Rom 5:1) as well as its future eschatology that looks forward to the coming of Christ (Heb 9:28; 10:37). In this way the concept of being in the heavenly presence of God here and now with the privilege of prayer to him would seem to correspond with the concepts of present union with Christ that are so prominent in Paul and John.

*Exodus theology.* The question of the background and origins of this unique theology have been fully discussed by other writers, and it would be difficult to add anything significant to their work. L. D. Hurst in particular has surveyed the field.[9] His summary has shown that despite some superficial resemblances that suggest an indebtedness to Platonism and the kind of thought found in Philo, the main thrust of the theology belongs within Judaism. Attempts to link it particularly with the theology of the Qumran sect or other more esoteric groups, including the Samaritans, must be judged to have failed. Within the early Christian church it shows notable links to the way of thinking associated with Stephen in Acts 6—7 and with Paul. The hypothesis of Gnostic influence, developed especially by Ernst Käsemann,[10] is to be discounted; the links of Hebrews are more with Jewish apocalyptic. Rather, Hurst sees the writer as a student of the Septuagint who uses the Old Testament in a similar way to what we find in Acts 7 and has been exposed to Jewish apocalyptic and to what he calls a "Paul-like" theology, and he claims that this "mix" will account for much of the letter. He recognizes, however, that it does not fully explain the develop-

---

[9]L. D. Hurst, *The Epistle to the Hebrews: Its Background of Thought* (Cambridge: Cambridge University Press, 1990).

[10]Ernst Käsemann, *The Wandering People of God: An Investigation of the Letter to the Hebrews* (Minneapolis: Augsburg, 1984).

ment of the motif of the heavenly high priest and leaves this question as the unanswered riddle that calls for fresh light.

What can be said is that exodus theology, in which the typology of the story of Israel's redemption from Egypt is explored, is a basic part of early Christian thinking; what we have in Hebrews is a specific development of this particular line of thought which could have been catalyzed by the existing concept of Christ's death as a sacrifice. The concept of Christ as heavenly Lord was closely linked to Psalm 110, and from there the development of the priesthood of Christ was fairly natural. The jump from a Melchizedekian priesthood to a levitical one in the typology is not so great a riddle as Hurst suggests, since the language of sacrifice was already in use. To be sure, it required an original, creative thinker to make the links and do the development, which is precisely what the writer of Hebrews was. I doubt whether any further explanation is needed.

*Missionary theology.* The missionary character of the theology may at first sight be less obvious in Hebrews. This letter is concerned more with the danger of Christian believers falling away from their faith than with the winning of new converts. Its appeal is to people to hold fast to their faith and to persevere. Nevertheless, it reflects the situation in which people become believers with its description of how the readers heard the message that was first spoken by the Lord, then confirmed to the readers by those who had heard the Lord, while God supported them and backed up their message with signs and wonders and gifts of the Holy Spirit (Heb 2:3-4). The recognition that the church owed its origin to the apostolic mission is thus clear. What is of particular interest here are the echoes of 1 Corinthians 12 with the reference to the Spirit giving gifts as God wills (1 Cor 12:11) and of Luke-Acts. W. C. van Unnik claimed that this short statement in Hebrews is an admirable summary of Luke-Acts, capturing precisely its structure and atmosphere.[11]

*Conclusion.* These observations show that with all its individual theological developments Hebrews has strong connections with the other main expressions of early Christian theology. The roots of its thought do lie in widely held Christian convictions. With the other documents that we have yet to consider in this chapter it adds a richness to the manifold witness to this theology and demonstrates yet again how individual New Testament writers were able to be creative

---

[11]W. C. van Unnik, "'The Book of Acts,' the Confirmation of the Gospel", *NovT* 4 (1960): 26-59.

and innovative in their theologizing.

## The Letter of James

Our analysis of James showed that there was a much more considerable theological substratum to it than is often realized. James is essentially concerned with the living of the Christian life in the midst of temptation. It stands in the tradition of Jewish wisdom and has its own characteristic way of expressing its teaching. We saw that James was concerned with practical problems in the church; what we do not know is whether he preached doctrinal messages, and, if so, how he did it. One might dare to say that his letter resembles what Ephesians or Colossians would have been like if we had only the second halves of these letters.

The background influence on the theology of James is to be found in Judaism. Indeed, the theory was once advanced that James is really a Jewish document lightly revised to give it a Christian veneer. Its concept of God is thoroughly Jewish, down to the echo of the Shema in James 2:19. The Old Testament is the source for the style and content of much of the teaching, the illustrations and the proverbial sounding paraenesis. Much of the exhortation could be at home in the Jewish piety of Tobit or the *Testaments of the Twelve Patriarchs*. This specific Jewish background, which is more obvious in James than elsewhere in the New Testament, gives it much of its characteristic color.

A major argument against this hypothesis of the basically Jewish character of the letter is the way in which it, more than any other New Testament letter, implicitly refers to the teaching of Jesus and is thereby stamped as being fundamentally Christian rather than Jewish. Strong echoes of the teaching of Jesus, rather than direct quotations, are to be found. These echoes come primarily from the Sermon on the Mount. Thus, as in 1 Peter, we have a Jesus tradition that sits alongside a Jewish tradition that is based on the Old Testament and appeals to its theology and its ethics. One might say that an important function of James within the New Testament as a whole is to remind people who attach great weight to the significance of Jesus as Lord not to neglect his down-to-earth teaching out of an overconcern with mouthing the right confessions concerning him.

Further, we have seen that at numerous points James reflects the common theology of the early church. His understanding of God as one, as lawgiver and judge, and as the gracious giver of gifts who hears the prayers of his people is fully in line with the central understanding of God. His concern for the poor reflects the teaching of Jesus. Although little is said about Jesus, his exalted, glorious position is assumed, and his future coming is awaited.

For James the Christian life begins with a new birth and is a continuing life of faith. He offers his own analysis of the nature of temptation and sin, and he is a realist in recognizing the temptations and trials that come to believers. He assumes that to be a Christian is to be a believer, but he corrects any misapprehension that belief is a mere matter of the head and does not affect behavior. We have already seen that, although James has often been thought to take up a different, indeed an opposing, position to Paul on the issue of faith and works, their positions are harmonious.

James writes to Christian groups with a keen eye on their life as congregations and comments on their life, particularly as regards the need to honor and care for the poor, to pray for one another and to exercise pastoral care particularly for those in danger of falling away from their faith. He affirms the reality of divine healing of illness in response to prayer. All of this clearly ties in with teaching elsewhere in the New Testament.

*A truncated theology?* Yet despite the undoubtedly Christian character of the letter there are astonishing silences. There is nothing on the incarnation, death and resurrection of Jesus. There is no reference to the Holy Spirit. There is none of the deeply theological teaching on the nature of the spiritual life that we find especially in Paul and John. We lack here any development of spiritual communion with God or of a life in Christ, in which believers are identified with him in his death and resurrection. James is primarily concerned in a down-to-earth manner with how people behave in the world and how they may suffer, and whether they pray.

Part of the explanation is no doubt that James is writing a practical letter to deal with specific anxieties about Christian behavior. There is, however, no lack of what we can legitimately call theological grounding of his message closely meshed with something more like proverbial wisdom. It is all very down to earth; it would get across to congregations who might find Paul or John or Hebrews hard going.

So the theological accents lie elsewhere than we might have expected. The question is whether the theology is compatible or incompatible with what we have elsewhere in the New Testament.

*James and Paul.* The main issue here is that of faith and works (Jas 2:14-26), where it is often thought that James is attacking the Pauline understanding of justification by faith and not by works.

In my view the use of the language of justification by faith to express the nature of Christian conversion originates with Paul or at least has no significant history prior to him. Certainly there are many scholars who think that it is a pre-Pauline motif that Paul then developed greatly. However, none of the texts (except perhaps Lk 18:14 and Rom 3:24-25) can be shown to be pre-Pauline. In any case, what James is discussing here is a concept that was at least brought to the center of Christian theology by Paul, and it is therefore most likely that what is going on here is some kind of reaction to Paul's teaching. But this does not mean that James was contradicting Paul or was his theological opponent. This assessment is sometimes found among German theologians, perhaps out of respect for Martin Luther's denigration of James. They argue that James knew the writings of Paul (Romans), understood what he was saying and protested against it, claiming that Paul had separated what belong together, namely, faith and works.

But this is probably not the case. Recently, Richard J. Bauckham has questioned whether James has Pauline teaching in his sights, and he argues that what we have in Paul and James are two parallel and independent developments of the same motif that arise out of Jewish teaching.[12] However, the coincidences in language weigh more heavily with me and make it difficult to accept that there is no relationship between them here. One possibility is that what James is contesting can have arisen out of a superficial understanding of Paul, and he saw the need to administer a corrective. The attack is then on a misunderstanding of Paul by some of his followers rather than on Paul. More probably, however, James and Paul stand back to back defending the gospel against different misunderstandings. Paul was contesting the misunderstanding that obedience to the Jewish law, especially circumcision and its ritual aspects, was necessary in order to be justified here and now; whereas James is contesting the misunderstanding that if you have faith in God, this need not express itself in the love that Paul also saw as the indispensable expression of faith (Gal 5:6). For Paul justification is primarily what made a person a Christian—note the wording of

---

[12]Richard J. Bauckham, *James* (London: Routledge, 1998), pp. 113-40.

Romans 5:1: having been justified! For James the focus may be more on justification as the action of God at the last judgment when the reality of faith is assessed; it corresponds to future salvation in Paul's thinking, as illustrated in Romans 5:9.

Further, James does not place works in antithesis to faith, which was the view that Paul combated so fiercely in Galatians and Romans. What Paul condemned was the view that works of the law were required instead of or in addition to faith in order to be justified. But James is concerned with the kind of good works that indicate the change of character that should accompany Christian conversion. It is entirely possible that some hearers of Paul took his insistence on faith alone as an excuse for lack of effort to do good actions.

The common argument, therefore, that James is opposing Paul and that Paul would have rejected what he says here is quite unconvincing. According to Rudolf Bultmann, Paul could not have agreed "with the thesis that faith works along with works (2:22)".[13] This may well be true, but only so far as the formulation is concerned. James, after all, is not Paul and puts things in his own way. Paul would certainly not have been happy with the slogan "faith and works" ripped out of its context, because for him "works" meant "works of the law", whereas for James it means something different; nevertheless, Paul would have agreed with the point that James was making.

*The individualism of James.* At the risk of being overanalytical I suggest that two things can be observed. One consists of the distinctive theology of James, this way of thinking largely based on the wisdom tradition and the teaching of Jesus. The other is material held in common with the early church; the glimpses that we have are surely the tips of an ice floe just showing above the water rather than a few pieces of scattered flotsam. But what does it say about a writer that he shows so little of this underlying mainstream theology (if we may so term it) and that he does not take up issues of a more theological character concerning the Christian life? Part of the answer is that James offers a very practical corrective regarding Christian practice because the nature of the situation apparently demanded it.

---

[13]Bultmann, 2:163.

But there is something more to be said. It is also the case that James has developed a theology that stands in the wisdom tradition with its stress on the piety of the righteous sufferer and its concern for the practicalities of fair and loving behavior. We have taken up the suggestion that wisdom as God's gift to believers may function in the same way as the Holy Spirit in Paul and John. If this proposal or something like it is valid, then James's understanding of the life of the believer is close to that of other New Testament writers than is sometimes thought.

But the effect of this observation is to pose a problem. It is one thing to identify what is going on in the letter of James. It is more difficult to explain how and why this particular individualistic strand of theology developed, a theology that does not naturally use the typical language of the rest of the New Testament, although we have kept on hearing echoes of all kinds, and that appears to say similar things in a somewhat different idiom. Why does James talk about wisdom rather than about the Spirit? Why does a Christian writer make so little direct reference to Jesus? Why is there no direct reference to his death and resurrection?

Maybe this is an unreal problem. There is an analogous situation in the marked difference in idiom between Paul and John, and perhaps still more between the ways in which the Synoptic Evangelists and John thought it proper to express the teaching of Jesus. The effect is to suggest that there was more individual creativity inspired by Jesus in the early church than we may have thought.

A plausible theory is that James, the leader of the Jerusalem church, wrote to Christian congregations that were probably mainly Jewish in character. It can be assumed that they found life difficult, just as the Jews did, and he wrote to strengthen them in their Christian faith by encouraging them to press on to perfection, to resist temptation and not to be disheartened by oppression. He was aware of standard problems within the church: partiality to the rich; a faith that did not issue in loving actions; the sins of speech, quarrelsomeness, the temptation to succumb to worldly desires, the temptation to get rich and to be arrogant, the need for prayer, and the need for loving pastoral care by the members for one another. His letter is primarily concerned with these pastoral matters, but it rests upon an individual theology that is deeply inspired by the Jewish wisdom tradition and by the teaching of Jesus but betrays some knowledge of the development of Pauline theology and has links with Peter.[14]

We have, then, to recognize a strain in Christian theology that shared the basic convictions that we find elsewhere in the early church but developed its own characteristic way of thinking that owed more to a kind of wisdom tradition and stressed Christian maturity shown in the development of character rather than the concept of spiritual life in Christ. In this respect James may be thought to stand closer to the kind of theology that we find in Acts rather than in Paul and John.

## 1 Peter

We have observed some similarities and contacts between James and 1 Peter, particularly in their use of the Old Testament and the teaching of Jesus. But the general character of the two letters is rather different. It might be summed up somewhat sharply by saying that in the context of 1 Peter it would make sense to be asking the question of a reader "Do you love Jesus?" (cf. 1 Pet 1:8), but it might seem odd to ask the same question of a reader of James. No doubt it is at least a trifle unfair to base a verdict on the limited evidence that the short letter of James, written for specific practical purposes, can give us for a full understanding of the spirituality of its author and readers. Nevertheless, with respect to the letters as we have them there is a broad distinction here.

There is considerable use of early Christian material in the letter. As in the case of James we find significant echoes of the teaching of Jesus. The theology is also strongly influenced by the use of the Old Testament. Peter has a clear theology of the way in which God worked through his Spirit in the formation of the prophetic writings (1 Pet 1:10-12). There is a remarkably high amount of quotation from and allusion to passages from the Old Testament; some of these passages are used independently by other New Testament authors, suggesting that there was a common pool of material that was known to early Christians. Analysis of the doctrinal and practical teaching also reveals signifi-

---

[14]The impression I gain is of an earlier date for the writing of the letter rather than a later date, by which time we might perhaps have expected more reflections of a consensus view. Wiard Popkes, *Adressaten, Situation und Form des Jakobusbriefes* (Stuttgart: Katholisches Bibelwerk, 1986), p. 120, estimates that the church life is less advanced than in the Pastoral Epistles. He draws attention to the parallels with the situation reflected in 1 Corinthians.

cant contacts in form and content with other New Testament writings and demonstrates that I Peter stands in close contact with the common teaching of the church; after all, this is precisely what one would expect from a letter of Peter.

The general theological character of the letter has been perceived to be not dissimilar to that of Paul's writings rather than to Hebrews, James or John. This suggests that a brief comparison with Paul may be the appropriate way to see how I Peter fits into the New Testament spectrum of theology.

Peter shares the common New Testament understanding of God as the gracious and faithful Father of Jesus Christ (I Pet 1:3; 2 Cor 1:3) and of believers, who is also the sovereign and impartial judge of humankind (I Pet 1:17; Rom 2:11; 14:11-12). His statements about God's foreknowledge of his people (I Pet 1:2) place him alongside Paul, who uses similar language to indicate that the creation of God's people, to which the readers belong, rests on God's purpose and initiative (Rom 8:28-30; Eph 1:3-6); the church is not a humanly created society of like-minded individuals.

Jesus Christ is the Son of the Father, and language is used that at least points in the direction of his preexistence. God's purpose of salvation through Jesus was conceived before the creation of the world but only now revealed to the world (I Pet 1:20; cf. Eph 1:4; Col 1:26). The Old Testament designation of "Lord" is applied to Jesus (I Pet 2:3, 13; 3:15; I Cor 10:26). The understanding of Jesus as the Suffering Servant of Yahweh is thematized (I Pet 2:21-25), although the actual term is not used of him by either writer, and the concept of self-emptying employed in Philippians is absent from I Peter.

The Holy Spirit is active in the inspiration of the prophets (I Pet 1:11; cf. 2 Tim 3:16) and in the empowering of preachers (I Pet 1:12; I Cor 2:10; I Thess 1:5). The Spirit also is at work in the sanctification of believers (I Pet 1:2; I Thess 4:8) and is present with them in their sufferings (I Pet 4:14; cf. Rom 8:26-27). All of this is amply paralleled in Paul.

Peter's understanding of salvation is likewise close to that of Paul. The death, resurrection and exaltation of Jesus constitute the saving event, but Peter is alone in developing the significance of the period after his death when Jesus visited the spirits in prison. The death is understood as sacrificial (I Pet 1:2, 19; Rom 3:25; Eph 5:2), the means of redemption (I Pet 1:18; Rom

3:24; Gal 3:13), the bearing of sin (I Pet 2:24; cf. 2 Cor 5:21), and the means of reconciliation whereby sinners are brought back to God (I Pet 2:25; 3:18; Rom 5:10). The hostile forces arrayed against them are subjugated to the exalted Lord (I Pet 3:22; I Cor 15:25-27). Christians are people characterized by faith, hope and love directed to Jesus (I Pet 1:3-9; I Thess 1:3). They have died to sin and live to righteousness (I Pet 2:24;[15] Rom 6:1-11), and their new life is in Christ (I Pet 3:16; 5:10, 14; I Thess 2:14; 4:1). Corporately they constitute the people of God, in continuity with Israel to which they now belong (Gal 6:16), and they are a royal priesthood and temple (I Pet 2:4-10; 2 Cor 6:16). They are God's flock and household (I Pet 2:25; 4:17; 5:2; cf. I Cor 3:9; Eph 2:21).[16] They are endowed with spiritual gifts to speak and serve in the congregation (I Pet 4:10-11; Rom 12:6-8; I Cor 12). Though they are afflicted by opposition and persecution, they put their trust in God to keep them and will finally attain to sharing in the glory of God to which they have been called (I Pet 1:5-9; Rom 8:31-39; 2 Cor 4:16-18; 2 Thess 2:14).

Although what has just been presented is a summary of Petrine teaching, reflecting his characteristic vocabulary, it will be clear from the references how close it is to Paul's way of expressing Christian doctrine not only in wording but also in essential structure. For our present purposes it matters not whether this is distinctively Pauline teaching or the common teaching that Paul shared with other Christians; the significant fact is that Petrine teaching manifestly fits into this context. Peter brings his own distinctive contribution within a theology that we can term broadly Pauline.

Further comparison is unnecessary. By establishing that I Peter exhibits a Pauline type of theology, we have demonstrated adequately that this letter fits comfortably within the parameters of one of the main streams of early Christian thinking. Some scholars take the argument further and claim that it really belongs to a Pauline school rather than to Peter or his circle.[17] This hypothesis is unlikely and unnecessary. The historical contacts between Paul and Peter and the background of both apostles in early Christianity are a

---

[15]Note, however, the different vocabulary used here.

[16]The image of the flock is not found in Paul's letters, but cf. Acts 20:28-29.

[17]Cf. Bultmann, 2:142.

fully adequate explanation of the resemblances in their theologies.[18]

## Jude and 2 Peter

We can conveniently consider these two letters together. Despite their differences they have much in common with one another. In both cases a major element in the situation is the activity of pseudo-Christians among the readership, false teachers who live immoral lives and propound false doctrines. The writers are concerned not to just to expose them and condemn them but also to preserve believers from their bad influence and enable them to persevere in their faith.

*Jude.* Jude concentrates on this one theme. He makes use of Jewish literature and traditions to place the heretics and to prophesy their fate. His employment of such materials places him out on a limb, although it must be remembered that parallels to the apocalyptic passages elsewhere in the New Testament can easily be found in extracanonical literature (particularly in I Enoch, from which Jude quotes), and there is no reason in principle why reference should not be made to such sources.

The brevity of the letter curtails the amount of evidence provided for Jude's theology. In our analysis we saw that what he has to say about God, Christ and the Spirit is in line with other early Christian writings. If the aspect of judgment emerges strongly, this is traditional language for the fate of rebels against God, and the picture of God in relation to believers is of a merciful and loving being. Christ is described as functioning in the same ways as the Father and thus as being equal with him. Salvation depends upon God's calling and perseverance is related to his love and mercy and also to the faith and prayer of believers.

The description of the readers as "called" is a designation also used by Paul, but, although he tends to link it with the goal of the action—"called to be saints"—the term can stand as a name for Christians in virtue of an essential characteristic, that they have been summoned by God to be his people and have

---

[18]Michael D. Goulder, *A Tale of Two Missions* (London: SCM Press, 1994), has argued that the historical Peter (who for him was not the author of I Peter) had significant theological differences from Paul. However, with the sole exception of the occasion described in Galatians 2 when Peter slipped back temporarily into the ways of the Judaizers, there is no compelling evidence whatever that the two apostles differed significantly in their understanding of the faith. Even if Goulder's hypothesis were correct, it would not affect the theological relationship of I Peter to the writings of Paul.

responded to the summons (Rom 1:6-7; 8:28; 1 Cor 1:2, 24; cf. Rev 17:14).[19] When the congregation are urged to build themselves up in their faith, this most naturally refers to a mutual activity, similar to what Paul describes in 1 Corinthians 12 and 1 Corinthians 14 when he insists that the purpose of the activities in Christian meetings is the promotion of the spiritual growth and good of the congregation as a whole and not simply of isolated individuals in it.

The goal of appearing blameless before God is precisely what we find in Paul; believers will be able to stand before God without fear of blame since they will be made holy by him (1 Cor 1:8-9; Phil 1:9-11; 1 Thess 3:13; 5:23). The motif of intense joy is reminiscent of 1 Peter 1:8. The use of the doxology, in which these motifs appear (Jude 24-25), probably mirrors the practice of the church in its prayer language, and the closeness of the language to that of Romans 16:25-27 is indicative of Jude's relationship to mainstream Pauline Christianity.[20]

The general impression made by this letter is thus of a theology that is very similar to that of mainstream Christianity. The references to the apostles as figures of the past (Jude 17) and the use of pious language (your "most holy" faith; cf. Mt 27:53; 2 Pet 1:18) may suggest a developed stage in the life of the church. However, the former of these points is not compelling, since the apostles are not to be seen as belonging to a distant point in time. There is nothing in the theology itself that can be regarded as early catholic. Bauckham has developed the hypothesis that Jude preserves an early form of christology associated with the family of Jesus in which Jesus is the agent of God's salvation and judgment, and this is summed up in his title of Messiah and in the attribution to him of God's name of "Lord".[21]

*Second Peter.* This letter appears to have much the same concerns as Jude. The fact that 2 Peter can take over so much of Jude should be taken as evidence that the two writers were dealing with much the same kind of problem rather than

---

[19]Only in Mt 22:14 is the term apparently used of people who have been invited but have not necessarily responded positively.

[20]Although many scholars hold that the doxology is a late addition to Romans, there are good grounds for regarding it as an integral part of the letter. But even if the doxology is not by Paul, it represents his theological understanding.

[21]Richard J. Bauckham, *Jude and the Relatives of Jesus in the Early Church* (Edinburgh: T & T Clark, 1990), pp. 281-314.

that they were engaging totally different phenomena. The major new element here as compared with Jude, where the emphasis was almost entirely on the immoral lifestyle of the false teachers, is the scoffing at the Christian hope of the parousia of Christ and the associated end of history. The Christian hope is in danger of dying out in this context. A further point is that the false teachers twist the Scriptures, including the letters of Paul. They pay lip service at least to Scripture but twist it in an antinomian manner to allow what Peter regarded as sinful license and to deny that it will come under judgment. These two characteristics evidently belong to one and the same group of people. Second Peter 3:3-4 is based on Jude 18, which suggests that the same people are in view. The denial of the parousia could well be due to influences from outside the church altogether.

The theology developed in this context is similar to that in the Pauline tradition. Jesus Christ ranks alongside God the Father and is probably named as God (2 Pet 1:1) in a manner that is found elsewhere in the New Testament (Tit 2:14). His function is summed up as that of Savior, again a term whose currency is seen particularly in the Pastoral Epistles but also in Luke-Acts. His saving activity consists in redemption (2 Pet 2:1), a term that probably carries a reference to his death, and there may be a reference to his righteous act that brings release from sin (2 Pet 1:1). We noted the very similar use of this motif by Paul and Revelation (1 Cor 6:20; 7:23; Rev 5:9; 14:3-4).

The reference to the transfiguration of Jesus is unusual, but there is nothing strange about it. The real puzzle is rather why the resurrection appearances of Jesus are not appealed to instead (cf. Acts 1:11), but the point may simply be that Peter wished to appeal to the majestic appearance of the transfigured Christ, which does not figure in the resurrection appearance stories in the Gospels.[22] Despite the lack of explicit reference to the resurrection, this is implicit in the references to his present existence alongside God the Father.

The readers are characterized by faith, stated to be a gift of God (as in Eph 2:8), and the Christian life is regarded as one of growth in grace and knowledge; we saw that this understanding has close links to Pauline teaching on the fruit of the Spirit.

The considerable stress on knowledge requires comment. The usage here is

---

[22]Admittedly the appearance of the resurrected Lord to Paul was of a glorified figure.

more personal than in the Pastoral Epistles and Hebrews, which use the stereotyped phrase "knowledge of the truth" for the experience of conversion. Usage elsewhere in the New Testament indicates that *epignōsis* increasingly came to be used for a personal relationship with God and hence of shared knowledge of his purposes. This use is found in the later Pauline letters (Eph 1:17; 4:13; Col 1:9-10; 2:2; 3:10).[23] It is also paralleled by the rich usage in John and 1 John for personal relationships involving God the Father and Christ. At the risk of oversimplification we may hazard the suggestion that the usage is not all that different from the common English use of "I know her" to express a personal relationship of greater or less depth. Thus the terminology does not indicate an intellectualization of Christian faith but rather something that is perhaps more mystical or, rather, personal (cf. Phil 3:10).

The language of sharing in the divine nature is unique to this letter. However, the substance of the idea is expressed by Paul and John. For Paul believers are linked so closely to Christ as to be fellow heirs of the glory that is his and sharers in his resurrection, receiving glorious bodies like his (Rom 8:17, 30; 2 Cor 3:18; Phil 3:21; cf. Eph 3:19). Similarly, in the language of John the relationships between believers and the Father and the Son are described in the same way as those between the Son and the Father (Jn 17:21). Moreover, humanity is made in the image of God, and this image is also found in Jesus, whose image will also be borne by redeemed humanity (1 Cor 15:49). It is not too much to say that closely related expressions are well and truly present elsewhere in the New Testament and that 2 Peter is essentially making the same point but in an unusual manner.

Another unusual motif is the replacement of the perishable world by a new heaven and earth. This is most closely paralleled in Revelation (Rev 21:1), and this is confirmed by Romans 8:21, which says the creation is liberated from decay and shares the glory of the children of God. The motif may be implied in 1 Corinthians 15, where the provision of spiritual bodies for believers might suggest the need for a new spiritual environment for them.

The basic theology of the letter is thus fairly categorized as mainstream. Nevertheless, some of the distinctive features are often taken as indications that

---

[23]The earlier Pauline use of the terms is more of intellectual knowledge or of personal relationships between human beings.

the letter is late and has undergone some major shifts in theology. A number of scholars invoke the category of early catholicism to typify the letter. The difficulty in evaluating this claim lies in the fact that the category is so vague. If it refers, as it normally does, to the stereotyping of the church's message, the control of the church over what was becoming a set of orthodox beliefs rather than a personal relationship with Christ, a theology resting on tradition that is fixed and unchanging, and the development of a hierarchical concept of office with the church as the dispenser of salvation, then it is hard to recognize this tendency in the letter. There is certainly the appeal to the authority of Peter the apostle and of Paul, and the denial of the freewheeling interpretation of Scripture practiced by the false teachers. But is this really any different from the apostolic authority to which Paul appeals? The wholly negative characterization of the letter by Ernst Käsemann, for whom "early catholic" was a strongly pejorative term,[24] has been increasingly rejected in recent scholarship for the very good reason that its exegetical basis cannot be sustained.[25]

True, there are signs of later language. The use of superlative adjectives such as "holy" with the "mountain" (2 Pet 1:18) and the "commandment" (2 Pet 2:21; cf. "most holy faith" in Jude) and "precious" (2 Pet 1:1, 4) is typical of this. There is also the backward look to the teaching of the apostles (2 Pet 3:2) and to a collection of Pauline letters regarded as Scripture (2 Pet 3:16), but both of these references are perfectly possible in the first century.[26] But that is all that there is. There is nothing here to suggest early catholicism, no exaltation of the church as the institution controlling and providing salvation, no replacement of a living relationship with Jesus Christ by mere intellectual assent to a set of doctrines

Without going so far in this direction Ralph P. Martin has detected a danger that "2 Peter represents a Christianity that is on the road to becoming tradition-bound, authoritarian and inward-looking". On the one hand, the letter is characterized as rigid and offering a "somewhat mechanical reaction to innovation and theological enterprise"; but on the other hand, it was necessary to defend the faith against the errors of the false teachers and so preserve it for the

---

[24]Ernst Käsemann, *Essays on New Testament Themes* (London: SCM Press, 1964), pp. 169-95.

[25]Representative is Jonathan Knight, *2 Peter and Jude* (Sheffield: Sheffield Academic Press, 1995), pp. 81-83.

[26]Cf. Bauckham, *Jude, 2 Peter,* pp. 287-88, 333.

future.[27] This characterization is perhaps not altogether fair. There is no evidence that the false teachers were offering a creative development of the faith, and in response to them 2 Peter develops some fresh argumentation (the appeal to the flood and to the Lord's sense of time) and uses a new vocabulary that would probably be appropriate for them.[28] It is important to bear in mind that from the beginning the theology of the early church rests firmly on tradition, and that a period of consolidation is inevitable and necessary.

More to the point might be the query whether 2 Peter retains the missionary character that is fundamental to New Testament Christianity. The charge of being inward-looking is best responded to by recognizing that the author saw the danger of the false teachers as being so great that (like Jude) he had to concentrate his message on that particular problem. It is true that he seems to foresee little chance of them abandoning their error and writes in the most powerful terms of the judgment that faces them and of the fear that people who lapse from the way of righteousness can scarcely be brought back to it. Nevertheless, the context of the letter is a church composed of people who have been rescued from a way of life that leads to destruction, and the dominant motif in the picture of God and Christ is that of a God who does not want anybody to perish but rather that all people should come to repentance.

## Conclusion

The documents that we have considered in this chapter are very varied in their character, but there is great value in their diversity. No doubt the most valuable are Hebrews and 1 Peter. The former gives us the essential typological understanding of the relationship of the Old Testament sacrificial system to the self-offering of Jesus and also the crucially important understanding of the life of the believer as an ongoing pilgrimage and growth to maturity. The latter sees life in the world as an opportunity for believers to demonstrate their faith and love despite the hostility that they experience. James has a particular place with its intensely practical wisdom that picks up on an aspect of Old Testament thought that might be thought to have little to offer to believers but here is seen

---

[27](Andrew Chester and) Ralph P. Martin, *The Theology of the Letters of James, Peter and Jude* (Cambridge: Cambridge University Press, 1994), p. 163.

[28]It is noteworthy how, despite its reliance on the material in Jude, 2 Peter has a developed vocabulary that situates it comfortably in the Hellenistic world.

to retain its relevance and importance. Jude and 2 Peter are somewhat slighter in weight, but have a significant message for a church that is confronted by the evils of hedonism and false values. They present the Christian faith in different ways, but we have not seen any evidence of serious differences in their central understanding, granted that in the case of the shorter writings the available evidence is limited. Here we have valuable, indeed indispensable witnesses to the richness of theological thought in the early church.

## Bibliography

Bauckham, Richard J. *James*. London: Routledge, 1998.

————. *Jude and the Relatives of Jesus in the Early Church*. Edinburgh: T & T Clark, 1990.

————. *Jude, 2 Peter*. Waco, Tex.: Word, 1983.

Bruce, F. F. "The Kerygma of Hebrews". *Int* 23 (1969): 3-19.

(Chester, Andrew, and) Ralph P. Martin. *The Theology of the Letters of James, Peter and Jude*. Cambridge: Cambridge University Press, 1994, pp. 65-86.

Käsemann, Ernst. "An Apologia for Primitive Christian Eschatology". In *Essays on New Testament Themes*. London: SCM Press, 1964, pp. 169-95.

Knight, Jonathan. *2 Peter and Jude*. Sheffield: Sheffield Academic Press, 1995.

Schreiner, Thomas R., and Ardel B. Caneday. *The Race Set Before Us: A Biblical Theology of Perseverance and Assurance*. Downers Grove, Ill.: InterVarsity Press, 2001.

Tasker, R. V. G. *The Gospel in the Epistle to the Hebrews*. London: Tyndale Press, 1950.

# PART 6

## CONCLUSION

# 31

# DIVERSITY AND UNITY
# IN THE NEW TESTAMENT

⮜⚬⮞

The purpose of this book has been to offer a presentation of the theology in the New Testament in a manner that would include doing justice to four main concerns.

First, it is essential to see the New Testament writings as part of the canonical Scriptures of the Christian church and therefore to undertake a biblical theology of the New Testament in which proper attention is paid to the substructure provided by the Old Testament.

Second, we were concerned to locate the theological activity that comes to expression in the New Testament in the context of the missionary situation in which it took place.

Third, we considered it essential to begin with examining the theology of each of the documents individually. Even where, as is the case with Luke-Acts and with the generally acknowledged letters of Paul, some writings can be ascribed to the same authors, it is still of value to look at these writings separately to see what contribution each has to offer to the total picture. In other cases the scholarly uncertainty regarding authorship requires us to look at each writing by itself without making assumptions about authorship. In this way we can hope to do better justice to each book of the New Testament than if we look simply at each separate author.

Fourth, we were concerned to see whether the several writings can be said to show any kind of theological unity. It could be said that the thesis that we have been testing here is that we can proceed through a recognition of the diversity in the documents to a recognition that there is a fundamental unity between them.

There are one or two other concerns that might have been addressed but that have been given little or no attention. I have not attempted to reconstruct the history of the development of New Testament theology, showing how ideas may have been born and then changed as they passed through many Christian minds. To some extent questions of the relationships between writers are essential to the understanding of theological ideas in their contexts: a consideration of James 2 with no reference to its relationship to Paul would not be fruitful. But I have made no attempt to create a global picture of development, an enterprise that is difficult and speculative.[1]

Nor have I undertaken the task of relating New Testament theology to the systematic, dogmatic theology of the Christian church today.[2] Rather I have tried to give an analysis of the theological thinking and ideas of the New Testament writers that will serve to help people to understand New Testament texts in their theological context and to have a systematic presentation that can form the starting point for a biblically based systematic theology. There is a dialectic or hermeneutical circle between apprehending the theology expressed in the New Testament texts and using that theology as a context for the understanding of those texts.

### The Biblical Context

Nothing more needs to be said at this point about the importance of understanding the New Testament writings as documents whose worldview is shaped by the faith expressed in the Old Testament and that draw heavily on the Old Testament for their motifs, concepts and theological vocabulary. The account of the exodus and new exodus terminology particularly in Isaiah 40—55 are used by several authors in bringing out the continuity between the old and new covenants. The fact that a New Testament theology must be a biblical theology of the New Testament has been so thoroughly demonstrated by such scholars

---

[1]See the varied treatments of Klaus Berger, *Theologiegeschichte des Urchristentums* (Tübingen: Francke, 1994), and Walter Schmithals, *The Theology of the First Christians* (Louisville, Ky.: Westminster John Knox, 1997).

[2]The forthcoming "Two Horizons" commentary series, edited for the New Testament by Joel B. Green and Max Turner, aims to meet this need.

as Hans Hübner and Peter Stuhlmacher that it requires no further demonstration here, and we have been content to assume this approach rather than to justify it.

## The Missionary Situation

The situation of the early Christians was one in which they were communicating the good news about Jesus to people who were not yet believers. It is worth remembering that people were believers only if they had become believers. The good news was news, something fresh that had not been heard before. Therefore, any people who became believers did so only as a result of the gospel being communicated to them. Whether deliberately or otherwise, whether consciously or otherwise, the early Christian church grew through sharing the message of Jesus with people who were not yet believers. There was no other way in which it could happen.

Inevitably, therefore, the church was active in mission, or else there would have been no church. Jesus was engaged in mission and called followers to share his work, and they knew that after his death and resurrection they must continue that mission. Consequently, the writings that we have arose out of that mission. While the majority of them were written to people who had become believers, some of them may have been intended to be evangelistic, the kind of writings through which readers might be brought to faith (Jn 20:30-31). Others of them described the mission of Jesus (the Gospels) and of his followers (Acts), and in both cases part of the purpose was to confront the readers with their heritage and set an example to encourage and direct them in their own mission. For the most part, however, the books were written to help those who had become believers and needed fuller instruction in their faith and practice. It is a narrow view of evangelism that confines it to the activity whereby people are brought to faith; the nurture of converts and the establishment of the congregations that they comprise are equally important as part of the task. In particular, the rise of false beliefs and evil practices creates dangers as a result of which people may make shipwreck of their faith and congregations may lapse, and therefore the New Testament books have to deal with these problems, even if the writers would gladly have written about other things (Jude 3). Consequently, it can be affirmed that mission is the origin of the New Testament documents. At the same time, the documents are concerned in part with the forwarding of the actual evangelism and contribute to a theology of evangelism.

Inevitably, however, a central area of interest is the theology that expresses the experience of believers and the new beliefs that they come to hold. Focusing on this activity can carry with it the temptation to ignore the task of mission as the sharing of the gospel with those who have not yet heard it or believed it. It is possible to remember how one became a believer, to carry on the activities expected of believers, individually and in a congregation, and yet to ignore mission and evangelism. Particularly in time of hostility and persecution believers may maintain a low profile and withdraw from mission and evangelism for entirely understandable reasons. Even today believers may find their attention diverted to the study of theology and other aspects of Christian living to the detriment of evangelism, and this presupposition may give them a skewed reading of the New Testament. Therefore, it has been my aim in this book to take note of the missionary character and implications of New Testament theology without exaggerating this element or giving it undue attention alongside the other characteristics of the theology.

The theological status of the mission is important. I have drawn attention to the essential role of Jesus as the One sent by God to act as his agent in the establishment of his kingdom and the associated blessings of salvation. Jesus then sent his followers to continue the same task. In the theology of Paul we saw how there is a consciousness that the Christ event and the apostolic proclamation of the gospel are the two inextricably linked parts of the one saving event in which God sends his Son to act as Savior, and his followers make known and interpret his coming, death, and resurrection, and call on people to believe the good news and accept Jesus as Lord. The ongoing mission is thus given its proper status as an integral part of the one saving action of God.

### Through Diversity to a Common Theology

Our presentation has shown something of the distinctiveness of the different books of the New Testament. A historical approach cannot assume that the writers would necessarily be in full agreement with one another in their manners of expression. Can we find a unity in their presentations? There are two complementary ways of investigating the matter. One is to compare the letters with one another to see if we can establish a common core of teaching that is expressed in or that manifestly underlies them all, a set of ideas that are held by all or by a reasonable majority of the writers. The other approach recognizes that the writers will express different facets and different implications of the basic theology in the several writings, but it investigates whether it is possible to formulate a full statement of their theology that will contain many motifs that may be peculiar to individual writings but that fit coherently together. For example, Paul's motif of the heavenly intercession of Christ is found only in Romans 8:34, but it would be foolish to assume that it was not part of Pauline theology because it is attested only the once, and the presence of the element elsewhere (Hebrews; I John) shows that it was not peculiar to Paul. The construction of a New Testament theology must pursue both the greatest common factor and the least common multiple approaches. Neither of these projects is easy to undertake, partly because the documents are shaped by their contexts, and again partly because they may be operating at different levels or with different modes of understanding.

Another kind of approach, taking account of the diversity, might be to try to categorize the New Testament writings, or rather the theological ideas that they express, into different types or streams that may have been flowing alongside one another. However, the complexity of the interrelationships, synchronically and diachronically, defies neat analysis. A fashionable scheme of some forty years ago saw three stages in the development of the early church and its theology—Palestinian Jewish Christianity, Hellenistic Jewish Christianity and Hellenistic Gentile Christianity, so clearly defined that one could plot the development of theologoumena in terms of these stages and assign different texts to each of them.[3] Although this interpretative grid has dropped silently out of use, this emphatically does not mean that it has to be replaced by a scenario that sees no developments and assumes that all parts of the New Testament bear testimony in the same kind of way to the same beliefs; that kind of easy harmonization is simply not possible. Rather, we have to recognize that the theological languages and concepts used by the early Christians developed and diversified. But to what extent were they still recognizably bearing testimony to the same things and the same experiences despite all the diversity?

---

[3]This methodology was applied especially to the study of christology by Ferdinand Hahn and Reginald H. Fuller, but it is open to various objections and has fallen from favor. Cf. p. 29 n. 18.

In an important discussion of the topic, James D. G. Dunn argued for a common core to the four categories of New Testament Christianity that he identified. These categories were Jewish Christianity, Hellenistic Christianity, Apocalyptic Christianity and Early Catholicism; the common core in them all could be represented somewhat abstractly as the affirmation of the identity of the man Jesus with the risen Lord.[4] That affirmation may sound very meager, as indeed it is, but it does encapsulate the fundamental affirmation of early Christians that "if you declare with your mouth, 'Jesus is Lord,' and believe in your heart that God raised him from the dead, you will be saved" (Rom 10:9). Certainly it would not be at all difficult to demonstrate that this affirmation is common to all the various kinds of New Testament Christianity and that anything less would not be Christian. All writers assume the lordly status of Jesus and implicitly accept that God raised him from the dead. But the implications of this are much wider, in that Paul's statement refers to *God, belief* and *salvation* in ways that are characteristically Christian and, it may be claimed, are as fundamental and as widely accepted by early Christians as the point that Dunn has isolated.[5]

Here we should not overlook the work of C. H. Dodd, who made a distinction between the preaching of the early Christians to nonbelievers and the instruction given within the congregations to those who had come to faith. He offered a reconstruction of what he called the "kerygma", the message preached by the early Christians to nonbelievers, on the basis of the evidence of the sermons in Acts and the traces of earlier, preaching material in Paul and elsewhere in the New Testament. Despite considerable questioning as to whether there was one kerygma or several, Dodd's approach seems to be fundamentally sound, although his conclusions need some refinement. It is not too difficult to show that the features that he and subsequent scholars, such as Robert H. Mounce, isolated as typical of early preaching, can be seen to underlie at least some of the New Testament documents. Dodd did not tackle the question of the so-called *Didache*, the instruction given to new Christians with equal intensity, but this theme was taken up by Edward Gordon Selwyn in a study of the sources

---

[4]James D. G. Dunn, *Unity and Diversity in the New Testament* (London: SCM Press, 1977).

[5]Moreover, all of the terms in Dunn's statement and in the Pauline text carry an enormous weight of theological content that cannot be separated off from them. There is thus far more in the statement than might appear at first sight.

lying behind the instruction in I Peter. Selwyn deserves the credit for identifying the common contents and structures in this material, even if his attempt to be more precise about the nature of the sources has not been so fruitful.[6]

All of these approaches are essentially concerned with the preliterary stages in the development of New Testament theology, the oral preaching and teaching of the church in its earliest days that has been dispersed and deposited piecemeal in the written documents and can be recovered from them only with some difficulty. The story of the initial efforts of scholars in this area was chronicled by Archibald Macbride Hunter some fifty years ago in a book on *Paul and his Predecessors,* and the task of identifying and analyzing such material has continued apace. But this approach is concerned with the preliterary material and not with the written texts that have been our concern. It is clearly relevant to our discussion if it can be shown that there was a common pool of material behind the documents and that the writers shared a basic package of theological understanding. It is not surprising that Hunter also wrote a very short book on *The Unity of the New Testament,* in which he demonstrated at a simple, but nonetheless convincing, level that there is a considerable measure of agreement between the texts.[7]

So what about the texts themselves? In his study of New Testament theology Werner Georg Kümmel placed side by side the teaching of Jesus, Paul and John whom he identified as the three principal New Testament witnesses. At the end of the book he asked whether there was a commonality of theology between them despite the manifest differences in expression. Jesus' message concerns the approaching end of the world and era of salvation, both of which were already beginning. The presence of salvation is closely bound up with the person of Jesus, and he is able to offer a share in it to his hearers. After the death of Jesus, his followers believed that he was raised from the dead and exalted as the heavenly Lord. They experienced the Spirit, who was promised for the end time, and saw themselves as the community of the end time. Thus like Jesus they believed that the end time had already begun, although they still looked forward to the

---

[6]Edward Gordon Selwyn, *The First Epistle of Peter: The Greek Text with Introduction, Notes and Essays* (London: Macmillan, 1946), pp. 363-466.

[7]Hunter analyzed the material under the three broad headings of "One Lord", "One Church" and "One Salvation". See Archibald Macbride Hunter, *The Unity of the New Testament* (London: SCM Press, 1943).

imminent coming of the kingdom of God. This experience provided the presupposition for the theology of Paul. He developed this understanding theologically, expecting the near end of the world but also conscious that through the sending of God's Son the time of salvation is already a reality. The living Christ and the Spirit are active in the Christian community. As for John, we find the same juxtaposition of the hope of the future coming of Jesus and the final revelation of the children of God in glory beside the reality of salvation here and now for believers. John emphasizes the presence of salvation more than Paul.

From this comparison Kümmel concludes that the three witnesses all know of the imminent coming of the final era of salvation and of the present reality of this future event in Jesus, the human being and the risen Lord. But Paul and John are more conscious of the presence of salvation, and the expectation of future salvation is less prominent. At the same time common to all three witnesses is the belief in the condescension of God in Jesus. In Jesus the love of God comes to fulfillment. The early church came to the recognition that Christ had died for their sins and that God had wiped out their sins. Paul took this further by seeing that Christ delivered people from their sin and guilt and also from the hostile powers in the world. John is said to follow a somewhat different route, in that he emphasizes the realization of God's saving purpose in the person of Christ to such an extent that the significance of his death almost disappears; salvation is much more the result of the love of God who gave his Son.

> Thus in spite of the development of thought exhibited in them, the three
> major witnesses of the theology of the New Testament are in agreement
> in the twofold message, that God has caused his salvation promised for
> the end of the world to begin in Jesus Christ, and that in this Christ event
> God has encountered us and intends to encounter us as the Father who
> seeks to rescue us from imprisonment in the world and to make us free
> for active love.[8]

This is a somewhat different and fuller account of things from Dunn's, but I cannot imagine Dunn doing anything other than essentially agreeing with it. Kümmel is especially conscious of the tension between the present realization

---

[8]Werner Georg Kümmel, *The Theology of the New Testament According to Its Major Witnesses* (Nashville: Abingdon, 1973; London: SCM Press, 1974), p. 332.

of the kingdom of God and salvation and the future consummation as a major structural element in New Testament thought, but he also emphasizes that God has acted in Christ in order to bring about salvation through his incarnation and death. This account of things seems to me to get nearer to the heart of New Testament theology than Dunn's rather formal statement.

Kümmel's statement is concerned only with the three principal witnesses to the theology of the New Testament. In the course of this study I have outlined the views of each writer, and my proposition is that what Kümmel established for three witnesses can be extended to cover all of them. The evidence for this has already been provided. We began by looking at the way in which the mission and message of Jesus are presented in the Synoptic Gospels. I argued that Matthew and Luke present essentially the same picture as Mark with greater detail and with some changes in emphasis that do not significantly alter the general impression. Further, I stated that there is every reason to believe that the substance of this presentation faithfully reflects the earliest traditions about Jesus, which in turn reflect what Jesus did and said. The Gospels reflect the earliest memories about Jesus, which there is good reason to see as being based on actual memories of him. Within the confines of this book, which aims to be reasonably compact, I did not develop a case for this assumption and refer readers to treatments of the historical Jesus.

I then brought the account of the early church in Acts into the picture. We saw that the presentation there fits within the general framework provided by the Gospels and specifically by Luke, and that it presents a picture of the beliefs and theology of early Christians that appears credible as the development of the message of Jesus in the light of Christian experience of the resurrection of Jesus, the outpouring of the Spirit, and the ongoing mission of the church. Although the picture is to some extent molded by Luke, it is generally coherent and convincing. Here, again, I did not attempt to justify this position in detail, being content to state my agreement with those scholars who have argued for a positive view of Luke's reliability over against the skepticism of an earlier generation.

We were thus able at this stage to bring together the theologies of the Synoptic Gospels and of Acts and to establish the harmonious development that can be seen between the theology of Jesus, as presented by the Evangelists, and the theology of the early church, as presented in Acts.

The next stage was to examine the letters in the Pauline corpus following a probable chronological order that conveniently enabled us to consider first those letters generally considered to be from his own hand and, second, those that are either later compositions by him or produced by his followers who presented his theology in ways appropriate for their situations. On the basis of this examination we were then able to produce a synthesis of Paul's theology based on the generally accepted letters. Throughout this section we were able to include evidence from the later letters that fit into this presentation, and then we looked at the later letters separately to compare their distinctive ideas with those of Paul. Again we were able to see that they developed Paul's theology in various ways, but what was produced was clearly in basic harmony with the earlier letters, in some cases fruitful further developments and in other cases an insistence on the importance of holding fast to Pauline teaching in the face of other, dubious theological and behavioral tendencies in some of the congregations.

We were then able to make a comparison between the theology of the early church in Acts and the theology of Paul. The effect was to show that there was a clear identity in basic matters, but the Pauline letters offered a much fuller picture in terms of the range of material covered and in the depth of the treatment. The greater depth of the Pauline material is not in the least surprising. The significant point is that the two theologies show so much identity. And this is the case despite the fact that although Luke presents himself as a partisan of Paul, nevertheless he has been suspected of misunderstanding Paul. Certainly he does not give expression to the finer points of Pauline theology, but on basic matters there is no conflict.

The next stage in the study was to bring in the third major area, the Johannine literature. The theology of the Gospel is expressed in a very distinctive fashion with its use of a dualistic framework. The theology of the Letters is closely related to it in the manner of expression and the content. The theology of Revelation suggests the work of a writer who belongs to the Johannine circle but who feels the need to make use of the apocalyptic traditions and style of expression that also occur in the Synoptic Gospels and to a limited extent in the Pauline corpus. The theology of the Gospel and Letters needs to be analyzed in comparison with the other Gospels and the Letters of Paul. The results of these comparisons show that once again we have a form of theology that shows the same basic content as those of both of the groups of writings. Of course, the manner of expression and the areas of discussion are different, but the central concerns and the understanding of them are essentially the same.

Finally, we brought into the discussion the remaining books of the New Testament, Hebrews and the so-called catholic letters, and looked at each in turn. The letter to the Hebrews produced its own remarkable angle on the person and work of Christ, and on the nature of the Christian life in order to deal with a specific danger of Christian fatigue and the threat of apostatizing, but once again, the fundamental understanding of the faith is the same as elsewhere. James is unusual in its concentration on Christian behavior, but there is more theology in it than is often noticed, and it reveals an author in close touch with the tradition of the teaching of Jesus and in critical contact with some misunderstanding of Pauline theology. Nevertheless, the manner of expression is remarkably different, thanks to its indebtedness to a wisdom tradition, although the thrust is that of early Christianity generally. The first letter of Peter is a gem in its extraordinarily dense and deep expression of theology in a brief space, and its similarities to Pauline theology, though not such an identity as to make us assign it to a follower of Paul, evidence how closely it belongs to the mainstream of New Testament theology. Jude and 2 Peter are often neglected in accounts of New Testament theology, but we discovered that they both demonstrate an underlying theology akin to that found elsewhere with a particular use of apocalyptic traditions to understand and evaluate the false teaching that they felt obliged to oppose. In short, there is considerable variety in this area of the New Testament, but the individual writings can be included without difficult in the map of New Testament theology rather than being relegated outside its boundaries.

Thus in broad terms our analysis suggests that there is a significant core of agreement and identity within the theologies of the individual constituents of the New Testament.

Is it possible to give an account of this core?

*The main theme.* Throughout the New Testament we are presented with a religion of redemption. The same four stages are common to all the writers: There is a situation of human need that is understood as sin that places sinners under divine judgment. There is a saving act by God that is accomplished through Jesus Christ, who is the Son of God manifested as a human being and whose death and resurrection constitute the saving act that must be proclaimed to the world, to Jews and to Gentiles. There is a new life for those who show faith in God and Jesus Christ, and this new life, mediated by the Holy Spirit, is experienced individually and as members of the community of believers. God will bring his redemptive action to its consummation with the parousia of Christ, final judgment and the destruction of evil, and the establishment of the new world in which his people enjoy his presence for evermore.[9]

*The framework of thought.* All our theologians work within the same Jewish framework of understanding the world as the creation of God and history as the narrative of the ongoing relation of God with the people whom he has chosen out of the nations, initially the Jews but then the people, Jewish and Gentile, who have a spiritual relationship with him. They tend to accept the apocalyptic understanding of history, and some writings make use of a cosmic and ethical dualism between God and the sinful world. They accept the Jewish Scriptures (the Old Testament) as the divinely authorized and inspired account of God's dealings with his people and as the record of his communications with them through his prophets who foretold what he would do in the future.

*Developing the theme. The context of mission: God the Father.* God is understood as the sovereign Creator and Ruler of the universe, holy and righteous, loving, compassionate and faithful. He is both the Judge of human sin and the Savior of sinners. In the New Testament he is characteristically the Father of Jesus Christ and of believers. He is the author of salvation. The concept of fatherhood is marginally present in the Old Testament, is developed by Jesus and taken for granted by the other New Testament writers. There is thus a fuller and deeper understanding of God as entering into personal relationships with individual believers.

*The context of mission: The story of God and humanity.* The New Testament writers assume the biblical story of the creation of human beings who were expected to love and obey God, the fall of humanity into rebellion and sin, God's calling and appointment of the patriarchs and their descendants to be his people, with whom he made a covenant, and the subsequent checkered history of the covenant people, a cyclical story of rebellion, judgment, repentance and redemption

---

[9]Here I use the categorization suggested by David Wenham; p. 36 n. 26.

repeated over and over again. They pick up the promises that God would make a new start with his people, and their story is the story of the establishment of this new covenant.[10] There is thus a profound continuity between the acts of God in both Testaments.

*The center of mission: Jesus Christ.* All our theologians understand Jesus to be the only significant mediator between the world and God. They are all agreed that Jesus is a human being, and yet they assign to him a status that also puts him alongside God the Father. At the very least he is the appointed agent of God, with authority and insight that make him the supreme prophet. The concept of Messiah or Christ expresses this role. The Jewish hope of an agent of God who would rule over his people, that is, inaugurate or revivify the rule (kingdom) of God, was believed to be fulfilled in Jesus, and there is good evidence that he saw himself as acting out this role, although he radically transformed it in doing so. To some extent "Christ" became a name for Jesus that carried less meaning for Gentile Christians, but the significance conveyed by it was not lost and was expressed in other ways. Jesus was conscious of a relationship with God as his Father in what was at least an unusual and probably indeed a unique manner. In the light of his resurrection, understood as exaltation to be with God, he is understood more and more by early Christians to be God's principal agent, is accorded the title of Lord, which was also the Old Testament title for God, and is recognized as the Son of God (other related expressions include Wisdom and Word). This status was understood to be something that for want of a better word we might call an ontological relationship that places him within the identity of God,[11] and occasionally the term God is used of him. Accordingly, he is understood as a being who was with God before he became incarnate as a human being.

*The center of mission: The saving event.* The death of Jesus and his resurrection are highly significant. All sorts of ways are explored to develop the significance of these events, with varying emphases. The basic idea of a death on behalf of other people is found throughout the New Testament. The fact that the death delivers people from sins and their consequences and reconciles them to God is again

---

[10]The old covenant-new covenant distinction is not all that prominent on the surface of the New Testament, but it seems to underlie Christian thinking on the understanding of the progress of salvation history.

[11]This is the helpful formulation offered by Richard J. Bauckham, *God Crucified: Monotheism and Christology in the New Testament* (Carlisle: Paternoster, 1998).

common to all. Different sets of images encapsulate different facets of the saving act. Common to them all is that Christ died for or on behalf of human beings and that his death deals with the sin(s) that separate them from God, enslave them in evildoing and place them under divine judgment that is active now and in a final rejection of those who reject the gospel. His death is understood in categories taken from the Old Testament understanding of sacrifice to remove the barrier caused by sin between humanity and God. Forgiveness, justification, redemption and reconciliation are the key categories of interpretation.

Likewise the fact that God raised Jesus from the dead and exalted him to a heavenly position alongside himself (a glorification) is common, basic Christian belief. The death and resurrection of Jesus are seen as one, single saving event, the action of God raising Christ rather than Christ raising himself. Through this action the forces of evil are defeated and death is overcome for God's people.

The saving event is made known through the proclamation of the gospel, which lies at the heart of the mission entrusted by Christ to his followers. Whether people can be saved without having heard the gospel is not a question that is discussed in the New Testament; what is emphasized is the divine command to the church to go and make disciples. This mission is itself an integral part of the saving event.

*The community of mission: The renewed Israel.* God originally chose the nation of Israel/Judah to be his people, and membership within it was on the basis of birth, ratified by male circumcision and expressed in obedience to the law. The Jews were in many ways not fulfilling their side of the covenant. Jesus came as the Messiah, and the Messiah's role in at least some Jewish minds was to rid Israel of its enemies and free the people from their oppression, and also to purge Israel so that the people might be holy (*Ps. Sol.* 17). Jesus accordingly had a mission to Israel. On the assumption that he believed himself to be fulfilling the role of the Messiah, it is not surprising that he called people to respond to him. Whether or not he did this, his followers certainly saw him as the Messiah and pleaded with the Jews to accept him as the Messiah and Lord. There thus developed a new people, standing in continuity with the faithful Israel of the past, who were the continuing people of God, whereas those who rejected Jesus as Messiah were excluded from this people, just as was the case in Old Testament times with those who rebelled against the law and went after idols. The racial qualification was dropped as believers became more and more aware that the mission of Jesus was not confined to racial Jews and that God was not the God of the Jews only but also of the Gentiles. The tree (a vine or olive) thus gained engrafted branches.

There are only intimations of this in the Synoptic Gospels, and for the most part it appears that the practice of Jesus was confined to Jews. Yet the three Evangelists are aware of the implications. The gospel is to be preached to all nations. Gentiles will come into the kingdom of God. Luke especially develops the theme in Acts. The fullest thematic treatment is in Paul, who knows himself as the apostle to the Gentiles. John also knows that the flock will be increased by other sheep not belonging to the original pen and that the appeal of Jesus will be to all people and not just to the Jews. There is thus not so much a supersession of the ancient promises to the Jews that they will be God's people as rather a spiritual renewal of those promises in the new covenant, whereby the spiritual element of faith and love toward God (that was always fundamental to the maintenance of the covenant) is now given fresh expression in the revelation of God's Messiah, Jesus, and the extension of the covenant people to include all who are spiritually descendants of Abraham through their faith in the Messiah.

The theologian who travels furthest on his own in this theme is Paul, who had to face the problem of the place of the Jewish law being applied to Gentiles in his churches, and who recognized that the law had become something in which people placed their confidence rather than in Christ. Although there were groups in the church who insisted that Gentiles should keep the Jewish law, especially circumcision, none of the New Testament writers adopt this position. This led Paul into a profound discussion of the place of the law in the purpose of God that is one of his major individual contributions to New Testament theology. Paul shows the deepest understanding of sin as it affects and takes control of humanity from Adam onward.

*The community of mission: The response of faith.* The understanding that because of what Jesus has done people can be delivered from sin and put right with God is also basic. The gospel is about a divine initiative, a divine offer that leaves no room for any human actions as a means of being saved. Nevertheless, it is crucial that for salvation to be received there must be a human response. Such a response is not something that human beings do to make themselves acceptable but rather is acceptance of what God has done for them through Jesus, an acceptance that requires a total, ongoing commitment from them, expressed in steadfastness and perseverance. Such faith is an acceptance of what God has done and is doing to save his people without any reliance on whatever human beings might try to do to gain acceptance. Hence *faith* is a defining characteristic of Christianity in a way that distinguishes it from other ancient religions.

Even faith can be thought of in some contexts as a gift of God in that it is aroused and made possible through the Spirit-empowered proclamation of the gospel. This has led some scholars to argue that behind the New Testament writings generally lies a concept of a purpose of God to save only specific individuals out of humanity in general, put into effect by sending Christ to die specifically and only for them (although his death is sufficient for all humanity), calling these foreordained individuals by the preaching of the gospel, creating faith in them and giving them the gift of perseverance so that God's purpose for them will not fail but be brought to completion. Although some texts may appear to support such a position, it does not do justice to the passages that indicate that Christ died for all and that the gospel is truly offered to all people who hear it. It would appear to reduce the New Testament language of personal relationships between God and his people to some kind of determination of people's willing and acting by God so that they do exactly what he wants, and despite their appearance of freedom to respond one way or another to the gospel they are in fact doing what they have been programmed by God to do. What they do, of course, includes their evil choices and actions, and this seems to make God in some sense the author of evil rather than its opponent engaged in a real conflict with it. We do better not to force the New Testament teaching into a tight, logical system that does not sufficiently recognize the mysteries and paradoxes that run through it.

Even less likely is the proposal that the New Testament teaches that God's plan is that ultimately all people will inevitably be saved. However congenial such a thought may be, there is no clear evidence that God will act to achieve this, and the overwhelming trend of the New Testament writers is to warn against the danger of judgment and call people to faith here and now.

*The community of mission: The Holy Spirit.* Although the Synoptic Jesus had little to say about the Spirit, it is recognized that his work was done in the power of the Spirit. The Synoptic Gospels do not say very much about the life of disciples after Jesus has left them, beyond warning of the difficulties and tribulations that lie ahead and calling for watchfulness and steadfastness. Only Matthew preserves the promise of the presence of Jesus with his assembled disciples. Thus for the most part the Spirit and the presence of the risen Jesus lie outside the horizon of the Synoptic Gospels. Nevertheless, the work of Luke culminates in the book of Acts, which does refer to the power of the Spirit in the disciples and to their experiences of the risen Lord. Luke, therefore, saw no problem in the contrast between the limited amount of coverage of these experiences in the Gospel and the new experiences that dominated Christian consciousness after Pentecost.

The place of the Spirit in the life of individual believers and in the congregations is developed most fully in the Pauline corpus and in John and I John. Paul sees the Spirit as the agent that transforms believers to be holy and loving, and empowers them for their struggle with evil. Yet the power of the Spirit is not such that it cannot be resisted and thwarted. The paradox of the relationship between human willing and divine transformation is not lightly resolved. The Spirit gives his gifts to believers to be used in the community for upbuilding one another as well as themselves. John sees the Spirit especially in his role as the Comforter to take the place of Jesus after his resurrection, bearing witness to him and conveying eternal life to them.

*The community of mission: The church.* The goal and result of the work of Jesus is the redemption of individuals and their formation into a community. These two aims belong closely together, since the purpose of redemption is not simply to deliver individuals from the consequences of their sinfulness but to create a new life characterized by righteousness and love. But since righteousness and love cannot be practiced in a vacuum but only in a community, it follows inevitably that redemption should result in a new community characterized by the mutual exercise of love and righteousness. Thus God's purpose of creating a people who will honor him is brought about.

There is little about the followers of Jesus forming what we might call an organized community in the Synoptic Gospels. During the lifetime of Jesus there was no need for organization beyond the fact reported by John that the traveling group had a common purse held by Judas and that there were arrangements for their keep from various women who evidently had material resources. Matthew does have some instructions applicable to a more formal group. Luke was not organization-minded, and the organization of the congregations in

Acts is dealt with rather casually. The Pauline letters reveal the development of various forms of ministry and types of activity within the groups of disciples with a mix of formal and less formal assignments of tasks within the congregations. Here the congregations meet together, and the meeting is the characteristic Christian activity. Contrast the Gospels, where there is no telling whether, let us say, the disciples of Jesus in Capernaum had any common gatherings or activities when Jesus was not there. We have a picture of disciples gathered around Jesus to be taught and presumably to pray, but that is all; in any case, at this point, they presumably still go to the synagogues for the normal religious activities expected of Jews. In John the picture resembles that in the Synoptics, and there is no anticipation of the life of Christian congregations.

Entry into salvation and into the community of believers is symbolically expressed in baptism, a rite that is eloquent of being cleansed from sin, sharing in the death and resurrection of Jesus, and receiving the Holy Spirit. The continuing relationship of believers to Christ is also symbolically expressed in the Lord's Supper, which is eloquent of the sacrificial death of Jesus, spiritual nourishment and the bond of unity and love between those who share in the one loaf and cup. The common life of believers further includes the manifestation of gifts of the Spirit intended to build up believers in their faith, especially through teaching, practical love and care for one another, and worship, thanksgiving, and prayer to God.

*The community of mission: The love commandment.* The clearest common motif in many of the sources, especially in Jesus, Paul and John, is undoubtedly the love command. Its centrality in the behavior of disciples and believers is obvious in all three cases. It appears in its most radical form in the sermon of Jesus where love of enemies is enjoined. But this motif is also present in Paul (Rom 12). In John the emphasis is more on love within the Christian community (Jn 13:34-35); as noted above, John is thinking of mutual love as the mark that distinguishes the Christian community. Loving care for the poor outside the community is hard to detect, although concern for the poor brother and sister is emphasized in 1 John. John too is more aware of the enmity of the outside world toward the believers. Granted these differences regarding the scope of love, there is still no denying the centrality of the motif as lying at the heart of Christian behavior.

Of a piece with the love commandment is the concept of leadership as humble service and not as the self-serving exercise of power and authority. The Son of Man came to serve, and he commended humility to his followers; true greatness lies in serving, not in being served. John presents the example of the Lord and Master washing the feet of the disciples. The motif may not be so obvious in Paul, but it is there also. The church certainly has leadership, and there is authority attached to it, but the authority is exercised for the benefit of the others and not for self-aggrandizement, and this transforms its character.

*The consummation of mission: The fullness of salvation.* Finally, in all our sources we are conscious of the imminent end of the present age and the overlap of the ages. It is notorious that in the Synoptic Gospels the kingdom of God is presented as a very near future entity and as something that is already exercising its power in the here and now. The kingdom is now and not yet. Equally, the Messiah is here now and yet not fully recognized. His power is seen in mighty works, but he can be arrested and put to death. The resurrection undoes the opposition and leads into the era preceding the parousia when the Son of Man will reign and judge. Equally salvation is here to be experienced, but it is not yet consummated. This broad picture can be accepted despite disagreements on the finer points. It is also the picture in Paul, who can speak of salvation in the future tense but also speak of the present realities of Christian experience of justification and reconciliation. Ephesians 2:8, whether Pauline or not, accurately sums up a theology that insists that believers have been saved and can therefore look forward with confidence to being saved from divine wrath at the final judgment. The belief in the imminence of the end is also there in the Pauline hope of the parousia and the resurrection of the dead; there should be no controversy over the affirmation that for Paul the end was certainly something that could come in the near future, whether or not he committed himself to saying that it must do so. As for John, we have seen that he is particularly concerned with the present experience of eternal life by believers but without forgetting the resurrection of the dead. John 11 in particular depicts the tension between eternal life now and the continuing experience of death until the time comes when the dead are resurrected; between the present coming of Jesus to his people and the future parousia.

None of our sources makes the error of thinking that believers are already living in the fullness of the new world; they insist on the preliminary, incomplete mode of Christian experience in the midst of suffering, temptation and physical weakness and death, but equally they insist that this experience is a genuine anticipation of the consummation. Consequently, there is a tension between strength and weakness, so that in the midst of utter human weakness the power of God may be manifested to believers. Tensions of this kind are to be found throughout the New Testament, although naturally they are more apparent in some writings than in others.

*Conclusion.* On the basis of this analysis, it can be claimed that our witnesses do bear testimony to what is palpably the same complex reality. We have found a far greater range of areas of agreement than Dunn's statement might have suggested. Hence a synthetic New Testament theology is a real possibility, but it must begin with seeing each writer in his own terms. Here we may refer again to the achievement of Ferdinand Hahn, who has shown how, despite all the variety to be seen in the individual writers, a comprehensive theology of the New Testament as a whole can be constructed. In this book I have attempted the more limited objective of establishing that there is a common, basic theology that can be traced in all our witnesses, but without developing this theology in detail. Perhaps, therefore, it should be emphasized that the various elements in the theology of the early Christians are to be found not just in this summary of the key essentials but also and above all in the detailed expositions of the individual books of the New Testament.

## Unity or Diversity?

Our survey so far has indicated that it is possible to construct a summary of theological teaching that is essentially shared by the New Testament writers. Some parts of it are multiply attested, while others have less explicit support. Nevertheless, it is a reasonable conclusion that if something like the summary just offered were put before the different New Testament writers, they would all be prepared to recognize it as being close to the essential core of beliefs that inform their individual theologies. But once this has been said, it must again be emphasized that we must not flatten out the teachings of the various writings in such a way as to suggest that they all saw absolutely everything in exactly the same kind of way. The unity is expressed in diversity. The issue is rather whether the diversity amounts to significant difference or even contradiction.[12]

---

[12]As has been indicated, there were manifestly differences between different groups in the early church, most conspicuously the groups of Judaizers anathematized or rejected by Paul. Our concern here is whether the New Testament authors stand together.

To illustrate the problem we may consider one important contribution to the discussion. Arland J. Hultgren has argued that there are a number of different understandings of Jesus and his work in the New Testament and has attempted to classify them into four distinguishable categories.

*Redemption accomplished in Christ.* This type of christology is found in the seven acknowledged Pauline letters and Mark. Basically it is theopractic in that God is the principal actor and Jesus is primarily obedient to God. It is the God of Israel who performs the redemptive act in Christ, who acts as his agent or instrument; Christ dies on behalf of humanity by taking upon himself the divine judgment upon sin, and his death and resurrection are the clues to his meaning as the Christ. There is variation between the documents in the metaphors used and in the presence or absence of preexistence in their varied christologies. The resulting christology is more functional than ontological, and the cross is central. Redemption is an accomplished fact, and the scope is universal. The church is essential in proclaiming redemption and as the community in which salvation occurs. No part of creation is outside its scope.[13]

*Redemption confirmed through Christ.* This understanding is found in Matthew and Luke-Acts. Through Jesus, God carries out or confirms his redemptive purpose, making salvation possible for humanity. Here Christ is rather more fully involved in the work of redemption than in the first view. On this view the cross is almost incidental to the resurrection and exaltation of Christ; it is as the risen Lord that he has authority to forgive sins. Redemption is now essentially a future prospect of which the gospel is a pledge. But the time in between is significant in that forgiveness of sins is available, although believers must persevere to the end to be saved. If there is less stress on the cross, there is now more recognition of the church as the community in which salvation is experienced. The benefits of salvation include guidance and teaching concerning conduct. No thought is given to those who have not heard the gospel.[14]

*Redemption won by Christ.* This perspective belongs to such diverse works as Colossians, Ephesians, the Pastoral Epistles, I Peter, Hebrews and Revelation. Here Christ is more obviously the redeeming figure as the One who comes from

---

[13]Arland J. Hultgren, *Christ and His Benefits: Christology and Redemption in the New Testament* (Philadelphia: Fortress, 1988), pp. 47, 64-67.

[14]Ibid., pp. 69, 85-89.

above to secure redemption through his cross and victorious resurrection and
then return to his former glory, after which he will be revealed at the parousia.
This christology is accordingly christopractic, with Christ as the center, and
forms the basis for *Christus Victor* theories. He is not merely sent by God, like a
prophet might be, but he is preexistent. The nature of Christ is beginning to be
the basis for his work. Several of the writings move to ontological unity between God and Christ. Christ acts to liberate from sins; he does not appease
God but rather ransoms human beings. Future liberation from the evil powers
and the devil is envisaged. The effects of Christ's work are accordingly essentially future, and the present life of the Christian is essentially preparatory for
the salvation that is to come. There is a tendency to universalism. The exalted
Christ already exercises his reign through the church. To some extent this later
perspective is already anticipated in Philippians 2:6-11, and the picture shows
some conscious contrast to the emperor cult.[15]

*Redemption mediated by Christ.* This view is found in John and to some extent
in 1-3 John. Christ, who is in union with the Father, reveals him and mediates
salvation from him to those who believe in him. So salvation is based in the
purpose of God but is essentially christopractic. The cross and resurrection of
Jesus are the presupposition and foundation of redemption. The message is
pronouncedly one of gospel and summons. The mediation of salvation takes
place when and where persons believe in the Son. It is very exclusivistic. In 1-3
John there is a return to the concept of the atoning significance of the death of
Jesus.[16]

Hultgren poses the questions that arise for discussion. Why are there different types of understanding? Is there unity within the diversity? What differences remain between the various views, and can they be harmonized? What cri-
teria can be used to assess their relative strengths, weaknesses and adequacy?
Hultgren thinks that these four views cannot be harmonized, and he finds the
first (the Pauline model) the most satisfactory.[17]

Hultgren is to be commended for this pioneer work in attempting to explore
the subtle differences there may be between different understandings of the

---

[15]Ibid., pp. 91, 135-43.
[16]Ibid., pp. 145, 160-64.
[17]Ibid., pp. 179-80, 181-89.

person and work of Jesus in the New Testament writings. The task is peculiarly difficult because of the very considerable overlaps between the different writings.[18] Hultgren has to recognize that there are some examples of "mixture" where elements of one type of understanding are found in writings that he assigns to another type. The effect of this may be to show that the different views are not as incompatible as he suggests. It has often been commented that the character of the gospel is such that it cannot be contained within any one, single model and that we need pictures taken from various angles in order to appreciate the fullness of its content. We have constantly had occasion to note the existence of paradoxes and tensions even within single documents in the New Testament as they grapple with the difficulty of expressing Christian beliefs, and we should not assume too swiftly that different presentations are necessarily incompatible with one another. There is also the danger of assuming that what is not mentioned in comparatively brief documents was not essential in the thought of the writers.

So, for example, it is difficult to accept his contention that the cross is less emphasized as the means of redemption in Matthew compared with Mark, or conversely that the resurrection is less significant in Mark.[19] And the God who saves in Matthew and Luke-Acts is the same God of Israel as in Paul. The christology of Paul is as ontological as that of these other documents, where Christ's preexistence is a matter of inference rather than of explicit statement. To say that no thought is given to those who have not heard the gospel in Matthew and Luke-Acts is to fly in the face of the commands to universal mission in both works and to assume wrongly that we are told about the salvation of those who have never heard or will never hear the gospel elsewhere in the New Testament. Again, to affirm that teaching and guidance concerning behavior is more characteristic of Matthew and Luke-Acts than Paul would have sorely puzzled readers of I Corinthians, to say nothing of Paul's other letters. As for redemption won by Christ, most of the features of this mode are to be found

---

[18]For a contemporary example of a similar problem one might compare the attempts to characterize the distinctives of the different generations of young people in the Western world. Much is shared between the different generations, and it becomes a case of trying to discover which features are more obvious in one group than in another. Cf. David Hilborn and Matt Bird, *God and the Generations: Youth, Age and the Church Today* (Carlisle: Paternoster, 2002).

[19]See Morna D. Hooker, *Endings: Invitations to Discipleship* (London: SCM Press, 2003), pp. 11-30.

explicitly and characteristically in Philippians as well as in other earlier Pauline letters. In particular, it is hard to believe that the triumphant resurrection of Jesus is any less prominent in Paul than it is here. Finally, the gospel presented in the Johannine writings is essentially at one with Paul in its emphasis on the message and on the response of faith, and the universality of the provision of salvation for the whole world is clearly expressed.[20]

These considerations show that there are good grounds for contesting whether the four types of christology identified by Hultgren are all that distinct from one another and incapable of being seen harmoniously. Hultgren certainly recognizes that there is a real unity within the diverse categories that he has identified. He lists four points: (1) Redemption is based in the purposes of the God of Israel. (2) Consequently, Christ does not act on behalf of humanity against God, but God is at work in him.[21] (3) Redemption is always seen as taking place in the death and resurrection of Jesus, however these may be understood. (4) With the death and resurrection of Christ a new age has begun in which redemption is a reality, even if there is tension regarding the extent of its fulfillment. I would suggest that the extent of the unity is rather greater than the content of these points and that the various authors are bringing together different elements that contribute to a fuller understanding of the many facets of christology and soteriology rather than setting up models that are incompatible with one another.[22]

Two points made be made in conclusion. First, we must recognize that there may be considerable differences in religious ethos that are compatible with a basic identity in experience. There is a distinct difference between a high Anglican liturgy and the informality of a charismatic celebration, and yet each of them may testify equally faithfully to the same gospel. How far was what went

---

[20]Hultgren, *Christ*, pp. 56-57, creates what I regard as an artificial difference by arguing that Paul teaches a universalism according to which all people will eventually be saved.

[21]Here it would be important to ask why Christ as the agent of God needed to become human. Hultgren is attempting to avoid any suggestion that some kind of appeasement of God's wrath against sin was needed, but the fact of divine wrath is not to be evaded.

[22]The major tension in the New Testament is probably that between the preaching in Acts with its concentration on the exaltation of Christ to be a Savior and its lack of attestation of the significance of his death as a means of atonement. Yet the Last Supper sayings and Acts 20:28 are adequate evidence that what we have is at most a shift in emphasis rather than a contradiction of the saving significance of the death of Jesus.

on in a typical meeting of the congregation in Corinth comparable with a traditional Jewish-Christian synagogue in Galilee? Such differences are tolerable, although even today Christians may find it difficult to adapt to them.

Second, in an important essay David Yeago has shown how the recognition of a distinction between judgments and the conceptual terms in which they are expressed can help us to recognize that the same judgments can be made in different conceptual terms. So, for example, Nicene dogma can be an expression of the same judgment as is made concerning the person of Jesus in the New Testament.[23] The same principle may be applied to the different conceptualities that are used to express the judgments concerning Jesus and the gospel that we find in the New Testament. Once we recognize that different conceptualities can be used to express the same judgment, the next question is whether we can recognize whether the same judgments are being made in the different bodies of evidence that we are examining. Thus, for example, it is not difficult to recognize that the judgment that there is a spiritual relationship between the risen Jesus and his followers is expressed using different conceptualities in Paul, John and other New Testament writers. Similarly, the judgment that Christ's death sets believers free from the consequences and the power of sin is conceptualized in a variety of models, each of which helps to enrich the total picture.

We close, then, with a recognition of a unity that is expressed through diversity. The quest is not complete. There is much theological detail that we have not been able to explore in a book that is intended to be an introduction rather than a comprehensive treatise. And it is part of the inspiration of Scripture for Christian readers that it constantly speaks in new ways to people in different generations and situations even if the message is still the same; compare how a Taizé chant, for example, remains the same even if the instruments and voices, the harmony and counterpoint, are infinitely variable. So, when we have reached the end of this book, we have not brought our study to a final conclusion but rather accepted an invitation that will lead us on further to a continuing engagement with the God who continues to speak to us in Scripture.

---

[23]David Yeago, "The New Testament and the Nicene Dogma: A Contribution to the Recovery of Theological Exegesis", in *The Theological Interpretation of Scripture: Classic and Contemporary Readings*, ed. Stephen E. Fowl (Oxford: Blackwell, 1997), pp. 87-100.

### Bibliography

*New Testament Theologies:* (German) Hahn, 2.

Dodd, C. H. *The Apostolic Preaching and Its Developments.* London: Hodder & Stoughton, 1936, 1944 (2nd ed.).

Dunn, James D. G. *Unity and Diversity in the New Testament.* London: SCM Press, 1977.

Hooker, Morna D. *Endings: Invitations to Discipleship.* London: SCM Press, 2003.

Hultgren, Arland J. *Christ and His Benefits: Christology and Redemption in the New Testament.* Philadelphia: Fortress, 1988.

Hunter, Archibald Macbride. *Paul and His Predecessors.* 2nd ed. London: SCM Press, 1961.

————. *The Unity of the New Testament.* London: SCM Press, 1943.

Mounce, Robert H. *The Essential Nature of New Testament Preaching.* Grand Rapids, Mich.: Eerdmans, 1960.

Selwyn, Edward Gordon. *The First Epistle of Peter: The Greek Text with Introduction, Notes and Essays.* London: Macmillan, 1946.

Yeago, David. "The New Testament and the Nicene Dogma: A Contribution to the Recovery of Theological Exegesis". In *The Theological Interpretation of Scripture: Classic and Contemporary Readings.* Edited by S. E. Fowl, pp. 87-100. Oxford: Blackwell, 1997.

# Author Index

References to the chapter bibliographies are given in **bold**. References to works on NT theology in the chapter bibliographies that have been already listed in the general bibliography are not included in this index.

## Subject Index

Aaron, 135, 612, 684

*Abba*, 193, 425, 472

Abraham, 96, 115, 213, 216-17, 219, 226-27, 230, 232, 311-13, 324, 326, 338, 430-31, 442, 447, 502, 614-16, 638, 640

Adam, 132, 279, 315-16, 339, 355, 427, 429, 434, 474, 594

adopt, adoption, 218, 321, 381, 451

adoptionism, 175, 426

advent, 149, 193, 301, 664

age (present, future), 78, 87, 91, 107, 116-17, 123, 146, 168, 173-74, 181, 186, 213-14, 223, 228, 240, 393, 511, 544, 559, 577, 612, 615, 618, 725, 730

agent, 36, 63, 68, 83, 103, 115, 122-23, 131, 141, 143, 146, 149, 152, 160-61, 166, 171, 175-76, 189, 199, 201, 205, 270-71, 273, 276, 179, 284, 286, 292, 294, 349, 368, 380, 395, 408, 440, 464-65, 486, 492, 494, 509, 512, 514, 535, 557, 562-63, 577, 580-82, 584, 634, 653, 664-65, 699, 710, 719, 723, 727, 730

angel, 76, 139, 143, 162, 245, 563, 665

anoint, anointed, 57, 59, 74, 82, 132-33, 146, 537, 545, 547, 569, 599, 607, 634, 639

antagonism, antagonistic, 36-37, 390, 648

apocalypse, apocalyptic, 73, 78, 86, 117, 137-38, 143, 188, 204, 245, 421, 482, 548-49, 551, 560-61, 570-72, 574-77, 582, 590-91, 668, 679, 688, 698, 712, 716-18

apostasy, 178, 228, 310, 406, 412, 541, 544, 547, 555, 563, 568, 574, 619, 664, 686, 717

apostle, 41, 60, 158-61, 166, 179-81, 186, 195, 211, 214, 237, 238-39, 241, 254, 258-60, 264, 266, 269-71, 273, 277, 284-85, 288-89, 291, 293, 297, 301, 364, 384-86, 390, 392, 394, 398-99, 405, 416, 431, 457-59, 464, 466, 472-74, 481-82, 564, 570, 600, 663, 672-73, 697-99, 702, 721

Aramaic, 27, 83, 158-59, 265, 472

ark, 310, 624, 647

ascension, ascent, 134, 160, 174-76, 394, 429, 673

assurance, 178, 193, 233, 247, 262, 289, 291, 323, 350, 406, 478, 508, 536, 550, 555-56, 560, 564, 575, 591, 618, 646, 653, 661

atone, atonement, 196, 230-31, 310-11, 437, 448, 476, 607, 611, 624, 684-85, 730

authority, 62-63, 67, 72, 79, 84, 85, 92, 105, 107, 111, 113, 115, 126, 147-50, 152, 160, 175-76, 179, 181, 188, 191-92, 197, 199-200, 211, 213-16, 237, 254, 257, 266, 270-71, 288-89, 306, 316, 318, 324, 327, 330, 355-56, 364, 368-69, 372, 374-75, 382-83, 385, 388, 394, 398, 401, 407, 418, 427, 431, 451, 457, 463, 481, 499, 512, 515, 551-52, 584, 586, 594-95, 662, 664, 665-66, 673, 702, 718-19, 724-25, 727

baptism, baptize, 58-59, 69-71, 82, 88, 96-97, 108, 111, 121, 132, 143, 159-60, 162, 167, 177, 181, 196, 199-201, 226-27, 233, 254, 264, 275, 316-17, 371-72, 393, 455, 457, 480, 487, 495-96, 505, 523, 541-43, 564, 625, 634, 640, 647, 652, 655, 678, 724

belief, believe. *See* faith

beloved, 97, 363, 529

*berakah*, 380, 643-44

birth, 96-97, 111-13, 126, 130-31, 143, 145-46, 149-50, 152, 175, 187, 190, 200, 227, 269, 348, 408, 412, 493-94, 498, 520-21, 543, 582-83, 637, 639, 644, 646, 657, 691, 720

bless, blessing, 35, 54, 61, 79, 82, 92, 99, 116, 146, 176, 195, 217, 226-27, 229, 232, 257, 259, 272, 290-91, 351, 353, 357-59, 380-81, 390, 393, 425, 427, 430, 451-52, 471, 493, 550, 573, 581, 594, 611, 615, 618-19, 644-45, 653, 664, 710

blind, 65, 71, 82, 90, 138, 144, 147, 285, 293, 498, 502-3, 505, 514

blood, 74, 80, 110, 139, 164, 167-68, 176, 197, 261, 266, 277, 310, 381, 437, 439, 441-42, 475, 501, 534, 536, 540-43, 550, 569, 587-88, 609, 624-25, 644-45, 649-50, 675, 684

boast, boasting, 220, 254-55, 269-70, 284, 289, 297, 302-3, 309, 326, 350, 384, 447, 475, 631

body, 74, 80, 176, 188, 227, 248, 256-57, 261-62, 265-66, 272, 274-75, 277-80, 285, 299-300, 320-21, 327, 346, 354, 355, 369, 371, 374-75, 383, 386, 388, 391-93, 416, 429, 434, 451, 453, 455, 457, 460, 463-67, 479-80, 487, 497, 532, 588, 598, 652

bread, loaf, 74, 139, 261, 274, 298, 457, 480, 487, 494, 500-501, 505, 514, 519-21, 525, 572-73, 581, 584, 588, 724

brother, brotherhood, 109-10, 188, 238, 328,